WE ARE BETTER THAN THIS

EDWARD D. KLEINBARD

WE ARE BETTER THAN THIS

HOW GOVERNMENT SHOULD SPEND OUR MONEY

OXFORD
UNIVERSITY PRESS

OXFORD
UNIVERSITY PRESS

Oxford University Press is a department of the University of Oxford.
It furthers the University's objective of excellence in research, scholarship,
and education by publishing worldwide.

Oxford   New York
Auckland   Cape Town   Dar es Salaam   Hong Kong   Karachi
Kuala Lumpur   Madrid   Melbourne   Mexico City   Nairobi
New Delhi   Shanghai   Taipei   Toronto

With offices in
Argentina   Austria   Brazil   Chile   Czech Republic   France   Greece
Guatemala   Hungary   Italy   Japan   Poland   Portugal   Singapore
South Korea   Switzerland   Thailand   Turkey   Ukraine   Vietnam

Oxford is a registered trademark of Oxford University Press
in the UK and certain other countries.

Published in the United States of America by
Oxford University Press
198 Madison Avenue, New York, NY 10016

Library of Congress Cataloging-in-Publication Data
Kleinbard, Edward D.
We are better than this : how government should spend our money / Edward D. Kleinbard.
    pages cm
Includes bibliographical references and index.
ISBN 978-0-19-933224-3 (hardback); 978-0-19-049668-5 (paperback)
1. Fiscal policy—United States.   2. Finance, Public—United States.   3. Government spending
policy—United States.   4. United States—Appropriations and expenditures.   I. Title.
HJ257.2.K595 2015
336.3'90973—dc23

                2014024466

9 8 7 6 5 4 3 2 1
Printed in the United States of America
on acid-free paper

To the memory of my father, who delayed my entry into academia by 30 years—
just long enough for me to have something useful to say

CONTENTS

PART II STARVING OUR FISCAL SOUL

PART III RECLAIMING OUR FISCAL SOUL

LIST OF FIGURES

LIST OF TABLES

ACKNOWLEDGMENTS

This book exists because of the indefatigable enthusiasm and counsel of my agent, Peter W. Bernstein, to whom I am profoundly grateful. I also am grateful for the support and interest shown by the editorial staff at Oxford University Press, including Terry Vaughn, who originally committed to the book, and to Scott Parris and Cathryn Vaulman, who shepherded it to completion.

A great many colleagues, friends, and relatives have been pressed into service to read portions of the manuscript, or of earlier papers on which the manuscript relies, and I thank them all. I would, however, like to acknowledge here some deeper debts, to the men and women who guided my transition to academia, and who have unstintingly offered remedial tutoring whenever a gap in my learning was exposed. I begin with the late David Bradford, the dean of public finance economists of his generation, and a man so kind that I used to joke that he was the Tax Mahatma. He was the first person to whom I confided my hope of making the transition to the academy, and he was so encouraging that I found the courage not to instantly abandon the idea as preposterous. Since then, many economists, including Rosanne Altshuler, Alan Auerbach, Thomas Barthold, Leonard Burman, Kimberly Clausing, and Michael Devereux, have taken turns tutoring me on various points. They are unanimous that they should not be blamed for any mistakes found in this volume. From the legal academy, Joseph Bankman, Edward McCaffery, and Daniel Shaviro were my great intellectual benefactors. Again, they beg the reader not to hold them responsible for my idiosyncratic worldviews. Finally, the Dean of the University of Southern California Gould School of Law during this book's gestation, Robert K. Rasmussen, was unstinting in his enthusiasm and support for the project.

I was blessed by the support of terrific research assistants as I worked on this book. Unlike a PhD program, where professors and graduate students work together for years, the productive lifespan of a law school research assistant is as ephemeral as a mayfly's. Nonetheless, each year's asssistants threw themselves into the project and made major contributions. I wish to acknowledge in particular the work of Richard Bohm, Ashley Elnicki, Juan Carlos Olivares, and Olga Zolotnik. Among other contributions, Rick Bohm was the principal chartmeister for the book, and Ashley Elnicki did the original research for Chapter 12's comparisons of the relationships among a tax system's size, progressivity, and impact on inequality.

INTRODUCTION

A NATION OF JERKS?

Let me ask you a question: What do you believe our government is good for?

I can almost hear the chortling—the nearly irresistible urge to answer my question with a hearty "Nothing!" and then to turn back to one's private pursuits. But I ask that you consider for a moment the possibility that the answer is not quite this obvious, and that in fact government—which is to say, all of us, acting collectively—can make our country healthier, wealthier, and happier, if we put government to useful work in those areas where it most productively complements our private markets.

That is what this book sets out to demonstrate. Its purpose is to encourage readers to resist the gravitational pull that naturally tugs us in the direction of becoming what one recent opinion piece termed a nation of "jerks."[1] That short article summarized research suggesting that the fraction of Americans who believed that government should guarantee each person enough to eat and a roof over her head fell by 10 percentage points over the five-year period since the onset of the Great Recession, declining to fewer than three out of five Americans in 2012. It would be nice if this disenchantment with government were a consequence of government's displacement by nationwide movements that actually funded and operated community-organized food banks and shelters sufficient to the national task, but the data contradict this convenient claim. Millions of American citizens are hungrier today than they were in 2007, and the reason is simply that those of us who are not acutely hungry are more anxious about ourselves and our own economic security.

As I write this in late 2013, our economy still underperforms for most Americans. As a result, this personal economic anxiety is understandable. But

We Are Better Than This shows that the path forward to a better economic environment for all of us lies through more government involvement, not less. When we
starve government of resources, it turns out that we largely are starving our own
long-term prosperity.

We are inundated today by economic noise and fog designed to generate superficially plausible rationales for what at bottom are simply jerk-like instincts. You
see this machinery at work, for example, when you read editorials making the
"leveling down" argument: you cannot make the poor rich, the writer sadly notes,
by making the rich poorer—there's just not enough money to go around to do
that. In your naïve ambition to level up the poor, you will only succeed in leveling
down the rich. The regrettable slaughter of the goose that laid the golden eggs
is sometimes invoked. The writer then typically draws from this purported iron
law of economics the conclusion that, since the rich cannot shoulder the whole
burden, why ask them to do anything at all?

We Are Better Than This refutes these and similar exercises in false economic
syllogisms. The book demonstrates that we effectively leave long-term prosperity
and happiness off the table through our current penchant for minimalist government. And it makes the economic case for a more muscular federal government
that complements the private sector through sensible investment and insurance
programs.

In making the economic case for government investment and social insurance functions that work with, not against, the private sector, *We Are Better Than
This* shows that we can afford to pay for government to take on a larger role, and
that our semi-annual budget emergencies are largely false fiscal crises. It calls
for somewhat higher federal income tax rates than those in force in 2013 (except
at the top!), but not materially higher than those in 1999, when the economy was
humming. There is nothing terribly radical in the book's programmatic aims
(except perhaps in its fundamental business tax reform suggestions, all the way
at the end of the book). I am not a closet Trotskyite. I am, in fact, a friend to business—in a Dutch uncle sort of way.

Along the way, the book marshals a great deal of evidence, and assists readers
in becoming much more sophisticated consumers of claims regarding tax and
budget policy. The reader who makes it all the way to the end may well not agree
with me at every turn, but he or she will be a better informed citizen, and much
less likely to be a fiscal jerk.

TAXING AND SPENDING, OR SPENDING AND TAXING?

As the actor Edmund Kean lay on his deathbed, a tactless friend inquired whether
dying was difficult. "No," Kean replied, "Dying is easy; *comedy* is hard."

And so it is with fiscal policy—that is to say, the art of government spending and taxing. Households find it difficult to earn money and easy to spend it. But for governments, taxing—the side of fiscal policy that seems so difficult and abstruse from the outside—turns out to be relatively easy as a technical matter; it is the policy underlying government spending that is maddeningly difficult.

This conclusion is something of an embarrassment to me, as I have spent 35 years meditating on federal tax matters, as a practitioner, government official, and academic, but it nonetheless is true. Colbert—not contemporary pundit Stephen, but rather Jean Baptiste Colbert, finance minister to King Louis XIV of France—explained the essence of tax policy neatly 350 years ago: "The art of taxation," he wrote, "consists in so plucking the goose as to obtain the largest possible amount of feathers with the smallest possible amount of hissing." All of contemporary tax policy analysis is just an elaboration.

Since the time of Colbert, we have learned a great deal about how to pluck the goose as quietly as possible. Public finance economists (the subspecies who study the effects of tax and government spending policies) now have a reasonably clear idea of which tax policies lead to the fewest squawks, in terms of unintended economic consequences. Government spending, on the other hand, is completely different. There are no generally agreed-upon technical solutions to the question, what is the proper role of government? This question, it turns out, ultimately does not even reside solely in the domain of economics (although many economists resist this). Instead, the issue implicates questions of moral and political philosophy with which thinkers since Aristotle have wrestled.

So all of our technical knowledge on the economic side effects of taxation cannot resolve the fundamental fiscal issue that dominates contemporary political discourse, which is how much tax revenue our technical expertise should be harnessed to collect in the first place. But in turn, government taxing and spending are completely bound to one another, so that policies in respect of one side cannot be developed without considering the other.

The famous economist Milton Friedman summed things up with the maxim, "to spend is to tax." That is, every decision by government to spend money necessarily requires an offsetting commitment to raise the revenues to pay for that spending. Friedman's aphorism is as close to a Newtonian law as economics gets.

Of course, government has a few choices of how to relate taxing to spending, some of which are more disreputable than others. Its honorable choices are to tax now to pay for current spending, or to issue bonds (IOUs) today, and collect taxes tomorrow (or the day after tomorrow) to repay those borrowings. Government's seedier options include borrowing today and then relying on inflation to minimize the tax burden tomorrow, but that is just a way of saying that inflation itself is a hidden and pernicious sort of taxation, in this case on lenders. And finally government can amaze the world by borrowing today and defaulting tomorrow, but this tactic turns out to be so cataclysmic in its implications that only a modern Nero would contemplate it.

Tax policy is the handmaiden, and spending policy the sovereign: we need to decide on what projects to embark collectively through the intermediation of government before we can design a tax system to meet those needs. Our greatest public finance policy mistake over the last few decades has been to obsess over tax policy, while simultaneously failing to have serious and rational debates over spending policy. We quibble over tactics without really engaging in the more difficult enterprise of forging a national consensus on our strategic objectives.

And therefore this book, which in its embryonic form was an explanation of the tax policy choices that confront us as a nation, necessarily has evolved into a more discursive inquiry into what we fairly should ask our government to do by way of spending our money. It is also a confession by a longtime tax geek that I, like many others, have elevated the tactical issues of tax system design beyond their ultimate importance to our society. Instead of arguing about tax rates or even levels of tax revenues in the abstract, we must focus instead on the real question, which is what we think our government is good for.

WHAT'S MORAL PHILOSOPHY GOT TO DO WITH THIS?

Fiscal policy recommendations in the end always are normative—they embody a point of view about our values, our relationships to each other, and what those values and relationships should be. Spending may be the sovereign, and tax policy the handmaiden, but *what* we choose to spend on is determined by our values and belief systems. And these in turn should be discussed more directly than they usually are, even by those of us whose inclinations tend more toward action than rumination.

This means that this book necessarily must touch on moral philosophy. To be clear, I hate philosophy just as much as does the next red-blooded American. Most philosophical texts are too convoluted and abstract to gain much traction with me, and I have the urge to tell any philosopher I meet that he should just lay off the word games, get outside, and throw a football around with the other fellows. But it turns out that all fiscal policy recommendations rest on a foundation of moral philosophy: the only question is whether we are conscious of that fact.

My values are old-fashioned progressive values. I internalize these values for two reasons. First, I believe that almost all of us embrace the dignity of work as a central organizing principle in our lives. I do not accept the picture of America that some like to paint, of a vast underclass interested only in leeching, or mooching, or whatever the verb of the moment is, off a virtuous super-class of authentically productive people. And because I believe that government serves all of us,

I tolerate the occasional counterexample, if rooting him out comes at the cost of failing to help thousands or millions of others to achieve as much as possible out of their lives.

Second, I see the pervasive hand of fortune—of simple luck—at work everywhere. I am very industrious, and I have achieved some success and material comforts, but I could fill a book longer than this one with all the good fortune that has come my way, starting with my native intelligence. Those who ascribe everything they are and have achieved to their "native" talents, and who view with derision those who have not achieved comparable success in the world, not only willfully overlook the good luck that has come their way, but more fundamentally fail to consider why it is they are blessed with those congenital qualities that the world rewards. Their fiscal thinking—usually articulated as a confusion of personal financial freedom with a society's political freedoms—ultimately rests on thinly veiled narcissism, or the embrace of a cartoon version of Calvinist predestination. Both are distasteful and un-American.

We Are Better Than This focuses mostly on economic claims and arguments, because that is the arena where modern fiscal debates actually take place. But I do think it worthwhile to hold up our moral premises for examination from time to time. I do this in particular by exposing readers briefly to the moral philosophy of Adam Smith. He would have been appalled by the affixing of his name to a belief system in which personal selfishness entirely explains individuals' behavior and life goals, and in which government exists principally to get out of the way of market transactions. By glancing occasionally at what Adam Smith actually thought, we can see how impoverished our moral discourse has become.

A DUTCH UNCLE TO ALL

I am a friend to business, even if the affection is not always reciprocated. I worked for decades on Wall Street, and my own conversion on the road to Damascus lay in the direction of engagement with fiscal policy in a broad sense, not in a repudiation of Big Business, or anything as silly as that. There are no rants in this book about the inherent evils of business, or business people. I fully accept that all else being equal, it is better to be richer than poorer, and that it is natural and appropriate to aspire to wealth.

But that does not mean that life revolves around these themes alone, or that they justify structuring our society as a winner-take-all contest fought in the marketplace rather than the forests of Panem.[2] As Adam Smith said, "When the happiness or misery of others depends in any respect upon our conduct, we dare not, as self-love might suggest to us, prefer the interest of one to that of many."[3] As chapter 2 demonstrates, Smith was vitally concerned with living a life of virtue, one in which rational self-centeredness in the marketplace plays only a small part.

On the other hand, I also am not a cheerleader for the Democratic Party, President Obama, or some standard tropes popular in progressive political circles. I do not think very highly of the fiscal implications of the Affordable Care Act. And I certainly do not propose to apologize for the October 2013 rollout of the infamous website by which citizens engaged with their new health insurance options. It was inexcusably awful, of course.

But by the same token, I do not draw any particular inferences from that debacle for the themes of this book. New Coke was a disaster, but it did not prove the futility or incompetence of capitalism in general. Similarly, the healthcare. gov website screw-up is not a particularly persuasive indictment of the utility of government in all cases, although it does suggest some concrete lessons for how large-scale IT rollouts should be handled in the future. As chapter 11 discusses, we often are quick to make a classic error of logic when we abstract from one concrete instance to a general claim about large-scale institutions. The only larger lesson to be drawn from the healthcare.gov rollout is that there are costs to decades of deprecating government service in general, and failing adequately to maintain agencies' infrastructures.

We Are Better Than This in fact argues that the progressive movement in the United States has made three fundamental strategic blunders over the years. First, the movement allowed conservatives to corner the market in encomia for the virtues of thrift, hard work, and personal responsibility. Progressives also embrace these virtues—they just are sensible enough to see the pervasive role that luck plays in actual outcomes. Because outcomes are uncertain, the collective purchase of reasonable levels of social insurance promotes socially useful risk-taking and enhances the overall welfare of society.

Second, the progressive movement allowed "redistribution" to be viewed as a value-neutral term, when it is not. You can observe this when reading a passage by substituting "social insurance" for "redistribution" every time the latter appears, and then noting how the sense of the passage changes.

Third, and most surprisingly, progressives have been fixated for over 100 years on the progressive income tax as their policy objective, when in fact what they should focus on is promoting a progressive fiscal system—that is, the net of all the "gives" and "gets" between a citizen and her government. Again, spending, not taxing, is the real purpose of government in its fiscal capacity, and it turns out that regressive taxes can and do fund genuinely progressive spending programs that, net, lead to more progressive outcomes.

THE BOOK'S AMBITIONS

Beyond its overarching goal of encouraging resistance to the gravitational pull of fiscal jerkdom, *We Are Better Than This* incorporates several congruent ambitions, all filtered through my unbridled enthusiasm for tax and budget policy. Rethinking what we ask of government requires our active engagement in the political process, armed with accurate information about what we are doing today, how well we are doing it, and how much it might cost to do it better. I therefore situate the United States as one country among many, and I construct report cards for the current health and performance of our society and our government across a range of important functions. When these report cards are examined objectively, we emerge as much less exceptional than we pretend to be, except in some unhappy ways, like our insistence on spending much more on healthcare (nearly $1 trillion every year in excess spending) than we would if we were to spend the same per capita as the next most profligate country in the world—without materially better outcomes in most cases.

Second, I present in an accessible manner current academic research into fundamental questions about the structure of our society and the trade-offs we face when a government tries to intervene. Who really pays the corporate income tax? Is inequality really growing, or is that just an artifact of how we measure it? Do tax cuts pay for themselves? There often are consensus answers among academics to these sorts of question, but the fruits of the research are poorly disseminated. More disturbingly, our information channels are choked with disreputable rascals who employ sophisticated rhetorical sleights of hand to make superficially plausible arguments to advance political agendas, rather than to increase understanding of our tax and budget policies. I therefore do my best to dissipate the fog of our fiscal wars. The result often is not one inevitable answer, but at least a narrower range of sensible options than our current overheated debates might suggest.

With this grounding in economic facts and analytical methods, the book turns to how government might usefully make things better, in ways that reflect our deepest values. These values include our strong commitment to private enterprise, both because private enterprise in general is the path to greater national wealth and because the circumstances in which it flowers also are conducive to the preservation of personal liberties. I therefore look for channels where government can productively complement the private sector, not replace it. I emphasize two: public investment and social insurance. The second in particular is conceptually important, because it brings into focus the important question of the role of luck in life's material outcomes, and what inferences we should draw from that.

Finally, the book returns to the area of my own academic work, which is the design of our tax system. Again, government does not exist to tax: it exists to spend, and tax design is just a question of how efficiently to raise the necessary revenues to support productive government spending. But of course there are smart and dumb ways to impose taxes, and I therefore suggest how we might move past some of the bad ideas that we currently embrace.

THE BOOK'S DATA SOURCES

Writing a book like this sometimes has the feeling of chasing one's own tail, because governmental agencies regularly update the data that they publish on our government's spending and taxing, and because new studies come out constantly. Whenever possible, I draw my data from the most reliable nonpartisan resources, such as the Congressional Budget Office, the staff of the Joint Committee on Taxation, and the Organisation for Economic Co-operation and Development. The book's data generally are current as of December 2013. Nonetheless, the fiscal trends that the book describes and the fundamental tensions that bedevil our public discourse surrounding our conception of government will not disappear in the immediate future, and I therefore hope that the book will be found useful even after the bloom is off the rose of the data I present.

Since this book entered production, a new book by Thomas Piketty, *Capital in the Twenty-First Century*, has rightly attracted enormous interest. Piketty's new volume appeared too late to be incorporated directly into this book's arguments, but I do rely on several of his earlier papers. Serendipitously for me, the two volumes are complementary in their objectives. Piketty studies long-term historical trends in inequality, and emphasizes that in low-growth eras capital, if left unchecked, can grow to levels where "patrimonial capitalists" dominate society and erode democratic values. Piketty's solution, which he himself acknowledges to be unrealistic, is a global wealth tax.

This book also recognizes the central importance of economic inequality, but paints a somewhat broader picture of the welfare of contemporary Americans. Instead of looking back through history, I emphasize cross-country comparisons across a wide range of welfare metrics among contemporary affluent countries. I do this to puncture the narcissistic bubble of American exceptionalism in which so many Americans live. I also focus on the vagaries of American political rhetoric and budget processes, which of course are not germane to Piketty's magisterial exploration of economic history.

Ultimately, this book tells a more optimistic story than does Piketty's major contribution. Early on, I deliver our dismal national report card, but I then explain how all of us, working together through the medium of government, can complement private markets in ways that lead to better economic outcomes (in the narrow sense) and welfare for all Americans, not just the patrimonial capitalists—in other words, how all of us can participate in improvements in our country's future national report cards. This book thus is a principled call for the reinvigoration of government as a positive complement to private enterprise in contemporary America. Finally, my substantive proposals, and in particular my ideas about comprehensive tax reform, are targeted to the immediate needs of the United States, which again was not the goal of Piketty's volume.

A CLOSING APOLOGY

This is a long book, but one that covers a great deal of ground. I have endeavored to give useful citations to important academic contributions in each field that I discuss; in general, I err on the side of citing recent contributions, on the theory that they typically incorporate discussions of earlier foundational works.

To every academic who picks up this volume, checks the references in the back, fails to see his name, and therefore assumes the work to be useless tripe, I ask your forbearance. If I were to cite every paper that has any relevance to the topics I cover, the endnotes alone would occupy several volumes. I hope that I have captured the sense of current academic debates on the themes I develop, but I cannot possibly identify every contribution to those debates.

More generally, I am profoundly grateful to the academic community as a whole for the kind welcome I have received in academia, despite my *arriviste* status. Writing this book has been a forceful demonstration of just how demanding our discipline is, and I am filled with admiration for those who have pursued it productively for decades.

WE ARE BETTER THAN THIS

PART I

OUR FISCAL SOUL IN PERIL

CHAPTER 1

THE HAPPINESS OF SOCIETY

> *Nothing tends so much to promote public spirit as the study of politics.... [P]olitical disquisitions, if just, and reasonable, and practicable, are of all works of speculation the most useful. Even the weakest and the worst of them are not altogether without their utility. They serve at least to animate the public passions of men, and rouse them to seek out the means of promoting the happiness of the society.*
>
> —ADAM SMITH, *The Theory of Moral Sentiments*,
> Part IV, Chap. 1.

FISCAL POLICY AND OUR HAPPINESS

We are a nation consumed by one great imperative, which is to protect our freedoms. But somehow many of us have confused our personal wealth with our political liberties, and in doing so have precipitated both an endless series of arid political debates over the role of government in our lives, and one unnecessary federal budget crisis after another. These debates have obscured from view the real topic that should interest us, which is, what can we do to enhance what Adam Smith meant by "the happiness of the society"? To answer this question requires an inquiry into how states help their citizens to be happier within a society than they would be on their own.

The essence of a state as a political construct is that it exercises the power of coercion over its own citizens. Anything else is a club, or a charity. The great virtue of a democracy is that all citizens participate at least indirectly in how government's power is exercised over them, and each citizen's vote is weighted the same as every other's. These are the political liberties on which our government was founded. But even democracies compel their own citizens' actions.

Many in the United States today argue that government as a concept is fundamentally suspect for the very reason that distinguishes a state from a club or a charity. Personal economic liberty—in short, an unalloyed right to keep what is mine—is seen as the only value that leads to the happiness of society; the police function of protecting personal economic liberty in turn is seen as government's one proper role.

The irony is that the United States applies a particularly light touch in this regard to Americans not currently incarcerated—with one great exception, which is taxation, and one minor one, which is jury duty. But from this failure to distinguish a state from a club springs a hatred of taxation wholly disproportionate to the reduction in our personal consumption that taxes entail, because taxation is the only significant manifestation of direct government coercion that affects most of us each year.

This book argues that the strand of contemporary American political thought that defines itself through its hatred of taxation is narcissistic self-pleading wrapped in a flimsy sheath of economic lingo. Personal economic liberty, of course, is one foundational principle of our country and our economy, but it is not the only principle that defines us; and the emaciated government that this philosophy demands is not the way to promote the happiness of society, if by that we actually mean the society composed of all of us who identify ourselves as Americans. Our fixation on taxation means that we have turned our thinking upside down: instead of focusing on what government might usefully do, and whether we can afford it, we obsess over the taxing side of things, and ignore the purposes to which those tax revenues are applied.

This book responds to these narcissistic false syllogisms. Its purpose is to provide readers with a fair and comprehensive review of how we collectively are doing in promoting the happiness of our society, to explain fundamental economic and political precepts relevant to analyzing our options, and to propose programs by which government spending can enhance our welfare—meaning both our material prosperity and the intangible values that contribute to our society's tranquility and happiness. Finally, the book addresses how best to design tax systems to finance those spending programs, keeping in mind our national preferences for modesty in tax demands and the central importance of private enterprise.

In other words, this is a book about *fiscal policy*—the technical term for government spending and the taxes that finance that spending.[1] It is also a book about limits: every government intervention has costs, and not every moral imperative can be wholly honored. The art of fiscal policymaking lies in deciding these hard cases in rational ways that honor *all* the deep values of a society.

My metaphor is that of our "fiscal soul": it captures the idea that we choose to articulate many of the values that distinguish us as a country, and that advance our society's happiness, through the mediation of government. As former congressman Barney Frank was fond of saying, government is just the things we decide to do together. We give expression to the shared values we wish to promote in large measure by deciding to invest in them. We all kick in money into a central pot through taxes, and we spend that money to promote the happiness of our society. To breathe new life into the common themes that define us as Americans, we must reclaim our fiscal soul, by embracing opportunities where government (that is, all of us, acting together) can improve our collective welfare through thoughtful spending programs.

Our fiscal soul is malleable, and our articulation of it often aspirational. Nonetheless, most of us would agree that the shared values to which we aspire include a commitment to genuine freedom of opportunity for all Americans, which in turn requires access to adequate nutrition and to high-quality education, regardless of income levels. We are appalled at the thought of seniors, or children, or veterans, living in grinding poverty. We reject racism, sexism, religious intolerance, or other invidious distinctions among us. We love the American landscape, and embrace the importance of clean air and water. At the same time, our shared values include respect for individual autonomy, and impatience with centralized meddling without good cause. And to a large extent we Americans define ourselves by our work; as a result, we are committed to the idea that every working-age American should have the opportunity to find and prosper at a satisfying personal work career. Thoughtful fiscal policy—the spending we decide to do together—breathes life into these aspirational values.

Stephen Colbert (the comedian, not Louis XIV's finance minister of France) once remarked that the United States is the new Sparta, except less tolerant of homosexuality. It is true that we spend an extraordinary amount on our military—about 42 percent of the entire world's military budget—but the metaphor of our fiscal soul reminds us that we define ourselves as more than a standing army, and that thoughtful government spending and taxing actually advance the values we hold dearest, and thereby the happiness of our society.

THE INSTRUMENTS OF FISCAL POLICY

Moral imperatives and collective economic opportunities align particularly well in two broad categories of fiscal intervention: social insurance and investment. Social insurance (the subject of chapter 11) is the easier of the two to visualize, and is an instrument that we already employ in many instances, like Medicare or Social Security.

Insurance is fundamentally about risk transfer and risk distribution. An individual transfers the financial risks of some adverse fortuity—a car accident, a house fire, or dying prematurely, to take three familiar cases—to a larger group, thereby distributing the risk across the group. Risk distribution from an individual's perspective turns an uncertain but very large cost into a certain but small and predictable one—the insurance premium. So long as the adverse fortuities are uncorrelated with each other (my house fire is not causally connected to your house fire), insurance companies can rely on the law of large numbers and actuarial research to turn the unpredictability of a single adverse event into a predictable stream of outflows across the larger group, which enables insurance premiums to be priced.

Private insurance markets are not complete: we cannot insure through private markets against every adverse fortuity that we might wish to. In other cases, private insurance is essentially inefficient, because of the fundamental problem of adverse selection—the tendency of those with private information that they are more likely to need insurance to be the first to step forward to buy it. Voluntary private health insurance is riddled with adverse selection dilemmas, and the methods used by private insurers to address this problem make the market expensive and incomplete.

Governments are extremely effective at complementing private insurers, because the tools of insurance are right at governments' fingertips. Governments typically have available to them a large captive pool of risks (their residents or citizens), thereby making risk distribution possible. If the insurance pool is defined broadly enough and is mandatory, government can remove in one blow the problem that bedevils private insurers of adverse selection. Governments have available low-overhead mechanisms to collect the requisite premiums: taxes. Finally, a government insurance program is an exercise in the pure mutualization of risks: the government as insurer is in the game to administer the transfer of risks among the participants in the pool, and to pay out claims from the premiums collected, but not to make a profit for itself.

The case for government as insurer thus is often an easy one to make. Indeed, this is why most developed countries run health insurance as a government insurance program.

At a more fundamental level, we cannot insure in private markets against all the random allocations of bad fortune that drive many of life's outcomes. Those who are born with the requisite genes to grow up tall, handsome, and clever often are befuddled by why others seem to struggle so hard to accomplish so little, or worse yet give up struggling. If we think about things a bit, though, we should appreciate that our founding fathers really did not create a government premised on the belief that happy material outcomes are outward manifestations of inner good karma stored up from past lives. Good fortune makes prosperous outcomes much easier, as the discussions later in this chapter and throughout the book demonstrate.

To acknowledge the pervasive role of fortune in our material lives does not imply a conspiracy to "level down," or to "mooch" off the productive elements in society, but rather a commitment to offer all members of society a reasonably fair foundation on which to build productive lives. In the end, we as a society are richer, not poorer, through these interventions, and we also are more tranquil, and therefore happier. The question remains, however, just how much of this sort of insurance we can afford to buy. That is what makes fiscal policy interesting and challenging, once we get past the convenient mythologies that we invoke to shield ourselves and our assets from serious engagement with the issues.

Government investment (chapter 10) has a disreputable air about it, as if by this term I am going to advocate ersatz Soviet-style five-year plans, in which the federal government either props up private firms that cannot survive on their own or tries to pick the Next Big Thing in which to invest. Everyone understands this to be a loser's game, at least in normal times: the government is a mediocre venture capitalist, at best, and the case for this sort of intervention generally is difficult to make.[2] Where private markets function smoothly, there is, or should be, a heavy presumption against government investment. Indeed, the problem we confront in this regard is exactly the opposite: we use the tax code today to make all sorts of government interventions in private markets, by subsidizing one or another industry or type of private investment. The trick here is not for the government to intervene more, but for us to recognize how often, and how pointlessly, it intervenes today through the hidden mechanism of tax subsidies.

But not all government investments are disreputable. Education is one obvious and critically important example that I will return to several times over the course of this book.

Tangible public goods like infrastructure investments also can work very well as government programs. Governments can appropriately take a broader view than can a private firm of the returns to an infrastructure investment, because a government ultimately cares (or should care) about the well-being of its citizens. So infrastructure investments that generate good construction jobs (and perhaps in difficult economic times enable people to preserve work skills and avoid falling back on government safety net programs) have positive spillover benefits that a government—that is, all the people, acting together—can take into account along with the direct returns from the investment, but that would not show up on a private firm's profit and loss statement.

Governments also can take a longer view of an infrastructure investment's payback period than can most private firms, since a government's long-term viability is largely assured. Private firms must price into any "public-private partnership" infrastructure project the risks of future government administrations trying to renegotiate or cancel the deal, but the government does not have to charge a premium to itself to cover any possible future bad faith behavior by it. Governments typically have lower costs of debt finance than do private firms, particularly in the construction industry. And the government, unlike a private firm, does not need to earn a profit on its infrastructure investments. For all these reasons, it is unsurprising that private toll roads and the like remain a small fraction of public infrastructure investment in the United States.

OTHER TOOLS OF GOVERNMENT

Government can wield other instruments of coercion beyond the power to tax. In particular, government can choose the instrument of regulation. Regulation, under the rubric of "job-killing red tape" or the like, is possibly even more despised than is taxation. Much contemporary political rhetoric in this area has an odd Homeric quality, but without the hexameter: all the leading figures and institutions are everywhere preceded by their epithets. So, instead of "rosy-fingered dawn" and "wine-colored sea," we have "job-killing red tape." I sometimes imagine a missing chapter of the *Iliad*, in which swift-footed Achilles battles job-killing Red Tape below the towers of Troy.

Government also has available the instrument of conscription; that is how we used to staff our armed services, and how the pharaohs built the pyramids. Conscription, however, is not part of our current culture.

Regulation includes the quasi-police function through which government ensures that private markets in fact operate efficiently (e.g., through the disclosure rules of the Securities Exchange Commission). But more interestingly for this book, regulation also can function like a form of hidden taxation, but one in which private actors retain a bit of operational control.

This book is not about choosing among these different instruments as much as it is an exploration of how government spending (and the taxing necessary to fund it) can be restored to its rightful place as an instrument to promote the happiness of our society; regulation by itself does not lead to better government insurance or investment programs. Nonetheless, regulation and taxation can sometimes serve as substitutes for one another. The right place to begin in every case is whether a government intervention of some sort is warranted, and if so, what is the right tool to effect that intervention—regulation or taxation?[3] The usual questions are: Which is administratively easier? Which is fairer? Which is better targeted to solving the problem without unnecessary additional burdens?

A good example in the arena of fiscal policy is the theme known in policy circles as "making work pay." The idea is that there are substantial positive returns to society from helping adults to enter and remain in the workforce, through assisting them in overcoming some of the hidden costs (child care arrangements, bus fare, cost of uniforms) that make the first step from unemployment to employment surprisingly costly. One strategy is a subsidy delivered to low-income wage earners through the tax system (known as the earned income tax credit). Another is the minimum wage. One is nominally a tax solution (formally, a tax rebate), and the other a regulation, but the two point in the same general direction. The principal difference between the two is where the burden of the rule falls in the first instance—on all taxpayers (the earned income tax credit) or on employers (the minimum wage). (There are meaningful second-order differences as well: some portion of the intended tax subsidy can be captured by employers reducing employees's wages, and some beneficiaries of the minimum wage are the children of affluent families holding after-school or summer jobs.)

In some cases, direct regulation that either mandates some positive behavior or forbids some undesirable one is the right instrument. Immunization is a good example of this last category. To achieve "herd immunity" and thereby suppress a disease even among those not immunized, it is necessary that a large proportion (say 85 percent) of a population be vaccinated. In this case, your decision to forgo vaccination affects not just your health but that of your neighbors as well. For this reason, governments (under our Constitution, typically state governments) often require that individuals receive vaccinations. Even though vaccination rates can never reach 100 percent, the herd immunity effect can protect the minority of the population that is not vaccinated, but the government effectively must compel every member of society that it can reach to be vaccinated, to ensure that the herd immunity threshold is reached, and because it would be viewed as unfair for one citizen to declare that he is the only one who is permitted to opt out.

Fundamental civil rights legislation, or Title IX (requiring equal treatment of female and male athletes in school athletic programs), or the Americans with Disabilities Act (requiring that facilities open to the public be made handicap-accessible) are other examples of regulations that prohibit certain behavior, or that mandate new behaviors. As such, they do not contemplate the fine-tuning of responses that a pollution tax does, because our society decided that no one should buy his way out of compliance with these goals. But the out-of-pocket compliance costs of these sorts of programs, particularly in the case of mandated positive action, are similar in effect to a tax on the objects of the mandate. That is, just as with an explicit tax, affected actors in the private sector are compelled to part with cash, but in the case of regulations the money goes to pay for specific goods (handicap-accessible bathrooms, for example) whose acquisition is overseen by the taxpayer.

Different forms of regulation and taxation thus constitute a continuum of possible government interventions; often, one can substitute for the other, particularly in the commercial sphere. In such cases, it is accurate to see regulation as simply a different form of taxation (or for that matter, the other way around). But even when regulation and taxation are close substitutes, they do not receive identical treatment in government accounts. Our standard metrics for describing what government does (taxes collected, deficits incurred, government spending as a percentage of gross domestic product) do not track the cost of regulating one activity, or prohibiting another.

This fundamental difference in "salience"—in the visibility of government's hand on the marketplace or our individual lives—can sometimes lead to distorted decisions, when for example government chooses the low salience instrument (regulation) to accomplish a task more logically handled by the higher salience one (taxing). The difference in salience also means that it theoretically is difficult to make comparisons across radically different societies. A highly regulated low-taxed country may suffer more "deadweight loss"—the distortions in individuals' behavior induced by government intervention—than would be true of a higher-taxed country with more functional markets. In practice, however, the developed economies of the world are not so different in their choice of governmental instruments as to make such comparisons inaccurate.

NATIONAL WELFARE IS NOT NATIONAL INCOME

Years ago, in the midst of the Mexican sovereign debt crisis, James Carville famously remarked that in his next life he wanted to come back as the Bond Market. The Bond Market is remorseless, almost insatiable, and ultimately unbeatable, as the slow motion train wreck of euro sovereign borrowers in 2012 reminded us. From Ireland to Portugal to Greece to Spain to Italy, the market turns to prey on the weakest of the herd of borrowers, until its demands are satisfied, or no more blood can be drained from the borrower's corpse.

It sometimes seems as if in our public discourse we share a similar attitude toward another institution, which we describe as the Economy. We do this when we measure every policy proposal almost entirely in terms of its alleged contribution to the Economy, usually framed in terms of aggregate gross domestic product (GDP). GDP essentially totes up the value of all the goods and services we produce in explicitly transactional settings in the United States. Even within the domain of work, narrowly construed, GDP captures only a fraction of our real work contributions: work within the household, for example, is ignored.

To measure every policy by its alleged effects on GDP is a sophomoric understanding of the human condition and the role of government. What we should care about is our aggregate welfare, which is not the same thing at all. "Welfare" incorporates all the instances of happiness, well-being, satisfaction, contentment, or similar concepts that together add up to what we would describe as an authentic and good life.[4] It is exactly what the framers of our Constitution had in mind when they provided (Article I, Section 8) that the Congress had the power "to lay and collect taxes...to provide for...the general welfare of the United States."

This use of "welfare" is commonplace in modern economics and the social sciences generally, but it is very different from how the term is used in ordinary conversations, where it connotes a program designed to help the poor, usually in a derogatory sense. Of course the welfare of individuals in poverty is enhanced by "welfare" programs, but the use of the word in the second context confuses matters. Such programs more neutrally are "income support" programs, when viewed from the perspective of their objectives, or "means-tested" programs, when viewed from the perspective of their eligibility criteria.

The logical error of conflating a nation's GDP with its welfare is endemic. Consider, for example, the famous economist Milton Friedman, whose popular work emphasized the theme that capitalism and freedom were joined at the hip.[5] In Friedman's construct, unalloyed capitalism supported the cause of personal freedom, and near-absolute personal freedom in turn was the foundation of successful capitalist systems: to interfere with one was to jeopardize the other. This worldview leaves little room for government to articulate any shared values beyond those required to host laissez-faire economic tournaments.

Thus, Friedman was mystified by the existence of national parks: "If the public wants this kind of activity enough to pay for it, private enterprises will have every incentive to provide such parks. And, of course, there are many private enterprises of this nature now in existence. I cannot myself conjure up any . . . [reasons] that would justify governmental activity in this area."[6] Putting to one side the factual error—there are no private enterprises in the business of offering customers privately owned million-acre authentic mountain wildernesses—Friedman's argument boiled down to the claim that, because he did not understand the value of wilderness or the symbolic pull of the national parks as an expression of national pride, no such values could possibly exist.

Yet millions of annual visitors—four million a year at Yosemite alone—not to mention calendars and coffee table books, point otherwise: many Americans take solace in our common ownership of some of the world's most beautiful terrain, and enjoy the thought that we collectively maintain places where the wild things really are. We accept an apparent economic efficiency cost (a small increase in taxes, which means a constraint on our individual freedom to spend our money exclusively on our private pleasures), in order to fund a portion of the cost of these great commonly owned resources that are open to all of us. We pay for the rest through user fees, but we keep those fees to a reasonable level, and use the tax system to pay the remainder, precisely to ensure that access is within the reach of most Americans.

National parks are an example of how national welfare and national product do not always perfectly overlap. And we reach agreement that national parks or other instances of government spending beyond the narrowest possible police functions "promote the happiness of the society" through the mediation of the political system, which is the forum in which consensus is forged and national values are articulated.

As a more recent example, Britons in 2012 enjoyed not only the usual clutch of holidays, but also the Olympics and the Queen's Diamond Jubilee (conveniently organized to offer workers a four-day weekend). One business organization responded by urging that this sort of frivolity should cease, as it was sure to cut into Great Britain's 2012 GDP. *Financial Times* columnist John Kay nicely skewered this sort of thinking:

> One could analyse these effects indefinitely, but the only thing to be gained from the exercise would be insight into the conventions of national accounting. Measuring output is of interest only as a step on the road towards measuring something else....After all, we could raise GDP further by cancelling Christmas (though we would lose the expenditure on unwanted gifts), taking shorter vacations (though think of the impact on easyJet), and by working till we drop from exhaustion. But why would we want to? The idea that there is something called "the economy," which is separable from the welfare of society and its citizens, is silly. There isn't. What really matters is whether the holiday, and the celebration, makes [sic] us better off. That question answers itself without need of economic statistics.[7]

Throughout the study of fiscal policy, our metrics, like GDP, often come to frame our thinking: because hunger in America, for example, reduces national incomes in ways not visible from casual inspection of GDP data, and because the misery that follows from poverty is wholly ignored, we tend to give short shrift to these fundamental issues of welfare, unless they are recast in econometric terms.

The country of Bhutan recognized this framing problem, and at one point in time replaced GDP as its official measure of its year-to-year development with GHP—its gross happiness product (although recently it has returned to more conventional measurement norms).[8] This is an adorable conceit, but one perhaps not terribly practical when applied to the United States, which accounts for about one-fourth of the world's income. The idea behind this book therefore is not to urge the abandonment of GDP as a policy tool, but to invite meditation on the underlying assumptions behind metrics like GDP, and the limits they impose on our public discourse.

WHAT DOES GDP ACTUALLY MEASURE?

Deep in the bowels of every business is an accounting system, and at the foundation of that accounting system is the general ledger. The general ledger is the place where all of a firm's transactions are recorded (technically, recorded twice, in double entry bookkeeping). From the general ledger the firm's accountants distill more abstracted (and more useful) pictures of the firm's wealth at a point in time (the balance sheet) or its income over a period of time (the income statement).

The closest analogy that the country as a whole has to a general ledger are the dozens of accounts that together comprise the National Income and Product Accounts, or NIPAs.[9] The NIPAs are produced by the Bureau of Economic Analysis (a division of the Commerce Department). The NIPAs' star attraction for economic analysis and political wrangling is the calculation of GDP.

The NIPAs are complemented by the Federal Reserve Board's Flow of Funds Reports. These reports can be understood as tracking the flows of money from households, businesses, and governments with money to save or invest to other households, businesses, and governments in need of financing. The Flow of Funds Reports are the only government reports that give a comprehensive picture of the assets and liabilities of households, including net worth.

The two sets of data are now closely integrated, so that but for the accident of which government entity produces which, the NIPAs and the Flow of Funds Reports can be viewed as one comprehensive record of the value added by the economy and the modes of financing of investments in a specific time period.[10]

The federal government produces a great many other datasets beyond the NIPAs and Flow of Funds Reports that are relevant to understanding how we as a country are doing. The Bureau of Labor Statistics compiles employment data; the Census Bureau collects useful personal information through the census, and also publishes statistical compilations of median incomes and the like; the IRS Statistics of Information Division publishes aggregated data drawn from the 140 million tax returns filed every year (so that you can look up how many tax returns claimed a charitable contribution deduction, or the minimum income required for admission onto the list of the 400 highest-income taxpayers for a year); and so on. I sometimes suspect that the best reason to get a PhD in public finance economics is because somewhere along the line someone must hand you the secret handbook telling you which agency collects which data, under which name.

Notwithstanding this torrent of useful information, GDP is the right place to start, because it figures so prominently in all our thinking about our economic health. It turns out that GDP is a more exotic concept than most people realize, and does not even purport to measure what most of us think it does.

GDP does not measure income, in the same sense that the tax code or an accountant uses the term, nor does it measure the country's wealth, or even its change in wealth. And GDP certainly does not directly compete with Bhutan's former calculation of gross national happiness as a measure of our collective welfare, in any complete sense.[11]

There are many equivalent ways of describing what GDP does measure. GDP can be said to measure the total "value added" over a specified period of time by the visible market economy of the United States—the dollar value of all goods and services created in the United States for sale to final customers (that is, ignoring business-to-business intermediate sales). Another way of phrasing matters that may resonate with readers accustomed to corporate income statements is that GDP measures the sum of all compensation income for labor performed in the United States, plus what business people might recognize as a sort of mega-EBITDA— that is, the earnings of all US businesses, after compensation and other costs of earning that income, but before taking into account interest or other financing expenses, depreciation (the allowance for the wear and tear on the machines and structures used to produce goods for sale), and any tax costs. The first way of phrasing things looks to the value of production, the second to the gross income earned from producing everything.

The two formulations are conceptually equivalent. The value added through production must translate into income for someone as soon as the production is reduced to cash—either the workers who provide their labor or the owners of businesses. So by definition, aggregate gross incomes of labor and business must equal the value of aggregate gross production.

GDP has some of the same flavor in an eighteenth-century insight called Say's Law (after Jean-Baptiste Say), but Say (or at least followers of Say) took matters one step further. Say asserted that production creates its own demand—that once value is created, and labor or business owners realize income, then they must do something with that income, and the only two things that you can do with your income is to spend the money on current consumption or to invest it (ultimately in more means of production). So, said Say, creating value creates income, which creates demand, because that's all you can do with your income—you demand other stuff with it. In other words, build it, and they will come. Say's Law is the great-grandparent of supply-side economic logic.

At its logical extreme, Say's Law (or perhaps Say's Lore) argues that there can be no such thing as depressions or massive recessions, which we know do occur. John Maynard Keynes's contribution was to create a logical story as to why production does not always create its own demand, and why in fact demand is sometimes needed to prod the supply side along. Keynes's core prescription basically was that, since the private sector under-demands things in recessions, government should pick up the slack by borrowing and spending (demanding goods and services) until the economy recovers its equilibrium, at which point the government's borrowings can be paid down.

The national accounts from which GDP is drawn properly are agnostic on whether supply (production) creates demand, or vice versa, or whether the answer varies as economies, like spinning tops, sometimes list this way, and then the other. All that the national accounts do is to assert that aggregate gross incomes must equal aggregate value added, without inserting any kind of causality arrow into the picture.

It is worth teasing apart the limitations implied in the definition of GDP. First, as its name reminds us, GDP is a measure of *gross* value added in a period. This means that GDP ignores depreciation—the wear and tear or obsolescence over the same period of the existing "capital stock," which is to say the aggregate amount invested in greasy machinery, buildings, and important intangible assets like computer software, all of which are used to create the added value. Part of the gross domestic product needs to be set aside to replenish this erosion in investment, to get an accurate picture of how much value we actually have created in a period.

Think of the economy for a minute as a single farmer. If the farmer were to eat his seed corn in 2012, GDP would record that consumption as a boost to GDP in 2012. Of course, come 2013, the farmer would starve. The Bureau of Economic Analysis also tracks *net* domestic product (unimaginatively called NDP), which does set aside an amount each year to fund the seed corn for the future, but for whatever reason it has never been the headliner that GDP is.

Second, GDP is a measure of the productivity of economic activities that take place within the United States, regardless of who owns the income-producing assets. A US business owned by a mysterious Lichtenstein trust adds to the GDP of the United States, even if all the profits are distributed to Lichtenstein. And conversely, a German beer company owned entirely by US persons, who earn enormous returns on their investment, contributes nothing to GDP. When people talk about GDP they often really have in mind gross national product, which measures the value added by investments owned by US persons, wherever situated in the world, and excludes US-generated income streams that are owned by foreigners.

Third, GDP is firmly based in the market economy. It ignores illegal businesses, but more important, it ignores all the value created by human beings in the private sphere of their lives—housework, child care, or do-it-yourself projects done for yourself or for your family, rather than for money. (Economists describe this arbitrary demarcation as defining the "production boundary.") This leads to the old joke, no doubt still considered riotously funny at the Bureau of Economic Analysis, about the economics professor who wrecked the economy by marrying his housekeeper: what had been commercial activity (providing housekeeping services for compensation) moved over to the private sphere, and thereby disappeared from view for GDP purposes. The statisticians recorded a drop in GDP when all that had transpired was an increase in married couples.

In reality, the exclusion of the private sphere of human activity from official GDP statistics is no joke, and materially understates the sum total of value added during our waking hours. This limitation is widely understood, and attempts have been made from time to time to quantify it (including attempting to set a value on leisure itself), but obviously precise data on the value added by all the homeowners of America through their assembly of IKEA furniture is hard to come by.

Bureau of Economic Analysis professionals have recently published a fascinating study of the size of this extra-market economy.[12] The study concludes that in

2010 "nonmarket services"—basically, things we do in the private spheres of our lives that we could hire someone else to do (child care, housework, etc.)—had a value of roughly $3.8 trillion, against an official GDP for the year of just under $15 trillion. If included in the official accounts, these nonmarket services therefore would have increased GDP by 26 percent.

The same paper also determined that the value of nonmarket services for the family was a much larger percentage of official GDP in 1965, accounting for some 39 percent of official GDP. The value of nonmarket services as a percentage of GDP has gone down over the last 45 years because women in particular have entered the workforce in increasing numbers. As they did so, they crossed the production boundary and became visible in the official statistics.

But to the extent that families now have to pay outsiders for services that a stay-at-home spouse previously would have performed, crossing the production boundary means that the official data double count our incomes. If the second wage earner in a family earns $30,000 per year (ignoring taxes for simplicity), and the family spends $20,000 of that on services that the second wage earner would have performed for free in the private sphere of the couple's lives, the family really is ahead $10,000 in monetary value (ignoring other satisfactions that come from a career and the like). But GDP data record all $30,000 as a component of GDP—along with the $20,000 of services provided by others to the family.

Our official GDP data thus have behaved like the old joke about the professor, except in reverse: it is as if the professor got divorced and started paying his ex-wife to be his housekeeper. The double counting means that a measurable portion of the growth of incomes of Americans in the official data over the last 45 years just reflected a change in visibility, by virtue of crossing the production boundary—which means that in this respect we have overstated our actual economic growth by some 0.2 percent per year from 1965 to 2010.

GDP does incorporate the private sphere of our lives in one important respect, which is homeownership. The Bureau of Economic Analysis statisticians accept the problems inherent in excluding the private sphere (the production boundary) as a necessary evil, but they work very hard to avoid such artificial results where they can. Housing is the largest class of investment assets in the United States, and so measuring the annual value added by investments in housing is extremely important to our national statistics.

If you rent your home, things fit easily into the standard metrics. Your rent is an annual consumption expense—it is one of the ways you spend your money on yourself for the year in question. And on the other side, your landlord is running a business, and the rental income (net of maintenance and other business costs) shows up as part of total value added by the market economy.

But what if you own your own home? Then you suddenly have retreated to the private side of the production boundary, and if nothing more were done, the contribution of your investment in your home to annual value added would disappear beneath the surface of the GDP ocean.

To keep renters and homeowners on the same footing, the Bureau of Economic Analysis adopts a rule that makes a great deal of sense to economists, and almost none at all to generation after generation of first-year tax law students, where the concept (called imputed income in that context) is discussed at length. The statisticians pretend that a homeowner is in the business of renting her home to herself. They therefore create a hypothetical income statement, showing the rent that the homeowner (wearing her tenant hat) hypothetically paid to herself (wearing her landlord hat). They further treat expenses of earning that hypothetical rental income just like other business expenses. Now a homeowner shows up in the national accounts as both a renter and a landlord, simultaneously.[13]

The Bureau of Economic Analysis collects data on rental rates around the country, and uses that data to estimate (to impute, in their lingo) the hypothetical rental values of all the owner-occupied homes in America, but obviously those values assume a gigantic market that does not really exist. Moreover, as housing prices soared in the early 2000s, the statisticians assumed that rental values for owner-occupied homes would go *down* as a percentage of market value, because landlords would expect to capture a large part of their economic return in the form of capital gains. In turn, as explained below, capital gains are ignored in calculating GDP. But when housing prices collapsed in the Great Recession, that same logic would suggest that imputed rental values as a percentage of market value must go up, to give homeowners, wearing their hypothetical landlord hats, a better return on their investment. One therefore should expect to see owner-occupied housing making a larger contribution to GDP just at the time that homeowners were mired in economic despair.

So GDP overstates our annual increment to national well-being in the sense that by definition it does not reflect an allowance for setting aside next year's seed corn, measures domestic value added rather than value added by assets controlled by Americans, understates our total productivity to the extent that it ignores the private sphere of our lives, including that portion that we could plausibly hire others to do for us, and adds to GDP a large number of market transactions that do not actually exist, in the case of owner-occupied housing. And of course GDP does not purport to value any of the other things that give our lives meaning, like the time I spend cycling rather than teaching.

GDP also does not measure our annual income in another critically important respect, because it completely ignores capital gains and losses. The idea is that GDP measures the annual value added by the economy—the product created in the year—or alternatively the income generated *by that production*. Capital gains are not part of the engine of production; they simply represent someone cashing in on a change in price for an existing asset, but that asset will continue to produce the same added value in the hands of the new owner. And on the downside, capital losses (whether realized or unrealized) also are ignored, even though they represent an immediate loss in wealth. Viewed more abstractly, in economic theory, an increase in value for a productive asset logically represents a discounting to today of all the future income the asset is expected to generate; since GDP measures value added this year, including capital gains effectively would mix expected future incomes with current incomes. (Here is a place where the Federal Reserve's Flow of Funds Report complements the GDP data nicely.)

Of course, the things that money can buy, including money derived from capital gains, do end up in GDP, if those things are produced in the United States. So depending on consumption patterns, capital gains do indirectly feed into GDP. But things get very complicated very quickly if you want to tease apart how much GDP growth is a real (permanent) increase in productivity, and how much is just a temporary run-up in consumption goods purchases fueled by an asset bubble. This is highly relevant, because the United States has endured two great asset bubbles in the last 15 years—the Internet boom of the late 1990s and the housing bubble of the mid-2000s. So one can fairly ask, how much of GDP growth in the 1990s was a permanent uptick in productivity of the economy, and how much the side effect of an asset bubble flooding Americans with newfound (and in many cases very temporary) wealth?

You can see the difference between GDP and income, as we ordinarily use the latter term, if you ponder for a minute the consequence of an uptick in automobile accidents in light of the treatment of capital gains and losses, as well as the characterization of personal purchases of cars and other consumer durables as a form of immediate consumption. Any normal person would conclude that a rash of car crashes must lower GDP, because all those expensive cars have been destroyed, but a special sort of person, typically found only at the Bureau of Economic Analysis, would say no—more accidents mean more GDP, at least assuming that the occupants of all those cars return to the workforce promptly. The cars themselves already have been accounted for as consumption, or alternatively can be viewed as constructively sold for a large capital loss, and meanwhile the ambulance services and other healthcare professionals are busier than ever, generating more production (in this case, in the form of services rather than tangible things). As explained by the authors of a study analyzing the international standards to which our government accounts now adhere, "It may seem strange that GDP rises if there are more road accidents.... On the contrary, one would intuitively like to see GDP diminishing in such circumstances. But this would be to confuse a measure of output (GDP) with a measure of welfare, which GDP is not. At most, GDP is a measure of the contribution of production to welfare. There are a great number of other dimensions to welfare that GDP does not claim to measure."[14]

GDP includes the value added by government as well. The treatment of government in the national accounts gets complex, but basically the idea is that transfer payments, including social security payments, are recorded as neutral (neither creating nor destroying value, just moving money around), and government spending on "free goods," like roads, defense, public schools, or the whole range of government services (air traffic controllers, Food and Drug Administration oversight of pharmaceuticals) is recorded as adding value. Most of the data are determined by actual or estimated market value, but here even the best statisticians give up, and record government spending on free goods as creating value equal to the cost expended on them.

So those readers who worship at the shrine of GDP should remember that the data take government spending at face value. If you really believe that government spending is the same as taking money and burning it, then our GDP is substantially lower than the numbers you read in the newspaper.

Finally, GDP itself is not an entirely static concept. In July 2013, for example, the Bureau of Economic Analysis changed how it measured GDP in some important respects, for example by treating the cost of research and development as an investment in an asset, rather than a current expense. The result was to increase the 2013 GDP of the United States by about 3 percent—an amount equal in size to the economy of Belgium.[15] More directly relevant to this book, because the revisions did not change actual tax collections, the revisions had the effect of reducing the amount of federal tax collections as a percentage of GDP—itself the most common metric used in Congress when debating the overall size of the tax system. The difference moved the needle substantially—reducing tax collections as a percentage of GDP by about 0.5 percent per year, for all years covered by the new methodology.

Notwithstanding this uncommonly large revision to its methodology, the calculation of GDP is sufficiently uncontroversial and objective that observers from across the political spectrum rarely debate the accuracy of the resulting figure. It is GDP's *meaning* that should be the topic of more discussion.

ALTERNATIVE WELFARE MEASURES

To summarize, GDP and similar metrics are poor surrogate measures of welfare.[16] First, GDP excludes all interactions that take place outside the marketplace. So, for example, performing one's own household work is not measured by GDP. GDP tells us nothing about whether the drivers of middle class financial survival over the last generation—the arrival of women in great numbers into the workplace, and the improvement in the wages they receive—are viewed within every family as welfare-enhancing, or as a stern financial necessity that constrains their innate preferences.

From the other direction, market transactions that respond to degradations in welfare nonetheless are included in GDP, simply because they are market transactions. For example, if crime increases, and as a result more police are hired, or individuals spend more on house alarm systems, these "defensive" expenditures increase GDP, while at the same time signaling developments that are problematic for welfare.[17]

Finally, measures like GDP per capita make no effort to reflect issues of inequality or poverty. A nation in which most of us are groundskeepers to plutocrats may not be a society whose welfare is as high as a nation of shopkeepers with lower aggregate GDP.

These are not simply academic observations. Because it is ubiquitous, easily described in news reports, comparable across different countries and relatively uncontroversial in its measurement, GDP tends to frame our sense of progress. This gives rise to the phenomenon of framing fiscal policy discourse in terms of a GDP Olympics with other countries. The results are false political conflicts, as between "growth" and "the environment," or the obfuscation of important social issues, as when statistics about per capita GDP crowd out questions surrounding the distribution of that national income. It may be that we are what we eat, but to a surprising extent our society is what we measure of it.

Social scientists have struggled to address the problem of our excessive reliance on GDP as a surrogate for welfare. One approach has been to measure "happiness" directly, principally through surveys. Proponents argue that empirical research methodologies are sophisticated enough to make the survey results reliable and meaningful, but others strongly disagree, either as to the reliability of surveys or as to their relevance to real-world policymaking.[18] There also are issues of cross-country comparability: Are the dour Swiss as able to admit to their own happiness as are the fun-loving Portuguese?

Another approach is to develop broader measures of welfare within the constraints of more traditional data collection methods. The best-known example of this is the Index of Sustainable Economic Welfare (ISEW), but the fact that most readers have never heard of the ISEW tells you all that you need to know about its general acceptance in the professional econometric community, much less in mainstream news outlets.[19] Like happiness surveys, the ISEW has been robustly criticized as relying too heavily on subjective inputs to be a reliable complement to GDP.

The point to take away from all this is that our collective welfare, which is the reason we band together to act together through the medium of government—and the good we want to maximize to have happy, meaningful lives—by design is not captured in GDP. Moreover, even if you construe welfare in the narrowest possible market economy sense, GDP is quite different from income, which presumably is what people think it is trying to measure. But because no better metric is at hand, we fall back on it.

As a society, we should care about more than winning a GDP Olympics: there are other values that define us as a unique society. To be sure, we care about the GDP Olympics more than we imagine our counterparts in France to care—that is one of our defining characteristics—but even so there is more to us as Americans than that. To say this is not to deny economics, but rather to recognize that we measure national product because it is easy to do so, when what we really mean to focus on is the broader concept of our welfare.

Every reader of this book already has fully formed ethical judgments, and my advocacy in support of particular moral imperatives will not change many minds. I therefore adopt throughout this book a morally indefensible but nonetheless realistic focus exclusively on national rather than global welfare, and on welfare consequences that ultimately have measurable productivity implications.[20]

Since this is a book about *national* fiscal policy, and since government spending comes from taxes we impose only on ourselves, my focus on national welfare viewed through the filter of measurable productivity has at least some practical justification. In light of the sorry state of our own awareness of our obligations to each other inside the United States, we should be so lucky as to have the occasion to revisit this narrow focus at some future date, when our fiscal soul is less in peril of utter extinguishment.

EQUALITY OF OPPORTUNITY

It is a commonplace of political disputations to argue that all that we can fairly ask of government is equality of opportunity—that our government does not exist to guarantee equality of outcomes. This may be right: government cannot make the homely handsome, and in the end fortune plays favorites for reasons opaque to us. Nonetheless, government in fact can do a great deal to give real substance to the phrase "equality of opportunity." Government does so when it militates against the worst outcomes, and creates a more secure platform from which those not clever enough to have chosen wealthy parents can nonetheless achieve their full potential. Social insurance, broadly construed, is one instrument for doing so. And government investment is the other.

The data here cry out to be heard. When we fairly listen to what the data are saying, and what careful research has demonstrated, we understand that those who blow their horns the loudest to define fiscal policy in terms of equality of opportunity do not really mean it.

If they did, they would, for example, insist on the highest possible investment in public education for children from low-income households, but the United States turns out to be one of the few developed countries in the world that spends less on educating the children of the poor than it does on the children of the rich (see chapter 3). Education is the essential foundation of opportunity, but no matter how you slice it, there is no equality of opportunity in our educational system today.

Similarly, an important recent research paper showed that poverty impedes cognitive function.[21] That is, poverty, by itself, leads to people behaving as if their IQ were 13 points lower, because of the amount of mental energy constantly channeled into coping with that poverty. In effect, the brain turns out to have limited bandwidth, and poverty permanently absorbs a substantial fraction of it, beyond measures of the consequences of stress and the like.[22] There is a reason, after all, why one adjective invariably linked to "poverty" is "grinding." Of course, some individuals overcome this and every other handicap. Kobe Bryant, slowed by a nagging injury, still outplays me on the basketball court. But that does not mean that a society that accepts widespread poverty as normal is one in which equality of opportunity is genuinely honored.

Consider one more example. According to research published by Save the Children Fund, malnourishment during the first 1,000 days of a child's development (from conception through the child's second birthday) leads to irreversible cognitive impairment. MRI scans show cerebral atrophy—a shrinking of brain—due to protein deficiency, and micronutrient deficiencies inhibit myelination, a critical brain development process that enables complex brain processes.[23] As a result, compared to adequately nourished children, victims of early malnourishment are 19 percent less likely to be able to read a simple sentence at age eight, even after controlling for differences in background and schooling. What is more, the young victims of malnourishment suffer from other follow-on effects, such as lethargy and smaller stature, which can lead to lower parental investment in their development.

These consequences persevere over time, with economic as well as personal consequences. Save the Children Fund's report finds that early childhood malnutrition reduces a person's lifetime earnings capacity by roughly 20 percent—globally, a productivity shortfall of around $125 billion a year when today's malnourished youngsters have been absorbed into the workforce in 2030. "By improving cognitive abilities, health, physical strength and stature," the report concludes, "good nutrition in the early years can lead to greater wages in adulthood."[24]

Save the Children Fund's principal focus in its report was on very young children in the world's poorest countries, but malnutrition haunts the United States as well. The Johns Hopkins Children's Center estimates that one percent of American children (around 760,000 in number) suffer from malnutrition. The US Department of Agriculture found that in 2012, 14.5 percent of all American households, comprising 49 million individuals, suffered from food insecurity at some point during the year, and 5.7 percent of households—17 million Americans—endured "very low food security."[25]

The United States in fact is the world's great outlier in ensuring that its own citizens receive adequate nutrition. Despite living in by far the richest large country in the world, US households saw food security issues at levels associated with Indonesia or Greece (which has about one-half the GDP per capita as does the United States).[26]

As a result of the pervasiveness of food insecurity in America, the Center for American Progress in 2011 calculated that the annual *economic* cost of hunger in America amounted to at least "$167.5 billion due to the combination of lost economic productivity per year, more expensive public education because of the rising costs of poor education outcomes, avoidable healthcare costs, and the cost of charity to keep families fed."[27] Just as poverty affects cognitive ability, so too the food insecurity that accompanies poverty has its own measurable productivity costs.

Federal government programs like Head Start's breakfast component and the Supplemental Nutrition Assistance Program (what used to be called food stamps) are a response to problems of childhood and adult hunger in America, but of course the data summarized here reflect the facts on the ground after taking into account the modest ameliorative effects of all such programs. Chapters 7 and 11 look more at the state of federal income security programs, including these. But to put food stamps in particular into context, here is what it means in practice in contemporary America to rely on the $5 or less per person per day that food stamps provide:

> As a self-described "true Southern man"—and reluctant recipient of food stamps— Dustin Rigsby, a struggling mechanic, hunts deer, doves and squirrels to help feed his family. He shops for grocery bargains, cooks budget-stretching stews and limits himself to one meal a day.
>
> Tarnisha Adams, who left her job skinning hogs at a slaughterhouse when she became ill with cancer, gets $352 a month in food stamps for herself and three college-age sons. She buys discount meat and canned vegetables, cheaper than fresh. Like Mr. Rigsby, she eats once a day—"if I eat," she said.[28]

We leave a cancer victim to feed a family of four on less than $12 per day in food stamp assistance, and a working man to supplement his family's calories by hunting squirrels. Hard-working Americans now are reduced to selling their own hair, breast milk, or eggs to make ends meet.[29] And in return, a member of Congress calls this government program an act of theft from him and other affluent American taxpayers. Yet at the same time, this Congressman apparently believes that the millions of dollars in federal agricultural subsidies that he has pocketed are the just deserts of the virtuous, paid to him by the gods, rather than by his fellow Americans through their tax burdens.[30]

Is eradicating malnutrition in the United States a moral imperative? Of course it is, but what more can usefully be said along those lines? Instead, the idea behind this book is to sneak moral objectives in the back door, by emphasizing the *economic* case for collective action. In other words, I try to meet on their own terms those who dismiss government interventions as naïve or as "class warfare," and to demonstrate that the fundamental idea of equality of marketplace opportunity—the essence of what Milton Friedman and his ilk have assumed to be the case—in fact is systematically dishonored in America today.

Thus, the example of infant and early childhood malnutrition can be presented as an investment opportunity as well as a moral plight. This is what Save the Children Fund was doing when it emphasized the loss in future earnings power of children who have suffered cognitive impairment from malnutrition, or what the Center for American Progress meant by toting up the productivity costs of hunger in America. Each institution sees little point in the current political environment in appealing solely to ethical impulses—nor is it necessary so to limit the reasons for government intervention. The economic case for government spending to afford children born into poverty genuine equality of opportunity through education, or to address early childhood malnutrition or adult hunger—the case for collective investment in an area where private markets necessarily must fail—basically makes itself.

For argument's sake, resist for a moment the urge to dismiss every inconvenient study as redistributionist propaganda, and accept that the studies summarized above are at least roughly accurate and relevant to some cases in the United States. These studies show that poverty, if left uncorrected, slices 13 IQ points off a poor person's human potential, and malnutrition leads to stunted human development that in turn reduces the productivity—the income—of each of its victims by thousands of dollars a year.

A capitalist offered the opportunity to invest a few hundred dollars today in a machine that will yield thousands of dollars in profits for years to come would jump at the opportunity. But of course there is no market in human lives, nor should there be, and capitalists therefore cannot invest directly in the most productive and important generators of income in American society—its citizens (at least when those citizens are not yet in the workforce). In the absence of such a market, we as a nation are doomed to leave on the table the returns we collectively could reap by investing in the proper nutrition of our most vulnerable citizens—unless we acknowledge that government exists as the mechanism to enable all of us collectively to make just such investments. Government here complements private markets by offering forms of insurance and making completely sensible investments in areas that private markets do not and should not reach.

All that is required is to appreciate that the poorest Americans are still Americans—that we are part of one large community, one society. If that fact is truly internalized, then it is in our interests to make the investment, because doing so will increase our national welfare (and in this easy case our national income as well), even after taking into account the modest costs to us of implementing the program.

And if the clear positive welfare returns to our country are insufficient to motivate us, if we must be assured that we personally will benefit from this collective investment, well even that is easy to demonstrate here. The modest costs of better prenatal and early childhood nutrition, for example, will lead not only to lower government safety net expenses later in life (which will mitigate future tax burdens), but also to higher national income, which in turn means higher demand for the goods and services that we or at worst our children will produce, and therefore higher incomes for us or our children.

And so, given the powerful and straightforward economic case for investments in prenatal and childhood nutrition, what steps are we taking today? We are stepping backward, by cutting existing programs in this area. For example, 2013's federal spending "sequestration" (the arbitrary slashing of many government programs) reduced funding for the Supplemental Nutrition Program for Women, Infants and Children (WIC) by $353 million. As a result, over 600,000 low-income, nutritionally at-risk women, infants, and children will not receive nutritious foods, counseling on healthy eating, and healthcare referrals.[31] This is an astonishing step backward, in light of the program's successes in reducing infant mortality rates by an estimated one-quarter to two-thirds, while costing the federal government less than what the government saves in Medicaid outlays.[32] And if that is not perverse enough, the budget adopted by the House of Representatives in 2013, and closely identified with Paul Ryan, as chairman of the House Budget Committee, would cut such programs still further.

Behind the pious statements about what we can and cannot afford resides a darker picture, of smirking "haves" thinking that they can segregate themselves and their economic outcomes from the futures faced by large swaths of American society, and a Congress that has shown itself to be much more attuned to the opportuning of the affluent than to the needs of the poor.[33]

As this book demonstrates, there is no genuine hard budget constraint on our ability to invest where we have the opportunity to enhance our national welfare—and in this case, our national income. We demean such investments and our fellow Americans when we carelessly describe these opportunities as just government "spending," as if they were indistinguishable from the bill for the fireworks display at a Fourth of July picnic.

I emphasize the economic case for insuring and investing in ourselves because this presentation is substantively accurate, and also fits with the temper of our times. For whatever reason, our intuitive instinct to help our fellow Americans, to feel intimately connected to them as part of a single larger community, has grown feeble in the last few decades, and rhetorical appeals directly to this instinct will have little effect. The explicitly moral component of the book's argumentation therefore comes down to this: when there is a clear economic case for collective investment or insurance through the instrument of government spending (net of considering the costs of government taxing) that will enhance the country's welfare, ignoring that opportunity is profoundly immoral. We endanger our nation's fiscal soul when we leave such opportunities on the table.

Here is one last example. The Affordable Care Act (popularly known as Obamacare) has as its central goal universal healthcare insurance, but unlike most other countries, that insurance will be delivered through several distribution channels. Those who have private insurance through their employers typically will keep that. Those who have no employer-provided insurance will be required to buy it (the individual mandate), and the government generally will subsidize the cost of that insurance for lower-income individuals, based on a sliding scale of income. And finally, the poorest Americans who are without coverage will obtain healthcare insurance through an expansion of the existing federal-state partnerships that fund Medicaid—or so the drafters of the legislation expected.

When the Supreme Court upheld the constitutionality of the Affordable Care Act, it allowed states to opt out of the expansion of Medicaid. Fourteen states have indicated that they will do so, citing the costs of the expanded program. But this is simply false. For the first three years of expanded Medicaid, the federal government will pay 100 percent of the incremental costs; thereafter, it will pay 90 percent. When the costs of uninsured individuals' emergency room visits and other uncompensated care are considered, states opting out of Medicaid expansion will incur $1 billion of extra costs in 2016, compared to the outcomes if all states opted in.[34] And these numbers reflect only direct expenses, and therefore do not include the loss in productivity (incomes) from premature deaths or unmanaged chronic illnesses.

As Paul Krugman wrote, this is an exercise in spite, not in fiscal prudence.[35] We are left instead with the spectacle of a state like Tennessee, which twice a year holds a telephone lottery, in which tens of thousands of uninsured and desperately ill low-income citizens (but nonetheless above the state's very low Medicaid cutoff) compete to win one of about 500 slots in its Medicaid program.[36] Perhaps in the near future other states will stage *Hunger Games*–type spectacles, in which elderly residents, confined to wheelchairs or walkers, some hauling oxygen tanks behind them, are equipped with bows and arrows and set against each other. Here we see the degradation of our national fiscal soul, when self-evident moral imperatives and economic interests align, and yet our political processes yield perverse results.

CHAPTER 2

OUR DESCENT FROM MORAL PHILOSOPHY TO NARCISSSISM

When the happiness or misery of others depends in any respect upon our conduct, we dare not, as self-love might suggest to us, prefer the interest of one to that of many.

—ADAM SMITH, *The Theory of Moral Sentiments*, Book III, Sec. I, Chap. III.

A WONDERFULLY OLD-FASHIONED definition of philosophy is that it is the study of that which must be true. This is why, two hundred years ago, what we today call "science" then was termed "natural philosophy." In turn, moral philosophy of the sort relevant to contemporary fiscal policy choices is a normative inquiry into how we should behave toward each other, in light of a carefully articulated system of values that (hopes the philosopher) cannot help but achieve general assent, by virtue of the philosopher's logical powers in developing that system from a few basic postulates to which we all subscribe.

Any coherent fiscal policy ultimately is an exercise in applied moral philosophy. An internally consistent fiscal policy describes who should comprise the objects of our attention in developing useful collective insurance and investment opportunities, and it identifies national values that the proponent believes are widely shared and that can find expression in fiscal policy—the values that together compose our fiscal soul. One of the great mistakes that fiscal policy analysts (including me) have made in recent decades is to assume rather than debate the moral philosophy that underlies our recommendations.

To the extent that we engage today in any explicit discourse in this area, our conversations are dominated by one central organizing principle, which is satisfying the demands of Homo Economicus—"the self-interest-seeking individual in a competitive environment."[1] This chapter shows how this powerful metaphor, drawn from one sphere of activity, has today been overextended to answer questions in every corner of public policy, with results that actually are counterproductive to our prosperity and are inconsistent with any semblance of shared citizenship.

It takes hard work to overcome the gravitational pull of self-centeredness. We are very good at recasting our own "conveniencies," to quote Adam Smith, into our "necessities." We care more about our comforts and those of our family than we do those of strangers. These sorts of instincts have always been true, and are completely natural.

In response, it once was the custom to employ moral philosophy to train people through education and socialization to moderate these instincts. Now, however, neoclassical economics dominates moral philosophy in all spheres of practical life; the popular understanding of economics in turn presents self-centeredness, as personified in Homo Economicus, as the scientific key, not just to economic efficiency and growth, but to all public policy decisions. We are the poorer, literally and spiritually, for it. And ironically, Adam Smith would be among the first to tell us so.

THE VILLAINS IN THIS DRAMA

Our real-world markets are extraordinarily efficient at inventing, making, distributing, and improving the smartphones, automobiles, toaster ovens, and software that we all consume. The original insight that in the ordinary course of commerce the marketplace allocates goods and services more efficiently than does any other mechanism rightly is laid at the feet of Adam Smith. To quote George Stigler, the University of Chicago Nobel laureate who arguably did as much as any other modern economic thinker to make Homo Economicus the referee of all public policy decisions:

> Smith had one overwhelmingly important triumph: he put into the center of economics the systematic analysis of the behavior of individuals pursuing their self-interest under conditions of competition. This theory was the crown jewel of *The Wealth of Nations*, and it became, and remains to this day, the foundation of the theory of the allocation of resources.[2]

In Smith's famous phrase, "It is not from the benevolence of the butcher, the brewer, or the baker, that we expect our dinner, but from their regard to their own interest. We address ourselves, not to their humanity, but to their self-love, and never talk to them of our own necessities, but of their advantages."[3] The great genius of the American people in the commercial sphere has been our consistent embrace of Smith's proposition that private markets alone are sufficient to get our steak, beer, and bread on the table, without the helping hand of any central planning.

When a private market is humming along smoothly, without distorted price signals from dominant sellers or buyers, without trailing a plume of pollution or other "externalities," with perfectly transparent information, and without excluding new entrants (which in turn requires that they can obtain financing to enter the marketplace on reasonable terms), economists describe the market as "efficient" in a technical sense.[4] When a market is efficient, government meddling, however well intentioned, cannot improve the allocation of goods and services across the economy.

Smith's observations about markets were so powerful that there is a tendency in modern thought to extend those insights too far into the policy arena—to claim that the world in fact is populated only with rational "participants who maximize their utility from a stable set of preferences and accumulate an optimal amount of information and other inputs in a variety of [freely accessible] markets," and to draw from this the conclusion that there is no role for government as insurer or co-investor.[5] But as research and our own observations have demonstrated in many different contexts, in fact we live in a world of important market failures, incomplete markets (areas where markets just do not reach), and unlucky persons, where poverty, bad luck, or other factors demonstrably impede individuals from fully participating in that competitive environment, and who therefore cannot maximize their utility entirely on their own.

For example, private markets in fact fail to make efficient investments in public infrastructure, for a variety of reasons developed in chapter 10. And in other cases, like healthcare, we are up to our eyeballs in private market failures, which in this case follows from the nature of insurance markets (chapter 11).

More fundamentally, poverty itself pushes its victims largely outside the orderly world of efficient markets. Poverty erodes cognitive ability in application. It means that rational opportunities for self-improvement cannot always be pursued, because of an incomplete ability to borrow against one's future, and because of the skewed risk-return calculus that the resulting debt implies. And the children of poverty enter the competitive markets for human services as young adults with far less having been invested in their human capital (including not just through money, but parental attention) than do the children of the affluent.

Being poor thus is existentially worse than just not having much money. Reality is not just a rounding error away from an imagined world of perfect markets and perfectly rational agents, and relying on it to formulate actual policy leads to hor- ribly misguided, or malicious, advice.

To the same effect, and as chapter 1 has suggested, some pundits conflate national welfare with national product. The two often move in the same general direction, but they are not strictly synonyms for each other. Bigger pies are bet- ter than smaller ones, all other things being equal, but it is not inevitable that all other things in fact are equal in the two states under comparison. Systematic envi- ronmental degradation is one example, because it is not a deduction from national product, but does reduce our welfare. So too is economic growth in which large numbers of American citizens do not meaningfully participate.

This book therefore rejects the pinched and artificial propositions advanced by economic writers aligned with political claims that unalloyed real-world pri- vate market outcomes are the only road to national happiness. I call these pun- dits "market triumphalists." These individuals organize their thoughts around a model—a mental map—of reality, dominated by the high ground of perfectly competitive markets, open to all of us, as "participants who maximize their utility from a stable set of preferences and accumulate an optimal amount of informa- tion and other inputs in a variety of [freely accessible] markets." From this mental map, these practitioners draw the conclusion that government invariably is a ran- dom meddler in those orderly markets, and that government spending and taxing therefore are inherently suspect.

This conclusion follows from the foundational postulate that the ideal of per- fect markets maps accurately onto reality. But once this inaccurate organizing principle is abandoned, what follows is a vital role for government as a comple- ment for private capitalism in the world that we actually inhabit.

If market triumphalism were simply an unsophisticated economic claim that real-world markets in fact were generally efficient in the technical sense, it would be troublesome to good policy, but what makes the doctrine truly pernicious is that market triumphalists, following in the footsteps of their "neoliberal" prede- cessors, conflate marketplace freedoms with *political* liberties. Their central idea is to define our political liberties as congruent with our freedom of economic action in private markets. Market triumphalists recoil at taxation, not simply out of an overstated concern for its efficiency costs, but also as something that strips them of their political liberty, by depriving them of the rewards they have reaped in the private markets.

The conflation of the conditions required for ideal markets with the conditions on which political liberty rests is simply a false syllogism. It is a fundamentally different claim from arguing that taxation introduces frictions into markets, and thereby leads to inefficient outcomes, in the technical economic sense.

The next several chapters of this book elaborate on the idea that the pervasive influences of poverty and fortune yield imperfectly competitive markets, and the sensible response in this environment is to conclude that a robust government can lead to greater prosperity, not less. This book further argues that moral imperatives and economic analysis align in many such cases. This chapter, by contrast, addresses the *political* claims that spring from market triumphalists' defective mental map. I outline the intellectual poverty of the core market triumphalist claim that political liberty rests on unalloyed market freedoms. In doing so, I try to rescue Adam Smith from his Babylonian Captivity as the mascot of libertarian values. Unlike his modern acolytes, Adam Smith understood perfectly well the limits of the marketplace as an organizing principle for how to conduct one's life, or one's government.

ADAM SMITH, MORALIST AND MENSCH

George Stigler described himself as Smith's "good friend," and argued that *The Wealth of Nations* demonstrated that "the efficiency property of competition" was "the crucial argument for unfettered individual choice in public policy."[6] The more I read of Adam Smith, however, the less confident I am that Smith would have returned the gesture of friendship, except, perhaps, out of the generosity of spirit that marked much of his thought.

Adam Smith was not the cartoon spokesperson for laissez-faire market outcomes into which we pigeonhole him.[7] Smith was a professor of moral philosophy at Glasgow University. At the time of his death, Smith had just completed a revised edition (the sixth), not of *The Wealth of Nations*, but of *The Theory of Moral Sentiments*, a book devoted to how we go about developing our internal ethical compass and regulating our appetites so as to reflect its direction.

Several first-rate biographies and monographs have been published in the last 15 years that together illuminate Smith's moral philosophy and its relationship to his economic insights.[8] These books demonstrate that what Stigler dismissed as "idiosyncratic" about Smith (his distaste for the relentless pursuit of wealth as if it were congruent with happiness or virtue) in fact was central to Smith's thinking, and that the "Adam Smith problem" posed by earlier scholarship (the belief that Smith had somehow put moral philosophy aside when writing *The Wealth of Nations*) was simply fatuous.

The Theory of Moral Sentiments is a long book, and one rich in insights into human behavior. A few paragraphs cannot do it justice, but perhaps can give some flavor of the issues that motivated Smith.

Smith begins the book with an extraordinary sentence: "How selfish soever man may be supposed, there are evidently some principles in his nature, which interest him in the fortune of others, and render their happiness necessary to him, though he derives nothing from it except the pleasure of seeing it."[9] Smith's basic point is that we are social animals, and our happiness *and our prosperity* are inextricably bound up in the happiness of the society in which we are situated:

> Man, it has been said, has a natural love for society, and desires that the union of mankind should be preserved for its own sake, and though he himself was to derive no benefit from it. The orderly and flourishing state of society is agreeable to him, and he takes delight in contemplating it. Its disorder and confusion, on the contrary, is the object of his aversion, and he is chagrined at whatever tends to produce it. He is sensible too that his own interest is connected with the prosperity of society, and that the happiness, perhaps the preservation of his existence, depends upon its preservation.[10]

We begin developing our moral intuitions (our "sentiments") by sympathizing with the pleasures or pains of others through imagining what we would feel in their place. As we become aware of these sentiments, we recognize that we approve of a man's behavior when his behavior accords with the emotions we imagine that we would feel were we in his place. When his actions and our imaginations coincide, we approve of (sympathize with) his actions.

We then observe how others see our own behavior. We learn which behaviors elicit sympathetic responses in others—which of our actions seem to others to be appropriate to the circumstances—and we adjust our own behavior, so as to cultivate praise from others:

> Virtue is not said to be amiable, or to be meritorious, because it is the object of its own love, or of its own gratitude; but because it excites those sentiments in other men. The consciousness that it is the object of such favourable regards, is the source of that inward tranquillity and self-satisfaction with which it is naturally attended, as the suspicion of the contrary gives occasion to the torments of vice. What so great happiness as to be beloved, and to know that we deserve to be beloved? What so great misery as to be hated, and to know that we deserve to be hated?[11]

Finally, we internalize the mechanism. We develop our own "impartial spectator" inside us. We no longer seek the praise of others, but rather to be praiseworthy in the eyes of our own internal impartial spectator. Only at this point have we developed the ethical compass to equip us to become fully functioning members of society.

The Theory of Moral Sentiments is an inquiry into how we go about becoming better persons, living more meaningful lives, and therefore the book focuses only a little on "the propensity in human nature to exchange," to use Smith's opening line from his most famous passage in *The Wealth of Nations*, where he explains that we do not rely on the benevolence of the butcher for our dinner, but rather his self-interest.[12] When our self-interest conflicts with the dictates of the impartial spectator, it is our self-interest that must yield:

[T]o indulge...at the expence of other people, the natural preference which every man has for his own happiness above that of other people, is what no impartial spectator can go along with. Every man is, no doubt, by nature, first and principally recommended to his own care; and as he is fitter to take care of himself than of any other person, it is fit and right that it should be so.... But though the ruin of our neighbour may affect us much less than a very small misfortune of our own, we must not ruin him to prevent that small misfortune, nor even to prevent our own ruin. We must, here, as in all other cases, view ourselves not so much according to that light in which we may naturally appear to ourselves, as according to that in which we naturally appear to others. Though every man may, according to the proverb, be the whole world to himself, to the rest of mankind he is a most insignificant part of it.... When he views himself in the light in which he is conscious that others will view him, he sees that to them he is but one of the multitude in no respect better than any other in it. If he would act so as that the impartial spectator may enter into the principles of his conduct, which is what of all things he has the greatest desire to do, he must, upon this, as upon all other occasions, humble the arrogance of his self-love, and bring it down to something which other men can go along with.... In the race for wealth, and honours, and preferments, he may run as hard as he can, and strain every nerve and every muscle, in order to outstrip all his competitors. But if he should justle, or throw down any of them, the indulgence of the spectators is entirely at an end. It is a violation of fair play, which they cannot admit of.[13]

The Theory of Moral Sentiments therefore ultimately is a guidebook to achieving happiness, not wealth.[14] Smith in fact consistently deprecates wealth-seeking as an empty pursuit, incapable of resolving the anxieties at the bottom of our souls:

[I]n the languor of disease and the weariness of old age, the pleasures of the vain and empty distinctions of greatness disappear.... Power and riches appear then to be, what they are, enormous and operose machines contrived to produce a few trifling conveniencies to the body, consisting of springs the most nice and delicate, which must be kept in order with the most anxious attention, and which in spite of all our care are ready every moment to burst into pieces, and to crush in their ruins their unfortunate possessor....They keep off the summer shower, not the winter storm, but leave him always as much, and sometimes more exposed than before, to anxiety, to fear, and to sorrow; to diseases, to danger, and to death.[15]

The ultimate aim of a good life is personal happiness and the happiness of society. To Smith, "happiness" has a very specific meaning. It is not the sum of simple consumption pleasures, but rather the tranquility (a word that he regularly used in immediate conjunction with "happiness") that comes from living a life of virtue.[16] (In modern fiscal policy discourse, we might replace Smith's term with "welfare.") In turn, governments "are valued only in proportion as they tend to promote the happiness of those who live under them. That is their sole use and end."[17] Government is but an "imperfect remedy" for our failure to achieve an ideal society, one dominated by "the general prevalence of wisdom and virtue."[18] People who lack virtue, and who therefore dismiss any commitment to "the happiness of the society," in fact are a danger to the society in which they hope to advance: "The person under the influence [of avarice, ambition, or vain-glory]. . ., is not only miserable in his actual situation, but is often disposed to disturb the peace of society, in order to arrive at that which he so foolishly admires."[19]

When Adam Smith wrote, "government" meant a small, barely democratic and often corrupt legislature, and a fellow named the king, who really was one. It therefore is foolish to extrapolate directly from what Smith wrote 225 years ago to what we imagine he might write today about the Affordable Care Act, but the point that I hope comes through clearly is that Smith expected adults to have a strong ethical compass and a commitment to the happiness and tranquility of the entirety of the society in which they lived, because we all are deeply connected to each other. As Smith observed, "How disagreeable does he appear to be, whose hard and obdurate heart feels for himself only, but is altogether insensible to the happiness or misery of others?"[20]

We live in a secular society, and we think of Smith as a hardboiled student of self-centeredness, so it is easy to overlook that Smith relies on his religious beliefs to explain what he saw as man's natural inclination toward "happiness" in the specific way he uses the term. But we cannot hope to understand the most famous passage in *The Wealth of Nations*, as discussed below, without appreciating the role of the Deity in Smith's thinking, as explained in *The Theory of Moral Sentiments*:

> The happiness of mankind, as well as of all other rational creatures, seems to have been the original purpose intended by the Author of nature, when he brought them into existence.... [B]y acting according to the dictates of our moral faculties, we necessarily pursue the most effectual means for promoting the happiness of mankind, and may therefore be said, in some sense, to co-operate with the Deity, and to advance as far as in our power the plan of Providence. By acting other ways, on the contrary, we seem to obstruct, in some measure, the scheme which the Author of nature has established for the happiness and perfection of the world, and to declare ourselves, if I may say so, in some measure the enemies of God.[21]

To summarize, *The Theory of Moral Sentiments* contemplates that man's happiness and prosperity are tied to the happiness and prosperity of the society in which he finds himself. Mankind develops a strong internal ethical compass through education and socialization. The mature individual pursues happiness, meaning a life of tranquility achieved through virtue. And by developing and exercising our moral faculties, we cooperate with God.

What on earth does this have to do with *The Wealth of Nations?* Not that much, on every page, because the two books are complements, not competitors, to each other. But that is the point: if you draw your fiscal policy action plan solely from a casual reading of *The Wealth of Nations,* you are looking primarily in the wrong instruction manual.

The Theory of Moral Sentiments accepts that men are self-interested, and explicitly rejects any criticism of self-interest, provided, critically, that it is channeled and expressed in ways that do no harm to others. The fruits of "the propensity in human nature to exchange" simply are not the subject of the book, which instead focuses on how individuals promote their own true happiness and that of society by developing their ethical compasses, and how government is charged with protecting the happiness of all of society. For its part, *The Wealth of Nations* rests on exactly the same premises about human values, although the subject matter of the book is different. That more famous book is not primarily about the ordering of society or the sources of its happiness, but rather is a positivist and historical explanation of the factors underlying economic growth, and a plea that government abandon its heavy-handed direct manipulation of markets through its mercantilist trade policies. It is, after all, *The Theory of Moral Sentiments,* not *The Wealth of Nations,* that from its title onward presents itself as ambitious *theory* of human behavior, in the same way that Newton proposed a theory of gravity, or modern economics posits its own theory of behavior, predicated on Homo Economicus.

The Wealth of Nations assumes the importance of the inculcation of internal virtue to all those individuals trucking, bartering, and purchasing to their hearts' contents, just as *The Theory of Moral Sentiments* assumes that there will be a whole lot of trucking, bartering, and purchasing going on. Smith makes this point in *The Wealth of Nations,* for example, in the context of expressing his admiration for the golden age of Greek philosophy:

> Wherein consisted the happiness and perfection of a man, considered not only as an individual, but as the member of a family, of a state, and of the great society of mankind, was the object which the ancient [Classical Greek] moral philosophy proposed to investigate. In that philosophy the duties of human life were treated of as subservient to the happiness and perfection of human life.... In the ancient philosophy the perfection of virtue was represented as necessarily productive, to the person who possessed it, of the most perfect happiness in this life.[22]

The Wealth of Nations criticizes governments extensively for their mercantilist meddling in areas that should be left to "self-interest-seeking individuals in a competitive environment" (to use modern terminology). This criticism, however, has really nothing to do with the larger questions of moral philosophy—of right actions toward others—that motivate *The Theory of Moral Sentiments*, and only a little to do with the questions of fiscal policy with which this book engages.

On those relatively infrequent occasions in *The Wealth of Nations* when Smith has reason to think about how to advance "the happiness of the society," his solutions are entirely consistent with *The Theory of Moral Sentiments*:

> [W]hat improves the circumstances of the greater part can never be regarded as an inconveniency to the whole. No society can surely be flourishing and happy, of which the far greater part of the members are poor and miserable. It is but equity, besides, that they who feed, cloath and lodge the whole body of the people, should have such a share of the produce of their own labour as to be themselves tolerably well fed, cloathed and lodged.[23]

This finally brings us to Smith's famous "invisible hand" metaphor, which he employed only three times in his voluminous publications.[24] Once was in his history of astronomy, where in a discussion of ancient beliefs Smith used the term to refer to the hand of the mythological god Jupiter. Smith most famously used the phrase in *The Wealth of Nations*, in the course of arguing that domestic trade necessarily benefits a society more than international trade (a proposition not consistent with modern economic thinking):

> First, every individual endeavours to employ his capital as near home as he can, and consequently as much as he can in the support of domestic industry,...and to give revenue and employment to the greatest number of people of his own country.... He generally, indeed, neither intends to promote the public interest, nor knows how much he is promoting it.By preferring the support of domestic to that of foreign industry, he intends only his own security; and by directing that industry in such a manner as its produce may be of the greatest value, he intends only his own gain; and he is in this, as in many other cases, led by an invisible hand to promote an end which was no part of his intention.[25]

When read in the context of Smith's complete oeuvre, the hand in question is rendered invisible, not because it belongs to Mr. Marketplace but because it is the hand of God, who wishes for the happiness of His people.[26] That is why Smith writes in *The Theory of Moral Sentiments* that "[t]he happiness of mankind, as well as of all other rational creatures, seems to have been the original purpose intended by the Author of nature, when he brought them into existence."

This connection between the invisible hand and Providence is made explicit in Smith's third use of the term, in *The Theory of Moral Sentiments*:

> The produce of the soil maintains at all times nearly that number of inhabitants which it is capable of maintaining. The rich only select from the heap [of agricultural

bounty] what is most precious and agreeable. They consume little more than the poor, and in spite of their natural selfishness and rapacity, they divide with the poor the produce of all their [agricultural] improvements. They are led by an invisible hand to make nearly the same distribution of the necessaries of life, which would have been made, had the earth been divided into equal portions among all its inhabitants.... When Providence divided the earth among a few lordly masters, it neither forgot nor abandoned those who seemed to be left out in the partition. These last too enjoy their share of all that it produces.[27]

It is a long and painful journey from Adam Smith's moral zeal, distaste for "natural selfishness and rapacity," emphasis on propriety in personal comportment, and concern for the poor to the uses to which his good name are put today. The remainder of this chapter sketches out this descent in our public discourse to our current cartoonish understanding of what Adam Smith actually stood for, and, more important, what should be important to us in thinking about what government can do for us.

NEOLIBERALISM

Like some sort of new avian flu, the modern market triumphalist school of thought is the result of the unexpected fusing of four vectors. In order of their first appearance, these are the economic/political movement of "neoliberalism"; the Reagan-Thatcher reaction against an often complacent and sometimes bloated government; a relatively recent tendency in society more generally to embrace public displays of narcissism, in this case by lauding rewards accrued in the market economy as due entirely to an individual's personal merit; and finally the Tea Party movement, which added its random faith-based zeal to the virus.

Each vector in turn justifies itself as an articulation of fundamental principles of individual liberty. This invocation of personal freedoms resonates particularly well in the United States, where many Americans still like to imagine that we can return to an America of self-sufficient pioneers, free of any government interference. Market triumphalism takes its final virulent form from this over-determined combination of plausible but vastly overstated economic claims, distrust of government, admiration for others' personal success, and quasi-religious fervor, in each case amplified by appeals to a simplistic understanding of freedom.

Neoliberalism is the intellectual foundation of market triumphalism. The term has nothing to do with modern political liberals. Rather, the "liberalism" portion of the term refers to the term's original meaning, as denoting a political philosophy that emphasizes the freedoms of the individual in different spheres, and equality among individuals, as crucial to a society's welfare.

Neoliberals begin from a base of neoclassical economics, which is simply the proposition that private markets generally do a terrific job of bringing buyers and sellers together (more formally, of allocating goods and services in the most efficient fashion) when individuals and firms are able to deal with each other freely, without any external constraints. In perfect markets, prices really do have a magical sort of quality of channeling consumers' wants and producers' costs into a single metric that by itself leads to efficient allocations of goods and services. Neoclassical economists (the dominant tribe among economists today) thus emphasize the central role of marketplace freedoms.

What made neoliberalism new ("neo") when it first was developed was its conflation of marketplace freedoms with political freedoms into a unified but off-base political economy story. Central to this story is the idea that taxation is necessarily immoral as well as economically undesirable, because it undermines the capitalist ethos that fuels both our country's economic success and our political liberties. The critical contribution of neoliberal thought is a political, not an economic, one: it is the idea that our political liberties are defined by our freedom of economic action in private markets.

Of course, and as the first half of this chapter showed, Adam Smith never intended that the marketplace serve as the organizing ideal for our personal conduct or our political thought. To the contrary, the great organizing principles in his worldview were three—prudence, justice, and beneficence:

> [N]o man during, either the whole of his life, or that of any considerable part of it, ever trod steadily and uniformly in the paths of prudence, of justice, or of proper beneficence, whose conduct was not principally directed by a regard to the sentiments of the supposed impartial spectator, of the great inmate of the breast, the great judge and arbiter of conduct. If in the course of the day we have swerved in any respect from the rules which he prescribes to us; if we have either exceeded or relaxed in our frugality; if we have either exceeded or relaxed in our industry; if, through passion or inadvertency, we have hurt in any respect the interest or happiness of our neighbour; if we have neglected a plain and proper opportunity of promoting that interest and happiness; it is this inmate who, in the evening, calls us to an account for all those omissions and violations, and his reproaches often make us blush inwardly both for our folly and inattention to our own happiness, and for our still greater indifference and inattention, perhaps, to that of other people.[28]

The political genius of the neoliberal movement was to take Smith's insights into the operation of the marketplace, rip them from the context of Smith's actual thoughts about moral and political behavior, and to use them to claim that neoliberals spoke for a two-hundred-year-old tradition of equating market freedoms with political liberties.

In the neoliberal political economy story, our welfare is derived entirely from our participation in the marketplace, and the great enemy of our welfare is creeping collectivism, against which absolute political and economic freedoms are the only defense. Markets depend on absolute personal and political freedoms, and markets in turn guarantee these freedoms; the two can only prosper in each other's company:

> Neoliberal thought began...with a reductive reading of Adam Smith's premise of man as a rational, self-interested actor. Human liberty depended on the economic individual, whose freedom in the marketplace, in the neoliberal view, was commensurate with human freedom more generally....It was a virulent faith in the individual and his economic behavior under market conditions rather than any conception of cultivated behavior, manners, or Smithian moral sympathy that was important to neoliberal thinkers.[29]

Friedrich Hayek's *The Road to Serfdom* is one of the canonical texts, Milton Friedman's *Capitalism and Freedom* another. Both authors were consumed by the risks inherent in big government, because collectivism, even if arrived at through democratic processes, was said to erode freedom of choice both in the marketplace and in the political arena. Years later, neoliberalism found political voice in great politicians like Ronald Reagan and Margaret Thatcher.

The intellectual innovations in neoliberalism (the conscious conflation of personal, political, and economic liberties, and the belief that those liberties hung by a thread) turned out to be contradicted by events, along two margins. China has demonstrated that at least some economic freedoms can exist inside a totalitarian political regime (not that I am recommending that theirs is a path worth emulating!), and of course Western democracies have not rolled down the slippery slope into suffocating collectivist societies.

Hayek at least had the excuse of staring into the maw of terrifying totalitarian regimes when he wrote his book, but Friedman, for all his accomplishments as an economist, reads today as a political and social simpleton. His insensitivity to the value of national parks (and his perplexing belief that market substitutes were at hand) has already been mentioned, but he did not stop there. He thought that markets would assure the full dissemination of political dissent, without the need for any further protections, and that racial discrimination would wither in the face of market competition for the best and the brightest.[30] His predictions have been uncanny in their inaccuracy.

Classic neoliberal texts today read as consumed by fear of totalitarian threats that at the time sounded plausible, but that now have largely receded. They also read as naïve about the ability of markets to solve all social problems. In this, neoliberalism draws continued intellectual energy from academic economic work that deprecates (or assumes away) values not shared by the model of a human as an essentially free and equal agent motivated entirely by a highly sophisticated and consistent calculus of utility maximization—or worse, academic work that purports to assimilate into economics entire fields of inquiry that emphasize other motives or concerns. In this way the political economy of neoliberalism is presented as resting on an unassailable bedrock of science.

Neoliberal enthusiasms lead some economists to betray contempt for other insights into human behavior, as if, for example, neither Freud nor Jung had anything the least bit interesting to say.[31] Other fields of study do not deny the importance of economic thought, and the reciprocal disdain shown by some economists reflects a stunted understanding of human motivations and a distasteful lack of cross-field comity. Economics has a longer history than some other social sciences, its basic insights offer powerful explanations for many human interactions, and its modern expression is a domain of highly sophisticated mathematical modeling. But none of these reasons justifies the conclusion that neoclassical microeconomics is the only window into our fiscal soul.[32]

In sum, neoliberal thinkers reject any interference with the marketplace, for three reasons. First, they see private markets as complete and entirely sufficient to address a society's allocative needs (how goods and services are allocated among individuals). Because private markets are thought to be complete, the proper role of government shrinks near to the vanishing point, and taxes in turn should become inconsequential. It is true that many markets with which we regularly interact are competitive—say, the markets for televisions or automobiles—but that does not mean that *all* markets are complete and perfectly competitive.

Second, because in their telling markets are perfectly complete, neoliberals argue that individuals face no significant barriers to entry into the labor markets or to the pursuit of careers commensurate with their abilities and ambitions; in other words, everyone of equal natal ability is thought to face equal opportunities. In turn, "redistributive" policies (policies that use taxes from the rich to fund some activity of the poor, to put matters bluntly) are thought to be wrongheaded, because they interfere with market-clearing wage rates (or other price signals), by blunting the work incentives that come from being broke and hungry.

Finally, and critically important to their larger political economy message, neoliberal thinkers believe that market freedoms and political liberties are necessarily the same concept. The result is the proposition that, because *ideal* markets are more efficient than government in allocating scarce resources among a population (all other things being equal), our political liberties are eroded when government plays any role in *actual* market outcomes—and what is more, market solutions should be extended to domains previously thought best to deliver through other mechanisms.[33]

But as chapter 1 already has suggested, and as the rest of this book amplifies, dire poverty is not simply a kick in the pants to get going and get a job. It strips Americans of basic freedoms, by immobilizing them, making it impossible to pursue opportunities that those with some money in their pockets can pursue.

The theory of efficient private markets presupposes genuine freedom of access to those markets, but that freedom requires more than a nominally open door.

So, too, do coherent theories of the meaning of political freedom.[34] To turn neoliberal claims on their head, our abilities to exercise our political liberties depend in practice on minimum conditions of economic sufficiency. Being free to hunt squirrels for your dinner is not in fact the exercise of market or political freedom in a modern democracy, because your hunger crowds out your ability to participate fully in either. People are not free and equal citizens, and markets are not in fact efficient, if individuals enter the marketplace on terms fundamentally skewed against them. This is what happens when infant malnutrition leads to neurological damage, or when systematic underinvestment in public education means that millions of young Americans enter the workforce with their human capital underdeveloped, because they were not able to buy their way into the superior educational experience routinely available to even the most mediocre student in an affluent household.

MARKETPLACE FREEDOMS, POLITICAL LIBERTIES

The neoliberal political economy story relies on both an artificial extension of ideal markets to describe all of reality and an impoverished understanding of the meaning of "freedom." Many decades ago, Franklin Delano Roosevelt reminded us that the "freedom" we cherish (or should cherish) is more nuanced than a simplistic freedom to keep what is "ours" unburdened by taxation. In his Four Freedoms address to Congress, Roosevelt briefly outlined other implications of the concept, including "freedom from want—which, translated into world terms, means economic understandings which will secure to every nation a healthy peacetime life for its inhabitants—everywhere in the world."

Our political liberties rest on two foundations: a core set of inviolable personal liberties, and a democratic process through which we debate what our government is good for, and implement our consensus conclusions. We all stand equal in the marketplace of political ideas, because our votes all are weighted equally. But the political mechanism for allocating governmental responsibilities is fundamentally different from the private marketplace's mechanism for allocating private goods and services. One by definition is centralized, and the other is not. One relies on consensus, and the other does not. And a democratic political process, even in an ideal form, ultimately exercises coercive power, while an ideal marketplace does not.

We are fully endowed with a full complement of our political liberties even when the consensus conclusion requires our participation in a policy with which we disagree, so long as our core personal liberties are not violated. Again, this is how a state is different from a club or a charity. The power of coercion that the state wields over each of us, in the form of taxation, is not an instance of an unconstitutional violation of our inviolable personal liberties—it is exactly what the Constitution contemplated.

Article I, section 8, of the Constitution grants to Congress the "Power to lay and collect Taxes, Duties, Imposts and Excises, to pay the Debts and provide for the common Defense and general Welfare of the United States." In addition, Congress is granted authority to "make all laws which shall be necessary and proper for carrying into execution" the powers enumerated in Article I, section 8.

What this basically means is that Congress can spend money any way it sees fit to advance our collective "general welfare," so long as in doing so it does not violate some fundamental individual right or express prohibition contained elsewhere in the Constitution (for example, by funding a national church). And Congress in turn has the plenary power to raise taxes to pay for that spending, subject only to some limitations that really are trivial in practice (like not taxing exports).

Many decades ago there was dispute over whether the Congressional power to spend and to tax was independent of the other enumerated powers also granted to Congress, or whether instead the spending and taxing power could only be exercised in aid of one of those other powers. The latter view was known as the "Madisonian" interpretation of the spending and taxing power.

On its face, the Madisonian interpretation is tautological, in that the Congress separately has the authority to pass laws "necessary and proper for carrying into execution" any of its enumerated powers. For this reason, as well as his fundamental disagreement over the scope of the federal government's powers, Alexander Hamilton (a principal author of the Federalist Papers) rejected the Madisonian interpretation in Hamilton's famous *Report on Manufactures* (1791). So did other framers of the Constitution and their contemporaries.

More relevant to the present day, the Supreme Court considered and rejected Madison's interpretation of the spending power and adopted Hamilton's in 1936, notwithstanding that at the time of its decision it was at the height of its resistance to New Deal legislative policies.[35] The Court explained that in contrast to Madison, "Hamilton...maintained the [taxing and spending] clause confers a power separate and distinct from those later enumerated, is not restricted in meaning by the grant of them, and Congress consequently has a substantive power to tax and to appropriate, limited only by the requirement that it shall be exercised to provide for the general welfare of the United States."[36] The Court expressly rejected Madison's reading as tautological, accepted Hamilton's, and held that "the power of Congress to authorize expenditure of public moneys for public purposes is not limited by the direct grants of legislative power found in the Constitution."[37] In turn, Congress can collect taxes to fund that spending.

Chief Justice Roberts neatly summarized this unbroken interpretation in the Affordable Care Act case as follows: "Put simply, Congress may tax and spend.

This grant gives the Federal Government considerable influence even in areas where it cannot directly regulate. The Federal Government may enact a tax on an activity that it cannot authorize, forbid, or otherwise control."[38] None of this was the least bit newsworthy to constitutional scholars.

The real substantive limitation on the spending and taxing power rests not in some list of constitutional "dos and don'ts," but with the people, in the form of our ability to throw the rascals out at the next election. The irony at work here, of course, is that the neoliberal movement and its degraded offspring, market triumphalism, are fundamentally anti-democratic, because they believe that the exercise of their political liberties in response to unfair or oppressive taxation to agitate to throw the rascals out invariably will prove insufficient to protect their personal interests from the rapacity of the people as a whole.

NEOLIBERAL THINKING IN ACTION

To make the previous discussion a bit more concrete, here are three quick examples of neoliberal thought in action.

First, consider the revisionist history that the federal government caused the Great Recession, through its alleged meddling in the mortgage markets to advance its affordable housing policies. This view unfortunately does not explain why the policies in question predated the crisis by several decades without precipitating an earlier financial crisis; why real estate markets collapsed in Ireland, Spain, and other countries as well as the United States; or why affordable housing policies should be blamed when the vast bulk of subprime lending, led by new market participants like Countrywide, took place outside the ambit of regulated entities covered by the Community Reinvestment Act and the ambit of the government-sponsored enterprises that guaranteed higher quality mortgages (although those enterprises did buy some AAA tranches of securitized subprime debt for their own investment portfolios).[39] Numerous analysts have rebutted the claim, but it persists, largely because the underlying belief system that markets can do no wrong—and governments no good—so thoroughly pervades the thinking of its proponents.

Now consider the widely held view that too many public schools are failing our children. The traditional response begins by embracing public education as a critical public good that we deliver through the collective mechanism of government (both local and federal in this case). If public schools are failing our children, then government agencies, as our collective agents, must be charged with doing better, through new standards, closer supervision, better teacher training, more money, or whatever.

The neoliberal response, on the other hand, is to deprecate the whole idea of public education, and to replace the role of government with that of markets, under which families armed with vouchers would shop for private schools competing for their education business. But this response ignores the social value of a public school as a place where children from different backgrounds learn to respect each other, and puts at risk millions of children who themselves are powerless (and whose parents for whatever reason are unable) to negotiate the education casbah on their own.

More fundamentally, the neoliberal impulse ignores the fact that the affluent can and will supplement those education vouchers with their cash, to buy better private educations. The result is that citizens' interest in investing in public education is dissipated, and voucher programs just serve as a discount for the private educations that the affluent would have purchased for their offspring anyway. In the wake of such programs lies systematic underfunding of wholly public education, and a further leg up for the offspring of the affluent into privileged positions in the next generation. It is a ploy for tribal schools couched in the name of market discipline.

As one final quick example of how neoliberal economists can take their abstraction of reality to extraordinary lengths in the pursuit of actual policy recommendations, consider a recent proposal to improve the performance of bank examiners by tying their pay to the value of securities of the banks they regulate.[40] Then, it is argued, the examiner's interests will be aligned with those of other investors, and the examiner will fiercely defend both those interests and his own wealth, by rooting out poor risk management or other problems at their earliest stages. Why the proponent would believe that the examiner would be more inclined to reveal problems than to cover them up, until such time as he could retire and sell those securities, is not explained.

DID SOUP KITCHENS CAUSE THE GREAT DEPRESSION?[41]

Neoliberal thinking's moral undertone, in which government "redistribution policies" or "entitlements" are seen as the great obstacle to prosperity, is particularly visible in analyses of labor policies. If you begin with a deep commitment to neoclassical economic models as descriptive of reality, "unemployment is a puzzle for economics."[42] There are many reasons that wages (the price of labor) are not as flexible as the prices of refrigerators, but the one on which neoliberal thinkers quickly settle is that the fault must lie on the supply side of the equation—with workers who do not adjust the prices at which they offer their services to reflect current circumstances. Labor unions often are trotted out as villains, because they are said to exercise monopoly power over the price of labor; for reasons unknown, the converse case—the monopsony power of many customers for labor services (i.e., employers)—rarely figures in neoliberal narratives. The other villain is government itself, which makes not-working too attractive through its safety net programs. The moral undercurrent emerges through the back door, in the form of arguments to the effect that not-working must be made less attractive (or union power must be eroded) if the market system for wages is to operate efficiently.

Consider as an example the book *The Redistribution Recession*, by University of Chicago professor Casey Mulligan, as well as his 2013 testimony on the same subject to a subcommittee of the House of Representatives' Ways and Means Committee.[43] Mulligan claims that legislative policies adopted at the outset of the Great Recession that were designed to ameliorate the hardships of the worst economic crisis in 70 years in fact had the perverse effect of encouraging joblessness and prolonging the collective economic pain. His fundamental argument is that there are costs to seeking employment and holding a job (commuting time and expense, forgone leisure, and so on), and that income maintenance programs that are available to non-workers, like the Supplemental Nutrition Assistance Program (SNAP—what used to be called food stamps) and unemployment insurance (UI) benefits, effectively raise the cost of working, because income from work leads to a phase-out or cessation of these benefits. Further, he argues, these income maintenance programs, particularly unemployment insurance, were greatly expanded at the beginning of the Great Recession, thereby making it affordable for workers effectively to opt out of the labor markets ("to opt to earn less") to enjoy all these benefits.[44] And finally, those individuals who opted to earn less also learned to make do with spending less, thereby damping down demand across the economy. One wag summed up the argument by suggesting that Mulligan had proved that soup kitchens caused the Great Depression.

The fact that many millions of Americans were unemployed at one point or another in the 2007–2012 period is incontestable; the issue with which Mulligan wrestles is causality. Did large numbers of workers opt not to work because newly increased income maintenance payments made it affordable for them to withdraw from the labor markets, or were they looking in good faith for employment, but not able to find any? Mulligan does not argue that unemployed individuals turned down great jobs; his claim is that people turned down not-so-great jobs—jobs they would have taken had the various income maintenance programs not been expanded by Congress.

Mulligan's book is an exercise in economic analysis, not propagandizing. But whether fully intended or not, there is a clear moral implication running through Mulligan's conclusions, particularly in the summary form in which he presented them to a Congressional committee in 2013. The message signaled by the book's title is that hard-working Americans who are gainfully employed now find their incomes "redistributed" to others who *choose* not to work, because the federal government has made idleness so comfortable that at the margin they have no reason to look for work. The moral implication is that we would do those who choose not to work a great favor by cutting safety net programs to the bone, because then they would face strong incentives to become productive economic contributors to society. As we will see, this message in turn has been amplified and rebroadcast by those who are closer to propagandists than to economists by predilection.

One response to Mulligan is to argue that Mulligan overstates the importance of "new" income maintenance programs; many of the changes he identifies (with the exception of the very short-term extension of unemployment insurance benefits in the depths of the Great Recession to 99 weeks for some covered workers) had been enacted in earlier years. This response emphasizes that aggregate benefit payments skyrocketed because of millions of new claimants, not because the programs themselves had become that much richer by design.[45] For example, at one point in the recent economic crisis one out of seven Americans was receiving SNAP (food stamp) assistance.

It is relevant to this line of inquiry that "take-up" rates for various benefits increased during the recent crisis[46] (many more people who were eligible in fact claimed benefits), because these facts militate against the claim that the existence of new programmatic features alone drove Americans to "opt to earn less."[47] It also is relevant that unemployment insurance benefits generally are conditioned on an individual's searching for work, because again this fact weakens Mulligan's claim that Americans have a simple choice between working and earning more, or going to the beach and earning less.

Mulligan's claims thus must be modulated to reflect this more nuanced reality. But having done so, the question would still remain, did income maintenance programs like unemployment insurance and SNAP (whether old or new) lead substantial numbers of workers at the margin "to opt to earn less" during the economic crisis?

Some economists who have engaged with Mulligan's thesis have done so at the level of macroeconomic arguments rather than the structure of the fiscal policies at stake. Some of these reasons to doubt the Mulligan hypothesis include the fact that employment collapsed in many countries around the world, not just in the United States; the 2007–2009 expanded benefits have largely expired, and yet employment has not surged; and perhaps most tellingly, that if labor suppliers (workers) left the market because sitting at home was made too cushy, then you would expect to see employers bid up labor rates to lure them back. But instead, exactly the opposite has happened: wage growth continues in 2013 to stagnate. Even a sympathetic reviewer in the Cato Institute's journal *Regulation* closed his review as follows: "If the decrease in work hours is due mainly to the drop in labor supply caused by the expansion of the welfare state that discourages work effort, why do so many people show up when jobs are advertised, even at Walmart?"[48]

Similarly, according to Mulligan's research, in the last few years senior citizens (who were not eligible for as many of the new benefits that he analyzes as were younger workers) have worked relatively more, not less, than younger cohorts. Mulligan believes that this supports his thesis that labor supply among those younger workers was dampened by their preference for lounging about. But the truth seems to be simpler, more obvious, and sadder: old people have been working more because they have lost much of their wealth (their savings, particularly in the value of their homes); they fear that Social Security will not in fact protect them; they fear that they will live longer than they originally had imagined (and therefore are more likely to run out of money); and saddest of all, because they are contributing a bit to the support of households that in another era would have been supporting them.[49] It is true that a family that sends Grandpa off to work at Walmart can preserve the unemployment benefits of Mom, the out of work engineer, but as discussed below, the answer to this concern lies in thinking more clearly about Mom's rational analysis of her lifetime opportunities.

Another line of disagreement with Mulligan's conclusions would suggest that Mulligan's model of rational economic behavior is incomplete; again, the point is to suggest that the arrow of causality points in the opposite direction to that suggested by Mulligan. Mulligan postulates the worker as Homo Economicus, carefully weighing the utility of government-subsidized leisure to the after-tax returns available in the marketplace, but he arguably ignores how a rational worker concerned about her lifetime employment actually would behave.

Imagine a recently laid-off engineer. She would know that being unemployed for long periods leads to an erosion of job skill and a stigma that affects future employers' hiring decisions, so her smart move from a lifetime earnings perspective would be to forgo leisure and return to the workforce as soon as possible. Further, the laid-off engineer might well decide not to take a job as a Walmart greeter, because that tarnishes rather than burnishes the resume of a mid-career professional who is further along her career path. (The same concern does not, of course, apply to her father, which is why he might be helping to support the family by working at Walmart while she does not pursue a similar job.) In other words, from a lifetime perspective, holding back from reentering the labor markets at the wrong level and instead waiting for a job commensurate with one's skills and experience arguably might be the most rational course of action. And finally, searching for a job might well be a full-time job in itself. All these are strictly rational economic reasons for the behavior we see all around us, without recourse to Mulligan's reverse causality claims.

In the same vein, if this hypothetical engineer is a typical American, she will have little choice but to get back to work if she can find employment. The reason is not the straw man that Mulligan sets up and knocks down (that some wage income always is better than none), but rather the reality that most Americans are highly leveraged. They have very little savings (the median family net worth in 2010 was $77,300, and the median value of family financial assets among families holding any financial asset was $21,500, without offset for financial liabilities[50]). At the same time, they have both mortgage debt service and car payments to meet, at a minimum. The life of a modern Huckleberry Finn rafting down a lazy river, making do on a reduced income for a year or two, would require most Americans to sacrifice both their homes and their automobiles.

The laid-off engineer also would be aware that unemployment benefits—by far the largest in dollar value of the various incremental cash "rewards" for not working that Mulligan identifies as tied to Great Recession legislation—are temporary in duration.[51] While the periods covered by UI benefits were extended at the depths of the recent economic crisis, a worker thinking in lifetime terms would be risk averse toward the prospect of letting go a job in hand against the hope of landing another one when benefits ran out.

Again, the question is not whether there was mass unemployment, but rather whether expanded safety net programs exacerbated unemployment levels by enabling individuals to pursue an alternative life of temporary leisure rather than reentering the job force in a relatively unattractive new position. The alternative perspectives suggested above are consistent with the idea that labor supply did not opt out in the recent economic collapse; labor demand collapsed.

Demand for labor initially collapsed as economic activity cratered, and demand for labor did not pick up as quickly as in past recoveries for two reasons. First, the severity of the financial component of this crisis, in particular the erosion of household net worth through the fall in home prices, has led households to pay down debt rather than ramp up spending.

Second, employers have in fact improved their productivity by investing in capital equipment and technology, and in doing so have permanently displaced workers.[52] Mulligan acknowledges that capital inputs went up in recent years, but seems to have drawn from it the wrong conclusion: he appears to see it as evidence of the fact that demand for labor did not decrease, because capital and labor inputs usually move in tandem, at least over the short run. What happened this time, however, was not the usual pattern, but a rapid and wholesale *substitution* of additional capital investment to replace labor.

Finally, consider Mulligan's thesis from the perspective of fiscal policy. Mulligan's fundamental methodology for quantifying the value of what he describes as government incentives *not* to work is to use an analogy to tax rates. Mulligan calculates the loss to a hypothetical worker reentering (or entering) the labor markets of forgoing his existing unemployment SNAP and similar income maintenance benefits. He then analogizes the benefits that the worker forgoes when reentering the workforce to a tax system that imposes high marginal tax rates on bands of relatively modest incomes: in this metaphor, the benefits that are forgone are the tax on returning to work.

The concept of marginal costs (or tax rates) is central to economics. An average (or "effective") income tax rate is just your tax bill divided by your income. A marginal tax rate, on the other hand, is the rate of tax that you will pay on your next dollar of income.

In a progressive income tax like that of the United States (and most other countries), your average tax rate goes up with your income; this feature of an increasing effective (average) tax burden as one's income increases in fact constitutes the technical definition of a "progressive" income tax.

The US income tax is progressive in part because of the rate structure of our tax code. We slice a taxpayer's income into several layers, and stack them one on top of each other. The first several thousand dollars of income is taxed at zero, the next several thousand dollars are taxed at 10 percent, and so on. The tax rate imposed on each bracket (or as I think of them, each level in an income ziggurat) remains unchanged, even as income that exceeds that bracket falls into a higher bracket and is taxed at a higher rate. Thus, millionaires get the benefit of a 10 percent tax rate on their first several thousand dollars of taxable income.

This last point often is difficult for people to absorb at first, but is very important both for tax revenues and for thinking about taxpayers' behaviors in the face of increasing income or tax rates. That last dollar of income might be taxed at a higher rate (that is, your marginal rate is higher than it was), but if you only have a few dollars of income in the new higher tax bracket, the effect on your total tax bill is very small. Which fact determines how you adjust your behavior? (There is a separate question, the subject of much recent research, as to whether people understand the actual consequences of our tax rate structures or whether instead they act on the basis of misunderstandings.)

Imagine that people are taxed at a 20 percent rate on the first $100,000 of their income, at 30 percent on their income from $100,001 to $400,000, and at 40 percent on income over $400,000. This is a classic progressive income tax rate structure, with different marginal tax rates for each layer of income. If you earn $99,999, your average and your marginal tax rates are both 20 percent (at least for just one more dollar of income). If you now earn $10 more, your average tax rate stays almost unchanged—your first $100,000 is still taxed at 20 percent, and only your last $9 at 30 percent. (Again, tax rate brackets are like climbing a ziggurat, not like falling off a cliff: your income in the lower-rate bracket remains taxable at the lower rate, regardless of how much income you have in higher brackets.) But now your marginal tax rate—the tax rate you face on your next dollar of income—is in fact 30 percent.

In very general terms, economists think of average tax rates as influencing what commercial activities you pursue, and marginal rates as influencing the scale of those activities. Economists tend to like tax systems that have a broad base (that is, few special deductions, exclusions, or exemptions) and a low marginal rate, because they emphasize that an individual's decisions at the margin are affected by her marginal tax rate, not her effective tax rate.

Imagine, for example, that Congress decides to encourage more people to become physicians by taxing the professional income of doctors at a flat 20 percent rate, while the rest of us are taxed under the rate schedule above. Looking at the return to your effort, you might decide that this is enough of a difference to cause you to enter medical school rather than law school. This is really an effective rate analysis, comparing two mutually exclusive investments of your time and tuition costs. Conversely, if you are a lawyer earning $100,000 per year, your decision as to whether to hold office hours on Saturdays might be affected by the fact that your incremental earnings will be taxed at 30 percent, even though your effective tax rate will be lower than that, because that first $100,000 remains taxed at only 20 percent.

Most government income maintenance programs are "means tested": you qualify for them based on having income and assets below a threshold, and you lose those benefits (usually through a phase-out mechanism that ramps down your benefits with increasing income) as your income climbs above the threshold. Unemployment insurance benefits are not means-tested, but that program has a cliff effect; anything more than *de minimis* wage income disqualifies you from continuing to receive unemployment insurance.

What Mulligan is arguing is that the phase-out of SNAP benefits, for example, that results from reentering the workforce and earning wages costs an employee real money in terms of the benefits forgone, and thereby acts in economic terms like a higher marginal tax rate on her band of income that falls within the phase-out range. If your household has zero cash income but receives $6,000 a year in SNAP benefits, and by virtue of taking a job paying $18,000 a year you lose those benefits, then without regard to any other taxes or policies, the net cash income pickup to you of taking that job is not $18,000 but $12,000.

What makes this use of the marginal tax concept different from our usual understanding of the term is that marginal tax rates ordinarily apply to your actual *last* dollar of income. Here the reverse is the case: the tax (the scaling back and eventual elimination of SNAP benefits) applies to your *first* dollars of income. This "tax" operates as a high-tax fog bank occupying the space near the ground—that is, your first dollars of income. Once you have earned sufficient wage income to forfeit all your former benefits, you suddenly revert to a relatively low marginal income tax rate environment, like a plane climbing through the clouds to the blue skies above.

This is a very old and very well-known phenomenon; it unfortunately is largely unavoidable if we are collectively going to fund any kind of means-tested safety net programs, where benefits are scaled back as your income rises.[53] And in turn, not means-testing programs makes them very expensive (as well as politically unpalatable to many).

For example, we could mitigate Mulligan's concerns about incentives not to work by providing that unemployment insurance benefits would be paid for a fixed period of time following an individual's becoming unemployed, regardless of whether that individual obtains a new job during that period. This design would be counterintuitive to most of us, and very expensive, but in Mulligan's terminology it also would impose a zero marginal tax rate on the act of reentering the labor force, beyond of course the higher regular income tax rates that all workers face as their incomes rise.

A more radical proposal along the same lines is a universal "negative income tax" (sometimes called a "demogrant"), in which all Americans would receive each year a fixed cash payment, regardless of need, in place of existing welfare and "making work pay" programs. (Milton Friedman in fact was the author of a major negative income tax proposal.[54]) The idea again is that, because you receive the demogrant regardless of whether you work, the demogrant imposes a zero marginal income tax on the decision to enter the workforce (that is, you do not forgo your demogrant benefits by working). The negative income tax would be a very hard sell to the American electorate, and contemporary neoliberals tend to shy away from the idea because they believe it would stifle the incentive to work too much, not for marginal tax reasons but because of the demogrant's "wealth effect." That is, by putting a significant amount of cash into people's pockets, a demogrant would enable Americans to patch together a life outside the regular full-time workforce.

One perfectly fair technical lesson that one can draw from social science inquiries like Mulligan's is that it is important to design safety net programs in ways that do not discourage work, including by considering how phase-outs can interact with each other to yield very large marginal tax rates for a particular band of income. This point, however, has been well understood for decades, and in fact generally has been taken into account in designing safety net programs.[55] But the basic problem is that there are only so many dollars to go around, and very slow phase-outs of safety net programs (which would bring down the marginal costs of entering or reentering the labor markets) are largely unaffordable.

Congress has wrestled for decades with the problem of the high marginal costs of entering the job market. This is the theory behind the Earned Income Tax Credit (EITC), which subsidizes low-income wage earners precisely to help with the twin problems of the out-of-pocket costs of holding a job and the forgone safety-net benefits that follow when income rises above poverty levels. The EITC offers very large cash rewards relative to entry-level wages—not just a zeroing out of tax liability but net cash payments to workers in many cases—but only for those individuals who in fact are in the labor market and have wage income. These net cash payments are called income tax "refunds," but of course are not, as there is no income tax payment to be refunded. (They can, however, be viewed as offsetting payroll taxes.) Stated simply, these are cash subsidies to "make work pay." The refundable portion of the child credit operates in much the same way.

Similarly, in the depths of the recent economic crisis, Congress did not simply reward featherbedding, as Mulligan's presentation implies. On a temporary basis Congress cut the payroll taxes that employees pay from their very first dollar of labor income, it effectively expanded the EITC on a temporary basis through the "making work pay" credit, and it extended permanently the refundable portion of the child credit (which is only available if a taxpayer has wage income). All of these steps were undertaken to "make work pay." As described below, Mulligan's story of a government encouraging a nation of incipient Huck Finns underestimates the importance of these countervailing policies.

There are three fundamental problems with Mulligan's marginal tax rate analogy. The first is that he treats as commensurate two income streams that in fact are temporally incommensurate: the very short-term income stream represented by unemployment insurance benefits in particular, and the presumptively long-term income stream that follows from taking a new job. To view forgoing the first as effectively a permanent burden on the first dollars of income from the second is simply not accurate. If instead Mulligan compared the present value of the short-term stream that an individual gives up to the present value of long-term employment, the marginal cost would have been much lower than the numbers he calculated. (In every case that marginal cost would go down even more the closer an individual was to the expiration of her unemployment insurance benefits, but the point is that the "marginal" tax would be far lower than Mulligan's calculations.)

Second, Mulligan has confused temporal margins in another sense. His marginal analysis really depends on looking at the date that legislation is enacted as the relevant margin, as if we pile one change in law on top of another, to see how the last revision affects behavior. In other words, he looks at new legislation as if it by itself had a marginal consequence. But unemployed people do not care when the various income support programs on which they are relying were enacted— they only care about the total package they are receiving while unemployed, compared with the package of compensation and "making work pay" subsidies they would receive if they were working. It is true, of course, that you can identify people who were working at a point in time, followed by a change in law, followed by a behavioral change in work patterns, but you cannot from this draw any sound conclusions about the marginal implications of the most recent legal change— other economic factors were at work in the actual case analyzed by Mulligan, such as the collapse of the nation's economy.

The third problem is that, despite the seductive nature of the metaphor, Mulligan is not engaging in a "marginal" analysis at all. Marginal analysis essentially is a continuous function—it applies to the next small increment of income, or whatever else is being studied. For example, the income tax rate on my next $1, or $10, is a marginal tax rate question. A plumber's marginal tax rate is relevant to his decision to work longer hours, and thereby generate a little more income.

The earned income tax credit (EITC), briefly mentioned earlier, is a tax subsidy for lower-income wage earners, and has an income phase-out range, where the tax subsidy is withdrawn as an employee's wages increase. For an employee at the cusp of the phase-out, and who is contemplating working overtime to earn a few extra dollars, it is perfectly fair to conceptualize the loss of the EITC subsidy as an additional marginal tax on that band of income. Returning to my earlier clouds and blue skies metaphor, this higher marginal tax rate actually disappears once the employee has lost all of her subsidy; from that point forward, her marginal tax rate is simply the marginal income tax rate (bracket) in which she finds herself. (The marginal tax rate terminology also often is used to describe the opportunity set confronting a non-working spouse whose partner is in the workforce, because the second spouse's income will sit on top of the first spouse's wages when they come to file a joint federal tax return.)

Unlike true marginal analysis, the phenomenon Mulligan is studying is profoundly *dis*continuous. His interest is in the binary choice between not working and working full-time. You must choose one or the other (the same hour cannot be spent working and not working). Mulligan is not really interested in what happens in the labor markets if I am unemployed and work a few hours on the side; his presentation is based on the idea that forgoing the "not working" income stream fully burdens the "working" stream for someone contemplating returning to the full-time workforce. This is an average tax rate comparison (more accurately, a comparison of the after-tax returns to my time), not a marginal tax rate comparison.

Mulligan's comparison really is analogous to holding one investment (the "not working" stream of income) and contemplating disposing of it to make a second investment (the "working" stream of income). Imagine that I had an actual investment in Acme Explosives and was considering swapping it for an investment in Wile E. Coyote Enterprises. I would look at the after-tax income stream I could expect from one, and compare it to the after-tax income stream from the other; I would choose whichever gave me the higher after-tax risk-adjusted return. If the two pre-tax income streams were otherwise identical, but had different tax rate schedules associated with them (for example, they are in different industries that have different tax rates), the comparison would boil down to the effective (average) tax rate on my projected income, not to any marginal tax rate comparison.

And so what? The reason to emphasize this point is that, on top of treating as commensurate two income streams of greatly different duration, Mulligan comes up with very high "marginal tax rates" on leaving the ranks of the unemployed and returning to the workforce through this confusion between marginal and effective rates. In particular, Mulligan ignores all of the subsidies that Congress has provided to "make work pay," whether enacted before or as a result of the Great Recession, mostly on the theory that they were not newly legislated, and so just formed part of the baseline tax environment.

So, for example, Mulligan argues that the Earned Income Tax Credit was in place before the Great Recession, and therefore is largely irrelevant to his analysis of incremental (marginal) changes.[56] He does the same for the child tax credit, and even the 2009 "making work pay" credit, where he argues that most taxpayers would have obtained that credit anyway (by working a few months during the year or having a working spouse), and so the credit is irrelevant to his marginal analysis.

In contrast, an effective (average) tax rate analysis of the consequence to labor markets of income maintenance programs does not take some subsidies off the table as old news; instead, it looks to the total tax burden on each of two competing streams, to see what the after-tax returns to each might be. As it happens, the EITC and other benefits lead to very low (indeed, often negative) *average* tax rates on entry-level labor income. Mulligan is giving Congress no credit for these important subsidies on the "working" side of the ledger, while toting up the forgone benefits of not working as pure costs to working.

Because the various benefit programs for not working and for working are complex and have different phase-out rules, depending not only on income but on family size, there is no single answer to the question that Mulligan poses. In this regard, his analysis can be faulted for not clearly and succinctly laying out the characteristics of his typical family unit, and presenting a number of differently situated hypothetical families. But consider one arbitrary example, recognizing that there are many other possible outcomes.

The year is 2010. A family of three (two parents and a child of 11) had a single working parent with wages of $24,000/year, who lost that job in 2009. They receive $925/month in unemployment insurance benefits and $300/month in SNAP benefits (the unemployment insurance benefits reduce the SNAP benefits payable). (If the other spouse was working and as a result the family was above the poverty line, no SNAP benefits would be available.) On January 1 a parent is offered a new job paying the same $24,000/year. Ignoring my point about the incommensurate duration of the two income streams, what is the fair comparison between these two opportunities (i.e., not working and working)?

Not working pays $14,700, until benefits run out. In the ordinary course, working would pay $24,000 before tax, and the family would incur an income tax of $165 (because the standard deduction and three personal exemptions would reduce taxable income to $1,650). There also would be about $1,500 in the employee's share of payroll taxes to consider, but paying those does convey future benefits in terms of Social Security eligibility, so for the moment put this aside.

My point is that Congress offered (and today offers) several important subsidies designed to "make work pay." The income tax associated with $24,000 in income would not actually have been $165, but rather would have been a large refund (really, a cash subsidy for working delivered through the tax system) of about $4,500 in after-tax cash subsidies for working ($165 of tentative tax liability, less $2,640 [EITC] + $1,000 [child tax credit] + $800 temporary "making work pay tax credit"). Again putting aside payroll taxes, the difference between non-work and work was not $9,300, but $13,800.

The $24,000 job almost doubled the family's economic income, from $14,700 to $28,500 after work-related subsidies are considered (assuming one thinks that a relatively low-income family like this gets fair value in Social Security benefits for the amounts its wage earner pays into that system). And again, the job-related income stream presumptively is of longer duration than the family's unemployment insurance benefits, in particular. Mulligan ignores all the legislative subsidies for working (on the theory that most were not "incremental") and the incommensurability in duration of different job strategies to reach his conclusions.

MARKET TRIUMPHALISM

Neoliberalism is a degraded interpretation of nineteenth-century classic economic and liberal political theories, mingling political fears of totalitarianism with an overstated confidence in private markets as the solution to all social problems. Market triumphalism in turn is a debauched form of neoliberalism, to which society's tolerance for public displays of narcissism and American popular faith-based belief systems have been added.

Market triumphalism dominates discourse on political economy issues today. Its twin messages are that taxes are the root of all economic evils and that government spending programs invariably constitute stupid and malicious interference with the smooth functioning of the markets. Its rhetorical devices include emphasizing the differences among us, rather than reminding us of the ties that bind us together into a single country[57]; claiming that financial success is an outward sign of inward superior character; and implying that financial distress is therefore the just deserts of laziness or character weakness.

Market triumphalists are fiscal policy absolutists. They ignore both the efficiency payoffs to well-chosen public insurance and investments that complement the private sector in instances where markets are incomplete and the moral tensions at work in any society, which have been the subject of serious introspection from Aristotle to Pope Francis. Instead, market triumphalists see lower taxes on the most affluent Americans as a sort of patent medicine that cures all ills. Their narratives emphasize their belief that we all work to promote GDP, rather than our welfare, and that taxation is inimical to growth, because it discourages private investment and entrepreneurship. The efficiency costs of taxation are real, but the question is, how big are those frictions? Chapter 5, "The Growth Fairy," addresses this; the short answer is that taxation at the levels practiced in the United States is not as toxic to growth as market triumphalists like to claim.

To market triumphalists, not all taxes are equally troubling: the taxes that cause the greatest distress are those on the rich and successful. Market triumphalists waste little energy urging lower taxes on middle of the pack Americans: to the contrary, they attack working class Americans for having no "skin in the game"— for not paying enough income tax. Market triumphalists also agitate for lower government spending, because that enables lower tax rates (since we use taxes to finance that spending), but their heart really is pinned to the supposed virtuous circle between lower taxes on the affluent and future happiness.

Market triumphalism confuses national income with national welfare; it ignores the positive returns to government insurance and government investment; it confuses life outcomes with the hand of Providence; and it justifies a distasteful narcissism and possessiveness toward all material goods. It enables the unreflective affluent to sleep at night, their consciences assuaged by its message that their success is explained by their own admirable virtues alone. And by virtue of its political messaging since the Reagan-Thatcher era and the anti-intellectualism exhibited by its recent influx of Tea Party enthusiasts, its arguments often are largely faith-based.

Market triumphalists fundamentally are false conservatives, because they deny that our country has common values that sometimes constrain the outcomes reached through the most literal adhesion to laissez-faire economic outcomes, and yet are worth conserving.[58] Margaret Thatcher could not have been more wrong when she said, "You know, there is no such thing as society. There are individual men and women, and there are families."[59] To the contrary, whatever our political persuasions, we all think that there is a unique genius to American society. I submit that whatever that genius is, it is more than, "You keep what's yours, I'll keep what's mine, and let's meet next Thursday to hire an army."

Real conservatives differ from progressives in three respects: real conservatives are less inclined to see market failures in how our society functions, they are more wary of government's abilities to address those failures that they acknowledge do exist, and they value stability and continuity with the past more highly. But all three of these dimensions lie along continuums, which is precisely why real conservatives and progressives were able to reach compromises in the decades before the Reagan-Thatcher revolution turned its back on national values as a component of *economic* policy. What is left is an empty, narcissistic sort of cult of market outcomes, practiced largely by those lucky enough to have obtained market success.

Casey Mulligan's work on employment was a genuine work of social science (albeit with the significant flaws I have tried to demonstrate). Nicholas Eberstadt's *A Nation of Takers: America's Entitlement Epidemic*,[60] on the other hand, is an instructive example of a market triumphalist interpretation of the same issues. Mulligan largely constrained his references to "redistribution" to his title, and makes no comments on individuals' characters, but for Eberstadt, "The dignity of work no longer has the same call on men as in earlier times....It would appear that a large part of the jobs problem in America is that of not wanting one." It follows from this that "[a]n unavoidable consequence of the noxious something-for-nothing thinking that lies at the heart of the modern entitlement mentality is the resort to redistributionist politics."

This is not just about rhetoric. Thinking along these lines provides the intellectual justification for measures like the infamous 2013 Southerland Amendment to the "Farm Bill," the gigantic Congressional appropriations package that includes federal funding for SNAP. The Southerland Amendment basically would have subsidized states to kick families out of the SNAP program, through a genuine Catch-22. Under the amendment, states would be permitted to limit SNAP benefits to adults who were working or enrolled in a training program for at least 20 hours per week. But of course the amendment provided no funding for such training programs, and in many states there are none available. So the able-bodied adult looking for work, at a time when unemployment remains very high by historical standards, would lose all SNAP benefits, as would mentally or physically disabled adults not able to hold a job or adults who stay at home to take care of children because no low-cost child care is available.

Why would a state take up this offer and impose such suffering on its residents? Because the Southerland Amendment would have given a state in cash, without restrictions of any kind as to how it might be spent, one-half the federal government's savings from removing individuals from the SNAP program. Many cash-strapped states would in fact take up this cruel offer. This is the great mischief that follows when pseudo–social science is enlisted to render simplistic policy recommendations.

There is a distasteful smugness to much market triumphalist literature, often manifested as a world-weary observation that the iron laws of economics require that the writer (or the objects of his prose) be successful, and others not. For example, Richard Epstein, a New York University law professor, wrote recently in praise of income inequality.[61] He argued that if the rich get richer, who can object, so long as the poor do not as a direct consequence get poorer? It therefore follows that "low, flat, and steady tax rates offer the only way...to sustainable overall growth":

> The blunt truth remains that any government-mandated leveling in society will be a leveling *down*. There is no sustainable way to make the poor richer by making the rich poorer. But increased...taxation will make both groups poorer. Negative growth hardly becomes equitable if a larger fraction of the decline is concentrated at the top earners....Only higher productivity [from investment presumably funded by the affluent] secures long-term higher wages.

This view argues that we must accept unequal marketplace outcomes in the greater service of growth and rely on some unspecified mechanism for the sharing of that economic growth to spread the returns to growth more broadly. The narrative presupposes that we will give up, for example, on incremental public investments in education today and, in return, somehow produce more wealth, more broadly shared, tomorrow.

This is the "leveling down" argument, one of the favorite tropes of market triumphalism. You will poison the goose that is laying all those golden eggs, goes the argument, if you tax high incomes at higher rates, because taxation is toxic to golden geese. Then there will be no more golden eggs and only one dead goose to go around. Chapter 4 unravels this vast overstatement.

The mechanism by which the golden eggs in turn are enjoyed by the laborers in the field, rather than the owner of the goose, usually is not well developed, but boils down to the theme that more business investment leads to greater productivity, which in turn leads to higher wages for workers—that is, capital and labor fairly share the productivity gains between them. In fact, it turns out that for a number of years productivity has been rapidly increasing in the American economy, but those productivity gains have *not* been shared with working Americans.[62] Instead, the economic returns to investment ("capital income") have gone up significantly as a share of total national income, while the economic returns to working ("labor income") have declined. Chapter 5 analyzes in more detail this important phenomenon, which directly contradicts the fable.

Moreover, as chapter 1 has suggested, and as will be further developed in the next few chapters, there is strong evidence that our country's rapidly increasing inequality has profoundly negative welfare consequences. That is, the rich getting richer is not necessarily a "Pareto improvement" (the idea that a move that makes one person better off and no one worse off is always desirable) because large-scale inequality itself has negative welfare consequences.

More directly, the leveling down argument misapprehends the economically efficient work that government can do as investor and social insurer. Markets are incomplete and imperfect in important ways—for example, the skewing in the market for human capital development (education) that directly follows from family income differences. This specific instance follows from both the cognitive impairment research already mentioned, and the distressing differences in investment (both financial and time commitments) in early childhood development among children from parents of different economic backgrounds. As chapter 10 further develops, the United States is one of only a handful of developed economies that spends less on the public education of poor children than on those from affluent homes. Finally, take into account the concept of the declining marginal utility of income—the fundamental idea that $1,000 more of after-tax income means less to the millionaire than to the Walmart clerk. In essence, this book develops why each of these assertions is a sound foundation on which to build policy inferences.

With those facts as foundation, consider the possibility that government has available to it a set of investment opportunities that are complementary to private market activities, that address those incomplete markets, *and that yield positive economic returns*—for example, by investing more than we currently do in the education of children from poor families, to help them overcome the handicaps already mentioned, and developed further in chapter 10. (A similar point can be made about the government as insurer, but it is easiest to see when thinking about the investment side of things.) Children with a better education will do better in their future work careers, and as such will earn more money for themselves and create value for the larger economy as a whole. (The current vogue is to call these sorts of productive social investments "trickle up" economics in action.) Such investments cost money, however. As Epstein notes, it is the affluent who have money to invest (that's what it means to be affluent!), and so they are the logical investors in these highly profitable investments. The mechanism by which the investments are made, though, is a little different from the usual investment decision, because it relies on tax revenues.

The result is a powerful case for the opposite policy recommendation to that argued by Epstein—significant tax revenues (including but not limited to a progressive income tax) used to fund the real and complementary investments that in practice only government can make. The alternative policy that this implies would mean that the poor in fact do get richer, because someone has invested more completely in developing their full human capital. The rich get a little cash-poorer at first, but their immediate welfare loss is swamped by the welfare gains of many more Americans, and ultimately even the rich share in the trickle-up consequences of more robust consumption across a broad swath of American society.

As one final example, consider an opinion piece published in 2011 in the *Wall Street Journal* by Harvey Golub, a wealthy man who had previously been the chief executive officer of American Express (and briefly the chairman of AIG).[63] In his op-ed, Golub directed his umbrage at Warren Buffett and President Obama for suggesting that the rich in general, and by implication Golub in particular, should pay somewhat more in income tax:

> I deeply resent that President Obama has decided that I don't need all the money I have not paid in taxes over the years....I certainly don't feel "coddled" because the various governments have not imposed a higher income tax. After all, I did earn it.

Golub's article accurately reflects the ethos of a large swath of the affluent classes, but in doing so reveals unexamined forms of arrogance that lie at the heart of our deteriorating ability to govern ourselves.

Referring to his many tens (hundreds?) of millions of dollars, Golub observed that "I earned it." No doubt this is true, in the sense that he apparently inherited very little wealth, is highly intelligent, has worked very hard his whole life, and in return has been paid extremely well for his labor. But is it really possible that Golub and his ilk are blind to how lucky they also have been? In other words, do they not realize how contingent the process of wealth accession really is? Many Americans without tens of millions of dollars also work very hard, and many are as smart as Mr. Golub. The nature of life is that we do not control it; both our native talents and our good fortune are distributed through processes that we cannot fathom and do not "earn."

The income tax in this respect operates as a kind of insurance policy. Following the famous metaphor of John Rawls, imagine that we are all sentient disembodied beings, waiting to be born. We know the full range of possible paths that any new life might take, including the great probability that we will end up struggling to make ends meet. But we know nothing about our future selves. We do not know who our parents will be, how healthy we will be, or with what native endowments we will embark on life. We are offered insurance in the form of a promise of some minimum level of support if we are unfortunate—but being disembodied beings, we have no cash with which to pay the premium. The deal is that we can pay in arrears—if we hit the jackpot, we kick in a fair chunk of money, and if we end up with the short end of the cosmic stick, we get helped out enough to mitigate the most abject misery. Who among us would be so foolish as not to sign up?[64] (Chapter 11 returns to this metaphor, in the context of the role that government should play as an insurer.)

Finally, Golub wrote that the federal government today violates "the implicit social contract between me and my government that my taxes will be spent— effectively and efficiently—on purposes that support the general needs of the country." Here he betrayed the unconscious great arrogance that he shares with many other successful people. There is no contract, express or implied, between the United States of America and any one of us. "The consent of the governed" does not mean that any citizen gets to pick and choose which government spending programs are smart, and therefore deserve his funding, and which are dumb, and from which he therefore can opt out. Again, the essence of governments, including the purest democracies, is that they coerce their own citizens, and to reject this principle is to repudiate government entirely.

Niccolò Machiavelli, that sublime analyst of all political instincts, understood Harvey Golub perfectly. In his greatest work, *The Discourses on the First Ten Books of Titus Livy,* Machiavelli wrote that truly admirable men remained constant in temperament through good fortune and bad. By contrast, "[n]ot so do weak men behave; for by good fortune they are buoyed up and intoxicated, and ascribe such success as they meet with, to a virtue they never possessed...."

Not much has changed for the fortunate affluent in the intervening 500 years. Wall Street is the perfect laboratory in which to observe the contemporary conflation of success with personal virtues, but it is only the most extreme example. The preferred stock trading desk, for example, might be a sleepy backwater, until some change in securities regulation or tax law, or an unexpected market development, makes preferred stocks the hot thing. Then the head preferred trader will demand (and receive) a huge bonus for his acumen, and will lecture other business units on their many failings when compared to his unquestioned genius, as demonstrated by the incontrovertible results his desk has achieved in the marketplace. Only once in my 30 years of working with Wall Street professionals did a senior Wall Street executive confess to me that he was, in his words, "the luckiest Irishman alive."

Of course, most great success stories contain large elements of hard work and sacrifice. But so do many stories of only middling material accomplishments, or even outright failure. Those of us who have achieved material success have been fortunate in ways great and small, visible and forgotten. We overlook the fact that our native intelligence, or good looks, are not karmic rewards for past lives well lived, that our good health is not due entirely to our superior self-discipline, and that the parent or teacher or boss who inspired or mentored us found us for reasons not entirely within our control. Instead, we emphasize the risks we took and the sacrifices we made along the way, and believe through our weakness of thought that we overcame the randomness that defines all of life solely through personal perspicacity.

As Machiavelli wrote, great republics, like great men, do not allow prosperity to make them arrogant. Yet in our political discourse as well as our personal lives we habitually ascribe to those fortunate to achieve great material success virtues that they do not necessarily possess, at least in the magnitude we imagine, and therefore treat them as beyond the proper scope of governmental inconvenience.

If we believe that our material success is ours alone—a reflection of our personal virtues, or perhaps the special benevolence of some Higher Power—and not in part the outcome of the unpredictable caprices of fortune, then we intuitively find repugnant the idea that we should be willing to share those gains through the intermediation of the tax system with those to whom fortune's wheel has been less kind. We reflect this in our tax policy by demanding still lower marginal tax rates on high-income taxpayers, to release their creative juices, or some similar simile. We view it as an innocuous consequence of our various virtues in operation that our society today is more unequal in incomes and in wealth than it has been at any time since the 1920s. We reject the original reason for the income tax, which was to rely on the principle of the diminishing marginal utility of money to "increase the happiness of the society." In doing all of this, we become like Tolkien's Gollum, holding onto "our precious" as if it were life itself.

It is not surprising that the affluent have always slipped into the convenient habit of mistaking good fortune for great virtue, and therefore into believing that higher marginal tax rates were a confiscation of the rewards that come naturally to those imbued with virtue. What is new is that the rich seem to have convinced the poor and middle class to believe this as well. As a result, we have drifted dangerously close to the citizens of Erewhon, the fictitious land of the nineteenth-century satirist Samuel Butler. In their country, Butler wrote, "if a man has made a fortune...they exempt him from all taxation, considering him as a work of art, and too precious to be meddled with; they say, 'How very much he must have done for society before society could have been prevailed upon to give him so much money'; so magnificent an organization overawes them; they regard it as a thing dropped from heaven."

Has ever any satirist better foreshadowed contemporary fiscal politics?

CHAPTER 3

OUR DISMAL REPORT CARD

The industrious knave cultivates the soil; the indolent good man leaves it uncultivated. Who ought to reap the harvest? Who starve, and who live in plenty? The natural course of things decides it in favor of the knave: the natural sentiments of mankind in favor of the man of virtue.

—ADAM SMITH, *The Theory of Moral Sentiments*,
Book III, Sec. I, Chap. V.

GRADING OUR PERFORMANCE

Whatever angst they induce in children and their parents, report cards provide useful insights into a child's intellectual and emotional development. In a similar vein, we can construct report cards for our country, to give us some sense of how we are doing in advancing the collective well-being of our citizens. Do government policies increase our welfare—not just America's total wealth, but the satisfaction that all of us derive from being members of our unique society—or does government just make everything worse? Are there alternative policies that might enhance our collective well-being more?

International organizations regularly publish studies benchmarking how their member countries' performances compare to one another, and many domestic government agencies produce highly reliable data about how the United States today is faring, compared with a few years ago. When these different studies are used to construct a composite report card for America, we should be distressed to learn that, by many measures, the United States is no longer a world leader in economic growth or social contentment. Those studies show us as in the middle of the pack, at best, across many important metrics relevant to the fundamental questions of our collective well-being.

This chapter summarizes much of this cross-country research by developing a report card on the economic health of Americans, both from a historical perspective and as measured against peer economies. I pay particular attention to labor markets, because work is a central vehicle by which we define ourselves. Because this chapter focuses principally on economic outcomes, it introduces one of the standard tools for measuring income or wealth inequality, the Gini Index. (Technically, this should be the Gini Coefficient, but the word "coefficient" is intimidating to some, and unnecessary here.)

Our report card suggests that American society as it is lived diverges wildly from the American values and practices that we think our society reflects. Compared to our peers, we are a small-government, low-tax country, not a laboratory of unbridled socialism. We are the richest large economy in the world, but an extraordinary number of Americans live in poverty. We are the most unequal society of all large peer economies, and even more shocking, we are nowhere near the top in income mobility—the ability to climb from poor to rich (or to slide down the opposite side of that hill). Our healthcare system, pre-Obamacare, was by far the most expensive in the world, without a commensurate payoff in medical outcomes. In short, if the United States were a third grader, it would be heading for a parent-teacher conference, sulking all the way.

While other countries also grapple with deficits and unemployment, the United States now for the first time in generations must confront long-term structural unemployment, particularly of men. And our economic anxiety is very high, because we impose so few constraints on the ability of firms to fire employees at will, and because we all stared into the chasm of economic free fall in the darkest days of 2009.

Ironically, the one bright spot is our penchant for budget deficits, which drives so much contemporary political bluster. Our deficits are not a very serious problem at all, at least for the next few years, if we choose to approach them with an intelligent long-term plan.

We thus have our conception of ourselves almost completely backward. We are not a world leader in terms of a robust middle class or in economic equality or mobility. And from the other direction, our apparently overwhelming deficits are false crises of our own design, well within our powers to correct if we choose to do so.

In making cross-country comparisons, here and elsewhere in the book, I look to the following reasonably large and affluent countries: Australia, Canada, France, Germany, Italy, Japan, Norway, Sweden, Switzerland, and the United Kingdom. American exceptionalists argue that none of these is strictly comparable to the United States, and of course that is true to some extent. It also is the case that each of these countries relies on a somewhat different mix of private and public sector contributions to its economy and its citizens' welfare. Nonetheless, quotidian life in each is not as terribly different from life in the United States as the most fervent adherents of American exceptionalism would like to believe, and to the extent there are differences, they can be useful in illuminating whether we have struck the right balance in our own policies.

Later chapters will extend the analysis along several margins. Chapter 4 takes a closer look at the contentious issue of how one measures income inequality and economic mobility. It considers an array of arguments intended to downplay the conclusions reached in this chapter. Part II of the book (chapters 6–9) reviews our current fiscal policies; we learn there, for example, how the United States is a comparative tax haven in relation to its economic peers, and how, without regard to the Affordable Care Act, the United States has become the most reckless healthcare spender in the world. Chapter 10 examines how we underinvest in education and other critically important areas, and chapter 11 demonstrates how we buy very little for all our extravagant healthcare spending. Again, the idea is to see how well we are doing, through whatever means, at delivering these core services to ourselves.

For now, however, my purpose is only to suggest that, like the third grader with promise but a bad attitude, we could be doing much better, if only we were to get serious about tackling the work in front of us.

WHO GRADES US?

Many think tanks and academics publish papers analyzing the performance of the United States along various metrics, but wherever possible I prefer to rely in the first instance on several national and supranational institutions endowed with the requisite skills, access to data, and commitment to nonpartisan truth-telling to deliver reliable conclusions. At the national level, the most important of these is the Congressional Budget Office (CBO). The CBO is an "office" (effectively, a wholly owned subsidiary) of Congress, but unlike Congress it is scrupulously nonpartisan in its mission and in its record over the 40 years since its formation. The CBO is the official scorekeeper of the national budget, both in measuring our fiscal performance today and in formulating the government spending and revenue projections on which Congress relies in shaping policy over the budget "window" (in general, the next 10 years). In addition, the staff of the CBO publishes helpful reports on fiscal policy topics; these are not advocacy pieces, but rather are designed to distill reams of data generated deep in the bowels of the government's accounting systems into more digestible presentations.

The staff of the Congress's Joint Committee on Taxation (JCT, the organization for which I worked) is joined to the CBO at the hip. Like the CBO, the JCT staff is fiercely nonpartisan, and an arm of Congress. The JCT staff traces its foundation back to the earliest days of the income tax. By law, the CBO relies on the JCT staff to estimate the revenue consequences of proposed tax legislation—to determine whether a tax bill will bring in more or less money than the status quo law would have produced over the 10-year budget window. Unlike the CBO, however, the JCT staff is actively involved in serving as a nonpartisan resource to both political parties and to both houses of Congress in drafting the precise wording of tax legislation, to express whatever policy outcome a member wishes. The JCT staff also produces detailed explanations—often running hundreds of pages—of tax legislation under consideration by the Congress's two tax-writing committees. As a result, the JCT professional staff comprises both lawyers and PhD economists, in roughly equal numbers; CBO's professional staff, by contrast, consists almost entirely of economists.

Other important nonpartisan Congressional institutions include the economics staff of the Congressional Research Service (CRS), an arm of the Library of Congress, and the Government Accountability Office (GAO). The CRS in particular produces reports by individual authors who are recognized experts in public finance, and whose work meets my working definition of nonpartisan, which is that their conclusions tend to annoy both political parties about equally.

The Federal Reserve System is the central bank of the United States. It is an independent institution that is not under the direct aegis of either the legislative or the executive branches. The Federal Reserve's researchers produce a wide array of important data, of which the most relevant to this book is their triennial *Survey of Consumer Finances* and the *Flow of Funds* reports.

By definition, executive branch agencies are not nonpartisan in a technical sense. Nonetheless, the professional staffs of the agencies relevant to measuring the economic and fiscal policies of the US government, for example the US Treasury Department's Office of Tax Policy and its Office of Tax Analysis, the Census Bureau, the Commerce Department's Bureau of Economic Analysis (BEA), and the Bureau of Labor Statistics (BLS), all have a reputation for highly professional work, performed consistently from year to year.

At the supranational level, the most important scorekeeper of the economic and fiscal performance of the United States in comparison to that of other countries is the Organisation for Economic Co-operation and Development (OECD). The OECD effectively is the trade association for the national governments of the developed economies of the world, along with a few second-tier economies. In 2013 its membership comprised 34 countries, including the United States, Canada, Australia, New Zealand, Japan, and all of Western Europe. (The BRICS—Brazil, Russia, India, China, and South Africa—are not members.) The OECD has a large budget (about $500 million/year) and a professional staff that collects data from the member states and benchmarks the membership's respective economic performance against one another. The OECD's data collection efforts are designed to ensure consistency in application from country to country, and its status as an association of national governments means that it has access to the same data that those countries use themselves. As a result, their benchmarking work is particularly useful in understanding the relative strength and weaknesses of US fiscal policy.

The International Monetary Fund (IMF) also is a multinational governmental trade association of sorts, although its membership comprises most countries in the world. Its principal focus is on monetary policies and currency exchange rate stability; it also plays the central role in international "bailouts" of countries in financial distress. The IMF prepares an annual report—really very close to a narrative report card—on the budgetary and economic health of each of its 188 members. Again, for those willing to listen, those reports offer useful advice on what the United States is doing well, and where it needs improvement.

SAGGING MEDIAN INCOMES, COLLAPSING WEALTH

We Americans define ourselves in large part through our work. Work provides us with material resources, of course, but it also gives dignity, structure, and purpose to our lives. Few Americans are constitutionally equipped for life as a *café habitué* debating existentialism with other idle friends. For all these reasons, the welfare of the *median* worker—the worker in the middle of income distributions—is closely bound up with the health of American labor markets.

As a reminder of the difference between average (mean) income and median income, consider the little country of Freedonia. It has an economy comprising five individuals, four of whom have incomes of $10,000/year, and the fifth an income of $5 million/year. In Freedonia, the average (or mean) income of its citizens is slightly above $1 million/year—but there would still be four poor Freedonians hustling to make ends meet. To calculate the median Freedonian personal income, imagine that you line up the country's citizens in order of their income, from lowest to highest. The income of the person in the middle of the line is the median income. In Freedonia, where average annual incomes are over $1 million, the median income is $10,000.

It might seem intuitive to begin our inquiry into median incomes and welfare by looking at trends in per capita GDP, but this actually is a poor measure of middle class economic progress or welfare, for two reasons. First, as the Freedonian example implies, it confuses means (averages) with medians (the guy in the middle). Second, as discussed in chapter 1, the standard method of presenting GDP is not a measure of the sum of all personal economic activity: it ignores, for example, the economic contributions of work in the home.

Every three years, the Federal Reserve publishes a detailed study of the financial health of the American consumer. The most recent edition of that work in turn tells a gloomy story, one completely invisible to observers who focus only on GDP. The current survey, released in mid-2012, examines 2010, and compares that year with 2007, 2004, and 2001.[1] These were very difficult years for the middle class.

From 2007 through 2010, median pre-tax constant-dollar incomes (the income of the family in the middle of the pack, adjusted for inflation, and before paying taxes) fell almost 8 percent.[2] What is more, median income also declined a bit from 2004 to 2007. The collapse in median constant dollar incomes wiped out the modest gains that the middle class recorded from 2001 to 2004. As a result, if measured over the 10-year period from 2001 to 2010, median family incomes declined from $48,900 to $45,800 (all in 2010 constant dollars)—a drop of about 6.3 percent (see Figure 3.1).

The collapse in real incomes described in the Federal Reserve's *Survey* did not apply evenly across all income levels. Mean (average) incomes dropped more from 2007 to 2010 than did median (middle of the pack) incomes, which suggests that higher-income Americans suffered proportionately larger drops in incomes than did regular folk from the collapse of the financial markets in 2008–2009. But higher-income Americans also had enjoyed much larger gains earlier in the decade. And as discussed at the end of this chapter, the incomes of the most affluent Americans have since rebounded sharply.

In 2010, the income of the family in the 95th percentile, ranked by incomes, was $205,000; it had been $217,000 in 2004 (all in constant 2010 dollars). But in 2001 the income for this group was $208,000, so from 2001 to 2010 the drop in incomes for families occupying in that year the 95th percentile, ranked by

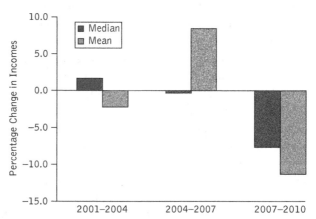

Note: Changes are based on inflation-adjusted dollars.

FIGURE 3.1 Change in Median and Mean Incomes (2001–2010)

Source: SCF Survey, 2.

incomes, was only about $3,000. This is not nearly so large a decline in percentage terms—*or even in absolute dollars*—as it was for the median family of the entire population, who earned less than one-quarter as much as did the family in the 95th percentile.

The Census Bureau's statistics for comparable periods basically tell the same story.[3] According to the Census Bureau, the constant dollar median income of all American families declined slightly from 2000 to 2009, and grew only 11 percent in total over the 19-year period from 1990 to 2009.[4] As described below, this 11 percent gain over 19 years was primarily attributable to more women within families entering the workforce, and women's wage rates climbing somewhat relative to men's (but still to levels substantially lower than men's).[5]

According to the Bureau of Labor Statistics, average hourly wages for all workers in the private sector increased in nominal terms from $14.54 to $19.07 from 2001 to 2010[6]; on an inflation-adjusted basis, that represents a raise of only about $0.75/hour (in 2010 dollars) over all nine years.[7] Since wages are expected to grow over time, as the productivities of workers increase, this suggests that in real terms either the average worker's productivity increased at a rate of only about 0.44 percent per annum over these nine years or workers did not capture a large share of real productivity growth. The answer turns out to be the second.

In constant dollar terms, the median (middle of the pack) full-time, year-round American male worker earned less in 2010 than did his father 37 years earlier, in 1973—$47,715 in 2010 versus $49,065 in 1973.[8] (The only good news here is that we have worked ourselves up from the lowest level recorded for these data over the last 40 years, which we hit in 1996.) Similarly, the Congressional Budget Office has calculated that the constant dollar hourly wage of the median American male worker remained essentially unchanged from 1979 to 2007.[9]

Income growth in the American middle class family over the last several decades has come almost entirely from the participation of women in the workforce. Between 1979 and 2007, approximately 85 percent of males ages 25 to 54 worked each year, while women in that age range increased their participation rate from 66 to 74 percent during the same time period.[10] While in 1973 there were more than 2.25 male full-time workers for every female worker, in 2010 there were only 1.32. And from 1979 to 2007 the median working woman's constant dollar hourly wage increased about 50 percent, from $10.50/hour to $15.60/hour.[11] So the market workforce includes far more women than was true a generation ago, and those women in turn have made significant (if still incomplete) gains in their returns to market labor.

A later section of this chapter discusses changing patterns in income inequality, but some mention of the topic is necessary here to put the dispiriting results obtained by median workers into context. After all, if the United States as a whole posted a consistently terrible record of income growth for several decades, one would not expect median workers to be doing materially better. The short answer is that there has been significant aggregate real family income growth over time, but the great bulk of that growth has been captured by the very topmost incomes in America. The most prolific private researcher into income and wealth inequality probably is Emmanuel Saez at the University of California, Berkeley. Chapter 4 discusses at length his methodologies and data sources, but in brief, in September 2013 he published a paper updating his earlier research.[12] Saez found that the real incomes of the top one percent of families grew by 86.1 percent over the period 1993–2012, while the incomes of the bottom 99 percent (which by definition includes families that are doing very well) increased by only 6.6 percent. The top one percent harvested 68 percent of the entirety of real income growth over this more extended period.

Any increase in middle class *consumption* over the couple of decades is largely the story of families relying increasingly on the incomes of secondary (predominantly female) wage earners and of spending funded by borrowing against the rising bubble of home prices. This borrowing did not simply maintain a constant level of mortgage debt to alleged value; instead, homeowners' equity consistently declined as a percentage of market value, even prior to the collapse of housing prices in the Great Recession.[13] For this reason, arguments focusing on the consumption patterns of the middle class over time tend to be highly misleading. For a decade or more leading up to the Great Recession, consumption was financed through borrowing against assets that in retrospect did not exist. In the end, consumption is the aim of earning income, but at the household level it is income that finances consumption, not the other way around.

The increasing importance of secondary wage earners to the incomes of middle class families raises difficult interpretative issues when moving beyond income measures to a consideration of the broader (and more appropriate) question of the welfare of middle class Americans. Many women have entered the workforce because they want financial independence and satisfying professional careers, just as many men do. But some women (and men) with a spouse or partner no doubt have left the home to join the workforce out of economic necessity; if offered the choice, these individuals might have preferred careers within the home.

Children complicate the calculus in both directions. On the one hand, when both parents work, they now must pay for child care, which reduces the secondary wage earner's returns to working outside the home. On the other, the parents may feel compelled to both pursue market-based careers to permit them to invest more money in their children, in the form of a better education, for example.

Similarly, it may be the case that even today many American males, whether through lack of social evolution, class conditioning, or otherwise, would prefer to live in a world where their spouse works (if at all) out of choice rather than necessity. The complete stagnation of male full-time, year-round wages puts the lie to that fantasy, and means that many families are compelled for purely financial reasons to abandon, in particular, their desire to organize matters so that one parent can stay at home to care for their children. Perhaps the intuitive understanding of this reality explains some of the undifferentiated male anger that seems to dominate current political debates.

Standard economic data cannot distinguish among these situations. The data instead treat every case as if the increase in a couple's market income occasioned by the second adult in the family entering the commercial labor market necessarily is also welfare enhancing for the couple in question.[14]

The effects of the Great Recession (and in particular the collapse of the housing and stock markets) on wealth are even more dramatic than those it reported for income. In constant dollar terms, the net worth of the median American family (the family in the middle of the wealth distribution) fell 39 percent from 2007 to 2010; if you instead use 2001 as your reference point, the median American family's net worth fell 27 percent over nine years. In 2010, the median family's net worth was about the same as it was in 1992,[15] which can be rephrased (only slightly inaccurately from a technical perspective) as saying that the middle of the pack family worked 18 years for no net increase in wealth. Even the mean (average) net worth of American families, which is pulled up by the vast wealth of the most affluent Americans, was flat from 2001 to 2010.

At the other end, the top 10 percent of American families, ranked by incomes, emerged from the 2008–2009 crash in much better shape than the middle class. The wealth of families in the 95th percentile (ranked by incomes) increased 17 percent over the nine-year period. The *average* wealth of the top 10 percent of American families is much greater than the wealth of the median (95th percentile) family within the top 10 percent, because of the extraordinary wealth of the very richest Americans, but during the nine-year period the average wealth of this group increased less than did the median (6 percent rather than 17 percent), pulled down (relative to the median for that group) by the loss of wealth incurred through the collapse of the financial assets held by the most affluent Americans.

Wealth is much more concentrated than is income, because only higher income households are able to save anything at all. One of the most sobering aspects of the Federal Reserve *Survey* is its implicit reminder of how little wealth most Americans have, particularly after the recent collapse of the real estate and financial markets. The 2010 net assets of the median family in America, ranked by their incomes (not by wealth), was $66,000, against an income of $45,800. And of course, even after the crash, much of this wealth was illiquid, in the form of investments in homes and automobiles. Only about one-half of families at or around the median of incomes had any direct or indirect ownership interest in stocks (including through pension claims), and of that half, the median value of those stock investments was $12,000. And by definition, of course, one-half of all

Americans had lower savings than did the median family. Most Americans walk a razor's edge every month between paying their bills and a liquidity crisis.

HOURS WORKED

The family in the middle of the pack worked in 2010 for less money (in real terms) than that family did at the turn of the millennium. There is no evidence of which I am aware that the explanation is that Americans have chosen to emulate the French, by voluntarily taking long vacations to enjoy more leisure, or now are kicking back three days a week rather than two, to tend their rose gardens.

To the contrary, the Congressional Budget Office in 2009 examined the income and employment characteristics of American workers between the ages of 25 and 54. The average annual workload of a middle of the pack (median) full-time, full-year male worker in 1979 was 2,260 hours. By 1989 that workload had increased to 2,290 hours, and in 2000 to 2,310. The figure for 2007 was 2,290 hours—the same as in 1989, and down only slightly from the high water mark a few years earlier.[16] The median full-time, full-year female worker increased her workload over the same time period, from 2,080 hours in 1979 to 2,140 hours in 2000, which figure remained unchanged in 2007. These numbers are a bit higher than one might expect because the underlying Bureau of Labor Statistics data on which CBO relies treat paid vacations as time worked.

Looking more closely at the effects of the Great Recession on labor incomes in the United States, the Department of Labor's BLS tracks weekly hours worked by industry; in conjunction with the Census Bureau, the BLS further separates that data between workers who usually work full-time and those who work part-time. As in the CBO study, the data show a relatively constant average hourly workweek for nonagricultural full-time workers over the last decade, until the Great Recession hit in 2008, followed by a partial recovery since. The difference, though, in average hours worked in 2007 compared with 2010 or 2012 for those lucky enough to have a full-time job was less than 0.5 hours/week (see Figure 3.2).

In sum, middle of the pack American families had materially lower incomes in real terms in 2010 than they did in 2001. Those who were employed full-time were working about as hard as they were 10 years earlier, but wage earners in many families had become unemployed, or had dropped from full-time to part-time employment.

INTERNATIONAL COMPARISONS

Good data comparing workers' incomes in different countries are hard to come by, but the BLS, the OECD, and a UN agency, the International Labour Organization (ILO), have endeavored to produce comparable data that enable cross-country

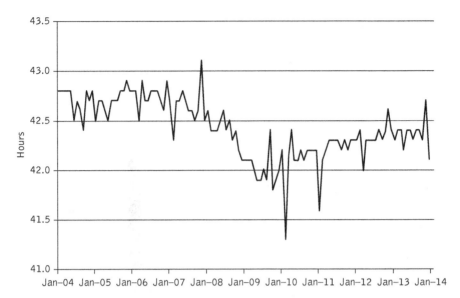

FIGURE 3.2 Average Hourly Workweek for Nonagricultural Full-Time Workers (2003–2013)

Source: BLS, *Average Hours, Persons Who Usually Work Full Time, Nonagricultural Industries Employed Full Time (Seasonally Adjusted)* (accessed 2013), http://data.bls.gov/timeseries/LNS12533120.

comparisons. Unfortunately, the BLS's efforts in this area recently have been discontinued, presumably due to budget cuts.

American workers in manufacturing (where the data are best) are not particularly well paid by the standards of the other peer countries considered in this book. Figure 3.3 compares the cash wages and benefits directly paid to workers across those countries in 2011. "Benefits" include paid vacations, bonuses, contributions to workers' savings plans, and the like.

In every country, employers pay more in total compensation costs than employees receive, due to Social Security taxes and the like. As Figure 3.4 shows, when viewed from employers' perspectives, the United States is not an expensive place, compared to its peers, to hire a manufacturing worker. This suggests that high labor taxes are not the explanation for the relatively modest wages received by US manufacturing sector workers.

Some economists have argued that differing wage rates fairly compensate workers for the risk that their jobs will disappear. This conclusion certainly does not translate across borders, because the United States manages to combine some of the lowest wages with by far the highest job insecurity of any of the peer countries considered here (see Figure 3.5).

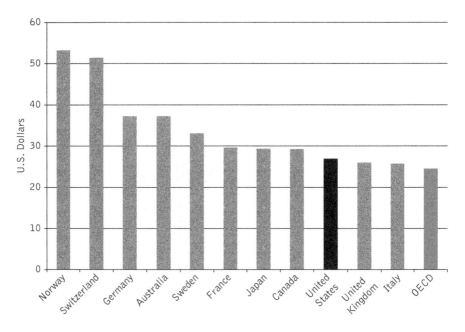

FIGURE 3.3 Hourly Manufacturing Wages + Direct Benefits in US Dollars (2011)

Source: BLS, *Charting International Labor Comparisons 2012* (2012), http://www.bls.gov/fls/chartbook/2012/chartbook2012.pdf (and supplemental data tables).

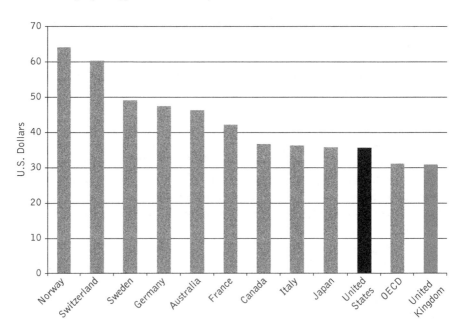

FIGURE 3.4 Hourly Manufacturing Compensation Costs in US Dollars (2011)

Source: BLS, *Charting International Labor Comparisons 2012* (and supplemental data tables).

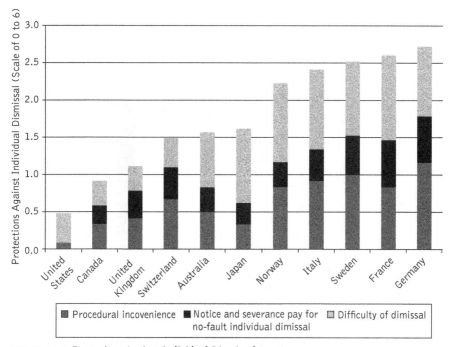

FIGURE 3.5 Protections Against Individual Dismissal (2013)

Source: OECD, *OECD Employment Outlook 2013* (2013), doi:10.1787/888932852694.

This is an important point when thinking about the welfare of the middle class. The United States arguably has the most flexible labor market among its peers, but what this "flexibility" means on the ground is that middle class workers rightly live in fear of losing their jobs without fault at a moment's notice, and receiving in return by way of a termination package what economists of the borscht belt school would have called "bupkis."

OECD data suggest that Americans who have jobs generally work longer hours than do residents of the peer countries considered throughout this book. The OECD data here can be misleading, however, because the OECD simply divides total hours worked over the year by the average number of people in employment.[17] This means that a population where a relatively large number of workers have part-time jobs can make the working hours of those with full-time jobs look lighter than is the case. (By contrast, US data from the BLS separate full-time, year-round workers from others.) For example, Germany and other countries have adopted "job sharing" strategies to maintain employment in face of the economic difficulties of the Eurozone, and this has the effect of driving down the OECD reported hours. Overall, looking at individuals with full-time, year-round jobs, Americans do not work terribly longer hours than is the norm in the OECD.

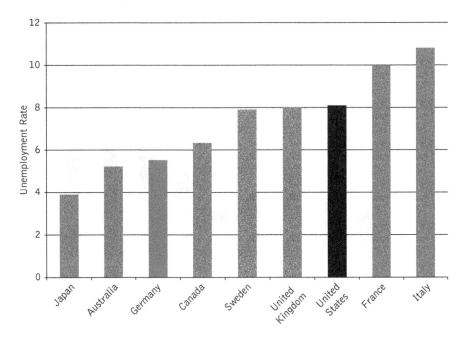

FIGURE 3.6 Unemployment Rates (2012)

Source: BLS, *International Comparisons of Labor Force Statistics, 1970–2012* (June 7, 2013).

Cross-country unemployment comparisons can be problematic, because business cycles in different countries are not precisely in sync with one another. Italy, for example, was doing quite well on the unemployment front in 2011, but its unemployment surged in 2012. Nonetheless, it is instructive to look at 2012 unemployment across the peer countries considered in this book.

The United States in 2012 had much better unemployment data than did Italy or France, but performed worse than every other peer country. (Data for Norway and Switzerland were not available in this comparison and so are excluded from the figure.) Again, the point is that in return for median wages that are not particularly high by peer standards, and for much worse job insecurity in general, the median US worker who lost her job also faced the prospect of a larger cadre of similarly situated out of work compatriots (see Figure 3.6).

LONG-TERM EMPLOYMENT TRENDS

There are two disturbing trends that go directly to the economic security of the middle class. First, the economic return to work has not kept pace with workers' contributions to national income. Second, long-term structural unemployment is on the rise.

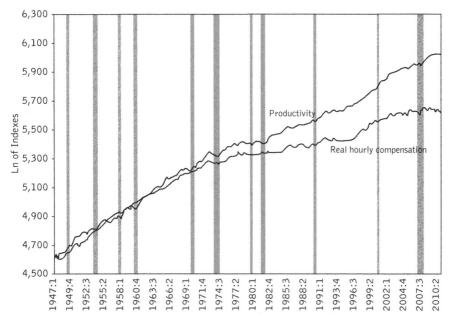

FIGURE 3.7 Hourly Productivity and Compensation in the United States (Q1 1947–Q1 2012)

Source: International Labour Organization, Global Wage Report 2012/13 (2013), 46.

Economists ordinarily expect that wages (the economic returns to labor) should keep pace with the productivity of that labor. Our incomes today are higher than those of workers 100 years ago because we leverage our labor through all the capital that stands behind us, which enables us to create more goods or services in an hour than earlier generations could. But something has gone wrong with this simple syllogism: in recent decades labor productivity has continued to grow, but workers have not captured the returns to those productivity gains (see Figure 3.7). Instead, business owners have. (In fairness, this is a global phenomenon, not a unique aberration of the US labor markets.)

The CBO calculated that labor's share of gross domestic income averaged 62.4 percent between 1950 and 2000, but since 2001 it has exhibited a downward trend, reaching 59.4 percent in 2012, the lowest value recorded since 1950.[18] The Bureau of Labor Statistics reported that from 1947 to 2000, labor share of income averaged 64.3 percent but had been falling since, reaching a record low of 57.8 percent in 2010.[19] This is one reason for the growth in income inequality discussed in the following chapter, but more directly it explains in large measure the stagnation in American middle class family wages just described.

The United States for decades has been blessed by an economy that invents new jobs as fast as it destroys old ones, so that long-term unemployment has

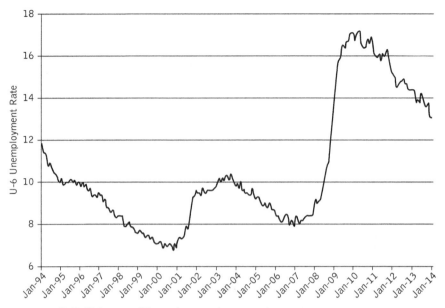

FIGURE 3.8 U-6 Measure of Unemployment (1994–2013)

Source: BLS, Total Unemployed, Plus All Marginally Attached Workers Plus Total Employed Part Time for Economic Reasons, as a Percent of All Civilian Labor Force Plus All Marginally Attached Workers (accessed July 2013), http:// data.bls.gov/timeseries/LNS13327709.

been a much less important issue in the United States than in Europe. But recent data are disturbing, and suggest that even as the Great Recession recedes, the United States may be entering a period of long-term structural unemployment. Figure 3.8 shows the 20-year history of U-6, the US government's broadest measure of unemployment. It adds to the official unemployment rate (technically known as U-3) individuals who want to work but who have become "discouraged," and therefore have not actively sought work in the last month, individuals who are "marginally attached" to the labor markets (individuals who want to work and have tried to find work in the last year, but not in the last month, and who may be unemployed for reasons that go beyond "discouragement"), and the underemployed—those who have part-time jobs when they desire full-time ones.[20] U-6 and the other unemployment figures do not count in their denominators those who are completely unattached from the civilian workforce, including institutionalized individuals, active military personnel, and happily retired individuals, so the data are not simply an artifact of an aging population.

The data speak for themselves. The jump in unemployment in the broadest sense is unprecedented in the last 20 years, and 2013's figures, while better than the worst days of the Great Recession, are still far higher than any seen before 2009.

Another relevant statistic is the civilian labor force participation rate—the percentage of noninstitutionalized civilian Americans who are employed. ("Institutionalized" here incorporates incarcerated Americans and those in long-term medical facilities.) The raw rate has trended down, but to be fair this is misleading, because it is not adjusted for the aging of the population. The Bureau of Labor Statistics does tabulate data for subsets of the population, including a series tracking Americans at the heart of the labor force, those ages 25–54.[21] Even within this group, labor participation in 2013 is 2.4 percentage points lower than it was in 2007. For those over 50 who have lost a job, the job market is particularly grim, yet these are individuals who by dint of their inclination and energy ordinarily would have years of labor force participation ahead of them.[22]

Recent OECD analysis suggests that US long-term unemployment is now comparable to that in many European countries (see Figure 3.9).

This is a very troublesome trend, particularly when coupled with the stagnation of real wages described above. The United States has always been a country where everyone works, and where labor receives the lion's share of national income. But now labor's share is declining, and not everyone who wants to work can find work commensurate with her training and experience. We are not yet a country of *rentiers* and proletariat, but we are pointing in a dangerous direction.

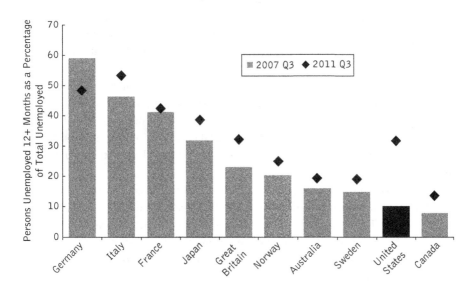

FIGURE 3.9 Persons Unemployed 12 Months and Longer as a Percentage of Total Unemployment (Q3 2007–Q3 2011)

Source: OECD, *Economic Surveys: United States 2012* (June 2012), fig. 1.7, doi:10.1787/eco_surveys-usa-2012-en.

POVERTY

The study of poverty in America is a fraught discipline, often consumed by definitional debates (absolute poverty or relative poverty? Cash income poverty or post-tax and benefits poverty?). There are poverty deniers (some of the so-called poor have refrigerators and televisions!) and poverty spinners (it is the poor's own fault, or they are the temporary victims of the creative destruction that drives economic growth). Exactly the same sorts of issues arise when one examines income inequality or mobility (the prospects for moving up, or sliding down, the income ladder relative to others in one's age cohort). Chapter 4 addresses these arguments in more detail.

For the moment, OECD data suffice to make the point that the United States is a remarkably unequal society—a land with a substantial poverty problem, and one where it is much more difficult to move from the bottom of the economic heap to the top than we would like to believe. The OECD applies the same measurement methodologies to every member country, assuring reliability and consistency over time. Those methodologies in turn are documented and vetted. And of course the OECD is an association of many national governments, with no agenda to agitate for one US domestic political outcome or another.

The United States is the richest large economy in the world. Its *average* national income per citizen (GDP divided by population—technically referred to as per capita GDP) substantially exceeds that of Germany, the United Kingdom, or France. Our per capita income is about 50 percent higher than the EU average. Within the OECD we lag behind only tiny Luxembourg, with its large "offshore" (i.e., tax evasion) banking sector, Norway, with its North Sea oil, and Switzerland (see Figure 3.10).

So one might start by thinking that if, on average, a US citizen is so well off, poverty must be a rare thing. But this is a misunderstanding of what "average" incomes conceal. Starting with total or per capita GDP demonstrates that the United States as a whole is rich, whether in total or taking into account the size of its population, but it tells us nothing about how that wealth is distributed among the population.

The OECD's standard measure of poverty, and one used by many academic researchers as well, is income less than one-half that of a country's *median* (midpoint) income. This is a relative measure of poverty—the poor in a very rich country might be better off than the poor in a poorer country—but it is thought to most accurately capture what life is like when competing with others for the goods and services necessary to make a life. The OECD also calculates poverty after taking into account government transfer payments designed to ameliorate poverty itself; this accurately captures how many resources a poor family has available to it, but from another perspective contaminates the data by making it more difficult to get a picture of how much government already is doing to ameliorate poverty.

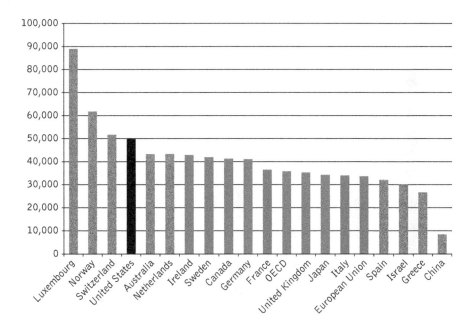

FIGURE 3.10 Gross Domestic Product (Expenditure Approach), per Head, US Dollars, Current Prices, Current PPPs

Source: OECD, *StatExtract: GDP per Capita in 2011 US $* (accessed 2013).

Finally, poverty data can reflect the extent of a country's social security system, as the elderly in many countries, including the United States, rely heavily on the government to provide them with market resources. A country with a weak social security system is likely to have great poverty among the elderly. It therefore is important to look at poverty among the elderly separately from poverty among working-age citizens.

When one looks at the official OECD data for poverty among working-age citizens, the results are appalling. The United States has the highest poverty level of any OECD country; even Mexico does better, relative to its more limited national resources (see Figure 3.11).

There are far more American households in dire straits than is commonly appreciated. In 2011, 1.6 million American households, with over 3.5 million children in those households, got by on less than $2 per person per day in cash income in any given month.[23] (These estimates include cash income amounts received from the Temporary Assistance to Needy Families and similar programs.) "Households in extreme poverty constituted 4.3 percent of all non-elderly households with children."[24] In such a household, bus fare might be an unaffordable luxury. This in turn has profound implications for the pursuit of labor market opportunities.

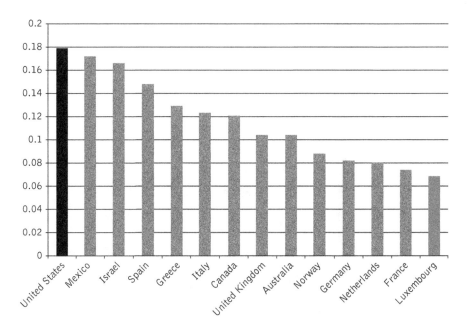

FIGURE 3.11 Poverty Rate after Taxes and Transfers, Poverty Line 50%, Working Age Population: 18–65, Current Definition (2010)

Source: OECD, *StatExtract: Income Distribution and Poverty MetaData: By Country—Poverty* (accessed 2013).

The US Census Bureau publishes extensive data on poverty in the United States. The official US measure of poverty essentially calculates the cost of a minimum food budget and multiplies that by three, to cover all other costs of living. The result is adjusted by family size; families with cash incomes below that threshold are classified as living in poverty.[25] In 1980, 13 percent of Americans lived below the poverty level; 18.1 percent lived below 125 percent of the poverty level.[26] In 1990 Americans living below the poverty level had increased slightly, to 13.5 percent of the population, but those living below 125 percent of the poverty level had stayed about the same. By 2000, the picture was very much happier: 11.3 percent of Americans lived below the poverty level, and 15.6 percent below 125 percent of the poverty level.

And now all those gains have been lost, and more. In 2011, 15 percent of Americans lived below the poverty level, and 19.8 percent below 125 percent of the poverty level. In absolute numbers, these are the highest levels ever recorded—46.2 million Americans living in poverty, and 60.9 million below 125 percent of the poverty threshold. To put this in perspective, a single person was below the poverty threshold in 2011 if his income was lower than $11,702/year; the members of a two-person family unit were below the threshold at $15,063/

year.[27] These are the conditions in which over 46 million Americans lived in 2011. Focusing just on working-age Americans, 13.7 percent (26 million) struggled with incomes below the poverty line. Perhaps even more shocking is that in 2011 over 20 million people (almost 7 percent of all Americans) lived in "deep poverty," with incomes less than one-half their poverty threshold.[28]

It is true of course that poverty data are notoriously complex to interpret. For example, these figures do not mean that 44 million Americans live in chronic (year in, year out) poverty. For the majority, poverty is a temporary status, and the Census Bureau's figures are a snapshot in time, not a movie of all 44 million affected Americans' life stories. But the same was true in 1980, and so on.

The Census Bureau has recently begun to publish an additional "Supplemental Poverty Measure," which updates the traditional metrics in a number of respects, including by taking into account payroll taxes on the one hand and various government benefits, like refundable tax credits and food stamps, on the other. This Supplemental Poverty Measure shows about three million additional Americans—another one percent of all Americans—living in poverty.[29]

INCOME AND WEALTH INEQUALITY

Income inequality is as contentious a topic as is the measure of poverty. One usual methodological starting place, however, is the Gini index. Imagine a box, where the horizontal (X) axis represents all Americans lined up in order of their incomes, from lowest to highest. The vertical (Y) axis represents the share of national income earned by people up to any given point on the horizontal axis. If all incomes were perfectly equal, then the "bottom" 20 percent of the population would earn 20 percent of national income, the bottom 60 percent would earn 60 percent, and so on. The line showing income shares would be a straight line drawn at 45 degrees (see Figure 3.12).

In reality, of course, incomes are not equal; the bottom 20 percent of the population, arrayed by incomes, receives nothing close to 20 percent of total national income. In fact, for 2010 (the most recent year available), the Census Bureau calculated that the bottom 20 percent of American households, ranked by households' shares of "market incomes" (basically cash income before considering government taxes paid or cash transfer payments received), captured only 3.3 percent of national income. The top 20 percent received about 50 percent of national income (15 times more per household),[30] and the top one percent earned over 15 percent of national market income—more than the bottom 40 percent of the population combined.[31]

The Gini index takes these miscellaneous distressing facts and reduces them to one inequality measure. The Gini index is just a measure of the shaded area in Figure 3.12 (technically, times two); the more unequal the distribution of incomes,

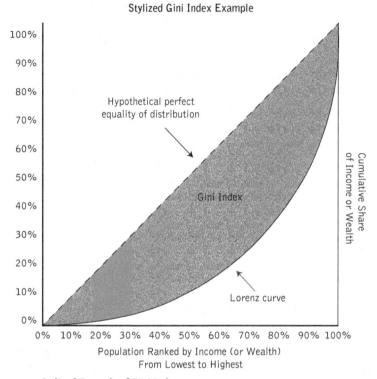

FIGURE 3.12 Stylized Example of Gini Index

the more the distribution curve will sag down toward the bottom right corner, and the larger that shaded area will be.

By world standards, the United States is a very unequal place. Among major industrialized countries, OECD data show the United States as near but not quite at the top of the inequality derby by reference to household *market* incomes—the income of a household before taxes and government transfer payments (including Social Security payments). But when the OECD measures inequality by reference to household *disposable* income—household income after payment of taxes and receipt of cash transfer payments (again including Social Security)—the United States moves up to first place in this distasteful contest (see Figure 3.13).

What this means is that the United States is in general a very unequal place, but that, unlike other major economies with similarly unequal distributions of household market incomes (such as France, Italy, or the United Kingdom), the combination of the US tax and transfer payment systems does very little to address those unequal market outcomes.

The Gini index is a handy single number, but it does not convey much information about exactly how inequality is distributed: Is it that the bottom of the

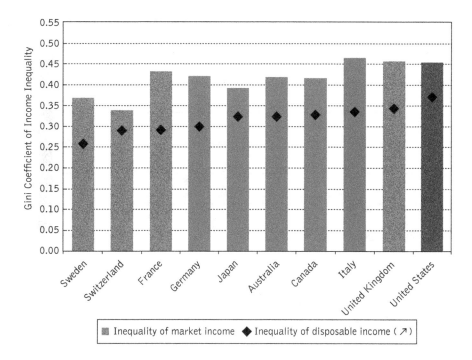

FIGURE 3.13 Redistribution Through Taxes and Transfers

Source: OECD, *Divided We Stand: Why Inequality Keeps Rising* (2011), Country Note: United States.

population does really badly, but the middle class is doing OK? Or is it that the bottom and the middle each are treading water, and the top of the population (by incomes) is running away from the rest? To get a handle on these sorts of questions, it is helpful to look at the ratios of incomes at different points along the income curve.

The most telling is the S90/S10 ratio, the ratio of the average income within the top 10 percent of households to the average income within the bottom 10 percent. You can see again (Figure 3.14) that the United States has by far the highest ratio among its peer countries.

The same is true if one compares upper incomes to the household in the middle (the median income household). The standard metric for this is the P90/P50 ratio—the ratio of the income of the household at the 90th percentile (that is, the household at the bottom of the top 10 percent) with that of the household at the 50th percentile. Again, the United States leads all its peer countries in this dismal contest (see Figure 3.15).

Even if one includes in a comparison all of the OECD countries, the United States's performance ranks at the very bottom by every measure. According to the most recent OECD data ranking 31 of its member countries across a variety

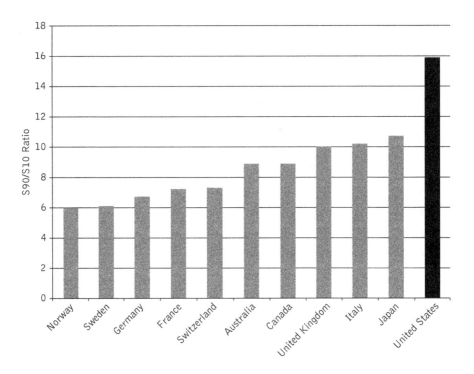

FIGURE 3.14 S90/S10 Ratio (2010)

Source: OECD, *OECD Factbook 2011–2012: Economic, Environmental and Social Statistics* (2012), doi:10.1787/factbook-2011-en.

of inequality measures, with the most equal country by each metric at the top of that contest, the best the United States finished was in 29th place (in the P90/P50 ratio, as it happens). In the other events, we were last or next to last.[32]

Not only does the United States have the most unequal distribution of incomes of any of the world's large economies, but that inequality has grown rapidly, and has done so mostly through an unprecedented concentration at the very top of the economic ladder. Inequality growth in the United States (measured again by the Gini index of household disposable incomes) has outstripped the trend in the OECD as a whole (see Figure 3.16).

Drilling down to the source of US inequality growth over this period, the CBO chart in Figure 3.17 shows growth in real (inflation adjusted) incomes over a 28-year period, ending just before the onset of the Great Recession.[33] The median household (the household right in the middle, with half doing worse and half better) increased its income by about 35 percent over that period, a bit better than one percent per annum growth in real income. (As previously described, this is largely attributable to increasing labor participation, and wage gains, by women.) The broad swath of Americans from the 20th to the 80th percentile in income

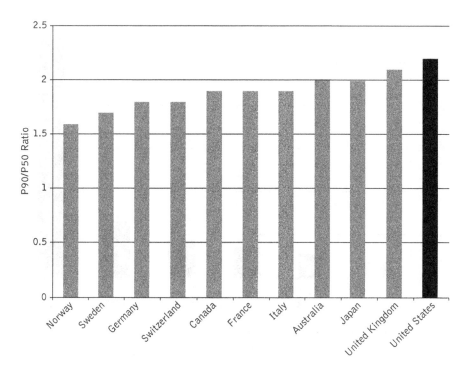

FIGURE 3.15 P90/P50 Ratio (2010)

Source: OECD, *OECD Factbook 2011–2012: Economic, Environmental and Social Statistics.*

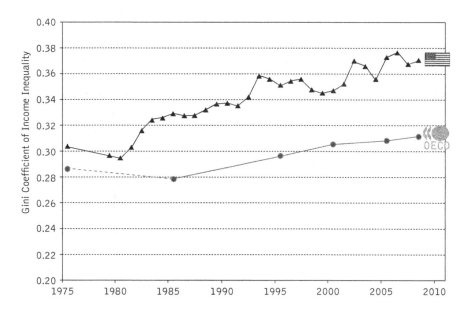

FIGURE 3.16 Trends in Inequality of Disposable Income

Source: OECD, *Divided We Stand: Why Inequality Keeps Rising*, Country Note: United States.

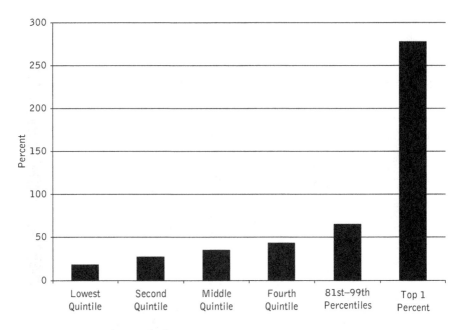

FIGURE 3.17 Growth in Real After-Tax Income (1979–2007)

Source: CBO, *Trends in the Distribution of Household Income Between 1979 and 2007.*

distributions saw their average real incomes grow less than 40 percent over that period. The top one percent, however, enjoyed income growth of 275 percent.

This extraordinary concentration in income growth among America's most affluent households means that, when comparing 1979 to 2007, *every* economic group lost ground in terms of their share of total national market income (basically, pre-tax cash income, like wages and investment returns), except for the top one percent. Even the 81st to 99th percentile of incomes—the top fifth of economic winners, save the top one percent—saw their share of national market income decline. The top one percent, however, actually doubled their share of national income, from 10.5 to 21.3 percent of the country's entire national market income, as the CBO's analysis demonstrates (see Figure 3.18).

Emmanuel Saez's research points in the same direction. As mentioned earlier, Saez found that during 1993–2012, the real incomes of the top one percent of families grew by 86.1 percent, while the real incomes of the bottom 99 percent increased by 6.6 percent. Further, the top one percent harvested 68 percent of all real income growth over this period.[34] Looking more narrowly at how the recovery from the Great Recession affected family incomes over the period 2009–2012, Saez found that the real (inflation adjusted) incomes of the top one percent of families grew in that period by 31.4 percent, while the incomes

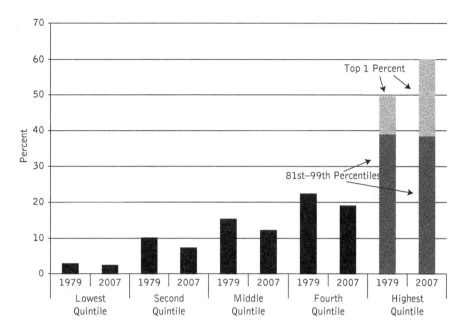

of the bottom 99 percent were essentially flat, increasing only 0.4 percent over that period. In other words, the top one percent captured 95 percent of all income gains over this period.

According to Saez's research, the top 10 percent of families, by market incomes, in 2012 captured more than 50 percent of all such income in the United States. This is the highest fraction in the history of his database, which goes back to 1917.

In sum, no other wealthy country has the kind of income inequality that the United States does. To the contrary, the traditional rule of thumb has been that as countries become wealthier they become more equal, not less. The position of the United States as a high-income, high-inequality outlier is obvious in Figure 3.19.

Looking just at domestic data, both US Census and CBO analyses show that income inequality in the United States is increasing. Using Census data, the P90/P10 ratio—the measure of the multiple of incomes enjoyed by the household at the 90th percentile of income distributions, compared to the household at the 10th percentile—increased from 10.22 in 1991 to 11.97 in 2011.[35] And it should be emphasized that the 90th percentile does not represent an exorbitant income, at least by the standards of major metropolitan areas on the two coasts: the 2011 cutoff point to qualify as a top-10 percenter was a household income of about $144,000.

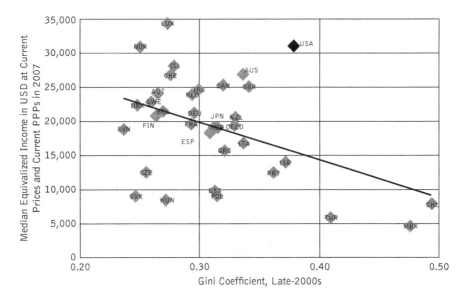

FIGURE 3.19 Median Income and Inequality

Source: OECD, Society at a Glance 2011 (2011), chart EQ 1.2.

CBO data, which for technical reasons tend to be superior to that of the Census Bureau in capturing topmost incomes, demonstrate that the Gini Index for household market incomes (pre-tax, pre-government transfer incomes) increased by 22 percent from 1979 to 2009, and by 4 percent from 1999 to 2009.[36] These are very significant changes in the composition of household incomes for a large country like the United States.

Wealth is generally more difficult to measure than income, because most individuals around the world are not required to file annual wealth tax returns or the like detailing the current market values of their assets, net of their liabilities. Wealth often is invisible on income tax returns; an increase in the value of one's stock portfolio is income in an economic sense, but is ignored for income tax purposes until the securities are sold, which might be many years after they first appreciated in value.

In general, wealth is much more concentrated than is income, for the simple reason that most people spend almost all their income as they earn it, and therefore add very little to their stock of wealth from year to year. Moreover, older citizens typically spend down what wealth they have; for example, 46 percent of senior citizens own less than $10,000 in financial assets at the time of their deaths.[37]

Probably the most current and comprehensive analysis of worldwide wealth is the Credit Suisse Wealth Databook, published annually by the research arm of the eponymous Swiss bank. The Databook's findings are surprising, even to one inured to income inequality data. First, American adults are not as rich on average as are the adult citizens of several other large economies, including Japan, Norway, Switzerland (the highest average wealth per adult in the world), Australia, and finally (and this one will really hurt) France.

But more distressingly, the *median* wealth per adult in the United States is by far the lowest of these countries. (Again, median wealth measures the wealth of the person in the middle of the wealth lineup, from poorest to richest; by contrast, average wealth measures effectively pretend that poor Americans are able to spend Warren Buffett's money.) In 2012 the average wealth of an American adult was $262,000, but the wealth of the median adult was only $39,000. A relative handful of very rich people brought up the average, but did not change the modest resources of the person in the middle.

By contrast, Canada's average wealth per adult was lower ($228,000), but the median wealth in Canada was $82,000. The middle of the pack Canadian had more than double the wealth of the middle of the pack American. And the median wealth of Italian adults in 2012 was $124,000—*three times* the wealth of the median American. The middle of the pack American in 2012 controlled less wealth than did his counterpart in Taiwan.

The result is that the United States has the most unequal distribution of wealth among all the large economies in the world, other than Russia.[38] No other OECD member has close to the levels of wealth inequality that we do. In 2012 the Gini index of our wealth (the measure of inequality in wealth distribution) was greater than the Gini index of wealth in Kazakhstan or Zimbabwe, at least as best Credit Suisse's researchers were able to measure them.

Money may not always buy happiness, but it does alleviate a great deal of pain. Most Americans have few resources to rely on should they lose their jobs, or to fund their children's education, or to supplement the meager life provided by Social Security benefits alone. Free markets and a vibrant economy do not require Russian-style oligarchic wealth amid general poverty to prosper; indeed, all the evidence points in the opposite direction—that great inequality in wealth ultimately destabilizes democracy and retards growth. And as the next section makes clear, outsized incomes and wealth in fact are somewhat hereditable in practice. Is the best that we can say about ourselves, as seen through the prism of our economic values, that we are not quite Russia, yet?

ECONOMIC MOBILITY

Plausible arguments can be offered that it is more important to focus on income mobility than on income inequality. After all, our collective psyche is engrained with the nostrum that the United States is a land of *opportunity* (the possibility of upward mobility), not a land of equal distributions. But here the data again tell a dispiriting story—the United States is not only more unequal but is also less mobile a society than most of us like to imagine.

Of course there is economic mobility in the United States—this is not twelfth-century Europe, after all, and we are not serfs tied to a nobleman's land. The right question is, do we compensate for our much greater income inequality with unusually high income mobility, so that everyone has a fair opportunity to capture those disproportionately large payouts? The consensus answer to date has been that we do not—inequalities persist over time.[39] Chapter 1 touched on this theme already, in terms of the disabling behavioral impacts of poverty; here, I look at work that measures directly evolving trends in income mobility.

Economic mobility is even more difficult to measure than inequality, because individuals naturally follow a progression over their working lives, joining the workforce as young adults at relatively low incomes and then moving up the income ladder as they develop skills, experience, and contacts. Then, on retirement, most Americans' incomes fall significantly. What we want to measure, therefore, is not the natural age progression of labor income, but the relative change in incomes of one individual compared to others in the same age cohort. But such "panel data" (following the same individuals over an extended period of time) are difficult to construct, because of privacy constraints on what information researchers can see.

Another approach is to look at intergenerational mobility—how do children end up faring economically compared to their parents? This is an important perspective, because it addresses the extent to which income inequality might become institutionalized over time. That is, the United States today is not an oligarchy, but if having affluent parents is highly predictive that you also will be affluent, then there is a risk that American society will become more oligarchical in the future. In this way, income inequality today can operate like a gene that is passed down to future generations. In areas like education and the productivity costs of poverty (which in turn color the next generation's starting point and likelihood of escaping poverty), inequality unfortunately does behave to a surprising extent like a gene.

Academic work in income mobility is rapidly evolving. A group of economists at the US Treasury Department with access to tax returns have been able to construct very interesting data following their subjects' actual tax returns over a period of decades.[40] In their most recent study, the authors constructed tables showing the changes in relative incomes among taxpayers within one age cohort as they matured from younger to older workers over the period 1987–2007. They also showed how teenagers claimed as dependents on their parents' returns in 1987, and classified in that year according to their parents' incomes, fared against each other 20 years on. In each case, mobility is clearly visible, but so is persistence: the teenager who was a dependent in 1987 of parents in the top quintile (the top 20 percent) of incomes in that year had a 41 percent likelihood of being in the top quintile of his peers 20 years further on; a child in the lowest income quintile in 1987, on the other hand, had an 11 percent chance of reaching the highest income quintile in 2007. The more affluent children had strong winds at their back.

The strength of the Treasury economists' papers is also their weakness, in that their data are drawn entirely from people filing tax returns, and are limited to income reported on those returns. Another study using different measures of income concluded that "mobility is lower in more recent periods (the 1990s into the early 2000s) than in earlier periods (the 1970s). Most notably, mobility of families starting near the bottom has worsened over time."[41]

Three researchers with access to Social Security data undertook another important recent income inequality study that followed one group of subjects over a period of time, in this case relying on the subjects' Social Security earnings history.[42] Basically, the authors found that income inequality increased over the study period 1937–2000, whether measured in terms of year-by-year earnings or by looking at 11-year spans of income.[43] This means that income inequality is not the result of random year-by-year fluctuations in earnings. Since the 1950s, however, men and women have exhibited completely different earnings patterns; income inequality worsened only a little for women, but soared for men.

The authors' analysis of long-term upward earnings mobility found that men lost some upward earnings mobility, but that women gained substantial upward income mobility over the same period. The great gains by women in this regard meant that the upward earning mobility of all workers improved somewhat over the study period.

There is also some relevant research at the top of the income ladder, where again there is some evidence of income mobility over time. This should not be completely surprising: "the" one percent are not a feudal aristocracy whose membership is fixed.

Upward and downward mobility is most vividly on display in the case of the top 400 taxpayers in the United States, whose redacted and amalgamated tax information the IRS publishes every year.[44] About 73 percent of those taxpayers fortunate enough to have joined this stratospheric club at some point over the 28 years that data have been published did so for one year only, and only 87 out of the 3,869 taxpayers who have ever earned enough to have made this list have done so for 10 years or more. This turnover reflects the fact that many taxpayers appear on this list only for the year they have sold a business or investment that they had cultivated over many previous years.

On the other hand, in 2009 membership in the Top 400 club required an income of $81 million, down from the all-time high water mark of 2007, when the cutoff was $131 million. Most of us therefore should agree that membership in this club even for just one year is sufficient to be treated as a very high-income individual indeed.

The Treasury economists' research that I just described also looked at the top one percent of income earners. The authors found, for example, that since 1991, only about one-quarter to one-third of taxpayers who are in the top one percent of incomes in any given year remain in the top one percent for five consecutive years. This actually is not terribly surprising, since so many members of the bottom rungs within the top one percent reach that income level through labor incomes: legal fees, investment banking bonuses, and similar large items of remuneration that fluctuate from year to year.

Nonetheless, when examining the incomes in 2007 of taxpayers age 35–40 in 1987, the Treasury authors found that 70 percent of those in the top one percent in 1987 were still in the top 10 percent in 2007, and 24 percent were in the top one percent. This suggests a good deal of persistence in incomes over time at the top end.

So while it is true that things change, and nothing is certain in life, there nonetheless is good evidence to suggest that the traditional year-by-year snapshot view of inequality has a significant correlation to long-term inequality outcomes. Results are heavily influenced by gender differences, attributable to the evolving participation of women in the workplace. If one tracked only male workers, the analyses would show a much steeper rise in income inequality and worsening of long-term income mobility over time. Results also are influenced by starting points: there seems to be greater persistence in outcomes for those starting either at the top or at the bottom of the income hierarchy.

Very recent work by academics at two institutions demonstrates that intergenerational mobility in the United States varies widely by geography: a child raised in Atlanta in the bottom income quintile (the bottom 20 percent) has a 4 percent chance of growing up to move into the top quintile, while a child born in the bottom quintile in Boston has a 9.8 percent chance. But even in the most mobility-friendly setting (San Francisco), the odds of climbing from the bottom to the top quintile in one generation are lower than 1 in 9.[45]

Recognizing that all the recent academic work is not perfectly reconcilable with each other, it does appear that a family's perch at the very bottom or top of the income distribution (the bottom and top quintiles) is stickier over time than is consistent with the most extravagant claims for the United States as an entirely fluid society. And the cross-country comparison work to date does not support the idea that the United States is exceptionally mobile compared with peer countries.

Intergenerational mobility depends heavily on investment in the human capital of young people, which is to say, in their education. As children and young adults we build up human capital through investments made in our education; we then can deploy that human capital in satisfying and remunerative future employment.

Chapter 10 presents our education report card in detail. In this context, however, it is important to refer to research conducted by Sean Reardon at Stanford, which shows that the academic achievement gap between children from high-income families and those in low-income families has grown dramatically in the last few decades, and is now 30 to 40 percent larger for children born in 2001 than it was for those born 25 years earlier.[46] Reardon concludes:

> At the same time that family income has become more predictive of children's academic achievement, so have educational attainment and cognitive skills become more predictive of adults' earnings. The combination of these trends creates a feedback mechanism that may decrease intergenerational mobility. As the children of the rich do better in school, and those who do better in school are more likely to become rich, we risk producing an even more unequal and economically polarized society.

The reasons are complex, and to some extent (for example, differing degrees of direct parental involvement in educational enrichment) not perfectly replicable through public spending. But tangible family financial investments in educational enrichment (e.g., computers and books) do vary directly with incomes, and therefore can be complemented by public investment in enrichment tools for children whose families cannot afford them.[47] And top-flight public education can develop the human capital of young people much further and more quickly than we sometimes imagine. Genuinely efficient private markets require large-scale public investment in education if we take seriously the premises that underlie the intellectual edifice of an efficient private market economy.

Alan Krueger recently introduced the idea of the "Great Gatsby Curve," showing the correlation between income inequality and intergenerational mobility across countries. Miles Corak of the University of Ottawa has plotted the curve, as shown in Figure 3.20.

Inequality is often described as a "static" snapshot of income distributions, but Corak's work shows that inequality and income mobility are intimately related through the instrument of opportunity:

> Inequality lowers mobility because it shapes opportunity. It heightens the income consequences of innate differences between individuals; it also changes opportunities, incentives, and institutions that form, develop, and transmit characteristics and skills valued in the labor market; and it shifts the balance of power so that some groups are in a position to structure policies or otherwise support their children's achievement independent of talent.[48]

Corak's work shows how income inequality in the United States (more particularly, affluence) operates as a quasi-gene capable of transmission from one generation to the

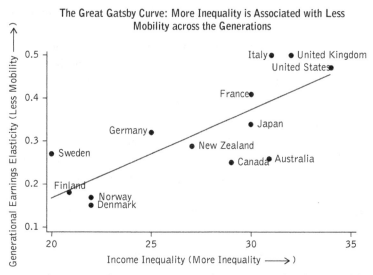

FIGURE 3.20 The Great Gatsby Curve: More Inequality Is Associated with Less Mobility across the Generations

Source: Miles Corak, "Income Inequality, Equality of Opportunity, and Intergenerational Mobility," *Journal of Economic Perspectives* 27, no. 3 (2013): 82.

next, by driving economic opportunity, and therefore ultimately calcifying income mobility. The most important mechanism of transmission is the large economic return to a college education, and the even larger returns to education at a select educational institution.[49] Affluent Americans understand these basic economic facts, and so invest in their children's human capital at levels that lower-income Americans cannot match. Thus, Corak finds that families in the top income quintile spend almost $9,000/year on their children's "enrichment" (private schools, computers, etc.), while families in the lowest income quintile are able to spend only $1,300. Affluent Americans are familiar with select college institutions, and are not intimidated by them in the way that many lower-income families are. Educational spending in the United States is heavily weighted toward "tertiary" (college and beyond) education, and 60 percent of that spending is private.[50] And of course college itself is costly, even after scholarships are considered, if for no other reason than the opportunity cost of not holding a full-time job while attending college.

The net result is that the children of affluent Americans begin their working lives with a large stock of human capital (or at least the opportunity to have amassed that human capital). This stock of human capital might not be immediately visible in income distribution tables the day after graduation, but ultimately explains the persistence across generations of children of the affluent being much more likely themselves to be affluent as they mature.

This is not an inevitable artifact of capitalism. Corak's work is particularly useful here because he directly compares the United States with Canada, which is a country with many similar values to our own. Corak's analysis shows how much more persistent inequality is across generations in the United States than in its neighbor to the north (see Figures 3.21 and 3.22).

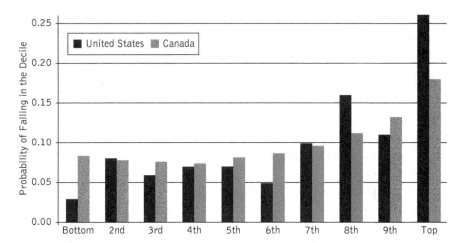

FIGURE 3.21 Earnings Deciles of Sons Born to Top Decile Fathers: United States and Canada

Source: Corak, "Income Inequality, Equality of Opportunity, and Intergenerational Mobility," 84.

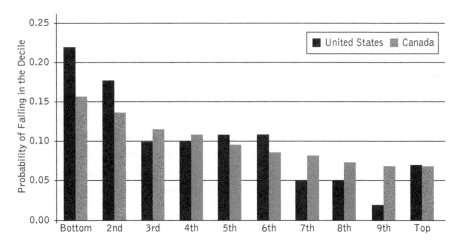

FIGURE 3.22 Earnings Deciles of Sons Born to Bottom Decile Fathers: United States and Canada

Source: Corak, "Income Inequality, Equality of Opportunity, and Intergenerational Mobility," 84.

Table 3.1 Intergenerational Mobility across the Earnings Distribution

	Denmark	Finland	Norway	Sweden	United Kingdom	United States
Probability of the son being in the same earnings quintile as his father						
1st Quintile	0.25	0.28	0.28	0.26	0.30	0.42
2nd Quintile	0.25	0.22	0.24	0.23	0.23	0.28
3rd Quintile	0.22	0.22	0.22	0.22	0.19	0.26
4th Quintile	0.22	0.23	0.22	0.22	0.25	0.25
5th Quintile	0.36	0.35	0.35	0.37	0.35	0.36

Source: OECD, *Growing Unequal* (2008), 205.

The OECD's work in this area across several countries reaches the same conclusion, but compares more countries. Affluent American parents are more likely to pass on their economic status to their children than are parents in other countries (see Table 3.1).

Again, the point is not that the economy of the United States is feudal in its structure: in a country of 310 million, it is not difficult to find examples of individuals who overcame great hardships to achieve extraordinary success, or conversely wastrel children who squandered every opportunity afforded them. There is mobility within the US economy, and no one's economic fate is wholly preordained. But the evidence is overwhelming that it is pleasanter and much easier to navigate the seas of economic uncertainty in a shipshape schooner whose sails catch the stiff wind blowing over its stern than it is to face constant economic headwinds in a leaky old scow. Who captains which ship is not simply a matter of chance.

WHAT HAVE WE BOUGHT FOR ALL THIS?

The United States has the highest poverty rate, the greatest income inequality, and the greatest wealth inequality of any major developed economy in the world. Our parents' incomes play a larger role in our personal economic fortunes than is true for other peer countries. Our long-term unemployment rate, once the envy of the world, has now sagged badly. Our education system is mediocre, and our healthcare is unaffordable to many, and too expensive for almost all of us. And what, in turn, have we bought in exchange for all this?

Not growth, at least over the last generation. The first refuge of the economist when this question is asked is to claim that inequality is a necessary consequence of free markets and a prerequisite to economic growth. This is true, but only to a point; inequality is not the nectar of the economic gods. Some is necessary, but

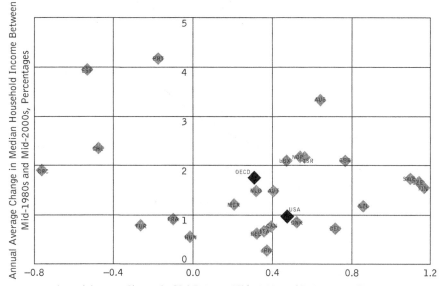

FIGURE 3.23 Change in Household Income and Change in Inequality

Source: OECD, *Society at a Glance 2011*, fig. EQ 1.3.

more is not necessarily better. No other developed country is as addicted to poverty and inequality as are we, and yet somehow they prosper.

US per capita GDP, measured in real (constant dollar) terms, grew 69 percent over the 30 year-period of 1982–2011. (It is important to look at per capita GDP to control for population growth.) That sounds pretty good, and indeed it is, but our results were precisely the same as the average performance of the OECD member countries over the same period. Sweden did a bit better (71 percent per capita real growth), Germany a little bit worse (66 percent growth—still extraordinary in light of the costs of German unification). Our outsized inequality did not buy outsized growth.

Another way to visualize how inequality does not drive extraordinary growth is to compare changes in median incomes (the income of the household in the middle of the range of incomes) to changes in the Gini index, which measures increasing inequality. Our preexisting high inequality, as measured by the Gini index, increased at an above average rate, but US median household incomes did not increase nearly as much as did the average OECD household. In return for greater and greater inequality, all we really have to show is a more and more unequal society, not a disproportionately wealthier one (see Figure 3.23).

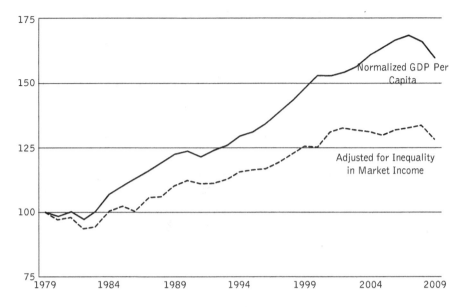

FIGURE 3.24 Gini-Adjusted GDP per Capita

Source: CBO, *The Distribution of Household Income and Average Federal Tax Rates, 2008 and 2009*, supplemental tables; U.S. Bureau of Economic Analysis, *National Economic Accounts* (accessed 2013).

WELFARE IS THE ULTIMATE METRIC

The national report card assembled in this chapter has emphasized standard economic measures, like GDP per capita, median income growth, or Gini index measurements of inequality. As emphasized several times already, this is a very incomplete picture of what really should command the attention of policymakers, which is our welfare—the things that satisfy us, that make us happy, that give us purpose and a sense of authenticity.[51] Money is a very important component of welfare, because we can buy lots of satisfying things with it, but money is not coextensive with the concept.

Nonetheless, I think it is possible to give some sense of the ways in which welfare and GDP might diverge through a simple exercise, which is to plot what I call "Gini-Adjusted GDP." The idea is to compare two curves of national income growth (see Figure 3.24). The first shows the growth in "real" (inflation adjusted) per-capita GDP (so as to control for population growth) over time; the second is the same curve multiplied by [1—the Gini index for market incomes for that year]. (I also normalize the curves to a starting index of 100 in the first year.) The thought is to give some sense of what per-capita income growth would look like if the country maintained a consistent level of inequality over time, rather than the increasing inequality documented earlier.

This is still a very incomplete measure of welfare, because it addresses only one example of the many shortcomings of GDP. Nonetheless it is, I think, a useful reminder that much of what we take to be the steady march of economic growth is not progress at all, when considered from the broader perspective of the sum of the life satisfactions of all Americans.

The sharp difference between GDP growth per capita and inequality-adjusted GDP growth per capita stands as a reproach to our juvenile fascination for the GDP Olympics, rather than our collective welfare. The standard explanation for why we should focus solely on the former is that all growth ultimately redounds to everyone's collective benefit. But when over a period of decades that growth is concentrated in fewer and fewer hands—and that is what it means for the Gini index to increase over time—there is reason to doubt the power of the argument, as applied to the vast majority of our citizens. They capture only a little of the overall income growth of the country, while in turn inequality has real and pernicious consequences that erode the value of the modest real income gains they do garner. A GDP Olympics is not a happy metaphor when most citizens are reduced to being cheerleaders rather than participants.

CHAPTER 4

INEQUALITY DEFENDERS, DENIERS, AND DISSEMBLERS

> *[W]hat improves the circumstances of the greater part [of society] can never be regarded as an inconveniency to the whole. No society can surely be flourishing and happy, of which the far greater part of the members are poor and miserable. It is but equity, besides, that they who feed, clothe and lodge the whole body of the people, should have such a share of the produce of their own labor as to be themselves tolerably well fed, clothed, and lodged.*
>
> —ADAM SMITH, *The Wealth of Nations*, Book I, Chap. VIII.

CHAPTER 3 PRESENTED SOME of the basic facts about income and wealth inequality, drawing its data from the work of consensus-driven nonpartisan institutions, not Trotskyite academics. Under the standard metrics employed by these institutions, inequality in the United States has increased substantially in recent decades; moreover, the United States has outstripped its peer countries in the rate at which disparities in income and wealth have grown.[1]

Our political discourse today is riven over the issue of inequality. For that reason, this chapter considers some of the objections typically raised to the standard presentation of the inequality facts, as summarized in chapter 3. In particular, I address the perspectives of commentators who embrace inequality as an inevitable byproduct of free markets, observers who claim that inequality is greatly overstated by the standard metrics, and disreputable folk who seem to earn a livelihood by presenting half-true arguments to an audience all too willing to suspend disbelief.

INEQUALITY DEFENDERS

The defense of inequality begins with an incontrovertible fact: free markets rely on inequality. Inequality is what inspires those who have less to work to get more, and inequality is a measure of the rewards captured by those who have achieved market success. Perfect markets yield unequal outcomes, both by reason of differing ability and by virtue of brute luck.

But this truism does not tell us how much inequality is enough. To the contrary, people worked hard and lusted for more a generation ago, yet inequality then was much lower, as measured by the standard metrics. In 1979, chief executive officer pay was 29 times as high as that of the typical worker in that firm's key industry; in 2011 it was 231 times as high—an eightfold increase in a generation.[2]

Figure 4.1 reminds us of how inequality has grown, measured in this case by two leading researchers, Thomas Piketty and Emmanuel Saez, using tax return data. Tax return data are particularly useful when looking at changes at the highest income levels, because Census Bureau data is "top-coded"—that is, it treats everyone over a certain threshold (currently, $250,000) as earning the threshold amount. (The next section discusses this in detail.) All data are in constant 2011 dollars, in each case include capital gains, and cover the same period (1979–2011).

The lowest line in Figure 4.1 shows average incomes per tax unit (i.e., on the basis of how tax returns are filed, so married couples filing joint returns are one

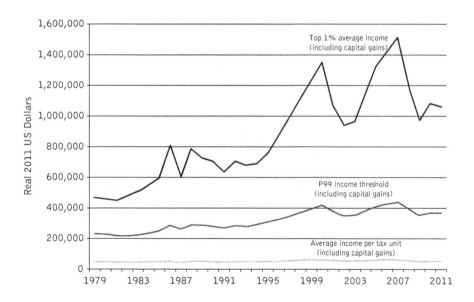

FIGURE 4.1 Top Income Shares and Average Incomes in the United States (1979–2011)

Source: Facundo Alvaredo, Anthony B. Atkinson, Thomas Piketty, and Emmanuel Saez, *The World Top Incomes Database* (accessed July 2013), http://topincomes.g-mond.parisschoolofeconomics.eu/.

tax unit, and so on). (Median income data, which would have been more appropriate, are not available in this dataset.) The middle line shows the minimum level of income required each year to get into the top one percent of income earners. The upper line shows the average incomes of the top one percent; the upper line of course is much higher than the middle line, because it shows the average of everyone in the one-percent club, not the minimum required to join.

Average incomes in constant dollar terms increased 15 percent over the 33-year period. The minimum income required to join the one-percent club increased 62 percent over that period. And the average income of members of the one-percent club more than doubled, increasing 129%. "The market made me do it" is not a complete response to these sorts of facts.

So the question really is, what defense can be mounted, not to inequality in general, but to current levels of inequality, which at least when measured by the standard metrics are at or near record levels?

N. Gregory Mankiw, a well-known economist and the author of very popular university economics textbooks, took on this challenge in a paper titled *Defending the One Percent*.[3] Mankiw does not dispute the surge in inequality documented by Piketty and Saez. Instead, he explains inequality as a consequence of well-documented economic trends, namely the globalization of the economy and the rising demands for "highly educated and exceptionally talented" individuals to meet the demands of the new digital economy. Globalization in particular is often said to drive larger rewards to those at the very top by virtue of the amalgamation of the world's economies into a single economic stage. After all, a singer in local clubs simply cannot command the appearance fees of one filling football stadiums with her fans. Mankiw offers as an example the late Steve Jobs of Apple, who created tremendous value for customers and shareholders throughout the world, and who became very rich in the process.

There is certainly a grain of truth in this explanation for the surge in incomes of the top one percent. The trouble is that there are just too many of them for this explanation to be very convincing. There are over 1.5 million Americans in the top one percent of the civilian labor force. Based on those I know, I doubt very much that the preponderance of them are Steve Jobs clones. Most are finance types, lawyers, doctors, and second- and third-tier business executives; the numbers essentially require as much. By definition, all the CEOs of the Fortune 500 put together are only 500 strong. What are the other 1.4995 million doing?

As Piketty and Saez observe, "the composition of income in the top income groups has shifted dramatically over the century: the working rich have now replaced the coupon-clipping rentiers."[4] As a group, the working rich are hard working and intelligent, but so too were their immediate predecessors a generation ago. The work of a Wall Street lawyer has not changed *that* much over one generation.

What is more, as Piketty and Saez pointed out, if technological change and globalization alone explained the surge in American income inequality, one would expect to see similar rates of inequality growth in other developed economies. Instead, one sees much more modulated growth in income inequality. Piketty and Saez plausibly hypothesize that "other factors, such as changes in labor market institutions, fiscal policy, or more generally social norms regarding pay inequality may have played important roles in the determination of the wage structure."

A more complete telling of the inequality surge would include a topic that Mankiw raises and dismisses, which is the idea of "rent seeking." Rent seeking is an extremely important contribution by political science to how we think about behavior in a wide range of settings. The idea at its broadest is that people look for shortcuts to wealth or power, by finding ways to advance their interests through whatever levers are available to them, without really creating any new economic value. A narrower sense of the term is that individuals who nominally are agents of others (a politician representing her constituents or a CEO his shareholders) are themselves active actors who seek to turn their situations to their own advantage. In either case, rent seekers enrich themselves without creating any new economic value.

For example, imagine that you are the CEO of a firm seeking a new tax benefit for your kiwi farming business, on the theory (or pretext, take your pick) that such an "incentive" will stimulate American kiwi farmers to hire lots more workers. You hire a tax lobbyist and head for meetings with members of Congress. Money is never discussed when you plead your case, but the lobbyist explains to you what is expected from you, your firm, its various political action committees, and so on. Finally the lobbyist calls you to announce with great fanfare that he has secured for you the tax break you have lobbied for, but only for two years. After all, the lobbyist explains, the tax break is expensive, and people want time to see if all your promises about new job creation come to fruition. Two years later, you have to start the process again, this time as an "extender"—the periodic rollover of "temporary" tax breaks that in fact are never expected to die.

Everyone in this story is engaging in rent seeking in the broadest sense in which the term is used, but you at least were transparent, and were a faithful agent of your shareholders' interests. The lobbyist and Congressmen who became your champions are the real masters of rent-seeking in this story, because you will have to pay them both, not just one time, but rather every couple of years as your tax break comes up for extension. They have created annuities for themselves out of your single tax break. Perhaps this sheds some light on how the tax code came to be littered with over 100 such business tax "extenders."

Joseph Stiglitz's book *The Price of Inequality*[5] argues that the surge of top incomes in the United States is largely explainable as instances of successful rent seeking. With the benefit of hindsight, it is difficult to see much of what went on in the finance industry in the early 2000s as anything but rent seeking, and even Mankiw acknowledges that perhaps behaviors (and resulting income windfalls) in this industry were problematic. But Mankiw rejects rent seeking more generally as an explanation. He does so by defining it very narrowly, as simply political lobbying for monopoly rights or the like.

In reality, everyone, or almost everyone, engages in rent seeking when the opportunities arise. Mankiw argues, for example, that rent seeking in the form of special pleadings and excessive coziness between public firms' CEOs and their boards of directors cannot explain the extraordinary surge in CEO incomes relative to average workers' incomes. Private firms as well as public ones pay their CEOs handsomely, he argues. But this misses one of the most obvious instances of rent seeking, which is the leveraged buyout (LBO) firm that essentially overcompensates a public target company's CEO as an inducement to obtain his active participation in facilitating the leveraged buyout.

Mankiw also overlooks the extent to which boards are populated with executives drawn from similar backgrounds and with similar interests in their own compensation, as well as the central role of compensation consultants. These consultants are paid handsomely by Firm A's executives (or the compensation committee of Firm A's board of directors) to poll Firms B and C, all to show how underpaid Firm A's executives are by comparison, whereupon Firm A's executives seek and receive pay bumps, and the compensation consultants move to Firm B, whence they poll Firms A and C, and so on, in a spiral of compensation inflation.

Mankiw queries why rent seeking would be something apparent in the data now and not a generation ago. That is a fair question. It certainly is not a novel concept: Adam Smith wrote that "[t]o widen the market and to narrow the competition, is always the interest of the dealers. [By doing so they] levy, for their own benefit, an absurd tax upon the rest of their fellow-citizens. The proposal of any new law or regulation of commerce which comes from this order, ought always to be listened to with great precaution...."[6]

A large part of the answer probably lies in eroding social norms, so that such behavior is no longer listened to "with great precaution." But in addition to this, Piketty, Saez, and a third co-author, Stefanie Stantcheva, argue that old-fashioned economic incentives are at work.[7] Their hypothesis is that lower tax rates increased the economic return to rent seeking, and thereby set many off on the path to finding their own stream of rents. In the 1970s, the top marginal individual tax rate was 70 percent; the Tax Reform Act of 1986 lowered the top rate to 28 percent. While the rate then crept back up, it remains very low relative to the tax rate environment in 1979. Through cross-country comparisons, the three authors find a strong correlation between tax rate cuts on top labor incomes (salaries) and increasing shares of national income captured by the top one percent. In turn, these increasing shares of national income captured by the top one percent did *not* correlate with higher GDP growth, which suggests that the higher incomes were the result of successful rent seeking, not the creation of greater real economic value.[8]

Mankiw moves from his unsatisfactory defense of rising income inequality (a nation of 1.5 million Steve Jobs) to the more vexing problem of equality of opportunities. There he veers very close to truly dangerous ground, as he appears to argue that, since under his general theory of income inequality very smart people are capturing all the top incomes, and since intelligence is hereditary, one must expect that children of high-ability parents are very likely themselves to be highly able.

In so arguing, Mankiw simply ignores the role of brute luck in market outcomes in the first place: our incomes are not in fact calculated by cosmic clerks down to two decimal places as direct returns on our abilities and efforts. But wealth, however obtained, can profitably be plowed into investments in the human capital of one's children. Mankiw thus understates how much can be accomplished on behalf of a moderately able child who is coached, prodded, cajoled, and bribed all the way into a top tier university, and then introduced to her affluent parents' circle of friends in order to find a first job.

By the same token, Mankiw also ignores the magnitude of the handicaps that poverty imposes. As chapter 1 already introduced, the poor are not just like us, only with less stuff. At every turn poverty erodes actual cognitive ability, the healthy physical and mental development that comes from adequate nutrition, and anything approaching equality of educational opportunity in practice.

Adam Smith had the perfect rejoinder to Mankiw here. Smith wrote:

> The difference of natural talents in different men is, in reality, much less than we are aware of; and the very different genius which appears to distinguish men of different professions, when grown up to maturity, is not upon many occasions so much the cause as the effect of the division of labour. The difference between the most dissimilar characters, between a philosopher and a common street porter, for example, seems to arise not so much from nature as from habit, custom, and education.[9]

Phrasing matters more directly, before we institutionalize eugenics as a social norm, we might want to bend over backward to invest comparable amounts in the human capital of children whose parents lack the disposable wealth to do so themselves.

Finally, Mankiw has no answer at all to the obvious question of why the United States should be such an outlier in the rate at which income inequality has grown. There is something about the United States that is unique: I submit that the answer lies not in its markets, which are largely indistinguishable in operation from those of other countries, but rather in its comparatively parsimonious programs of government investment in its citizens.

Mankiw concludes with some philosophical musing, arguing that the average person in the top one percent pays about a third of her income in taxes (including state and local taxes). He argues that this is enough to compensate the United States of America for the institutions—the rule of law, the supervision of markets, and so on—that in the aggregate form the largely unexamined foundation on which all economic activity sits. But not only does that argument assume its conclusion, it also poses the wrong question. The right question is, are there collective investment opportunities that we are failing to exploit, and by doing so failing the 99 percent of Americans who are not so fortunate as to find themselves among the top one percent?

Mankiw closes by urging on his readers his "just deserts" theory of moral philosophy. Unfortunately this is not a theory that we all would prefer just to eat dessert, please—that actually might gain adherents among philosophers. It is instead an embarrassing and circular paean to unalloyed market outcomes, now presented as a moral imperative: market outcomes are morally just because they are the outcomes reached by the markets. As Mankiw explains in his philosophical summa, *Spreading the Wealth Around: Reflections Inspired by Joe the Plumber*:

> Let me propose the following principle: People should get what they deserve. A person who contributes more to society deserves a higher income that reflects those greater contributions. Society permits him that higher income not just to incentivize him, as it does according to utilitarian theory, but because that income is rightfully his. This perspective is, I believe, what Robert Nozick, Milton Friedman, and other classically liberal writers have in mind. We might call it the Just Deserts Theory.
>
>
> One implication of the Just Deserts Theory is that it gives a new normative interpretation of the equilibrium of a competitive market economy. Under a standard set of assumptions, a competitive economy leads to an efficient allocation of resources. But we economists often say that there is nothing particularly equitable about that equilibrium. Perhaps we are too hasty in reaching that judgment. After all, it is also a standard result that in a competitive equilibrium, the factors of production are paid the value of their marginal product. That is, each person's income reflects the value of what he contributed to society's production of goods and services. One might easily conclude that, under these idealized conditions, each person receives his just deserts.[10]

In short, people should get what they deserve, so what they do get must be what they deserve. Apparently fortune, good or bad, plays no role in the Mankiw household, although it plays a large role in market outcomes. And in Mankiw's mind alone, perfect markets rule, and opportunities are not at all skewed by the accident of birth or other contingencies. Mankiw has no theory of justice beyond the claim that whatever the market bestows is the natural order of things.

But for his forays into philosophy, N. Gregory Mankiw is an intelligent and industrious man who has written excellent university textbooks, and who as a result of their sales alone no doubt finds himself comfortably among the one percent. But can Mankiw really be so blind to how lucky he also has been? As I observed earlier, the nature of life is that we do not control it; both our native talents and our good fortune are distributed through processes that we cannot fathom and do not "earn." Our loud proclamations that what we take from the market is our just deserts is just noise made against the darkness, trying to still the voice inside that asks, why me and not them?

Adam Smith wrote:

> We frequently see the respectful attentions of the world more strongly directed towards the rich and the great, than towards the wise and the virtuous.... Two different roads are presented to us...the one, by the study of wisdom and the practice of virtue; the other, by the acquisition of wealth and greatness. Two different characters are presented to our emulation; the one, of proud ambition and ostentatious avidity; the other, of humble modesty and equitable justice. Two different models, two different pictures, are held out to us, according to which we may fashion our own character and behavior.... They are the wise and the virtuous chiefly, a select, though, I am afraid, but a small party, who are the real and steady admirers of wisdom and virtue.[11]

How very disappointed Smith would be in what passes for philosophical insight among those who believe themselves his direct intellectual heirs.

INEQUALITY DENIERS

Chapter 3 and the beginning of this chapter laid out the facts surrounding income inequality and mobility. In fact people simply do not have equal opportunities—this is what it means to say that markets are systematically incomplete in fundamental areas, like investment in human capital. And markets are imperfect in other respects as well.

This is not simply an ethical or social issue: systematic underinvestment in human capital leads to lower productivity, which is to say, lower national income. Comparative data show that America today offers less social and economic mobility than do many of its peer countries—a startling rebuke to the reflective mythology too often invoked in American political discourse. Moreover, especially since the *Citizens United* case, it is now apparent that vast fortunes can buy special relationships and privileges with government, which further act to turn today's great fortunes into dynasties.

Our current enormous income inequality creates social tensions in two directions. From the point of view of the majority, it is not just a question of envy, although that is real—it also is the distortion in prices of important assets, like houses in good school districts. And from the point of view of the extremely affluent, it becomes all too easy to disengage from any contact with the rest of America, and to see one's great wealth as some sort of divine award for one's special genius, rather than for many factors, including blind luck. That sense of difference in turn leads to the absurd sort of narcissism and insensitivity to one's fellow Americans that we see played out in the media and in the "just deserts" school of moral philosophy.

So contrary to market triumphalist rhetoric, rapidly accelerating income inequality is not a badge of honor. Perhaps recognizing how poorly this message plays, very recently some economists and web pundits have shifted to arguing that the phenomenon of widening income inequality does not really exist, because the metrics used in the leading income inequality studies overstate the problem.

I use as an example of the new school of inequality denial papers one widely cited study by Richard Burkhauser, Jeff Larrimore, and Kosali Simon, A "Second Opinion" on the Economic Health of the American Middle Class.[12] This paper concludes that the work of Piketty and Saez, in particular, overstates the growth of income inequality in America, and that the middle class actually showed good income growth over the period 1979 to 2007. More specifically, the Burkhauser paper finds that the median income of "tax units" (on which more below), calculated in a manner analogous to the work of Pitteky and Saez, was only 3.2 percent over the entire period, but that under the Burkhauser group's preferred method, the median income of "households" grew about 37 percent.

As developed below, it is not the numbers in the Burkhauser group's paper with which I take issue, but rather the authors' conclusions that their research shows a healthy and prosperous middle class. A more complete inquiry into the data leads to the opposite conclusion, that the middle class rows against the tide of dramatically increasing income inequality, and has fallen behind over the last generation in important respects.

The paper and their lead author have received a great deal of attention, because the paper's conclusions are highly convenient for the market triumphalist school of thought, and in particular those affluent souls who dread that some of their high incomes will be siphoned off for "redistribution" to the 99 percent. As a result, the paper has been touted by conservative blogs, and its lead author has appeared on news media and podcasts to broadcast his conclusions.

How can studies of the same topic—income inequality—come to such different conclusions? The answer in large part comes down to two basic variables: the definition of "income" and the definition of whose income is being measured.

First, a word about data. Piketty and Saez, on the one hand, and the Burkhauser group, on the other, measure income starting from two different data sources. The Piketty and Saez work relies on actual federal income tax return data. As a result, Piketty and Saez have available by far the best detail on all the components of market income (wages, self-employment income, income from investments) in each year, particularly at the very highest income levels. But tax return data are incomplete in an important respect, which is that the data do not include forms of economic income that are not relevant for tax purposes. Supplemental Nutrition Assistance Payment (food stamp) benefits, for example, are not included in the Piketty and Saez data.

The Burkhauser group, on the other hand, relies on the March Current Population Survey (CPS), an annual face-to-face survey of about 60,000 house-holds conducted by the Census Bureau. (CPS surveys are conducted in other months as well, but the March survey is the most detailed inquiry into a house-hold's sources of income.) The CPS is the basis for official national unemploy-ment data, and contains a wealth of other information as well; if you want to know something about incomes broken down by education level, for example, the CPS is the place to turn. CPS data also include all sorts of government transfer payments.

Nonetheless, CPS data suffer from two large problems. The first is that they make no effort at all to capture capital gains (profits from selling investments, one's business, or one's home). The higher up the income ladder you go, the more important capital gains become, especially after 2001. The Burkhauser 2012 paper simply is missing all data relating to capital gains.

The second problem in using the CPS to study income inequality is that public-use CPS data are "top-coded" on an item-by-item of income basis. This means that for those interviewees whose income in a particular category exceeds a stated maximum, the CPS data substitute that maximum, to protect individuals' privacy. The current top-coding cutoff for "usual hourly earnings," for example, is $150,000/year; for total income, it is $250,000/year. In 2007, about 6 percent of subjects were top-coded in respect of at least one income category; this obviously is a large number if you are studying incomes at the top of the ladder.[13]

To enable researchers to have more useful information on higher incomes, the Census Bureau since 1996 has also provided "cell mean" data; basically the idea is to look past the public top-coded number, calculate the actual average income in each category for all households that have been top-coded, and then substitute that average number for the top-coded number. Burkhauser and Larrimore, who held special status as "special sworn researchers," were the principal developers of the historical datasets applying this "cell mean" approach to years before 1996.

There is little doubt but that IRS tax return data are more complete measures of money income than are CPS data the higher up the income ladder one looks. At the outset there is an obvious question of whether high-income Americans are more likely to be forthcoming about the exact amounts of their various items of income on their tax returns (where noncompliance can lead to large civil or even criminal penalties) or through a Census Bureau interview. In fact, about

9 percent of households contacted for the CPS survey do not participate, either because they do not respond or refuse to do so. But putting both these concerns to one side, there are still strong reasons to prefer IRS data.

Mean cell data are better than top-coded data, but they have their own limitations, in that they treat every household that is top-coded in respect of one item of income as earning the average of all top-coded households in respect of that single item. This has the effect of producing total income figures that tend to be closer together than might be the case if actual household-by-household data were employed. In addition, Census Bureau data are subject to a hidden second level of top-coding (reminiscent of super-secret double probation in *Animal House*), under which the Census Bureau stops counting income in a particular category for all purposes, including their internal nonpublic databases, if that income exceeds the second cutoff. For example, until 1994 the Census Bureau kept no record at all of primary labor earnings over $299,999; that was the internal top-coding cutoff.[14] The Burkhauser et al. paper must work with this limitation.

Finally, the CPS is designed to capture the incomes of working America, and its survey size is probably too small to give accurate information about the top one percent of incomes. By definition, if the survey size is 60,000, and it perfectly mirrors the country's income distribution, only 600 surveyed households will be in the top one percent of national incomes. The problem compounds once one moves to even more rarified income levels.

For these reasons, the Piketty and Saez datasets are fundamentally superior to the CPS datasets on which the Burkhauser group relies at measuring the top end of market incomes, and the Piketty and Saez data include capital gains. On the other hand, Piketty and Saez do not purport to capture the effects of most government transfer payments and the like, and have the problem at the bottom end of missing data on individuals who do not file returns. (In this regard, however, remember that the working poor invariably do file tax returns in order to claim the refundable portion of the earned income tax credit and the child tax credit.)

To many observers, the Congressional Budget Office's recent large-scale studies of income inequality in America are the "gold standard" of income inequality research.[15] (This is why I relied on CBO data in the discussion in chapter 3.) The CBO, working with the staff of the Joint Committee on Taxation, can draw on both CPS data and actual tax return data. In preparing its major income distribution studies, the CBO therefore did exactly what one hoped would be done, which was to combine CPS and actual tax data. This required complex statistical matching of tax and CPS data on a household-by-household basis: as CBO modestly explained, "Each pairing resulted in a new record that took on the demographic characteristics of the CPS record and the income reported" on tax returns.[16] For this reason alone, it is fair to approach the CBO's work as the gold standard in this area.

Comparing the Burkhauser papers to the CBO studies helps to draw the differing methodologies into sharper focus. Specifically, we can look at the underlying assumptions and data sources on which the Burkhauser group's 2012 paper relied to see why its results are so different from those reached by Piketty and Saez. The place to start is by specifying how we define the concept of "income." It turns out that this is not a self-evident exercise. There are three broad contenders for what we want to measure when we are examining income inequality, and then various optional extras that can be piled on top of each.

The first broad approach to the measurement of income for purposes of studying income inequality is what the CBO calls "market income." This tells us what the world would be like in the absence of tax liabilities, on the one hand, and many government transfer payment receipts, on the other—in particular, not just food stamps or unemployment benefits, but Social Security benefits. The name "market income" captures the idea that this is the state of play before most government interventions. It is not strictly a government-free perspective on the world, because federal and sub-national governments in the aggregate account for almost 30 percent of GDP, but it is as close as one can get in practice.

The second broad approach to the measurement of income for purposes of studying income inequality is what the OECD calls "disposable income," and what the CBO sometimes calls "after-tax income." The idea is that this income measure includes the cash value of all government transfer payments received (again, not just food stamps, but Social Security payments and the statistical value of participation in Medicare or Medicaid), and subtracts taxes paid. It is a good measure of the market resources you command, *after* taking into account the role of government in your life.

The third broad approach, and to my mind the least useful, is what CBO calls "before-tax income." Both CBO and the Census Bureau use this as their base case measure of income for income inequality study purposes, although if you hunt around you can find the data on the other approaches as well. It is not useful because it reflects one-half of the role of government in our lives (transfer payments we receive, including Social Security and Medicare) but not the other (the taxes we pay to fund those transfers).

"Before-tax income" is not at all the same as market income or "taxable income," which is what you pay tax on. CBO's base measure of "before-tax income" is the sum of your market income and the value of any government transfer payments you receive in cash or "in kind"—not just food stamps, but also broad-based entitlements like Social Security payments, Medicare and Medicaid benefits, unemployment insurance, and much more. Many of these transfer payments, like the statistical value of Medicare benefits a participant receives, or Social Security benefits received by the majority of elderly Americans, are not includable in the taxable income of their recipients.

Needless to say, transfer payments are bottom-weighted, just as one would expect. According to the landmark CBO 2011 report on income inequality, households in the bottom 20 percent, ranked by market incomes, received 40 percent of transfer payments (an average of $23,000 per household). Almost two-thirds of that came from Social Security and Medicare, not some imagined welfare programs.

The inclusion of transfers significantly changes the percentage of national income claimed by different income groups. For example, the top 20 percent of households in the income distribution in 2009 earned 51 percent of aggregate "before-tax" incomes, but 57 percent of market incomes.

Transfers also are very heavily weighted toward older Americans. This point is not strictly relevant to the methodological arguments reviewed here, but it is so important, and so inconsistent with market triumphalist mythologies of a country overwhelmed by young and able "takers," that it is worth making again (see Figure 4.2).

The answer to the question of which income metric is correct depends on what you are trying to measure. If the question is, how are people doing today? then disposable income is probably the most useful single metric. The problem with stopping here, however, is that think tanks and politicians often use conclusions

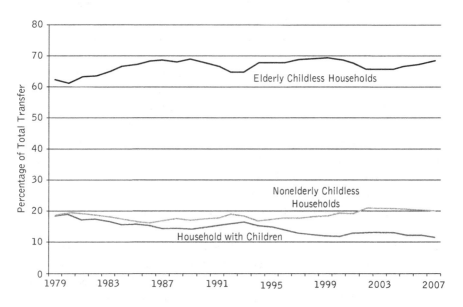

FIGURE 4.2 Shares of Total Transfers by Type of Household

Source: CBO, *Trends in the Distribution of Household Income Between 1979 and 2007.*

reached through studying disposable income as reasons to cut the very transfer programs that partially explain the results on which they rely.

So if the question is, how is *government* doing today at mitigating market income inequalities, you need to start by ranking households by their market incomes, and then compare their shares of total national market income with their shares of total disposable income. In other words, you need to start with outcomes as they would be in the absence of government intervention, and then compare them to outcomes in the world with both sides of government intervention—the tax and the spending sides. Each side has its own distributional consequences. (Chapter 12 expands on this theme.)

CBO's base case measure of "before-tax" income therefore is fundamentally muddled, because it chases its own tail. It takes the spending side of government intervention into account in the "before" picture of well-being, as if the increments to personal wealth that come from government programs are free goods. But government spending exists only by virtue of the taxing side of things. Our taxes fund the very transfers (principally, Social Security, Medicare, and Medicaid) that CBO labels as components of "before-tax" income, even though these programs cannot exist in the absence of those taxes.

In other words, we can have taxes without transfer payments, but not transfer payments without taxes. When it comes to considering the distributional impact of current or proposed fiscal policies, what we want to capture is the *net effect* on individuals' well-being of both sides of government intervention. For this reason, one should measure the status quo ante and the status quo post, but not a midstream position that cannot logically ever hold. And conversely, if we want to consider what distributional results would obtain if government went out of the business of providing Social Security, Medicare, Medicaid, and all the other, smaller, transfer programs, we should look at market incomes alone.

CBO's landmark 2011 study, as augmented by online additional data and a 2012 supplemental publication, provides information on all the different measures of income. The Burkhauser group's 2012 paper also is constructed with an additive approach, starting with market incomes, then going to before-tax incomes, and finally considering disposable incomes. Piketty and Saez focus entirely on market income. This is driven by their use of tax data, because most transfer programs are not reflected as income for personal income tax purposes. But in turn, Piketty and Saez, unlike the Burkhauser group, obtain granular detail about the very top of the income distribution. Here CBO's unique ability to combine the two competing datasets shows its strength, by enabling comparisons of market income inequality to disposable inequality while retaining the same level of granular detail that Piketty and Saez capture.

You can conceptualize the definitions of market incomes and disposable incomes as answering "when" questions—when in the process of acquiring disposable resources should we take a snapshot of how people are doing? But that leaves unanswered some very difficult "what" questions—what exactly should we include in the measure of income? Cash compensation, of course, and interest and dividend income, but what else?

Capital income—income from investments, including one's share of net business income—is famously top-heavy in its distribution. In particular, capital gains are realized predominantly by the most affluent Americans. Going to the very top of the heap, the IRS publishes each year consolidated data on the 400 highest-income taxpayers in the country. In 2007 (the last year before the Great Recession), it took $138 million in income in that one year to join this exclusive club. The group averaged about $9 million in compensation income, but over $90 million each in capital gains. Moreover, the early 2000s saw a boom in efforts by private equity managers and others to convert what economically was compensation income into capital gains, to take advantage of the very low capital gains tax rates. So if you want to say something useful about how the most affluent Americans are doing relative to the rest of us, you should want to include capital gains in your measure of income.

But it turns out that the Census Bureau does not collect information on capital gains, and therefore the Burkhauser group's 2012 paper simply ignores them, and makes only one laconic reference to that fact in its summary of the March CPS data. This is a very troubling omission. The Piketty and Saez papers generally include capital gains in their measure of incomes, and their continually updated website gives researchers the opportunity to view data with and without capital gains.[17] The CBO definition of income includes capital gains.

From the other direction, one of the biggest complaints that the Burkhauser group has about the results published by Piketty and Saez is that those conclusions ignore important forms of what might be called "invisible" compensation income—economic income that is not paid in cash, and is not reported on your tax return. By far the most important source of invisible income is your employer-provided health insurance, if you are lucky enough to have it. The street value of that policy—more accurately, what your employer pays—might be in the neighborhood of $12,000/year for a family plan. Your employer deducts that expense in figuring out its own taxable income, just as it does other business expenses, including in particular your cash salary. If your employer paid you a bonus of round-trip plane tickets to Hawaii, or a new car, the value of those items would be included in your annual W-2 statement as income to you. But if you look carefully at your W-2, you will see that the value of your employer-provided health insurance is *not* included in your wage income reported to the IRS.

It turns out that this hidden federal subsidy for employer-provided healthcare insurance explains in large measure why existing healthcare markets do not function properly, and puts the lie to the idea that government has not been subsidizing the healthcare of middle class and affluent Americans all along. The amounts involved are staggeringly large—perhaps $1.3 *trillion* in federal subsidies over the next five years. This hidden subsidy is an example of what specialists call "tax expenditures" (that is, government spending programs hidden in the tax code as special deductions or credits, or in this case exclusions from income). Chapter 9 addresses in detail the operation and consequences of this hidden form of government spending, as delivered through the tax code, but for now the point is, simply, what should be done with this large item of invisible income in figuring out the relative economic performances of different economic strata of our society?

Piketty and Saez ignore the invisible income of employer-provided health insurance, because it is not reported to the IRS. The Burkhauser group, by contrast, adds this item back in, through what economists call "imputations" of the missing data. (That is, they do their best to estimate what the missing number might be, and use their estimates to populate the data fields of the populations they are measuring.) CBO also includes this invisible income item.

You can see intuitively that, since healthcare insurance premiums do not rise linearly in cost with incomes (million dollar executives do not hold healthcare insurance plans with premiums of $120,000/year), including this invisible income in your calculations of how incomes are distributed across the American population will tend to bring up the middle class relative to the most affluent. In turn, because healthcare costs have skyrocketed much faster than the base rate of inflation, the premiums paid by employers on behalf of employees also have increased rapidly. Thus, the Burkhauser group argues, cash wages may have basically stagnated in real terms, but that is because employees are getting paid more and more in invisible currency.

There is logic to the idea of using a comprehensive measure of income, including invisible income like employer-provided healthcare, but there are issues as well in imputing these employer-paid premiums to workers. Some are technical, but at least one is conceptual: there are good reasons to suspect that the value to employees of employer-provided healthcare is not the same as the amounts employers pay. The basic points are that most employees have no choice but to take the healthcare program given them, so that they cannot decide how to allocate their wages as they see fit, and that rapidly increasing healthcare costs in turn are in large measure the result of overconsumption of healthcare (and indifference to its cost) caused by the mistaken belief that the programs are free or nominal in price.

In other words, in return for healthcare costs that rise at rates that substantially outstrip the rate of inflation, are we really getting more and more healthcare value each year? If you conclude that we are not getting fair value for the skyrocketing premiums paid on our behalf, then including the imputed amount of healthcare premiums at face value to some extent confuses income and welfare. Imagine that your employer makes annual charitable contributions of 10 percent of your salary in your name to a charity whose mission you abhor, without your ability to refuse. Would you think that these contributions should be counted as your income for statistical (or any other) purposes on a dollar-for-dollar basis?

As this fanciful example suggests, it is possible for costs paid and value received to diverge. This observation is inconsistent with standard economic thinking, which treats the market price of something as conclusive evidence of its value to the buyer, but healthcare as delivered in the United States through employers is simply different from most consumer decisions.

The other problem with imputing income items that are not actually available to be spent this year in cash is that it becomes difficult to know where to stop. For example, high-income Americans often enjoy large pension accounts that build up every year during their working careers, as well as the increasing cash values of their life insurance policies. None of Piketty and Saez, the CBO, or the 2012 Burkhauser et al. paper includes these items.

The CBO's definition of market income goes further in one respect, and includes as income earned by individual Americans their imputed shares of the income taxes paid by corporations. Why is an expense seen as income? The theory is that if there were no corporate income tax, then household income would be higher to that extent. But the CBO here is very odd in its imputation theorizing, as it does not impute to individuals the other side of this coin, which is the after-tax increase in retained earnings of corporations: that is reflected only when stock is sold and capital gains or losses toted up. This is a methodological error, plain and simple.

Finally, when it comes to thinking about income, one must ask not just when and what, but also who? That is, whose income are we measuring? There are about 310 million Americans, and we form all sorts of different living arrangements. Since Piketty and Saez use tax data, they deal with the issue by following tax law definitions—treating a married couple filing a joint return as one "tax unit," for example. There are roughly 140 million tax units in America.

The CBO and other institutions organize Americans by "households," which is a different concept. A household includes all people living in a single housing unit. For the years covered by the studies discussed here, for example, gay couples could not file a joint income tax return, so they would be counted as two tax units, but one household. Or as another example, a husband and wife whose house is shared by another adult relative (like a mother-in-law) typically will constitute two taxpayer units, but only one household.

The Census Bureau organizes income data by households, but simply stops there. If you think about it for a moment, though, a family of six with a household income of $50,000 is not as well off as a household of one adult with the same income. CBO therefore goes one step further, and for purposes of figuring out where every household stands in the line of household incomes from lowest to highest, adjusts incomes to reflect differences in household size. CBO's rule is that the cost of running a household goes up roughly by the square root of household size; so, for example, a family of four needs twice the income (2 is the square root of 4) as a single person to have the same standard of living. (This gives rise to that stock phrase from old movies and romance novels, "But honey, two can live as cheaply as the square root of two.") The Burkhauser 2012 paper and many other researchers follow the same general approach, by adjusting March CPS data for household size.

The choice of tax units versus households and the decision to size-adjust household incomes have very large consequences for looking at income growth and distributions over time. The Burkhauser paper, for example, finds the results shown in Table 4.1 for median income growth (ignoring capital gains income, as mentioned earlier) in the period 1979–2007—that is, the income growth from year to year of the middle unit (tax unit or household) in the population.

The difference in median income growth rates between Columns (1) and (2) is due to the switch from tax units to households over the relevant period. Adjusting for household size and taking into account taxes and transfers gets to the results in Column (4). In each case the growth rate is measured in respect of the same definition of income over the specified period.[18]

In some respects, households are clearly preferable to tax units as the basis for measuring income. A gay couple who were unable to marry in the years under study is a paradigmatic example. But there is another side to this question as well. One reason for changes in household composition in recent years has been that elderly adults and young adult children find it increasingly difficult to support themselves; nonetheless, they bring some income into the household. Since adjusted household size goes up only by the square root of the number of household members, a third or fourth adult member of the household does not need to bring with her huge sums of income to increase adjusted household income levels.

Table 4.1 Annualized Median Income Growth Rate in Percent, 1979–2007

(1)	(2)	(3)	(4)	(5)
Tax Unit/ Pre-tax/ Pre-transfer	Household/ Pre-tax/ Post-transfer	Household Size-Adj./ Pre-tax/ Post-transfer	Household Size-Adj./ Post-T&T + Health Ins.	Household Size-Adj./
0.12	0.54	0.84	1.05	1.31

Source: Burkhauser, Larrimore, and Simon, "A 'Second Opinion' on the Economic Health of the Middle Class" (2012).

Using adjusted household size as the relevant unit means that you are saying to the fellow whose mother-in-law moves in with him and his wife, because she cannot afford to support herself on her own, "Congratulations! Your household just got richer." The point is not that the authors are wrong about the rule of thumb for adjusting household costs to reflect household size, but that they think that adult children, or their parents, view returning to the parental nest as implicitly welfare-enhancing, rather than what it really is, which is an acknowledgment of failure to establish an independent and self-sufficient next generation.[19]

Where does all this leave us? The Burkhauser group argues in their 2012 paper that their "second opinion" shows that the middle class enjoyed healthy economic growth in the 1979–2007 period.[20] CBO's work also finds long-term growth in median disposable income—about a 35 percent increase in constant dollar terms over 29 years, or a little over one percent per year.

Even with the substantial limitations identified here, the Burkhauser group's paper in fact shows a substantial increase in inequality from 1979 to 2007, as measured by changes in the Gini Index; the paper also shows that, using its preferred measure of income (household size-adjusted, post-tax, post-transfer, plus health insurance income)—which as it happens is the same concept used by CBO in measuring what the OECD calls disposable income—the top 5 percent's mean income growth from 1979 to 2007 in nominal dollars was 63 percent, while the middle quintile grew only at 37 percent.

The CBO 2011 and 2012 papers eclipse the Burkhauser group's research, by providing more data about differences among the different measures of income and by providing information missing from the Burkhauser group's paper in respect of the very top of the income distribution. Its conclusions leave us with the dismal report card that we took home from school in chapter 3, as amplified by the next few paragraphs.

The CBO, like the Burkhauser group, includes the value of employer-sponsored healthcare insurance in market incomes, but unlike Burkhauser, CBO also includes capital gains, which are particularly relevant at the top end. The CBO, like the Burkhauser group, works with size-adjusted household income, for better or worse. The CBO, like Burkhauser but unlike Piketty and Saez, captures the estimated value of government transfer payments and in-kind programs. And most important, the CBO, like Piketty and Saez, has the best possible data for the very top end of the income spectrum, which is where the extraordinary growth in incomes has occurred.

This last point is one elided over by inequality deniers. Looking at incomes by quintiles, for example by drawing comparisons between the top 20 percent and the median 20 percent, is a way of hiding what has gone on in America over the last few decades. For example, in 2009 the top 20 percent of households had an average market income of $218,000, which sounds pretty flush. But as the CBO carefully noted, "that average masks wide differences between subgroups [within the top 20 percent]; households in the 81st to 90th percentiles received $125,000, on average, compared with $1.2 million for households in the top percentile [i.e., the top 1 percent]."[21]

Working with the supplemental data posted by CBO in connection with its 2012 update to its income distribution research, we can learn by comparing 1979 to 2007 that the market incomes of all households in the aggregate grew about $6 trillion, from $4.6 trillion to $10.6 trillion, in constant 2009 dollars. The middle quintile of households—the middle class—captured about 10 percent of this total income growth. The top one percent, by contrast, captured over 28 percent of the growth in total household market incomes.[22] In other words, the top one percent captured nearly three times as much of the total increase in the household economic pie as did the population 20 times as large and in the middle of income distributions.

The same data show that in 1979 the middle quintile of households earned 77 percent *more* total market income than did the top one percent—just as one would expect in a functional democratic market society. In 2007, however, the top one percent earned 61 percent more in market income than did the entirety of the middle quintile. This is an unprecedented and extraordinary reversal in less than 30 years.

Median real (inflation-adjusted) household *market* income—the market income of the household in the middle, taking into account size adjustments and the value of employer-sponsored healthcare—grew all of 19 percent from 1979 to 2007, with one-third of that gain coming in the pre-crash bubble. In the entire 31-year period from 1979 to 2009 (that is, including the crash that began the Great Recession), median real household market income grew a miserable 14 percent.[23]

Median real household market income growth over this period is largely the result of four related stories: fewer individuals in each household; more tax units in each household; more women in the workforce; and higher remuneration for those women. The Burkhauser group's paper gives useful insights into the changing dynamics of households. Basically, what one sees on average is fewer individuals in each household, but more tax units. This means that on average there are more adults earning income in each household, beyond a husband and wife filing a joint return, and fewer mouths for those income-earning adults to feed, for example through a decision to have fewer children.

Again, some of these shifts capture welfare-enhancing moves, as when a gay couple decides to cohabit rather than maintain separate households, because society has become more tolerant of that decision. But some reflect deterioration in income security, as when the mother-in-law moves in, or the post-college son cannot be induced to move out. The Burkhauser group is insensitive to the ambiguous welfare implications of these developments.

In 2009, the CBO published a large study of changes in the distribution of labor earnings from 1979 to 2007.[24] The CBO's paper looked at the population of men and women aged 25 to 54 who had at least some labor income, and further ranked that population by sex and earnings.

The percentage of men in the 50th percentile of the earnings distribution who were employed full-time and for the full year increased 5 percentage points, from 87 percent in 1979 to 92 percent in 2007. Meanwhile, the percentage of women who were so employed increased 16 percentage points, from 67 to 83 percent.

Over the same 28-year period, the constant-dollar hourly wages of men in the 50th percentile of the earnings distribution were almost precisely flat. Despite large productivity gains per worker, male workers in the middle saw no improvement in real wages. But women in the 50th percentile of women workers saw large gains in real wages, from $10.50/hour in 1979 to $15.60 in 2007 (all in 2007 dollars). That wage rate still lagged the wages paid to men in the 50th percentile of men, but not nearly as badly as had been true in 1979.

So the very modest gains in median real household market incomes from 1979 to 2007 were mostly the results of more women in those households working, and getting paid more fairly for their work. Male workers in the middle basically saw no gains in the rewards to their labor. Does this not explain a great deal about political and social unrest in America today?

Market income is the measure of how households actually are doing in terms of the rewards for their labor and investments. As measured by the CBO, market income probably overstates the welfare benefits from the increasing healthcare costs paid through employer plans, and the ambiguous welfare consequences of changing household compositions, but it is a reasonable measure of how people are doing in the actual economy. Disposable income is a creature of politics, of government transfer programs and taxes. If you want a healthy middle class, what you want is a middle class that makes great strides in market incomes, not one whose disposable income depends on more government transfers and tax relief.

But as the CBO research shows, almost half the growth in median real disposable income was the result of lower taxes or larger government transfers, *not* real economic gains. Median disposable income grew about 35 percent over the 1979–2007 period, while median household market incomes grew 19 percent.

A moment's reflection will reveal that one cannot trumpet the advances in available resources of the middle class when those advances are driven to such a large extent by government tax and transfer policies, unless you also are willing to entertain ever-increasing government transfers, and steeper taxes on the highest income Americans to fund them. But market triumphalists use the work of Burkhauser and others to make precisely the opposite argument, that everything is fine, and that there is no case for increasing taxes on more affluent Americans. And in turn, observers of all stripes now agree that over the long term, our tax and transfer policies are unsustainable. The buoyant middle class that Burkhauser and others purport to have discovered is a creature of a decades-long fiscal policy of borrowing against the future by delivering more transfer benefits than our current level of tax collections can support.

INEQUALITY DISSEMBLERS

One stock answer to my picture of inequality is that it is an exercise in envy. If the middle class is doing fine, the argument goes, then who cares if the top one percent are doing spectacularly well?[25]

There are two answers to these sorts of claims. The first is that, viewed in isolation, the middle class is not doing at all well: chapter 3 and the previous section of this chapter made this point. Real median household market incomes increased only 19 percent over 28 years, and did so largely because the average household contained more income-earning adults, principally due to women's larger participation in the workforce. Median male wages in constant dollar terms have not increased in decades. The somewhat better record for disposable income is a story of political cravenness, in which median households have received more and more transfer benefits (principally Medicare), while being asked to pay less and less in taxes. This is a fiscal policy of propping up the middle class by borrowing against a future that draws increasingly near.

The second answer is that inequality is and always has been about relative wealth. Housing, education, and medical care are all instances where the buying habits of the most affluent Americans crowd out those on the next rung down, and so forth. The great economic success of the top one percent may not trickle down, but their impacts on housing or education costs do ripple outward, in ways that play to the great disadvantage of the middle class.[26]

A related line of argumentation is that the so-called poor have refrigerators, televisions, and often cell phones, which means that they are really rich in comparison to previous generations, or to the poor in the worst-off countries in the world.[27] Adam Smith made fun of this point nearly 250 years ago, when he mentioned the "common complaint that luxury [now] extends itself even to the lowest ranks of the people," because the prices of potatoes, turnips, carrots, and cabbages had fallen over the previous several decades.[28]

This claim not only ignores the fundamental idea that inequality is a relative concept, but also is highly selective in the basket of consumer goods that it holds up as exemplars. Household electronics are cheaper, but education, housing, and healthcare costs all are much higher than a generation ago.

This is what it is like actually to be poor in America today:

> There have been days, since her son Ezekiel was born 11 months ago, that Los Angeles mom Beth Capper has gone without food to keep up her supply. One friend was arrested for stealing some.

It's not drugs or alcohol or even baby formula that has put her in such a bind. It's diapers.

"There's no way around buying them," said Capper, a 41-year-old single mother who doesn't work because of a disability.

Across the country, mothers like Capper are facing the same predicament. According to a report published...in the journal *Pediatrics*, diaper need—the inability to afford to keep a child in clean diapers—affects a "substantial" number of low-income Americans, with nearly 30% of mothers questioned in New Haven, Conn., reporting that they did not have enough for their children.

Keeping a young child dry and clean can cost a pretty penny; the average is $18 a week. A single mother earning $15,080 a year in a minimum-wage job would need to devote more than 6% of her pay to diapers, according to the Pediatrics study.

Add in the fact that many lower-income families can't afford to buy diapers in bulk at stores like Costco and Target and the expense becomes prohibitive.[29]

And so low-income mothers stay at home because they cannot afford the diapers that they must provide to send their child to day care, or reuse dirty diapers because they cannot buy clean ones. Hundreds of other examples can be offered, but the simple message is that being poor in America is a hard life, and focusing on the relative cheapness of televisions, or of turnips and cabbages, is as distasteful an argument now as it was 250 years ago.

Adam Smith in fact envisioned completely different economic outcomes from those that obtain today. He wrote:

[I]t is in the progressive state, while the society is advancing to the further acquisition, rather than when it acquired its full complement of riches, that the condition of the laboring poor, of the great body of the people, seems to be the happiest and most comfortable. It is hard in the stationary, and miserable in the declining state. The progressive state is in reality the cheerful and the hearty state to all the different orders of the society....

The liberal reward of labor [i.e., high wages]...increases the industry of the common people. The wages of labor are the encouragement of industry, which, like every other human quality, improves in proportion to the encouragement it receives.[30]

As a final, slightly ridiculous example of inequality dissembling, consider the claims of Mark Perry, an economics professor at the University of Michigan. In 2013 he published an online opinion piece on the American Enterprise Institute's website claiming that the middle class has largely disappeared, all right, but that was because they are all rich now.[31]

Perry's logic underlying this extraordinary conclusion went as follows: 2009 incomes of $25,000 to $75,000 sound sort of middle class, so using Census Bureau data let us consider family incomes in that range in 1967, applying 2009 constant dollars to nominal incomes in that year (which the Census Bureau help-fully calculates). How many families fell into that band of income? About 62 per-cent of families. Now, jumping forward to 2009, how many families fell into that same band of income in actual 2009 dollars? Only about 39 percent. The number of families with incomes below $25,000 in constant 2009 dollars had declined from 22 percent in 1967 to 18 percent in 2009, and the number above $75,000 had increased from 16 percent in 1967 to 43 percent. So voila, concludes Professor Perry, the middle class in 1967 had migrated to the upper class in 2009.

Perry's presentation is a rich smorgasbord of methodological error. Let us begin with the most important. In constant dollar terms, the GDP of the United States more than tripled in the period 1967–2009; per capita real GDP more than doubled. Although CBO data do not go as far back as 1967, CBO's analysis of household incomes, discussed earlier, shows that aggregate real household mar-ket incomes more than doubled from 1979 to 2009, increasing from $4.6 tril-lion to $10.6 trillion in constant 2009 dollars. Professor Perry has forgotten that at least some crumbs of this increased wealth fell to the slice of the population he identified, and so by concluding that in constant dollar terms many families had pierced the arbitrary $75,000 income barrier, he shows nothing at all about whether they have moved to the "upper class."

Perry also starts with the wrong population. In Census-speak, "family" means two or more individuals living in a single household who are related by blood or marriage. Single people or cohabiting adults are completely excluded. What you want to start with are "households," for all the reasons described earlier. And Perry's income cutoffs for "middle class" are in fact very low in 2009 terms, given that the poverty line for a family of four in 2009 was $22,000.

If one starts instead with household incomes, one discovers that in 1967, 30 percent of all households (not 22 percent) had incomes below $25,000, and that in 1967 the $25,000 to $75,000 band of incomes occupied the 30th to 86th percentiles of household incomes.[32] Jumping to 2009, the range of household income distributions falling in the income band of $25,000 to $75,000 had shifted profoundly downward, and now covered the 25th to 68th percentiles of household income distributions. The data thus demonstrate precisely the oppo-site of what Perry claims: individuals who remained locked in place somewhere in the constant-dollar $25,000 to $75,000 band gained nothing from the trebling of real GDP, and got somewhat poorer, not richer, in relative terms, from 1967 to 2009.

Adam Smith should have the last word on the inequality defenders, deniers, and dissemblers who daily gather on the electronic battlefields, under the banners of the *Wall Street Journal*'s editorial page, the American Enterprise Institute, the Hoover Institution, and similarly directed organizations:

> This disposition to admire, and almost to worship, the rich and the powerful, and to despise, or, at least, to neglect persons of poor and mean condition, though necessary both to establish and to maintain the distinction of ranks and the order of society, is, at the same time, the great and most universal cause of the corruption of our moral sentiments. That wealth and greatness are often regarded with the respect and admiration which are due only to wisdom and virtue; and that the contempt, of which vice and folly are the only proper objects, is often most unjustly bestowed upon poverty and weakness, has been the complaint of moralists in all the ages.[33]

CHAPTER 5

THE GROWTH FAIRY

The great mob of mankind are the admirers and the worshippers, and,
what may seem more extraordinary, most frequently the disinterested
admirers and worshippers, of wealth and greatness.

—ADAM SMITH, *The Theory of Moral Sentiments*, Book I,
Sec. III, Chap. III.

THE REDISTRIBUTION OGRE

This book's fundamental political economy claim is that government insurance and investments that complement private markets lead to greater welfare for all Americans, and that opportunities abound for just such productive collective activities. But government spending of all sorts in practice is funded by one source—taxes. User fees and sales of government-owned property (surplus military bases, for example) raise trivial revenues. Government borrowing is just an indirect form of taxation, because government debt must eventually be paid back from future government revenues. As a result, government debt just shifts the imposition of tax burdens forward. (Government debt thus has the unique property of being the only way that the current Congress can bind the tax policy of future Congresses.) My cheery predilection for focusing on the positive returns to government investment cannot ultimately mask the fact that some people will be assigned the obligations to make those investments, possibly over their objections, and that the tax system is the device by which we allocate those obligations.

Market triumphalists jump off the train even before it has left the station. First, where is the money for that government investment to come from? And second, how are we going to enhance the welfare of all Americans without engaging in pernicious "class warfare" and "redistribution"?

There are in fact at least four competing demands that underlie the practical determination of sensible fiscal policy. Well-chosen social insurance and investment programs can have large positive economic returns, but require capital, which comes through the coercive mechanism of taxation. Coercion is a serious business, not to be undertaken lightly. What is more, taxation introduces its own frictions, so that not all the money transferred from private market opportunities to these collective opportunities reaches those public goods. By itself, this tension would suggest a traditional cost-benefit analysis, but there are moral philosophy tensions as well. The more we invest in sensible public opportunities, the more we increase the happiness of large numbers of Americans relatively quickly, but in doing so we make those who fund the collective investments unhappier faster. How do we weigh those against each other? Welfare economics cheats here, by assuming one or more answers to the moral philosophy questions (embodied in the "social welfare function") and concentrating on the cost-benefit trade-offs once the social welfare function is specified. But real life fiscal policy cannot do this, and must consider and balance all these competing demands simultaneously.

Market triumphalists reject the entire enterprise of balancing these competing demands, because they see taxes as an infringement of their personal liberties, and because they claim that taxation is a hugely inefficient undertaking. Chapter 2 touched on the confusion between marketplace freedoms and political liberties. This chapter focuses on this second claim—the efficiency cost of taxation.

Perfectly competitive markets do not yield perfectly equal outcomes. To the contrary, whether through luck or differences in native endowments, individuals' outcomes vary all over the place. Those who for whatever reason enjoy great material rewards in the marketplace do not directly benefit in the short term from many of the complementary collective investments on which I focus, like public education—the rich can buy the goods directly. In turn, one cannot expect those who have few assets and little income today to fund those collective investments, because they do not have the money to invest, and in the absence of perfect markets cannot borrow to make these otherwise-compelling investments.

As a practical matter, investment in complementary collective goods or collective insurance programs requires the mechanism of state coercion to take from the rich and invest in—not give to—the rest of America, in ways that ultimately redound to everyone's benefit. In modern political discourse, this notion that we collectively should make highly productive investments in those without the resources to invest in themselves quickly is dismissed as "redistribution," as if that label disposed of the matter, because "redistribution" in turn is viewed as the battle flag of "class warfare."

The logical error should be obvious. Market triumphalists who have made "redistribution" into the battle hymn of the underclass treat social insurance and investment as a forcible and quickly consumed "gift" to the poor, like a Christmas goose (perhaps the one that laid the golden eggs?), when in fact the purported redistribution should be analyzed as money spent on economic programs (insurance or investment) with measurable short- and long-term economic returns. Those programs must be judged on the basis of those returns, while giving appropriate weight to the coerced nature of the investments. The market triumphalist view is profoundly non-economic, because it brooks no possibility of making investments with very high economic returns shared by society as a whole, whenever those investments are made through the mechanism of the state.

I argue in chapter 11 that one of the three great strategic errors of the progressive movement in America over the last several decades was to allow the highly charged term "redistribution" to creep from social science literature to common discourse, as if it were a neutral concept. It is anything but neutral, right from the "re-" in "redistribution," which implicitly asserts a claim that the market outcomes reached in a world dominated by imperfect markets and random acts of fortune are imbued with a legitimacy that "redistribution" upsets.

Our vocabulary here betrays us. You can see this if, when reading any article on fiscal policy, you substitute a term like "social investment" or "social insurance" for "redistribution"—the entire tenor of the passage changes. In 2011, for example, Rebecca Blank was a top candidate to become the chairwoman of President Obama's Council of Economic Advisors, but then the White House discovered that Ms. Blank had once written in a paper on poverty issues that "[a] commitment to economic justice necessarily implies a commitment to the redistribution of economic resources, so that the poor and the dispossessed are more fully included in the economic system."[1] That one use of the toxic term was enough to disqualify her from consideration. Perhaps she would have become the chairwoman had only she written that a commitment to justice implies a commitment to "productive complementary social investments," or the like.

Social scientists made "redistribution" a commonplace term, but perhaps did not think very carefully about all the word's implications as they did so. For example, welfare economics is devoted to the theme of maximizing economic efficiency in light of other specified non-economic values—in this field's academic models, a shared social preference for more egalitarian outcomes—encapsulated in an assumed "social welfare function."[2] That social welfare function in turn often is summarized as implemented through "redistribution" via the tax system. My intuition is that if you were to poll Americans today to find what percentage of those queried favored "redistribution" to achieve "more egalitarian outcomes," you would be lucky to find those in favor reaching the double digits. But if you asked, who is in favor of more collective investment in productive opportunities, or the like, those in favor would be a much higher number.

In short, this book rejects the idea that the identification of "redistribution" in action ends a debate even before it begins. But from the other direction, the book's claims ultimately are founded in economics, which means that I embrace the importance of economic growth. Even if one were to believe that any country would ever declare itself to be plenty rich enough, economic growth remains imperative. In a country without per capita economic growth, our individual striving for economic success quickly does degenerate into a war of all against all, because the only way for Harpo to become richer is for Groucho to become poorer. This is a very bad idea, especially from Groucho's perspective. So economic growth is not an optional feature.

Economic growth is the product of investment in physical and human capital, new production technologies, and new products.[3] As discussed in this chapter, taxation introduces at least some frictions into marketplace transactions, and in doing so slows down private market growth. The principal question for this chapter, then, is just how much does taxation hurt growth?[4]

THE GROWTH FAIRY NARRATIVE

Chapter 1 introduced the theme that our welfare—the happiness of society, as Adam Smith would phrase things—depends on more than our national income. Market triumphalists reject this elementary proposition of moral philosophy. To them, the purpose of life is for the United States to win the gold medal at the GDP Olympics every year. In this quest for GDP gold, the performance-enhancing drug of choice is the Growth Fairy, and she in turn subsists entirely on a diet of low taxes.

The supply-side economics rhetoric of the Reagan years was an early iteration of this meme that tax sparing the rich is the key to growth. In those market triumphalist foundational myths, low tax rates at the top end were said to spur so much economic growth so quickly that the IRS would quickly recoup the momentary loss of tax revenues, through the lower taxes collected on a much larger economic base. Even apologists for the supply side point of view have tempered their remarks somewhat in this one respect, but their core message remains that tax rates on the labor income of the most successful Americans, and taxes on the investment income of the wealthiest Americans, must be kept extremely low for the economy to prosper.

The market triumphalist belief system thus rests on two pillars. The first has a crystalline clarity about it: a light tax touch on the rich is the key to economic growth. The intimate connection between taxes on the affluent and economic growth is seen as a physical law of the universe, as inescapable as gravity. The second is mentioned sotto voce: it is that the ever-increasing wealth of the rich will trickle down to the rest of us, in ways that do not need to be specified. Being cabana staff to plutocrats is the best the rest of us can hope for, but if we have mobile phones and our parents did not, what is there to complain about?

I think of these pillars as laying out the ground rules for a visitation from the Growth Fairy. In the more extreme economic models, human beings behave toward taxes as if we all had the fiscal equivalent of a deadly allergy to shellfish, where the slightest exposure to higher taxes will send us into anaphylactic shock. Conversely, lower tax rates will act like a performance-enhancing drug, causing us to throw off the mantle of laziness under which our native talents have slumbered, and propelling the country to enormous gains in economic growth.

Market triumphalists always see a Growth Fairy hovering in the distance, just waiting to shower wealth upon us, if only we would demonstrate that we deserve her blessings by lowering tax rates on the affluent some more. The Growth Fairy offers empty promises of something for everyone, at the immediate price of enhanced inequality, delivered in the form of disproportionately light tax burdens on the most successful.

Some observers on the left claim that market triumphalists use the Growth Fairy narrative and their preoccupation with GDP as pretext to cover their real agenda, which is low taxes for themselves (or for the affluent people they hope to be). Unlike these commentators, I take market triumphalists at their word; I believe that they believe that GDP is everything. I reject that worldview, however, because it repudiates any sense of national community, ignores the immediate costs of poverty for cognitive development and educational opportunities, and overlooks how contingent the outcomes of our lives really are.

In market triumphalist narratives, tax policy must be used to encourage people to become rich, so that they take big risks, and so they can amass great stocks of capital, which when saved can fund new productive investments by businesses, thereby generating greater business profits, which profits in turn will somehow be shared with workers. These narratives thus emphasize the alleged growth-strangling consequences of higher taxes on the highest-income Americans. In this political economy story, there are no plausible tax increases, just "job-killing tax hikes." For example, market triumphalists predicted that allowing the Bush tax cuts to expire for the most affluent Americans at the end of 2012 would lead our most productive citizens to throw up their hands and retire to the beach, thereby depriving us of the fruits of their future services. But that did not happen. More generally, as this chapter demonstrates, the economic consensus points in the opposite direction: there is a relatively weak relationship between work effort and labor tax rates, for both technical and practical reasons.

Like good science fiction, the Growth Fairy narrative is grounded in superficial plausibility. Since the time of Adam Smith we have understood that business investment is a critical driver of economic growth. Lower taxes can possibly lead to higher private investment. And it is possible to imagine circumstances where tax rates are so high as to stifle current economic activity, much less future growth. It is just that ours are not those circumstances.

Why is the Growth Fairy story not a credible guide to fiscal policy? Five reasons, which I discuss further in this chapter:

1. The United States today is a low-tax country.
2. Empirical studies have shown little connection between tax rates and critical inputs into economic growth, like labor participation or individual savings.
3. More theoretical economic models reach many different conclusions; the modeling of the relationship between tax policy and growth is not yet reliable enough to base policy recommendations on it.
4. The Growth Fairy narrative is fundamentally incomplete by its own terms. It does not consider the positive growth effects of public investment that complements private markets.
5. The Growth Fairy story confuses welfare and income, in particular by not offering a convincing story as to how the growth it posits will be broadly shared without violating its own central premise that inequality is the key to growth.

In sum, the market triumphalist ode to the Growth Fairy is an exercise in wishful thinking, missing thoughts, and hyperbole. The story is wishful, in that it invariably is a message delivered by the affluent to the rest of us, explaining why the iron laws of economics require lower tax burdens on them, so that they can get richer at ever-increasing rates. The fable is missing a critical part to make its story hang together, which is how all of us will share in the increasing wealth stored up by the most affluent. This in turn raises the question of which government programs are financed by the taxes that the affluent are so eager to shed. And the argument is hyperbolic, because the evidence on the relationship between growth and taxes is far more ambiguous than Growth Fairy devotees claim.

The place to begin is to ask how taxes might affect the overall economy. This is not an entirely vapid question, because economists do not think about the burden of taxation in the same way you do. You measure the burden of taxation by the size of the check you write. Economists, by contrast, do not see the cash taxes we pay as particularly problematic, at least at a macroeconomic level: the nation as a whole is not made poorer, because the money has not disappeared, it is just in someone else's pocket. What economists care more about is "excess burden," or "deadweight loss" (the two terms are synonymous), which very simply is the measure of how behavior changes in response to taxation.[5]

The basic problem is that most taxes affect you along two different margins. First, a new tax makes you poorer. That is a tax's "income effect." From the perspective of the overall fiscal system, though, which encompasses not just the taxes raised but government's spending of those tax revenues, someone else somewhere in the system is better off by virtue of the taxes you pay. From this broader perspective, the pluses and minuses of individual income effects more or less cancel each other out, at least in simple and moderate cases.[6]

In response to being made poorer by a tax, you might choose to work more to earn more money to undo the income effect, or you might learn to make do with less. But this income effect is the unavoidable bedrock of tax-induced behavioral distortions: no one has yet invented a tax that sends money to the government but makes no taxpayer poorer.

Second, a new tax changes your behavior in ways that go beyond just making you poorer, because *for all practical taxes you can change your tax liability by changing your behavior,* through substituting other goods or activities that are less heavily taxed.[7] If apples are taxed and pears are not, you may increase your pear consumption relative to apples; if mobile phone services are subject to new excise taxes, you might rely more on e-mail or Skyping from your desktop computer, and so on.

This is the "substitution effect"—the idea that you change your behavior away from what is taxed more highly to something that is taxed more lightly. In the case of the income tax, the thing that is taxed lightly is the one other use to which you can put your time besides participating in the market economy—leisure. (Economists use "leisure" to denote all activities on the private side of the production frontier. To an economist, doing household chores is time spent at leisure.)

Deadweight loss is a measure of the substitution effects induced by taxation. In the case of the income tax, deadweight loss is the measure of your instinct to chuck it all and head to the beach, or more realistically to work less overtime or take a less strenuous job, to reflect the fact that taxes have made not working (leisure) more attractive compared to working.

Think of a perfectly competitive private economy as transferring water from one spot to another in a watertight bucket. Deadweight loss is the measure of trying to do the same job with a leaky bucket—not all that is put into the tax system reaches the other end.[8] That is, taxpayers suffer greater economic burdens in respect of their tax liabilities than the cash that gets delivered to the government at the other hand.

This is not because government necessarily spends money stupidly (although that of course sometimes happens), but rather because the economic burden of taxation is not measured in the first place by the cash the tax raises for the government. On a national scale, if taking $100 of my income from me via an income tax and giving it to you changed nothing about how you or I otherwise behaved, the bucket would be watertight—aggregate national income would be unchanged. I might be unhappy, but you presumably would be happier, and nothing else would be different. This is the pure income effect.

The economic measure of the deadweight loss of taxation lies not in the $100 paid to the government, but rather in the fact that, in light of the tax, I might choose to work less, or differently. The deadweight loss of taxation is thus the measure of what I choose *not* to do in a world with a distortionary tax, that I would have done in a world where the same tax revenues were raised by a perfect (and entirely hypothetical) lump sum tax.[9] In a more practical sense, it is the deal not done, the apple not bought, or to paraphrase Arthur Conan Doyle, the dog that does not bark when one expected that it would.

Consider a change to the personal income tax rate tables. There is no theoretical answer to how taxpayers will resolve their inner conflicts between income and substitution effects. All that we can observe is the unitary action ultimately taken by a taxpayer, which might be on balance to work more, because the income effect of the tax predominates, or to work less, because the substitution effect predominates. This decision will depend on how rich the taxpayer already is, how old she is, how large the tax change is, how much debt she has, how flexible her labor market opportunities are, and many other factors. You can begin to see already why it is so challenging to model the economic consequences of a change in tax law.

A BACKGROUND OF LOW TAX RATES

What we need to focus on, then, are the behavioral distortions induced by taxation. The deadweight losses from a proposed tax hike in turn depend not just on the magnitude of the proposed increase but on the tax structures already in place.

You can intuit why deadweight loss is a function of the existing level of taxation simply by focusing on the after-tax returns to working. Taxpayers in fact do not respond to tax rates as such, but rather to the effect of taxes on their after-tax income. Because tax rates today are so low, a tax rate increase has a lower impact than would be the case if we were starting with the tax rates that applied in the 1970s and 1980s.

Imagine that a high-ability taxpayer who in 2012 enjoyed a 35 percent marginal tax rate finds that in 2013 her marginal tax rate has jumped (for simplicity) to 40 percent. As a result, she will now keep $60 of every $100 earned, rather than $65.[10] That $5 difference represents a 7.7 percent reduction in after-tax income on the taxpayer's last dollar of income.[11] (Her effective tax rate will be affected even less.) Perhaps this decrease in after-tax returns from her last hour of labor will lead the taxpayer to chuck it all in, or even somehow to negotiate a life in which she works only 92.3 percent as hard, but given the volatility in pre-tax returns to labor (and to capital) that we all have endured in our roller coaster economy over the last 15 years, this would seem to be an extreme reaction. Conversely, if marginal tax rates were 65 percent, the same 5 percentage point increase in marginal tax rates, now to 70 percent, would reduce the after-tax return to a taxpayer's last dollar of income from \$35 to \$30, a 14.3 percent reduction—close to double the dollar effect when compared with 2012 tax rates as the starting point.

As it happens, the US personal income tax rate today is roughly in line with the first example, not the second. In the 1970s, however, the maximum personal income tax rate was 70 percent, while from 1986–1988 the maximum rate was 28 percent.

More generally, as will be described in chapter 7, the United States today is an extremely low-tax country. In fact, the United States in 2012 had the lowest tax burden as a percentage of GDP of any country in the OECD.[12] So one should not expect deadweight losses to overwhelm us.

For these reasons, current levels of taxation do not necessarily impose devastating deadweight losses. One standard public finance textbook gives an example of a wage earner with an annual income of \$40,000 who moves from a world of zero tax to one where the taxpayer faces a 40 percent income tax rate. Using values that the authors believe to be realistic, they calculate a deadweight loss of taxation of \$640, about 4 percent of the tax collected.[13]

This is not a very troubling figure in the great scheme of things. The point is not that \$640 in the pocket of a wage earner with a \$40,000 income is trivial; it is that deadweight loss is unavoidable, period. The alternative is not \$640 more in take-home pay, because there always will be some deadweight cost to government, and because deadweight loss is not a measure of lost income in the first place—it is a measure of the more abstract opportunity cost of taxation. To discover that deadweight loss amounts to a bucket that leaks 4 percent on the way from income producers to the government is actually pretty good news—particularly in this example, which contemplates a 40 percentage point swing in tax liabilities, from zero to 40 percent.

EMPIRICAL STUDIES: INDIVIDUAL LABOR AND SAVINGS

Tax policies might affect economic growth by discouraging some key behavioral input into that process. Do workers change their behavior very much in the face of fluctuating taxes? Do individuals save more when tax rates on their financial income goes down? Do entrepreneurs flourish only in low tax climates? And finally, are business investments burdened by high taxation? These are the principal channels by which tax policies might conceivably affect the rate of economic growth.

A great deal of empirical work has examined the real life responsiveness of taxpayers to changes in tax rates.[14] Some of these economic studies focus on the responsiveness of workers to changes in the personal income tax rate applicable to their labor income.[15] Others focus on the responsiveness of individual savers to changes in the tax rates imposed on savings. And a third group looks at the responsiveness of business investment to changes in the taxation of those investments.

The nonpartisan Congressional Research Service in 2011 reviewed both the historical record and empirical studies. The CRS concluded that tax rates did not have much of an effect on labor income, and actually pointed in a direction opposite to what one might expect with respect to savings:

> Historical data on labor participation rates and average hours worked compared to tax rates indicates little relationship with either top marginal rates or average marginal rates on labor income. Relationships between tax rates and savings appear positively correlated (that is, lower savings are consistent with lower, not higher, tax rates), although this relationship may not be causal....
>
> A review of statistical evidence suggests that both labor supply and savings and investment are relatively insensitive to tax rates. Small effects arise in part because of offsetting income and substitution effects (which make the direction of effects uncertain) and in part because each of these individual responses appears small. Institutional constraints may also have an effect.[16]

In determining the overall effect of a change in tax rates on labor supply (particularly the labor supply of high-ability taxpayers, who might plausibly be in a position to buy more leisure through reduced labor effort), economists analyze whether the "substitution effect" (the urge to chuck it all in and head for the beach) in fact would outweigh the "income effect" (the urge to work even harder to restore one's after-tax income to its pre-tax increase level). In very general terms, most research suggests that labor effort (particularly of the primary wage earner in a household) is relatively inelastic (does not respond all that much) to changes in tax rates of the magnitudes we witnessed when crossing from 2012 to 2013.[17]

To the same general effect, two leading academic economists concluded: "The consensus among economists is that the evidence shows that aggregate labor supply responds little to its after-tax return, that the evidence is not clear on whether saving responds to its after-tax return, and that the evidence regarding investment is somewhat mixed."[18]

The ambiguity as to whether an individual's saving responds to tax rates is an example of the internal struggle between income and substitution effects. A lower tax rate on savings means that an individual with a predetermined retirement goal will reach that goal more quickly, and therefore actually could choose to save less and still stay on target (the income effect), but on the other hand the payoff from saving rather than consuming has gone up (the substitution effect), which would argue for saving more. Neither effect invariably dominates the other.

What is more, a great deal of individual savings today takes place through tax-deferred retirement accounts, like IRAs.[19] Those arrangements would not be directly affected by tax rate reductions, except that their relative advantage to saving outside the tax-preferred vehicle would diminish. If tax reform had the effect of lowering pre-tax interest rates, that could actually reduce tax-preferred savings.[20]

The analysis of labor supply responsiveness ("elasticities," in economists' jargon) can be refined by dividing labor income into job seekers (the "extensive" margin) and job holders looking to change their hours or effort level (the "intensive" margin), and further by reference to income levels (high-income workers do not show the same elasticities as low-income workers). One also can distinguish between the primary wage earner in a household and "secondary" wage earners. Although the gap in responsiveness has greatly narrowed, secondary wage earners (which in the literature are sometimes reduced to married women) still are thought to be more responsive to tax rates than are primary wage earners.[21]

When all is said and done, however, the conclusion remains that changes in tax rates, at least at the moderate levels seen in the United States for the last several decades, do not have very large effects on total labor supply or on individuals' savings.[22] The first of these thoughts in particular should not be very surprising: few of us can afford to quit our jobs because tax rates go up, and most jobs are not so flexible in hours for which we are paid as to allow us to trim our work effort to correspond precisely to fluctuations in the tax rates we face.

This consensus view angers market triumphalists. They argue that the maximum tax rates now in effect on the highest income Americans will crush the souls of high-ability taxpayers, leading them to retire to the beach, no doubt to read *The Fountainhead*. But arguments of this nature border on the preposterous. The fictional Gordon Gekko in the movie *Wall Street* (1987) was comfortable with the thought that "greed is good," even though he faced 28 percent capital gains tax rates—not the 20 percent rate for post-2012 years.[23] And the highest marginal tax rates on labor income are now comparable to the same rates that applied in the 1990s, when the economy was booming, and high-ability individuals swarmed the canyons of Wall Street and the corridors of the first Internet start-ups.[24] Even Fox News commentator Bill O'Reilly stayed at his post when personal income tax rates went up on January 1, 2013.

Direct measures of labor participation and intensity, or rates of saving, bear directly on the effects of taxation on the real economy, but arguably are incomplete in a number of respects. For example, if tax rates go up I might choose to work the same number of hours, but just not try very hard, because I no longer care quite so much about getting a raise; alternatively, I might choose to accept a lower-paying job in a nicer climate. Or if I am a corporate executive, I might ask to take my compensation in a more tax-favored form: doing so would not change my actual work habits, but would have a real impact on the tax revenues raised by the tax increase. Or I could read up on tax-evasion techniques. Some of these responses take place in the real economy but are not visible by looking at labor participation and hours (choosing to take a lower-paying job in a nicer climate); others are relevant only between me and the IRS (taking more tax-free fringe benefits and less taxable cash compensation).

In response, the economist Martin Feldstein proposed a new metric for measuring the distortions in behavior induced by taxation: the elasticity of taxable income (ETI).[25] Feldstein's contributions were two. First, he convinced most analysts that simply toting up the number of hours an individual worked did not fully capture his responses to tax rate changes, because it ignored the kind of responses suggested immediately above.

Second, Feldstein argued that you could lump all of these responses together in a simple single measure, the "elasticity of taxable income"—that is, the extent to which a one percent rise in tax rates will affect the taxable income I report on my tax return. ETI thus combines real behavioral changes and tax return responses to taxation in a single number. It is *not* an alternative measure of how responsive my labor effort is to taxation, but rather a measure (in this example) of how responsive the wage income number I put down on my tax return is to changes in tax rates.

Feldstein then basically went on to conclude that ETI is very high, particularly for high-income individuals. This would imply that we should tax the highest incomes very lightly, because otherwise we reduce aggregate welfare much more than the incremental tax revenues that are transferred from taxpayers to government might suggest.

Feldstein's ETI concept was a huge success; economists loved it because it was tractable (easy to work with in their models), and because it made empirical work easier: all possible behavioral effects, both real and entirely tax-motivated, were combined into a single number that could be derived from existing tax return data.

More recent work brought some of Feldstein's bolder claims down to earth.[26] From the perspective of this book, however, the point worth emphasizing is that it is unproductive to lump together all sorts of different responses to changes in tax rates if the goal is to guide real-world fiscal policymaking. Closing tax loopholes is not the same as choosing one tax rate schedule over another.

Imagine a poorly advised government that increases marginal tax rates, and at the same time radically reduces the penalties for outright tax evasion. The new rules come into effect and tax collections do not budge. My goodness, Feldsteinites might say, look at the dramatic elasticity of taxable income response here—that new higher rate certainly implies huge deadweight loss, because it changed taxpayer behavior so dramatically that their taxable incomes fell enough that the higher tax rates didn't collect an extra dime. But in fact nothing at all has changed in the real economy. What we really are bearing witness to is simply evidence of poor tax system design.

And that is the basic problem with Feldstein's ETI construct: it gives no direction to actual policymaking. The current Internal Revenue Code is an overflowing fountain of lawful tax minimization strategies; as a result, a meaningful taxable income response to even modest tax rate increases can plausibly be described as in large measure evidence of the structural defects of the tax system itself. It is possible to address the porosity of the current tax system head on. If the tax system were improved, and tax evasion suppressed, then in fact we would be left more or less where we started, which is that labor and savings are not terribly responsive to tax rate fluctuations. ETI does not distinguish real deadweight loss from the artificial losses we impose on ourselves through our loophole-ridden tax system.

I take the real message of the ETI research to be that there are a great many virtues to a tax system with as broad a base as possible (few deductions, exemptions, or exclusions) because by definition a broad base eliminates many unproductive avenues for responding to higher tax rates—and of course with a broad base you do not need as high a marginal rate in the first place. Chapter 13 returns to this point.

EMPIRICAL STUDIES: BUSINESS INCOME

To summarize to this point, it turns out that economists of all stripes broadly agree that neither the supply of labor nor the supply of savings is very responsive to fluctuations in tax rates in the range that we have experienced in the United States. Martin Feldstein identified labor responses other than labor participation and labor hours that might be sensitive to tax rates, but a great many of his examples really point to loopholes in the current income tax system that could easily be addressed, were there political will. The best case for the Growth Fairy should be more persuasive than the circular argument that we must reduce tax rates, because if we do not we are compelled to have a tax system riddled with loopholes that induce taxpayers to engage in self-help to reduce their tax bills.

Unless we are satisfied with faith-based fiscal analysis, the case for the existence of the Growth Fairy relies on identifying a plausible channel by which tax policies materially affect an important factor that supports economic growth. Through what tax-related channels can the Growth Fairy transmit her blessings, if not through increased labor supply or savings? We are left with an inquiry into the responsiveness of risk-taking and business investments to changes in tax rates. (Economists usually refer to individuals' financial portfolios as "savings," and business's spending on physical capital as "investments." Personal savings ultimately fund business investments, but the savings do not have to come from US individuals; foreigners also can supply savings to US firms.[27]) Since the Growth Fairy does not hover around the supply of labor or savings, risk-taking and business investment are where she must make her home, if she is to have any effect at all.[28]

Entrepreneurial activity is important to growth: it is the spark of inspiration, and the will to carry that idea forward notwithstanding collective indifference, that creates the next big thing. We really do not know very much about the relationship between tax rates and entrepreneurial risk-taking. The logical relationship is precisely the opposite of most peoples' intuitions. A theoretically ideal business tax would apply symmetrically to income and loss: if you make money, you pay tax, and if you lose money, the government mails you a check equal to the tax rate multiplied by your loss. In such a system, the IRS is a business's full silent partner, regardless of how the business performs. (US law actually offers businesses a partial risk-sharing mechanism; net losses are not immediately reimbursed, but those losses can be carried forward and claimed as deductions against future years' profits.) Because government is sharing the risk of loss, the effect of taxation is to reduce the riskiness of investments—to modulate returns.

The very fact that this argument appalls most entrepreneurs suggests that there is more going on inside the head of an entrepreneur than can be explained by logic. I suspect that in almost every case an entrepreneur has an irrationally exuberant opinion of himself and his venture; he is fixated on the profits he believes he will capture, not on the possibility of failure. It is not at all clear how tax policies map onto the consciousness of such an individual. One possibility is that if the basic story of entrepreneurship is that of irrational optimism, then it follows that from the perspective of the entrepreneur, imposing a silent partner (the tax system) on her is fundamentally unfair, because the entrepreneur (irrationally) values the silent partner's absorption of a percentage of possible losses much less than she values the silent partner's slicing off of a share of profits. The optimism leads to an asymmetrical view of risk, and therefore of the cost to the entrepreneur of her silent partner, the tax system.

On the other hand, we know that the first great Internet bubble, circa 1997–1998, took place at a time when overall tax rates were higher than they are in 2013, and the maximum personal tax rates closely comparable. We also know that the 1990s were a decade of strong economic growth overall. And irrational exuberance has the great virtue of being, well, irrational, and therefore not necessarily much affected by tax rates. Moreover, as chapter 9 explains, the capital gains tax is not a targeted reward for entrepreneurial courage, and the business tax system today already offers a great many incentives to small business.

In the end, access to capital and other nontax matters are infinitely more important to an entrepreneur's first steps than is the tax system that might apply years down the road. The relationship between capital supply and tax policy in turn is a very attenuated one, given the importance of Fed monetary policy, the role of tax-exempt investors, and other factors. We see this relative indifference to tax planning in operation in the fact that many recent great success stories (Facebook, Google, etc.) did not organize themselves from the get-go in business structures that a sophisticated tax planner would have preferred.[29] I therefore discount the idea that tax rates are a principal driver of entrepreneurial ambitions.

Within the moderate band of actual US tax rates over the last several decades, the evidence is at best ambiguous that tax policies drive labor supply, savings supply, or entrepreneurial fervor. A plausible case for the existence of the Growth Fairy therefore comes down to this: Will lowering tax rates spur business investment?

Business investment is central to economic growth. Human beings are not natively smarter or stronger than they were 50 or 100 years ago, but workers nonetheless are more productive today, because their productivity is leveraged by all the business investments, both past and present, on which they draw in performing their jobs.[30] These investments in tangible business capital (greasy machinery), business intangibles (patents, know-how, goodwill), and human capital (education or job training) explain why wages today are higher in real terms than wages 50 years ago.[31]

Textbook economic growth models attribute growth to technological progress, so that a dollar of capital invested today is more productive that the same dollar in real terms invested 50 years ago. But these technological improvements in turn are the results of prior business investments of the sort just identified. Labor incomes and national wealth benefit in the long term through these twin mechanisms of technological progress and sufficient new investment funded by our savings to maintain real levels of investment as assets wear out and the population grows.

You can intuit a high-income individual's marginal tax rates on his wage income by looking at the published tax rate schedules. Business income, however, is much more complicated to measure. As a result, the most direct place to begin is to examine the actual burdens that our federal tax system imposes on incremental business investments. This is an exercise in diving deep into the plumbing of the tax system. Unfortunately, many economists gloss over the need to roll up one's sleeves and understand the tax system as it actually is lived.

Are business investments today highly taxed? For market triumphalists, the answer is self-evident. Yuri Vanetik, a private equity professional writing in the *Los Angeles Times's* op-ed pages in July 2013, identified the impediment to growth as "the abnormally high statutory U.S. tax rates and the mind-boggling complexity and opacity of the code itself.... The rate itself crushes countless businesses and hurts U.S. competitiveness."[32]

It is true that in July 2013 the United States had the highest statutory corporate tax rate of any major economy in the world (35 percent at the federal level)—but virtually no firm pays tax at that rate. The day before Vanetik's op-ed appeared, the nonpartisan US Government Accountability Office (GAO) publicly released a study of the tax burdens of large corporations, drawn from actual tax return and financial accounting data.[33] That study concluded that in 2010, profitable large corporations paid an *effective* federal corporate tax rate (their tax bill divided by a comprehensive measure of their income) of 12.6 percent. If one includes foreign income taxes actually paid on foreign income, the worldwide effective tax rate was 16.9 percent. There are reasons that 2010 may have been an exceptional year, but the fact remains that firms' effective tax rates are much lower than the nominal headline rate might suggest.

Vanetik also claimed that the best way "to encourage businesses to translate growth into new jobs is to reform the corporate tax code." This hardy perennial among Growth Fairy buffs, that high business tax rates are "job killers," is particularly difficult to square with reality, given that firms deduct from their income the compensation they pay their workers. In other words, firms are taxed on the profits left over *after* paying workers' salaries. So long as a new worker can be expected to generate a positive return (more than cover her salary), why would a rational firm not hire that individual? The more nuanced argument is that every new hire implies a concomitant capital investment to support that worker, but here Vanetik conceded the issue without being aware that he had done so, when he wrote that even under the current corporate tax system, firms were expanding operations and accumulating capital.

The United States is unique in having a large fraction (roughly half) of all business income earned in entities that are not subject to the corporate income tax: partnerships, "S" corporations, limited liability companies, and sole proprietorships. The key tax fact is that these entities do not pay tax; instead, the firms' owners report on their personal income tax returns their share of an entity's profits. (For this reason, partnerships, "S" corporations, and limited liability companies often are referred to as "pass-through" entities.) The effective tax rate of profitable pass-through entities is higher than 12.6 percent, but nowhere near the maximum individual income tax rate.

More important, closely held pass-through entities have no tax reason to pay salaries to their owners (since their net income and their salaries are lumped together at the owner level in paying individual income tax). As a result, pass-through firms' "profits" often are a muddle of an entity's stand-alone performance with an owner's inchoate labor contribution, which in a large corporation would have been paid out as salary. Complaints about high effective rates of tax imposed on the pass-through sector in many cases therefore boil down to unhappiness over the tax rate structure imposed on this form of labor income. More bluntly, such complaints are just a call for lower tax rates on the labor income of the self-employed, relative to the tax burdens imposed on employees.

Overall effective tax rates are one important benchmark, but economists generally believe that growth is fueled by *marginal* investments—the next investment—and that in turn requires us to consider what tax rates actually are imposed by the current business tax system on a prospective marginal business investment. (Economists call this the effective marginal tax rate, or EMTR— "effective" because it compares actual taxes paid to a comprehensive measure of income from the investment, and "marginal" because the calculation applies to a prospective and hypothetical incremental investment, not to the firm's entire tax bill.)

As previously observed, business investment takes three basic forms: investment in intangible assets (patents, processes, software development, goodwill), tangible assets (greasy machinery), and human capital (education and worker training). Investments in intangible assets are heavily tax-favored today: the costs of developing intangibles are immediately expensed by a firm, and in addition, qualifying expenses are eligible for a tax credit—a dollar for dollar reduction in the firm's tax liability. The combination means that the tax system today *subsidizes* rather than taxes investments in intangible assets.[34]

Investments in human capital also are partially tax-subsidized. Employers expense the costs of training workers, but workers do not reflect in their tax returns the value they receive (their superior skills and productivity). Academic scholarships also are tax-free to recipients, although again the education adds to future income potential.[35] And finally, full-time post-secondary education involves a hidden investment, which is the labor income the student could have earned in lieu of enrolling in a full-time program. Economists (admittedly, *only* economists) see the forgone income, which of course is not taxable, since it was never earned, as a form of implicit tax subsidy for investing in human capital.

That leaves investments in physical capital—greasy machinery of all shapes and sizes. The effective tax rate on a marginal investment in an asset depends primarily on the nominal tax rate, how the asset is financed, and the depreciation schedule for that kind of asset. (Depreciation is an annual deduction for the decline in value of a productive asset over time as it is used in a business. If I invest $1,000 in a machine used in my business, and that machine wears out at a predictable rate of 1/10 of its value each year, for 10 years, I would take as an expense on my tax return a $100 depreciation allowance each year for those 10 years.)

In 2005 the Congressional Budget Office undertook a herculean analysis of the effective marginal tax rates actually applicable to marginal investments in a wide range of asset types.[36] The CBO analysis demonstrated that our current business tax system imposes wildly divergent burdens on marginal investments, depending on funding source (debt vs. equity) and asset class. Holding funding sources constant, the CBO found that effective marginal tax rates varied as a result of the depreciation schedules mandated by Congress for various assets, but since Congress's general inclination is to encourage investment through accelerated tax depreciation schedules, the effective marginal tax rates on most business investment were significantly lower than the statutory rate. Debt-financed investments in fact faced a *negative* 6.4 percent tax rate (because of the tax deduct-ibility of interest expense combined with accelerated depreciation on the asset being acquired), which means that under our current tax system all of us actually subsidize every corporate business investment in tangible equipment financed with borrowed money—we pay more in taxes so that the tax system can give busi-nesses the economic equivalent of a cash handout every time they buy equipment.

Since the date of that study, Congress has regularly enacted various "bonus" depreciation schemes, amounting to an immediate write-off of 50 percent or in some years 100 percent of an investment, even if the economic life of that invest-ment is measured in decades. Those bonus depreciation schemes were designed to encourage business investment even more in light of economic weakness, but they had the effect of driving the effective marginal tax rates on business invest-ments down as low as zero, in the case of equity-financed investments, and to even larger negative rates (i.e., hidden cash subsidies) in the case of debt-financed investments.

In short, the effective tax burdens imposed on marginal business investments are far lower than our statutory tax rates imply, although admittedly our current tax system induces misallocations of investments across different asset classes and forms of financing. Perhaps for this reason, and as noted earlier, empirical studies on the effects of taxation on business investment have been "somewhat mixed."[37] Nontax data are clear that in the years since the bottom of the Great Recession busi-nesses have been very profitable and have picked up the pace of their investment activity.[38] Where then can the Growth Fairy alight, if business investments are already lightly taxed, and firms in fact are investing with both fists?

To be clear, our current business tax system is a mess. As the 2005 CBO study implies, our tax rules distort the financing decisions for investment (by offering a tax subsidy for borrowing money) and the choice of investments (by imposing different effective marginal tax rates on different types of investment). These dis-tortions have real economic costs.[39]

This distortion in the allocation of investments between tax-favored and tax-disfavored assets could be addressed by adopting a more uniform system for taxing returns from business investments. Moreover, there are sound reasons to recommend that the US statutory corporate tax rate should be reduced. The United States today has the highest nominal corporate tax rate in the world, and given our global economy and internationally mobile capital markets, that fact does distort investment locations and encourages tremendous investments in tax avoidance technologies, rather than productive investment.[40] I go further, in fact, and argue in chapter 13 that we should tax all capital income at lower rates than labor income.

Corporate tax reform that lowers the statutory tax rate while broadening the definition of income subject to tax probably will have some long-term positive growth implications, by reducing distortions in investment decisions in the types and location of investments. But this is not a net tax reduction: it is classic "revenue neutral" reform. A close examination of the tax rates actually imposed on business investment today leads more to the inference that the Growth Fairy has already come and done at least some sort of half-assed magic, than to the conclusion that her further intercession is urgently required. What we really need now are fewer incentives and more rationalization of the business tax system.

TOP-DOWN ECONOMIC MODELS

The previous section reviewed the principal transmission channels by which tax policies could be expected to influence economic growth, and did not find large and obvious economic behavioral bonanzas that could be unleashed by lower tax rates. This approach of analyzing the major levers that influence growth is termed a "bottom-up" analysis of the issue. At this point, it is worthwhile to switch to a higher-level review of some of the conclusions reached by economists who study the overall effect of taxes and the economy—the "top-down" perspective.

At one level, historical or cross-country economic analysis is easy, in the sense that it is straightforward to plot GDP per capita against tax revenues as a percentage of GDP, either for one country over time or across countries. The problems come when one tries to control for variables other than tax effects (for example, monetary policy), and in interpreting which is cause, and which effect.[41]

Nonetheless, it is at least somewhat relevant that a cross-country comparison along these lines finds no evidence of a correlation between lower total tax burdens and higher growth. Figure 5.1 relies on OECD data to examine 28 countries in the period 2004–2006 (a relatively stable economic period, before the Great Recession). The figure compares a country's total tax revenues as a percentage of GDP with its average growth rate during this period. There is no apparent correlation between lower tax burdens and higher growth rates, contrary to what one might expect if the Growth Fairy performed her magic on market economies generally.

The nonpartisan Congressional Research Service (an arm of the Library of Congress) has undertaken analyses of the historical correlations between US tax rates and economic growth. In two recent (and controversial) studies, the CRS concluded, first, that "periods of lower taxes are not associated with higher rates of economic growth or increases in investment," and second, that "the reduction in the top [personal income] tax rates [prior to 2013] has had little association with saving, investment, or productivity growth."[42]

Market triumphalists reacted angrily to the second of these reports in particular; shortly thereafter the author resigned from the CRS and took a post at a private think tank. Objectors complained that the CRS historical analyses did

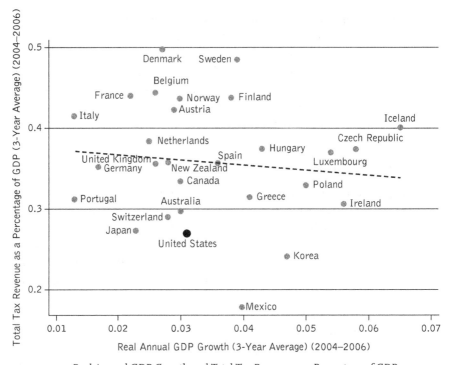

FIGURE 5.1 Real Annual GDP Growth and Total Tax Revenue as a Percentage of GDP

Sources: OECD, *Revenue Statistics: Comparative Tables* (2010), doi:10.1787/data-00262-en; OECD, *OECD Factbook 2009: Economic, Environmental and Social Statistics* (2009), doi:10.1787/factbook-2009-12-en.

not consider a wide range of other matters (Fed interest rate policies, government deficits, and so on) that might affect growth in any period—the authors did not control for all the relevant factors.

But those objections actually make my point. Measuring the impact of taxes on the overall economy is like watching the mating habits of butterflies alongside a freeway—what seems like a fascinating new behavior often is just the downdraft from a passing tractor-trailer. So too the effect of taxes on actual behavior in the field may be overwhelmed by other more fundamental drivers of the economy and human behavior.

For example, the behaviors of the investment markets in the first half of 2013 owed much more to the interventions of the Federal Reserve than they did to the modestly higher top income tax rates rolled out at the beginning of the year; the equity markets were up significantly over the first few months of 2013 for reasons largely ascribable to the Fed's policies, but in June, the Dow Jones Industrial Average lost 550 points in two days as a result of the Fed's announcement that it would begin to wind down its quantitative easing program. The economy is too big, and exogenous shocks (oil crises, globalization, climate change, Federal

Reserve policies) are too large (and by definition unpredictable), for moderate changes in tax rates to drive growth or affect investment rates in clearly definable ways.

A recent paper by Christina Romer and David Romer takes a more nuanced approach toward the historical record, by setting out to control for some of the factors that might muffle the tax story.[43] They start from a place similar to the point I just made, without the butterfly metaphor:

> That views of the effects of tax changes vary so radically largely reflects the fact that measuring these effects is very difficult.... Because the factors that give rise to tax changes are often correlated with other developments in the economy, disentangling the effects of the tax changes from the effects of these underlying factors is inherently difficult.

In response, the authors develop a "narrative record" approach to historical correlations: by studying the reasons for particular tax legislation, they attempt to isolate instances of tax changes undertaken for reasons unrelated to the state of the economy, and limit their analysis to these "exogenous" cases. They basically then compare the state of the economy following these tax law changes with a hypothetical baseline of how the economy would have performed had it stayed on pre-legislation trend.[44] Romer and Romer conclude that a tax increase of one percent of GDP reduces output over the next three years by roughly 3 percent. (Over a longer time horizon, the output gap gradually dissipates.) This is a very substantial response, and indeed is larger than that obtained in other studies.

The Romer and Romer analysis no doubt will foster a small ecosystem of further critical examinations and reexaminations of their narrative record approach. One subsequent paper, for example, has come to very different conclusions by applying different statistical methodologies to the same set of tax legislation.[45] Further, the Romer and Romer analysis focuses on short time horizons. It therefore arguably tells us more about the near-term consequences of fiscal stimulus programs than it does about whether changes in tax collections move the economy to a permanently higher or lower growth path.

In addition, Romer and Romer observe that the effects they observe are substantially smaller after 1980 than before that date, and are smaller for deficit reduction legislation than for other tax bills. And finally, as chapter 6 describes, there is a large cost today to *not* raising taxes, particularly against the backdrop of our current low levels of taxation in the United States, in the form of much higher interest costs to finance increasing federal debt. Those higher interest costs have both financial stability and "crowding out" implications. (The latter term refers to the idea that increased Treasury borrowing raises the cost of debt finance for private firms as well as the federal government, thereby making it prohibitively expensive to finance projects that would have been feasible in lower interest rate environments.)

Actual tax legislation is rarely as simple as across the board rate changes; Congress typically mixes a great many individual items, each pointing in a somewhat different direction, into one tax legislative gumbo. Thus it is entirely possible to have legislation that overall is a tax cut, but that raises the effective marginal tax rate on certain classes of investment, or vice versa. All this will need to be teased out in further work.

In addition to work drawn from the historical record, there are a great many economic papers that rely on theoretical models to predict the relationship between tax law changes and economic growth. The results are all over the map.[46] Perhaps most surprising, the field of "endogenous growth models"—abstract models of how tax policies might affect growth—is really only a couple of decades old.[47] Many of these studies include only one "representative agent" (that is, everyone is assumed to behave identically). Others reduce tax policies to overly simplified characterizations that ignore the details of tax law as it is lived. By definition, none has been tested for generations.

We are confident today that we have the laws of Newtonian physics pretty well scoped out. It is just not realistic to ask today's theoretical economic tax and growth models to carry the same weight when it comes to fiscal policymaking that we ask of Newtonian mechanics when we come to aim a missile.[48] The general import of the models is clear in most instances—keep marginal tax rates as low as possible, typically by broadening the base (eliminating exemptions and tax subsidies). Beyond that, one should proceed with great circumspection before asserting that one or another academic paper proves much of anything when it comes to immediate tax legislative priorities.

One particularly troubling problem with many such studies is that they do not adequately focus on the revenue consequences of the tax medicine they ask us to swallow. Whatever opportunities there are for the Growth Fairy to alight as a result of a tax cut depend absolutely on cutting government spending concomitantly; the models' growth effects follow from shrinking both sides of the government's ledger.[49] But many models ignore the issue entirely, or assume that the tax cut will in fact be undone by a later tax increase.

In other words, even within the terms of a typical theoretical model, the growth effects observed from cutting taxes depend critically on the assumptions one makes about the magnitude of the positive returns to the spending programs that as a result must be trimmed; the more productive the forgone government investment, the smaller the theoretical total productivity gain.[50] Some economists have an unfortunate tendency to make this analysis too easy for themselves, by assuming that there are never any positive returns at all to government programs, by not specifying which programs will be cut, and by not considering the distributional consequences of the resulting package.

GROWTH EFFECTS OF GOVERNMENT INVESTMENT

We do not collect taxes just for sport: we do so to fund government programs. The deadweight loss of taxation therefore is only one part of a larger question, which is, what is the net benefit to society of collecting the tax (taking into account the spillage from the leaky bucket) *and then spending the money?* A somewhat inefficient tax that funds collective investments that complement private markets is still welfare-enhancing on balance. In other words, in thinking about the economic cost of government intervention, one must examine the spending/taxing system in its totality.

The Growth Fairy narrative completely ignores the positive economic growth that comes from government investments in education, infrastructure, or other areas that are complementary to private markets. This point is critical, yet constantly missed in the literature: *there is no meaning to the growth effects of taxes as such, only to fiscal policy taken as a whole.* (Chapter 12 expands on this theme.) Focusing on the deadweight loss of taxation alone ignores the positive economic returns to public investment—education, to take one example. Taxes fund those investments, and they in turn yield direct economic returns, not just abstract social goods.

Growth Fairy acolytes stack the deck in their favor when they frame the debate as exclusively about the costs of taxation without considering that those costs go to pay for public investments that complement private markets in arenas that the private sector does not reach. In those cases, the opportunities for high-return public investment abound. What is more, those returns usually are much more broadly shared than the returns from private investment, without the need to rely on trickle-down hypotheses to explain how those investments will enhance "the happiness of the society."

For example, consider the little country of Freedonia, which in this example is blessed with large hydrocarbon reserves. Under its constitution, those reserves belong to all the people and can be exploited only by the national oil company. (This actually accords with practice in many countries other than the United States.) If the Freedonian National Oil Company needs tax revenues to fund the development of hydrocarbon production, the income from which will go to reduce future tax burdens, and Freedonia raises the necessary funds through a personal income tax, the deadweight loss of that tax by itself would not be a useful measure of the net welfare gains enjoyed by Freedonian citizens from the overall fiscal policy.

INCOME GROWTH OR WELFARE GROWTH?

Finally, Growth Fairy devotees tell a logically incomplete story, because they do not explain how their vision of economic growth will enhance the welfare of all Americans. This is not the result of forgetfulness on their part. To the contrary, the driving force behind their narrative—the very ambrosia on which the Growth Fairy sups—is that growth is fueled by inequality. Inequality in wealth and income is not just a marketplace byproduct in the neoclassical economic model of private markets. Like the two terminals of a battery, inequality is the potential energy that motivates peoples' ambitions to work to better themselves.

There is much truth to the idea that inequality fuels economic growth, but the question is, whose growth? For one hundred years, the United States, along with every other major economy, has tried to balance the value of inequality as a motivation with institutions that ensure that the resulting growth benefits us all. The most important such mechanism turns out to be government investment and insurance programs funded by adequate tax revenues, through which the most affluent disproportionately fund the collective investments that enhance our national welfare—including, ultimately, their own.

Narrators of the Growth Fairy fable have a superficially plausible story to tell of how a gentle touch in taxing the rich might spur economic growth (and accelerating wealth for those who already are affluent), but beyond mumbling about trickle-down effects they have no explanation at all for how that increasing wealth will do the rest of us any good. Their mumbling cannot be helped, because the entire theory rests on the idea that more inequality (through a light touch in taxing the affluent) yields more growth. But this becomes a vicious circle, in which the only response to low taxes today on the rich—and therefore minimal public investment—is still lower tax burdens tomorrow, so that their great wealth can accumulate still faster. There is no institutional trickle-down mechanism so much as there is some unavoidable leakage when the most affluent look to spend some small fraction of their wealth on lawn care and personal trainers.

The alternative—one completely ignored by Growth Fairy proponents—is a sprinkle-up model. Reasonable levels of taxation (including the progressive income tax) can fund public investments that directly generate higher levels of prosperity for a broad swath of Americans. In turn, the accelerating wealth and purchasing power of most Americans ultimately boosts the returns to the most affluent Americans from their labor and from their savings. This second model is fundamentally welfare-enhancing for the nation as a whole in ways that the Growth Fairy fable is not.

We collectively want economic growth, but only to the extent that it corresponds with increased welfare for the nation as a whole. Growth itself should not be our only objective, as if the country were engaged in a GDP Olympics with other nations. Our welfare depends on all of us participating in growth, mostly through work that conveys dignity as well as fair remuneration. But as chapters 3 and 4 demonstrate, this is one place where the data are unequivocal: as tax rates have generally declined over the last 30 years, wages of men have stagnated, and income inequality has soared. While Growth Fairy acolytes fear that we will become as burdened by social programs and taxation as is France, their own economic policies point us in the direction of oligarchic Russia.

PART II

STARVING OUR FISCAL SOUL

CHAPTER 6

....

A FIELD GUIDE TO FALSE FISCAL CRISES

> *The leader of the successful [political] party,...if he has authority*
> *enough to prevail upon his own friends to act with proper temper and*
> *moderation. . ., may sometimes render to his country a service much*
> *more essential and important than the greatest victories and the most*
> *extensive conquests. He may re-establish and improve the constitution,*
> *and from the very doubtful and ambiguous character of the leader of*
> *a party, he may assume the greatest and noblest of all characters, that*
> *of the reformer and legislator of a great state; and by the wisdom of*
> *his institutions, secure the internal tranquility and happiness of his*
> *fellow-citizens for many succeeding generations.*
>
> —ADAM SMITH, *The Theory of Moral Sentiments,*
> Part VI, Sec. II, Chap. II.

IS THE UNITED States of America the next Detroit, headed for inevitable bankruptcy as we collapse into an ocean of Treasury debt? So claimed R. Glenn Hubbard, former chair of George W. Bush's Council of Economic Advisors, and Tim Kane in an opinion piece in the *New York Times* in August 2013.[1]

The short answer is no, for two obvious reasons. First, the creditworthiness of any enterprise is a reflection of its capacity to generate revenues. In the case of a government, those revenues take the form of tax collections. Detroit was a city whose population collapsed, whose industry shrank dramatically, and whose tax base therefore evaporated. We remain a rich country with a vibrant economy, and with a potential tax base to match; we could reach deeper into our pockets to fund our national government if we needed to do so. Second, the United States of America controls the medium by which it settles its debts, while Detroit did not.

There is no short-term crisis in financing the national debt. Treasury borrowing rates remain at near-record lows. Indeed, a strong case can be made that this is an ideal time for the federal government to stretch out the average maturity of its debt, to lock in today's very favorable rates. Nor is there a general crisis in the availability or cost of capital for the private sector.[2] (Of course, small or less creditworthy firms may continue to experience difficulties in borrowing at reasonable rates.) We can see the plentiful supply of credit for strong borrowers in the recent boom in debt-financed mergers and acquisitions.

Nonetheless, our current fiscal trajectory—the net effect of government spending and taxing—is not sustainable indefinitely. Part II of this book attempts to reconcile the apparent conflicts among our unsustainable long-term fiscal path, the demands we all place on government today, and the forgone opportunities that surround us.

The economic and social issues outlined in Part I are not inevitable, yet we do not respond to them by investing in ourselves or implementing more comprehensive social insurance programs. The reason for our inaction is that we are paralyzed by false fiscal crises. Regardless of our political persuasion, we all know that the US government's current fiscal policies are unsustainable over the long term, but our fiscal panic attacks have left us immobilized by the seeming insolubility and indivisibility of the issues. We argue that taxes are too low, or insufficiently progressive—or perhaps the opposite. We maintain that we should slash government spending, unless perhaps we should increase it. But our tax debates cannot be separated from our views on the size of government, and how can we decide which should determine the other? And overlaying all these thoughts is the paralyzing fear that keeping to our current course will lead to fiscal collapse in the foreseeable future, so that something dramatic must be done, immediately.

These debates are dominated by abstract disagreements over income tax rates, or how progressive the tax system should be, as if these were goals in themselves. But taxes are means, not ends. Collecting tax is not the point of government; taxes are simply how we divide up the bill for the goods and services we collectively deliver to ourselves through the medium of government. Government spending is the logical predicate to taxation, not the other way around.

At the same time, we do not engage in rational discourse about the desired size of government, because we allow those discussions to loop rapidly into debates about how to finance that government spending—that is, our tax policies. And those debates play out against the backdrop of the unsustainability of the net consequences of our current spending and tax policies—that is, our budget deficits. And so the circular arguments repeat themselves.

As a result, we are unable to see that our fiscal problems are not insurmountably large, and that there is a logical order in which the issues might be teased apart, to enable our political discourse actually to reach rational conclusions. What we need are some reference points. When we benchmark our government insurance programs or investments in ourselves—in our future welfare and wealth—we see that the problem is not too much spending, but rather too little collective insurance and investment, as a result of inadequate funding (tax revenues). We ask too little of ourselves by way of chipping into the collective investment pot. We do not need nationwide Kickstarter projects, we need a collective kick in the pants.

Part II elaborates on these themes. In it, I demonstrate that whether measured by historical precedent, comparative norms, or by reference to the opportunities surrounding us, our federal government is too small, not too large, and our tax collections are too small even for the parsimonious course we have set for ourselves. The last chapter in Part II introduces the critically important theme of "tax expenditures"—government spending programs lurking beneath the surface of the budget seas in the form of tax subsidies. Many of these hidden spending programs are enormously costly, economically inefficient, and palpably unfair. If those subsidies were presented as explicit government spending, their proponents would be laughed out of office. Addressing them is the key to finding the fiscal resources to reclaim our fiscal soul.

In this chapter, I first introduce some basic budget terminology and explain the complicated fiscal variants on Russian roulette that so intrigue some of our legislators. I next consider why the federal budget deteriorated so quickly during the Great Recession; the largest single factor turns out to be the collapse in tax revenues, which actually showed that the country's fiscal system was operating exactly as it was designed to do. I then examine our budget looking forward over the next 10 years, and find—even with "sequestration" and other constraints on spending in place—that our revenue base will be too low to support even the hollowed-out government it implies. I turn next to the other side of the fiscal coin, by briefly reviewing the spending side of things, as a reminder that cuts at the levels already budgeted are the fiscal equivalent of trying to squeeze blood from a stone.

The following two chapters elaborate on the spending and taxing sides of our current fiscal policy, respectively. Chapter 9 focuses on our tax expenditure addiction. Part III then follows by exploring how we can put fiscal policy to better use to address the economic and social issues we confront, and the opportunities we are forgoing.

OUR PROCRUSTEAN FRAMING OF FISCAL POLICY

In January 2001, immediately following the election of George W. Bush as president, the Congressional Budget Office prepared its annual *Budget and Economic Outlook* for fiscal years 2002–2011. The first sentences in its Budget Outlook summary expressed an optimism that the CBO has had little opportunity to express again: "The outlook for the federal budget over the next decade continues to be bright. Assuming that current tax and spending policies are maintained, the CBO projects that mounting federal revenues will continue to produce growing budget surpluses for the next 10 years." The CBO further predicted that the economy would grow at 5 percent per year during the coming decade (3 percent in real terms).

In fact, matters looked so rosy that the CBO in January 2001 projected that by 2006, the US Treasury would have retired the *entirety* of the public debt available for redemption.[3] As a result, instead of the government incurring net interest expense on the order of 2 percent of GDP (as today), the CBO envisioned a world in which the Treasury would *earn* about one percent of GDP on its rainy day fund.

The primary driver of this sunny picture was the tax system: the CBO in 2001 anticipated that throughout the next decade the government would take in tax revenues averaging about 20.4 percent of GDP; the average rate over the previous few decades had been roughly 18.3 percent. (The actual figure for 2000 was 20.6 percent.) To be clear, the CBO's felicitous expectations for economic growth took into account any negative implications (through adverse incentive effects) of this level of tax collections. By contrast, in 2012 the federal government collected tax revenues of only 15.8 percent of GDP, attributable to both the implications of the Great Recession for tax receipts and a decade-long political program to "starve the beast" by reducing tax rates. The 2013 projection for average tax revenues in the decade 2014–2023 is 18.9 percent of GDP.

This chapter shows that political decisions to slash our tax collections are the root of our current fiscal difficulties. The CBO's 2001 projections for discretionary spending six years in the future were almost exactly the same as a percentage of GDP as were its 2013 projections for 2019. The CBO in 2001 underestimated the coming decade's surge in mandatory spending, attributable to excess cost growth in healthcare, in some part to the unfunded extension of Medicare prescription drug benefits, and at the end of the decade to the deployment of safety net mechanisms to arrest the fall of the Great Recession (but not, of course, to the Affordable Care Act, which did not come into effect during this period). But in turn, the projected difference in interest costs to carry the national debt between the two scenarios was even larger. Of course, the CBO could not have foreseen the events of September 11, 2001, or the wars that followed, but the basic point remains that we have created false fiscal crises for ourselves by not collecting sufficient tax revenues to provide for the government that we in fact want, much less the one we really need.

In short, our modern fiscal policy debates all rest on the foundation of an irrational Procrustean assumption. We have arbitrarily set projected tax revenues to excessively low levels, and now argue about which spending programs should be lopped off to fit into the revenue constraints we have imposed on ourselves. To a large extent, both "sequestration" and the budget caps of the 2011 Budget Control Act (explained below) are efforts to recoup on the spending side monies that should have been collected on the revenue side.

Whatever the future for entitlements programs like Social Security and Medicare, tax revenues are the only way to finance our gradual transition from here to there. It is for this reason that bipartisan majorities on deficit reduction panels (for example, the Bowles–Simpson and Rivlin–Domenici commissions), major nonpartisan studies (for example, the Peterson–Pew Commission on Budget Reform's report), the staff of the OECD, thoughtful budget experts like Robert Greenstein at the Center for Budget and Policy Priorities, and prominent economists like Alan Greenspan and Martin Feldstein have all agreed that tax revenues must rise from their current levels in order to finance our government.

Bluntly, there is no rational alternative. The need to repay the revenue shortfalls of the Great Recession, the rapid increase in the number of elderly Americans, the continuing needs of the many Americans who are unemployed or in poverty, our oversized and inefficient healthcare system, our large military expenditures, and the costs of supervising the world's largest, most complex, and most sophisticated economy collectively require government revenues greater than those we currently are on track to collect.

The conclusion that tax revenues must rise sits badly with market triumphalists. They argue that high taxes impede economic growth and job creation. These sorts of nostrums have as much policy utility as the adage that, all other things being equal, it is better to be rich and healthy than poor and sick. Chapter 5 reviewed the evidence and concluded that somewhat higher personal income taxes do not have as large an effect on real economic activity as market triumphalists typically claim. Tax revenues need to increase not because higher taxes are desirable as an independent goal, but because there is no other choice. Whether viewed from the perspective of world norms or our own recent history, it is simply not credible to argue that the US economy cannot sustain higher levels of tax collections than the historically low levels of the last few years, or even slightly higher levels than historical averages.

THE FEDERAL BUDGET, DEBT, AND DEFICITS

Because the United States uses unintuitive (and inaccurate) terms like "mandatory" spending to explain what government does, it helps to set the stage for the discussion that follows by quickly reviewing some key budget concepts.

The budget of the United States is basically a cash flow statement: the budget totes up cash receipts (essentially, tax collections) and subtracts cash disbursements (government spending, whether to pay salaries or to build new infrastructure). If, as was true for the last four years of the Clinton administration, the government has cash left over, it runs a surplus; if, as has been true over the last several decades in every year other than at the end of the Clinton administration, the government does not have enough cash receipts to cover its disbursements, it incurs a deficit for that year.

The federal government runs on a fiscal year that begins on October 1 and closes on September 30. At the beginning of every calendar year, the president proposes a spending and taxing plan called the budget for the upcoming fiscal year—in early 2014 for the fiscal year beginning October 1, 2014. (This means that the first fiscal year for which a new president has any ability to shape fiscal priorities comes almost a year after his or her election.) The president's budget is tremendously detailed, but in constitutional terms is just a wish list.

Congress takes the president's budget and does with it whatever it will. The process by which Congress is supposed to create and implement its budget is laid out in detail in various budget laws and internal rules of the two houses of Congress. These rules can be called Byzantine only if one imagines the Byzantines having a very pissy day. Since every schoolchild knows that Congress fails each year to follow its own required processes, spelling out the procedure in detail is pointless.[4]

In the end, Congress alone controls the purse strings of the government; the president's only power is to veto spending legislation. The executive branch cannot spend what Congress has not directed the executive to spend, and *must* spend whatever monies Congress has legislated to be spent.[5] If you think that the federal government spends too much, blame Congress, not the president.

By convention the budget is divided into three major categories: interest on the national debt, mandatory spending (also called direct spending), and discretionary spending. Interest on the national debt is the only true mandatory spending program (assuming, as convention does, that the Treasury will always be able to borrow new money to pay back the principal of outstanding Treasury debt as it matures). Failure to pay interest would trigger a default on the national debt, with catastrophic consequences.

So-called mandatory spending primarily comprises the "entitlement" programs like Social Security, Medicare, and Medicaid. Mandatory spending might better be called "autopilot" programs; these are programs that by the terms of their enabling legislation continue from year to year without the need for Congress to reauthorize them or specifically legislate their funding for the year. The food stamp program (the Supplemental Nutrition Assistance Program, or SNAP) is an outlier; it is classified as a mandatory program for budget accounting purposes, but its funding must be appropriated by Congress annually.[6]

Mandatory spending programs like Social Security are called "entitlement" programs because Congress specifies the criteria by which individuals qualify for the entitlement program's benefits; if an individual satisfies those criteria, he or she is paid whatever those benefits might be. Nonetheless, individuals have no vested claim to "entitlements" or to any other government-spending program (other than interest on the national debt). Congress could repeal Social Security tomorrow; if the president were to sign the legislation into law, no one would have legal recourse to demand a refund of his years of payroll tax contributions. This means that there is nothing mandatory at all about mandatory spending; these programs instead simply rely on Congressional inaction to continue from year to year, while discretionary programs must be funded every year through new legislation.

Tax revenues for certain of the big entitlement programs, like Social Security, are paid into separate "trust funds," while other tax revenues go to the Treasury's "general fund," but less turns on this than most people believe. Positive balances in a trust fund are not stashed away in the form of gold bullion in Fort Knox. Instead, monies paid into the trust funds are immediately "lent" by the trust fund's managing trustee (the secretary of the Treasury) to the Treasury's general fund, whence the money flows out to any and all government spending programs. The trust funds receive "interest" on these loans, and can ask the Treasury's general fund for their money back when they need to pay out benefits, but all of this is invisible to the public. The trust funds' nominal assets can be converted back into cash only through general tax revenues, because those revenues are the only source of money from which the Treasury's general fund can pay the interest and principal of the debt held by the trust funds. In effect, then, the trust funds are more like an accounting concept than an actual pool of assets; the nominal balances are relevant for determining whether scheduled entitlement payments can be made under the terms of the original authorizing legislation, or instead must be scaled back, but otherwise have no operational consequence.[7]

Finally, discretionary spending comprises all the government programs that Congress wrangles about every year. Discretionary spending is divided into defense and nondefense spending. Discretionary spending includes not only outlays to fund particular projects (a new highway or a new aircraft carrier, for example), but also outlays for running the courts and all the government agencies that together comprise the entirety of the legal and regulatory apparatus that keeps our economy working.

Discretionary spending programs go through a two-step process designed primarily to befuddle outsiders. First, the program itself is "authorized." Then, moneys to be spent under the program are "appropriated." If Congress "authorizes" the construction of a $10 billion dam, not a shovel can be lifted until money is "appropriated" for the project.

Appropriations are made on a year-by-year basis. Thus, Congress can choose in 2015 not to appropriate any money to be spent on a multiyear program it proudly authorized in 2014. The annual nature of appropriations, the size and complexity of the discretionary budget as a whole, and the specificity and inflexibility of Congressional appropriations all conspire to make the budget procedures mandated by law almost impossible to satisfy for even the most functional of Congresses.

Mandatory (that is, autopilot) spending comprises the bulk of federal government outlays—roughly 60 percent of all government spending for fiscal year 2014. The "big three"—Social Security, Medicare, and Medicaid—absorb three-fourths of this amount. All "income security" programs combined (food stamps, unemployment compensation, child nutrition programs, cash outlays for "making work pay" tax credits, etc.) account for 15 percent of total mandatory spending in 2014, or 9 percent of the total federal budget. Interest expense is not projected to be very large in the near future (perhaps 7 percent of total spending), but to roughly double as a percentage of total federal spending in a decade's time, as interest rates climb and the outstanding amount of government debt rises.

Discretionary spending comprises about one-third of the federal budget in 2014; this in turn is divided roughly 50–50 between defense and nondefense spending. So the entirety of nondefense discretionary spending (including the budgets for the agencies and courts that keep planes in the air, inspect our food, supervise our securities and banking markets, and administer the justice system) is about one-sixth of the total budget.

The Congressional Budget Office's standard overviews of the federal budget follow the divisions summarized above among interest expense, mandatory spending, and discretionary spending. Figure 6.1 summarizes the allocation of government spending in FY 2013 along these lines. It graphically shows the relative sizes of different programs, and gives their size as percentages of GDP.

One difficulty with this sort of presentation is that it tends to harden people's beliefs that mandatory spending programs are quasi-constitutionally inviolate, rather than simply autopilot spending. The other problem is that similar functions are not grouped together, because those functions often straddle the mandatory/

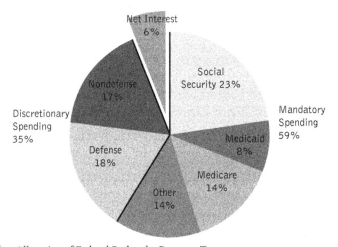

FIGURE 6.1 Allocation of Federal Budget by Program Type

discretionary boundary. The Center for Budget and Policy Priorities (CBPP) therefore usefully recasts the budget into functional terms, without regard to the mandatory/discretionary distinction.

Figure 6.2 follows the CBPP methodology to summarize federal government spending by function for 2013, expressed as percentages of total spending. Since federal government spending is about one-fifth of GDP, you can roughly approximate the size of each functional category as a percentage of GDP by dividing by five.

The government borrows money from investors to fund deficits, and total Treasury debt outstanding in the hands of lenders therefore represents the net accumulated deficit of the federal government over its entire life.[8] If the United States runs a surplus, about the only thing it can do with the money is to retire (pay back) some of that outstanding debt. One of the big concerns at the beginning of George W. Bush's administration was that the United States was on a pace to pay back all of its outstanding debt within a relatively few years, and then what would the government do with its annual surplus? Start buying stock of private companies? The vast deficits created by President Bush's tax cuts quickly resolved this dilemma.[9]

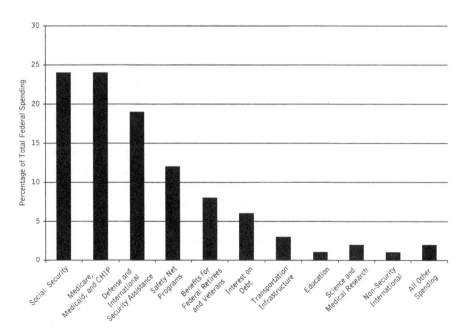

FIGURE 6.2 Allocation of Federal Budget by Functional Groupings, Fiscal Year 2013, as a Percentage of Total Federal Spending

There are three useful budget rules of thumb helpful to all honorary budge-teers, as budget wonks are called. First, do not think about deficits or other budget numbers in terms of dollars, but rather in percentages of gross domestic product (GDP). As chapter 4 described in more detail, GDP essentially measures the size of the entire US market economy in a year. Budget and deficit numbers grow more or less automatically from year to year, both because of inflation and because GDP itself usually grows in real (inflation-adjusted) terms every year. As a result, you cannot compare year-to-year budget performance very accurately unless you think in percentage terms.

Second, like a large successful company, the US government can afford to carry plenty of debt on its national balance sheet, because it has a large potential rev-enue base (taxes on the private economy) from which to service that debt. The United States did not lose its "AAA" credit rating because its revenue base is too small relative to its debt, but rather because the rating agencies correctly perceived that Congress is dysfunctional and cannot be trusted to take the steps necessary to avoid formal default. Nonetheless, we do not want government debt to mus-cle private borrowers out of the way when competing for lenders' money; such "crowding out" hurts economic growth over the long run, by siphoning invest-ment capital away from private businesses.[10]

No scientific rule defines how much government debt (accumulated deficits) is too much, but one common rule of thumb is that government debt should not exceed 60 percent of GDP.[11] In the United States, that ratio was over 100 percent at the end of World War II; it was about 40 percent just before the financial collapse at the start of the Great Recession. It currently is a little over 70 percent.

Third, deficits do not necessarily add to the debt-to-GDP ratio. Imagine that the federal debt-to-GDP ratio is 50 percent and the economy is growing at 4 per-cent a year. If the federal government runs a deficit equal to 2 percent of GDP, the debt-to-GDP ratio will remain a constant 50 percent—the denominator goes up by 4 percent, and the numerator by 2 percent (from, say 50/100 to 52/104). Many economists therefore do not lose sleep over deficits that average no more than 2 percent of GDP over the long haul; if one assumes that the long-term US economic growth rate hovers around 3.5 percent per annum, this would imply a stable debt-to-GDP ratio in the neighborhood of 60 percent. This is just one of many reasons that balanced budget amendments are silly.

BUDGET BRINKSMANSHIP

The federal budget deficit has declined dramatically since the worst days of the Great Recession. In 2009, the deficit was over 10 percent of GDP—a level not seen since World War II. In 2013, the deficit fell to 4 percent of GDP. And because tax revenues are rising as the economy recovers from the Great Recession, the deficit will continue to decline, to roughly 2 percent of GDP by 2015, before beginning an upward trajectory again.[12]

Against this backdrop of improving fiscal conditions, a powerful business case for government to invest today in job opportunities for the millions of Americans still unemployed or underemployed, and a longer-term fiscal imbalance that should be addressed on the revenue side of the equation, members of Congress continue to apply their Procrustean assumptions to every fiscal issue, through threats to "shut government down," through "sequestration," and through holding the "debt ceiling" hostage to demands by the most radical members that spending programs not to their liking be jettisoned. The reason is that both parties are trying to seize every possible opportunity to reset the long-term direction of American government, not to pass a budget resolution for the next year.

Each threat takes advantage of a different vulnerability in Congressional procedures. Government can be "shut down" through the device of not passing appropriations legislation to fund discretionary spending. As previously described, all discretionary spending, including the spending necessary to operate the various administrative agencies of the federal government through which government acts, is appropriated on an annual basis. Congress rarely succeeds in keeping to the ambitious procedural timetable contemplated by the Budget Act of 1974 for developing and enacting appropriations legislation. And as explained in the preceding section, the president has no independent spending authority: Congress alone determines every penny that the government spends. Finally, under the terms of the Anti-Deficiency Act, the core of which dates to 1884, executive branch agencies cannot create new obligations of the government when those obligations have not been authorized by Congress. This means that the executive branch cannot use IOUs to avert a government shutdown.

The normal solution is to rely on "continuing resolutions," which is a fancy way of saying that Congress enacts short-form (usually very short-term) legislation authorizing discretionary spending to continue on the same course that it was on for the prior period. If the process breaks down for any reason, and a continuing resolution or other appropriations legislation is not enacted, then almost all of government must effectively shut down, as there then is neither money available to pay for it to function nor legal authority to incur new obligations to pay in the future for goods or services provided on a current basis.

There are some exceptions to the reach of the Anti-Deficiency Act. Congress has authorized (or the attorney general in legal opinions has inferred) a few emergency functions that may continue in the absence of appropriations to fund them. As summarized by the Congressional Research Service, these are (1) activities "necessary to bring about the orderly termination of an agency's functions"; (2) administration of benefit payments provided through funds that remain available in the absence of new appropriations (e.g., Social Security benefits);

(3) activities financed with prior year funds and ongoing activities for which funding has already been obligated; (4) activities undertaken on the basis of constitutional authorities of the president; and (5) activities related to "emergencies involving the safety of human life or the protection of property," which are understood to include core military functions.[13]

A government shutdown actually happened in 1995–1996, when the House of Representatives, led by Speaker Newt Gingrich, formulated spending legislation unacceptable to President Clinton, who vetoed the bills, and again in 2013, but for a much shorter time. At the nadir of the earlier crisis, 800,000 federal government employees were furloughed. The standard version of the history of that event recounts that the shutdown was extremely damaging to the economy, and politically disastrous for the Republican Party, but as always there are revisionist opinions at the margins.

A debt-ceiling crisis is even more serious in its economic and institutional implications. Under the Constitution, Congress must authorize Treasury's borrowings. Originally, Congress did so on a borrowing-by-borrowing basis, but that obviously is infeasible in light of the amount of outstanding Treasury debt and the speed at which financial markets move. As a result, Congress for many decades has given the Treasury blanket authority to borrow money, up to a specified ceiling.

As described earlier, the federal budget is basically just a cash flow statement, and a deficit arises when outflows (spending) exceed inflows (tax revenues). This means that whenever the government runs a deficit (almost every year in memory, other than at the end of the Clinton administration), that deficit must be financed by new borrowing, to fund the gap not covered by incoming tax revenues.

The problem is that the debt ceiling is not operationally tied to the amount of spending and taxing that Congress has enacted. At the same time, the executive branch is *required* to spend whatever Congress legislates; that is, the president may not constitutionally refuse to implement lawful spending legislation.

The trap that Congress set for itself when it moved away from bond issue-by-issue authorization for Treasury borrowings to a blanket authority is that Congress might (indeed, regularly does) enact spending legislation that yields deficits, which once legislated cannot be avoided (except through serendipitous increases in tax revenues resulting from a stronger economy), but at the same time Congress does not necessarily raise the debt ceiling. The crisis comes when the executive branch spends the money it is required by law to spend, collects the revenues it is authorized by law to collect, is left with a completely predictable shortfall, and then cannot borrow the funds to pay for the bills that have been incurred at the direction of Congress because Congress has not authorized the borrowing by raising the debt ceiling.

It is easy to confuse an artificial and avoidable government shutdown crisis with an artificial and avoidable debt-ceiling crisis. A government shutdown arises when Congress fails to authorize and appropriate the funds necessary to keep government services functioning. A debt-ceiling crisis arises when Congress remembers to authorize and appropriate funds necessary to keep government running, but neglects to allow the Treasury Department to borrow the money to pay the resulting bills.

It cannot be emphasized too strongly that a debt-ceiling crisis is both artificial and entirely the creature of Congressional processes. A debt-ceiling crisis is artificial because it has nothing to do directly with controlling government spending. Borrowing is the result of spending, not the other way around, and the spending in question is designed and made mandatory by Congress's own legislation. The crisis is entirely the creature of Congressional processes because the Constitution mandates that Congress is responsible both for all spending decisions and for all borrowing decisions.

The obvious solution is to include in all spending legislation the authorization to borrow funds necessary to pay for the spending so required. Instead, Congress deals with the implicit conflict internal to its rules by regularly raising the debt ceiling, sometimes several times a year. In the past, these laws were never ultimately controversial, but did allow marginal actors to huff and puff on a national stage for a few days before the inevitable enactment of a higher debt ceiling.

During 2011, the debt ceiling became a weapon used by the Republican Party in Congress to extract major concessions from a Democratic president. The predictable results were public disgust with the political process, still further polarization of the two political parties, and the first downgrade of the credit of the United States by a commercial credit rating agency. That downgrade was a reflection on our political process, not our ability to pay our bills as they came due.

The failure to raise the debt ceiling to enable the United States to borrow the funds necessary to honor its obligations would trigger global financial and economic crises, as well as domestic constitutional ones. The role of the US dollar as the global reserve currency would be quickly eroded, and the price paid by the United States to borrow once the crisis was resolved would surely increase significantly. Meanwhile, the executive branch would find itself on the horns of a constitutional dilemma, because it would be required to spend money it did not have, and would be prohibited from borrowing the money to pay for that spending.

Presumably for strategic reasons, the Obama administration in 2011 and 2012 did not articulate what it would do if a debt-ceiling crisis actually were triggered. One idea mooted by Republican legislators eager to downplay the impact on ordinary citizens of the crisis they wished to precipitate was that the executive should prioritize payments, so that Treasury bonds and Social Security checks, for example, would be paid on time and in full. But prioritization rests on an uncertain constitutional footing, as all claims against the US government, whether for a federal employee's salary, rent owed to a landlord of property occupied by a government agency, Social Security benefits, or interest due on Treasury debt, are equally valid and probably have equal priority as a constitutional matter. Treasury's computer payment systems distinguish between payments on Treasury obligations and everything else, but within that second category do not distinguish payments by the character of the underlying claim, just by the amount due. As a result, it is not clear that a prioritization program could be implemented as a mechanical matter, beyond prioritizing Treasury bond payments over all other "full faith and credit" obligations.

From the other direction, Democratic pundits argued that the president could ignore the debt ceiling as itself unconstitutional, because the Constitution directs the president to do nothing to question the "validity" of the national debt. But not paying debt is not the same as questioning its validity. Bankrupts acknowledge their debts to be valid—they just cannot pay them. And this suggestion ignores the fact that the Constitution vests in Congress the power to authorize borrowing. Other ideas were still more fantastical in their thinking, such as the idea that, because Congress authorized the Treasury to create collectible-style coins out of certain rare metals, the Treasury could strike a single $1 trillion dollar platinum coin, and carry it (very carefully) to the Fed for deposit in the Treasury's account there.

Were a debt-ceiling crisis actually to precipitate, the least awful course of action would be to follow the example of hard-up states and municipalities over the years, by announcing that the Treasury would issue scrip—"registered warrants"—in lieu of money to large classes of claimants.[14] Recipients could include defense contractors, Medicare service providers, federal employees, and Social Security recipients. The scrip would not pay interest (except in certain exotic cases where required to do so by virtue of a preexisting law). Most important, the scrip would explicitly disavow that it constituted debt of the United States. Instead, the scrip's operative language would provide that it constituted an acknowledgment of a preexisting debt that the Treasury was not currently able to pay, and that it would become immediately redeemable in cash only when the Treasury was able to certify that there was enough money available in the Treasury's general fund to cover it.

Scrip with these terms has three great advantages over other ideas. First, there would be no confusion in the marketplace between valid Treasury bonds and this new paper, which would have a completely different name and operative legal language. The scrip by its terms would not constitute a currently enforceable claim against the United States, and could ripen into one only on Congressional action to resolve the crisis and, in effect, adopt the scrip at that point as valid debt.

Second, the scrip would not explicitly ignore any constitutional allocation of powers. Issuing scrip would not require the president to ignore the debt ceiling, and at the same time the scrip could be used to pay for the goods and services that Congress had previously authorized and appropriated.

Third, the scrip would be transferable. Financial institutions would buy the scrip at a high percentage of its face value, knowing that the crisis could not continue for very long. In that way, claimants forced to accept scrip would have a low-cost way to turn their scrip into immediate cash in private markets, even while the Treasury was unable to issue new debt. The federal Anti-Assignment Act generally prohibits the transfer of claims against the United States from one private actor to another, but the government could waive the act's application, which is what the president would do here.

The scrip strategy may sound far-fetched, but it has been used before: in fact, California relied on it as recently as 2009. Beginning in July of that year, California addressed its budget crisis by issuing 450,000 registered warrants, totaling $2.6 billion, to individual and business claimants, including recipients of aid programs, recipients of tax refunds, and government contractors. Those holders who needed immediate cash were usually able to sell their registered warrants to banks at face value, though some institutions limited such purchases.

Whether as a result of public shaming, pressure from banks, or a newfound sense of responsibility, the California legislature quickly worked out a budget deal, and the scrip was then redeemed for cash. Throughout the ordeal, California continued to pay its public debt service in cash and on schedule and never lost an investment-grade credit rating.

THE GREAT RECESSION

What really went wrong in 2008–2012? Deficits soared to unprecedented levels in the 2008–2012 period, and as a result so too has the national debt, essentially doubling in five years as a percentage of GDP. Why did a deficit that previously had troubled only policy wonks suddenly turn into a terrifying chasm of debt that has paralyzed the country's political processes?

This recession was different because it came breathtakingly close to collapsing into an authentic second Great Depression. Chapter 3 already has laid out some of the sad consequences of this extraordinary economic calamity, for example in respect of unemployment. In this section I emphasize what the Great Recession meant for federal government budget receipts (tax revenues) and outlays (spending).

Less went wrong than the usual narratives would suggest. There is no story here of exploding socialism, or a permanent government takeover of anything much. Instead, there is the standard story of all recessions, that tax revenues fell and preexisting emergency safety net spending (for example, for unemployment and Supplemental Nutrition Assistance Program—food stamp—benefits) rose.

These consequences are known as "automatic stabilizers"—just by the design of these programs, they operate without any new legislative interventions to mitigate the consequences of a recession, by leading to smaller tax bills and more payments to individuals who qualify for some modest assistance toward meeting current living expenses.[15] Of course, automatic stabilizers also generate deficits until the economy recovers and the programs in question return to normal levels. Because we have not endured an economic collapse of this magnitude in the living memory of most Americans, we have generally underappreciated the role that automatic stabilizers played in our surge in national debt.

Congress enacted three large spending initiatives in the context of the Great Recession: the Troubled Asset Relief Program (TARP), enacted under President Bush's administration; the American Recovery and Reinvestment Act (ARRA), enacted a month after President Obama took office (February 2009); and of course the Affordable Care Act, enacted in early 2010. The CBO's analyses have demonstrated that TARP has cost the American taxpayer essentially nothing, because we made a tidy profit on the investments made to prop up the banking sector. And although few seem to be aware of it, the CBO scored the Affordable Care Act as reducing, not increasing, government deficits, because the legislation contained revenue-raising measures designed to pay for its new spending.[16]

The ARRA was a one-time spending program that added about $880 billion to our annual deficits, mostly in 2010–2012. In return, that program substantially increased employment and GDP—boosting GDP, for example, possibly as much as 4.1 percent in 2010.[17]

As just noted, government debt held by the public doubled from 2007 to 2012, from 36 percent of GDP to 72 percent at the end of 2012, the result of several years of trillion-dollar deficits. If the three large legislative spending initiatives can explain less than $1 trillion of net new deficits, what was the source of the hemorrhaging?

The answer is that during the Great Recession, tax revenues collapsed further, and preexisting emergency spending programs were called on to spend more, than in any other recession in the last 70 years. The villains in the piece really were weak public finances coming to the end of the last expansion, so that there was no financial cushion in the fiscal system, and the depth of the economic collapse in 2008–2009. The automatic stabilizers (reduced tax revenues, increased unemployment and SNAP benefits, etc.) are what the public saw and reacted to, but they were artifacts of the problem, not the problem itself.

Safety net spending increased dramatically during the Great Recession—just as it was designed to do in times of economic calamity. And by design, this spending is on a steady downward trend as the economy slowly recovers, as Figure 6.3 shows. Safety net spending will remain somewhat higher than pre-2008 levels in

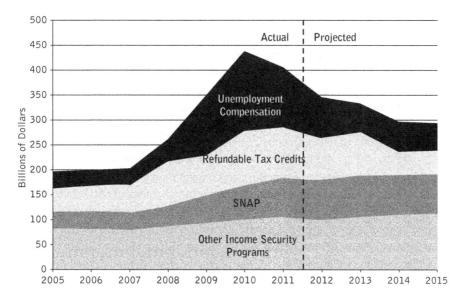

FIGURE 6.3 Outlays for Income Security Programs

Source: Congressional Budget Office, *Budget and Economic Outlook: Fiscal Years 2012 to 2022,* fig. 3-3.

nominal dollar terms because of the effects of population growth, inflation, and the lingering effects of the Great Recession itself.

But the biggest story, and one largely unappreciated, is the collapse in tax revenues during the Great Recession. A quick review of tax revenues during the 2008–2013 period illustrates this point. For the decades leading up to the crisis, and using the pre-2013 restatement of historical GDP, federal tax revenues averaged 18.3 percent of GDP.[18] (This of course does not mean that revenues approximated this number each year; revenues topped out at 20.6 percent of GDP at the end of the Clinton administration, for example, and revenues fell significantly in earlier recessions.) During the current crisis years, by contrast, federal revenues fell precipitously, to about 15.1 percent of GDP in 2009 and 2010, for example. To be fair, not all of this decline in revenue was the result of the automatic stabilization properties of the income tax, as Congress implemented new temporary tax reductions to stimulate the economy, but a significant portion was attributable to the automatic stabilization function.

To make this more concrete, I calculated what the federal government's tax revenues would have been in the 2008–2013 period, if revenues each year totaled 18.3 percent of that year's GDP, and compared those hypothetical revenue figures to the revenues actually collected (or in the case of 2013, the revenues that are projected to be collected). The difference is a gap of $2.1 trillion—without regard to the increased interest costs incurred to finance this contribution to the deficit.[19]

In short, forgone revenues (compared to historical norms) are the largest single explanation for where our most recent deficit problems have arisen. In very rough terms, ARRA and other new discretionary spending programs cost no more than $1 trillion; existing safety net programs (some of which, like unemployment benefits, were extended as a result of the severity of the economic collapse) cost about another $1 trillion over baseline levels, and forgone tax revenues cost over $2 trillion. In the absence of these three items, Treasury debt held by the public at the end of 2012 would have been about 47 percent of GDP, not 72 percent.

In past years (e.g., the 1990s) we used years of strong economic performance to pay back the "missing" revenue from recessionary periods, by allowing tax revenues to rise above the long-term average. After all, 18.3 percent of GDP could not have been the average revenues collected over many years if some years fell below that number, and no year rose above it. The reason that we are paralyzed by false fiscal crises today is that we are not willing to use the economic recovery to allow tax collections to rise sufficiently to pay down the deficits unavoidably incurred during the economic collapse of the Great Recession, and to provide for the demographic pig in the snake, in the form of our aging population.

WHERE ARE WE HEADING?

Fiscal year 2013 actually was a success story from a deficit perspective, as the recovering economy and concomitant higher tax collections meant that the annual deficit fell from about $1.1 trillion in 2012 to $680 billion in 2013. The CBO projects that fiscal years 2014 and 2015 will show continued improvement; because tax revenues are rising as the economy recovers from the Great Recession, the annual deficit will continue to decline, to roughly 2 percent of GDP by 2015.[20] The automatic stabilizers that pulled us back from the brink of complete economic collapse are unwinding, just as they were designed to do.

By 2016, however, the positive trend is expected to reverse, as increasing mandatory spending and Treasury debt interest costs begin to dominate. As a result, under the CBO's relatively optimistic baseline assumptions, federal debt held by the public as a percentage of GDP will dip for a few years, but then slowly will climb to roughly 77 percent of GDP in 2023 (a bit higher than its 2013 level), at which time it will be trending up at an accelerating pace. Under plausible alternative assumptions, the 2023 ratio would be 87 percent.[21] This is a disquieting trajectory. And if one were brave enough to chart our very long-term budget trends, the projections of outstanding Treasury debt as a percentage of GDP a few decades from now become unimaginably large.[22]

Something must be done, of course. But the numbers tossed around are so large as to be paralyzing. Like deer caught in the headlights of an oncoming car, policymakers cannot comprehend any way to move forward productively. The trick here is to divide our problems into three time tranches: short, medium, and long-term. Each requires a different approach.

Our short-term focus should be on the fact that the United States is still mired in an immense jobs crisis, not a government-spending crisis. The February 2013 edition of the Congressional Budget Office's *Annual Budget and Economic Outlook* predicted that the United States would record unemployment rates exceeding 7.5 percent for six consecutive years (through 2014), for the first time since the Great Depression.[23] Our actual performance since that date in the baseline unemployment statistic has been somewhat better than expected, but in part that reflects a greater than anticipated number of Americans giving up on job searches altogether. (Chapter 3 described the different measures of "unemployment.") The corrosive effects of long-term unemployment are impossible to overstate: they include a degradation of skills, an awkward re-entry to the labor markets when younger workers have passed one by, and severe stresses on family structures. This actually is an ideal time to spend more, not less, to take advantage of a large potential labor pool without triggering wage inflation, and while government financing costs are so cheap.

Longer term, the analysis necessarily shifts to considering whether government spending can usefully be reduced, or tax revenues increased. For the reasons developed in the remainder of this chapter and in the rest of Part II, the inescapable conclusion is that tax revenues must rise. Even if you reject my case for increased insurance and investment programs, tax revenues must rise. Indeed, even if your dream is to slash entitlements programs, after one takes into account the long transition rules that have always accompanied changes in such programs, tax revenues must rise.

A TALE OF TWO BUDGETS

Around January of each year the Congressional Budget Office releases an eagerly awaited volume, its annual *Budget and Economic Outlook*. Each *Outlook* contains detailed federal budget projections for the next 10 years, as well as an analysis of overall economic trends and special narrative discussions of issues of particular importance in that year. By law, the CBO assumes in preparing each year's projections that the tax law then in effect will remain the law, even when that assumption is politically improbable. But this convention also affords us the chance to see where the deficit problem really comes from, at least over the next 10 years or so.

The CBO's January 2012 projections of budget trends for the coming decade were surprisingly rosy, particularly when viewed a year later. The CBO 2012 baseline budget projections showed the federal government running deficits averaging only 1.5 percent of GDP for the entire 2012–2022 period (and in the range of 1.0 percent at the end of the period), and Treasury debt held by the public falling to 63 percent of GDP by 2021.

One year later, in early 2013, the CBO projected much higher deficits 10 years out, and Treasury debt at 75 percent of GDP in 2021—a full 12 percentage points higher than the 2012 base case. What changed? Not the economy—it continued to heal during 2012, more or less as predicted.

To see where the deterioration in our budget future comes from, we can look at fiscal year 2021, which is not so far in the future as to be irrelevant to most readers, but which is expected to be fully out of the shadows of the Great Recession. I use 2021 to demonstrate that we have the wherewithal to bring government back into our lives in useful and complementary ways to what we can expect from private markets, without subjecting ourselves to ruinous taxation or a death spiral of budget deficits. To the contrary, it is current policy, notwithstanding all its spending caps and sequestrations, that plainly is unaffordable, for the simple reason that current policy is designed to starve the government of the revenues necessary to accomplish even the bare bones tasks that we currently ask of it.

Table 6.1 shows the CBO's two projections for what our federal budget will look like in 2021, drawn from the 2012 and 2013 editions of the annual *Budget and Economic Outlook*. Both reflect the Budget Control Act of 2011's "caps" on

Table 6.1 CBO Budget Projections for FY 2021 (Billions of USD)

	2013 Projection	2012 Projection
GDP	23,842	23,614
Revenues		
Individual Income Taxes	2,282	2,664
Social Insurance Taxes	1,433	1,447
Corporate Income Taxes	493	452
Other (estate tax, excise taxes, etc.)	288	364
TOTAL	4,496	4,926
Outlays		
Mandatory	3,263	3,272
Discretionary	1,356	1,344
Net Interest	730	590
TOTAL	5,350	5,205
Deficit	-854	-279
Percentage of GDP		
Revenues as a Percentage of GDP	18.9%	20.9%
Outlays as a Percentage of GDP	22.4%	22%
Deficit as a Percentage of GDP	-3.6%	-1.2%
Treasury Debt Held by Public as a Percentage of GDP	75%	63%

discretionary spending, and that law's additional automatic spending cuts that were triggered when the Budget "Supercommittee" was unable to reach an agreement on a budget path forward to present to Congress. The automatic cuts are usually referred to as "sequestration," although technically the cuts are only partially effected through sequestration pathways.

The fact that the 2012 *Budget Outlook* predicted that in FY 2021 we would be running a deficit of 1.2 percent of GDP was not problematic. In a growing economy, the government can run at least some deficit every year, while debt held by the public remains constant as a percentage of GDP. (As explained earlier, so long as the deficit as a percentage of growth in annual GDP is no greater than total debt outstanding as a percentage of GDP, total debt will not grow as a share of GDP.) Debt as a percentage of GDP is the relevant benchmark, because that is what tells you how the government's obligations stack up as a fraction of total national market income, which is what GDP approximates.

As it happens, GDP growth of 3 percent per year is about what our economy currently seems capable of delivering in normal times, and a debt-to-GDP ratio of around 67 percent is somewhere near the upper end of debt ratios to which most public finance economists would signal assent. This suggests that we should see deficits above 2 percent per annum in normal economic conditions as cause for further inquiry. Moreover, many economists would prefer to see the United States pay down its overall debt level to a lower ratio—say, 50 percent of GDP—to leave some cushion for the inevitable next crisis.

The 2012 projections for FY 2021 show a frankly cheery *deficit* picture, although one premised on inadequate spending levels. The CBO's 2012 *Budget Outlook* showed the debt-to-GDP ratio at 63 percent and trending down, with a deficit in 2021 of a bit more than one percent. But the 2013 projection for FY 2021 is horrifying, with deficits three times as large—at a time in the future when the economy is projected to be humming along (because that is how the CBO always projects the future more than five years out), and therefore no special stimulus argument can be made. Why? What terrible event explains the gloomy 2013 forecast?

The explanation for the gloomy 2013 forecast was not a sudden change of heart about the productivity of the economy—projected FY 2021 GDP is almost identical in the two years' forecasts.[24] Nor did the CBO materially change its projections of future mandatory (Social Security, Medicare, etc.) or discretionary government spending. What *did* change between 2012 and 2013 were the CBO's projections for FY 2021 tax revenues, on the inflow side, and Treasury debt interest expense, on the outflow side. The second, it turns out, is attributable entirely to the first, because in its 2013 presentation the CBO predicted a long string of much larger deficits in the years from 2013 to 2021 than the CBO had predicted in 2012, all as a result of weaker expected tax revenues.

As a result of these larger projected annual deficits, the CBO predicted in 2013 that Treasury debt in the hands of the public would amount to 75 percent of FY 2021 GDP (and trending up), a sharp increase from an expected 63 percent of FY 2021 GDP (and trending down) in 2012's *Budget Outlook*. More borrowings mean more interest expense, even if those borrowings do not increase average borrowing rates (an implausible assumption, over the long run).

The FY 2021 deficit picture and trends in the 2013 *Budget Outlook* should terrify the reader. They plainly terrify the CBO, as evidenced by the message carefully and dispassionately delivered in that agency's 2013 edition of its annual publication, *The Long-Term Budget Outlook*, which comes every summer. The CBO's concern is not that the United States will default on its publicly held debt at some point in the immediate future. Instead, the CBO's principal concern is that increasing levels of government debt as a percentage of GDP—which is to say, substantial deficits (because government debt rises as a percentage of GDP only when deficits exceed a fraction of the economy's growth rate, as just described)— will "crowd out" private investment:

> Large federal budget deficits over the long term would reduce investment, resulting in lower national income and higher interest rates than would otherwise occur. The reason is that increased government borrowing would cause a larger share of the savings potentially available for investment to be used for purchasing government securities, such as Treasury bonds. Those purchases would "crowd out" investment in capital goods, such as factories and computers, which make workers more productive. Because wages are determined mainly by workers' productivity, the reduction in investment would also reduce wages, lessening people's incentive to work. In addition, both private borrowers and the government would have to pay higher interest rates to compete for savings, and those higher rates would strengthen people's incentive to save. However, the rise in private saving would be a good deal smaller than the increase in federal borrowing represented by the change in the deficit, so national saving would decline, as would private investment.[25]

Foreign lenders will fund the difference, but this in turn will mean that a larger share of national income will be owned by those foreign investors.[26]

Increasing levels of federal debt as a percentage of GDP will have other adverse repercussions as well. As the CBO recently observed:

> [H]igh and rising amounts of federal debt would have significant negative consequences for both the economy and the federal budget. Those consequences include reducing the total amounts of national saving and income relative to what they would otherwise be [i.e., the "crowding out" phenomenon]; increasing the government's interest payments, thereby putting more pressure on the rest of the budget; limiting lawmakers' flexibility to respond to unexpected events; and increasing the likelihood of a fiscal crisis.[27]

To be clear, the CBO's implied message was not that it expects that the wheels necessarily will come off the bus in the next decade—just that they will at some point in the next 25 years.

The specific event that took our budget deficit path from rosy to catastrophic, at least over a 10-year horizon, was the January 1, 2013, "fiscal cliff" tax deal, the American Taxpayer Relief Act of 2012. This deal was packaged as a tax hike on the most affluent, but in reality it operated as a massive tax cut for most Americans, against the backdrop of already low tax collections.

The CBO in its 2013 *Budget Outlook* projected that *the 2013 fiscal cliff tax deal by itself* would add about $4.6 trillion to our accumulated deficits over the 2013–2022 period (comprising $4 trillion in lower tax revenues, and $600 billion in higher interest costs), which would more than double the size of the 10-year projected deficits, compared with the 2012 baseline.[28] This means that the budget cost of the fiscal cliff tax deal over the period 2013–2022 is more than double the amount of all the spending caps and sequestrations imposed by the Budget Control Act of 2011, as discussed in the next section.

Attributing our newly depressing budget fortunes to the "fiscal cliff" tax deal will surprise many readers, as that tax deal was presented to most Americans as largely a tax hike on the most affluent, which sounds good for deficit hawks, even if it saddened the wealthy. This widespread intuition rests, however, on a misunderstanding of how CBO budget projections are prepared.

In constructing its 10-year budget forecasts, the CBO assumes that the laws governing mandatory spending will remain in place without amendment, and that as a result mandatory spending will follow whatever path the empirical data suggest, taking into account demographic trends, healthcare cost trends, and similar variables. The CBO assumes that discretionary spending (which must be reappropriated annually) will grow with inflation, but then will be subject to any statutory spending caps, as are in place right now.

On the revenue side, the CBO projects future tax collections on the basis of "current law," which means that the CBO assumes that any "temporary" provisions will expire, even if those temporary provisions have been consistently renewed for decades. This is the case, for example, with a large package of business tax subsidies known colloquially as "the extenders"; if the CBO were to assume that the extenders in fact would be extended yet again (and again), its revenue forecasts would be lower, and projected deficits higher, than is reflected in the official baseline forecast. The CBO does not make this assumption because it is stupid or politically tone deaf, but rather because, first, the law establishing how CBO forecasts are to be constructed specifies this assumption, and, second, it would be impossible for the CBO (or the staff of the Joint Committee on Taxation, who are in the same pickle) to maintain its nonpartisan status if it were simultaneously handicapping the outcomes of future political decisions.

But what does this have to do with our suddenly sagging fiscal fortunes? Many people forget that our entire personal income tax rate structure from 2001 through 2012 was governed by temporary tax legislation. "Permanent" law here meant the tax system applicable at the turn of the millennium. As a result, in 2012 the CBO's forecasts for years after 2012 assumed the lapse of the temporary rate environment we had all grown accustomed to conceiving as the norm, and the reversion to the across the board higher rates (and other ancillary revenue-enhancing measures) that had prevailed in 2000. The CBO understood that this was an improbable political outcome, and in its narratives stressed the differences between what became known as "current law" versus "current policy" forecasts, but the official baseline 10-year budget forecast was rosy specifically because it assumed the return to pre-2001 tax law.

Of course, this was not to be. Instead, the American Taxpayer Relief Act of 2012 provided that only the top regular income tax rate would revert to its pre-2001 level of 39.6 percent, and then only for incomes greater than $450,000/year (for joint returns). Capital gains taxes reverted to 20 percent, but again only for incomes greater than $450,000/year (for joint returns), and dividend income tax rates were raised, relative to the 2012 rules, or from another perspective lowered, relative to the pre-2001 rules, by preserving permanently their coupling to the capital gains rate. (In addition to the income tax, top incomes in the United States generally are subject either to a Medicare tax or a new complementary tax on "unearned income"; as of 2013 the rate for either is 3.8 percent. As a result, the highest combined statutory marginal tax rate for ordinary income is now 43.4 percent, and for capital gains or dividends 23.8 percent.)

The fiscal cliff deal in fact gave *every* taxpayer an income tax discount relative to what would have been the case had those temporary tax cuts fully expired. The source of the discount, as will be explained in chapter 8, is that the first dollars of income a taxpayer earns keep the benefit of the lower tax brackets; as a result, even the highest-income joint filers enjoy the benefit of the Bush tax cuts on their first $450,000 of income. Other regular income tax brackets were protected, and the dreaded alternative minimum tax (AMT) was "patched" permanently, so as to limit its application more or less in accordance with the annual temporary patches on which Congress had been relying. To give a sense of scale, this AMT patch alone was estimated to cost $1.8 trillion over 10 years, relative to the pre-2001 law that otherwise would have sprung back to life.

As a result of the "fiscal cliff" tax deal, the 2013 CBO baseline projection now contemplates that federal government revenues will reach a bit less than 19 percent of GDP during the coming 10 years. Conversely, the 2012 CBO baseline projection contemplated that revenues slowly would climb to about 21 percent of GDP. (As elsewhere in this book, these figures are based on GDP estimates before the mid-2013 restatement of GDP; under the new methodology, tax revenues are consistently about 0.5 points lower as a percentage of GDP.)

In short, on January 2, 2013, most of us felt that we had dodged a bullet. But what we dodged at a personal level now has boomeranged back to slam into our collective rear ends, in the form of improvidently large government deficits in the immediate future. And of course our future deficits probably will be worse than projected. First, it is likely that many of the tax "extenders" in fact will be extended (or their costs rolled into comprehensive business tax reform), just as they have been extended in the past. Second, and more important, government spending is implausibly constrained by the budget caps and automatic spending reductions (sequestration) imposed by the Budget Control Act of 2011. The next section amplifies this last point.

To summarize, if the federal government had collected its historic average of 18.3 percent of revenue during the 2008–2012 recessionary period, and then switched to the higher revenue levels contemplated by the 2012 CBO baseline (i.e., the expiration in particular of the 2001–2003 tax cuts in their entirety) for 2013–2023, deficits over the 2008–2023 period would have been on the order of $7 *trillion* lower (taking into account debt service savings). That $7 trillion in lower deficits represents a 35 percent reduction in projected levels of Treasury debt outstanding a decade from now.

So both looking forward to projected revenues after the fiscal cliff tax deal, and looking back to the revenues forgone through the automatic stabilization function of the income tax (as well as various temporary tax relief measures), we see a consistent story of missing revenues that to a large extent explains our recent worrisome fiscal trends. The fiscal policy chasm that has brought our political discourse to a state of paralysis is simply whether tax collections should average 19 or 21 percent of GDP over the next decade (about $4 trillion in total, before interest expense savings). We currently are on course to collect about 19 percent of GDP, but as the CBO's 2013 10-year projections show, these revenue levels now baked into the tax code will lead to unsustainable deficits and a weaker economy in the foreseeable future.[29]

Conversely, revenues running at roughly 21 percent of GDP, which are the levels that would have obtained had all the Bush tax cuts expired, would have paid down our outstanding debt to more reasonable levels, would have led to a stronger economy over the next decade, and would have bought us the time we need to begin a transition to a more fiscally responsible approach to healthcare policy. The tax rules that would have applied had we fallen off the dreaded fiscal cliff would have been the same as those that prevailed in the year 2000. It is not particularly credible to argue that a step-up to tax revenues at this level—a level that we imposed on ourselves less than 15 years ago—would choke our economy or erode our fundamental liberties.

SPENDING: SQUEEZING BLOOD FROM THE STONE

This section briefly summarizes current budget trends in respect of government outlays (spending). Chapter 7 completes the picture by looking more closely at the substance of the major spending programs.

Discretionary Spending

The across the board cuts in defense and nondefense discretionary spending contemplated by the Budget Control Act of 2011, amounting by 2021 to roughly 25 percent of all discretionary spending, as a percentage of GDP, would mean that the federal government would be required to abandon not only its current levels of protecting our markets, our rule of law, and our domestic tranquility, but also all our ambitions as the dominant military presence in every strategic theater of operations in the world. Magical thinking about slashing mandatory spending cannot solve the problem, because even if that magical thinking were to be reflected in law, history suggests that it would need to be phased in over decades, and in the meantime, the deficits must be financed. And all the while the United States would slide down the slope toward a meaner, less successful country, on a slower growth path, and with less authentic freedom for the bulk of its citizens.

"Sequestration" is an ugly word for an uglier policy, one requiring a roughly $100 billion annual haircut to discretionary spending in each of the next 10 years ($1 trillion total). Congress of course designed sequestration in 2011 as a sort of mutually assured destruction, the price to be paid if it were unable to agree to a long-term deficit reduction path. The theory was that sequestration's consequences were so self-evidently destructive and stupid that Congress would reach some compromise long-term path to avoid triggering this fiscal weapon that it had aimed against itself, but once again Congress surprised even itself on the downside.

Although largely unknown to the public, sequestration sits on top of another set of haircuts to discretionary spending enacted as part of the Budget Control Act of 2011. As a result of the interaction of these two limits, discretionary federal government spending is estimated to be $1.5 trillion less over the next 10 years than would be the case if it simply grew at the projected rate of inflation.[30] What this means is that in 2023 defense and nondefense spending would each fall to roughly 2.8 percent of GDP—only 60 percent of the 40-year average for defense, and 67 percent of the average for nondefense spending (which of course was not inflated by the various wartime buildups in budget on the defense side).

These are unrealistic and unwise projections. As Martin Feldstein, a prominent conservative economist, concluded in an opinion piece in the *Wall Street*

Journal, "The truth is that federal finances cannot be stabilized by reducing discretionary outlays alone."[31]

To take a few examples, in mid-2013 one already can see the consequences of the sequester in 57,000 fewer children accommodated in Head Start programs,[32] in healthcare funding initiatives scaled back, and in federal museums shuttered.[33] Low-income families have lost rent subsidies,[34] NASA scientists were unable to travel to the National Space Symposium in Colorado Springs to meet counterparts from France, Germany, and China who had traveled there, and trips by government geologists to keep tabs on Alaska volcanoes have been cut in half.[35] A federal laboratory testing new therapies for human retinal degenerations was forced to fire a postdoctoral fellow and euthanize the expensive genetically modified rabbits that it had purchased with the prior year's budget.[36] Nor could the laboratory have held back some prior spending to keep the rabbits going: by law, each year's authorized funding must be spent by the end of that fiscal year.

It also must be remembered that "discretionary" spending covers not just spending on the poor—as already shown, that is a small fraction of the federal budget—but spending on the administrative machinery that keeps government functioning, from federal courts to the Securities and Exchange Commission's oversight of the financial markets, to the Environmental Protection Agency's vigilance over our air and water, and to our Homeland Security agencies. Federal workers across the board have been forced to take unpaid furlough days to meet sequestration's requirements.

Very little of this has been visible so far to citizens who do not rely on programs directly affected by sequestration. The one exception was the 2013 disruption in air travel as a result of mandatory furloughing of air traffic controllers. This inconvenience was intolerable to Congress, whose members fly to their home districts almost every week, and so was promptly reversed by emergency legislation. But over time the degradation in government services, like any instance of deferred maintenance, will become more and more obvious.

Focusing simply on fiscal performance for the moment, sequestration is also poor economic policy. The International Monetary Fund (IMF) concluded in July 2013 that America's economic growth in 2013 would be roughly 0.5 percentage points lower than otherwise would have been the case by virtue of America's "excessively rapid and ill designed" sequestration. Elaborating, the IMF wrote that sequestration policies "not only exert a heavy toll on growth in the short term (reducing this year's growth by some 0.5 percentage points of GDP), but could also reduce medium-term potential growth by reducing infrastructure, science, and education spending."[37]

The Congressional Budget Office agreed that sequestration hurt our current economic performance. In July 2013 the Congressional Budget Office analyzed what it would mean for the economy, as measured by GDP, if sequestration and the Budget Control Act's spending "caps" were repealed. The CBO's central esti-mate was that by the end of September 2014 (the end of the government's fiscal year) repeal of these odious constraints would increase inflation-adjusted GDP by 0.7 percentage points and increase employment by 900,000 jobs.[38] Of course the increase in deficits would need to be addressed over time, but the clear implica-tion was that our basic budget priorities were backward: 2013 should have been a time for more, or at least constant, government spending if Congress wanted to support the slow recovery from the Great Recession.

A principal reason that sequestration and the Budget Control Act's other caps on discretionary spending have such a deleterious immediate impact on the economic performance of the United States (without regard to any other consid-erations relating to the happiness of society) is that the economy itself is still performing well below its full potential, as summarized in the CBO graphic in Figure 6.4. In such circumstances, debt-financed government spending actu-ally leads to a virtuous circle of more economic activity, without risk of inflation. Such a policy of course cannot continue forever; in a rational world, however, short-term additional deficits would be addressed, as the IMF pointed out, "with a back-loaded mix of entitlement savings and new revenues." What this means is that the United States should have in place a plan today to raise additional taxes and limit the growth in entitlement payouts over the middle and long term,

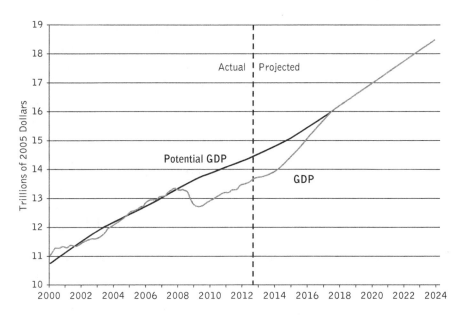

FIGURE 6.4 GDP and Potential GDP

Source: Congressional Budget Office, *The Budget and Economic Outlook: Fiscal Years 2013 to 2023.*

thereby giving comfort to the capital markets that our long-term fiscal trajectory is sustainable.

In 2013 the Budget Control Act caps did not fully apply to defense spending, as they do beginning in 2014, at which point the howls of pain will become bipartisan. The Department of Defense apparently believes that the various caps will never actually apply to it—its Future Years Defense Program exceeds the maximum allowed under the caps by about $500 billion over the next 10 years.[39] If the Defense Department's view were to prevail, this $500 billion would need to be financed, either through higher current taxes or deficit financing, which is just another way of saying higher future taxes.

If Congress were to repeal all the caps and sequestrations introduced by the Budget Control Act of 2011, and if one made the further assumption that in the absence of such constraints discretionary spending would grow with the rate of inflation (i.e., be flat in real terms), then in fiscal year 2021 discretionary spending would be about $180 billion higher than the CBO forecast in 2013, and over the 10-year period 2014–2023, discretionary spending would be some $1.5 trillion higher.[40] In addition, mandatory spending would be about $100 billion higher, as some of the Budget Control Act applies to a small slice of mandatory spending. This additional spending would need to be financed, of course, through higher taxes, either on a current or on a deferred basis (in the latter case, through debt financing).

Mandatory Spending

Sequestration applies only our discretionary budget. Our projected long-term growth in mandatory spending is attributable to two factors: the greying of America and the continued growth in medical costs over and above the rate of inflation ("excess cost growth").[41] The CBO projects that from 2013 through 2038, 75 percent of the growth in federal healthcare spending will be attributable to these two items.[42]

Even if you have an instinct to scale back our large social insurance programs embedded in our mandatory spending—which would be a terrible idea, for all the reasons developed in chapter 11—change in this area must come slowly, because individuals have settled expectations that can be addressed only by long transition periods. As Senator Max Baucus of the Senate Finance Committee was fond of saying, in such situations it is important that you "boil the frog slowly."[43] This means that we must rely on long transition periods to move from where we are to where we need to be without unfairly upsetting settled expectations and modes of healthcare delivery systems. *In the meantime, however, the resulting costs must be financed.*

The long-term fiscal picture reflects the intersection of two independent unsustainable vectors: systematic undertaxation and overindulgent healthcare spending. The Congressional Budget Office has projected that government spending on Social Security and the major healthcare programs will amount to 11.7 percent of GDP in 2023. In 2007 that figure was 8.2 percent, and in 1970 3.8 percent. As described in chapter 7, Social Security needs a nip here and a tuck there: the big driver of these accelerating numbers is healthcare. The further out one projects, the more healthcare crowds out most every other imaginable use to which we might put our money.

The government's long-term *fiscal* health therefore depends directly on grappling much more fundamentally than we have to date with how we provide healthcare services to our citizens.[44] The Affordable Care Act did too little, not too much, in this regard, as chapter 11 demonstrates. There will be fewer uninsured in 2014, but the absurd pricing of medical services will be only slightly more constrained in the future than it was before the act took effect, because the act leaves largely unchanged the government-subsidized world of employer-sponsored health insurance.

The medium term—say, from 2015 to 2023—is the critical period on which fiscal policy should focus, because it must serve as the bridge from the unsustainable path that we currently are following to a more sensible long-term fiscal trajectory. What this means is that we must use the time to adopt and slowly phase in much more radical healthcare policies, and to establish a revenue base more consonant with running a first-world country.

Healthcare is a mess as a fiscal matter, but will take a very long time to heal. In the meantime, we cannot ask other explicit government spending programs to carry the load. There is no future in tough love for those receiving income security payments, when all such programs combined are on track to cost only about 1.3 percent of GDP 10 years from now. Nor is it remotely feasible to imagine cutting discretionary spending more, unless we declare peace and disband the army.

Spending Summary

Figure 6.5 summarizes our expected federal government spending over the next 10 years. The most remarkable aspect of the spending forecasts reflected in this figure is the proposition that we should slash discretionary spending over the coming decade while countenancing increasing our spending to pay interest on the national debt by roughly the same amount. This is a form of institutional madness, or blindness. The principal reason that interest expense on Treasury debt held by the public is expected to increase is that there will be a lot more of such debt, even with the spending constraints factored into the CBO's budget projections. But we control this prediction, in ways that we cannot control the aging of America, or the settled expectations of Americans toward existing social insurance programs, or the need for all the discretionary programs that

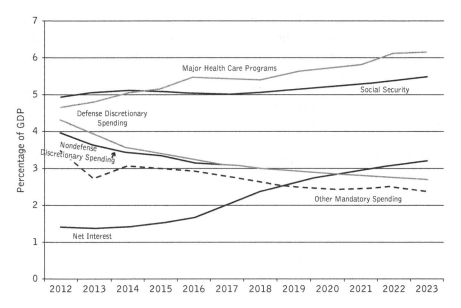

FIGURE 6.5 Historical and Projected Federal Government Spending, 2012–2023

Source: CBO, *Updated Budget Projections: Fiscal Years 2013 to 2023* (May 2013), fig. 3.

will go unfunded. We control it by choosing not to tax ourselves sufficiently to pay on a current basis for even our pinched and parsimonious proposed spending programs.

The lesson is plain: the United States cannot run a federal government on a tax base of 19 percent of GDP. Revenues will need to be about 2 percentage points higher—about the levels that would pertain if on January 1, 2013, we had reverted to pre-2001 tax rates. The simple fact is that we cannot afford as a country to see our government's discretionary spending wither to the levels contemplated by the Budget Control Act's fiscal corset. At least some of us do not wish to see our military's capabilities eroded through spending constraints amounting to some $500 billion over the next 10 years, and others of us appreciate that nondefense discretionary spending translates directly into the welfare of our society—through funding the agencies that keep markets honest and efficient, through a variety of social insurance programs funded through this channel, and through investment in infrastructure. The result is a slightly disjointed but ultimately bipartisan realization that the budget caps must go. Doing so would restore spending to historically normal levels, and would not trigger orgies of new government programs.

There is an often-advanced view that the Budget Control Act's caps are necessary to control federal deficits, or—to deal more frankly with the underlying political objectives—the caps should be replaced with spending cuts in mandatory social spending programs. But as chapter 7 demonstrates, our social insurance programs already are among the smallest in the OECD, and as chapters 11 and 12 develop, there is powerful empirical evidence for the proposition that a country not consumed by economic anxiety is both happier and more productive. We do not have to accept the false proposition that our only choices are to starve our discretionary spending programs or to cancel without transitions of any kind large swaths of our social insurance programs. The missing fiscal instruments in this mix are revenues—in particular, revenues at levels similar to that contemplated by the CBO's 2012 budget forecasts, which is to say, at levels comparable to pre-2001 tax law.

CHAPTER 7

AN OVERWEIGHT GOVERNMENT?

> *The orderly and flourishing state of society is agreeable to [man], and he takes delight in contemplating it. Its disorder and confusion, on the contrary, is the object of his aversion, and he is chagrined at whatever tends to produce it. He is sensible too that his own interest is connected with the prosperity of society, and that the happiness, perhaps the preservation of his existence, depends upon its preservation.*
>
> —ADAM SMITH, *The Theory of Moral Sentiments*,
> Part II, Sec. II, Chap. III.

A TWO-FISTED SPENDER?

An annual government deficit is the consequence of government spending exceeding revenues. This means that deficits can be addressed from two different directions—spend less or tax more. International comparisons and the work of our own nonpartisan record keepers point to the most productive path to follow. For better or worse, that path contemplates higher tax burdens.

Why not slash spending? The simple answer is that the United States actually runs a relatively lean government when compared with its own history and with peer countries, with two large exceptions: healthcare and the military. Historical and projected trends in federal government spending show that the federal government has not ballooned out of control. And OECD data that combine *all* national and sub-national government spending, both mandatory and discretionary (including social security), confirm that the United States is not the victim of government spending run amok. (When making international comparisons, total government spending at *all* levels is the more useful comparison, because countries vary widely in how they divvy up responsibilities between central and sub-national governments.)

All of the numbers that follow in this section are based on the pre-2013 restate-ment of GDP[1]; as a result, they overstate government spending as a percentage of GDP. But even with these older, lower GDP figures, our government is a lean spender.

The Congressional Budget Office projects that federal government spending will increase substantially over the next 10 years in only two categories. Net inter-est expense on Treasury debt will rise significantly as the total amount of debt outstanding increases and prevailing interest rates rise. Social Security spending will trend up a little bit, which reflects the unavoidable demographic fact that the number of Americans age 65 or older will increase by one-third over the next 10 years (and by 50 percent over the next 20).[2] But government outlays for health-care are projected to increase substantially. Importantly, as Figure 6.5 summa-rized, all discretionary spending and all mandatory spending on income security programs are projected to decline.

Discretionary spending has been so contentious a topic that it deserves closer examination. The long-term historical budget trend has been for less and less dis-cretionary spending, particularly on the nondefense side, interrupted principally by the American Recovery and Reinvestment Act, enacted early in 2009 at the depths of the economic crisis engulfing the country. This program spent about $880 billion in a one-time infusion of money to stabilize the economy; when mea-sured by its own objectives, it was a rousing success.

Figure 7.1 excludes funding for America's twenty-first-century wars, which have been conducted through appropriations outside the regular budget process, but makes the point that the federal government's outlays for discretionary spend-ing have been on a long-term downward slope, and in fact are heading for unsus-tainably low levels. Our nondefense discretionary spending today in particular is modest by world standards.[3] The CBO projects that the federal government in 2023 will spend 2.7 percent of GDP on all nondefense discretionary spending, but will run a deficit of 3.8 percent of GDP. This means that the federal government would run a significant deficit in that year even if it were to spend *zero* on all non-defense discretionary spending programs. Long-term deficits are not going to be addressed through further cuts here.

The federal government's income security programs include the Supplemental Nutrition Assistance Program (formerly food stamps), Supplemental Security Income, unemployment insurance, the earned income and child tax credits, fam-ily support, child nutrition, foster care, and miscellaneous tax credits.[4] Impressive though this list may sound, our government's total outlays for all of these pro-grams combined is much smaller than many observers realize. Congressional Budget Office projections contemplate that government outlays for income secu-rity programs will decline as a percentage of GDP from 2.0 percent in 2014 to 1.3 percent by 2023.[5] For the largest and most successful economy in the world,

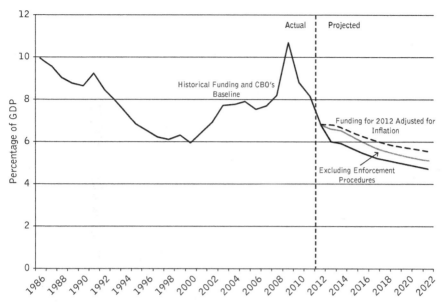

FIGURE 7.1 Total Discretionary Budget Authority as a Percentage of GDP (Excluding War Funding, Disaster Relief, and Program Integrity Initiatives)

Source: CBO, *An Update to the Fiscal and Economic Outlook: Fiscal Years 2012–2022* (August 2012), fig. 1-2.

this level of support for Americans struggling with unemployment or in poverty cannot in any way be described as lavish.

In fact, the OECD graded the United States in 2009 (the most recent year for which data were available) at 28th out of 34 countries in the generosity of its income-support programs for the working age population, as a percentage of GDP. (As a reminder, OECD data include federal, state, and local governments.) The countries less generous than us, with one exception, were not those we think of as peer economies: they comprised Turkey, Mexico, Chile, Korea, Greece, and Japan. We spent just about exactly one-half as much as did Canada or the United Kingdom on such programs, as a percentage of GDP, and about 60 percent of the OECD average.[6] Similarly, our 2009 public social spending in its entirety (including Social Security, Medicare, and Medicaid) put us in 29th place among the OECD-34.[7]

As shown in Figure 7.2, the United States ranked 5th from the bottom in 2013 among the 34 OECD member countries in total government spending as a percentage of GDP.[8] We keep company with the Slovak Republic, not most of the developed economies that we might grudgingly acknowledge as peers. Canada, for example, spends 2 percentage points of its GDP more for government than we do, and the United Kingdom spends in excess of 9 percentage points more.

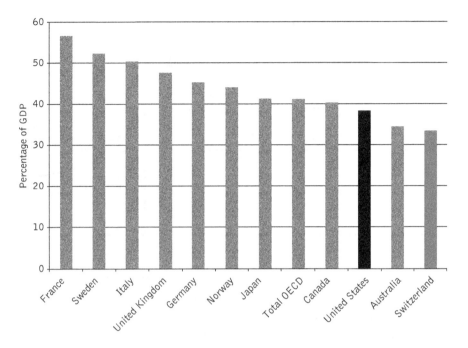

FIGURE 7.2 Projected Total Government Outlays: Percentage of GDP (2014)

Source: OECD, *Economic Outlook, Analysis and Forecasts* (May 2013), Annex Table 25.

Similarly, our 2009 public social spending (which includes Social Security and Medicare) put us in 29th place among the OECD-34.[9] Given our outsized military and healthcare spending, as described below, this implies that the United States is a very parsimonious government spender in all other respects, when compared with our world peers. If we were to spend what Canada does as a percentage of GDP, we would spend about $300 billion more every year on government services.

MILITARY SPENDING

The United States is a spending outlier today only in two areas: military and healthcare spending. The United States contains about 5 percent of the world's population, but in 2011 we spent almost exactly as much on our military services as did the next 14 largest militaries *combined*—in fact, 41 percent of the world's total military expenditures.[10] We spend more per capita than does Israel, whose existential threats arguably are much more immediate.[11] In 2012 we spent about 4.4 percent of GDP on military expenditures, including the war spending bills not considered through ordinary budget channels; countries like France and the United Kingdom spend around 2.5 percent of their GDP.

The most expensive mobile manmade object in the world no doubt is a nuclear-powered aircraft carrier with its air wing of 60 aircraft, together with the support ships that protect and service it. There are 11 of these in the world: the US Navy sails 10 of them (having decommissioned the USS *Enterprise* in early 2013). (The 11th of course belongs to France; if that is not obvious, you are not a careful student of French cultural history.) The first of a new class of nuclear-powered carriers (the USS *Gerald R. Ford*) is under construction, at a cost of around $14.5 billion (not including $5 billion in research and development costs for the new class as a whole), and the Navy has plans to build five additional Ford-class carriers over the next 30 years, for a total cost for the six new carriers of around $75 billion (in 2013 dollars).[12]

The point here is not to quarrel with US defense policy, but rather simply to point out that it is not possible to run a government on a shoestring when, on the one hand, the number of citizens over age 65 will increase by one-third over the next decade, and, on the other, we outspend Israel in per capita military spending.

HEALTHCARE

Overview

While our military spending is much larger than that of peer countries, healthcare spending is the heaviest fiscal weight dragging us down. Healthcare is the largest *fiscal* problem that the United States faces, because our country's healthcare spending is so outsized, and so much of the cost is absorbed by the government. Putting to one side the moral failings of a society in which 45 million Americans had no healthcare insurance before the Affordable Care Act's adoption, and looking instead at matters purely from an economic perspective, healthcare spending is where our dollar bills go to die—all too often followed by us, prematurely.

This observation has nothing whatsoever to do with the Affordable Care Act: healthcare's central role in our fiscal pickle long predates the new law, and what is more, the new law is projected to reduce government spending on healthcare somewhat. The great failure of the Obama administration here was in failing to explain to Americans why healthcare reform was a fiscal as well as a moral imperative, and how heavily "private" health insurance in fact has been subsidized by the federal government—a theme addressed in chapter 9.

This section begins the discussion of the central role of healthcare costs as a principal vector of our *fiscal* malaise. Chapter 11 returns to the topic, from the point of view of the failure of our current muddle of healthcare delivery systems to function as a coherent healthcare insurance mechanism.

A substantial part of the fiscal challenge we face relative to historical levels of government spending and taxing follows from the demographic pig inside the snake, in the form of the baby boomer generation.[13] The number of Americans age 65 or older will increase by 37 percent from 2013 to 2023, and by 85 percent from 2013 to 2038.[14] In 2010, the population of elder Americans was about 21 percent of the population of "working-age" (18–64) Americans. In 2035, the population of elder Americans will be 38 percent as large as the working-age population.[15]

Demographic trends, along with the long-term trend of medical costs increasing from year to year more rapidly than GDP ("excess cost growth"), have inevitable large fiscal implications, in particular through the claims that older Americans will make on Social Security, Medicare, and other government programs. This demographic trend of a population that is aging much more rapidly than most observers appreciate by itself means that historical levels of government spending on Social Security and healthcare cannot possibly be sufficient over the next couple of decades, as the demographic pig is being digested by the snake of our economy. In the case of Social Security, this follows automatically, because the program's benefits flow primarily (but not exclusively) to elder Americans. In the case of healthcare, the aging of America is highly relevant both because Medicare in particular is aimed at elder Americans and because it is the sad nature of life that older people get sick more often than do young ones. Social Security, however, is the smaller and much more tractable policy issue of the two, as the next section of this chapter explains.

The problem does not disappear by repealing the Affordable Care Act (which in any event was self-funding, so that the repeal would generate no net revenues for other purposes), because the problem is more fundamental: it is an inescapable attribute of the human condition that old people make more claims on healthcare and safety net systems than do young ones. And as developed below and in chapter 11, the demographic trend lies on top of what is (and was before the Affordable Care Act) the most inefficient healthcare delivery system in the world.

Healthcare policy debates can easily spin into abstruse arguments, but there are really only three points to remember:

1. Healthcare spending in America is unimaginably high, and largely uncorrelated with favorable health outcomes. Our excess spending, over and above what our most generous peer countries spend, will soon top *$1 trillion* per year.[16] Because government ultimately pays so much of the national healthcare bill, and because our population is rapidly aging (and therefore almost by definition is consuming more healthcare), healthcare is America's largest fiscal problem.

2. The reasons for our outsized spending are principally our fragmented healthcare delivery systems, the insertion of private firms in monopoly or monopsony positions, and a general failure to implement a coherent theory of healthcare insurance—a theme to which chapter 11 returns. (Monopoly refers to outsized market power wielded by a seller that dominates its market; monopsony is the converse, when the dominant market player is a buyer of the good in question. In either case, market prices can be distorted.)

3. The Affordable Care Act has been a tremendous distraction from the urgent fiscal problems associated with our compulsive healthcare spending behaviors. The ACA does too little, not too much, by way of changing our fragmented healthcare delivery systems. The ACA was, however, self-funding, through new taxes, so the ACA by itself is not an enabler of further fiscal deterioration. (By contrast, the 2005 extension of Medicare to cover prescription drugs, which was wholly unfunded through new tax receipts, did have an adverse effect on our fiscal picture.)

The United States today spends vastly more on healthcare than does any other developed economy in the world, whether measured as a percentage of GDP or as per capita healthcare spending (see Figure 7.3). The numbers are almost beyond comprehension. Applying consistent OECD metrics, in 2011, the United States spent 17.7 percent of GDP on healthcare from public and private sources combined; the next most profligate country, the Netherlands, spent 11.9 percent.[17] *If the United States spent the same percentage of GDP on healthcare as did the Netherlands, our total public and private healthcare spending combined would have been $869 billion lower in 2011.*

Healthcare overspending remains evident even when measured as dollars spent per capita. In 2011, the United States spent $8,508 per capita on healthcare, by far the highest in the world; the next most profligate country, Norway, spent $5,600 per capita.[18] The aggregate excess of our total public and private spending per capita on healthcare over what Norway spends per capita is *by itself* about 6 percent of our GDP. *If the United States were to spend per capita what Norway does on healthcare, our aggregate healthcare spending (public and private) would immediately decline by over $900 billion/year.*

In return for all this profligate spending, we do not buy ourselves extraordinarily happy medical outcomes. It is true that you are more likely to survive breast cancer, a major heart attack, or stroke in the United States than in most other OECD countries, particularly if you have good medical insurance and choose to have your heart attack on the sidewalk in front of a major medical center, in a season other than summer, when the new interns arrive.[19] Where we fail, however, is in consistently

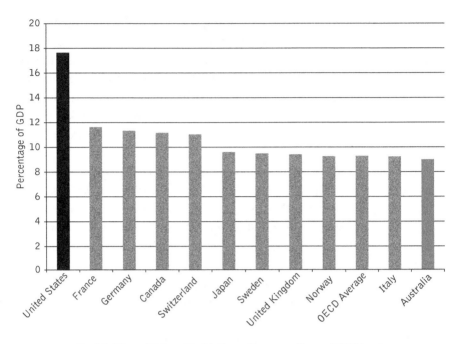

FIGURE 7.3 Total Public and Private Health Expenditure as a Share of GDP (2011)

Source: OECD, *OECD Health Data 2013: How Does the United States Compare* (2013), 1.

delivering good health, as opposed to responding to acute crises, because healthcare in America is so disproportionately costly for many, and so fragmented in its delivery.[20] Chapter 11 reviews further some of the evidence for just how inconsistently we deliver basic medical services, and how as a result Americans die sooner and are sicker than their counterparts in other high-income countries.

Public Healthcare Spending

Ignoring private spending on healthcare, the United States today—before the full implementation of the Affordable Care Act—is second in the world (only to Norway) in *government* spending per capita on healthcare (including all levels of government).[21] In 2010, US federal, state, and local governments combined spent more per capita on healthcare than did the governments of Germany, Denmark, Switzerland, France, or Canada. Our extraordinary profligacy in government spending on healthcare has nothing whatsoever to do with the Affordable Care Act, which had no impact on 2011 healthcare spending (the year covered by the data in Figure 7.4), and which in fact is projected by the CBO to mitigate somewhat the growth rate of government healthcare spending.

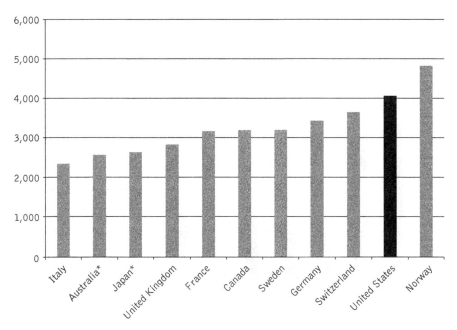

*Australia and Japan Data from 2010

FIGURE 7.4 Public Spending on Healthcare Per Capita in US Dollars (2011)

Source: OECD, *Public Expenditures on Health Per Capita at Current Prices and PPPs.*

In short, the government's long-term *fiscal* health depends directly on grappling much more fundamentally than we have to date with how we provide healthcare services to our citizens.[22] The great failing of "Obamacare" was not that it socialized medicine—this is untrue both as to the operation of the new law and as to how healthcare has been funded in the recent past—but rather that the president failed completely in opening the public's eyes to how inefficient healthcare services are today, and how completely unaffordable they will be for the government to finance tomorrow.

Very recent data suggest that healthcare costs no longer are accelerating from year to year as quickly as was true over the last several decades. Nonetheless, those costs are continuing to grow. De-acceleration in healthcare cost growth by itself will not resolve our fiscal dilemmas unless those costs grow materially more slowly than the economy as a whole for an extended period. The Obama administration's Council of Economic Advisors has argued that the Affordable Care Act and other developments in fact are now pointing us in the direction of just such a sustained period of slow growth in healthcare costs.[23] Another recent analysis, however, concluded that about three-quarters of the slowdown in medical cost increases

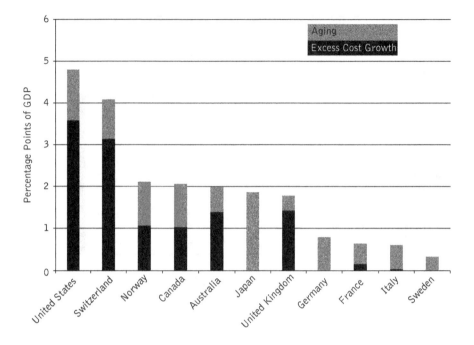

FIGURE 7.5 Projected Increases in Public Health Spending (2013–2030)

Source: IMF, *Fiscal Monitor: Taxing Times* (World Economic and Financial Surveys, October 2013), fig. A.1.3.

was simply a function of the weak economy following the crash of 2008.[24] And many observers feel that the Affordable Care Act's cost-containment measures are helpful but ultimately inadequate without further legislative reforms. For these reasons, it is premature to assume that the overwhelming fiscal problem of healthcare is on a trajectory to heal itself.

In October 2013, the International Monetary Fund projected future governmental healthcare cost growth across many countries. The IMF's conclusion is grim reading for those intent on believing that our future healthcare cost growth path will moderate. Not only does the United States start at the top of the heap in terms of governmental expenditures on healthcare today, but under the IMF's projections our costs will grow more quickly than those of any other country in its survey (see Figure 7.5).

Private Healthcare Spending

What makes the United States truly remarkable is the private spending on healthcare that we pile on top of our public spending. For example, French public healthcare spending as a percentage of its GDP is a little higher than that of the United

States (although we pull well ahead on public per capita spending, because our per capita national income is greater). But France spends only 2.7 percent of its GDP on private healthcare spending, while private spending in the United States is more than three times as much, at 9.1 percent of GDP. The contrast with the United Kingdom is even greater: that country's private healthcare spending is only 1.6 percent of GDP.

Ordinarily, we think of private spending as pure personal consumption decisions. By this standard, a discussion of private healthcare spending seems out of place in a chapter devoted to the size of government. If (by way of an entirely hypothetical example) I were to present data on private spending on automobiles as a percentage of GDP, and the United States were to outstrip its peer countries, you might conclude that cars matter a lot to Americans. Of course, we could speculate as to whether this preference reflected different tastes in how we express social status, or limited investment in public transportation in the United States, or simply the large size of our country. But for the most part (and recognizing the possible trade-off in this example between public transportation and private spending on automobiles), how we spend our money—our bundle of consumption decisions—is usually separable from what government programs do.

Healthcare is different. With the exception of some cosmetic surgery, like LASIK eye surgery, most of us generally believe that we spend what we do on healthcare because we must. We may buy too much healthcare, because we are not sophisticated enough on medical issues to make highly refined decisions on how much is enough, and because none of us is terribly objective about our own mortality, but if asked to explain our decisions, we typically would aver that we had no practical choice in the matter. We end up paying too much because of the price opacity of the healthcare delivery systems, their fragmented design, and because healthcare ultimately is an existential imperative.

We have designed our fragmented healthcare systems in such a manner that even after the full implementation of the Affordable Care Act, most employed Americans under the age of 65 will obtain healthcare largely through private spending (either their own spending, possibly mitigated through government subsidies for exchange-purchased insurance, or, more frequently, their employer's spending). As a result, private healthcare spending is an ersatz sort of tax that we impose on ourselves. For this reason, we can view all of healthcare spending as quasi-public: about half is spent directly by government, at a level roughly commensurate with other peer countries as a percentage of GDP. Then we spend about the same amount all over again through private spending, because the governmental lacunae in healthcare services compel us to tax ourselves.

The same might be said of food or other existentially unavoidable expenses, yet we do not view these as quasi-taxes. The difference is that the food markets are healthy competitive markets; private health insurance markets are not, and as a practical matter can never be. Chapter 11, on government's role as an insurer, elaborates on this theme.

As will be described in more detail in chapter 9, most "private" healthcare spending in the United States in fact is heavily government-subsidized. The subsidy is hidden from view because it is delivered in the form of tax breaks on employer-sponsored health insurance, which is how most Americans obtain health insurance. This hidden subsidy runs at a rate of over $250 billion a year. Individuals who agitate to keep the government out of private healthcare markets should contemplate where they will come up with another $250 billion or so every year, if they were to get their wish.

FIFTY SHADES OF GREY . . . AMERICANS: SOCIAL SECURITY

Social Security is the federal government's largest single spending program, and arguably its most misunderstood one. Those misunderstandings color how we perceive not only Social Security but also other major spending programs.

In 2012 Social Security's cost was $768 billion, far exceeding the total spent on all defense programs combined. It is impossible to overstate the reach and importance of Social Security. Ninety percent of Americans age 65 or over receive Social Security benefits. In 2013, 58 million individuals (including disabled individuals and other eligible recipients under age 65) will receive Social Security benefits. Those benefits constitute 39 percent of the aggregate cash income of all elder Americans. And almost one-quarter of all married Americans age 65 and older, and one-half of unmarried elder individuals (to be blunt, the widows of America), rely on Social Security for 90 percent or more of their cash incomes.[25]

The "full retirement age" for new Social Security beneficiaries (i.e., the age at which one can retire and claim full benefits) today is 66; it is scheduled to rise to age 67 for Americans born after 1959. Workers can retire as early as age 62 (the "early eligibility age") and obtain discounted retirement benefits.

Notwithstanding these impressive figures, the United States' spending on Social Security is at the low end of the OECD's scale. Of course, comparisons here are made more complicated by the existence of a wide range of tax-favored (i.e., government subsidized) private savings plans across different countries, but as the data above suggest, Social Security remains the dominant retirement income security vehicle for millions (see Figure 7.6).

The most interesting aspect of Social Security is figuring out what it really does and who benefits, as in operation it defies any simple categorization.[26] We all have a vague intuition that Social Security is some sort of retirement plan to which we contribute while working, and from which we receive a retirement annuity when we retire, but this is true in only the most approximate sense. Social Security is not an "actuarially fair" retirement plan (that is, the sort of deal one might find

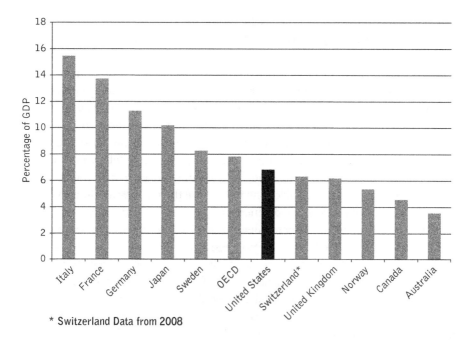

* Switzerland Data from 2008

FIGURE 7.6 Public Spending for Old Age and Survivors' Benefits as a Percentage of GDP (2009)

Source: OECD, *Social Expenditure—Aggregated Data: Public Expenditure on Old-Age and Survivors Cash Benefits, in % GDP* (OECD, July 2013).

offered on commercial terms by an insurance company). Nor are one's contributions dedicated to funding one's retirement. Instead, Social Security combines elements of long-term disability insurance, life insurance (that is, insurance against the risk of dying young), longevity insurance/annuity arrangements (insurance against the risk of dying too old and thereby running out of money), regressive taxation, progressive payout schedules, intergenerational compacts, and outright welfare payments, all intertwined in almost incomprehensible ways.[27]

Less than 70 percent of Social Security benefits go to retirees and their families. The rest goes to disabled workers and their families and to survivors of deceased workers. These latter two categories resemble long-term disability insurance and ordinary life insurance, although the benefits payable are determined by a worker's earnings history, not a contractual fixed amount.

Social Security retirement benefits are quite different from a normal commercial pension plan. Payments into the system are determined by the regressive tax formula described earlier, where all workers (and employers) pay as payroll taxes a fixed percentage of wages up to an annual wage ceiling. Benefits reflect the average of a worker's wages (up to the ceiling) during the worker's 35 highest-income years (indexed to inflation so that earlier years are weighted equivalently to later years) and the worker's age at retirement, but do *not* reflect any investment returns on contributions.

Unlike a commercial funded pension plan, Social Security retirement benefits are largely paid by the next generation of workers. Under the 1983 revisions to Social Security, the memorandum accounts we call the Social Security "trust funds" were designed to run a surplus over the last few decades to help fund the retirement of the baby boomer generation. Even when the trust fund surplus is exhausted (roughly 2039 under current predictions, following the convention of treating the two trust funds as one unified one), today's prediction is that current-year payroll tax collections from those then in the workforce will pay about 80 percent of the scheduled benefits of then-retired workers.[28]

Retired workers receive benefits determined as percentages of their indexed average wages, calculated under a progressive payout scale. What this means is that a retired worker basically receives each year as Social Security benefits 90 percent of her first few thousand dollars of average annual past wages, then 32 percent of the next few thousand dollars of average past wages, and finally 15 percent of her remaining average past wages, up to the wage ceiling. When the dust settles, the maximum payout is in the neighborhood of $25,000/year. In turn, these benefits are increased if the retired worker is married or has dependents. Elaborate rules enable workers to switch midstream from benefits determined under their earnings history to benefits measured by those of a spouse, or to collect survivor's benefits for a long-divorced spouse, and so on.

As a consequence, the core retirement features of Social Security do not constitute a "defined contribution" retirement plan, in which an employee makes specified payments into the plan while working, those payments earn investment returns, and the balance effectively makes actuarially determined annuity payments on retirement. Nor is Social Security a "defined benefit" plan, because the benefits are a function of a worker's wage history over his working career and his particular family situation, and those benefits in turn become less and less actuarially fair the higher his income.

More plausibly, but impoliticly, Social Security is an odd kind of income security program designed to ensure that elder Americans have some minimum financial resources—what most Americans would describe as a "welfare" program. It is a sad commentary on the current state of political discourse that most readers will think my description of Social Security as "welfare" is deprecatory, but the welfare of its citizens is an honorable aspiration for a government. Adam Smith urged us to seek the happiness of society, and perhaps I would cause less unintended offense here were I to describe Social Security as a program designed to afford some minimal level of happiness to elderly or disabled Americans.

Describing Social Security as an honorable exercise in welfare enhancement explains such features as the highly progressive nature of benefits, in which the poorest working Americans receive almost as much in retirement as they earned while working, benefit payments to survivors, and the increase in benefit payments to reflect family size. This explanation also fits with the history of Social Security's original adoption in the middle of the Great Depression, when older Americans often lived in appalling poverty. But this characterization runs smack into Social Security's oddest feature of all, which is that it is not "means-tested." As a result, every former worker receives Social Security benefits, regardless of current need.

Higher-income retirees must pay income tax on a fraction of their Social Security benefits, but the right way to think of this is as a further adjustment to Social Security's progressive benefits schedule, because the income tax liability on the receipt of those benefits simply operates to reduce the net benefits that higher-income retirees retain. As it happens, this characterization is consistent with Social Security intragovernmental cash flows, as the income taxes received by the Treasury are forwarded to the Social Security system as additional revenues from which to pay benefits. In the end, income taxes on benefits account for only 3 percent of the revenues received each year by the Social Security system.

Given how the Social Security system actually operates, why do we treat it as analogous to private retirement plans? The answer lies in the fiscal metaphors through which the program has been presented since its original adoption. Thus we make contributions, rather than pay taxes, and those contributions do not go to the Treasury, but instead to "trust funds" to fund our future benefits. Were it not for this fiscal language, we might more clearly see Social Security as a vitally important income security (welfare) program for the disabled and elderly, and in turn ask whether it really is necessary to pay benefits under this program (and Medicare), but not others, without regard to need. The overall program is referred to as "insurance"; in this case, however, the insurance is not analogous to an annuity contract sold by an insurance company, but rather a more existential insurance against the vicissitudes of life leaving a wage earner in desperate circumstances in her old age. What else explains the rights of long-divorced surviving ex-spouses?

As described briefly earlier, the Social Security trust funds are really just memorandum accounts that keep track of program inflows and outflows.[29] Substantively, the mechanism caps the total benefits payable each year, because benefits can be paid only out of a positive balance in the memorandum accounts (the trust funds). This function could be accomplished in fact by a simple memorandum account. For example, when Congress operated a severe form of spending constraint known as PAYGO, we relied on a PAYGO scorecard, not a separate trust fund, to keep track of whether revenues and spending satisfied the PAYGO legislation's constraints.

More important, the mechanism acts in the popular imagination to reinforce the annuity metaphor and to invest wage earners with a proprietary interest in their contingent future claims to Social Security benefits. But to reiterate a point made earlier, these benefits are not contracts between workers and the government.[30] Congress is free to change the benefits available, or to abrogate Social Security entirely, without incurring any obligation to return wage earners' "contributions." This is another income security (welfare) program in the end.

Reflecting in this manner on the underlying role of Social Security is important for two reasons. First, it helps us to focus on whether the program design best accomplishes its purpose. Second, separating the fiscal metaphor from the actual program reveals a great deal about attitudes toward government. The fiscal metaphor explains why Tea Party enthusiasts could carry placards demanding that government keep its hands off "their" Social Security and Medicare without even a hint of irony. And more perniciously, it explains why it is so easy for many Americans to view the official means-tested income support programs as free handouts for underserving others, while Social Security and Medicare are described as our receiving benefits that we have paid for.

The long-term fiscal challenge for Social Security of course is the surging number of elder Americans, attributable principally to the aging of the baby boomer generation. These are a lot of elderly mouths to feed. As a consequence, over the next two decades Social Security's cost as a share of GDP will rise from around 5 percent to more than 6 percent.

Unlike healthcare, Social Security's fiscal imbalances are not difficult to fix, at least as a technical matter.[31] Today, legislation caps the wages against which Social Security "contributions" (more accurately, taxes) are measured at about $113,000/year. (The number goes up with inflation.) In the not very distant past, 91 percent of all wages were below the then-applicable ceiling; by 2009 that had declined to 83 percent. This is an oddly regressive way of running a program: not only are wages taxed from the first dollar of wages, but the effective rate goes down for those Americans with incomes above the ceiling. Eliminating the ceiling by itself basically balances Social Security for many decades to come, even if doing so were accompanied by permitting high earners to enjoy larger benefits under the current payout formula.[32]

FIFTY SHADES OF GREY ... AMERICANS: MEDICARE

I have already described how healthcare spending constitutes the great fiscal dilemma facing America, and that our outsized spending comprises roughly equal private and public spending components. The federal government spends about $1 trillion/year on the health of Americans. In doing so it subsidizes virtually everyone who has health insurance of any kind, including the majority of

Americans who believe that they have entirely private employer-sponsored health insurance.[33]

The largest single federal healthcare program, and the second largest single item in the federal budget, of course is the Medicare program.[34] This is not surprising, given the fact that most Medicare spending supports the elderly (it also encompasses a smaller program for permanently disabled Americans younger than 65), and that being elderly and being sick, particularly with chronic illnesses, are unavoidable fellow travelers.[35]

Medicare has many problems, but administrative inefficiency is not one of them. To the contrary, the administration of the Medicare program is much less costly than is true of private insurers, and of course Medicare does not seek to earn a profit from its operations. Instead, the issues are much more fundamental. As the CBO noted in 2009:

> Perhaps the most compelling evidence about the extent of inefficiency in the health sector is that Medicare spending varies widely across different regions of the country, but the variation is not correlated with available measures of the quality of care or health outcomes. Researchers affiliated with the Dartmouth *Atlas of Health Care* have compared the Medicare spending for enrollees across the nation, controlling for demographic characteristics such as age, sex, and race. According to those researchers' calculations, Medicare spending could be reduced by almost 30 percent if outlays in medium- and high-spending regions were reduced to the average level in the lowest-spending decile.[36]

Future historians will win Pulitzer Prizes for their explanations of how the United States descended into institutional madness on the subject of the Affordable Care Act, but one overlooked casualty is that for several years now policymakers have abandoned all efforts to rethink in a fundamental way how healthcare services are delivered through Medicare and other programs. (Chapter 11 elaborates on this.) The Congressional Budget Office, which did important analytical work along these lines before 2010, has now wisely abandoned the field, beyond fulfilling its mandated responsibilities to estimate the budgetary consequences of current law or new legislative proposals. All I can do here is to observe that an unconstrained fee-for-services model is no way to run a national healthcare system, that many plausible alternative ideas have been suggested, and that a few are being implemented in tentative ways through the Affordable Care Act.[37]

The trust fund metaphor is even more frayed when applied to Medicare than it is when invoked to explain Social Security. Like Social Security, Medicare is not means-tested. But unlike Social Security, general tax receipts in fact are used to fund 43 percent of Medicare's total operating revenues. Medicare payroll taxes—the contributions that go into the Medicare "trust fund"—finance only about 36 percent, and premium contributions another 13 percent. This means that today the income taxes of the young go directly to pay the Medicare benefits of the elderly. (Chapter 12 expands on this by demonstrating that, when all government taxes and spending are considered, the elderly are heavily subsidized today.) Technically, the allocation of these streams to Medicare's major subdivisions varies, so that Part A (hospital coverage) is presented as largely funded by the payroll taxes, while Parts B (Supplementary Medical Insurance) and D (outpatient prescription drugs) are paid predominantly from general tax revenues, but this allocation again is more rhetorical than substantive. If the government were in fact to keep its hands off your Medicare, the system would collapse overnight.

C. Eugene Steuerle of the Urban Institute regularly analyzes the lifetime costs and benefits of Social Security and Medicare.[38] Because the relevant payroll taxes paid before age 65 and benefits enjoyed thereafter by design are only loosely correlated, the analysis varies with incomes and family situations. Steuerle therefore presents a number of hypothetical cases, but in general they demonstrate that many individuals take out more from Social Security, and most take out much more in Medicare benefits, than they contribute in payroll taxes and Medicare premiums.

Steuerle's summary tables include both the employer's and the employee's share of payroll taxes (for the reasons explained in the next chapter). Steuerle further discounts taxes paid and future expected benefits to the year the couple in question turns 65 (so that lifetime benefits and taxes can be directly compared), and treats Medicare premiums as reductions in Medicare benefits.

Steuerle's research shows that a one-earner couple earning the average wage is heavily subsidized by other taxpayers (see Table 7.1).

A two-earner couple where one earns a higher than average wage, and the other an average wage, does not on balance profit so handsomely, but still comes out far ahead on Medicare, which more than compensates for its negative return on Social Security contributions (see Table 7.2).

The positive returns reaped by the hypothetical families in these examples did not (or will not, as the case may be) materialize from thin air, but rather constitute subsidies that have been or will be paid by younger cohorts—each retiring generation's children, in effect. This is particularly true of Medicare, even today. It was true for Social Security a generation ago, but, as Steuerle notes, "The most recent waves of retirees getting Social Security can make a stronger case that they have paid for their benefits. The complication is that their Social Security taxes mainly supported their parents in retirement, and the only way they can do as well in a money-in-money-out (at times partially funded) system is to foist higher tax rates on their children."[39]

Finally, I have made the point before, but it is so important that it bears repeating: the Affordable Care Act made the *fiscal* picture for healthcare spending somewhat better, not worse. The Congressional Budget Office originally projected that

Table 7.1 One-Earner Couple Earning the Average Wage
($44,600 in 2012 Dollars)

Year cohort turns 65	Annual Social Security benefits	Lifetime Social Security benefits	Lifetime Medicare benefits	**Total lifetime benefits**	Lifetime Social Security taxes	Lifetime Medicare taxes	**Total lifetime taxes**
1960	14,200	214,000	41,000	**255,000**	18,000	0	**18,000**
1980	23,100	377,000	151,000	**528,000**	98,000	9,000	**107,000**
2010	26,900	467,000	387,000	**854,000**	300,000	61,000	**361,000**
2020	28,400	508,000	499,001)	**1,007,000**	350,000	77,000	**427,000**
2030	30,800	564,000	664,000	**1,228,000**	404,000	90,000	**494,000**

Table 7.2 Two Earner Couple: High Wages/Average Wage ($71,400/$44,600 in
2012 Dollars)

Year cohort turns 65	Annual Social Security benefits	Lifetime Social Security benefits	Lifetime Medicare benefits	**Total lifetime benefits**	Lifetime Social Security taxes	Lifetime Medicare taxes	**Total lifetime taxes**
1960	20,000	278,000	41,000	**319,000**	42,000	0	**42,000**
1980	35,000	534,000	151,000	**685,000**	230,000	21,000	**251,000**
2010	45,000	693,000	387,000	**1,080,000**	765,000	156,000	**921,000**
2020	48,000	756,000	499,000	**1,255,000**	909,000	199,000	**1,108,1100**
2030	55,000	840,000	664,000	**1,504,000**	1,050,000	234,000	**1,284,000**

the Affordable Care Act in its entirety would reduce, not increase, the budget deficit, and in 2012 reaffirmed that conclusion, by advising House Speaker Boehner
that repealing the Affordable Care Act would raise the federal deficit by over $100
billion over the next 10 years.[40] Opponents of the Affordable Care Act point out that
it will increase federal spending (how else would the act increase the number of
Americans with health insurance by some 25 million?[41]), but neglect to acknowledge that the legislation paired the additional spending with new taxes more than
sufficient to cover those costs. The Affordable Care Act also made Medicare's Part
A (the hospital insurance part) somewhat more fiscally sustainable.[42] The fiscal
challenges posed by healthcare remain very grave, but the Affordable Care Act
was a small step in the right fiscal direction.

MEANS-TESTED INCOME SUPPORT PROGRAMS

The federal government operates 10 major "means-tested" income support programs designed to help low-income households. The largest of these programs
is Medicaid; the Supplemental Nutrition Assistance Program (SNAP, formerly
food stamps) is the second largest, but is one-third the size of Medicaid (see
Figure 7.7).[43]

The Congressional Budget Office's standard presentation of data (as in
Figure 7.7) understates the size of the earned income tax credit and the child tax
credit, because the standard presentation counts only the "refundable" portion
of those credits—that is, the portion paid in cash rather than the portion used to
reduce an individual's tax liabilities. The latter portion is treated as a reduction
in tax revenues for governmental accounting purposes. The portion of the total
earned income tax credit used to reduce tax liabilities is only about 10 percent of
the total value of that credit, but the child credit basically doubles in value once its
tax-reduction component is included.[44]

The existence of 10 programs costing hundreds of billions of dollars annually
sounds very generous, but as observed earlier, the United States in fact spends
much less to support low-income households than do its peer countries. For
example, Figure 7.8 relies on OECD data to summarize public spending intended
specifically to support families (not including health, housing, or employment

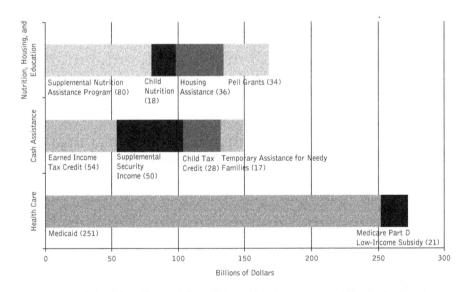

FIGURE 7.7 Federal Spending on Selected Means-Tested Programs and Tax Credits (2012)

Source: CBO, *Growth in Means-Tested Programs and Tax Credits for Low-Income Households* (February 2013), fig. 2.

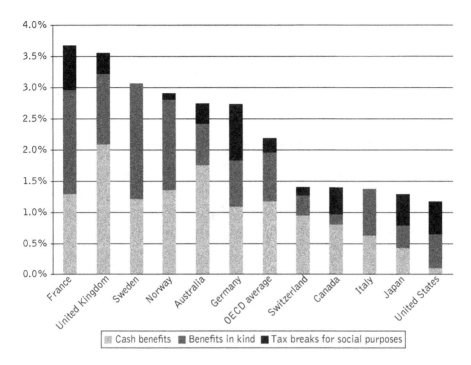

FIGURE 7.8 Total Public Spending on Family Benefits as a Percentage of GDP (2007)

Source: OECD, *Social Expenditure—Aggregated Data: Public Expenditure on Family by Type of Expenditure, in % GDP* (OECD, July 2013).

support). Because countries deliver these services through different mechanisms, this chart includes cash payments, in-kind benefits (for example, direct provision of child care), and subsidies delivered through the tax system. (Unfortunately, the OECD does not regularly collect data on all three delivery mechanisms for every kind of expenditure, but obviously in-kind benefits are more relevant for family support than they are for military expenditures.) The United States finishes dead last among the peer countries considered in this book.

Figure 7.9 looks at all explicit cash public spending for all forms of social services, other than health and old age benefits, at all levels of government. Again, the United States finishes at the bottom.

In 2012, federal government expenditures for all 10 means-tested programs (including Medicaid) totaled less than half of government spending on the elderly through Medicare and Social Security. Moreover, as pointed out earlier, Congressional Budget Office projections contemplate that federal government outlays for income security programs will decline as a percentage of

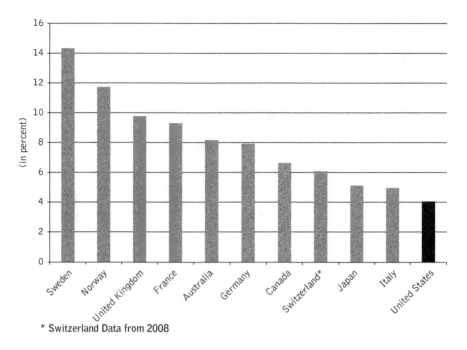

* Switzerland Data from 2008

FIGURE 7.9 Total Public Social Spending as a Percentage of GDP, Excluding Social Security and Healthcare (2009)

Source: OECD, *Social Expenditure Database* (OECD, 2013) and OECD, "Social Expenditure," in *OECD Factbook 2013: Economic, Environmental and Social Statistics* (OECD Publishing, 2013).

GDP from 2.0 percent in 2014 to 1.3 percent by 2023.[45] In brief, the United States is and will remain a parsimonious provider of assistance to low-income households.

Notwithstanding these data, many observers are obsessed with our means-tested programs. The programs are described as rife with waste, fraud, and abuse; or as "unearned" benefits, in contrast to Medicare or Social Security; or as subsidizing individuals not to work. All of these criticisms are overstated or wrong.

Some people do defraud or abuse the means-tested programs. It also is possible to find examples—infinitely larger examples, as it happens—of waste, fraud, and abuse in the private sector. Bernie Madoff defrauded investors of $65 billion, nearly as much as an entire year's budget for the SNAP program. All programs need proper administration, but if we shut down all activities in which waste, fraud, or abuse were ever discovered, there would be little left for any of us to do to occupy ourselves.

Means-tested programs are "unearned," in the sense that recipients receive more in benefits than they may have paid in federal income tax, but the same is true of Medicare. Most Medicare recipients today receive benefits far exceeding the payroll taxes they paid in the past, or the negligible income taxes and Medicare premiums they pay today. Our fiscal rhetoric gives Medicare recipients a free pass from the opprobrium of being "takers" or "moochers," because we allow ourselves to believe that our "contributions" have somehow fully purchased our benefits, but this is factually untrue. And as chapter 8 shows, everyone pays taxes. The federal income tax is just one of a large suite of taxes; by design, the income tax comes into effect relatively late in the income hierarchy, but other taxes, like payroll or excise taxes, apply from the first dollar of earnings or consumption.

More forcefully, the means-tested programs largely support children, the elderly, and disabled individuals. Three out of four households receiving SNAP benefits had a member in one of those categories. The remainder for the most part are just extraordinarily poor; the average income of households receiving SNAP benefits in 2010, for example, was $9,000.[46]

Similarly, one-half of Medicaid enrollees are children. Another one-quarter of the enrollees are parents of those children or pregnant women. And the final one-quarter are elderly or disabled.[47] The means-tested programs are not the refuges of millions of able-bodied loafs.

I considered in chapter 2 some of the arguments to the effect that unemployment benefits or the SNAP program encouraged people not to seek employment. Again, the SNAP program, by way of example, pays recipients between $4 and $5 a person a day to supplement their food budgets; the allowance is provided through a credit card type mechanism that ensures that the money is spent in fact on qualifying food. The Department of Agriculture's Thrifty Food Plan, from which SNAP benefits are calculated, contemplated in July 2013 that a young family of four could feed itself adequately on $18.24/day.[48] That plan allows men ages 19–50 to feast over the course of a week on 2½ pounds of potatoes, about 3 pounds of all meat and poultry products, and two eggs, along with various grains, dried beans, and the like.[49] It is profoundly distasteful to imagine distinguished professors of economics spending a day's SNAP benefits or more on a cup of latte at their local espresso bar, all the while declaiming why the poor will never look for work once given such princely benefits.

It is true that SNAP benefits were expanded as part of the 2009 emergency legislation designed to ameliorate the worst harms of the depths of the Great Recession, but those modest expansions expired in the fall of 2013, with serious repercussions for the food security of poor Americans. And in point of fact SNAP participation increased by 40 percent between 2002 and 2007, before the onset of the Great Recession.[50] Of course it is true that SNAP costs (and beneficiaries) increased another 60 percent during the Great Recession, as did unemployment benefits, but in each case they did so for the same reason: millions of Americans lost their jobs, and as a result also lost their sources of income from which to buy basic necessities. The countercyclical costs will diminish as the economy continues to recover.

Medicaid is largely paid for by the federal government, but operates as a federal-state partnership, and each state therefore can set its own eligibility levels for access to Medicaid. Those rules are complicated, but as a rule of thumb, unemployed healthy adults without children can obtain Medicaid benefits in only a handful of states. Pre-Affordable Care Act federal law applicable to years before 2014 required that children up to age 6 be covered if their family income was below 133 percent of the federal poverty guidelines, or 100 percent of federal poverty levels for older children. (For a family of four, the federal poverty guideline was $23,550 in 2013.) Parents of dependent children are largely in the hands of state legislators. In Connecticut, parents are covered up to an income of almost double the federal poverty levels, while in Missouri, Medicaid benefits are available only if family income is below 35 percent of the federal poverty level, for working adults, or 18 percent, for jobless ones.

Federal Medicaid costs are very high, and projected to climb. Taking current program costs first, 30 percent of Medicaid spending goes for long-term care; Medicaid in fact pays for 40 percent of the nation's total nursing home costs.[51] Because of program design constraints, Medicaid today has a bias in favor of institutionalized long-term care. The Affordable Care Act fixes this, and encourages greater use of home care where feasible, but for reasons inconsistent with reducing government spending, political operatives have mischaracterized this feature in order to fan the flames of Obamacare anxiety.[52] Medicaid also has been the victim of gaming by many states, which have redesigned their own health programs in ways that enable them to shift a large portion of costs formerly borne by them onto the Medicaid program.[53] And of course Medicaid, like all other health insurers in the United States, has confronted rapidly rising per capita healthcare charges.

Looking forward, Medicaid costs will climb as the Affordable Care Act is implemented, because Medicaid is the vehicle by which 12 million low-income Americans who nonetheless are above the Medicaid income ceiling will obtain medical insurance in the future. But this cost was fully paid for when the Affordable Care Act was enacted, through companion tax increases.

The Affordable Care Act as originally enacted was designed to expand Medicaid to serve as the health insurance vehicle for all families with incomes at or below 138 percent of federal poverty levels who do not obtain health insurance through their employers. By virtue of the Supreme Court's 2012 decision in *National Federation of Independent Business v. Sebelius*, however, that expansion has become optional, with each state entitled to decide whether to accept the additional coverage for its lower-income residents.

As of late 2013, about half of the states are on a path to expand Medicaid coverage, and half either are not or have not resolved their plans. For those states that do go forward, the federal government will pay 100 percent of the incremental costs incurred for the first three years, and 90 percent thereafter. Most of the states that have determined not to move forward with expanded Medicaid had very low Medicaid eligibility cutoffs for pre-2014 years. In the South, 85 percent of all non-elderly individuals with incomes at or below 138 percent of federal poverty levels who do not today have health insurance will be precluded from obtaining Medicaid, because they live in states that have elected not to expand their programs.[54] Those with incomes at least equal to the federal poverty level will be eligible to receive subsidies to buy insurance in the new health exchanges, but those below that level yet above state cutoffs for Medicaid eligibility will remain wholly without insurance.

Rational arguments to justify a state's decision to behave so spitefully to its own residents do not leap to mind. Exquisite sensitivity toward federal budget costs seems a quite improbable explanation, and the federal sharing ratio means that the costs to states in many cases will be less than the ongoing costs to them of providing minimal services to uninsured patients. It is difficult to overcome the supposition that race might have something to do with this, given that nearly 60 percent of non-elderly uninsured African Americans with incomes at or below 138 percent of federal poverty levels live in states that have chosen not to move forward.[55]

CHAPTER 8

ARE HIGH TAXES KILLING US?

Every new tax is immediately felt more or less by the people. It occasions
always some murmur, and meets with some opposition.
—ADAM SMITH, *The Wealth of Nations*, Book V, Chap. III.

THE UNITED STATES IS A LOW-TAX PARADISE

Chapter 6 has briefly described our troubling medium- and long-term deficit trends. A deficit in any year simply means that the government has spent more than it collected in taxes in that year. In turn, if deficits are at troubling levels, we can theoretically approach the problem from either of two directions: cutting outflows or increasing inflows. But as chapter 7 just demonstrated, the problem does not lie with overall spending levels.

The great programmatic spending exception is healthcare, where the Affordable Care Act rests on a fundamentally unaffordable foundation of profligate but not very effective government-subsidized spending. Change in this last area will be challenging, and in such situations it is important that we rely on long transition periods to move from where we are to where we need to be without unfairly upsetting settled expectations and modes of healthcare delivery systems. In the meantime, the resulting costs must be financed.

And like it or not, that brings us to tax revenues. Overall government spending is low by the standards of our peer countries, and too low in many important areas, yet the federal government is running deficits that are not sustainable over the next decade or more. The only policy lever that remains is the revenue side of things—which is to say, taxation.

Fortunately, we begin with such a low level of tax collections in the United States that it is feasible to raise tax collections over the next several years without unduly disrupting the US economy. The United States is an extraordinarily low-tax country by world norms, and in recent years the "automatic stabilization" properties of the income tax (discussed in chapter 6) have mitigated even those modest levels of tax burdens.[1]

Here OECD comparative data (which combine all national and sub-national taxes) are again extremely helpful. *Those data show that for 2012, the United States had the lowest total tax collections at all government levels combined as a percentage of GDP of any country in the OECD.*[2] Yet at the same time, we finance a military as big as that of the next 14 countries combined, and the most expensive and inefficient healthcare system in the world. Why are we then surprised that we are running budget deficits?

Of course, the United States raised its tax rates on the highest-income Americans in 2013, and additional taxes to finance the Affordable Care Act take effect in 2014. But even taking these new taxes into account, the OECD projects that the United States will remain a low-tax environment in 2014 and beyond (see Figure 8.1).

To emphasize, these charts include *all* levels of government taxation—federal, state, and local. What is more, they include all payroll taxes and other similar

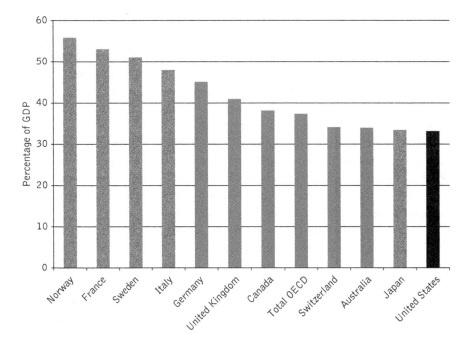

FIGURE 8.1 Projected National and Sub-national Tax Revenues as a Percentage of GDP (2014)

Source: OECD, *Economic Outlook Annex Tables*, Table 26.

mandatory "contributions." And as implied by chapter 6, the difference between the unsustainable path on which we have embarked, and one that is fiscally prudent, basically comes down to whether federal tax revenues should be 19 or 21 percent of GDP over the next decade or so. That is the entirety of the bid-ask spread, to use Wall Street jargon, that has paralyzed all political discourse in the country for the last several years. But as the charts show, were we to raise federal tax revenues by 2 percentage points of GDP, we still would be at the low end of all our peer countries in the tax burdens we place on ourselves.

Imagine that I were to offer you the opportunity to live in the United States, but to enjoy the same tax burdens as those imposed on the happy burghers of Switzerland, that famously well-run low-tax paradise. I could in 2012 have *increased* federal tax collections by the 2 percentage points of GDP we need to address our medium-term deficit issues, and still kept my side of that bargain, with change left over. In 2014 the Swiss would come out ahead, but only by about one percent of GDP, notwithstanding all the imagined fiscal horrors of implementing the Affordable Care Act. We are taxed about as lightly as the Swiss, but believe that we carry burdens as heavy as do the French.

Another way of getting a sense of our modest current tax burdens is to look at the "tax wedge" on labor—the difference between the costs to an employer of hiring an employee (including the employer's share of payroll taxes, like Social Security contributions) and what an employee takes home as after-tax wages (net of any cash benefit payments from the government).[3] Here again, OECD data demonstrate that the United States is at the low end of developed country norms. Figure 8.2 looks at a couple with two children, where one spouse earns the national average wage. It records the percentage of gross wages paid by an employer (including the employer's share of payroll taxes) that is taken by government, and therefore does not reach an employee's pocket.

The tax wedge varies across countries according to family composition, number of wage earners in the family, and family incomes. Figure 8.3 shows the same sort of tax wedge calculations for a higher income family, where one spouse earns 100 percent of the average wage, and the other 67 percent. The total tax wedge of course increases, but the United States remains a low-wedge country.

The other side of the tax wedge is the "all-in" tax rate imposed on workers. Here the OECD data again show the United States as a low-tax environment. As in 8.2, Figure 8.4 shows the tax rates imposed on a one-earner couple with two children, where one spouse earns the national average wage. The tax rates include both the income tax and the employee's share of payroll/retirement taxes; as described later in this chapter, a more complete picture might include the employer's share as well, but this issue cuts across the countries considered. The chart nets cash tax refunds or other transfer payments against taxes paid, to get a more complete picture of the net burden to this hypothetical couple.

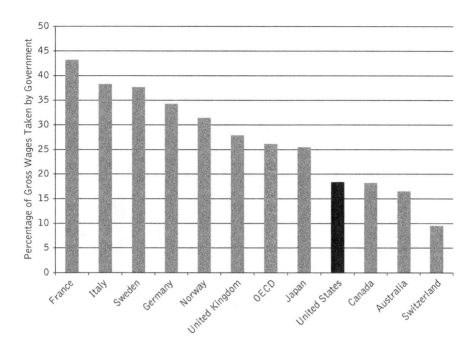

FIGURE 8.2 Tax Wedge for One-Earner Married Couple with Two Children and Earnings at the Average Wage Level (2012)

Source: OECD, *Economic Outlook* (2012).

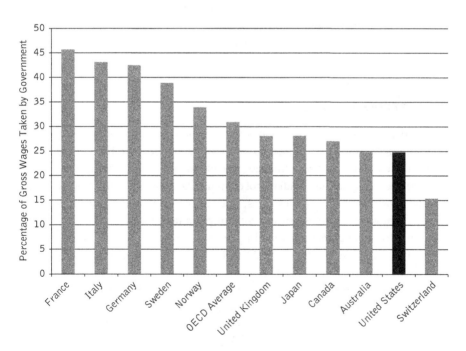

FIGURE 8.3 Tax Wedge for Two Earner Married Couple with Two Children (100% + 67% of Average Wage) (2012)

Source: OECD, *Taxing Wages 2013* (Paris: OECD Publishing, 2013).

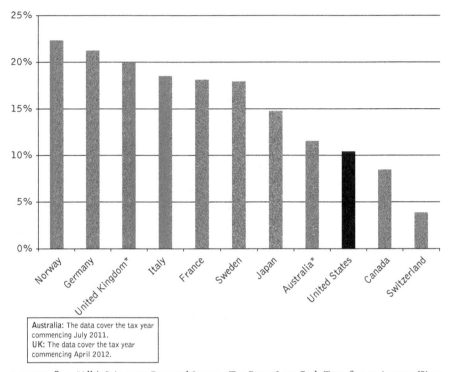

FIGURE 8.4 "All-in" Average Personal Income Tax Rates Less Cash Transfers at Average Wage for a One-Earner Married Couple with Two Children (2012)

Source: OECD, *OECD Tax Database* (accessed August 2013), Table 1.6.

COMPOSITION OF TAXES

The relatively low combined income/payroll tax burdens imposed on US workers relative to peer countries are particularly remarkable because the United States stands alone among its peers (indeed, in comparison with virtually every other developed economy in the world) in not coupling its income tax with a broad-based national consumption tax. (Sales taxes, value added taxes, and excise taxes are all just different ways of implementing consumption taxes; their differences are relevant only for tedious technical tax implementation debates. From an economic perspective, they are identical.) In 2010, US national and sub-national governments combined collected less than 4 percent of our GDP in all varieties of consumption taxes, well below that of our peer countries (see Figure 8.5).[4]

By looking at how different countries collect their taxes at all levels of government in relation to their total tax collections, it becomes apparent that the United States is an outlier in three respects. Table 8.1 demonstrates that, to collect our

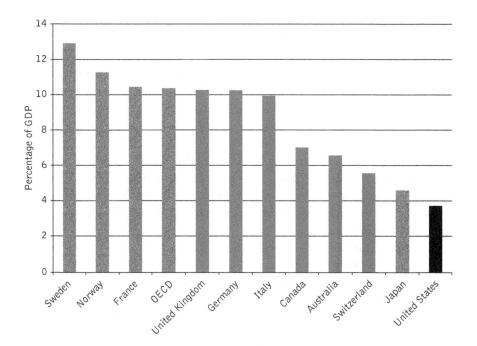

FIGURE 8.5 Consumption Taxes as a Percentage of GDP (2010)

Source: OECD, *Revenue Statistics: Tax Ratios Changes Between 2007 and Provisional 2011 Data*, Table 25.

Table 8.1 Tax Revenue of Major Categories of Tax as a Percentage of Total Taxation (2010)

	Income and Profits	Social Security and Payroll	Property	Goods and Services	Other
Australia	57.1	5.2	9.2	28.4	0.4
Norway	47.0	22.5	2.9	27,6	0,4
Canada	46.8	17.4	11.5	24.3	0.0
Switzerland	462	23.8	7.4	22.6	0.0
United States	42.6	25.7	12.8	18.0	0.0
United Kingdom	37.5	19.0	12.1	30,8	0,4
Sweden	35.6	32.1	2.4	29.4	0.1
OECD	33.2	27.4	5.4	33,1	0,6
Italy	12.0	21.1	4.8	25.9	4. 8
Japan	30.2	41.1	9.7	183	0.3
Germany	28.7	39.0	2.3	295	0.0
France	21.9	42.0	8.5	25.0	2.4

Source: OECD, *Revenue Statistics*, Table 6.

total tax intake at all levels of government, we rely more heavily on income taxes than do most (but not all) of our peers; we rely much more heavily on property taxes than do most of the others; and we are at the bottom of the list in our reliance on consumption taxes. The data are presented as percentages of total tax collections, not GDP, because its purpose is to compare our mix of tax instruments with those of other countries. This means, however, that identical percentages in the table from one country to another do not translate into identical dollar values or percentages of GDP.

Our reliance on property taxes reflects how localities in the United States fund schools, police, and basic services. One consequence of this is greatly different spending on public education across localities with different levels of affluence.[5] Chapters 3 and 10 expand on the implications of this for the varying quality of public education in America.

The relative unimportance of consumption taxes in the United States is highly relevant when thinking about the share of our total tax burdens imposed on workers, because as an economic matter, to a first order of approximation, consumption taxes of all species are just more income taxes on wages.[6] It is not obvious at first glance that a sales tax, a payroll tax, and an income tax on wages are economic equivalents, but the underlying logic is straightforward.

The basic insight is that money ultimately is only good for buying things. For a worker who spends all of her wages, it obviously does not matter in an economic sense whether she suffers payroll or income taxes on her wages, and then spends her after-tax dollars without further tax, or alternatively receives her wages income tax-free, but then faces sales taxes on every good or service that she purchases, so long as the tax rates are equal. And for a worker who saves some of her income, the results economically also are identical, because the hypothetical income tax described here applies only to labor income.

In the labor income tax case, the worker will pay taxes up front, but then her savings will grow tax-free. In the sales tax–only case, the worker has more savings to start with, but then her sales-tax liability will grow at the same rate as her savings do; conceptually, she is in the same position as if she set aside in a separate savings account in the first year sufficient cash to pay her sales tax, and then used that set-aside to pay her future tax bills.

This economic equivalence of different-sounding taxes was the heart of the fiscal hocus-pocus underlying 2012 presidential candidate Herman Cain's "9-9-9" campaign plan. That plan proposed what seemed to be three small taxes on different things, but their economic effect was to impose one much higher combined tax rate on the wage incomes of average working Americans than is true under current law.[7]

As an example of what this means in practice, imagine that you want to compare the total tax burdens imposed on an average worker in the United States with one in the United Kingdom. You would start with the "all-in" income and payroll tax burdens on their wages, but then you would need to continue, by accounting for the much higher consumption taxes that the UK worker faces when he goes to put his post-income tax wages to use by buying things. For this reason, the low tax wedge faced by the American worker compared to his counterpart in the peer countries considered here becomes even lower in its full context, once the American's lighter consumption tax burden is included.

EVERYONE PAYS TAXES

Harvey Golub, the former chief executive of American Express, and a man whose self-interested opinions on fiscal policy were described in chapter 3, echoed market triumphalists everywhere when he wrote in a 2011 *Wall Street Journal* opinion piece that about half of all income tax filers "pay no income taxes at all." From this Golub argued that nonpayers "should [be required to] pay something and have a stake in our government...too."[8] Mitt Romney made similar claims in the midst of the 2012 presidential election campaign when he famously assailed "the 47 percent" who pay no income taxes, and who "are dependent upon government, who believe that they are victims, who believe that government has a responsibility to care for them, who believe that they are entitled to health care, to food, to housing, to you name it. That that's an entitlement. And the government should give it to them."[9]

The trope that half of Americans have no "skin in the game," to use another popular phrasing of the argument, is meant to imply that these individuals have not fully earned their citizenship, because they have no "stake in our government." This is simultaneously a stunted understanding of citizenship and a factually incorrect claim about tax burdens. We do not restrict citizenship to property owners, or income earners. Poll taxes, one explicit purpose of which was to keep those with no skin in the game from participating in the core privilege of citizenship, which is the right to vote, were declared unconstitutional at the federal level through the 24th Amendment in 1964, and at the sub-national level through a 1966 Supreme Court decision.[10] When Golub argues that a citizen must pay tax to have a stake in our government, he is just trying to recreate poll taxes in another guise, and for all the same tired reasons—that without such constraints the rootless have-nots will seize power and plunder the deserving haves. But the United States is not modeled on the *Serenissima Repubblica di Venezia* in the seventeenth century, and in this country citizenship is not tied to those who can demonstrate that they are people of economic substance.

The argument that half of Americans have no "skin in the game" thus stands on shaky historical and moral grounds. But at the risk of honoring the argument too much by debating it on its own terms, it also is simply false as a factual matter.

The income tax is simply one of a suite of federal taxes imposed on rich and poor in different proportions and collected through different mechanisms.[11] In 2013, the CBO projected that the Treasury in 2014 would collect about $3 trillion in tax revenues. That amount breaks down approximately as follows:

Personal income taxes: $1.4 trillion
Social insurance taxes: $1.0 trillion
Corporate income taxes: $0.4 trillion
Other (including excise): $0.3 trillion.

Each tax has its own rate schedule, persons subject to it, and point in the economic stream of value creation where it is collected. To focus on the personal income tax alone as the badge of true citizenship is to miss the majority of federal tax impositions.

Both the Congress's staff of the Joint Committee on Taxation and the Congressional Budget Office have looked at this question. Their nonpartisan research demonstrates that, once one includes *all* the federal taxes to which individuals are subject, everyone has skin in the game.

In 2010 the JCT staff found that every stratum of society—even those making less than $10,000/year—bore federal taxes in that year.[12] The CBO came to the same conclusion in respect of 2009 (and earlier years).[13]

More recently, the JCT staff updated its research for the tax rates applicable in 2013. The JCT staff's work here (following their modeling of distributional issues generally) calculated Americans' average tax rates in 2013 as a percentage of their "expanded incomes."[14] This is a term of art employed by the JCT staff: it starts with adjusted gross income as defined in the tax code, and then adds tax-exempt bond interest, untaxed Social Security benefits, untaxed income-support governmental benefits, the employer's share of payroll taxes paid on behalf of the employee, and some smaller items.[15] The result is a very broad measure of income, which in turn drives down the effective (average) tax rates that the JCT staff reports, when compared to narrower measures. The taxes that the JCT staff took into account included, in addition to the personal income tax, both the employee's and the employer's share of payroll taxes, all excise taxes, and the corporate income tax; I explain the reasoning behind including these items in the next section's discussion of tax "incidence."

The JCT staff's 2013 "baseline" distribution of incomes and tax burdens again showed that Americans at every income level pay federal taxes (see Table 8.2).

When one includes state and local taxes, many of which are notoriously regressive, the effective tax rates actually imposed on the poor are surprisingly high. The federal nonpartisan institutions do not collect this data, but Citizens for Tax

Table 8.2 JCT Baseline Distribution of Income and Federal Taxes (2013)

Baseline Distribution of Income and Taxes (2013)			
	Number of Returns (thousands)	Expanded Income ($ millions)	Tax Liability ($ millions)	Average Tax Rate
0 to 10,000	18,506	80,476	6,513	8.1
10,000 to 20,000	18,328	277,369	7,879	2.8
20,000 to 30,000	20,427	503,472	34,666	6.9
30,000 to 40,000	15,853	554,348	56,225	10.1
40,000 to 50,000	14,654	657,243	82,227	12.5
50,000 to 75,000	24,357	1,503,844	213,051	14.2
75,000 to 100,000	16,860	1,459,798	237,769	16.3
100,000 to 200,000	24,334	3,303,188	682,788	20.7
200,000 to 500,000	6,094	1,708,978	439,925	25.7
500,000 to 1,000,000	743	497,484	148,679	29.9
Over 1,000,000	362	1,173,450	375,042	32.0
Total	160,518	11,719,650	2,284,763	19.5

Source: JCT Staff, Modeling the Distribution of Taxes on Business Income, Table 9.

Justice calculated that in 2013 those in the lowest income quintile of cash incomes (with an average cash income of just $13,500) would pay 18.8 percent of their cash income in taxes to one tax authority or another. These very low-income Americans pay roughly twice as much in state and local taxes as they do in federal taxes.

According to the Citizens for Tax Justice analysis, Americans in the middle quintile of cash incomes face an effective tax rate on their cash incomes of 27 percent. The top one percent, with an average income of $1,462,000, pay at an all-in rate of 33 percent. It is remarkable that the top 60 percent of Americans pay total taxes as a percentage of their cash incomes at rates that vary by only about 6 percentage points, once *all* taxes are considered (see Table 8.3).

You also can see in the second column from the right in Table 8.3 the steep regressivity of state and local tax burdens—that is, the poor pay an even greater percentage of their incomes in these taxes than do the affluent. The lowest quintile of income earners incur an effective state and local tax burden of 12.4 percent of their incomes, while the top one percent pays an effective state and local tax rate of only 8.7 percent.[16]

Understanding, then, that the question itself is fundamentally unfair, who are the "47 percent" who pay no federal *income* taxes? In 2011 the Tax Policy Center, a

Table 8.3 Incomes and Federal, State, and Local Taxes (2013)

	Shares of			Taxes as a Percentage of Income		
	Average Cash Income	Total Income	Total Taxes	Federal Taxes	State and Local Taxes	Total Taxes
Lowest 20%	$ 13,500	3.3%	2.1%	6.4%	12.4%	18.8%
Second 20%	27,200	6.9%	5.1%	10.9%	11.6%	22.5%
Middle 20%	43,600	11.2%	9.9%	15.4%	11.2%	26.6%
Fourth 20%	71,600	18.4%	18.2%	18.8%	11.0%	29.8%
Next 10%	109,000	14.0%	14.6%	20.4%	11.0%	31.4%
Next 5%	154,000	10.1%	10.7%	21.4%	10.6%	32.0%
Next 4%	268,000	14.3%	15.3%	22.0%	10.2%	32.2%
Top 1%	1,462,000	21.9%	24.0%	24.3%	8.7%	33.0%
All	$ 75,100	100.0%	100.0%	19.7%	10.5%	30.1%
Addendum: Bottom 99%	$ 61,100	78.2%	75.9%	18.3%	11.0%	29.2%

Source: Citizens for Tax Justice, *Who Pays Taxes in America in 2013?* (April 2, 2013).

nonpartisan and research center in Washington whose work is highly regarded, undertook a detailed analysis of this question.[17]

Within the population of those individuals who pay no federal income taxes (that is, the "47 percent" derided by Mitt Romney), about 60 percent are workers who pay federal payroll taxes.[18] As chapter 6 explained, payroll taxes are not the economic or moral equivalent of putting one's own money aside to fund one's retirement or health benefits. That fiscal metaphor may have made payroll taxes more politically palatable, but the metaphor in turn allows for the systematic misimpression that payroll taxes somehow do not count when totaling up the tax burdens imposed on lower-income Americans. They are in fact taxes like any other, and do not by themselves purchase, or even cover the cost of, retirement benefits for lower-income Americans.

Some of these workers get cash income tax refunds attributable to the refundable earned income tax credit and child credit. These credits are described in a bit more detail in chapters 4 and 11, but basically they are critical components of the long-term reorientation of income-support programs in the United States from old-fashioned "welfare" to "making work pay" programs, in which the government subsidizes low-income workers to make the returns to working more attractive. In this regard, it sometimes is imagined that large numbers get earned income tax credit refunds that wipe out their payroll tax burdens, but such calculations typically ignore the one-half of the payroll taxes nominally paid by employers (a tax that in economic substance actually is borne by workers, as described below). These assertions further often are artifacts of the Great Recession, when "making work pay" credits were temporarily expanded.

More fairly, in 2007, immediately before the Great Recession, almost four-fifths of working Americans had a net federal tax liability, looking only at income and payroll taxes, even after taking any refundable tax credits into account.[19] If it would make Messrs. Golub and Romney happy, we could follow the example of other countries and require the working poor to pay income tax, but then mail them checks to supplement their incomes, but that simply does in two steps what our tax code today does in one.

Of the remaining 40 percent of those individuals who pay no federal income taxes (that is, 40 percent of the 47 percent), about half are elderly Americans living primarily on Social Security benefits, and a little less than half are students, disabled individuals, or long-term unemployed.[20] They pay no income tax because they have no income. Nonetheless, as the JCT and CBO analyses show, once all federal taxes are considered, every income stratum pays federal tax.

ECONOMIC INCIDENCE OF TAXATION

The most important federal tax for most workers is not the income tax, but rather payroll taxes, which apply to the first dollar of a worker's wages, without exemptions, deductions, or exclusions of any kind. Federal payroll taxes are imposed at a total rate of 15.3 percent on a worker's first $113,700 of income (in 2013), and then drop to a 2.9 percent tax (the Medicare tax component) on income above that amount. (For wages over $200,000, or $250,000 in the case of a married couple filing a joint return, the Medicare tax kicks up by another 0.9 percent, for a total tax on income over that threshold of 3.8 percent.) And of course payroll taxes apply to every member of a household that earns wages. Payroll taxes are thus relatively unimportant to very high-income workers (because the largest component is capped), but they are extremely important to workers with more modest wages—just the opposite of the income tax's pattern of burdens.

Payroll taxes actually are collected in two bites. Employees pay one-half through withholdings from their cash wages (which the employer then forwards to the IRS on the employee's behalf), and the employer pays a matching amount. (The 0.9 percent incremental Medicare tax on high wage earners is paid just by the employee.) The payroll tax rates just summarized include both the employee's share and the employer's share of these obligations. This reflects an extremely important economic concept, which is the *economic incidence* of a tax. An inquiry into the statutory incidence of a tax simply asks, who writes the check to the tax authority? Economic incidence asks, who really bears the burden in the end? The concept is not new—Adam Smith wrote about it, when arguing that a tax on agricultural production ultimately was borne by landowners—but it is surprisingly easy to overlook.

The employer bears the statutory incidence of its share of the payroll tax, but virtually all economists agree that the economic incidence of that tax rests on the shoulders of employees. That is, an employer does not reduce its profits by the "employer's share" of payroll tax. Instead, it reduces employees' wages by that amount. As a result, employees ultimately bear the economic burden of both parts of the payroll tax, or in economists' lingo, the incidence of the tax falls on employees. In the same way, federal gasoline or cigarette excise taxes ultimately are borne by consumers, even though the firms that actually mail in the excise tax payments are far upstream in the line of production and distribution.

The JCT staff, the CBO, and most economists treat the economic incidence of payroll taxes (or any other tax measured directly by wages) as falling on workers, regardless of who has the obligation to mail in the check to the taxing authority, and the economic incidence of excise taxes as falling on the consumers of those products. By contrast, the economic incidence of personal income taxes generally is assumed to follow the statutory incidence: the personal income tax ultimately is borne by the individuals obligated by law to pay it. (Very recently, the JCT staff broke with this assumption to a very modest extent in respect of personal income taxes imposed on net business income earned by self-employed individuals; the point is developed a few paragraphs below.)

Where debates among economists get interesting, and in fact downright ugly, is in figuring out the economic incidence of the *corporate* income tax. Mitt Romney actually was correct, in his clumsy way, when he said that corporations were people, too. Corporations pay income tax on their income, but you have never seen a corporation walking down the street. Ultimately, some individuals must suffer the economic burden of those corporate payments. The only question is, which individuals? Shareholders? All owners of investment capital? Employees? Consumers?

Some academics think that workers bear all or nearly all the economic burden of the corporate income tax. Much of that work, however, fails to distinguish between corporations that are earning "normal" (plain old boring run of the mill) returns on corporate investments and corporations that control patents, software, brand names, or trademarks that enable them to earn supersized returns (technically, "economic rents").

Unseemly scuffles break out when the question is posed at academic conferences.[21] Everyone agrees, however, that some groups of individuals bear the burden of the corporate income tax. As a result, in order fairly to answer the question of how tax burdens are shared in America, one must "distribute" the corporate income tax to those individuals on whom the incidence falls.

Corporate income tax collections are much smaller than personal income tax collections, but still are very large in absolute terms. The CBO projects, for example, that in 2015, after the effects of the Great Recession have largely dissipated, corporations will pay about $450 billion in US corporate income tax. This means that the economic incidence of the corporate income tax has real relevance to all Americans.

The nonpartisan Congressional Budget Office recently changed its methodology for "distributing" the corporate income tax to individuals. It now assumes that the economic incidence of the corporate income tax falls 75 percent on all owners of investment capital (in proportion to each owner's capital income) and 25 percent on workers (in proportion to their wages).[22] (The Treasury Department, by contrast, treats 82 percent of corporate taxes as borne by investors and 18 percent by labor.)

Until 2013, the nonpartisan staff of the Joint Committee on Taxation dealt with the issue by ignoring it; that is, the staff declined to opine on which individuals bear the economic incidence of the corporate income tax, because it believed that the academic literature was too unsettled. Since Congress officially relies on JCT staff "distributional tables" to examine how a tax law change might affect the relative distribution of tax burdens across the income spectrum, the JCT staff's agnosticism indirectly shaped legislative disputations over this contentious issue.

In 2013, however, the JCT staff reversed course and proposed a methodology for "distributing" the corporate income tax that essentially follows the CBO's results.[23] But in a move destined to create complexity and esoteric budget gamesmanship for years to come, JCT one-upped the CBO by introducing a different and altogether novel rule for distributing a slice of the economic incidence of business income taxes imposed on *unincorporated* businesses, like partnerships.[24] The income of unincorporated businesses is reported directly on the individual owners' tax returns—for example, the personal tax returns of the partners in a partnership. The JCT now treats 95 percent of any unincorporated business income taxes as falling on the individual owners of those businesses, and 5 percent as burdening the labor incomes of workers. This means that for the first time a government agency has shifted the economic incidence of a slice of personal income away from the individual on whose return that income is reported.

The economic incidence of the corporate income tax is important for tax policy, for two principal reasons. First, when policymakers argue about raising or lowering the effective corporate income tax rate, they need to have an opinion on economic incidence to conclude which individuals are being gored or rewarded, as well as the efficiency costs of the change in law.

More directly relevant to the discussion here, the economic incidence of the corporate income tax is relevant when one wants to figure out which taxpayers bear which percentage of the total federal tax burden. The JCT staff and the CBO both prepare this sort of analysis, in the form of a table showing what portion of an existing or proposed tax is borne by which individuals, arrayed in order of their incomes. When they do so, the organizations are said to be "distributing" the burdens of the taxes they are analyzing.[25] Because the JCT staff until 2013 was agnostic on corporate tax incidence, it did not include that tax when it distributed the total burdens of federal taxation among individuals. The CBO, by contrast, has done so for many years.

A related but ultimately different issue is the hardy perennial of the "double taxation" of corporate earnings. Here the idea is that shareholders suffer not only the direct cost of dividend or capital gains taxes in respect of their shares, but also the indirect burden of the corporate income tax. In 2012, for example, this argument was advanced as a defense to the claim that Governor Romney paid only a 14 percent effective tax rate on his 2010 income. Instead, it was claimed, his true effective tax rate on his investment income was closer to 45 percent, comprising a 35 percent corporate rate and (for 2010) a 15 percent rate on dividend income or capital gain attributable to an investment in corporate stock.

There are many reasons that this line of argument was inapposite to Governor Romney's situation, or to that of any private equity investor.[26] At a more general level, the argument suffers from several important flaws that illustrate some common differences between tax politics and tax policy. First, its underlying theory of the incidence of the corporate income tax is that the tax is borne entirely by shareholders, which economists do not accept. (As described above, many do think that the burden falls primarily on all capital investment, but this is a much broader category.) Second, as a tax rate matter, US firms today enjoy effective tax rates much lower than the statutory rate of 35 percent. As a general rule of thumb, the more multinational the firm, the lower its all-in federal and foreign tax burdens are likely to be.[27]

Finally, the argument is often used to justify low capital gains taxes in particular, but this is not how the capital gains tax operates. Instead, the capital gains preferential rate is available for profits recognized from the sale of virtually any investment asset, including investments that by their terms cannot be subject to double taxation under any stretch of the imagination. For example, gains from selling appreciated US Treasury bonds are taxed at the low capital gains rates, and the United States of America certainly does not impose the corporate income tax on itself!

SHARES OF TOTAL TAX BURDEN

Analysts use distributional studies of the sort just described to compare the relative tax burdens of different individuals along the income distribution continuum, in order to draw some conclusions about whether tax burdens are being shared fairly among different income levels. For example, it is theoretically possible that, while every income stratum pays a little bit of tax, our tax burdens nonetheless are so disproportionately top-weighted—that is, imposed almost entirely on individuals with the highest incomes—that even those of us clustered in the middle of the pack could muster momentary empathy with the most affluent. It turns out, however, that this is another fable, constructed through the same selectivity in the taxes considered as was evident in the story of the rootless 47 percent.

The JCT staff's "baseline" 2013 distribution of incomes and taxes, presented earlier (Table 8.2) already has made the point—the average (effective) federal tax rate imposed on 2013 incomes of over $1 million was about 32 percent—including high-income earner's share of the corporate income tax. In fact, if you look back at Table 8.2, you will see that all federal taxes, combined, yield a moderately progressive federal tax structure, with one dip very far down the income strata, representing the subsidy effects of the earned income tax credit.

To take one example of many misleading presentations, Harvey Golub wrote in the same 2011 opinion piece discussed earlier that the 250,000 American families who earned $1 million or more paid 20 percent of all federal income taxes; this was intended to suggest that they paid a disproportionate amount of federal taxes. The 2010 JCT staff study referenced earlier actually projected the number of 2010 tax returns showing incomes of $1 million or more to be 336,000 (good news for Mr. Golub!). That group (just 1/500 of all returns) was projected to earn about 11 percent of total personal income in the United States, and pay 26 percent of all federal *income* taxes—but less than 14 percent of all federal personal taxes in the aggregate. (JCT staff data at the time ignored the corporate income tax, as described above.)

The lesson here again is that the income tax is just one of a suite of taxes; by design, it burdens higher incomes in particular, just as others are borne disproportionately by the poor or middle class. It is the aggregate tax burden that is relevant. In fact, at least before 2013, taxpayers with incomes in the $200,000 to $500,000 range, not Mr. Golub and his crowd, got the worst of the deal; their all-in effective federal tax rate was significantly higher than that borne by those earning over $1 million. That incongruity has now been ironed out, with the reversion of tax rates on the very highest incomes to the 39.6 percent rate that had applied before 2001.

The Congressional Budget Office has undertaken comprehensive analyses of the distribution of household incomes and federal taxes. As described in chapter 4, the CBO's standard presentation ranks households in order of their "before-tax" income, which includes the very government transfer payments that tax revenues finance. These transfer payments are very bottom-weighted, but generally do not change the taxes that individuals pay. In addition, the CBO treats cash transfer payments in the form of "refundable" earned income tax credits and child credits as negative taxes, rather than as transfer payments.[28] (For annual budget purposes, by contrast, the refundable portion is scored as government spending. I am not aware of a logical basis for the different treatment.) This had the effect for 2009 of reducing the share of total federal taxes (in this case, payroll taxes) paid by lower-income households by more than $100 billion. Both points operate to shift the apparent share of tax burdens to higher market income households; I discuss them again in the context of debates over the progressivity of the tax system.

Notwithstanding these methodological biases, the CBO's standard presentation for 2009 showed that federal taxes, taken as a whole, were shared in *moderately* progressive ways across the income distribution. The bottom 80 percent of households, ranked by before-tax incomes, all shouldered smaller fractions of the total national federal tax burden than their shares of before-tax incomes, but each income quintile paid a higher effective tax rate than the quintile below it. The top 20 percent of households paid a higher fraction of the total tax burden than their share of before-tax income, but the differences were not very great by world standards. Focusing on the percentage of tax paid by different groups is a meaningless exercise when stripped of the contexts of the relative pre-tax incomes of those groups (see Figure 8.6), and the overall size of the tax system.

Figure 8.6 in fact overstates the practical progressivity of the tax system, because the overall US tax system is simply very small when compared with those of other countries. A more meaningful way to look at things is to ask, how did taxation affect after-tax incomes? A highly progressive but very small tax can make for an impressive looking bar chart along the lines of the one presented here, but have no great impact on individuals' after-tax resources.

When we look at how taxation affects different groups' relative shares of after-tax disposable resources, the picture comes into sharper focus: in 2009, the bottom 80 percent of households—four out of five—enjoyed slightly larger shares of after-tax income than of before-tax income, but even within the top quintile the sacrifices in relative wealth were quite small (see Figure 8.7).

Citizens for Tax Justice undertook a distributional analysis for 2013 comparing individual incomes and the total taxes paid in respect of those incomes, including state and local taxes and corporate income taxes. That analysis concluded that, once all taxes were included, there was surprisingly little variation across the income distribution in the proportion of taxes paid relative to each group's share of total income (see Figure 8.8).

EFFECTIVE AND MARGINAL TAX RATES

Another way of examining relative tax burdens across income distributions is to consider effective tax rates faced by individuals at different points along that spectrum. As a reminder, the effective tax rate is just the tax paid divided by some

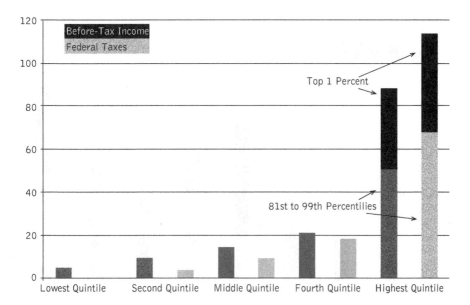

FIGURE 8.6 Shares of Before-Tax Income and Federal Taxes, by Income Group (2009)

Source: CBO, *Distribution of Household Income and Federal Taxes*, 8–9.

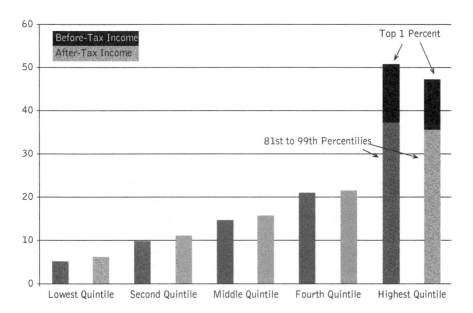

FIGURE 8.7 Shares of Before- and After-Tax Income, by Income Group (2009)

Source: CBO, *Distribution of Household Income and Federal Taxes*, 11.

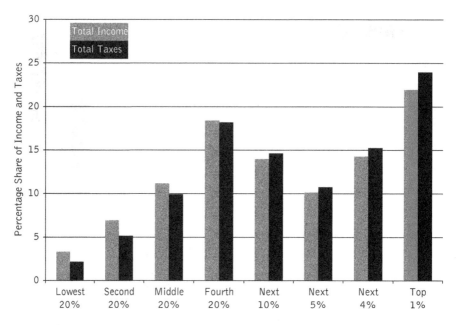

FIGURE 8.8 Shares of Total Taxes Paid and Shares of Income, by Income Group (2013)

Source: Citizens for Tax Justice, *Who Pays Taxes in America in 2013?*.

measure of pre-tax income. The art of constructing or deconstructing such presentations is to understand the measure of income being employed.

Effective and average tax rates are the same, except that economists usually use the word "effective" to signal that the measure of pre-tax income they have in mind is broader than the measure used in the income tax statute itself. For example, when the staff of the Joint Committee on Taxation measures effective tax rates, they typically use for their measure of pre-tax income their concept of "expanded income," defined earlier in this chapter.

By contrast, the marginal tax rate is the rate imposed on the next small increment of income. As an important rule of thumb, economists are made very unhappy by high marginal tax rates. Their reasoning is that an individual typically is faced with discrete economic decisions—Should I work longer hours to collect overtime? Should I join the workforce if my income will be taxed at rates on top of my spouse's? Should I spend or invest this money I just inherited? When confronted with these sorts of choices, a rational individual thinks in terms of the tax on the incremental activity, not the effective (average) tax she incurs. Interesting work in behavioral economics has questioned whether individuals really are this sophisticated in their internal deliberations, or for that matter whether they have any clear understanding at all of the tax environment in which they live.

The US personal income tax is structured differently from those of most of our peer countries in two important respects. First, our marginal tax rates are not terribly high. Second, and more important, most peer countries apply their highest personal income tax rates much further down the income ladder than we do. For years before 2013, our top statutory marginal income tax rate was 35 percent; as of 2013, it is 39.6 percent—but that rate only applies to a married couple in respect of their income over $450,000. By contrast, other countries begin to impose their top rates on income levels one-third or even one-quarter as high. (In addition to the income tax, top incomes in the United States generally are subject either to the Medicare payroll tax or a complementary tax on "unearned income"; as of 2013 the rate for either is 3.8 percent.)

The first column in Table 8.4 shows for each country for 2012 the highest statutory personal income tax rate (national plus sub-national), combined with the employee's share of any payroll taxes applicable to incomes at that level. (Thus, for example, the US figures do not include Social Security payroll taxes, because they roll off before the top income tax rate is reached, but do include Medicare payroll taxes, because they are uncapped.) The third column shows the average wage, in

Table 8.4 Top Statutory Personal Income Tax Rate and Top Marginal Tax Rates for Employees at the Earnings Threshold Where the Top Statutory Personal Income Tax Rate First Applies

	Personal income tax &. employee social security contributions	The gross wage earnings threshold at which the top statutory rate first applies (Measured as a multiple of the average wage)	Average wage in US dollars based on PPP
Sweden	56.60%	1.5	43,685
United Kingdom	52.00%	4.2	52,720
France	51.20%	5.1	42,494
Canada	48.00%	10.7	38,291
Japan	47.80%	4.7	46,086
Norway	47.80%	1.6	55,350
Australia	47.50%	2.4	48,199
Germany	47.50%	5.8	56,058
Italy	47.30%	10.4	36,563
United States	43.20%	8.4	47,650
Switzerland	41.80%	3.5	61,048

Source: OECD, *OECD Tax Database*, Table 1.7.

US dollar purchasing power parity terms—that is, adjusted for exchange rates as well as differences in the cost of goods.

The second column is the most interesting: it shows the income level at which the top income tax rate first applies. In Australia in 2012, for example, the top income tax rate applied to all incomes greater than (2.4 x $48,199), or about $116,000. In the United States in 2012, the top rate applied only to *taxable* incomes over $388,350—or over $400,000 in wage income, before standard deductions and personal exemptions are considered.

Thus, compared with many other countries, an important feature of the US tax system is that very few families actually ever encounter the top tax rate. This is often overlooked when "top tax rate" comparisons are made.

Looking at federal income taxes alone, the JCT staff found that in 2010 the over $1 million club faced effective income tax rates of a little over 24 percent—hardly the punitive rates implied in Golub's op-ed piece. In 2013, that rate was 32 percent, reflecting the January 1, 2013, "fiscal cliff" tax rate deal. The Citizens for Tax Justice analysis chart of taxes as a percentage of income presented earlier in this chapter projected a similar federal effective rate for 2013 for the top one percent of incomes.

When one gets to the really super-rich, effective federal income tax rates actually decline, because so much of their income is taxed as long-term capital gain. The data published annually by the IRS on the 400 highest-income tax returns for the year is particularly helpful here. For 2009 (the most recent year), their effective federal income tax rate was under 20 percent. If one measured their tax liabilities against their true economic income (including items like tax-exempt municipal bond income and capital gains not yet harvested through a sale), that rate would decline still further.

A PROGRESSIVE TAX SYSTEM?

The US personal income tax is designed to be "progressive." Chapter 3 briefly described the term in the context of introducing the importance of marginal tax rates to economic decision-making, but it is now necessary to explain the concept in a little more detail. I defer to Part III the defense of the progressive income tax as a social good; in the remainder of this chapter I am concerned only to explain the mechanics of what the term actually means, and to consider whether the United States has a very progressive tax system, or not so progressive a tax system, or perhaps whether that question as normally formulated is meaningless. I come down on the side of meaninglessness.

The technical definition of a progressive income tax is one where a taxpayer's effective (average) tax rate increases as his income goes up. In a proportional income tax, by contrast, a taxpayer's effective tax rate remains constant. Under either design, taxes paid go up as income increases: high-income individuals pay more than low-income individuals.

In other words, in a proportional tax system, the tax paid is a constant proportion of income at all points on the income ladder. For example, a flat 20 percent income tax with no standard deduction or personal exemption is a proportional tax: an individual with an income of $10,000 pays $2,000 in tax, and one with an income of $100,000 pays $20,000: ten times the income, ten times the tax bill. The fact that an individual's tax bill increases with income does not tell us whether the tax is proportional or progressive.

Market Income	Tax	Effective Tax Rate
$10,000	0	0
$20,000	$2,000	10 percent
$40,000	$6,000	15 percent
$100,000	$30,000	30 percent

By contrast, in a hypothetical progressive tax, we might see a schedule like this: Here, the tax bill climbs more quickly than does income, which is what it means to say that in a progressive tax the effective tax rate increases as income increases. $100,000 is five times as great as $20,000, but the taxpayer with $100,000 in income pays in this case 15 times as much in tax as the taxpayer with $20,000.

I constructed this hypothetical tax as follows:

1. All taxpayers receive a $10,000 standard deduction. This reduces a taxpayer's "taxable income," which is the base on which a tax bill is calculated. The standard deduction is not a real expense, and so does not reduce economic income; this is relevant when we calculate effective tax rates, as economists use the term.
2. Taxable incomes (market income less standard deduction) up to $30,000 are taxed at a rate of 20 percent.
3. Taxable incomes above $40,000 are taxed at 40 percent.

This construction illustrates three critical concepts in progressive income tax design. First, the standard deduction operates to give a taxpayer a layer of zero-tax income: we could just as well call this a "zero rate bracket" or the like.

Second, each layer of income—usually called an "income bracket"—has a tax rate associated with it, but the tax imposed on a higher layer does not affect the tax imposed on a lower layer. A taxpayer with a market income of $20,000 always enjoys a zero rate on his first $10,000 of income, and for that matter so does a taxpayer with $100,000 of market income. I mentioned earlier that many people misunderstand how tax rate brackets work in our income tax system, but for just this reason it bears repeating: when you move into a "higher bracket" only the income in that bracket is taxed at the new higher rate. Bill Gates enjoys a layer of income taxed at zero, a layer of income taxed at 10 percent, and so on—it is just that in his case those low-taxed layers are inconsequential relative to his large amounts of income at higher tax rates.

Third, a taxpayer's effective tax rate is a weighted average of the tax rates imposed on his income in each layer. The taxpayer with $100,000 in market income faces a *marginal* tax rate of 40 percent, because all taxable income over $40,000 is taxed at 40 percent, but the taxpayer's effective (average) tax rate is 30 percent. That figure is composed of a bottom layer of $10,000 of market income taxed at zero (thanks to the standard deduction), a second layer of $30,000 (that is, from $10,000 to $40,000 in market income, or zero to $30,000 in taxable income) taxed at 20 percent (i.e., $6,000), and a third layer of $60,000 taxed at 40 percent (or $24,000). The total tax bill is 0 + $6,000 + $24,000.

In contrast to a proportional or progressive tax, the Social Security payroll tax is an example of a regressive tax. The tax is a flat 6.2 percent of wages paid by the employee, plus another 6.2 percent paid by the employer. If we stopped there, the tax would be a proportional tax. (The 2.9 percent basic Medicare payroll tax actually is an example of this, ignoring the new 0.9 percent incremental tax on high wages.) But in fact the Social Security payroll tax applies only to the first $113,700 (in 2013) of wage income: the marginal tax rate can be said to drop to zero for the income bracket of all income above that amount. This means that the more you make, once you pierce the $113,700 barrier, the lower your average Social Security tax rate (total tax, capped at 6.2 percent x $113,700, divided by total income). Excise taxes on cigarettes are another example of a regressive tax, but for a different reason: cigarettes are a larger share of the consumption budget of a poor person than of a rich one.

Overall, our federal tax system is moderately progressive in the aggregate. You can see this again in Table 8.2: the over $1 million/year club has an effective (average) federal tax burden of 32 percent, the $500,000–$1 million crowd a rate of 29.9 percent, the next tranche down a rate of 25.7 percent, and so on down the income ladder. Each income group bears an effective tax burden a little higher than the next lower income group, with the exception of the second-lowest rung of the ladder, where the earned income tax credit's subsidy effects (i.e., cash income tax refunds) push down those individuals' total tax bills.

In sum, our federal tax system actually is a mix of progressive taxes (the personal income tax), proportional taxes (the basic 2.9 percent Medicare payroll tax and the corporate income tax, in practice), and regressive taxes (Social Security payroll tax and excise taxes). From this you can see that focusing on just the personal income tax can paint a misleading picture of the progressivity of our tax system.

And yet people cannot resist the temptation to do just this. For example, did you know that the Congressional Budget Office demonstrated in 2012 that the top one percent of American taxpayers "pay too much" in federal taxes? This came as news to me, and no doubt to the CBO itself. We have Ari Fleischer, President George W. Bush's former press officer, to thank for this startling claim, made in a 2012 opinion piece in the *Wall Street Journal*.[29]

Fleischer relied for his claim on the CBO's July 2012 report, *The Distribution of Household Income and Federal Taxes, 2008 and 2009*. I refer to this report several times in this book, because it is an important and reliable window into the growth of income inequality in the United States as well as the distribution of tax liabilities among different income levels (notwithstanding my quarrel with some of its methodology).

Fleischer began by asserting that the tax system—by which he means the personal income tax—is "incredibly progressive." Of course the *income* tax is progressive—that has been a hallmark of its design since its adoption in 1913—but again, it is only one of a suite of federal taxes, others of which are regressive or proportional. Fleischer further reports, as if it is news, that those with higher incomes pay a larger share of the nation's total tax bill than do the poor, but does anyone really recommend the contrary? Finally, Fleischer observes that those with higher incomes pay a larger share of total federal taxes than their share of total national income. In fact, Figure 8.6 makes clear that this last point is true only of the top 20 percent or so of American households, and Figure 8.7 (comparing before and after-tax income shares) demonstrates that the system is only moderately progressive—there is nothing particularly incredible going on.

But drilling down, what is the basis for the conclusion that the system is "incredibly" progressive? Fleischer consistently presents selective data relating to the tax burdens on those Americans in the top 20 percent of the income distribution. This group in 2009 had an average "market income" of $218,000, which sounds pretty flush. But as the CBO Report carefully notes, "that average masks wide differences between subgroups [within the top 20 percent]; households in the 81st to 90th percentiles received $125,000, on average, compared with $1.2 million for households in the top percentile [i.e., the top one percent]."

This point is important, because our political economy debates are not about how the top 20 percent of Americans by income should be taxed, but rather the top 2 or 3 percent. What Fleischer does is weave an argument on behalf of the very affluent while hiding their actual tax and income data behind the skirts of a much larger class of reasonably but not extraordinarily successful taxpayers, whose tax rates are not the subject of much controversy.

Fleischer elided over another critical point, which is that the CBO's base measure of income for its distributional analyses is "before-tax income." As described in chapter 6, "before-tax income" is the sum of your market income *and* the value of any transfer payments you receive—not just "food stamps" (technically, the SNAP program), but also broad-based entitlements like Social Security payments, Medicare and Medicaid benefits, unemployment insurance, and much more. Most of these transfer payments are *not* includable in the taxable income of their recipients.

As pointed out earlier in this chapter, transfer payments are bottom-weighted, just as one would expect. Households in the bottom 20 percent, ranked by market incomes, received 40 percent of all transfer payments (an average of $23,000 per household). Almost two-thirds of that came from Social Security and Medicare, not some imagined "welfare" programs. The inclusion of transfer payments radically changes the percentage of national income claimed by different income groups. In particular, the top 20 percent of households in the income distribution in 2009 earned 51 percent of aggregate before-tax incomes, but 57 percent of market incomes.

Fleischer thus argued that the US tax system is "incredibly progressive," by presenting data on how much tax the top 20 percent actually pay, and comparing that, not to their share of aggregate market incomes, but rather to their share of national income *after* taking into account the very transfer payments that are funded by the tax system. By doing so, he made the average tax rate shouldered by the top 20 percent seem higher.

The CBO in this report thus inadvertently helped Fleischer overstate reality by using its odd construct of "before-tax" income (which again actually is after the transfer payments funded by taxes), and also by treating the refundable portion of the earned income tax credit (and other refundable tax credits) as negative taxes, rather than as income. (This presentation is particularly odd, because as explained earlier it conflicts with how refundable tax credits are presented in the federal budget.) This further drives down the aggregate tax burden (as presented in this report) on lower income Americans. Again, if you want to talk about tax burdens and progressivity, you should do so before taking into account tax refunds that exceed taxes paid, because those are transfer payments by another name.

Progressivity is actually a tricky thing to measure, because it is a comparative thought—one system is "very" progressive only in comparison to another system.[30] But in light of Fleischer's assertion that the CBO report demonstrates that the top 20 percent of Americans pay "too much," one might fairly begin with the obvious question, does the tax system, taken as a whole, tax the top 20 percent of taxpayers more harshly than it did in 1979 (the beginning of the CBO's data)? There the data are clear: the average tax rate for the top 20 percent of taxpayers (measured by before-tax incomes) *"reached a new [modern era] low in 2009, about*

4 percentage points below its 1979 level." A roughly similar story applies to the top one percent crowd—their effective tax rate in 2009 was much lower than it was in 1979.

Now consider the progressivity of the income tax system by itself. Some public finance economists are fond of something called the Kakwani index, which is analogous to a Gini index (that is, the index of income inequality, as introduced in chapter 3) applied to tax rates in the abstract. The Kakwani index shows the deviation of any given tax system from proportionality. A Kakwani index of zero means that taxes are perfectly proportional to income; a positive Kakwani index signals a progressive tax system, while a negative one signals a regressive system.[31] The Kakwani index is indifferent to the size of the tax system being measured: a small tax that is collected only from the rich is treated as more progressive than a large tax that is imposed on a somewhat broader base.

I view the Kakwani index as positively pernicious in policy discourse, because in the hands of pundits it is misused to assert conclusions that are simply untrue. The problem is that the Kakwani index tells you nothing about how much tax is being collected, which in turn informs the question of how much real impact a tax system can have. If the entire tax system collected $1,000 in tax revenues, total, and all of that from America's highest income individual, this tax would score on the Kakwani index as a hugely progressive tax system, when in fact 310 million of us would pay nothing, and in turn government could do essentially nothing with its $1,000 of tax receipts actually to address market income inequality.

You can see this problem by looking at movements in the Gini index for different measures of income over time. Between 1979 and 2007, the Gini index for pre-tax market incomes (the right starting place, as it happens) increased by 23 percent, which means that more and more of total national market incomes were captured by the highest earners. But the Gini index for income after all transfers and taxes increased even more, by 33 percent. Because after-tax and transfer income inequality rose more quickly than did market income inequality, this means that taxes and transfers were doing *less* at the end of this period to address market income inequalities than they were at the beginning.

The primary reason for this extraordinary development from 1979 to 2007 was that the distribution of transfer payments and benefits became less progressive over time, because a larger share of these benefits took the form of Social Security, Medicare, and other broadly distributed items, in which the middle class, not just the poor, participate.[32] If used to make a statement about the progressivity of our government's interventions taken as a whole (as often is the case), the Kakwani index by itself thus would simply miss what actually was going on.

A more meaningful tax progressivity index is an index that compares the progressivity of before-tax and after-tax incomes; technically this is known as the Reynolds-Smolensky index. The reason is simply that it does what the Kakwani index does not, which is to consider how much of a difference a tax system actually makes to people, which requires considering how large the tax system is.

The most meaningful index would compare before-tax market incomes with incomes after taxes paid and transfer payments received. The CBO's definition of "after-tax" income corresponds to the second of these, but the CBO does not publish data starting from market incomes. Instead, and as pointed out earlier, the CBO's starting point for calculating a Reynolds-Smolensky tax progressivity index (what the CBO calls "before-tax" income) already includes the transfer payments funded by the very taxes whose effect the CBO is trying to measure. This is a pity.

The CBO's 2009 Reynolds-Smolensky tax progressivity index (which again compares "before-tax" and after-tax incomes to see the leveling effect of the tax system) was at exactly the same level as it was in 1979—and what is more, from 1994 to 2009 that measure of progressivity hardly fluctuated at all (except for 2007, when the tax system did somewhat less to reduce inequality than in the surrounding years). The tax system has *not* gotten more progressive in any meaningful sense, and at the same time the rich in fact are pulling away faster and faster from the rest of America, whether measured by market incomes, before-tax incomes, or after-tax incomes.

As the CBO explained in its report, what actually went on in 2008 and 2009 had nothing to do with the story Fleischer wanted to tell, and everything to do with the depths into which the economy fell. Essentially, the whole income distribution curve shifted dramatically to the left (toward zero, not toward Democrats): the very affluent made a lot less money, but still earned a lot, while millions of Americans lost their jobs and saw their market incomes plummet to near zero.

As one result, total federal tax collections as a percentage of total national income fell to a modern era low, and every segment of society, including the top 20 percent, paid a lower average tax rate than they did in the boom year of 2007. (The exception was the top one percent's tax rate; these fortunate individuals actually saw their average tax rate go up a little bit, because a smaller percentage of their total income came from capital gains, which at the time was taxed at a preferential 15 percent rate.) As another consequence, if millions are suddenly rendered jobless, of course their tax bills go down, because they have no incomes on which to pay tax. The result is that the much smaller total tax bill for the country looks like it is being paid disproportionately by the affluent, but again that is a meaningless statistic, because it is an artifact of total tax collections collapsing as a percentage of national income: as a percentage of their incomes, the affluent (at least below the top one percent) paid a lower tax rate, not a higher tax rate, in 2009 than in 2007.

The years 2008 and 2009 were exceptional in many other respects as well. Most important, in early 2008 President Bush signed the Economic Stimulus Act of 2008, which gave taxpayers bonus tax refunds of up to $600. The CBO in its distributional analysis (but not in its official budget scorekeeping) treated these bonus refunds as negative taxes, not additional transfer payments. The same was true for the emergency "making work pay" credit in 2009 of up to $800 for joint returns, along with other recession-fighting tax measures. These bonus refunds were a small matter to the affluent, but greatly reduced the percentage of taxes paid by lower income Americans in those years. By classifying these cash infusions as negative taxes, the CBO again inadvertently made the tax system both smaller and more progressive, in the limited sense that these emergency measures temporarily removed many low-income Americans from the tax rolls entirely.

In addition, the CBO decided in this report to make a fundamental change in how it calculates the value for transfer payment purposes of Medicaid benefits; this accounting change in the valuation of Medicaid benefits ("accounting," because it changed nothing about the government's actual costs or recipients' benefits) caused the CBO to show lower-income Americans as having $200 billion more in "before-tax" income in 2009 than would have been true under the old methodology.

In short, what happened in 2008 and 2009 is that incomes collapsed, and because the tax system is progressive, higher income Americans still had some positive tax liability, while millions of less fortunate Americans dropped temporarily off the income tax rolls. This apparent concentration of tax responsibilities was exacerbated by all the emergency measures adopted under both Presidents Bush and Obama in 2008–2009, and by the CBO's new methodology for accounting for Medicaid, because those benefits in aggregate were bottom-weighted in their distribution.

As a result, in 2009 the affluent were asked to swallow a larger share of the radically smaller tax pie than was the case in 2007, when the tax liability pie itself was larger. But either way, the real question is, how much tax pie did I have to swallow? And in this respect, the affluent (other than the top one percent), like other Americans, in fact paid less in tax as a percentage of their income than they had in the past.

Finally, Fleischer notes that the CBO report includes both payroll and income taxes, but overlooks (or fails to state) that the report carefully notes that its figures "distribute" not only taxes paid by or on behalf of individuals, but also corporate income taxes, in the manner I described earlier in this chapter. This means that wealthy taxpayers are credited not only with the taxes they actually pay, but also with the lion's share of corporate income taxes. But for reasons that continue to baffle me, the CBO does not "distribute" to shareholders or anyone else corporate earnings that are retained inside the corporation. The result is to distribute a tax bill without crediting individuals with the associated income.

I described earlier how economic incidence of the corporate income tax is hotly contested. It is ironic that those aligned with Fleischer's political views typically show great flexibility of mind on this conundrum, by arguing that corporate taxes actually fall on the wages of humble workers when those individuals are proselytizing for lower corporate tax rates, and then claiming that the taxes clearly are a burden to the wealthy when the question shifts to the tax indignities forced upon America's highest income families. Keep this in mind when you read an opinion piece in which the author argues that he is trying to do the working man a favor by reducing corporate income tax rates.

CHAPTER 9

THE HIDDEN HAND OF GOVERNMENT SPENDING

> *The interest of the dealers ... in any particular branch of trade or manu-*
> *factures, is always in some respects different from, and even opposite to,*
> *that of the public. To widen the market and to narrow the competition, is*
> *always the interest of the dealers. To widen the market may frequently be*
> *agreeable enough to the interest of the public; but to narrow the competi-*
> *tion must always be against it, and can serve only to enable the dealers,*
> *by raising their profits above what they naturally would be, to levy, for*
> *their own benefit, an absurd tax upon the rest of their fellow-citizens.*
>
> —ADAM SMITH, *The Wealth of Nations*, Book I, Chap. XI,
> Part III.

OUR SUBSURFACE SPENDING PROGRAMS

Government is the things we decide to do collectively, rather than individually through market decisions. Spending is the prime mover of government; it is the first step in much government action, and it determines how much we will be asked to chip into the collective pot to pay for all the goods and services that government purchases. And of course we live in contentious times, when the size of government (which is to say, its various commitments to spend money) is hotly debated.

You therefore would imagine that any sensible discussion of how and why government spends and taxes in the way it does would begin with a clear recitation of government's actual spending policies. You further might expect that a glance at the Congressional Budget Office's annual summary of government spending and taxes for the next decade (its annual *Budget and Economic Outlook*, released early each calendar year) would give you a pretty clear picture of where your money was going.

You would be wrong. Visible federal government spending is only about two-thirds of its actual spending in normal times. The rest—*amounting to as much as all defense and nondefense discretionary spending put together*—is buried in the tax code, where it appears as simply lower tax revenue. This spending through the tax code is vitally important, not only because it amounts to over $1.2 *trillion* in subsurface government spending every year, but because a large portion of that spending is extravagant, poorly targeted, and highly distortive. [1]

As a reader of this book, you almost certainly are a direct beneficiary of some of these largely invisible government subsidy programs, because about $1.1 trillion of these subsidies are aimed at individual taxpayers. The home mortgage interest deduction is one example, but so too are the tax preference for capital gains and the earned income tax credit. As developed below, this hodgepodge of different subsidies serving different purposes needs to be teased apart to say anything useful about whether particular subsidies are wasteful.

At the same time, "the sophistry of merchants," to quote Adam Smith, has led to around $100 billion of outright subsidies every year to various business interests—subsidies that never would pass muster as cash outlays. These ersatz business subsidies delivered through the tax code operate as if we were running a Soviet-style five-year plan underneath the table. We subsidize petroleum production, and then we subsidize renewable energy production, so that the newer industries can catch up. We give to the "wind" industry, and then, when solar complains, we give to them, too. These expenditures are so plainly inconsistent with any plausible theory of efficient markets as to fall of their own weight once held up for examination. Because these interventions in traditional private markets are so self-evidently dubious, this chapter spends little time on them. Instead, I focus mostly on the other $1.1 trillion of annual subsurface government spending programs, which accrue to the benefit of individuals like you and me.

Specialists use the term "tax expenditures" to describe these synthetic government spending programs that are delivered through the tax code. Tax expenditures are really spending programs, not tax rollbacks, because the missing tax revenues must be financed by more taxes on somebody else. If Congress were to pass a law giving blue-eyed Senators an extra $1,000 in cash salary, most of us would think that to be a mighty strange law, and we would wonder where the money would come from to pay those bonuses. But we enact programs that are only marginally more rational, in which we give narrow subpopulations subsidies in the form of tax deductions or credits, and call them "targeted tax relief" or the like. The difference is that when we award subsidies through the tax code, members of Congress actually say for the public record that they "are just letting the people keep what's theirs."

The late David Bradford, the dean of public finance economists of his generation, was fond of a joke that he constructed to illustrate this hidden hand of government spending that lies buried in the tax code. He proposed a marvelous new way to cut taxes without affecting government services: instead of wasting tax revenues on military equipment purchases, Congress could implement a "Weapons Supply Tax Credit," under which arms manufacturers would receive a tax credit (a dollar for dollar rebate against their income tax bill) for delivering to the US government weapons meeting certain specifications. The amount of the credit would equal what Congress might formerly have spent on purchasing those weapons. Then Congress could announce that, through this "targeted tax relief," taxes had been slashed without jeopardizing our security or increasing the deficit.

The joke, of course, is that nothing at all would have changed; the federal government still would obtain the same weapons and incur the same economic cost to do so. Our governmental accounting for the transactions, however, would differ. Instead of recording government revenues from taxes collected and government expenditures for national defense, we would just report net lower taxes collected. Before, the government took in $1,000 and spent $100 on fighter planes. After, the government would record just $900 in revenues, and some "free" planes would arrive at the Air Force's doorstep. On paper, the government had gotten smaller; in reality, it would be as large as ever.

Bradford's joke was meant as a gentle parody to illustrate the empty formalism of our categories of government revenues and expenditures. When the government subsidizes people or businesses by writing them checks, we all recognize that intervention as government spending. When the government subsidizes the same people or businesses to the same extent by giving them a targeted tax break, that action often is mischaracterized as "keeping what's yours" or "smaller government."

Like all parody, Bradford relied on hyperbole to make his point. How, then, would he have reacted to two Internal Revenue Service notices from 2009?[2] The first of those notices explained to taxpayers how to apply for $250 million in tax credits to be allocated by the IRS and the Department of Energy (surely a bureaucratic odd couple) for delivery of certain "Phase II [qualifying] gasification projects." The second announced $1.25 billion in tax credits to be awarded, again by the same two agencies, for certain advanced coal facilities. In effect, the notices announced the transfer of hundreds of millions of dollars from the federal government to selected energy companies.

Bradford's joke has lost its punch line. We now find ourselves living inside the parody and thinking it normal.

Tax expenditures have grown in importance to the point where they are now the dominant instruments for implementing new discretionary spending policies.

We spend more than twice as much through tax expenditures as we do through old-fashioned explicit nondefense spending programs.

Tax expenditures dissolve the boundaries between government revenues and government spending. In doing so, they reduce both the coherence of the tax law and our ability to conceptualize the very size and activities of our government. Our standard budget presentations are infected by misinformation attributable to large spending programs that for budget purposes are invisible, because they are scored simply as reduced tax revenues.[3] We do not appreciate how distorted and therefore imperfect our private markets are in critically important areas of the economy, like healthcare. Tax expenditures also skew the internal processes of Congress, again in ways that redound to our collective detriment.[4]

For example, the personal itemized deductions as a group disproportionately subsidize upper class families. The result is that individuals who believe themselves to be heavily taxed "makers" often are unaware that they simultaneously are large-scale "takers" from government as well. We can pretend that the home mortgage interest deduction, for example, is all about getting young families into their first homes, but as the discussion that follows demonstrates, this is self-interested puffery: the principal real-world application of that deduction and other subsidies for home ownership is to make it easier for affluent taxpayers to buy larger homes than they otherwise would.

To be clear, some tax expenditures make good sense; the earned income tax credit is an example, for the reasons described later in this chapter. But many tax expenditures cannot pass any sensible policy filter. Chapter 13 makes specific suggestions for cashing in some very expensive but low-value tax expenditures to fund a more efficient tax code.

Other countries also employ tax expenditures as a fiscal tool. Cross-country comparisons are difficult here, because different countries have very different tax systems, retirement systems, and so on, and because there are no internationally agreed standards for what constitutes a tax expenditure in the first place. The OECD has worked extensively on this comparability problem. In 2010 it published the results of a multiyear inquiry, which concluded that the United States ranked second only to Canada in its personal income tax expenditure appetites, measured as a fraction of income taxes collected.[5] But Canada eclipsed us in this dubious race only because of its unique mechanisms for accounting for transfers from the federal government to the provinces; if these intergovernmental transfers are removed, the United States emerges as the world's preeminent tax expenditure junkie.[6]

Like any other addict, the United States now uses tax expenditures indiscriminately and to excess. As described in more detail later in this chapter, our tax code is littered with about 250 of these hidden forms of government spending. We now spend as much in personal income tax expenditures as we collect in personal income tax revenues. In other words, it is as if we raised twice as much in personal income taxes as we think we do, and then spent another $1 trillion or so each year on subsidies that, in the aggregate, go predominantly to the most affluent Americans.[7]

GOVERNMENT-SUBSIDIZED PRIVATE HEALTHCARE

The United States prides itself on being a market-based economy, where market prices, not central planners, determine the allocations of goods and services. All too often, however, tax expenditures undercut this premise, and in fact represent a government thumb on the scale of market prices—with all the inefficiencies that this implies.

The two largest clusters of tax expenditures are those for healthcare and those for owner-occupied housing. Each has had a large and profoundly negative allocative effect on the economy—that is, each has distorted what goods and services we all purchase, by changing relative prices through hidden government subsidies. Each also is poorly targeted, in the sense that the subsidy often goes to taxpayers who would have purchased those goods or services without the help of the subsidy.

Our dysfunctional healthcare markets in particular are the result of government subsidies hidden in the tax code. The most important such subsidy is the treatment of wages paid by an employer in the form of healthcare benefits as tax-exempt in the hands of an employee. This one invisible government subsidy program will amount to 1.6 percent of GDP—roughly 9 percent of all federal tax revenues—over the next decade.[8] And in turn, more than one-third of these government handouts will go to the top 20 percent of households, by income.[9]

When you work for a business, you get a cash salary, which in turn is part of your taxable income. If the business were to pay a bonus in the form of a new car, you would discover (perhaps to your dismay) that the value of that car also was part of your taxable income. At the same time, the employer deducts the total value of the compensation it pays you in figuring out its income, on which it pays its own income tax. So the employer is in the same position whether it pays the bonus in cash or by surprising you with a new car of your own.

In short, the tax code does not care in what currency (cash, cars, rutabagas) your employer pays you, only the total value of your compensation in US dollars—*unless* your compensation takes the form of employer-provided healthcare. Then the tax code simply permits you to ignore this very valuable form of compensation, both for income tax and for payroll tax purposes.

Healthcare is the only significant form of employee compensation that can be delivered tax-free to the employee, while being treated as an immediate business expense by the employer. For example, bonuses paid in the form of cars, diamonds, free housing (with very narrow exceptions), or, for that matter, chickens, would all be taxable income to you.

The exclusion of employer-paid healthcare costs is a deliberate exception to the general rule that any form of compensation must be included in your income. This is not an instance of the government letting you keep what is yours. As anyone who has compared job offers knows, healthcare is just another part of your total compensation package, but one that uniquely can be delivered tax-free.

Imagine, for example, that you have a $50,000 salary at your job. Your boss offers you a big raise starting next year—say, $10,000. What's more, she offers you a one-time choice: you can take the raise as more cash income going forward, or in the form of a new health insurance policy costing $10,000 every year.

In a world without taxes, you should take the cash (assuming that the insurance policy was available to you at the same price), because that multiplies your options—you could buy the same healthcare coverage if you wanted to, or take the risk of going uncovered and spend the money on something else, or buy a cheaper insurance policy and spend the remaining cash elsewhere. If the healthcare policy were treated the same as any other compensation, you again would go through the same calculus, except here you would remember that if you kept the expensive healthcare policy you would have to pay the tax bill each year on its $10,000 value out of your cash income.

But by virtue of the special subsidy buried in the tax code, you simply get to ignore the $10,000 health insurance policy (but not a bump in your cash income) in calculating your taxable income. Now your preferences are reversed. Even if this is a bigger insurance policy than you might buy on your own, you will take it rather than the cash, because one is tax-free and the other is not. If income and payroll taxes sum up to a 30 percent rate, then your choice becomes one between a $10,000 insurance policy and $7,000 in cash (after tax). You'll take the insurance policy even if it's only worth $7,500 to you, because that still is better than $7,000 in cash. And the employer does not care, because its tax deduction for your compensation is the same $10,000 in either case.

This "exclusion" from employees' incomes of wages paid in the form of employer-provided healthcare will cost some $143 billion in forgone income taxes in 2014 alone,[10] but even these enormous costs understate the true picture, because they do not include the payroll tax revenues forgone by the exclusion, which amount to more than $100 billion every year.[11]

In short, the total value of this government subsidy for one mode of healthcare delivery is on the order of $250 billion per year.[12] Yet precisely because this subsidy is delivered as an income "exclusion," its recipients are largely unaware that they are the beneficiaries of a hidden government handout.

The core story line of healthcare policy in the United States over the last 50 years is a meditation on how the tax exclusion for employer-provided healthcare has impeded sensible policy. Employees have every reason to prefer oversized health-care plans over cash income, and employers have every reason to accommodate them. The result has been the relative overconsumption of healthcare insurance (that is, a relative insensitivity to its costs), the proliferation of employer-provided plans, and with the latter the collapse of the individual health insurance markets, because most people most of the time are covered through their employers. (The technical formulation here would be that the subsidy distorts "allocative" deci-sions—decisions about how and when we spend our money.)

And precisely because of the near invisibility of this subsidy, millions of Americans who railed against the Affordable Care Act as an unwarranted govern-ment intervention into private markets were completely unaware that those mar-kets had been shaped by a massive government intervention dating back decades, to which they themselves were the beneficiaries. Their vision obscured by the fog of fiscal illusion, these angry Americans thought they were firing on the adminis-tration, and did not realize that the targets of their ire should have been themselves.

The subsidy for employer-sponsored health insurance thus distorts our per-sonal spending patterns, by encouraging us to take compensation in the form of generous healthcare programs. The subsidy does so inefficiently, by subsidizing higher-income Americans more, since tax exemption is more valuable to them—the classic "upside down" subsidy pattern of many tax expenditures. That is, a $10,000 income exclusion is more valuable to someone in the 39.6 percent tax bracket than the same $10,000 exclusion is to someone in the 15 percent tax bracket: the first taxpayer enjoys a $3,960 tax savings, and the other, poorer, one only captures a $1,500 benefit. Finally, the tax subsidy for employer-sponsored health insurance is conspicuously unfair, because its availability depends on the programs offered by your employer, not consistent national standards available to everyone.

For these reasons, every health economist of whom I am aware believes that the tax subsidy for employer-sponsored health insurance is both unaffordable and bad policy. Many were acutely disappointed that the Patient Protection and Affordable Care Act left the subsidy largely intact (except for certain "Cadillac" plans).

The tax subsidy for employer-provided healthcare is the largest single tax expenditure, but taken together the several subsidies that comprise the "personal itemized deductions"—the deductions you claim for home mortgage interest and property taxes, charitable contributions, state and local income taxes, and so on—are just as large. These subsidies are even more "top heavy" than the health insur-ance tax expenditure—they go overwhelmingly to the most affluent Americans.

ECONOMIC IMPLICATIONS OF TAX EXPENDITURES

Tax expenditures serve many different purposes. Some (the earned income tax credit, the special tax rates on long-term capital gains) might be viewed as adjustments to the tax rate tables; others (the child credit, the refundable portion of the EITC) serve important social and distributional goals; still others (pension plan contributions) can be explained as moves toward a consumption tax rather than an income tax. But many fall into the category of inadvisable instances of Congressional meddling with our market economy, by subsidizing different forms of personal consumption or business activity. These latter sorts of tax expenditures typically introduce economic inefficiencies, miss the target of their intended beneficiaries, and waste a great deal of money.

To illustrate the economic costs of tax expenditures, consider a little example involving the small but self-reliant country of Freedonia. Its economy comprises 10 fruit and vegetable growers, each earning $1,000 pre-tax, for a total gross domestic product of $10,000. Each grower pays income tax to support the Freedonian army at a flat rate of 15 percent, for total tax revenues of $1,500.

Freedonia's sole kumquat producer is particularly resourceful. Armed with scientific reports showing the many health benefits of kumquat consumption, he convinces the Freedonian legislature that kumquat production deserves tax incentives, to bring kumquats within the reach of every Freedonian family. The legislature responds by effectively exempting kumquat production from its income tax through an innovative kumquat production tax credit.

But Freedonia is not a profligate state, and it believes in fiscal discipline in the form of "pay-as-you-go" budget rules. "Pay-as-you-go," or "PAYGO," is a self-imposed discipline that Congress has used from time to time to curb its instincts for profligacy. In a nutshell, PAYGO rules require that every new tax cut be paired either with an offsetting tax increase elsewhere or a decrease in entitlements programs of equivalent value. Bizarrely, relative to most people's expectations, Democrats reintroduced the fiscal discipline of PAYGO when they took over the House of Representatives after November 2006, and Republicans repealed the rule as soon as they became the majority after the 2010 elections.

Consistent with its PAYGO rule, and to keep the kumquat credit revenue-neutral, the legislature pairs the new preference with an 11.1 percent tax hike on the other producers, to maintain tax revenues at $1,500. (Freedonian tax policy allows for rounding error.) That means that the other fruit and vegetable farmers will each pay $167 (instead of $150) in tax on their $1,000 of income.

In a world without tax expenditure analysis, the Freedonian legislature can argue that nothing has changed: government revenues are constant, and there is no increase in government spending or borrowing. But this is plainly wrong; things have changed, in both the private and the public sectors.

First, the tax incentive increases kumquat production and consumption. The equilibrium price and quantities sold of kumquats will be different relative to other fruits and vegetables after the tax incentive. Economists believe that, in the absence of some identifiable market failure, markets set prices better than legislatures do, but the kumquat credit alters the quantity of kumquats sold relative to the case in which the tax burden of all fruit and vegetable growers was equal. Unless the overall health of Freedonians really is improved by the kumquat credit (perhaps because of prior rampant borderline scurvy among the population), the result will be a less efficient allocation of our collective resources.

Second, the introduction of the kumquat credit in an apparently virtuous "revenue neutral" fashion has another profound economic effect: tax rate increases on the incomes of all the fruit and vegetable producers who do not receive targeted tax relief. All taxes, no matter how beautifully implemented, impose deadweight losses. That is, some transactions that are rational in a world without taxes become too expensive in a world with those taxes and thus do not take place. And deadweight loss increases faster than the tax rate: in standard presentations, in fact, at the square of the tax rate.

What all this means is that, by virtue of granting "revenue neutral targeted tax relief," the Freedonian government may raise the same aggregate revenues as it did previously, but impose more deadweight loss on the remaining taxable Freedonian private sector. This result is one of the great ironies of many tax expenditures, particularly those that fall into the category of business incentives—once the incentive's impact on tax burdens for others is considered, it impoverishes the country even more than it enriches the beneficiaries of the legislative largesse.

Third, by virtue of its new kumquat credit, the Freedonian government just got bigger, even though aggregate nominal tax revenues remain constant. The best way to see this effect is to employ a mode of analysis pioneered by Louis Kaplow of Harvard and analogize the new kumquat credit to a uniform 11.1 percent tax hike on all of Freedonia's fruit and vegetable producers, followed by a $167 kumquat crop farm subsidy payment to the kumquat producer. By recasting the tax expenditure in this way, as a constant tax burden and a separate transfer payment, the two different functions of government are restored to their customary formal presentation, and the words "revenue" and "spending" can be applied consistently to economically identical (but formally different) modes of implementation. As so recast, it is easy to see that Freedonia's economic handprint on the private sector is no longer $1,500 in tax revenues, but rather $1,667 in economic terms. The government is bigger in every meaningful sense of the word.

Fourth, deadweight loss cannot be avoided by electing "targeted tax relief" without revenue offsets. This point may seem obvious to many readers, but I am confident that, without explicit discussion of the point, at least some members of Congress would conclude that the only problem with tax expenditures is trying to pay for them.

The simple fact is that, as the third lesson sought to demonstrate, the kumquat credit is a form of government spending. Once one acknowledges (as the more rational members of the tax triumphalism movement do) that tax cuts (or direct subsidies) cannot entirely pay for themselves, the government has only four choices as to how to finance this net spending. First, it can pay for its incremental spending on a current basis by raising taxes on someone else. Second, the government can borrow money today and repay it with future taxes. Third, the government can borrow today and inflate its way out of the problem—but inflation is just another kind of a tax imposed haphazardly and often cruelly on capital owners or claimants to fixed revenue streams like pensioners. Fourth, the government can borrow today and default on its debt in the future. No other options are available.

If you agree with me that the fourth way is a bad idea, then you are left with the realization that each new tax expenditure necessarily implies a tax increase. I can think of no more important principle of public finance for policymakers to absorb.

BUDGET PROCESS AND PRESENTATION CONCERNS

Because of Congress's pervasive use of tax expenditures, we cannot determine by inspection of our budget how much support the federal government provides to different sectors of the private economy. And in turn, because the facts are not presented in a straightforward manner, we cannot debate fairly the efficiency costs of a system in which spending and revenues are disguised from both citizens and many legislators.

Congress's consistent use of tax expenditures to achieve what Daniel Shaviro calls an "allocative" agenda (that is, these programs are designed to affect how goods and services are priced and sold in the marketplace) means that words like "spending" and "taxing" lose their significance.[13] This means that historical or cross-country comparisons are not as reliable as they could be, because the United States at different times, or different countries today, can choose a mix of how they deliver these allocative programs—either directly, as subsidies, or indirectly, through tax benefits.

Congress relies on the low visibility (the technical term is "salience") of tax subsidies to increase spending on favored policies, by decreasing the visibility of those benefits to most observers (but not, of course, to the beneficiaries) and simultaneously decreasing the visibility of the tax costs incurred to finance those spending policies. Low salience thus is associated with bigger government—that is, a larger tax base. The result is a classic example of *fiscal illusion*, in which both taxpayers and many members of Congress underestimate the real extent of government spending (and therefore the tax costs of financing that hidden spending).[14] Tax expenditures augment fiscal illusion, and fiscal illusion, in turn, drives poor policy.

The budgetary imperative to spend through the tax system also interferes with the internal workings of Congress. Tax expenditures are bestowed by the tax-writing committees, not the substantive authorization committees. Petitioners for federal largesse therefore can and do file claims with multiple committees: if the Farm Bill created through the normal authorization process does not contain what you want, just ask the Senate Finance Committee for a tax credit. The result is appropriated spending and tax credits that duplicate, overlap, or conflict with one another.

In the same vein, "permanent" tax subsidies are not subject to any sort of review or oversight by the Congressional committees charged with substance matter expertise, and no comprehensive Congressional review of tax expenditures exists. So tax expenditures, once implemented, are essentially unmonitored by any arm of Congress. Instead, they simply disappear below the surface into the mainstream of baseline revenues.

All of this would be interesting to those involved in creating the federal budget and almost no one else, except for the fact that tax expenditures unquestionably constitute by far our most wasteful government spending. Unfortunately for the cause of virtue, that spending is directed primarily at middle class and affluent voters, who rely on self-interest and self-induced fiscal illusion to insist that their subsidies be retained.

EVALUATING TAX EXPENDITURES ON THE MERITS

To be clear, the fact that a spending program is delivered to individuals through the tax system does not mean that the program necessarily must be poor policy. The point, rather, is that it in fact is a spending program, and its design and consequences should be explicitly debated and tested on that basis.[15] Our tax subsidies for owner-occupied housing (i.e., your home) are a perfect example. If I were to propose that the federal government should give higher-income Americans cash subsidies to enable them to buy bigger homes, my sanity would be suspected, but when we do exactly the same thing in the form of various tax deductions for housing, the thought never crosses most of our minds.

From the other direction, the earned income tax credit is an example of an instance where spending through the tax code is perfectly sensible. This credit, it will be recalled, is designed to "make work pay" for low-income Americans. Its generosity is keyed not only to income levels, but also to the number of children that a worker has. As a substantive matter, many economists think that the EITC is a great way to get people into the workforce, because it reduces the initial financial barriers to doing so (clothing, child care, commuting costs, and so on). And as a process matter, the tax system is the most efficient delivery vehicle. By definition, the tax system is already in the business of collecting information on a worker's income, and the number of her dependents also is part of the information already collected on every tax return. Finally, the IRS has the capability of issuing tens of millions of refund checks every year. Given that the necessary data already are being collected, and that mechanisms already are in place to get cash to the people who qualify, it makes sense to use the tax system to deliver the cash benefits of the earned income tax credit, rather than to invent a whole new federal agency to do so.

Every tax expenditure therefore must be evaluated on its own merits. Nonetheless, when one does perform this sort of evaluation, many tax expenditures, including some of the most expensive ones, fail miserably: that is, they represent extraordinarily costly government spending programs that do not deliver commensurate social welfare benefits.

In 2008, during my tenure as chief of staff, the staff of the Joint Committee on Taxation undertook a comprehensive review of tax expenditure analysis in a pamphlet titled *A Reconsideration of Tax Expenditure Analysis*. Its purpose was to assist policymakers in using tax expenditure analysis "as an effective and neutral analytical tool" to analyze tax proposals.[16] One of the principal contributions of *A Reconsideration of Tax Expenditure Analysis* was to urge that tax expenditures be grouped into different conceptual buckets, so that each could fairly be analyzed in accordance with its overall purpose, and compared to other expenditures serving a similar overall purpose. To my regret, the staff of the Joint Committee on Taxation later retreated from the presentation recommended in the pamphlet. I think that this reversal unfortunately weakened the utility of tax expenditure analysis in general.

Tax expenditure analysis traditionally has identified "tax expenditures" as those provisions of the tax code that are said to deviate from a hypothetical "normal tax" system. The fundamental problem, however, is that this "normal tax" system is itself a contentious normative assertion, rather than an economic fact. To mitigate the importance of the "normal tax" concept, *A Reconsideration of Tax Expenditure Analysis* recommended that items traditionally labeled as tax expenditures be divided into two main groups: "tax subsidies" and "tax-induced structural distortions." The former category contained the majority of tax expenditures; it comprised those items that a fair reading of the Internal Revenue Code would suggest were exceptions, not to some hypothetical ideal called the normal tax, but rather to the general rules visible on the face of the Code itself. Tax-induced structural distortions comprised important tax provisions traditionally categorized as tax expenditures, but where the general rules of the Code were not clearly visible, so that it was impossible to say which was the exception and which the rule. The treatment of the international income of US multinational corporations is a perfect example of an economically important tax provision that cannot fairly be described as a simple exception to a general rule of the Internal Revenue Code.

A Reconsideration of Tax Expenditure Analysis further recommended that the world of tax subsidies (which again comprised the vast bulk of tax expenditures) be subdivided into three conceptual buckets: Tax Transfers (refundable credits);

Social Spending (tax subsidies unrelated to the production of business income, which are intended to subsidize or incentivize non-business behaviors, such as the subsidy for charitable giving); and Business Synthetic Spending. Tax expenditures that fall into the last category in particular, in my view, are inherently suspect, as they represent direct Congressional meddling in the operation of our marketplace economy.

A Reconsideration of Tax Expenditure Analysis showed how tax expenditures could be analyzed under traditional tax considerations of equity, efficiency, and ease of administration. These considerations weigh differently across the different conceptual buckets described above. For example, one might expect a Business Synthetic Spending tax expenditure to be justifiable primarily on efficiency grounds, while equity considerations in general dominate the design of Tax Transfers.

Finally, *A Reconsideration of Tax Expenditure Analysis* offered some insights into how best to design a tax expenditure, once the decision to offer a tax subsidy had been made through the political process. The pamphlet emphasized the goals of designing subsidies that are transparent (so that costs are easily identifiable, and the identity of beneficiaries made clear), well-targeted (so that the subsidy goes to change behavior in the direction that policymakers intend, and not to reward people who would have engaged in the activity in any event), and certain (so that intended beneficiaries know that they qualify, and can plan accordingly).

Here is an excerpt from the report that applied some of these principles to the vexing question of our very large government subsidies for owner-occupied housing:

> To take a well-known example, the Federal income tax today contains several large subsidies (incentives) for home ownership. Most economists would agree that these tax subsidies are welfare-diminishing. The tax expenditures can be described as introducing inequality of after-tax treatment between otherwise similarly-situated home owners and home renters. The incentives can also be seen as introducing inequities in another sense, by virtue of what Stanley Surrey called their "upside down" design— that is, the fact that these tax expenditures, by being structured as tax deductions, give proportionately greater government subsidies to taxpayers with higher incomes (because the value of a tax deduction is determined by the taxpayer's marginal tax rate). Housing tax subsidies can also be viewed as inefficient, in at least three respects. First, they encourage private capital to be diverted into the housing sector from other investments that would have been made in a world without such incentives, thereby raising the cost of capital for the rest of the economy. Second, the revenues forgone by providing these tax subsidies must be made up by raising marginal tax rates, and those higher tax rates by themselves introduce distortions in behavior. Finally, current law's housing incentives certainly add significant complexity to our tax system.

Nonetheless, the political process has concluded that subsidizing home ownership is desirable. This conclusion can be explained as reflecting factors other than efficiency—for example, "externalities" such as the possible advantages to society of having its citizens feel more "invested" in their communities, and committed to the larger political system, that might stem from homeownership. Moreover, a simple application of tax expenditure analysis along the lines summarized above might be criticized in this context (when one is reviewing a longstanding tax expenditure) for assuming a world where decisions had not been distorted for many decades by these incentives; the technical analysis of what to do with those tax expenditures in light of that past history, or in light (in this case) of the market dislocations that this sector of the economy currently is suffering, might be completely different from the analysis that would be applied to a completely new proposed tax expenditure.

To conclude this example, tax expenditure analysis can shed helpful light on the costs (in the broad sense, including, as noted above, environmental costs and similar externalities) of tax subsidies associated with owner-occupied housing, or can propose ways of rethinking the subsidies that might reduce their costs (for example, the replacement of housing-related tax deductions with tax credits). The ultimate decision as to the net societal welfare to be gained by subsidizing home ownership, however, can only be resolved through the political process.[17]

The opponents of this subsidy have by far the better of the argument. The subsidy is inefficient, because it induces Americans systematically to overinvest their capital in homes, rather than in productive business investments; the subsidy is inequitable, in that its benefits go primarily to the highest-income Americans (the "upside down" subsidy problem associated with any subsidy that takes the form of a tax deduction); and the subsidy is poorly targeted, in that its benefits in many cases go to individuals who would have bought a home in any event.

HOW MUCH IS AT STAKE?

By any measure, tax expenditures represent an enormous part of the federal government's operations. Forty years ago, Congress charged the staff of the Joint Committee on Taxation to track tax expenditures and to estimate their magnitude. The JCT staff's first report, in 1972, counted 60 such items. In its 2013 report, the JCT staff listed around 250 instances of spending programs delivered in the form of tax subsidies. (The report also lists 30 *de minimis* tax expenditures, each of which can cost up to $50 million over five years.) Every two years, the nonpartisan Congressional Research Service summarizes the government's tax expenditure programs; the most recent such publication (from December 2012) runs for over 1,000 pages.[18]

The simple sum of the forgone revenues from the 250 major tax expenditures is about $1.2 trillion a year. Ninety-two percent of that money represented tax

THE HIDDEN HAND OF GOVERNMENT SPENDING 255

expenditures for individuals, while 8 percent represented a reduction of corporate income tax.

If all tax expenditures somehow were repealed (a sort of tax expenditure mass extinction event), the total effect on tax revenues would vary somewhat from $1.2 trillion, for a great many reasons, but that is not really the point.[19] The point rather is that the number would be an enormous one. Since no one has calculated a true "clean slate" revenue base, it is convenient to use the $1.2 trillion figure, so long as one remembers that it is only an approximation of the net cost of all tax expenditures taken together.

To put $1.2 trillion of tax expenditures into context, that sum is greater than the *entire amount raised by the individual income tax in 2012*, and is roughly equal to all federal discretionary spending in that year. Indeed, it is about twice as much as all nondefense discretionary spending in 2012. If tax expenditures were treated in our national accounts as what they are, rather than as reductions in tax revenues, we would have seen that 2013 spending was about $4.7 trillion rather than the $3.5 trillion officially listed. By the same token, 2013 tax collections in economic reality totaled $4.0 trillion, rather than the $2.8 trillion listed in the actual budget. And there is nothing at all special about 2013—the same point (with roughly the same orders of magnitude) can be made about any earlier or later year in the last decade or so.

In 2008, our nondefense, non–safety net annual spending through tax subsidies was about 275 percent of the amount of explicit government outlays in those areas. In other words, when looking at education, transportation, scientific research, and every other activity by which the federal government touches the day-to-day lives of middle class and affluent Americans under the age of 65, our official scorekeeping in that year captured only 27 percent of the government's actual spending—the remaining 72 percent was delivered by hidden spending in the tax code.[20]

So tax expenditures are enormous in absolute terms, are larger than explicit government spending in comparable areas, and have grown rapidly. As a share of GDP, tax expenditures are now at a much higher level than in 1974, when federal accounting for tax expenditures was first officially adopted. In 1974, for example, the simple sum of all tax expenditures amounted to 5.7 percent of GDP. The simple sum of all tax expenditures now totals about 8.5 percent of GDP, the highest percentage since the mid-1980s. To put this number in context, if tax expenditures in 2013 were the same percentage of GDP as was the case in 1974, the simple sum of current tax expenditures would have been some $465 billion lower than the actual estimates!

Official tax expenditure estimates by the Treasury Department and the JCT staff include only income tax expenditures. This estimate understates the importance of tax subsidies in some important areas, particularly energy policy.

A Department of Energy study, for example, found that tax expenditures for energy production amounted to $10.4 billion in 2007; of this amount, nearly $3 billion was attributable to excise tax credits for ethanol production alone, and therefore was absent from official JCT staff and Treasury Department lists of income tax expenditures. Consistent with my larger theme, that Department of Energy study also found that, in constant 2007 dollars, tax expenditures for energy production and conservation more than tripled over eight years, from $3.2 billion in 1999 to $10.4 billion in 2007, and made up an increasingly large share of total federal government financial support over this period.

In a wonderful display of fiscal schizophrenia, the federal government offers tax subsidies for alternative energy at the same time that it also provides tax expenditures for fossil fuel production. Oil companies are simply excused from tax principles that apply to other businesses (for example, through rules that allow certain oil companies to write off the cost of creating new wells, rather than recovering those costs over time as is true for other capital investments). In doing so, we offer the lucky beneficiaries discounted tax rates, which of course are the same as simply taxing the firms on the same terms as those that apply to every other business, and writing a check to the oil companies for the difference.

There is no plausible case to be made for these subsidies, which have been maintained for decades. There are no apparent market failures for which government intervention might be justified, and there is no disagreement about the relevant tax principles from which oil companies are excused.

It sometimes is argued that these subsidies "encourage" oil production, as if that were a free good, or enhance our energy security, or reduce prices at the pump, but these arguments fall of their own weight. First, in the absence of some externality or other market failure, our economy generally relies on markets to set levels of production, without an outside force putting its hands on the scales. (Ironically, of course, many of the same political voices that stand for the unfettered role of markets find themselves defending these particular interventions.) Second—and this is a problem with a large number of tax expenditures—most of these subsidies go to firms that would have done exactly the same things without being subsidized. As a result, the money does not advance any national security agenda, but rather is simply wasted. And third, lower prices at the pump (if such in fact is the case, and firms do not simply capture the value of the subsidy for themselves) are offset dollar for dollar by higher taxes on all of us (or larger deficits, which is the same thing).

WHO BENEFITS?

Every tax expenditure has its own distributional story to accompany its intended purpose. The earned income tax credit, for example, obviously benefits low-income households, and just as obviously the capital gains preference benefits high-income ones. On an overall basis, however, higher-income Americans capture the bulk of the benefits of these hidden spending programs.

In 2013, the Congressional Budget Office examined 10 major tax expenditures, amounting to some $900 billion in subsidies in that year (about two-thirds of all tax expenditures in dollar value). The CBO found that the top 20 percent of households (ranked by before-tax incomes) were awarded 50 percent of this honey pot, and the top one percent of households, 15 percent (see Figure 9.1).[21] In other words, in 2013 these selected tax expenditures amounted to $60 billion in synthetic transfer payments from ordinary Americans to the most affluent one percent of households in America.

This distribution reflects three facts. First, tax subsidies for investment income, such as the capital gains preference, are quite large in amount and very top-weighted in distribution. Second, the largest single tax expenditure, the income exclusion for employer-sponsored health insurance, increases in value with one's tax rate, and requires employment by an employer that offers such insurance.

And third, the largest cluster of income tax expenditures, taken as a group, are the personal itemized deductions—the deductions we claim that subsidize our homes (the home mortgage interest deduction, the deduction for local property

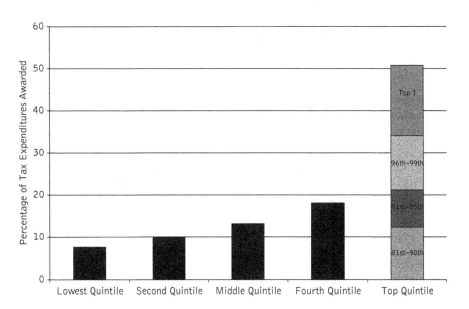

FIGURE 9.1 Household Shares of Top 10 Individual Income Tax Expenditures, by Incomes

Source: CBO, *The Distribution of Major Tax Expenditures in the Individual Income Tax System*, fig. 1.

taxes, etc.), our charitable contributions, our state and local income taxes, and so on. Personal itemized deductions are projected to cost at least $240 billion in forgone income tax revenues for 2013, and that cost will climb as the economy recovers.

The benefits from the personal itemized deductions go overwhelmingly to higher-income taxpayers. For example, a paper by Adam Cole of the US Treasury Department and others analyzed who obtained the benefits of the home mortgage interest deduction.[22] They found that approximately 80 percent of the value of the mortgage interest deduction went to the top 20 percent of incomes, and 50 percent to the top 10 percent.

Intuitively, this makes sense, for three reasons. First, mortgage interest expense does not reduce your tax bill at all unless you have enough income and sufficient expenses of the right type to itemize your personal deductions rather than to claim the standard deduction. Second, the value of the deduction increases with your tax rate. And third, the amount deductible increases with the size of your mortgage, and as a general matter higher-income Americans are likely to be able to afford larger mortgages. If the purpose of the mortgage interest deduction is to encourage homeownership among first-time homebuyers, it is a resounding flop; many first-time buyers do not even itemize their deductions, and therefore do not claim the mortgage interest deduction. If its purpose is to subsidize the acquisition of McMansions, it arguably is a success: but is that really the highest and best use of our scarce government resources?

The personal itemized deductions have important negative economic efficiency consequences, because they lead to a fundamental misallocation of capital in the private sector, in the form of our overinvestment in single-family homes compared to other forms of capital investment.[23] They also are classic examples of upside-down government subsidies, in which affluent Americans get a bigger subsidy from every dollar they spend than do lower-income taxpayers, because the value of the subsidy is determined by the tax rate of your top dollar of income, on which you no longer have to pay tax by virtue of the personal itemized deduction. And of course in a large number of cases we provide these subsidies to those who would have bought their homes (or made charitable contributions, or chosen to live in high-tax states) regardless of the tax incentives.[24] In these cases the subsidy is just manna from heaven—or more accurately, from all the rest of us who pay for the manna in the form of our higher taxes or reduced government services.

THE SACRED TAX COWS OF PERSONAL ITEMIZED DEDUCTIONS—IT'S THEM OR US

Chapter 13 makes some specific suggestions about fiscal reforms that we should undertake. Without my meaning to spoil the surprise, it turns out that curbing tax expenditures is the most powerful single fiscal instrument by which we can right our fiscal ship.

In very rough terms, the total federal government subsidy for "private" employer-sponsored health insurance will be on the order of $3 trillion over the next 10 years, including both income tax and payroll tax effects. Subsidies for personal itemized deductions—that is to say, the subsidization of personal consumption decisions of higher-income Americans through the tax code—will amount to something in the range of $2 to $2.5 trillion over 10 years.

I recognize that all of these items are frequently described as political "sacred cows," but they simply are luxuries that we no longer can afford. Either we corral these sacred cows, or they will stampede us.

The tax subsidy for employer-sponsored health insurance necessarily stands on its own, because any change here would only make sense as part of the migration to more rational provisioning of healthcare services generally, in which the tax revenues saved would be applied to mitigating the costs of whatever that new system might be. At the time of writing, however, the political environment is so toxic when it comes to government interventions in healthcare that it would be less realistic than a pipe dream's pipe dream to suggest actually touching the healthcare subsidy. For reasons of discretion rather than logic, therefore, I limit my thoughts here to the personal itemized deductions.

The personal itemized deductions should be converted into nonrefundable tax credits at a 15 percent tax benefit rate: that is, a $100 deduction would be converted into a $15 cash equivalent, in the form of a tax credit.[25] To ease the pain for those taxpayers living in particular at the margin of affordability of their homes, the new principles should be phased in over a few years.

A 15 percent tax credit leaves in place about one-half the aggregate value of the personal itemized deductions, which mitigates some of the transition concerns. If the process were to stop there, we would raise around $1.1 trillion over the next 10 years. If we phased down the 15 percent credit to zero over the second five years, revenues would rise commensurately, and going forward into the second decade after the reform we would by this one stroke alone have filled half or more of the revenue shortfall I described in the previous section.

Even if we were to stop at simply converting the itemized deductions into a 15 percent tax credit, we would not only raise very large revenues, but also strike a blow for economic efficiency. The result would be that these activities still would be subsidized, but to a much smaller degree, and the subsidy no longer would be "upside-down." In other words, all taxpayers who itemize would get the same $15 tax benefit from a $100 charitable contribution (or whatever), rather than getting a bigger subsidy if they are in a higher tax bracket.

Compared with other revenue-raising alternatives, our efficiency gains would come from the fact that we would raise this incremental revenue *without* raising marginal tax rates. (The right comparison is not to current law, because current law is unaffordable.) And as described in the previous chapter, we would undo the misallocation of capital in the private sector that stems from our overinvestment in single-family homes compared to other forms of capital investment. We also would eliminate the inefficiencies by which we provide these subsidies to those who would have bought their homes (or made charitable contributions, or chosen to live in high-tax states) regardless of the tax incentives.

Finally, the elimination of the tax preferences for these items also would add to the progressivity of the tax system, because itemizers generally have higher pre-tax incomes than do taxpayers claiming the standard deduction.[26] (Only about one-third of tax filers are eligible to claim itemized deductions today.)

In sum, the personal itemized deductions, as the name implies, are all *personal* expenses. Replacing them with scaled-back tax credits (ideally phasing down to zero) would make the tax system more progressive, more efficient, less distortive, and simpler. Doing so would also raise a great deal of a lot of money without adding unduly to the deadweight loss from taxation, and raising more tax revenue in general is something that we have no choice but to embrace, as chapters 6 through 8 already have emphasized.

The reason to scale back *all* of the personal itemized deductions is that it is impossible to choose among them. Each can be defended as an incentive for one desirable goal or another. Our only practical hope is to round up and eliminate all these tax sacred cows at once.

Others have made similar pleas, but often those are accompanied by a willingness to excuse charitable contributions from any scale-back. I understand the impulse to protect charitable giving, but I do not agree with it.

At one level, charitable giving at its best operates like an extension of government social services, but with a unique political economy story. There is something charming about the democratic way in which we subsidize culture in the United States. If I want to give to the Museum of String, all of you (acting of course through the intermediation of government) come along for the ride, in the form of the tax savings you award me. In other countries, state awards to the Arts with a capital "A" lose this democratic flavor, and often are criticized for institutionalizing particular aesthetic preferences (Rachmaninoff over Robin Thicke, for example).

Nonetheless, charitable giving must be included in the roundup of tax sacred cows. Charitable giving is not a substitute for government social services, as the objects of donors' affections typically reflect the donors' backgrounds, business connections, and desires for social status. To be blunt, the money pours into the nation's greatest private universities, opera companies, medical centers, and art museums, but the poor and disenfranchised from races or backgrounds very different from those of the largest donors are infrequently the beneficiaries of commensurate largesse. There also is an argument that charitable support is in some respects more degrading to recipients than government income maintenance programs; such support certainly is less reliable, as donors' preferences and financial resources fluctuate.

Charitable giving is very top-weighted by incomes, and leaving it protected vitiates much of the progressivity of the proposal to convert personal itemized deductions into credits. Moreover, charitable giving is rife with questionable practices (for example, donor-advised funds or the aggressive use of charitable remainder unitrusts) that have little to do with the eleemosynary purposes for which the charitable contribution deduction was intended. Excusing one personal itemized deduction also opens up impossible political economy problems, as proponents of the others explain why they too represent important public goods. Finally, the large institutional recipients of charitable giving in many cases get a double or triple subsidy: the subsidy for giving, the subsidy in the form of tax exemption in respect of their multibillion-dollar endowments, and the subsidies that come from government-financed research or similar activities that those institutions undertake, which have enormous spillover benefits for the institutions.

The incremental revenues that would result from eliminating or scaling back personal itemized deductions would fill a large fraction of the revenue hole from which we need to climb out, and would do so with as little economic harm as is possible, given the revenue constraints. Closing down these inefficient, poorly targeted, and unfairly top-weighted government subsidy programs would constitute a major achievement in fiscal reform.

LOW TAXES YET HIGH PAIN

Chapter 8 explained that in 2012 the United States had the *lowest* tax collections of any OECD country as a percentage of GDP. Yet we do not behave as if that is the case: to the contrary, all the evidence suggests that we are a nation of tax whiners. Are there reasons for this, beyond revealing an odd national personality trait, dating back to the Boston Tea Party?[27]

Tax expenditures are a large part of the explanation. Tax expenditures distort our understanding of the tax pain that we inflict on ourselves by reducing government tax revenues in the official scorekeeping, rather than being recorded in a manner consistent with their substance, as additional tax collections offset by government spending programs. And in turn, the United States is a tax expenditure junkie: as just explained, the United States spent more through income tax expenditures in 2012 than it collected in income tax. This means that our *tax rate structure* operates as if we collected more than $2 trillion in income tax, not $1 trillion, and then ran additional government spending programs that cost more than $1 trillion/year.

In other words, our low tax collections are raised through a tax rate structure whose marginal rates are appropriate to a much larger taxing function than the official scorekeeping suggests. And looking at matters from the opposite direction, if additional tax revenue is needed (and chapters 6 through 8 have already demonstrated that it is), the best way to raise that additional revenue is through "inframarginal" tax collections, which is the economist's way of saying that we should broaden the tax base rather than raise marginal rates. The reason, as described in chapter 2, is that marginal rates have a greater negative impact on our behavior—not just our propensity for tax whining, but the economic choices we make—than do average tax rates.

Scaling back tax expenditures raises tax revenues without any need to touch statutory tax rates. Admittedly, doing so can have marginal tax implications from the perspective of effective (rather than statutory) marginal tax rates—particularly for the earned income tax credit, which I conceptualize more as an adjustment to the tax rate scale for low-wage labor income than a true tax expenditure. Nonetheless, the effective marginal tax rate implications of scaling back tax expenditures in practice either are more muted when some of the largest and most inefficient tax expenditures are considered, particularly the personal itemized deductions, or simply are dominated by the efficiency losses of current law's subsidies.

This is why every major tax reform initiative begins by proposing a vast reduction in subsidies delivered through the tax code. By doing so, either the existing rate structure can be retained, and more revenues collected, or alternatively existing revenue levels can be maintained and tax rates lowered.

Chapters 6 and 13 explain why we have no choice but to follow the first path. We are the mirror image of the fellow in the old story who complains to his doctor that his wife thinks she is a chicken. "How long has this been going on?" asks the doctor. "About 10 years," says the fellow. "And you just came to see me now?" "Well, the fact of the matter," the fellow explains, "is that we needed the eggs." Going forward, we find ourselves in need of the eggs, and so must keep the revenues that follow from scaling back the many inefficient or downright perverse hidden spending programs couched in the form of tax breaks.

The second reason for our low tolerance for tax pain is that the federal government in particular collects its showpiece tax—the personal income tax—in the most painful way possible, by asking each of us to assess the tax against ourselves. For most Americans, that means starting from a blank form and a shoebox full of miscellaneous pieces of financial data.

Self-assessment is unavoidable, but the pain can be mitigated if the IRS were to send taxpayers a "prepopulated" tax return that reflects the data already furnished to the IRS. (Imagine, for example, receiving a partially filled-out tax Form 1040 in which all the information concerning your investment income contained in the

1099s thrown into your shoebox had already been entered for you on the appropriate lines.) Programs like this are feasible (and even exist in California and in other countries), but have been blocked in the United States in part through the vigorous lobbying of tax preparation companies anxious to protect their franchises. Here, the tax pain is the result of legislative sausage making at its most venal.

The third reason for our low threshold of tax pain lies deeper: We have allowed our fiscal debates to be framed in a way that highlights only the pain of opening our wallets. We can see this backward framing of the issues, for example, in the debate over sequestration, where it is claimed that because taxes cannot rise further, spending must be cut—without any examination of what purpose that government spending serves. By ignoring the uses to which tax revenues are put, these debates implicitly deprecate the very purpose of government.

When you set out to buy a house, you think carefully about how big a house you can afford, but in the end you are not poorer for the money you spent, because you acquired something useful, namely, a new home. Why then in fiscal debates do we look only at the cost of government, and not at the collective goods or services we thereby acquire? Unsurprisingly, once we phrase tax policy as a collective exercise in fiscal masochism, our threshold for tax pain turns out to be very low.

PART III

RECLAIMING OUR FISCAL SOUL

CHAPTER 10

GOVERNMENT INVESTMENT

The sovereign...[has] the duty of erecting and maintaining certain pub-
lic works and public institutions, which it can never be for the interest of
any individual, or small number of individuals, to erect and maintain;
because the profit could never repay the expence to any individual or
small number of individuals, though it may frequently do more than
repay it to a great society.
—ADAM SMITH, *The Wealth of Nations*, Book IV, Chap. IX.

PART II OF this book summarized what government does today to enhance the happiness of our society, and how we finance the activities that government pursues. Part III extends the analysis by considering more closely the opportunities available for us to invest in ourselves, and to provide better and cheaper social insurance, thereby benefiting our entire society. The case for more public investment and insurance is persuasive even when viewed through a narrow commercial lens, and it becomes even more compelling when one adopts a comprehensive construct of our welfare. What is more, we can afford to exploit these opportunities without radically changing our tax system.

This chapter focuses on the role of government as an investor in public goods, both in respect of classic "hard" infrastructure investments and in respect of investments in science and education. It analyzes the commercial as well as social returns to public investment and suggests how a national infrastructure bank can help to finance the investment opportunities that surround us. Chapter 11 argues for a more comprehensive understanding of what insurance is all about, and how government (that is, all of us, acting together) is well situated to offer social insurance that is cheaper and more comprehensive than what private markets can provide.

Chapter 12 addresses again the issue of progressivity, but this time to demonstrate that what we should care about is the progressive impact of the entirety of our fiscal system, not just our tax structures. Government investment and insurance lead to progressive fiscal systems, even when funded by mildly regressive taxes. Chapter 13 proposes how our existing tax system can be overhauled to raise the revenues required to seize the opportunities identified in the previous two chapters (and implicit in our unbalanced budget today), through a package of improvements I have dubbed the Better Base Case. Finally, chapter 14 concludes by returning to some of the moral philosophy themes with which the book began, and asks whether the path that we are following today really is consistent with the purposes of government that Thomas Jefferson identified when he wrote in the Declaration of Independence that our government should be organized "to effect [our] Safety and Happiness."

THE MANY FACES OF INVESTMENT

Government regularly invests in infrastructure (large-scale physical capital projects, like roads, sewage treatment plants, or hospitals), and in human capital, through public education. Public investment yields high returns, both in straight economic terms and in respect of the ultimate purpose of government, which is the happiness of society. These investments complement rather than compete with private markets, and do not get made if one relies on private markets alone.

Public investment in the United States is now at its lowest level since the demobilization following World War II (see Figure 10.1). On a net basis—that is, taking into account the depreciation (wear and tear) on our existing investments—we now are investing almost nothing in public infrastructure, even after adding state and local government investment with federal investment.[1]

As a result, we are leaving on the table today collective investment opportunities that would redound to all of our welfare, were we to seize them.

The first part of this chapter makes the case for larger commitments to public infrastructure, and argues that a national infrastructure bank can address many of the implementation issues that bedevil public projects, adding by bringing into the mix new sources of private financing. The second part continues the analysis by examining the importance of government investment in education. In each case, the basic point is that we can be a richer and happier society if government were to spend more, not less, because these investments have high economic as well as social returns, and will not otherwise be made.

The aims of this chapter are modest, in arguing only for more systematic public investments along familiar lines. Some recent academic literature goes further, and seeks to resurrect the idea of "industrial policy," by which government makes investments or policies designed to affect directly the allocation of

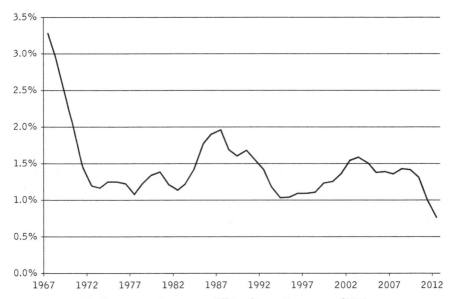

FIGURE 10.1 Net Government Investment (All Levels) as a Percentage of GDP

Source: St. Louis Federal Reserve FRED database; Bureau of Economic Analysis.

goods and services in the economy—by nudging private markets in a particular direction.[2] The underlying theories rest heavily on the problems arising from the same market failures on which this book relies, but the implementation of explicit industrial policy in the United States is famously fraught (for example, the excitement surrounding US Department of Energy loans to Solyndra, a photovoltaic cell manufacturer that went bankrupt), and in any event is made more uncertain by the size and complexity of our economy. In the end, I take the route that we should be so lucky simply to ramp up traditional forms of public investment, including in this category basic scientific research.

INFRASTRUCTURE

The Sorry State of Our Infrastructure

Since the construction of the Erie Canal (financed by the State of New York, notwithstanding Thomas Jefferson's famous objection that the project was "a little short of madness"), government has played a large role in infrastructure investment in the United States. The grant of public lands to nineteenth-century railroad companies to finance their transcontinental expansions, the Hoover Dam, the Tennessee Valley Authority, and the interstate highway system are all familiar examples of federal investment in critical infrastructure. And of course today water and sewage systems are most commonly owned by state and local government agencies, as is much electricity generation and distribution.

As our commitment to doing things together through the intermediation of government has eroded, so too has our ability to invest in new infrastructure, or to maintain the state of our existing investments. We celebrate the Hoover Dam as if it were completed yesterday, when in fact it will soon celebrate its 80th birthday. What civil engineering project in the last 30 years commands comparable national respect? Boston's "Big Dig"? That was a routine regional road improvement project, made to seem consequential only by comparison to the timidity of our other infrastructure commitments, and by its enormous delays and cost overruns. (Hoover Dam, by contrast, was finished two years ahead of schedule.)

The American Society of Civil Engineers (ASCE) regularly reviews the state of American infrastructure: their latest report card (2013) gave the United States a grade of D+, up from an F in 2009, thanks to the additional funding provided by the American Recovery and Reinvestment Act (ARRA).[3] The ASCE estimates that the amount of infrastructure investment that we require over the next eight years is $3.6 trillion, against total projected governmental funding (federal, state, and local) of about $2 trillion, leaving a funding gap in the neighborhood of $200 billion/year.[4]

By way of context, the entire nondefense discretionary budget of the federal government is projected to average about $600 billion/year over the next decade. While much routine infrastructure maintenance and investment is funded through state and local governments, this nonetheless gives a sense of the commitment that would be required to change our current dismal trajectory. And of course the ASCE does not even address investment in Internet access or "Big Science" projects, as described below.

By way of a concrete example, in August 2013, a new overpass opened in Southern California that eliminated the Colton Crossing rail intersection.[5] Colton Crossing dated from 1883, and had remained essentially unchanged (but for better signal equipment) for 130 years. It was the rail equivalent of a four-way stop intersection for two of the busiest rail lines in America: the north-south Burlington Northern tracks and the east-west Union Pacific line. Goods moving from the largest container port in the United States (Los Angeles/Long Beach), as well as passenger trains, were delayed for hours as trains waited their turn to cross the intersection. It cost less than $200 million to resolve this century-old problem, but this self-evidently necessary project had to wait for the American Recovery and Reinvestment Act of 2009 to scrounge up the requisite funding.

And of course other massive rail bottlenecks remain unaddressed. Indeed, one of the most obvious is that there is no direct rail connection to the Long Beach container port, with the result that containers must be offloaded from ships onto trucks, to be hauled a few miles on a traffic-choked highway to the rail yards. These are stories we expect to read about the rail system in Bangladesh, not the United States.

Passenger rail systems are in no better shape. Every day, nearly half a million unlucky souls—almost as many as inhabit all of Wyoming—descend into the windowless fluorescent hell of New York's Pennsylvania Station rail and subway hub. Almost from the day its transcendentally beautiful Beaux Arts predecessor was wantonly destroyed in the 1960s, planners have sought to create a new transportation center that would serve America's largest city more effectively and that would be an object of national pride, rather than shame.

About 20 years ago, the Mckim, Mead, and White Post Office building across the street was identified as ideally suited to be the new home of the station. The 2009 ARRA finally funded the first tentative scratches in the dirt to undertake phase one of the construction, which amounts to nothing more than some new elevators, escalators, and entrances, and which will not be completed before 2016.[6] The future construction of the train hall itself inside the shell of the old Post Office is entirely unfunded (with a projected budget in the neighborhood of $1.5 billion).

The new Penn Station was to have been the visible jewel in a major upgrade in passenger rail service from the mainland of America to Manhattan, including the construction of a desperately needed new passenger rail tunnel between New Jersey and Penn Station—the first new tunnel in 100 years. But in 2010 New Jersey's Governor Christie torpedoed the entire federal–New York–New Jersey project just as it was getting underway, for reasons having much more to do with national political posturing than New Jersey's financial commitments, which amounted to only about 14 percent of the project's cost.[7] It was not until the devastation caused by Hurricane Sandy that Congress, as part of the relief effort, provided some funds to Amtrak to protect part of a future tunnel's route from being made permanently inaccessible as a result of construction of new residential towers on Manhattan's West Side.[8]

Amtrak has now attempted to revive the project (renamed the Gateway Project), including the relocation of Amtrak's portion of Penn Station, the tunnel under the Hudson River, and the replacement of a century-old railroad bridge over the Secaucus River. The proposal is projected to cost about $15 billion, and might be completed by 2025, were it to be funded—but of course no funding has been made available.

A sensible dream born when I was a boy will not be realized before I die. The United States cannot muster the political consensus or money to build a new rail tunnel between Manhattan and the mainland of America, while at the same time the United Kingdom—a country in much worse financial shape—has scrounged up $23 billion to build London's Crossrail project, to improve transportation across that nation's largest city, and Turkey has found the wherewithal to build a major rail tunnel connecting Europe and Asia under the Bosphorus Strait in Istanbul.

The United States's inadequate investment in civil engineering infrastructure results in large hidden costs and dangers. According to a McKinsey study, our demand for roads exceeds capacity by 43 percent.[9] That study further estimated that 15 percent of our roads are in an "unacceptable" condition. Congestion resulting from our excess demand and poor road conditions results in $101 billion per year in excess fuel costs and time.[10] Additionally, the more time we spend on lower quality roads makes our transportation network one of the deadliest, with 33,000 Americans killed in 2010—a fatality rate that is 60 percent above the OECD per capita average.[11] Congestion and delays in our airports resulted in costs of almost $22 billion in 2012, which at current funding levels are expected to rise to $34 billion in 2020. Meanwhile, congestion on rail lines is costing the economy an estimated $200 billion per year. One of every nine bridges is rated as structurally deficient, and over 4,000 dams are classified as deficient, which includes 2,000 "high-hazard" dams.[12]

The four-lane Ambassador Bridge connecting Detroit to Windsor, Ontario, is said to be the highest dollar-volume international trade border crossing in the world; its traffic accounts for about one-quarter of all Canadian–American trade. The bridge was constructed in 1929, and is owned by one man. For years government leaders on both sides of the border have understood the need for a modern bridge that connects directly to the highway networks on both sides of the Detroit River, particularly given that the Ambassador Bridge dumps its Canadian-bound traffic onto local Windsor streets, but the project has been stymied by Michigan's inability to pay its $550 million share of the cost, as well as by lawsuits filed by the owner of the Ambassador Bridge. (The bulk of the financing would come from the federal government.) Only in 2013 did the project begin to lurch forward, and then because Canada has agreed to pay Michigan's share of the project's cost as well as its own.

In the 2013 World Airport Awards, the only American airport to crack the top-30 was the Cincinnati/Northern Kentucky International Airport, which came in at number 30.[13] Not a single train station in the United States made a list of the top 100 busiest train stations in the world. In addition, we are decades behind countries in Europe, Japan, and China when it comes to high-speed rail. The only passenger service in the United States than can charitably be characterized as high-speed is the Acela Express trains that run from Washington, D.C., to Boston; it occasionally reaches a speed of 150 miles per hour for brief segments, less than half the speed of the world's current fastest trains.[14]

Similar unmet needs can be told about every major city of the country; the Metropolitan Policy Program at the Brookings Institution has cataloged many good examples. These projects are not pipe dreams of supersonic people movers snaking through the mountains of California, but obvious and plainly productive projects that will enhance the quality of life for the millions of people that they collectively touch every day. But the opportunities are not limited to improved roads or better mass transit and intermodal transportation hubs. The country today suffers from large economic losses through the failure to fund and quickly implement the next generation of air traffic control, which by reducing airport delays would enhance productivity. Sewage treatment plants across the country regularly overflow with every hard rain, and 100-year-old water mains randomly burst with dismal frequency.

Many presentations of unmet infrastructure needs consider only civil engineering projects, but "infrastructure" encompasses much more than that. We all understand the importance of high-speed Internet services, but much of rural America still does not have twenty-first-century service available to it. In 2008, for example, the United States ranked 15th in the world among industrialized nations in high-speed Internet connectivity.[15]

"Big science" is another important example. The 2013 Nobel Prize in Physics was awarded to François Englert and Peter W. Higgs (of Belgium and the UK, respectively) "for the theoretical discovery of a mechanism that contributes to our understanding of the origin of mass of subatomic particles, and which recently was confirmed through the discovery of the predicted fundamental particle, by the ATLAS and CMS experiments at CERN's Large Hadron Collider." These theoretical insights might have been confirmed years earlier, had the United States not abandoned in 1993 (after $2 billion already had been spent) the Superconducting Super Collider (SSC) project then under construction in Texas.

It may be that the SSC was simply too gargantuan in concept, or too poorly managed, to be seen to completion, but the fact is that the United States for decades has enjoyed tremendous private sector productivity gains through serendipitous spinoffs from large-scale pure research projects, including the large ecosystems of scientists that surround the locations of the projects. We will not know for a generation if the construction of the Large Hadron Collider will have marked the beginning of the end of US dominance in physics research, but the fact is that there is little by way of new "Big Science" projects in the United States to which one can point. The International Space Station (ISS), which will absorb perhaps $100 billion of contributions by the United States, has only limited relevance to pure science, and its overall effectiveness has been reduced by the retirement of the space shuttle, which limits the number of scientists who can man the station at any one time. The James Webb Space Telescope is much more important from this perspective, but was nearly canceled in 2011, and may be yet, as it is still years from completion, and remains at risk in Congress's annual appropriations process.[16] Its $9 billion projected cost sounds gargantuan (except perhaps in relation to the ISS), but that cost will be spread out over many years, and still compares favorably to the cost of the Navy's newest aircraft carrier, the USS *Gerald Ford* (about $14.5 billion, not including nearly $5 billion in research and development costs[17]). Other NASA astrophysics projects are largely unfunded. Meanwhile, ITER, the international consortium building the world's first break-even nuclear fusion reactor (one that generates as much energy as goes into it to create the superheated plasma at its core) is located in Cadarache, France, and FAIR, the Facility for Antiproton and Ion Research, is under construction in Germany.

Pure research does not simply satisfy idle curiosity; it also opens up whole new fields of applied work. Almost by definition, those practical applications are unknown at the start, but they have followed all the pure research that has ever been done to date. By failing to invest in appropriate "Big Science" projects, the United States puts at risk one of the reasons for the great success of the American economy over the last several decades.

Another example of important infrastructure not encompassed by civil engineering is our system of polar-orbiting weather satellites run by the National Oceanic and Atmospheric Administration (NOAA) and the US Air Force. These satellites gather vital data on weather patterns that feed into complex models used by meteorologists to predict both mundane changes in the weather as well as life-threatening natural disasters. The average person who gets weather information from the nightly news likely does not realize the importance of government-run satellites in gathering the relevant data on which all weather predictions rely—including those of private services. In fact, so expensive are such endeavors that the United States has entered into partnerships with other countries to spread the costs.

How valuable is this information? A European weather organization ran forecasts of Superstorm Sandy without the data available from the NOAA polar-orbiting satellite.[18] Rather than giving residents four days' warning of the storm's size and predicted landfall (as actually happened), the models instead would have anticipated that Sandy would remain over the Atlantic. Yet a recent report by the Government Accountability Office added gaps in the availability of polar-orbiting satellites as an area of high risk to proper government operations.[19] The report anticipated a gap of 18 to 24 months between the retirement of the current NOAA satellite to the launch of its replacement. The costs—in dollar terms and in lives lost—remain to be seen.

International comparisons of infrastructure spending are difficult to come by because of numerous data limitations.[20] The OECD collects some data, but the latest available year that includes data for the United States is 2003. Looking at that year, the United States invested substantially less in inland transport infrastructure as a percentage of GDP than did our peers (see Figure 10.2).

Notwithstanding these limitations, one can get a sense of comparative infrastructure investment by looking to the World Economic Forum's Global Competitiveness Report, which in its 2013–2014 publication ranked the United

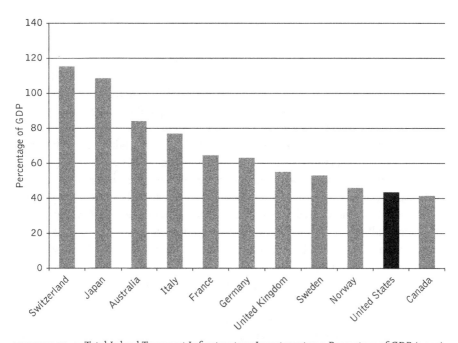

FIGURE 10.2 Total Inland Transport Infrastructure Investment as a Percentage of GDP (2003)

Source: OECD, *StatExtracts: Total Inland Transport Infrastructure Investment* (accessed October 2013) (and author's calculations).

States in 15th place in respect of its infrastructure—down eight spots since the first decade of the 2000s.[21] Obviously, if the United States were ranked in relation to our per capita GDP (the highest of any large economy in the world), we would have been far lower down the index than that. By any objective measure, our infrastructure lags behind that of most other comparable advanced nations, although we are not at the bottom of the heap.[22]

Why Public Infrastructure?

Every government makes large investments in infrastructure. In the United States, for example, all levels of government combined own non-military tangible infrastructure with a carrying value of a bit less than one-half the country's private capital stock—a ratio, as it happens, about the same as the median of our OECD peer countries.[23] Yet at the same time, the United States is a thriving capitalist society, with the world's deepest and most sophisticated capital markets. Surely, if profitable opportunities for investment exist, private investors should take them up. What reason is there for public investment in such circumstances?

The answers are neither obvious nor fixed for all time, and many real-world infrastructure investments actually are hybrids. Many infrastructure projects relate to natural monopolies—water, sewage treatment, or electricity services delivered to homes in a community. In cases like these, unalloyed market outcomes cannot work. My adopted hometown of Pasadena, California, has responded by owning and operating the local electricity generating and distribution company as part of the municipal government, while residents of adjacent communities receive electricity through a private utility. But the terms under which that utility offers electrical services in turn are heavily regulated by government, so that the private utility has no greater freedom to set electric rates wherever it pleases than does Pasadena's municipal operation. Given that both approaches coexist today throughout the United States, it is doubtful that one necessarily dominates the other in all instances; in fact, fashions for one solution or the other seem to oscillate with larger social trends and the pace of cleanup from the latest storm.[24]

One reason for public infrastructure is that such investment is required as a practical matter to deliver most public services. Public education requires school buildings; public medical care requires public hospitals; the regulation of automobile drivers requires that the DMV occupy a building somewhere, and so on. Assuming for the moment that one accepts that the service itself ought to be provided by government, public ownership of the ancillary infrastructure makes a great deal of sense. In general, public entities have lower costs of financing than do most private firms, longer investment time horizons, and of course do not need to earn a financial profit on their capital outlays. In these circumstances, public investment can be the low-cost alternative.

Other public infrastructure is an end in itself: roads or public rail transportation systems are examples. Why should government own these?

In many cases, the answer is that the infrastructure is intended to operate as a "public good"—an asset that can be shared broadly by many persons simultaneously, and from which it is difficult to exclude those persons who have not signed up to pay for it. A local street is a public good—it is there for the using by anyone, and we do not today have in place systems to charge individuals for their use of that particular street.[25]

Economists, determined to slightly misuse English, refer to goods that cannot be consumed by several persons simultaneously—a single hamburger, for example—as "rival goods," when they really mean "rival users of the good." Goods from which it is practical to exclude freeloaders are "excludable" goods. A particular Big Mac at McDonalds is a rival good and an excludable one—freeloaders have a tough time scoring Big Macs. Indeed, most goods furnished by private markets are both rival and excludable. (Commercial software and entertainment are very big exceptions, because they are non-rival but excludable, at least among law-abiding folk. Microsoft Office is not a rival good, because you and

I, and millions of others, all can use Microsoft Office simultaneously, but it is an excludable good, in that freeloaders cannot lawfully use it.) Clean air, by contrast, is neither rival nor excludable: I cannot stop you from taking a deep breath of it, even if I paid the cost of installing the pollution-control equipment that protected it, and your inhalation can coexist with mine.

But even here things exist on a continuum. An empty seat in a kindergarten built for 30 students arguably is a non-rival good when one new student and her family move into the neighborhood—one more child in the classroom does not materially change the educational experience of the others—but if 100 new students suddenly materialize, the analysis is completely different. And revelations about the scope of the National Security Agency's technological prowess remind us that, if we really wanted to, we could indeed keep track of every street on which you drove, and bill you accordingly. Both rivalry and excludability thus evolve with technologies and circumstances.

If a provider cannot exclude freeloaders from the use of an asset, we can expect that private capital will underinvest in that asset class, even if it is useful to society at large, for the simple reason that private investors will not be able to capture the full economic returns to their investments, and therefore will stop investing well before the classic microeconomic equilibrium point, where the marginal cost of the next profit just equals the marginal returns therefrom. This is a very important point: if private entrepreneurs do not capture all of the returns from a class of investment, the total private pool of such investments will fall short of the optimal level from the perspective of society as a whole.

Most economists therefore agree that public investment of one kind or another is justified in the pursuit of public goods (perhaps more accurately, non-excludable goods). In some cases, like research and development, public investment often takes the form of subsidies (in the United States, in the form of tax credits); the theory is that the subsidies compensate the firm for its inability to capture all of the value created by a new discovery as it ripples through the economy. In other cases, like roads and bridges, the more straightforward way to get to the socially optimal level of investment is through government directly funding and owning the asset.

The same rationales for public investment suggested earlier of lower cost financing, longer investment horizons, and absence of financial profit markups apply generally to all public infrastructure investments, including those in support of public goods. In addition, public infrastructure investment often yields "positive externalities," which just means that the investment benefits all of us indirectly as well as directly. If, for example, a new commuter rail line improves air quality by reducing automobile traffic congestion, that is a positive externality. A private investor contemplating building the rail line has no reason to include that indirect benefit in its profit and loss calculation, but government effectively can.

One important positive externality is that infrastructure investment means good quality construction jobs. As chapter 3 described, the United States today has a disappointingly low overall level of employment. This excess labor capacity erodes personal dignity and family structures, reduces individual welfare, and lowers national consumption, thereby holding back the overall economy. We can talk until we are blue in the face about the New Economy and knowledge-based jobs, but they are not for everybody. Infrastructure investment puts people to work in productive ways, and thereby supports a broader and more prosperous middle class. The jobs are there whether the investor comes from the private or public sector, but government fairly can take into account the positive spillovers from creating useful and remunerative jobs in judging the viability of a project.

The Lighthouse in Economists' Imaginations

When Nobel Laureate Ronald Coase died in 2013, at the age of 102, he left behind an important legacy in economics, and an even more outsized influence over discourse in American law schools, where his two seminal articles ("The Nature of the Firm" and "The Problem of Social Cost") continue to shape most work on the application of economic analysis to legal problems. Coase of course wrote more than these two papers; another, of which he was proud enough to include in a book of his collected papers, is directly relevant to this discussion. It is "The Lighthouse in Economics."[26] Fortunately for Coase, his towering reputation does not rest on this essay.

Prior to Coase, a long line of economists had used the example of a lighthouse as the quintessential public good. A lighthouse was costly to build, and its light was expensive to operate, yet its beacon was useful to all ships, regardless of whether they contributed in some fashion to its upkeep. From this economists argued that a lighthouse was exactly the sort of public good that governments should furnish, because the light was useful to all, but remunerative to none.[27]

Coase set out to undercut this claim, based on his reading of the history of lighthouses in Great Britain. Sparing the current reader a detailed summary of the financing and operation of British lighthouses over several centuries, Coase's argument boiled down to the assertion that, if only one closely studied the actual financial history of lighthouses, one would discover that private investors financed and operated most of the coastal lights on which ships in British coastal waters relied. "The role of government," Coase wrote, "was limited to the establishment and enforcement of property rights in the lighthouse."

It is impossible to tell from the face of Coase's essay whether his underlying purpose in writing the article was simply to tweak many illustrious predecessors, or to make a larger statement about the importance for economists of closely studying the actual commercial arrangements they purport to summarize (arguably the reading closest to his stated purpose), or a still grander agenda to undercut the general presumption of a primary role for government in providing public goods, but it certainly has been read as standing for the last of these. Yet careful readings of the facts adduced in Coase's own essay, together with two more recent papers, demonstrate exactly the opposite of Coase's claims: there was nothing particularly "private" about British lighthouse finance at all.[28]

The British model was at best what today we would call a public–private partnership. Originally, private owners would cajole or bribe their way to a lighthouse concession from the sovereign, and would build the light with their own funds, but were remunerated through a derogation of the taxing powers of the sovereign. In fact the freeloader problem proved to be insoluble through commercial means. Lighthouse tolls were collected in harbors, at rates set by the sovereign, by the sovereign's customs agents, who then remitted the tolls to the private owner. This is simply a tax by another name. Later, the authority to build lighthouses and to impose the harbor tax was shifted to what today would be called a government-sponsored enterprise (Trinity House).

The insertion of private lighthouse owners proved to be a consistently terrible idea. The sovereign, motivated mainly by bribes from prospective operators, did not allocate lights in an efficient manner, and many private franchise holders took the tolls (taxes) to which they were entitled, but did not maintain their lights, or built poor quality lighthouses that were regularly destroyed by storms. In other cases, private enterprise found it more profitable to extinguish a light and profit instead from plundering the resulting shipwrecks. The tolls collected generally far exceeded the costs of actually maintaining the lights, thereby converting private lighthouse franchises into vehicles for what economists call the capture of "economic rents"—supersized returns to the fortunate franchise holder beyond what was necessary to compensate the investor for the risks of the business.

In short, the insertion of private entrepreneurs into British lighthouse financing did not displace the role of the sovereign, which continued to tax ships for the alleged value of the light services. Instead, private operators used the instrumentality of the state to siphon wealth for themselves, while delivering far worse services than would have been the case had they never been allowed a role. Adam Smith of course warned about just this:

> The proposal of any new law or regulation of commerce which comes from…[business people], ought always to be listed to with great precaution, and ought never to be adopted till after having been long and carefully examined, not only with the most scrupulous, but with the most suspicious attention. It comes from an order of men, whose interest is never exactly the same with that of the public, who have generally an interest to deceive and even to oppress the public, and who accordingly have, upon many occasions, both deceived and oppressed it.[29]

Coase saw private funding, and from that inferred that lighthouse proprietors simply held the ordinary private rights of "ownership" (subject only to regulation of the tolls they could charge, like an electric utility today), without really thinking carefully about the meaning of "private" and "public" roles in this context.[30] If anything, the British lighthouse saga is a cautionary tale of the dangers of allowing private entrepreneurs to have a role in the provision of public goods, because in return for what today we would call the discipline of the markets they bring the risks of regulatory capture, of failure to fulfill the purpose of the underlying public good, and so on.

The larger point simply is this. The standard economic definition of a public good (one that is non-rival and non-excludable) is not very helpful in the modern world, where the categories themselves occupy continuums, and where there are many ways in which the state and the private sector can interact. The more useful distinction is that any activity that requires the direct application of the power of the state in a way not applicable to all private actors has an element of a public good in it. That state power might be the taxing power, or condemnation power, or the grant of an easement in property owned by the state, or a dozen other forms of government authority. In each such case, however, we cannot pretend that we are dealing with just another instance of private markets in operation, and the respective roles of the state and of private actors must be carefully delimited to assure that the public purpose underlying the state's targeted action is furthered.

As the examples of adjoining public and private electric utilities demonstrate, in some cases the result is government investment, while in others it is government-regulated private investment, but regardless, when the state brings its power to bear in a targeted manner, it must retain a major economic role. The decision of which path to follow really is a question of tactics, not normative concepts. In general, however, it seems sensible to start with a presumption in favor of government investment and ownership. This presumption aligns major incentives most neatly—that is, avoids the conflicts of interest that bedeviled the British lighthouse experience. Government, unlike private market participants, further has sufficiently broad societal goals, ample resources, and a lengthy investment horizon to address three major concerns associated with private investment in infrastructure: natural monopolies, large positive externalities (ancillary benefits), and high capital costs with deferred returns.[31]

Privatization

The spiritual heirs to Ronald Coase's interpretation of the lessons of British lighthouse financings are the proponents of "privatization" of public operations. Britain in particular indulged in a binge of privatizations during the Thatcher premiership, and again in 2013, when the Royal Mail (but not local post offices) was privatized. The overarching claim is that private markets left untethered provide services more efficiently than can the government, and as a result society benefits when public firms are subjected to the discipline of market competition.

The case for privatization is straightforward when dealing with steel companies, or airlines, or other businesses that generally are conducted through commercial firms, and where no natural monopolies are involved. But once one moves to operations designed to deliver or protect public goods, things get much more complex than these sorts of market triumphalist slogans would suggest. For example, in a long investigative report published in the *London Review of Books* in 2011, James Meeks examined the postal service in the Netherlands, where four different firms delivered mail to homeowners.[32] Mailing costs had plummeted for large businesses, but the reason in large measure was that the new mail carriers were paid on a piecework basis, with individual carriers sorting mail on their kitchen counters, or beds, and delivering the mail for compensation in the neighborhood of €3/hour, far lower than the statutory minimum wage. In one case described by Meek, a carrier for one of the new discount operators had simply given up, and hid dozens of cartons of undelivered mail in her apartment. It is not clear why the cost savings to bulk mailers of catalogs, at the cost of the disappearance of middle class jobs and missing deliveries, necessarily would enhance the happiness of society.

The actual financial performances of former government operations in the years following their privatization have been all over the map, and have depended on a host of factors: the nature of the business privatized, the operational health of the firm in public hands, the competitive environment, the extent of regulatory or contractual constraints on the privatized firm, and wholly exogenous factors, like fluctuations in the fuel prices that utilities were required to pay. Moreover, higher profits might be attributable to higher prices, or to fundamental degradations in the services offered by a newly privatized firm, rather than to greater productivity.[33]

For example, if following the privatization of the Royal Mail, domestic mail deliveries in the United Kingdom take on average one day longer to reach their destination, but the Royal Mail's profits are significantly higher compared with its pre-privatization results, is that a step forward or backward for the happiness of society? Owners of the Royal Mail's stock might in this case be pleased, while pensioners in remoter corners of Britain would see their welfare reduced, in ways not ordinarily measured in firm or national accounts.

The Royal Mail privatization also serves as a reminder that there are no truly private firms when it comes to the provision of traditional public services. The Royal Mail's postal rates will be regulated in the future. The Royal Mail is contractually obligated to use the government-owned Post Office for delivery to homeowners (the "last mile" of postal service) through 2022, and is required to continue universal postal service (delivery of mail anywhere within the United Kingdom for a flat rate), at least until 2016. Moreover, Royal Mail stamps will continue to display the head of the queen (or a future reigning monarch), but whether a monarch can in the future demand a royalty for the use of his or her likeness is unclear, at least to me. The idea that post-privatization of the Royal Mail, or for that matter a private operator in the United States running the county jail, is analogous to just another consumer business thus is a false one.

In the United States, the privatization debate has revolved around the United States Postal Service (USPS), which has the bad fortune to be both a semi-commercial enterprise, owned by the federal government yet held accountable as a private firm, and completely hamstrung in its day-to-day operations by Congress. As in the case of the Royal Mail, the most convincing reasons even to consider more complete privatization really are political ones: in Britain, to meet deficit reduction targets, to facilitate the sale of locally loved high street locations, and to insulate government from an unruly labor force inclined to periodic strikes, and in the United States, to force Congress to relinquish micromanagement of USPS operations.[34]

Other arguments have a makeweight quality to them. For example, the argument that postal services need investment to modernize is not a meaningful reason by itself to prefer private to public ownership, given that the national governments of the United Kingdom and the United States enjoy lower borrowing costs than will entirely privatized postal services.

In practice, private firms cannot simply substitute for public investment, if for no other reason than the fact that government participation is unavoidable in most important projects. From the sovereign's grant of lighthouse franchises to toll roads that rely on the state's condemnation authority and regulation of rates, private investors must in some fashion partner with—and therefore be exposed to the vagaries of—the public sector. Even without regard to differences in borrowing costs in the capital markets, the risks of partnering with the public sector mean that private investors must demand returns that the public sector need not charge itself.

The large costs associated with privatization in such circumstances (higher implicit financing costs, including a substantial return to equity investors, enormous monitoring and conflicts of interest issues, and the difficulties in internalizing all the positive externalities that government takes into account) are a high price to pay to address political dysfunctionality—and of course that dysfunctionality, if not addressed, still haunts the future operation of the privatized firm (and in turn is reflected in the risk premium that private investors demand). The political issues are real, but rather than eroding all the public goods that government investment throws off, we would be better served were we to devote more energy thinking about how we could restore some professionalism to the craft of politics, including career service in government administration.

Returns to Public Infrastructure Investment

Beginning with the work of David Aschauer (then at the Federal Reserve Bank of Chicago) in 1989,[35] economists have closely studied whether public infrastructure investment yields measurable economic returns in the form of higher productivity and wealth. Aschauer calculated very high returns to private productivity from public infrastructure, and further estimated that the growth-maximizing amount of public capital stock (i.e., investment in infrastructure) is 61 percent of private capital stock.[36] Yet the average level of investment among the 48 states in that study was 16 percentage points lower than that optimal amount.

Aschauer's early work showed such high returns to public infrastructure investment that one persistent strain of criticism has been that his results were "too good to be true."[37] That might be the case, but more recent research continues to show substantial productivity returns to public infrastructure investment, in the range of 8 to 10 percent.[38] One 2008 paper, for example, reviewed 76 earlier studies in this area.[39] The consensus results are surprising; as the 2008 meta-analysis concluded, "the true output elasticity of public capital is positive and significant."[40] Another 2012 review of the literature concluded, "In fact, the new research shows that public investment is *at least* as productive as private, and several strands of the research seem to indicate that it is substantially *more* productive."[41] In other words, public infrastructure investment is a highly profitable business for a society, even when social returns are calculated in the narrow sense of higher measurable productivity.

Of course public infrastructure is not inevitably productive—we can expect poor returns from building expensive bridges to remote Alaskan fishing villages—but on balance it is surprising just how large a productivity gain follows from even halfway sensible infrastructure investment. The underlying explanation is simple: public investment is complementary to private investment, and thereby leverages the returns obtained by private investors. Public investment in roads, for example, both reduces transportation charges as an intermediate cost of producing goods and increases the productivity of trucking firms; truckers and producers (and ultimately consumers) in turn divide the resulting surplus.[42]

The implicit financing costs of private investment in public infrastructure by themselves mean that public infrastructure investment should be expected to yield high productivity returns, because the investments are not made when the public sector does not make them. These risks include the risks inherent in partnering with the public sector, and therefore the requirement of high returns to investment, the very long lead times of projects (another kind of risk), and the very large sums of money involved (a third risk, exposing early investors to the uncertainties of future investments to complete a project).

The productivity case for infrastructure investment is a bit different from the economic arguments advanced in 2009 to support the case for the American Recovery and Reinvestment Act. That legislation was designed to deal with the near-collapse of the economy through stimulating demand, by taking up every "shovel ready" project that could be found. As Keynes himself waggishly noted, in the absence of actual productive projects, the goal of stimulating demand could be satisfied by the government hiring workers first to dig holes in the ground, and then to fill them up. Many projects with large productivity returns are not "shovel ready," because it costs a great deal of money and takes a long time to prepare a large infrastructure project for construction. But the productivity argument essentially is a permanent one, not a pleading relevant only in times of economic calamity.

The productivity case for public investment also is logically separable from the important question of how that infrastructure should be financed—for example, through general tax revenues or user fees (like highway tolls). I discuss that question below.

The total social returns to public infrastructure investment greatly exceed the measurable gains from such investment for private productivity (although to emphasize, those alone are very substantial). Cleaner air, more attractive parks, or simply a faster commute, thereby enabling more time to be spent on leisure, are all positive social returns that enhance the happiness of society, but that are not captured in standard productivity measures.

So, too, a commitment to public infrastructure investment implies a steady stream of remunerative and dignified work for large numbers of Americans who are not destined to be software engineers. These good jobs in turn have positive multiplier effects associated with them, because as those workers spend their wages, their spending provides income for those who provide goods and services to them, and so on. So in a narrow economic sense, well-chosen infrastructure yields a triple benefit, in the form of the returns to the investment, the returns to labor expended to build the investment, and the multiplier effect when those higher incomes are spent. And on top of this sits the more intangible social and psychological values that come from offering thousands of Americans new high-quality jobs.

To put matters crassly, which is better for both the wealth and the happiness of our nation: a small number of immensely wealthy Americans employing the underclass as dog walkers and topiary trimmers, or a larger commitment to publicly financed infrastructure that yields both direct productivity enhancements and a more robust middle class, through the jobs those projects create? Adam Smith in fact discussed the trickle-down benefits of the idle rich hiring poorer members of the society to perform menial tasks, but why not a flood instead of a trickle? That is, why not collectively hire fellow Americans to perform work that yields real productivity gains, and hence future wealth, rather than more perfectly manicured lawns?

Infrastructure investment also can function as a useful balance to secular trends in private investment. This is not the 2009 stimulus argument; rather, it responds to the fact that for a great many reasons private investment can be lumpy, in part because private investment is responsive to technological breakthroughs. Public investment can follow different cycles, and thereby smooth the lumpiness of economic investments.

In sum, public investment in infrastructure yields positive productivity returns, because those investments are complementary to private investment, and because private investment cannot by itself supply the projects, for the reasons described above. For this reason alone, a country that relies on the private sector to fund investments in infrastructure will systematically underinvest. When one adds to this all the positive externalities of public investment—the ancillary returns to society, from good quality jobs to non-monetary benefits from the investments to the smoothing of investment cycles—the case for public investment in infrastructure is extremely powerful.

The 2009 American Recovery and Reinvestment Act failed to amaze the world with the infrastructure projects it financed, because most "shovel ready" projects, like paving roads, are small in scale and technologically straightforward. (Nonetheless, it turns out that there are very large productivity returns, and large cost savings as well, from keeping up with preventive road maintenance.) And it also is true that the large productivity gains we recorded from completing the federal interstate highway network might not be replicated by simply building more highways. But there are highly useful major infrastructure projects waiting to be built, if only we had the vision to commit to them. The discussion at the beginning of this chapter points to some specific cases.

In fact, wherever one looks at current mega-projects around the world, what is most striking is the absence of American undertakings. The richest large country in the world is beggaring its own future by decades of systematic underinvestment in infrastructure. By doing so, we drag down our future productivity and deprive tens of thousands of Americans of attractive job opportunities. The investment opportunities are all around all of us, wherever in the United States we live.

Financing Infrastructure

Infrastructure projects are expensive, and the current shortfall in US infrastructure spending amounts to hundreds of billions of dollars per year. What is more, current public infrastructure financing programs are complex in their design, and exist at all levels of government.[43] Very generally, though, most public funds today come from state and local governments; federal government directly or indirectly provides about 40 percent of new infrastructure investment, and about 10 percent of maintenance costs (other than aviation, where the federal government pays about one-third of the public contribution toward operating costs).[44] Existing programs tend to be single-modal (e.g., either highways or rail, but not rails-to-roads), and investments are made through complex formulae that have only tangential relationships to where the biggest returns for the buck can be obtained. The confluence of fiscal federalism in funding sources, the need for much more funding, and the design of individual programs makes for an unsatisfactory state of affairs.

Obviously much good work can be done by rethinking how infrastructure is financed in the United States. In light of the complexity of the subject, I present here a few general observations.

First, the federal government should play a larger role in financing large-scale infrastructure projects. In our tightly networked domestic economy, the public goods that result from infrastructure projects tend to spill over across regions, and therefore will lead to systematic underinvestment by sub-national governments that see only a fraction of the gains. Moreover, states and municipalities are resource-constrained.

Second, the existing federal budget process is problematic in two important respects. The annual appropriations process is not consistent with funding long-term construction projects, and the budget presentation muddles maintenance costs with investment. A genuine capital budget would match up liabilities with the assets acquired with those liabilities, and move us away from incorrect "deficit" fixation in those cases where a new asset is being acquired. Moreover, a capital budget that shows the stock of government infrastructure net of depreciation more accurately presents the current level of infrastructure investment than does simply toting up gross flows.

Capital budgeting is periodically proposed, and then rejected, but the arguments against capital budgeting have an odd makeweight quality to them that in the end are unpersuasive.[45] For example, one recent nonpartisan summary reported that: "Critics of capital budgeting assert that shifting a significant portion of the budget to an accrual basis (in which costs are apportioned over the lifetime of an asset rather than accounted for up front) would unduly complicate the budget process and undermine the task of setting priorities over the full range of governmental activities."[46] Somehow accrual method accounting is within the purview of every medium-sized business in the United States, but is thought to be too puzzling for government accountants to figure out.

Third, existing programs at all levels of government are inadequately focused on objective measures of returns on investment, and instead reward entrenched business-political networks.

Fourth, new technologies make it more feasible than in the past to finance road projects in particular through user fees, as opposed to general tax revenues. The radio frequency transponders now in use in many places around the country enable congestion pricing, as well as lower-cost toll collections. Most economists prefer to see infrastructure projects relying on user-fee type financing mechanisms, because they align more closely the direct benefits of a project with those who are asked to pay for it.[47]

Fifth, "public–private partnerships" should be approached with great caution. When used to refinance existing public infrastructure, such ventures often generate immediate cash at extraordinarily high implicit financing costs to the government in question (through the redirection of large future revenue streams), and further raise difficult oversight issues for which many governments are underprepared. When used to finance new projects, the issue becomes the size of the risk premium that the private party requires, which premium a government would not impose on itself. One study, for example, found that the cost of European public–private partnerships to construct road projects averaged 24 percent more than for comparable public-only projects.[48] As described below, private *debt* capital in the right circumstances can be infused into public infrastructure without incurring disproportionate risk premiums, but it is much more difficult to insert private equity capital and still accomplish the public goals of a project.

Finally, there are good reasons to think that the time horizons and potential returns from infrastructure investment match up very well with the investment needs of insurance companies and pension funds. Dedicated revenue flows from infrastructure projects (through user fees) enable such investments to be financed through classic project finance structures.[49]

These observations all converge on one idea that could have a large positive impact on infrastructure development in the United States: a national infrastructure bank, modeled loosely on successful existing organizations like the European Investment Bank.[50] Such an institution is not a bank in the ordinary sense, of being regulated by the Federal Reserve and taking demand deposits (checking accounts). Instead, the national infrastructure bank would be an independent government-owned corporation charged with two complementary functions: to provide independent reviews of the economics underlying all major infrastructure projects referred to it by Congress or in which it might invest, and to invest in those projects it selects through objective criteria as having high national or regional public returns. A well-managed institution thus would not just introduce new funding sources for socially important infrastructure projects, but also would bring credibility to the projections on which funding decisions are made.

In general, the national infrastructure bank would become the preferred vehicle through which the federal government would invest in large-scale infrastructure projects; all other projects funded by Congress would be understood either as below the minimum size for which the bank's special expertise was required or as justifiable only on non-economic grounds. Even if my suggestion that the national infrastructure bank serve as the near-exclusive vehicle by which the federal government invests in traditional infrastructure is not adopted, the bank could serve a tremendously important role in validating the viability of proposed projects. Just as the Congressional Budget Office and the staff of the Joint Committee on Taxation effectively guarantee the reliability and objectivity of budget and revenue forecasts (but not their ultimate accuracy!), a nonpartisan government-owned national infrastructure bank can serve as a check on excessively politicized infrastructure initiatives. The idea would be that Congressional action on every project that receives federal funding (above some *de minimis* figure) would be required to proceed only after receiving a national infrastructure bank score. No "precommitment" device has ever been developed to protect Congress (and us) from Congress's willful stupidity or cupidity, but a published score from an objective source will over time modulate the worst political enthusiasms in this area.

Barring catastrophic investments or a Congressional determination to ramp up its size, the bank would not require annual appropriations from Congress. Instead, the bank would operate as a profit-making independent corporation, retaining its earnings and eventually paying market dividends to its owner (the federal government) when it had built up enough retained earnings to justify doing so.

The bank's investments would be leveraged at two levels. First, the bank itself would sell bonds (i.e., raise funds in the debt capital markets), relying on its own profitability (that is, the income streams from its investments, in the form of toll charges and other user fees) and the equity infusion made by Congress to capitalize the bank at inception. This would enable the bank to marshal four or five times as much money as Congress's initial equity contribution to invest in deals.

Second, as a highly professional independent lead investor in public infrastructure projects, the bank would vet every proposed project, oversee the disbursal of funds, and monitor the operation of a project. By taking on these roles, the bank would attract pension plans, insurance companies, and other institutional investors to provide loan financing to individual projects, through classic project finance structures.

Critics of a national infrastructure bank who recommend instead the expansion of existing programs within the Department of Transportation or the like completely miss the point. Only a genuinely independent institution will have credibility with the capital markets to raise money on its own, and to serve as the lead investor in project finance structures. By evaluating projects on the merits, a national infrastructure bank disciplines the formulation of project proposals, reduces the risk of misdirected government investment, and creates the environment necessary to attract private project finance capital.

The market discipline introduced by a national infrastructure bank responds to the usual objection that public infrastructure investment carries with it a trail of waste, fraud, and abuse. The bank structure insulates the project selection and funding process from the day-to-day politics of Congress, and further addresses the problem of Congress's short-term appropriations cycle, which matches badly with the very long construction timelines of major infrastructure investments. An independent bank also can address in a timely way (unlike Congress) whatever financing or operational exigencies might arise, thereby reducing the overall risk to private investors of excessive rigidity in a deal's financing structure.

To be sure, not every project financed by the national infrastructure bank will be a howling success, but that also is true of private financial institutions, no matter how well managed. That is why it would start operations with a significant layer of equity capital. But so long as it is well managed and allowed operational independence, there is every reason to believe that it would stand on its own two feet.

EDUCATION

We all understand that children are our future—except, apparently, when it comes to educating them. Our country's economic progress, and more crassly its ability to pay those of us now old enough to read this book the various old age benefits to which we believe ourselves accustomed, will depend on how successfully we invest in human capital today, because returns to labor are the principal drivers of economic wealth. Today's education yields tomorrow's economy.

In every country, investments in human capital are understood as properly the purview of government as investor, because every member of a society deserves a comparable level of investment, and because a broad commitment to public education (to investment in human capital) maximizes the potential of each citizen. As in the case of public infrastructure investment, public investment in human capital yields positive private productivity returns in the narrow sense, but equally important, happiness returns as well, because education is the key both to a productive career and to our ability to realize our native endowments, with all the satisfactions that implies. The middle class cannot buy its way out of poor public education, but their children when they mature will compete on a global stage in more and more instances as the world's economy evolves.

For all these reasons, public investment in human capital is indispensable to our country's future. The simple place to start, then, is to ask how are we doing in educating proficient youngsters, compared with other countries?

Our Education Report Card

The OECD conducts standardized tests in dozens of countries around the world, including non-OECD member countries, to assess the academic performance of students in core disciplines. The most recent cycle of assessments in this

"Programme for International Student Assessment" covered 2009.[51] The results were predictably depressing.

In reading, the United States scored a 500, right about average for OECD countries, but well behind Australia (515), Canada (524), and Japan (520) (not to mention Shanghai, which placed first with a 556 score).[52] On the other hand, we did manage to tie with Poland, and were only one point behind Estonia.

In mathematics, matters did not go as well. Our score of 487 was well below the OECD average of 496. We did, however, tie with Ireland, and nosed out Latvia. Asian economies like Shanghai (600), Korea (546), and Hong Kong (555) lapped the field. But again, Australia (514), Canada (527), and Japan (529) were well ahead of our children. Germany (513), whose children were no better at reading than ours, performed much better in mathematics (and in science).

In science, we again were about average for OECD countries. Again, the Asian economies that performed well in the mathematics test were far ahead of our children's performance, but so too were Australia, Canada, and Japan.

Overall, our performance was mediocre. We were not the only country to perform disappointingly: so did France, for example. But even French children performed meaningfully better at mathematics than ours. What is more, we did significantly worse in the 2009 tests than we performed in 2000. And the number of younger Americans who have graduated from college, which 30 years ago was far above the OECD average, is now only slightly above that average, and again is far behind Canada's performance.[53]

We are drowning in third-rate colleges offering essentially remedial classes for students who would not be admitted to universities in other countries, rather than investing in students earlier in their development. In many cases, families in turn bear a large percentage of the cost of attending these institutions. If you believe this assessment of undergraduate programs in the United States to be unfairly harsh, I urge you to administer to the high school seniors of your choice some of the UK "A-level" exam questions available on the Internet, keeping in mind that students matriculating at UK universities typically sit for such exams in no fewer than three subjects.[54]

In October 2013 the OECD released its first comprehensive comparative study of adult skills.[55] Adults in the United States ages 18–65 scored a bit lower than average in literacy proficiency, much lower than average in numeracy, and much lower than average again in proficiency in "problem solving in technology-rich environments"—which is to say, the modern competitive workplace. The problem is not technophobic geezers dragging down our test results; to the contrary, it was US young adults ages 16–24 who performed much worse than their peers in other countries. Our young adults were at the bottom of the heap in literacy, and lagged far behind the field in numeracy. Young American adults were near the bottom as well in working in technology-rich environments, where the percentage of US young adults in the top level of proficiency was far behind the percentage performing at that level, not just among German and Dutch young people, but also those in Estonia, Austria, and Poland, to name a few.

We are a much richer country than most of the economies that outperformed us, including in particular Australia, Canada, and Japan. One would expect that a country as affluent as ours would find a way to fund peerless education for our children, because that is the obvious keystone of future American prosperity. But we fail to deliver on this fundamental obligation to individuals unable to fend for themselves.

Public Investment in Education

Why does the United States fare so badly in these cross-country comparisons? The United States actually spends a good deal of money in the aggregate on public education, but as in the case of healthcare, we do not get very good value in return. The largest factors behind our mediocre returns seem to relate to the lopsided ways we spend on education in the United States. First, we penalize children in poorer communities relative to rich ones along two margins—the unavoidable fact that more affluent families spend more on education enrichment outside the classroom than do struggling families, and the fact that education investment is still determined in large measure by the affluence of the community in which a child resides. Second, we underinvest in earliest childhood education, even though a great deal of exciting new research suggests that educational and even life attainment is enormously affected by the environment in which very young children grow. On top of these first two lopsided policies, we spend disproportionately on college-level education.

As a percentage of GDP, our *public* spending on education is a bit below that of most of the peer countries that I use throughout this book as a comparison, but in absolute dollar terms we near the top, by virtue of our higher GDP per capita (see Figure 10.3).

When private spending on education is added to the mix, our total educational budget is very high—about 8 percent of GDP. We allocate about 60 percent of that to primary and secondary education, and 40 percent to college and post-graduate education.[56] Private educational spending, however, is disproportionately allocated 3:1 to college and post-graduate education over primary and secondary education.

Teacher pay is broadly correlated with student performance.[57] We pay our teachers well, but not lavishly. Unsurprisingly, given their children's test results, Canadian teachers are paid much better, and as just outlined, Canadian children perform at much higher levels. French teachers are paid poorly, which might explain why French children keep company with ours, except in mathematics, where they do meaningfully better (see Figure 10.4).

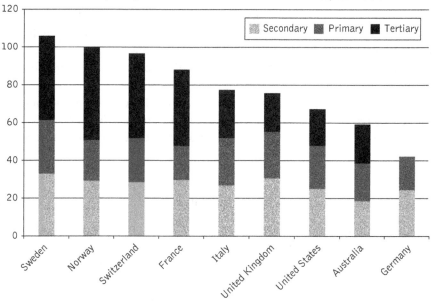

FIGURE 10.3 Per-Student Public Education Spending (% of GDP Per Capita) (2009)

Source: World Bank, *Expenditure per Student, (% of GDP per Capita)* (accessed October 2013), http://data.world-bank.org/indicator/SE.XPD.SECO.PC.ZS.

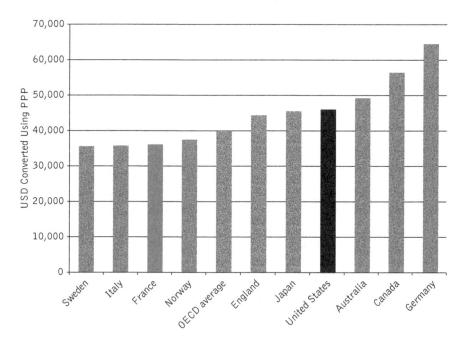

FIGURE 10.4 Average Teacher Salaries, Lower Secondary, 15 Years Experience (2011)

Source: OECD, *Education at a Glance: 2013*, doi:10.1787/teachsal-table-2013-1-en.

Skewed Education Investment Priorities

Let us begin by dispensing with the base canard advanced by economist Gregory Mankiw, that children of high-income parents perform better in school and in life because they have inherited a classier set of genes than the average baby. In fact, research shows that there are no cognitive differences among babies born to rich or poor parents.[58] There are, however, large differences in outcomes, which operate to turn current generation income inequality into semi-permanent caste distinctions. These differences are explained in large measure by differences in family expenditures in time and money in education enrichment (by itself an inevitable result of laudable parental instincts), combined with upside-down public spending, in which poorer children face lower public investment in their education, not the higher commitment that rationally is required to overcome their family situations.

Families in the top quintile of incomes spend on average seven times as much on education enrichment for their children as do families in the lowest quintile—in 2006, about $9,000 per year per student.[59] (These figures do not include private school tuition—just enrichment expenditures like tutors and music lessons.) This is normal, understandable, and in fact desirable. But what one would expect, given this entirely predictable expression of family love, is that public education would be designed to mitigate these sorts of differences.

But of course, the opposite is the case. The United States is an outlier in viewing public education as a sub-national expense, and indeed a local government one in many cases. Our children's results therefore were more influenced by socioeconomic factors than the OECD average.[60] For example, among regular public school districts in 2010, the median expenditure per pupil was about $10,000, but per pupil spending at the fifth percentile of school districts was only $7,400, while spending at the 95th percentile school district was over $19,000.[61] As the OECD drily noted, "Among OECD countries, only Israel, Slovenia, Turkey, and the United States favor socio-economically advantaged schools with access to more teachers."[62]

As a result, our comparatively high levels of income inequality exacerbate our poor student performance. A study by Martin Carnoy and Richard Rothstein analyzing the PISA 2009 results noted that the United States has more students in a disadvantaged social class than do similar post-industrial countries.[63] Since in every country students from lower socioeconomic environments were outperformed by those higher in the distribution, our relatively greater number of students in the disadvantaged class served to further depress our scores.

That report concluded that, once one adjusted for differences in social advantages, the United States did not perform as badly in the PISA 2009 tests as the raw scores might indicate. The right interpretation of this conclusion, however, is not that we should feel better about the quality of American education, but rather that, once one appreciates the long shadow that social disadvantage casts over educational attainment, we need to rethink our commitment to socioeconomically disadvantaged schools. Keeping company with Slovenia and Turkey in the design of our system for financing education is not where the United States of America should be.

In the United States, the public school that a student can attend is dictated by his or her home address. A family who lives in an underperforming school zone generally has only two options to try to improve their children's lot: pay for private schooling or relocate to an area with a higher performing school. Unfortunately, both options are likely unavailable for all but the affluent.

Across the United States, private school tuition averages over $6,000/year for elementary schools and over $10,000/year for secondary students; elite private schools of course cost several multiples of these numbers.[64] These costs are prohibitive for low or lower-middle income families, especially for those with more than one child.

At the same time, the option to relocate to a better performing school district often is circumscribed by the high price of homes in such areas. A prominent national real estate agency recently released a report comparing the cost between homes in high-performing school zones with homes in low-performing ones.[65] The report found that "housing prices in the zones of highly ranked public schools are remarkably higher than those served by lower ranked schools." As Figure 10.5 demonstrates, the difference can amount to "hundreds of thousands of dollars for similar homes in the same neighborhood," depending on the school test score percentile.[66]

The situation is summed up well by the OECD's report card for the United States on education. That publication makes for depressing reading, and emphasizes our skewed allocations of education expenditures:

> The US education system is less effective than those of other countries in helping children realise their potential, as illustrated by a much greater impact of the socio-economic background on education achievement. To reduce this impact, more resources need to be directed towards disadvantaged students. Currently, the United States is one of only three OECD countries that on average spend less on students from disadvantaged backgrounds than on other students.... These resource allocations reinforce the disadvantages of social segregation, which results in children in poorer schools having lower educational expectations and outcomes.[67]

Underinvestment in Early Childhood Enrichment

It turns out that investment in very early childhood education—more generally, environmental enrichment—pays huge dividends in education and even in life

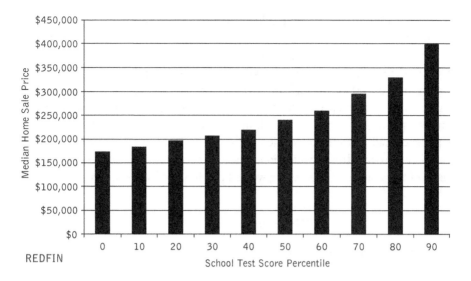

REDFIN

FIGURE 10.5 US Median Home Sales Price versus Elementary School Test Scores

Source: Unger, "Affording a House in a Highly Ranked School Zone?"

outcomes. In a very recent study, Anne Fernald, Virginia A. Marchman, and Adriana Weisleder demonstrated that children only 18 months old showed significant differences in their language skills based on the socioeconomic status of their families; by 24 months, there was a six-month gap between upper and lower socioeconomic status children. These differences persist into kindergarten, by which time the differences "are predictive of later academic success or failure."[68] Another research team earlier estimated that by the time they are three years old, children from advantaged families have heard 30 million more words directed to them than children in disadvantaged households. Fernald and her co-authors summarize the importance of all these research efforts as follows:

> [H]aving the opportunity for rich and varied engagement with language from an attentive caretaker provides the infant not only with models for language learning, but also with valuable practice in interpreting language in real time. Thus, child-directed talk sharpens the processing skills used in online comprehension, enabling faster learning of new vocabulary.

Terrific pre-K programs are probably not as effective as are perfect parents in creating "a rich and varied engagement with language" for a very young child, but in a world where many families are preoccupied by the issues attendant on grinding poverty and job insecurity, terrific pre-K programs can offer the children of such families a far richer and more varied environment than they otherwise would experience. We owe these children at least that much.

In an important recent study, Raj Chetty and his co-authors analyzed the long-term outcomes of a program in Tennessee that randomly assigned 11,500 kindergarten students and their teachers to different sized classrooms. The students remained in these randomly assigned classes through the third grade, and then returned to their normal programs. Class size turned out to be somewhat important in some respects, like the probability of attending college, but what was truly surprising was that the overall quality of a child's kindergarten education experience had a strong correlation with a child's future success as an adult.[69] This is an extraordinary validation, through a randomized large-scale experiment, of the adage that everything worth knowing one learns in kindergarten.

Post-Secondary Education

Sixty percent of post-secondary education is privately funded, which obviously works to the advantage of those from affluent backgrounds.[70] So, too, do family connections (and with them "legacy" admissions opportunities), general familiarity with the names and reputations of competitive colleges, and much better support networks for parsing the admissions and financial aid obstacle course. As a result, 70 percent of students at the most competitive colleges come from families in the upper quartile of the income distribution, and only about 5 percent from families in the bottom quartile.[71] There is a direct connection between our modest public investment in education at every level and our increasing income inequality, because children of the affluent acquire superior educational experiences throughout childhood, and find the sting of college tuition costs less painful.

Student loan programs make college affordable in a technical sense for some students, but they then graduate with tens of thousands of dollars of debt, which hangs over their future, dampening their appetite for entrepreneurial risk-taking at precisely the point in their lives when such risks should be least costly to them.

Privatizing Education

Public education in America is not perfect, although I have argued above that its principal problems lie more with our skewed educational expenditure priorities than with schools' sclerotic staff. Public education also has great social importance for a democracy, which is its fundamental inclusiveness. Public school is one of the few places in life (standing in line at the Department of Motor Vehicles is another) where we are thrown together with people of very different backgrounds and incomes, all of whom have just as valid claims to being American as we do. This is something to treasure, and therefore to work to preserve.

The current vogue, however, is to deprecate public schools. It is worth teasing apart some of the different ways in which the urge to insert private control over public education is manifested.

The most obvious alternative to public education, of course, is a private school. This term has radically different meanings in different parts of the country. To a reader in Manhattan or Pacific Palisades, it may mean The Brearley or Marlborough, or perhaps a New England boarding school—all schools costing upward of $30,000/year, and with intensely competitive admissions standards. Alternatively, the term may evoke traditional parochial schools of the sort run by the Catholic Church in particular, many of which are a century or more old and with their own competitive admissions policies.

These sorts of exclusive or long-standing institutions are a small part of the private school universe. The reality is that many private schools across the country are relatively recently established second-rate institutions affiliated with local religious organizations, offering education that is no better—and often worse—than that of local public schools. Whatever advantages these private schools show in terms of standardized test scores are attributable to the relative affluence of the families who send their children to them, not to some pedagogical magic inside their halls.[72] Many of these private schools really serve as tribal havens for the families that patronize them, assuring that their children will mingle only with children of similar socioeconomic, and in most cases religious, backgrounds. To encourage such enterprises as large-scale alternatives to public education is to promote the further tribalization of American society more generally.

Privatization is not the same as private education: privatization, at least in my view, should be understood as the derogation by the state to private parties of some of the public education responsibilities that are the state's obligation in the first instance. In effect, privatization here is to public education what the privately owned lighthouse is to infrastructure.

Diane Ravitch has effectively skewered the vogue for privatizing the delivery of public education in her book *Reign of Terror*.[73] Her case against for-profit institutions running public schools is completely persuasive, and some nominally not-for-profit outfits appear to be used to skim income in the form of outsized rents or the like to associates of the operators. Ravitch is, however, a bit unfair to the charter school movement, in lumping some of the sleazier operators with the best charter school networks, like Knowledge Is Power Program, Achievement First, and Uncommon Schools. The bottom feeders in the charter school world are for-profit outfits, or engage in the kind of cherry-picking of students out of public schools that rightly infuriates Ravitch. But the best-of-breed networks in fact are transparent and well-governed not-for-profit organizations that open their schools to all students through lotteries. Those networks distribute extra lottery chances to the lowest income or otherwise neediest families, and reach out to the community through door-to-door introductions and via social workers. Their success does not necessarily prove, as Ravitch implies, that they have rigged the game in their favor.

The way forward here is to embrace the charter movement more directly, by randomly assigning students to traditional or charter schools, and by budgeting from the start sufficient funds to study the outcomes. By doing so, the original impetus for charter schools, as laboratories for alternative pedagogical styles, can be honored, while answering the concerns of critics like Ravitch. The best ideas then can be harvested and deployed more widely. If the result is that more public schools in the future are organized like an Uncommon Schools network school, where teachers work 60 hour weeks, 48 weeks a year, and have no tenure, but are paid very well, so be it.

Education as Investment Summary

To reiterate, education is investment by another name—in this case, investment in the human capital that will power our country's economy in a few decades, and pay for the retirement benefits of those old enough to read this book on its publication. In this regard, consider the OECD's conclusion as to the long-term significance of our mediocre education system:

> The international achievement gap is imposing on the United States economy an invisible yet recurring economic loss that is greater than the output shortfall in what has been called the worst economic crisis since the Great Depression.... A recent study...suggests that a modest goal [of improving as much over the next 20 years as some countries have done in 10] could imply a gain of $41 trillion for the United States economy over the lifetime of the generation born in 2010.[74]

In infrastructure, the problem is insufficient public investment, period. In the case of education, the problems are subtler, but the overall thrust of our efforts should be threefold. First, we need to invest more at the earliest stages of childhood education. Second, we need in general to invest disproportionately more in lower-income community schools, to help students overcome some of the disadvantages that poverty implies, and to compensate partially for the many thousands of dollars spent by affluent families each year in education enrichment. It is never going to be easy for children of low-income families to themselves become affluent, but our current approach to financing education, which rewards children of affluent families with better public schooling, is perverse.

Finally, we need to rethink post-secondary education. The cost of post-secondary education must be lowered for most students, so as to make it more accessible and to reduce the financial leverage with which too many young adults begin their careers. And gifted students from disadvantaged backgrounds need more systematic assistance in finding and succeeding at elite institutions.

CHAPTER 11

GOVERNMENT AS INSURER

> *The trade of insurance gives great security to the fortunes of private people, and by dividing among a great many that loss which would ruin an individual, makes it fall light and easy upon the whole society.*
>
> —ADAM SMITH, *The Wealth of Nations*, Book V., Chap. 1, Part III.

Policy analyst Ezra Klein describes the United States federal government as an insurance company with its own standing army. This is exactly right, and exactly as it should be. Most federal government outlays can be categorized as different forms of insurance benefits, defense spending, or interest on the national debt. The remainder of federal government spending (basically, nondefense discretionary spending) is in the neighborhood of 15 percent of the entire budget: one can conceive of that spending in turn as in large measure basic overhead costs, and—as just described in chapter 10—a depressingly small amount of public investment.

The universal experience around the world is that as a country grows richer, the basket of insurance that its government offers its citizens—more accurately, the mutual insurance its citizens provide for each other through the intermediation of government—also grows in size. This is not the sure sign of decadence, but of common sense. Think back (or if you are young, project forward) to your own situation: the life insurance you carried when you were 25 probably was wholly inadequate to your requirements at age 45 or 50, in light of your increasing income and the needs of your family. The same is true for countries: as they become richer, they invariably find that outcomes that were regrettable but unavoidable when the country was young and poor are simply no longer acceptable as a social matter.

The United States today offers a wide array of insurance and quasi-insurance to its citizens. Before analyzing any of these programs, however, it is useful to describe briefly the essence of insurance as a concept, and to contrast it with the most odious term in fiscal language, "redistribution." Doing so puts our poli-cies on firmer foundations, sheds useful light on the failures of our approach to healthcare insurance in particular, and allows us to consider the insurance aspects of many programs that might not otherwise be couched in those terms.

WHAT IS INSURANCE?

Insurance is the queen of financial products. Putting aside Babylonian or Roman proto-insurance, true insurance, beginning with marine insurance in fourteenth-century Genoa, has a continuous history of 600 years or more.[1] Befitting its status as the queen of financial products, in 1936 marine insurance co-starred with Tyrone Power in a wonderful Hollywood movie, *Lloyd's of London*.

Classic marine, fire, or similar insurance is extraordinary because from the perspective of the insured, an insurance policy effectively causes risk to disappear. More accurately, insurance replaces the risk of a large but uncertain financial loss with a small certain loss—the premium. "Individuals in modern societies are unable to predict the magnitude of events that profoundly affect their well-being. Insurance, in all its guises, is the institution that mitigates the influence of uncer-tainty."[2] By eliminating some uncertainties, insurance allows people (who gener-ally are risk averse) to take on risks with which they are more comfortable—for example, the baker who can deal with changing tastes for baguettes or new com-petition, but who does not have the wherewithal to assume the uncertain prospect of his bakery possibly burning to the ground.

Traditional insurance of the sort celebrated in *Lloyd's of London* has four irre-ducible components. First, the insured must face a fortuity—an identified uncon-trollable and uncertain event with adverse financial consequences to the insured. The identified fortuity is described in insurance contracts as a "peril." The risk that fire might burn down the bakery is an insurable peril; normal wear and tear of the dough-kneading machine is not. Second, there must be many such risks, similar in general nature (fire) but largely unrelated in occurrence, such that the chance of loss can be calculated through empirical and statistical methodologies. Third, the consequence of the adverse fortuity must be reasonably ascertainable financial loss. Finally, the insurer must be able to control for the unique problems of adverse selection and moral hazard, described below.

When these conditions prevail, insurance is possible. Through contract, the insured shifts to the insurer the risk of financial loss arising from his bakery burning. In turn, the insurer distributes that risk among a large group of simi-larly situated insureds. The insurer pools all these similar risks in such a man-ner that, by application of the mathematical principle known as the law of large numbers, the insurer can predict with reasonable accuracy the losses that the pool as a whole will sustain. The insurer then can apportion those predictable losses to all members of the pool on some rational basis. From an insured's perspective, insurance thereby transmutes large but highly contingent losses into small certain ones.

Risk *shifting* (by the insured) and *pooling* (by the insurer) are the essence of insurance; the law of large numbers is the underlying theory under which the pooled losses can be predicted, such that each insured can pay her share, via the premium.[3] For fairly priced insurance, an insured's premium is simply an appropriate share of predicted losses to the pool, plus administrative fees and a share of any capital cushion. In this sense, all traditional insurance ultimately is mutual insurance, because the cost of insurance is driven by the loss experience of the pool of insureds of which one is a part. The theme of mutuality binding insureds to one another through a precommitment to share a fraction of others' losses in return for protection against bearing the entirety of one's own loss is the unique genius of insurance.

Insurance thus is fundamentally different from hedging.[4] Imagine that a US firm sells merchandise to a European buyer, and as a result holds receivables denominated in euros, but the US seller is unwilling to accept the risk of fluctuations in the dollar value of the euro. The firm can hedge that exposure by selling euros in the foreign exchange forward or futures markets, guaranteeing it a fixed number of dollars when the buyer pays its bills. By doing so, the US firm has *shifted* euro risk to the financial party on the other side of its hedge, but the US firm has not *pooled* the risk. The risk of a catastrophically large foreign exchange loss to one party or another somewhere in the system remains unmitigated. Similarly, when a firm puts aside liquid reserves against a contingency the firm is not insuring itself, because in this case there is neither shifting nor pooling of the risk.

Insurance also is fundamentally a financial product. Life insurance, for example, does not compensate the bereaved for the pain of losing the decedent, but rather for the loss of the decedent's expected income.

Life insurance is worth a brief explanation, because on reflection a reader might observe that death is not a fortuity—this outcome regrettably is certain. But the timing of death is a fortuity, and that is what life insurance addresses—the risk of dying in the coming year, and thereby depriving one's family of one's future income. This means of course that premiums to purchase a fixed dollar death benefit life insurance contract should rise annually, even without any other change in the insured's apparent health. Life insurance is made into an enormously complex product because people want level premium "permanent" life insurance, and because the tax code encourages saving through the vehicle of a life insurance policy. The result is that whole life policies and their more modern variants are combinations of traditional insurance (say, the shifting and distribution of the risk of 57-year-olds in the pool dying in the next year) with individual savings accounts embedded in each contract. Early year premiums exceed the insurance cost for the year, and become a sinking fund for meeting the cost of insurance in later years.

Obviously, modern insurance practices have mutated beyond boundaries cognizable by Tyrone Power. In many cases this represents the fact that insurers undertake financial trading through the guise of insurance, in various forms of regulatory arbitrage.[5] In others (e.g., mortgage credit insurance) it represents the extension of core insurance principles to new risk-pooling opportunities.

Any insurer faces two commercial problems that are unique (or at least apply most forcefully) to this industry: adverse selection and moral hazard. Both adverse selection and moral hazard feature prominently in the discussion of health insurance that follows.

"Adverse selection" refers to the fundamental asymmetry in information between a prospective insured and an insurer: that is, the prospective insured knows better than does the insurer why she wants insurance in the first place. Unsurprisingly, it turns out that those who volunteer to buy insurance often are more likely to need it than are others. A life insurer, for example, might deal with this risk by reviewing a prospective insured's medical records, and subjecting her to a medical exam, before agreeing to write insurance. Another way of looking at adverse selection, as applied to open-ended social insurance programs (such as health insurance with annual enrollment options), is that it invites free riding: an individual opts out of the insurance pool until such time as she needs the insurance, in which case she suddenly jumps in.

"Moral hazard" describes the effect on an insured's behavior that holding insurance from a peril might induce. The baker with fire insurance might be a bit more careless about ensuring that the oven's fire is extinguished than is the baker without such insurance. The existence of a "moral" hazard does not mean that the insurance in question encourages poor moral values; rather, it is simply the term of art used to describe the set of post-insurance incentives faced by a person.

Adverse selection and moral hazard make the practice of insurance much more difficult than the theory. The practice of insurance also is made difficult because the "underwriting" process—the construction of the pool of insureds—is itself somewhat uncertain. The ideal insurance pool must contain relatively homogeneous but uncorrelated risks, with relatively predictable outlays if the covered fortuities occur, and the probabilities of those fortuities must be resolvable. As the insurance pool moves away from the ideal, residual risks to the insurer increase, which must be compensated for in terms of higher premiums.

SOCIAL INSURANCE

The government of every developed economy offers a range of insurance products that are baked into that country's social compact. In the United States, Social

Security, Medicare, unemployment insurance, and the Supplemental Nutrition Assistance Program are all examples.

These instances of *social insurance* have in common the themes that every citizen is in the insurance pool (although of course not every citizen claims benefits at any given point in time), that premiums (which may or may not be determined through actuarially accurate insurance principles) are collected through the tax system, and that the purposes of the programs are to mitigate the harshness of unalloyed private outcomes—by offering minimum income to the elderly, a food budget to the impoverished, and so on. Social insurance in fact operates as true insurance, in that it relies on risk shifting and risk pooling to turn egregiously bad potential outcomes into more tolerable ones, at the cost of annual premiums collected through the tax system.

In their book on the history and design of American social insurance programs, Michael Graetz and Jerry Mashaw define the "essential social purpose" of social insurance as:

> [T]he provision of a degree of income security due to risks common in a dynamic market economy. Moreover, it seems clear that income security has two elements: the protection of income against absolute inadequacy, and the protection of income streams from sudden termination or massive diminution because of risks that are commonly shared but uniquely distributed.[6]

This chapter points in the same general direction, with two caveats. First, many instances of protection against "absolute inadequacy," such as Social Security, cannot fairly be laid entirely at the feet of our dynamic market economy: the frequent penury of the elderly long predates modern dynamic capitalism. Second, Graetz and Mashaw essentially rule out of order the use of social insurance to address differences in natal abilities. This might be sensible as a practical matter, but is not required by the theory of insurance or by moral philosophy, at least so long as one permits the use of retrospective premiums. For these reasons, I prefer to think of social insurance as insurance against life's fortuities rather than the risks of a dynamic market economy. The difference becomes meaningful, for example, when thinking about whether the structure of the progressive income tax can be described as an implicit form of social insurance.

Countries employ social insurance as a key component of the social compact because most people believe that to be a member of a society is to have an interest in the welfare of other members of that society. This impulse can be expressed in ethical terms, but it also is based on straightforward economic logic: healthy and adequately nourished citizens are more productive, and will contribute more to the prosperity of society, than will sick and emaciated ones. Finally, in many cases, such as health insurance or insurance against "absolute inadequacy," insurance is most efficiently delivered as mandatory social insurance (that is, as a government program), because this effectively addresses problems of adverse selection.

Implicit in social insurance are at least three separate thoughts. First, there is the observation that people will not always make decisions today that are optimal for their future selves—by saving enough when young, for example, to finance a comfortable retirement. This reflects the psychological reality that our future selves are largely unknown to us, and therefore do not always attract as much care as we would in hindsight wish we had expended on ourselves.

Second, regardless of foresight, some unalloyed market outcomes are simply inconsistent with the long-term interests of society—as when a young worker is suddenly fired because her employer has gone bankrupt. That young worker has not yet had time to build up a nest egg of her own, but through social insurance (in this case, unemployment insurance) the worker can pool the financial risk of an uncertain but devastating outcome (she loses her job through no fault of her own) with the same risk faced by all other workers, and thereby accomplish risk shifting and risk pooling. Private unemployment insurance would face large adverse selection problems, but because the unemployment insurance pool is universal, social insurance can complement private insurance markets by offering a useful product that private insurance firms cannot, at least on commercially reasonable terms.

Third, social insurance need not be priced on strict actuarially determined terms. Indeed, many social insurance programs, such as Social Security, seek to enhance the welfare of society by structuring benefits or premiums (whether called by that name, or "contributions," or "taxes") on some sort of progressive schedule, so that less affluent citizens end up with larger insurance benefits than their premiums would have purchased in an actuarially fair program. I offer a justification for this fact pattern (universally followed by countries) later in the chapter.

Social insurance directly implicates the issue of moral hazard—the concern that insureds will behave more carelessly or lazily in the presence of insurance than they would in its absence. This is the essential point of political contention today over many forms of social insurance—the argument that citizens have chosen not to contribute to their own advancement (and indirectly to that of society as a whole) because they prefer the comfortable hammock of indolence made possible by social insurance. This issue was discussed earlier in the book in the context of unemployment insurance, and is discussed again at the end of this chapter. The short answer is that the argument that members of society look forward to the hammock of social insurance benefits in lieu of exerting themselves fails on careful examination, when the purported hammock turns out to be closer to a bed of nails.

Social insurance by definition contains an "individual mandate" (the obligation to participate in the social insurance program) whether we are aware of it or not, because the insurance is hard-wired into the social compact. Despite all our collective agitation over the Affordable Care Act's individual mandate, as if such a mandate were an unheard-of thing, it is worth remembering how many insurance mandates we have been subject to all along. For example, in almost all states you cannot own and operate an automobile without holding automobile liability insurance. (New Hampshire and California allow you to avoid such insurance by making alternative arrangements with the state to assure your ability to meet claims.) Your mortgage lender will require you to carry fire and other casualty insurance on your home, and in many cases might require the assignment of a life insurance contract as well. And of course one is required to participate in Social Security and other government insurance programs. In the ordinary course of modern existence you are not allowed to be wild and crazy, accepting all uncertain risks to which you might be exposed.

In the most delicious irony of all, even before the Affordable Care Act, most individuals in the United States lucky enough to have had healthcare insurance obtained that insurance through mandatory programs. Medicare is a mandatory insurance program for elderly adults, and at least before the Affordable Care Act those working adults who were under the age of 65, not so poor as to qualify for Medicaid, and who had health insurance were overwhelmingly likely to have that insurance because it was provided through their employers in programs that were simply part of working conditions. Employers might have been free to drop such insurance, but most did not, because the tax subsidy for employer-provided healthcare and executives' desire for healthcare insurance for themselves were sufficiently powerful incentives for the employers to continue those programs. And employees in turn could not opt out and take the cost of insurance as cash compensation, although in some firms they were allowed to select among different options.

THE SOCIAL VALUE OF INSURANCE

Contemporary political discourse's fixation over moral hazard in the context of social insurance—of course usually phrased less genteelly, by relying instead of "moral hazard" on terms like "mooching" or "taking"—has completely obscured a far more fundamental point, which is that insurance, whether private insurance or social insurance, has tremendous social value. Insurance mitigates the catastrophic outcome—say, the financial loss incurred when one's cargo goes down with a ship sunk by storms—and replaces that outcome with a known alternative that can be priced and accounted for in the calculus of whether to undertake the voyage.

In other words, *insurance encourages risk-taking, not indolence*. Because of insurance, the docks of Genoa swarmed with shipowners and captains willing to risk their capital in long sea voyages. Imagine that a fair risk-free return on your investment—a sure thing, like a bond issued by a reputable government—is 10 percent. You are considering an investment that in fact has risk associated with it, like financing a trading vessel embarking from Genoa to Constantinople. In fact, there is a 5 percent (1 in 20) chance you will lose the entire investment—the ship will sink out of sight of land. Ignoring the time it would take to complete the voyage, a fair return on money invested in this activity might now be about 21 percent.[7] In that case, the returns on 19 successful trips out of 20 compensate for the one out of 20 catastrophe.

But to invest 100 florins in this risky investment makes no sense if this represents all of your capital, because then you literally are playing a form of Russian roulette, hoping that the shipwreck comes only after many successful voyages. If you had sufficient assets, you might make 20 such investments in different ships, but you can get to the same place more quickly and reliably through insurance, which by creating a very large pool of comparable risks makes it far more likely that the statistical probability (5 percent chance of shipwreck) describes the group's actual experience. As a result, the capital available to risk in voyages from Genoa to Constantinople, and the returns on capital that are demanded, will more closely correspond to underlying odds. Commercial activity will reach its market-clearing level, because capital owners can now afford to be risk-takers.

The same is true with social insurance, particularly once one sees that the progressive rate structure of the personal income tax functions in part as a form of social insurance premium (see chapter 12). Knowing that the tax-funded "social safety net" exists, a young person takes a gamble, and sets out to develop the next great app. She knows that if she succeeds, her returns will be reduced somewhat by a tax bill (the implicit insurance premium), but she also knows that if she fails miserably she will not starve in the streets. Because her downside is now tolerable, she takes the risk with her time and her life that otherwise would have been foolhardy.

Individuals are naturally and understandably risk averse. Indeed, academic study after study has shown that the risk of loss looms much larger in personal decision-making than does the possibility of gain. This is not a new phenomenon, or the sure sign of the collapse of a nation's moral fiber, but rather a completely rational conclusion, in light of the fact that each of us has only one life, not 20, with which to gamble.

In the absence of social insurance, personally rational risk aversion leads to socially suboptimal personal risk-taking, because again one cannot diversify one's life experience through assuming 20 separate avatars. The other side of the coin is moral hazard, but this is a side effect, not a purpose, and is mitigated through program design. Our obsession with moral hazard has led us to ignore the tremendous value of social insurance in enabling a socially desirable level of risk-taking through the classic insurance mechanisms of risk shifting and risk pooling.

HEALTHCARE INSURANCE[8]

How Private Are Our Healthcare Insurance Markets?

My simple summary of the conditions required for efficient insurance markets reads like a bill of particulars making the case that wholly voluntary private healthcare insurance markets either will fail or will include only a small fraction of citizens. There are good reasons that the fourteenth-century Genoese invented modern marine insurance, but not private healthcare plans.

In fact, our existing crazy-quilt system of delivering healthcare insurance has never been a wholly private market. Government's hand has long shaped and subsidized healthcare markets, for example in Medicare and Medicaid (which dominate how medical care is organized, delivered, and priced in America, even for care that falls outside their reach), or the requirement that hospitals treat the urgent care needs of indigents. Insurance products in the individual health insurance market were regulated by the different state insurance regulators before the Affordable Care Act, and to a limited extent by the federal government under the 1996 Health Insurance Portability and Accountability Act (HIPAA).

But the most consequential government subsidy is rarely mentioned or even noticed: government for decades has directly subsidized individuals' costs of employer-provided healthcare, to the tune of roughly $250 billion every year in income and payroll tax forgiveness—sums far greater than the annual costs of the subsidized insurance coverage provisions of the Affordable Care Act.

Chapter 9 outlined the concept of tax expenditures—forms of government spending baked into the tax code—and identified government subsidies to "private" employer-provided healthcare plans as the largest single instance of these subsurface spending programs. The government subsidies that undergird all such plans are delivered through the tax code, rather than through messy health exchanges or government checks, but they remain subsidies nonetheless. All that has happened is that we have become lost in the fiscal fog of our own rhetorical devices, so that those who receive these subsidies deny that they are the beneficiaries of government largesse, while decrying efforts to offer analogous but smaller subsidies to other Americans.

The vast majority of Americans get their healthcare through employer plans, which of course will continue under the Affordable Care Act. As chapter 9 explained, when your employer pays your salary, the employer deducts the cost of your compensation as a business expense in figuring its own tax bill. The same applies to healthcare that your employer buys for you—the insurance premiums or out-of-pocket expenses the employer pays are deductible expenses, because those costs, in fact, are simply more compensation paid for your services.

But—and here is the magic—while cash salary or bonuses paid to you are your taxable income, the tax code expressly allows you to ignore the value of the health-care costs that your employer pays on your behalf in calculating your taxable income. If your healthcare insurance costs your employer $10,000 each year, you are saving up to $4,000 or so on your income tax bill, plus saving payroll tax costs on that $10,000, as well. Conversely, if your employer paid you the $10,000 in my example in cash, and told you to go buy insurance if you wanted it, you would be hit with both income and payroll tax bills on that amount.

The healthcare exclusion is not a new government subsidy program—it has been the law for many decades. Like many other tax expenditures, its origins were largely accidental, rather than the implementation of some deliberate national health policy. During World War II, the government imposed wage and price controls on the domestic economy, to prevent profiteering from the surge in activity to support the war effort. Employers desperate to attract workers stumbled onto the fact that the Internal Revenue Service traditionally had not taxed fringe benefits to workers, and therefore those benefits were not included in the measurement of wages for wage control purposes. Employers began offering this additional fringe benefit, and the concept continued long after wage and price controls were lifted.

The poster child for fiscal obtuseness in this regard has been Senator Ted Cruz of Texas, whose health insurance is provided through his wife's employer (an investment firm). That insurance, which has a value of about $20,000/year, benefits from the federal subsidies described above to the tune of around $8,500/year. (State and local income tax savings would add to this estimate.) Yet because the policy is not obtained through a health exchange, the employer incorrectly explained to the *New York Times* that the plan "comes at no cost to the taxpayer."[9]

Senator Cruz thus is himself the beneficiary of a large federal healthcare subsidy, even as he works to deprive millions of other Americans who do not enjoy employer-provided healthcare from obtaining smaller government subsidies of their own. Why is the tax expenditure subsidy somehow lost in a fog of flag waving and free enterprise talk, and the explicit subsidy offered by the Affordable Care Act the sure sign of galloping socialism?

Can Efficient Private Healthcare Markets Exist?

In short, even without regard to the Affordable Care Act, we have absolutely no experience with genuinely private healthcare insurance markets in the United States. Nonetheless, let us try to imagine starting from a blank sheet of paper and creating an efficient private market.

Right at the start we would run into the fundamental problem of adverse selection. Illness often differs from fire, in that the onset may be sudden, but the condition can linger for days, months, or years. Without safeguards, the phenomenon of adverse selection would give individuals plenty of time to rush out to buy health insurance to cover their foreseeable upcoming expenses. And any safeguards would be difficult to police along several margins. For example, exclusions for preexisting conditions in turn lead to difficult controversies over the scope of the exclusion, as one medical condition can implicate another in diffuse chains of causality—or not, depending on each case.

To get a sense of what is at stake from an insurer's perspective in weeding out the most egregious adverse selection cases, consider a recent study by the Agency for Healthcare Research and Quality, part of the US Department of Health and Human Services. It estimated that the top one percent of healthcare consumers account for 21.4 percent of total healthcare spending in the United States; conversely, the bottom 50 percent account for only 2.8 percent (see Table 11.1).[10]

To be clear, the top one percent of healthcare cost consumers are not the same as the top one percent of income-earners. In fact, exactly the opposite is the case: today, many members of this one percent are the poor, the chronically ill, the mentally challenged, and sufferers of emotional and physical abuse, many of whom fear the cost and bureaucracy of the healthcare system, and therefore avoided it until their problems became acute.[11]

Medical insurance would do no good for hideously expensive long-term illnesses if an insurer had the right to cancel the contract on an annual basis, as is true for other casualty insurance. If the contract were constructed to include future costs of a condition diagnosed during the term of the contract, that of course would both raise the cost of a policy and lead again to controversy over what future expenses related to the covered condition.

Insurers also would have to address the problem of moral hazard. They might, for example, require insureds to obtain annual exams, or police various forms of

Table 11.1 Distribution of Health Expenditures for the US Population by Magnitude of Expenditure and Mean Expenditures (2010)

	Top 1%	Top 5%	Top 10%	Top 25%	Top 50%
Percentage of Total Expenditures	21.4%	49.9%	65.6%	86.4%	97.2%
Mean Expenditures	$87,570	$40,876	$26,851	$14,155	$7,960

Source: Agency for Healthcare Research and Quality, *Statistical Brief #421*, fig. 1.

risky behavior (smoking or excessive alcohol consumption), using such behavior as reason to cancel a contract or deny coverage for a claim.

Risk-averse individuals might like to obtain "permanent" health insurance, analogous to permanent whole life insurance. But permanent private healthcare insurance that covers the cost of future care for annual premiums fixed in advance is impracticable for an insurer to write, because the indemnity—the financial cost—is unknowable over time, due to rapid technological evolution in healthcare. (Conversely, the indemnity is straightforward to measure in the case of fire insurance or life insurance—it is the agreed value of the property or the face amount of the policy.) The best one could do is to agree in advance to pay annual premiums at then-current rates. This essentially is how the individual health insurance market worked before the Affordable Care Act: an insurer was obligated to offer you annual renewals of your insurance product, but the insurer could set whatever rates it wanted and could modify the product being offered.[12]

Finally, all of us incur medical expenses, particularly as we age, while most of us never make a claim on our fire insurance policies. "Permanent" health insurance therefore either would need to have steeply escalating premiums (even before taking into account technological evolution in the field) or to have very large savings accounts embedded into the contract, like permanent whole life insurance does. But that in turn would make such insurance unaffordable to most young people, leading to a smaller and sicker pool of potential customers, which in turn would require still higher premiums for the remaining insureds. Life insurance basically deals with this problem by paying "death benefits" to the survivors of an elderly individual who dies in the form of the decedent's own money—the savings account stapled to the true insurance policy. The actual true insurance coverage in whole life insurance dwindles to nothing as one ages.

In light of the adverse selection problem, the cost structure of private healthcare insurance (which in turn encourages the young and healthy to drop out of the insurance pool), and all the other problems quickly outlined above, it is straightforward to see that ordinary private markets and healthcare insurance make for a very bad match. And that of course is exactly what one saw before the Affordable Care Act for individuals seeking to purchase insurance in the individual market: denial of insurance for preexisting conditions, or prices so high as to be unaffordable.

Our Fragmented Healthcare Markets in Operation

Before the Affordable Care Act, about 15 million individuals bought retail individual healthcare insurance products. Most individuals did so as one or two-year gap coverage, in between work for employers that offered employer plans; 40 percent of those with private individual insurance moved to public insurance, such as Medicare or Medicaid.[13] Each insurer determined for itself the actual insurance products that it offered to customers; those terms were subject to wildly varying regulation by the 50 state insurance commissioners. Most states permitted insurers in the individual market to address adverse selection issues through an underwriting process, including a medical exam, and through differential "rating"—charging different subgroups different prices for the same product, based on factors like age, sex, or preexisting conditions.

According to industry data, in 2008 only about 73 percent of those individuals who began the insurance process ultimately were offered insurance. But even this figure actually overstates the number who qualified on their own, as it includes policies that insurers were required to issue on a guaranteed basis to HIPAA-qualified individuals (those who formerly had group coverage and met certain other conditions) in states that otherwise permitted medical underwriting.[14] Insurance products typically excluded preexisting conditions, even where those conditions were unknown at the time insurance was underwritten (for example, a slow-growing tumor).[15]

Among those offered individual healthcare insurance in 2008, the industry data reveal that roughly one-third received offers at premiums above standard premiums. Most coverage comprised Preferred Provider Organization plans (also the dominant approach among employer plans); about 55 percent of family PPO plans had deductibles in excess of $5,000/year. Most plans further required significant co-payments and co-insurance payments, and had lifetime benefits caps.

An individual insurance contract typically runs for 12 months. Before the Affordable Care Act, the actual medical care coverage offered varied from insurance product to product, subject only to state regulatory constraints; often, however, the coverage was very bare-bones. (For example, psychiatric or maternity care might not be covered.) Under HIPAA, insurers even before the Affordable Care Act were required to offer renewals of an insurance product to existing customers, but this arrangement for "permanent" insurance was subject to three gaping holes: insurers could amend the product itself (with state insurance regulatory authorization); they could set any new premiums for the product that they wished for the renewal period; and they were free to abandon offering the product, provided that in the last case they offered customers the opportunity to switch to any other product that they continued to offer in that state. (In fact, this is what happened in late 2013, as insurers withdrew from the market insurance products that did not meet the minimum standards introduced by the Affordable Care Act.)

This quick review of the actual individual healthcare insurance market before the Affordable Care Act demonstrates why private markets and healthcare are a bad fit. Many could obtain no insurance at all, others paid a great deal for very limited coverage (including deductibles that would bankrupt many families). Even after HIPAA's intervention in those private markets, all individual healthcare insurance participants were at risk of losing their insurance whenever an insurer chose to withdraw from a market, or to raise premiums beyond an insured's breaking point. From their perspective, insurers were often at risk of a "premium spiral," in which young and healthy individuals in the pool would exit, thereby forcing higher premiums on the remaining members of the pool, which would cause others to exit, and so on.

In 2013, about 140 million Americans held private healthcare insurance, but roughly 125 million did so through mandatory participation in employer-sponsored group plans. The mandatory nature of insurance obtained incident to an unrelated activity (employment) avoided the fundamental adverse-selection problem. In turn, we have widespread employer buy-in for such plans largely because of the massive federal government subsidies that encourage employers to structure employee compensation in this manner. These are not the outcomes of private markets.

In short, the situation applicable to Americans under the age of 65 before the Affordable Care Act relied on nominally private insurance arrangements, delivered through the logically unrelated mechanism of employer fringe benefits, and held together by the glue of massive federal subsidies. This system was intolerable for at least two reasons. First, an extraordinary number of Americans—nearly one in six—had no health insurance at all, because those individuals did not work for employers that provided it, and because they were priced out of individual markets, or thrown out due to insurers' aggressive application of preexisting conditions standards. Second, if you set out to try, you could not invent arrangements that would be more inefficient or more expensive.

In 2009, for example, only about 81 percent of Americans (including seniors) had basic healthcare insurance coverage, putting us in the embarrassing company of Turkey. Somehow 30 other OECD countries were able to provide all or almost all their citizens with healthcare coverage without all rolling down the slippery slope into socialist hells. Indeed, with the exception of Germany, all relied almost entirely on public insurance arrangements of one kind or another to do so (see Figure 11.1).

To be clear, foreign peer countries that have state-sponsored healthcare systems do not all rely exclusively on "single-payer" government plans (like Medicare), much less single-provider plans (like the Veterans Administration healthcare system, where medical providers are employees of the VA). In all such countries, however, healthcare insurance is mandatory, coverage is made available to low-income citizens through subsidies or similar arrangements, and both the scope of insurance coverage and the prices of medical services (and pharmaceuticals) are directly regulated by the government. No peer country allows healthcare to operate in the Wild West sort of atmosphere that still dominates US provisioning and pricing.

FIGURE 11.1 Public and Private Healthcare Coverage (2009)

Source: OECD, *OECD Health at a Glance 2011: OECD Indicators* (2011), fig. 6.2.1, doi:10.1787/888932525685.

Switzerland, for example, has a public healthcare system in substance (as the OECD data show), but that country's technical implementation takes the form of closely regulated private insurers. Each Swiss resident must obtain basic insurance (an individual mandate), but may choose her preferred private insurer. In turn, each insurance company must accept all residents in the canton in which the insurer operates, and must charge the same rate to all residents (community rating) for basic coverage. Low-income residents are subsidized. Crucially, the medical profession and related industries operate under a national tariff structure that controls prices. In France, to take another example, public health insurance covers about 75 percent of the nation's medical bills; most French citizens have supplemental private plans that cover about one-half of the remainder. Germany's system is similar to Switzerland's. Ninety percent of the population is covered by a large number of statutory sickness funds. These funds nominally are private, and compete for customers, but receive government funding that ordinarily covers all of a citizen's basic coverage premium costs. Higher-income citizens can opt into a unique form of private insurance, under which preexisting conditions must be covered; the insured must maintain that insurance for life, and the insurance company must renew the policy for the insured's life without premium increases, other than general expenditure increases for the entire pool. None of these countries operates a "market-based" healthcare delivery system, as that term is used in US political discourse.[16]

The inevitable consequence of America's large uninsured population was that the United States simply failed to deliver necessary healthcare to many individuals, including Americans with above-average incomes, because they could not afford it (see Figure 11.2).

Another study estimated that Americans receive "on average, about half of medical care processes" recommended by current research and evidence-based guidelines.[17]

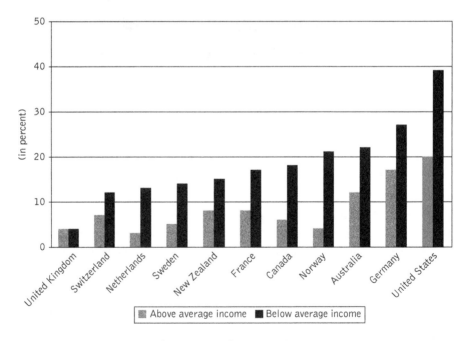

FIGURE 11.2 Unmet Care Need Due to Costs, by Income Group (2010)

Source: OECD, OECD Health at a Glance 2011: OECD Indicators (2011).

The nature and quality of healthcare also varies considerably among states. The National Academy of Sciences reported that if all states could have provided the quality of care delivered by the highest performing state, 75,000 fewer deaths would have occurred throughout the country in 2005.

Perhaps as a result, our life expectancy is at the bottom end of the OECD, well below that of countries we would recognize as even remotely our peers (see Figure 11.3).

The National Academy of Science in 2013 published a book comparing health outcomes in the United States to those of 16 other high-income countries. The study's conclusions are signaled by its title, *U.S. Health in International Perspective: Shorter Lives, Poorer Health.*[18] That book dissected in detail the mortality statistics reflected in Figure 11.3. A disproportionate number of Americans die prematurely from accidents and homicides, for example, but the most powerful indictment of our overall healthcare system is the number of Americans who die from communicable diseases, given that our per capita medical spending dwarfs that of any other country (see Figure 11.4).

The National Academy's study further demonstrates that we have the worst infant mortality rates, the most obese children, the most obese young adults, the highest birth rates to adolescent mothers, the highest rates of diabetes (save Spain, which barely edges us out among women, but not men), and the largest percentage of adults at high risk for cardiovascular disease, of any of the 16 other

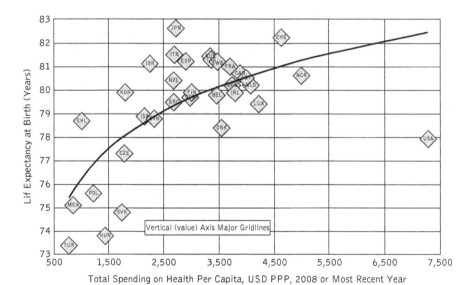

FIGURE 11.3 Life Expectancy at Birth in 2008

Source: OECD, *Society at a Glance 2011–OECD Social Indicators* (2011), chart HE1.2.

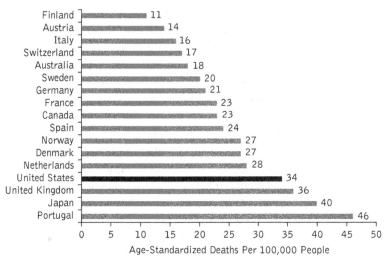

FIGURE II.4 Mortality from Communicable Diseases in 17 Peer Countries, 2008

Source: National Research Council, *U.S. Health in International Perspective*, fig. 1-2.

countries included in the study. The *only* areas where our death rates are noticeably better than the average of the 16 other countries are in respect of death from certain cancers (but not lung cancer, lymphomas, or leukemia) and respiratory infections.[19]

Again, these are appalling results when considered against the fact that we spend so much more per capita on healthcare than do any of these other countries. In chapter 7, I described at length how extraordinarily expensive US healthcare spending is. As a reminder, if the United States were to reduce its per capita spending to that of the second-most profligate country on earth (Norway), we would save almost $1 trillion every year in public and private funds.

Even in a world of ideally designed healthcare insurance, our healthcare programs would be very expensive, because our wealth enables us to spend heavily here, and because our unwillingness to allow government to make any decisions that could be characterized as rationing healthcare or regulating prices condemns us to do so. Nonetheless, our current patchwork delivery systems make things much worse along two margins: we waste almost unimaginable sums of money, and we have the terrible overall outcomes that follow from incomplete healthcare insurance coverage.

Our fundamental problem is that, by virtue of our patchwork delivery instruments, we do not in fact have a healthcare "system" in the United States. Most healthcare is not "tradable"—while there is some medical tourism, most individuals are treated near their homes, or where they suffer a catastrophic incident.

This means that prices for healthcare services 1,000 or even 100 miles away are less important than are prices for books, which we can easily have delivered to us.

As a result, we actually have a fragmented environment of hundreds or even thousands of geographically distinct mini-healthcare markets in the United States, each largely immune to competition from the others, and often dominated by one or two market sellers (healthcare providers, such as hospitals or preferred provider organizations). As George Halvorson, chair of Kaiser Permanente, wrote in 2007:

> We don't really have a health care delivery system in this country. We have an expensive plethora of uncoordinated, unlinked, economically segregated, operationally limited microsystems, each performing in ways that too often create suboptimal performance both for the overall health care infrastructure and for individual patients.[20]

The large preferred provider organizations are the dominant providers (sellers) of healthcare services. On the other side, there are nearly 40 major medical insurance companies in the United States today, and more reportedly are being created in response to the Affordable Care Act. (This count does not include public insurers such as Medicare, Medicaid, and the Veterans Administration; self-insured employers; or private issuers of Medigap insurance policies.) The immediate buyers—the insurance companies—are often themselves the victims of monopoly pricing by these sellers.[21]

From the other direction, there have been instances in the early rollout of the Affordable Care Act's exchanges where only one insurer offers coverage in a certain rural area. The insurers, which effectively buy healthcare from the PPOs or other organizations and sell it to consumers, then can act like monopoly sellers in their pricing of their products (the insurance contracts) to consumers.

In one such example uncovered by the *New York Times*, insurance in a rural county in Georgia cost exactly twice as much as the same policy in metropolitan Atlanta, where there is more competition at both levels.[22] Plans have been mooted to create new national insurers to create more competition at the insurance company level, but those plans do not address monopoly pricing at the provider level, and, to the extent they are effective, just beg the question, why do we not just stop torturing ourselves and move to a program that has the operative effect of a single payer system, as many other countries have done?[23]

To make matters worse, private insurers are largely indifferent to the prices they are charged by hospitals and other providers, because they in turn just pass those costs on to the ultimate purchasers, employers. From the other direction, employees are largely unaware of how much their employers spend per employee on the health insurance those employers provide, and therefore do not agitate for lower healthcare charges combined with greater cash compensation. Employers have incentives to control healthcare costs to the extent that those costs grow more quickly than explicit compensation would, but as a group are flummoxed by the complexity and opacity of the price information available to them, and so do surprisingly little.[24]

These factors encourage extraordinary inefficiencies. At an operational level, doctors often perform routine work that could be done just as well by nurses, nurses perform administrative tasks intended for non-medical staff, and the whole lot spend countless hours on unnecessary paperwork. One recent study estimated that each year the healthcare industry wastes $100 to $400 billion on administrative costs.[25] A RAND study estimated that the administrative costs incurred by physician practices simply to interact with insurance plans was over $68,000 per doctor.[26] And the Institute on Medicine estimated the waste existing in six domains—unnecessary services, services ineffectively delivered, prices that are too high, excess administrative costs, missed prevention opportunities, and medical fraud—to be $765 billion in 2009.[27]

Fragmentation of markets and the monopoly presence of major preferred provider organizations lead to price opacity and unconscionable markups that are unacceptable in any other commercial context. You can get a feel for the bizarreness of the US healthcare economy by pricing hip replacement surgery that is not covered by insurance. In many cases you will discover that it is almost impossible to get a price quote at all, but if you do, you will learn that the nominal retail price for the procedure (the so-called hospital "chargemaster" rate) is as much as 10 times higher in the United States than in Belgium, and that the discounted rate paid by large insurers is on the order of three times as great.[28] And as the *New York Times* demonstrated, hospitals' "chargemaster" billing systems produce starting bids for routine products, like a bag of salt water (saline solution) used to rehydrate a patient, of 100 or 200 times the manufacturer's price, not including separate charges for administering the water, already priced at the level of a first-growth Bordeaux.[29] This is what happens when private monopolies price goods and services that have existential importance to their consumers.

The OECD recently attempted to analyze why healthcare costs are so much higher in the United States than elsewhere, and basically found that medical services cost more at every stage: in-hospital or outpatient, pharmaceuticals, or administrative expenses—all outstrip OECD norms.[30] We actually have far fewer doctors per 100,000 residents than do other countries, we have fewer hospital admissions, and the average hospital stay is much shorter than the comparable statistics for most other OECD countries. Where we excel is in charging a lot of money, and in using a lot of machines. A famous article in the academic literature summed things up in its title: *It's The Prices, Stupid.*[31]

Finally, without regard to prices or inefficiencies, the current fragmented healthcare delivery "system" leads to poor medical care, because that care is largely uncoordinated. This includes referrals from generalists to specialists and back, discharges from hospital to outpatient care, admissions to hospitals (therefore outpatient to inpatient) or visits to emergency rooms, transfers within hospitals, communication among specialties within hospitals, and many other types of situations. For example, one nationwide study revealed that one in seven Medicare patients suffered harm from hospital care, of which 44 percent of those errors were found to be preventable.[32]

Thomas Bodenheimer summarized the results of a number of studies documenting and illustrating the ubiquity and seriousness of this problem. He reported that a study of referrals by pediatricians showed that information regarding a patient was sent by a referring pediatrician to a specialist only 49 percent of the time, and information was transmitted by the specialist back to the referring doctor only 55 percent of the time. He also described a study finding that fewer than half of primary care physicians received information about discharge plans or medications of their recently hospitalized patients.[33]

Both Medicare and the Veterans Administration have far lower administrative costs than does the private insurance sector, among other reasons because they do not have to negotiate with every provider in their network. They also are not at risk of gaming by other payers in the healthcare chain trying to shift costs to them, because they operate what are effectively single-payer (or in the case of the VA, single-provider) systems. Moreover, because they are open to all individuals who meet the relevant standards, neither program is at risk of adverse selection concerns, and therefore does not have to behave as if it were in a state of war with its customer base.

But the biggest cost-saving advantage that a single-payer system like Medicare has over the multiplicity of private insurers in place today is that the single-payer system is itself a monopsony, and so can negotiate reasonable prices. That is exactly what Medicare does today.

You can see the difference in the field of prescription medications, where Congress in its infinite wisdom has prohibited Medicare from negotiating prices, and where private insurers are largely helpless to control which medications are prescribed by providers, thereby effectively conferring monopoly pricing advantages on private producers of pharmaceutical products. The *New York Times* reported the example of an asthma medication that cost $250/month in the United States, but $7/month in Europe.[34]

American doctors often do not know the cost of medications they prescribe, whether inpatient or outpatient.[35] Since low-cost medications can be as or more effective than high-cost medications, and sometimes the best option is no medication at all, healthcare spending could be dramatically reduced without changing patient outcomes at all, and in some cases improving them, if there were any sort of external common sense brought to bear on the prescribing decision.

This can be demonstrated by looking at a single medication, Nexium (esomeprazole), a prescription medication used to treat and prevent gastroesophageal reflux disease. It was the top-selling medication by dollar cost in 2012, with sales of over $5.6 billion.[36] Pharmacologically its active ingredient is identical to that of its predecessor, Prilosec (omeprazole), now sold over the counter. Clinically they also are nearly indistinguishable. The average cost of a one-month supply of Nexium is $240, compared with an average cost of $22 for a one-month supply of Prilosec. If doctors had substituted Prilosec for every prescription of Nexium in the United States in 2012, the savings would been about $5.1 billion.[37]

For many years healthcare costs rose materially faster than the rate of infla-tion or GDP growth.[38] As chapter 7 described, during the Great Recession the pace of this "excess cost growth" unexpectedly moderated. For example, federal spending on Medicare and Medicaid in 2012 was about 5 percent lower than the amount predicted by CBO two years earlier (not lower in absolute terms, but not as much higher as had been expected).[39] While the President's Council of Economic Advisors report referenced in chapter 7 expresses great optimism, no one really knows what trajectory healthcare costs will follow as individuals' economic prospects recover, but there is no reason to believe that the trend of increasing healthcare costs will reverse, and that costs will come down.

The counterexample, frequently invoked by Senator Rand Paul and Congressman Paul Ryan, is LASIK eye surgery, which can correct one's vision so that eyeglasses are not needed. This surgery is not generally covered by private health insurance, because it is viewed as a purely elective cosmetic intervention. Prices for the procedure have steadily fallen over the last decade or so. Rand Paul and Paul Ryan have both touted this development as evidence that the problem with American healthcare is that it is not market-driven in its pricing, but this is a largely fatuous claim. Messrs. Paul and Ryan have confused a personal pure consumption item (elective cosmetic surgery) with the bulk of healthcare, which we understandably approach as an existential imperative.

The example Messrs. Paul and Ryan avoid with their easy case of a wholly elective cosmetic procedure is, what is the going rate for a surgeon to reattach a detached retina? There we suddenly discover both the opacity of price informa-tion and the impossibility of comparison shopping when our sense of sight is at stake. Healthcare is more than just another personal consumption decision.

The Business Case for Public Health Insurance

In summary, healthcare fits poorly with the general conditions for thriving private insurance markets. In turn, the unavoidably fragmented nature of healthcare, attributable to the fact that it is not a "tradable good" (as books sold by Amazon are), is a perfect breeding ground for monopoly sellers (the healthcare provid-ers) and price-indifferent intermediate buyers (the insurance companies). If Karl

Marx were alive, he would use our fragmented healthcare system, with its trillion dollar annual waste, as the paradigmatic example of a society so mesmerized by capitalist slogans that it not only sold itself the noose with which to hang itself, but stuck its neck in the noose without the slightest external provocation.

Shipowners buy marine insurance incident to their larger enterprise, which is profiting from shipping. Making insurance claims is not by itself a business model, because the indemnity offers no better than a break-even return, before considering the administrative costs of the insurance. (There of course is some modest amount of fraud in casualty insurance, but that relates primarily to the overstatement of the indemnity claim, and not to a genuine business plan.) Marine insurers can and do inspect the vessel and its cargo, and values for each ordinarily are easily set by reference to market prices. The event of loss and the amount of loss also ordinarily are easily identified—the ship is at the bottom of the ocean. And neither the insurance markets nor the salvage markets are dominated by monopoly or monopsony players, because insurance can be obtained from any-one, the indemnity paid anywhere, and the property that is insured replaced in well-functioning large-scale private markets.

Healthcare insurance is different along every margin. The insurance is not obtained incident to a larger financial objective, but to fund an existential neces-sity. Underwriting exams cannot identify every defect, and many expensive claims relate to conditions that take years to present, and then become chronic conditions. This begs for gaming through adverse selection.

The good being insured—health—is uncertain in scope, and the pathways to restoring it (the appropriate medical protocols for each situation, corresponding to the measure of indemnifiable loss) are not themselves well defined at all, so that the same condition can be addressed through interventions of widely different cost, depending on entirely endogenous circumstances (for example, your doc-tor's relative predilection for ordering CAT scans). Adverse selection and moral hazard are present at every turn, because for an insured this insurance is the ultimate objective, not an incident to a larger objective, like running a profitable business. And the indemnity—the provision of medical services—is delivered in hundreds or thousands of fragmented local markets dominated by monopoly sell-ers (the preferred provider organizations and other medical providers). Without more, these are not conditions under which one would anticipate robust private markets.

As an aside, life insurance is much simpler, because the event of loss and the amount of the indemnity (death, and the agreed death benefits) are easily speci-fied. Adverse selection and moral hazard can be mitigated through underwriting (to deal with the prospective insured at death's door) and with a limitation on death benefits in the first couple of years of the contract, because the mortality risk associated with new insureds who survive the first couple of years become statistically indistinguishable from the larger population.

More important, society as a whole has already undertaken to write some poorly defined base level of health insurance, in the form of emergency rooms open to all. In light of all the unknowns suggested above, private health insurance will always leave a large fraction of the population without explicit insurance. But this in turn weakens society, because it exposes the unlucky to bankruptcy risks having nothing whatsoever to do with their willingness to work or similar nostrums.

If the purpose of society is to advance our collective welfare (which encompasses our collective prosperity as one component), we do so most straightforwardly in this area by offering healthcare insurance to all—just as virtually every other country in the world does. Social insurance addresses adverse selection, because by definition everyone joins in the insurance pool. Socially provided healthcare insurance can have modest administrative costs, because we do not have to weed out the "uninsurable" through the underwriting process, and because we have already in place a very low-cost mechanism for collecting the explicit or implicit premiums: the tax system. Socially provided healthcare insurance is not a profit-making venture, and therefore does not need to earn positive returns beyond the loss experience of the pool. And socially provided healthcare insurance responds directly to the monopoly power of locally fragmented healthcare markets.

The benefits of a healthy population are almost too obvious to recite. A better national health quotient would save resources that today go only to staunch literal or metaphorical bleeding, thereby permitting the redeployment of those resources to more productive uses. And healthier citizens are themselves more productive than sickly ones. So along both margins a healthier population yields a more productive economy, as well as happier citizens.

The idea that redirecting resources from healthcare to other uses somehow would hurt "the economy" because the healthcare sector would decline in importance is a classic example of the broken window fallacy. This fallacy argues that when the sandlot baseball slugger breaks a butcher's window with his home run ball, the economy is enhanced, because now the butcher must hire a glazier to fix the window, and the glazier in turn can spend her incremental income at the baker's, and so on.

The argument is fallacious because it ignores the destruction of wealth in the first place. The butcher has suffered a loss through the breaking of his window, which loss reduces his wealth. The broken window requires the butcher to take money that otherwise would have been applied in the most productive direction that he saw, according to his own lights, and instead apply it only to restore himself to where he was before the tiny slugger unleashed his mighty shot. The butcher has lost the returns that his previous plans for the money would have brought.

The same is true of wasteful healthcare insurance. Spending money that we do not need to spend to restore us collectively to a state of health we could have obtained more directly and cheaply is not "good" for the economy, although it might be good for those exercising monopoly or monopsony powers inside this sector. From a social perspective this wasteful spending and incomplete protection of our health represents a diversion of resources from the higher and better uses to which we each individually would have put our portion. Our ersatz patchwork "private" healthcare insurance markets thus are not an engine of economic growth, but rather randomly distribute large losses throughout the economy.

We do not pursue the path of our society's happiness, including our collective prosperity, by pursuing abstractions like the sanctity of markets if by doing so we waste $1 trillion or so every year in healthcare spending, and further leave tens of millions of Americans without adequate healthcare coverage, thereby condemning them to worse long-term health outcomes and to risks of bankruptcy. To the contrary, the markets here are telling us something quite clearly, which is that healthcare for all members of a society is a load that private markets cannot lift alone. And what is true of healthcare of course is even more apt for broader forms of insurance against the vicissitudes of life.

The alternative—a national single-payer system—is so obvious, and so powerful in its logic, that it beggars belief that the Obama administration abandoned it in the debate leading up to the Affordable Care Act. There is a reason, after, all, why virtually all other developed countries rely on this solution (whether in those words, or through combinations of policy instruments that have the same effect), and why the United States itself relies on it for all its seniors (through Medicare) and all its veterans (through the VA system, which actually is a single-provider system). At one stroke, the fundamental problem of adverse selection disappears, because all members of society participate. Premiums are easily collected through the existing tax administrative machinery. A patchwork of largely monopolistic local sellers now faces a monopsonistic buyer. Operating administrative costs are reduced, as we see today in Medicare administration. There is more than enough value on the table here to compensate the medical community fairly and still reap hundreds of billions of dollars of savings every year.

For all the good that the Affordable Care Act may have done in extending the number of Americans with some form of medical insurance, it did very little to address the underlying fiscal crisis of healthcare, which is that our current fragmented form of delivering health insurance is unaffordable. Not even the United States can afford to squander $1 trillion a year in the name of free market sloganeering, particularly in this unusual arena, where free market principles cannot help but fail. Here is an instance where more government, in the form of a national healthcare insurance for all, would have meant both better outcomes and greater wealth—in short, a happier society.

OTHER SOCIAL INSURANCE PROGRAMS

Large-scale social insurance programs that insure against not just poor health outcomes but also other life vicissitudes are the universal practices among our peer countries. The difficult question, of course, is how much ought to be offered? That is, how much social insurance should we as a society choose to buy?

Private insurers must wrestle with the problems of adverse selection and moral hazard. Social insurance does not have an adverse selection problem, because by definition everyone is in the pool. For example, you do not elect into the Social Security system; by virtue of being a working American, you are enrolled. Social insurance does, however, face a moral hazard issue—the risk that people behave differently by virtue of having the insurance than they would without it, in ways that are inconsistent with the larger interests of society.

Social insurance further introduces a new adverse incentive effect, by virtue of the fact that social insurance premiums are imposed primarily on those who enjoy positive material outcomes, and who therefore bear the brunt of those premiums in the form of taxes. These taxes reduce the return to labor or investment, and further impinge on the absolute personal liberties that some Americans believe to be their due. For both reasons, then, tax revenues available to finance social insurance are not an inexhaustible well.

These two factors constrain the scope of social insurance that a society can usefully offer. Once healthcare is taken off the table and addressed separately, however, it becomes apparent that the United States is a very skimpy buyer of social insurance.

Chapter 7 reviewed the basic fiscal facts, but by way of summary, in February 2013 the Congressional Budget Office estimated that our entire federal budget for all income support programs combined (mainly, the refundable portion of the earned income tax credit and the Supplemental Nutrition Assistance Program) would decline from 2.0 percent of GDP in 2014 to only 1.3 percent of GDP in 2023.[40] The earned income tax credit, of course, is designed to have a direct positive economic incentive effect, because it is available only to those who work; as discussed below, it probably is best characterized as outside but complementary to social insurance programs. Including it here thus overstates the scope of our social insurance programs.

One useful way to think about the right level of social insurance to promote the happiness of society is to benchmark ourselves against peer countries. In this regard, it is useful to reprise one chart from chapter 7, which again includes all social spending programs, regardless of whether properly characterized as

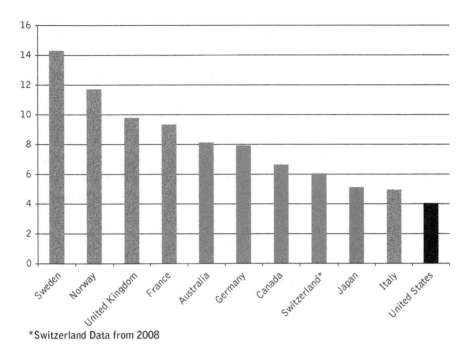

*Switzerland Data from 2008

FIGURE II.5 Total Public Social Spending as a Percentage of GDP, Excluding Social Security and Healthcare (2009)

Source: OECD, Social Expenditure Database (OECD, 2013) and OECD, "Social Expenditure," in *OECD Factbook 2013: Economic, Environmental and Social Statistics* (OECD Publishing, 2013).

insurance or investment (see Figure 11.5). Whatever moral hazards and other adverse incentive effects we are running must be much smaller than those of any other country we can imagine as a peer.

Chapters 2 and 7 already have described the best-known examples of social insurance and ancillary social investment programs, but to review, we can divide the standard forms of these programs outside the realm of healthcare into old age assistance (Social Security) and income support programs. Income support in turn can be subdivided into "making work pay" programs (principally the earned income tax credit), unemployment insurance (another form of insurance directly tied to work), and finally anti-destitution programs like the Supplemental Nutrition Assistance Program and Temporary Assistance to Needy Families, where the relationship to work is more attenuated.

Social Security is the best-known and largest single federal social insurance program.[41] (All healthcare programs combined slightly outdistance it.) As chapter 7 described, Social Security actually is an amalgam of different forms of insurance. About 85 percent of benefits go to the old age and survivors insurance programs, and 15 percent to disability insurance (which can be analogized to classic casualty insurance). The heart of Social Security—its old age benefits—function very much like private annuities, in that the amounts are paid for life, regardless of actual need at the time, and effectively guarantee against outliving one's resources. Unlike classic annuities, however, Social Security old age benefits are not technically returns on one's own money. Moreover, the terms of the annuity have a pure social insurance component to them, because Americans with consistently low labor earnings over their lifetimes get much better returns on their contributions than do Americans who consistently hit the annual wage cap on contributions. (In other words, the payment terms of the annuities are themselves progressive, even though the contributions that fund the program are regressive.)

The fiscal aspects of Social Security are out of balance in the long term. This has led many to urge that it be recast as a pure anti-destitution program, by denying benefits to higher-income elderly Americans. This idea has technical problems—for example, how does one handle the financially comfortable couple who give their assets to their children, so as to make themselves eligible for the income-restricted program? It also represents a profound and ultimately unnecessary recasting of the political economy presentation of Social Security for the last 70 years. It is true that my benefits are not literally paid from my contributions, but rather from those of the next generation, but so what? I made contributions, and now I get benefits—that is an internally consistent annuity story with important welfare consequences, because it means that each generation believes that it has earned its benefits. It is the accident of the start of the program, where the first generation of recipients had to be paid from somewhere, that explains the generational mismatch.

As it happens, the most straightforward way to address Social Security's fiscal imbalance is simply to lift the wage cap on contributions. This brings in sufficient revenues to fund Social Security for many decades into the future without changing the terms of the benefits offered. Doing so reinforces the embedded social insurance component of the program, because workers who consistently have very high labor incomes over their entire working careers will now have worse returns (more negative returns) on their contributions, but does so without asking the bulk of recipients to shed or hide their assets in order to qualify for assistance. The annuity rhetoric may be empty talk, but it has proved to be socially useful empty talk for the last three generations of Americans.

The earned income tax credit and similar "making work pay" programs administered through the tax code are very important in size and in effect. The "refundable" portions of the earned income tax credit and the child credit (cash payments to recipients) amount to over $80 billion/year, on top of tax reductions of about $125 billion/year.

Nonetheless, these programs do not really belong on a list of social insurance. They are best seen as subsidies, not insurance programs, whose purpose it is to bring into the above-ground private economy workers who might otherwise find the marginal cost of entering the workplace to be too great. In short, they are forms of social *investment* in our fellow citizens more than they are insurance. More generally, they can be seen as simply a special set of tax rates applicable to individuals with labor incomes at certain levels; even the refundable portion can effectively be characterized as primarily a rebate of payroll taxes borne by a low-wage worker.

The minimum wage fits squarely here as well. It is not usually counted among our social insurance or spending programs, but that is exactly what it is: a subsidy to low-wage workers, funded by society because the positive externalities of being part of the organized labor markets more than compensate for the social cost of the subsidy.

Unemployment insurance is a true social insurance program, designed both to ameliorate hardship and to have useful countercyclical effects from a macro-economic perspective. Chapters 2 and 3 discussed the claims advanced by Casey Mulligan and others about the negative incentive effects that unemployment insurance allegedly induces. There is no doubt that such insurance has some moral hazard risk associated with it, but for all the reasons developed in those earlier chapters, the risk is vastly overstated once one takes a more complete view of a rational unemployed worker's marginal calculus.

Finally, we have five anti-destitution social insurance programs (excluding healthcare programs for the poor), of which the two best known are the Supplemental Nutrition Assistance Program (food stamps) and Temporary Assistance to Needy Families.[42] (Pell Grants should be viewed as social investment in education, not insurance.) In 2012, deep in the Great Recession, these five federal social insurance programs had a combined cost of about $200 billion. In constant 2012 dollars, they are expected to cost less than that in 2023. These programs represented about 5.5 percent of federal government outlays in 2012.

Much of our current political discourse turns on the philosophical basis for these social insurance programs designed to mitigate the unluckiest of life outcomes. The next section therefore considers why such programs are economically rational and integral to the happiness of society, using food stamps as the principal exemplar.

SOCIAL INSURANCE AND "REDISTRIBUTION"

The federal government writes a little insurance of the sort celebrated in *Lloyd's of London* (for example, flood insurance), but it is an enormously important insurer of life outcomes more generally. It is these functions that Ezra Klein had in mind when he described the government as an insurance company with a standing army. It is also these functions that market triumphalists have in mind when they argue that government social insurance programs sap the able-bodied of the will to work, and the programs that Congressman Stephen Fincher of Tennessee no doubt had in mind when he explained that "[t]he role of citizens, of Christians, of humanity is to take care of each other, but not for Washington to steal from those in the country and give to others in the country." (Of course, when toting up all the government "stealing" going on around him, Congressman Fincher overlooked his personal status as a recipient of millions of dollars in federal farm subsidies.[43])

Fincher's description of social insurance programs as "stealing" is beyond the pale, but it is the logical downward tumble of a slightly more highbrow term that dominates both political discourse and the public finance literature. That term is "redistribution."

The progressive movement in America has made three fundamental strategic errors over the last several decades. The first is its failure to embrace explicitly and forcefully its best philosophical vantage point, which is the awareness of the importance of brute luck in life's outcomes, which in turn shapes policy. Progressives allow themselves to be caricatured as champions of moochers or takers, when in fact their point should be that, of course hard work is to be admired and encouraged, and of course great material success by itself is not problematic, but brute luck has more to do with both great successes and with lives of deprivation than we like to admit. We do not choose our parents, or our hair color, or our intelligence, or height, or any other birth attribute; nor do we control every twist and turn of our daily fortunes. When we recognize the contingent nature of our own outcomes, we also recognize our own face in that of our fellow citizens.

The second fundamental error of the progressive movement has been to confuse its real goal, which is a progressive fiscal system, with an incomplete means to that end, namely, progressive taxation: Chapter 12 addresses this confusion. And the third—the one directly relevant here—is to accept the word "redistribution" as a neutral and accurate description of social insurance in action. If the word "redistribution" were banished from political discourse as perniciously judgmental, and replaced instead with the term "social insurance," our debates would be both more civil and more productive.

In this regard progressives are following the public finance academic community. Indeed, the entire canon of welfare economics literature relies on the concept in defining a "social welfare function." The subfield of optimal taxation, for example, assumes that society has a given preference for redistribution, expressed mathematically in a social welfare function. It then asks, how do we go about instantiating that preference through taxation in the most efficient way possible?

It may be that welfare economists are sufficiently pure of heart that they use the term "redistribution" without any hint of moral opprobrium attached to it, but no one else does. In practice, the word carries with it an unavoidable suggestion that wealth is being taken from those who have it in order to "distribute" it to those who do not. Whether that amounts to "stealing" (to quote Congressman Fincher) depends on your views about the legitimacy of the state, but the clear implication, at a minimum, is that what is going on is a "taking."

One example of the dangers of "redistribution" as a label is the news story summarized in chapter 5, to the effect that a candidate to be chair of President Obama's Council of Economic Advisors was removed from consideration for the sin of having used the word "redistribution" in a 20-year old academic article. Another example is a long article in the *National Journal* (the most substantive of the inside-the-Beltway magazines aimed at policymakers and policy wonks—not the *National Review*) from November 2013.[44]

In that article, the author, James Oliphant, argued that the Affordable Care Act was an exercise in "redistribution," that this fact had been hidden from the American people, and that only in late 2013 was the truth revealed that there would be winners and losers. He acknowledged that Social Security, Medicare, public schools, and roads all have distributional implications, but somehow the Affordable Care Act's "benefits are diffuse and less tangible." This of course is an occluded view, impaired in part because the program has not been in place for a number of years, by which time most individuals will have experienced specific and tangible payoffs from it.

Oliphant seemed to have difficulty understanding what it means to be a "winner" in the insurance offered by the Affordable Care Act, by looking at one year's premiums, rather than a lifetime of assured enrollment and future benefits. He also seemed to think that the measure of winners and losers should be toted up by reference to fluctuating healthcare insurance premium costs, without much regard for differences in what the premiums are buying (including in particular guaranteed continued coverage in the future). Oliphant also overlooked that the legislation in fact was deficit-reducing, because it included a new progressive tax (the new tax on net investment income) that funded the cost of the expanded insurance programs. This of course means in one sense that the Affordable Care Act is more "redistributive" than the author suspected, but in another means that the act's funding mechanism is factually similar to that used for other social insurance programs (albeit less regressive in structure). A measure of "redistribution" also would require taking into account the distribution of existing healthcare subsidies, in particular the $250 billion or so of hidden tax subsidies that disproportionately benefit upper-income Americans. "Redistribution" hides all these analytical flaws, and impugns an entire program for functioning as what it is, which is social insurance.

The premises and implications of the word "redistribution" are fundamentally flawed. First, "*re*distribution" implies a natural order—a legitimacy—to the market distributions that are at risk of being distributed a second time. It is easy, however, to come up with examples of unalloyed market distributions that would give us pause. This is why local electricity companies and other utilities are regulated everywhere, and without objection from most of us: we do not accept the market distributions that would follow from the unalloyed application of monopoly powers.

Local utility company regulation thus is a form of "redistribution," although one hidden from view, as it is not implemented through transfers of cash back from utilities to customers. Yet this unseen expression of redistribution is not problematic to the overwhelming majority of Americans. Once you accept that the exercise of naked market power should not be rewarded in all circumstances all of the time, you have acknowledged that there is room for what we today call "redistribution."[45]

At a deeper level, moral philosophers and ethicists for millennia have concluded that market outcomes depend to a substantial extent on fortune—on luck—and as I discussed in chapter 2, in the context of Machiavelli, a claim to outcomes resulting from luck is a highly contingent one. This is a theme best addressed by highbrow moral philosophers, most famously in the dueling books of John Rawls and Robert Nozick, but the simple point for twenty-first-century fiscal policy is that good fortune breeds good fortune: that is the point of all the inequality research laid out earlier in this book. Children of the affluent grow up in a more language-rich environment, go to better schools, and are surrounded by more parental educational investment in computers and tutors than children of the poor can hope to obtain. In what way, then, are the relatively superior outcomes that those fortunate children enjoy as adults the universe's entirely natural distribution of things?

In more straightforward economic terms, private insurance markets, like education markets, will always be incomplete, because there are no practical private markets in which we can borrow secured only by the prospect of a better tomorrow, whether to pay for education when we are children or for anti-destitution insurance. In each case, society as a whole takes on the role of financing our future or insuring against destitution.

We do so not only out of moral compunction, or to avoid bread riots in the streets, but because doing so enhances the happiness and prosperity of society. If we want to increase our collective prosperity, we need to field adequately fed children and adults, so that they can devote themselves more effectively to improving their situations within our market economy, rather than being reduced to eating once a day and hunting squirrels to keep themselves alive. But as the *New York Times* reported in 2013, our social insurance programs are so modest in scope that this is precisely what some of our fellow citizens are reduced to.[46]

Congressman Steve Southerland of Florida has vigorously campaigned to cut back the Supplemental Nutrition Assistance Program, arguing that its barebones support interferes with the "gospel of work." He is proud of the fact that he began working at the age of 10. But he got that job, and his wealth, because his father took a liking to him, and brought him into the family funeral home business; the Congressman's grandfather started the firm. His political campaign paid for the upkeep on a family home that he inherited, and later sold for $550,000.[47] He believes that he stands with his two feet firmly on the ground, but in fact they rest high on the shoulders of the family members who preceded him.

None of this is to suggest that Congressman Southerland did not work hard. The point is simply that those of us who are successful in the material outcomes we obtain too often succumb to the comforting but false notion that our claims to those outcomes express the natural order of the universe, rather than a stew of personal effort and uncontrollable contingencies of all sorts. The more contingent our claim to our material outcomes, the less power the "re-" in "redistribution" has.

Now, the trouble with this line of argument is that it invites the counterattack that the only equilibrium that would satisfy John Rawls, or a closet Rawlsian like me, is a complete "leveling" of outcomes through fiscal policy. But I believe this to be an unfair reading of Rawls, and in any event an unnecessarily reductionist assertion in our quotidian world.

It is here that insurance comes into the picture. Insurance does not eliminate all risk—no one can afford the premium for insuring a wholly risk-free life, and it is not available in any event, because (as explained earlier) insurance is simply a financial product offering indemnity against financial loss. But insurance does usefully modulate outcomes. Fire insurance does so for fires, life insurance does so for the income lost by early death (but not the heartache of the grieving family), and social insurance does so for the financial aspects of individual life outcomes that are morally unacceptable or that simply reduce the aggregate happiness—and material wealth—of society.

The only interesting question is, how much social insurance can we usefully buy to maximize the happiness of society? In a sense, this is the question assumed in optimal tax theory when it postulates a social welfare function, but as reformulated it is couched in straightforward market terms (how much insurance is the right amount?), not in ways that smack of an ersatz Robin Hood function of taking and giving.

It is helpful here to return to a point introduced in chapter 2, by considering again Rawls's famous thought experiment, in which we are unborn disembodied but highly rational beings, and our representatives (I like to think of them as our lawyers) gather to debate the fundamental contours of the society into which we will be born. We know the full range of possible lives that we might assume once we take corporeal shape through birth—gorgeous and brilliant or homely and stupid; American or Bangladeshi; the children of rich parents or of poor ones; healthy or suffering from an incurable congenital illness; and so on. For what sort of society will we instruct our representatives to negotiate on our behalf?

The unfair summary of Rawls is that we will insist on absolute equality of outcomes, but this is not what Rawls actually claimed. Regardless, a more satisfactory way for this non-philosopher to continue the thought experiment is to recognize that, by agreeing in fact to be born at all, we disembodied beings have consciously chosen to embark on the adventure that is life, with all its perils and rewards.[48] We do not expect or desire equal outcomes any more than did the fourteenth-century Genoese mariner contemplating a voyage across the Mediterranean to Constantinople. That defeats the whole purpose of consciously undertaking life's adventures as sentient humans. But we are highly rational, and so before lining up in the birth queue, we each say to ourselves, damn, I had better buy some insurance against a really crappy outcome.

Of course, as highly rational but disembodied beings, we have neither pockets nor cash with which to buy insurance. Unlike other insurance, we can only pay our premiums for this financial insurance in arrears, which is to say, out of our material wealth, as and when we accumulate it. Social insurance, with its progressive benefit structure financed through premiums (taxes) collected on those of us who enjoy favorable material outcomes, is the result.

The Supplemental Nutrition Assistance Program has taken the brunt of criticism from the political right, in the person of individuals like Congressman Southerland, as imposing moral hazard concerns so unacceptable as to justify slashing funding for the program, but this is an inherently nonsensical argument. As chapters 2 and 7 explained, the supposed economic case that SNAP encourages people not to work is simply not there—nor should one expect it to be, given that benefits under this program amount to less than $5.00/day. Most recipients are children, the elderly, or the disabled. Participation soared as a result of the Great Recession, but that is what social insurance is supposed to do—to insure against dire personal financial situations in times of great economic distress for society as a whole.

In 2012 the Congressional Budget Office analyzed the SNAP program; it reported that 85 percent of recipient households had income below the poverty line, and that the SNAP program made a material difference to such households' abilities to feed themselves.[49] Almost two-thirds of the growth in the cost of the SNAP program from 2007 to 2011 was attributable to the economic collapse in the Great Recession; another 20 percent was the result of temporary boosts in benefits that have since expired. Military families claim $100 million in SNAP benefits a year at military base commissaries alone.[50] And in 2013 Bloomberg News reported on the large number of Americans who have resorted to selling parts of their bodies to make ends meet during the Great Recession: in every quarter save two from 2011 through late 2013, one of the top four autofill results in Google searches beginning with the phrase "I want to sell my. . ." was either "hair," "eggs," or "kidney."[51] This is not a picture of moral hazard in action, but rather of inadequate social insurance in the first place.

"Work is not a penalty, but a blessing," Congressman Southerland likes to say. But no rational person disagrees with that. What people lack are jobs, not a willingness to work. The solution is not a new and insidious individual mandate, in the form of a work requirement for SNAP recipients without assurance that jobs can be found, but rather new jobs, period. And that of course is something that, as the previous chapter demonstrated, government is good for, were only we to allow it to do so.

ARISTOTELIAN FALLACIES AND JASON THE SURFER

Aristotle described two logical fallacies that 2,500 years later continue to dominate political discourse. The fallacy of composition holds that it is logical error to assume that what is true of a part must be true of the whole. The fallacy of division is the converse: it is the error of inferring that what is true of the whole must be true of every part thereof. (For example, a boat floats, but that does not mean that its outboard motor by itself floats.)

And that brings us to Jason the Surfer.[52] Jason apparently claims SNAP benefits (as of mid-2013) and does not try very hard to land a job. Fox News broadcast a piece on Jason's relaxed lifestyle, and he quickly became a *cause célèbre* among conservative pundits. From Jason's existence the political right has inferred that an overwhelming number of SNAP recipients lead surfer dude–style existences and do not try to get jobs.

Invoking a Jason is a common rhetorical device, but it is both illogical and insulting to the group in question. (Alternatively, if one example defines the group, why not the hard-working mechanic interviewed by the *New York Times* who, in order to get enough to eat, has to hunt squirrels to supplement his SNAP benefits?)

Roughly 48 million Americans—more than one in seven among us—claimed SNAP benefits at the height of the Great Recession. Let us imagine that we set as a goal in designing the program a success rate of 999 out of every 1,000 beneficiaries—that is, that only one out of every 1,000 SNAP recipients would on reflection seem to us to be unworthy. This overwhelmingly successful program nonetheless would yield 48,000 Jasons for Fox News to hold up as exemplars of failure. Even if our "defect" rate in the implementation of our program were one in a million, Fox News with enough diligence could find 48 Jason-like individuals.

But so what? Do we really imagine that the welfare of 47,999,952 Americans should be ignored because we have been over-generous to the remaining 48?

Remember that the consequence here of "failure" is some unintended generosity, not summary execution. Is this really so great a moral hazard as to put the welfare of one in seven Americans at risk?

Recent voter fraud legislation has much the same quality. A single anecdote—or even the possibility of an anecdote—suffices to rewrite eligibility rules that disenfranchise thousands. What is true of the anecdotal case is not true of the group as a whole.

A program like SNAP must be analyzed *as a program*. When one does so (as for example the Congressional Budget Office did in its 2012 review), one discovers that this and other social insurance programs are actually fairly well designed. No doubt all such programs could be improved, as can all the works of man, but in every case the evidence suggests that our existing suite of social insurance programs errs principally in being too small to accomplish its purpose, not so large as to be dominated by adverse incentive effects.

CHAPTER 12

FROM A PROGRESSIVE TAX TO
A PROGRESSIVE FISCAL SYSTEM

> *The subjects of every state ought to contribute towards the support of the government, as nearly as possible, in proportion to their respective abilities; that is, in proportion to the revenue which they respectively enjoy under the protection of the state.*
>
> —ADAM SMITH, *The Wealth of Nations*, Book V, Chap. II, Part II.

PROGRESSIVE TAXATION VERSUS A PROGRESSIVE FISCAL SYSTEM

Chapter 11 argued that the progressive movement in the United States committed three long-term strategic blunders. First, the movement did not adequately communicate that progressives embrace the virtues of thrift, hard work, and personal responsibility—they just also are sensible enough to see that the collective purchase of reasonable levels of social insurance promotes socially useful risk-taking and enhances the overall welfare of society. Like you, I have automobile insurance, homeowner's insurance, medical insurance, and life insurance. I also carry social insurance, as do all other Americans, and for the same reason: social insurance does not interfere with individuals taking on all sorts of risks unique to their individual life adventures, but does enable them to pool those risks not central to their personal narratives.

Market triumphalists, by contrast, systematically confuse their totemic invocations of freedom with the smart thing for individuals to do, as if only those cocooned by excessively cushy safety nets and personal cowardice would carry automobile liability insurance, or ride a bicycle while wearing a helmet. The result of following their advice would be socially suboptimal levels of useful risk-taking, along with individual catastrophic outcomes that could have been avoided. Together these drag down the happiness of society far more than do the social insurance premiums we pay, or the moral hazards these programs expose us to.

Second, the progressive movement allowed "redistribution" to be viewed as a value-neutral term, when it is not. You can observe this when reading a passage by substituting "social insurance" for "redistribution" every time the latter appears, and then see how the sense of the passage changes.

These first two blunders are two sides of one coin, which is the failure by progressives to articulate what social insurance is and why it is desirable in economic as well as ethical contexts. Progressives' third blunder was more strategic. It was their myopic focus on the progressive income tax as their policy goal, to the exclusion of what really is important, which is a progressive fiscal system.

A fiscal system incorporates both the tax and the spending side of government. What progressives really should care about is whether government, taken as a whole, enhances the happiness of society by making socially useful investments and buying appropriate levels of social insurance. These goods are financed by tax revenues, but the tax revenues are not the point of the system—the goods are. And as this chapter demonstrates, it turns out that to finance the goods that should be at the heart of the progressive agenda, you do not need a progressive tax system—you just need a big one.

Insisting on progressive taxation as an independent desideratum has the unintended consequence of inevitably capping the size of the fiscal system at too small a level to support the really important social goods that we should be purchasing. It also distorts the analysis of why we might want a progressive tax system at all. The best reasons for progressive taxation are not found in examining tax systems in the abstract, but rather in asking which tax systems most neatly complement our collective investment and social insurance objectives?

This may sound a bit crazy, but that just demonstrates how pervasive is the erroneous view that progressive taxation is our objective. The Nordic countries figured this out a long time ago: their famously progressive fiscal systems, which actually do a great deal to reduce income inequality and to yield a happier society, are funded by mildly regressive taxes. It is the spending that matters most, not the taxing.

This chapter proceeds by first reviewing some of the history of our progressive tax system, and why academic debates surrounding tax system design might be more productive if we were first to begin with a clear idea of what we are trying to finance. At a more practical level, however, our policy discussions remain fixated on tax rate progressivity as an independent problem in need of solution. The second section therefore reviews the distribution of current tax burdens, some of the technical issues associated with measuring the distributional consequences of changes to the tax code, and the economic and political constraints on significantly higher marginal tax rates to finance government.

The final section of this chapter returns to the critical theme that the right measure of progressivity is with respect to our fiscal system taken as a whole, not simply our tax structures. That section reviews some recent preliminary efforts to measure the distribution of our fiscal system in its entirety, and demonstrates that progressive fiscal systems in practice invariably are financed with tax systems that are less progressive than ours, but much larger in absolute size.

WHAT'S SO GOOD ABOUT PROGRESSIVE TAXATION?

How Did We Get Here in the First Place?

2013 marked the one-hundredth birthday of the modern US personal income tax. In *Making the Modern American Fiscal State*, Ajay K. Mehrotra recounts the history of the progressive movement's early fixation on the progressive income tax.[1] Similar ground has been covered by other modern scholars, and Edwin Seligman, the leading public finance economist a century ago, authored several books that today offer insights into the contemporary justifications for the progressive income tax at the time of its adoption.

The income tax movement culminated in the very rapid adoption of the Sixteenth Amendment in 1913, overturning a famously wrong-headed Supreme Court case that had declared an earlier income tax unconstitutional on technical grounds of no great policy interest. As Mehrotra and other scholars have developed, the underlying populist clamor for an income tax rested on the idea that the rich were escaping paying tax on their "fair share." The last decades of the nineteenth century and the first of the twentieth century witnessed the birth of great fortunes of almost unimaginable size. The US government financed its (very small) needs through a potpourri of consumption taxes, particularly various import levies. The widely shared view at the time (not necessarily an incorrect one) was that all these levies ultimately were borne by consumers—that is, to reprise the technical language introduced in chapter 8, the economic incidence fell on consumers. And in turn, since the working class consumed essentially all of its income, while the new generation of capitalists did not, the view was that the working class was disproportionately bearing the brunt of taxation, while the Rockefellers, Mellons, Huntingtons, and other great fortunes could enjoy the rapid compounding of their wealth unencumbered by significant taxes. What was needed, instead, was a tax based on "ability to pay," which implied a tax base that comprised the entirety of a person's annual income, not simply the fraction of that income that a person might consume in any given year.

There are two remarkable lessons to be drawn from examining the dawn of the modern American income tax a century ago. The first is that in the years running up to the Revenue Act of 1913 the mainstream income tax movement was not primarily focused on using the tax to address income or wealth inequality directly. "The goal was not to radically redistribute wealth, but rather to ensure that those who had the greatest taxpaying capacity were contributing their fair share."[2]

The second remarkable fact about the early income tax movement is that this income tax based on "ability to pay" was conceived from the beginning as having a progressive marginal rate structure. Chapter 7 explained the meaning of a "progressive" income tax, but to recapitulate, a progressive income tax is one in which the average tax rate that you pay increases with your income. This means that your tax bill rises as a proportion of your income as your income increases. A proportional tax is one where your tax bill goes up as your income does, but stays at the same proportion of your income.

One of the ways the US tax system implements a progressive structure is to slice your income into different layers, called brackets; the bottom layer of your taxable income is taxed at a low rate, the next layer at a higher rate (without affecting the first layer's tax rate), and the third layer at a still higher rate, and so on. We also implement a progressive rate structure by exempting a certain foundational layer of income from any tax at all; we do that through personal exemptions and standard deductions, but we could just as well have called that foundational layer of income the zero rate bracket.

Technically, increasing marginal rates are not a necessary component of a progressive income tax. A "flat tax" with a relatively high single tax rate, a large personal exemption, and cash subsidies to the lowest-income households in fact can be more progressive in practice than a tax system that relies on increasing marginal rates alone.[3]

At the end of the nineteenth century the desirability of progressive taxation was the subject of independent vitriolic debate, but by the time the Sixteenth Amendment was adopted in 1913, most people seemed to understand that a vote for an income tax implied a vote for a progressive rate structure—that was what people understood an income tax to mean. Opponents objected to the idea of an income tax at all, wishing instead to preserve "the tariff" (import taxes) as the main source of federal revenue, but there was much less debate than a modern observer might expect over the relative virtues of proportional versus progressive (or "graded") income tax structures.[4]

Why as a matter of political economy did the income tax imply a progressive rate structure to most participants in the debate? Here a reading of Edwin Seligman is helpful. Today virtually no one reads Seligman, because some of his public finance economic analyses in hindsight border on the ridiculous, and because his writing style was long, discursive, and rooted in history, making his analytical toolset closer to Adam Smith's than the modern mathematical style of economics pioneered by his contemporary Alfred Marshall. But when the question is the history of ideas, Seligman cannot be ignored, because he was the dominant public finance figure of the time, and a staunch proponent of the progressive income tax.

In *Progressive Taxation in Theory and Practice*, Seligman argued that the concept of what comprised the "ability to pay" a tax (or one's "faculty," to use his preferred term) migrated from a theory of proportionality to one of progressivity as people began to conceptualize the faculty to pay tax as comprising only income above a level necessary for existence. This "entering wedge" implied a foundational layer of exempt income, and further instigated ruminations on the idea that perhaps not all wants were equally compelling:

> The conditions which limit faculty are to be found not only in the amount of the income, but in the demands that are made upon the individual in disposing of his income. In other words, the idea of burden, or sacrifice, was introduced....Taxes, in so far as they rob us of the means of satisfying our wants, impose a sacrifice on us. But the sacrifice involved in giving up a portion of what enables us to satisfy our necessary wants is very different from the sacrifice involved in giving up a portion of what enables us to satisfy our less urgent wants.[5]

From this followed the idea that taxation should embrace an ideal of equality of sacrifice. Given that our less compelling wants are sacrificed at lower cost to ourselves than our necessary ones, the case for progressive taxation was made. Seligman then recast this argument into the now-familiar language of the declining marginal utility of income, which is the most common justification to this day for our zero rate foundational bracket of income and increasing marginal rates thereafter. To his credit, Seligman also developed some of the conceptual difficulties in the argument, and concluded that progressive taxation was not inexorably required as a matter of economic logic.

Nonetheless, the intuition underlying the equal sacrifice theory appears to have been firmly grafted onto the general understanding of "ability to pay." And since the whole purpose of the income tax movement was to fix tax liabilities by reference to individuals' differing abilities to pay, the income tax and progressive rate structures seem to have been unalterably joined at the hip from the start. As a practical matter, of course, so long as we have a foundational layer of income on which we impose no tax, we technically will have a progressive income tax.

Progressive Taxation as Inequality Remediation

The idea that the income tax should be the vehicle for inequality leveling as a goal in and of itself came to the forefront later, in the New Deal era. According to historian Joseph Thorndike, President Roosevelt's economists "had repeatedly urged the president to lower taxes on the poor.... But the president cast his lot with a different group of advisers: Treasury lawyers more interested in soaking the rich than saving the poor."[6] These lawyers were led by Herman Oliphant, who believed that "[t]ax policy... could be made the vehicle for fundamental social reform, specifically targeting the accretion of economic power among a small group of companies and the people who ran them."[7]

In retrospect, the idea that high taxes on the rich should be a social desideratum in and of themselves—an income inequality remediation program—was an authentically terrible innovation. The idea reflects the same sort of instincts that have motivated sumptuary taxes over the centuries—a view that wealth, and how it is displayed, should be directly regulated by government. All sumptuary taxes fail, because the rich just choose unregulated ways of displaying wealth. (The most recent example in the United States probably was the 1990s luxury yacht tax, which was repealed after only a couple of years in place.) The theory runs directly against the grain of most economic work, which emphasizes the social waste attributable to deadweight loss that arises from very high marginal tax rates. It also plays directly into the hands of a long line of conservative thinkers, dating back to the nineteenth century, who have viewed progressive taxation as a stealth weapon of class warfare, waiting to spring upon the affluent if they let down their guard for a moment. As such, conceptualizing progressive taxation as a tool for leveling down just raises the tension level at the demilitarized zone that separates our different political movements.

More generally, in twenty-first-century America, even those of us who are self-described progressives would agree that cutting the rich down to size is not a very sensible business plan, whether for a political movement or for a government. It certainly is one that does not resonate with many Americans, who, if surveys are to be trusted, admire the wealthy and are proud that our country is a fertile environment for new fortunes to grow.

If our focus is on the happiness of society, the case for gratuitously making the most successful worse off is a difficult one to win. Robert Frank and others have reminded us that envy is a common and debilitating worldview, but progressive taxation by itself will not reduce envy in practice very much. Nor does progressive taxation, when used as an independent tool to directly regulate affluence, offer a very convincing response to affluent Americans' ability to insulate themselves from the failures of government, as by flocking to better school districts.[8] The more targeted answer in this last example is to bring up the quality of schools generally. Progressive taxation can be part of how that sensible goal is funded; it is not leveling down that is the agenda, however, but rather educating up.

Most important, using the tax system as a form of direct social regulation to remediate inequality both distracts from and limits the more useful questions of how government can complement the private sector through collective investments and social insurance, along the lines developed in the last two chapters. The use of progressive taxation to advance a deliberate agenda of remediating inequality puts the cart before the horse: government is useful for spending money in useful ways, and taxing is just how we finance those goods. Collecting taxes without regard to what the revenues buy is like Keynes's figure of speech of hiring thousands to dig holes and then cover them up again: that may serve a purpose in extreme times (in Keynes's example, to serve as economic stimulus during a depression), but in ordinary circumstances just destroys value. Instead of focusing political discourse on the social value that flows from smart government investment and social insurance, we become distracted by zero sum debates regarding how much inequality remediation is enough.

The inequality remediation theory of progressive taxation also unintentionally limits the amount of how much remediation actually can take place. The reasons are economic—the substantial social cost of the deadweight loss attendant on high tax rates—but also political: making the rich very, very angry is costly, in a political sense. As this chapter describes a little later, the secret of funding a progressive fiscal system—one that actually has a measurable impact on inequality as it is experienced—is not through quasi-sumptuary taxation in the form of high marginal tax rates. Instead, the secret sauce is a tax system that is only mildly progressive, or even regressive, but that is large enough to fund the government investment and social insurance programs that change lives.

Government spending is almost always steeply progressive—no government to my knowledge has ever enacted a No Polo Field Left Behind statute. Because the spending side is so progressive, the most important trick is to get the money to fund that useful spending, and so long as the taxing side is not truly wacky, its progressivity in the abstract is not terribly important.

Why Bother with Tax Progressivity?

From the other direction, it might be argued that if the case presented later in this chapter is convincing that a progressive fiscal system does not need to be funded by a progressive income tax, and if progressive tax rates are a very difficult political mountain to climb, why should we bother with a progressive structure to our income tax at all? One answer of course is that so long as we impose a zero rate of tax on some foundation level of income (whether through personal exemptions and standard deductions or by an explicit zero rate bracket), we technically will have a progressive tax structure, but that does not explain our deeply engrained preference for increasing marginal tax rate brackets.

The year 2013 was not only the one-hundredth birthday of the modern income tax in America, but also the sixtieth anniversary of the publication of the monograph version of a famous essay by Walter Blum and Harry Kalven, *The Uneasy Case for Progressive Taxation*.[9] Blum and Kalven reviewed the standard arguments for why progressive tax rate structures were desirable, and concluded that progressivity in fact is not easily defended as a theoretical matter, when compared to a proportional tax.

Blum and Kalven's monograph has been criticized for not making a positive case for proportional taxation, for not recognizing that a flat tax rate nonetheless could be employed to implement a progressive tax system, and for not carefully distinguishing their objections to "redistribution" as a social goal from their technical economic objections to progressive marginal rates. [10] At a more fundamental level, however, the proportionality–progressivity debate misses the point that all income taxes unavoidably are progressive along the one margin that distinguishes an income tax from consumption taxes, which is the treatment of capital income.

The essential distinction between an *income* tax—any income tax—and a well-designed consumption tax is that an income tax but not a consumption tax burdens capital income: that is, all returns to investment, however denominated.[11] This was not a side effect, but rather an important rationale motivating the nineteenth-century income tax movement in the first place: proponents of the income tax wanted to include capital income (including saved labor income) in the tax base so that the great new fortunes would be taxed according to their overall "ability to pay," not their current year's level of consumption.

One of the generally underappreciated aspects of the taxation of capital income is that all such taxation—even a "flat" or proportional tax on capital income—in fact is progressive along the margin of time. Since the only purpose of capital income from an individual saver's perspective is to fund future consumption (what else is money good for?), this is an important margin along which to examine the progressivity of capital income taxation.

That is, savers put capital aside to shift consumption from the present to the future, but the way annual capital income taxation works is that the longer your time-shift, the higher the income tax rate imposed on you. (Capital gains taxes are different, because they are imposed only once, when a capital investment is sold; the discussion here relates to the taxation of interest income today, or idealized capital income taxes more generally.) In turn, the ability to defer consumption for long periods of time is an attribute of those with ability to pay, because they have both surplus funds and the foresight not to spend them.

Imagine that you hold a savings account whose balance compounds at a fixed interest rate of 10 percent indefinitely into the future, and that the account's annual interest income is subject to a flat tax of 30 percent, which you pay out of the account's balance. Your pre-tax earnings compound at 10 percent, but your after-tax earnings compound at only 7 percent. What this means is that the longer your savings account grows and compounds, the larger becomes the difference between what would have been your account's balance had it not been subject to tax, and your actual balance. The tax takes a 30 percent bite if you save only for one year, but if you save for 20 years, the bite of this nominally "flat" tax grows to about 42 percent of what you would have earned had there been no tax imposed. Economists call this phenomenon the "tax wedge"; its significance here is that it means that *all* genuine income taxes (that is, taxes that burden capital as well as labor income, and do so consistently every year) are inherently progressive in this critical respect.

I think it fair to summarize Blum and Kalven as arguing that the two best justifications for progressive taxation in the traditional sense of the term (that is, increasing marginal tax rate brackets) are, first, the declining marginal utility of income point mentioned earlier (in Seligman's terms, the idea that a principle of equal sacrifice requires a high-income individual to pay a *disproportionately* larger number of dollars in tax than does a low-income individual), and second, the overt inequality remediation agenda described in the preceding section.

Blum and Kalven's principal reason for being dissatisfied with the declining marginal utility of income theory is the now generally accepted view that utility cannot be measured in cardinal terms, which is just a fancy way of saying that no one knows the quantum of utility I derive from my next dollar of income, according to some objective scale (like "pounds" or "yards"). As a result, interpersonal comparisons are impossible, which means that one cannot answer the question, how many dollars must we tax the rich fellow to make him feel the same pain that the poor one does when we tax her, say, $100?

In fact, in my prior life, when I worked a great deal with very affluent clients, I found the declining marginal utility of income theory to be violated at every turn. The affluent clients with whom I worked largely shared the view that they sincerely loved money, that money was attracted to them because it sensed their love, that they knew how to take care of money and give it a good home, and that other less affluent individuals would horribly mistreat that money. I sometimes thought that these fortunate individuals stayed up at night ironing their dollar bills, so they would look neat and tidy. If there is such a thing as the declining marginal utility of income, someone forgot to tell these folk.

Blum and Kalven did a good job (for that matter, so did Seligman decades earlier) showing that the declining marginal utility of income theory did not inexorably justify progressive taxation as a logical or economic matter. Nonetheless, there still is some utility, if you will pardon the play on words, to the declining marginal utility of income theory. We can recast it as an aspirational statement: as I explain to my students, it represents how we all would behave if we had good mothers, to whom we listened. Governments reflect and refocus society's values, and there is no reason to be ashamed of the idea that the declining marginal utility of income is one such value that reflects how most Americans believe that their lives would be ordered if their incomes suddenly jumped, even if economists staunchly deny that they can reduce the phenomenon to quantitative measurement. For that matter, economists also cannot measure the labor contribution of angels, but that does not stop a large percentage of Americans from feeling angels' presences in their daily lives.

Blum and Kalven did not have as strong a technical argument to rebut the inequality remediation hypothesis, because it rests explicitly on a value judgment that less inequality is a good thing. But as the previous section argued, the inequality remediation theory essentially is limited by its own agenda as a matter of economics (the deadweight loss problem) and political economy (incurring the anger of the rich has substantial political costs).

Conversely, if one can sneak in a bit of tax progressivity, why not? If it can be done without paralyzing political discourse, it certainly is a convenient way to fund government spending programs. And since we have today a certain amount of progressivity within the income tax, and that level is tolerable from a political discourse perspective, why throw it away? This leads to a highly practical view of progressivity, which goes back to Jean Baptiste Colbert's aphorism that one should pluck the goose until its squawking becomes intolerable.[12]

More recent work in the decades since Blum and Kalven's monograph, such as a well-known paper by Joseph Bankman and Thomas Griffith, has sharpened both the economic analysis of progressive rate structures and the moral underpinnings of different social welfare functions.[13] But even this more recent work largely operates within a closed model of tax collections and cash "redistribution." Indeed, that is the basic outline of how formal optimal tax models operate.

As a result, most of the literature in this area continues to consider tax system design as if that were what we are trying to optimize, when in fact it is simply a mechanism for financing government operations.[14] If instead we begin with the spending side of things, and in particular government's opportunities to make useful investments and to write useful social insurance, we can ask the right question, which is simply which financing decision—which tax structures— most effectively complement the purposes of that investment and insurance? In other words, the nature of the public goods a government seeks to acquire should inform the financing structures that it chooses.

To crystallize this fundamental difference in perspective, consider for a moment elementary corporate finance. Corporations do not first design the size and structure of the liability side of their balance sheets (the debt and stock they issue to investors), and then ask what assets they might acquire with the funds on hand. Instead, they look for investment opportunities and ask, which are affordable? And, what financing structures most effectively match up against those assets? When it comes to contemporary government, by contrast, we do things backward along two margins: we start with an arbitrary size of our financing (the amount of taxes to be raised), and we make no effort to design the structure of that financing to most effectively complement the purposes to which the money will be put.

This different perspective leads to several possible related arguments not considered by Blum or Kalven, or most of the subsequent literature, in support of progressive tax structures. The first simply would be a special application of old "benefits" arguments, in the form of a claim that progressive financing structures complement the purposes of government investment, if you begin with the assumption that high-income individuals derive a disproportionately greater benefit from investment in public goods than do lower-income taxpayers. I briefly discuss this question below in the context of some recent early steps at presenting a distributional analysis of all of government (the spending as well as the tax side), but intuitively this claim seems a bit far fetched: Taxpayer B, with an income 10 times that of Taxpayer A, may derive greater benefits from roads, schools, or our military than does Taxpayer A, but it is improbable that Taxpayer B enjoys 20 or 50 times the benefits. Even a proportional argument here is not intuitively obvious. When it comes to the investment side of government's operations, then, one is left simply with the argument that much of such investment (education, for example, but probably not roads or the military) is designed to enable lower-income Americans to overcome market failures that are not problematic for higher-income taxpayers, and so we should expect high-income taxpayers to finance the bulk of such market-curing investments.

The more convincing justifications for progressive taxation not developed in Blum and Kalven follow from the previous chapter, on social insurance. These begin with my dumbed-down application of John Rawls, in which our society's basic terms are discerned by imagining the bargaining among our noncorporeal predecessors, who agree to be born, but who further recognize the wide array of possible life situations into which they might be thrown, and who therefore have the good sense to sign up for some insurance just before embarking on the adventure of life. The only way those noncorporeal beings can pay for that insurance is in arrears, and since those who make insurance claims cannot generally afford the insurance premiums, those who do well will have to contribute disproportionately. Proportional taxation does not work well here, because in fact we generally excuse from tax those whose circumstances require them to make an insurance claim, even if they have a little income. The progressive rate structure more neatly describes the post-paid insurance model.

The final justification for a progressive income tax rate structure is similar to the argument just offered, shorn of Rawlsian pretense. My claim here is simply that the progressive rate structure by itself is a form of social insurance, in that it relieves those at the bottom of the income hierarchy of a cash expense they would face were income taxes collected on a proportional schedule, and does so simply because their material life outcomes have not been terribly successful. The money so saved in turn can be spent in enhancing the relatively modest material lives that these outcomes imply.

In other words, if one accepts the fundamental premise of this book, that material outcomes are determined by an undifferentiated porridge of personal efforts and brute luck, by virtue of which we all have a bit less control over our material successes than we like to pretend, then some tax rate progression functions as a broad social insurance program to address the brute luck component. It is a broad-brush sort of insurance, as its benefits (relative to proportional taxation) are not delivered with surgical precision only to the most appealing hard-luck stories, but under most any theory of the utility of income, this arrangement, if not carried to excess, increases the net happiness of society. And in contrast to other forms of social insurance, no one on the political right seems to argue that a progressive rate structure necessarily lulls the modestly successful (or downright unsuccessful) into lives of state-supported indolence. For this reason of political economy alone, a moderate approach to progressive taxation is a useful way of delivering some social insurance benefits to those who need it, when compared with the proportional tax alternative.

TAX PROGRESSIVITY IN CONTEMPORARY APPLICATION

How Much Tax Progressivity Do We Have?

Chapter 7 discussed various measures of progressivity. It argued that measuring the progressivity of a tax system in the abstract is a fool's errand. A tax of $1,000 imposed on each and every billionaire in the United States will score as very progressive—only the very most affluent Americans will be burdened by it—but the tax will raise trivial amounts of revenue. What consolation is there in being told that this tax, although too small to fund any useful government program, is really highly progressive? There is no virtue to such abstractions.

A better way of eyeballing progressivity in our current tax system is to reprise Table 8.2 from chapter 8 (repeated here as Table 12.1), which reproduced the work of the nonpartisan staff of the Joint Committee on Taxation in distributing the economic incidence of all federal taxes (other than the estate and gift tax) to the individuals who bear the burden of those taxes. The JCT staff table shows the effective (average) all-in federal tax burdens of Americans, by income class, as a percentage of individuals' "expanded incomes."[15]

What the JCT staff work product demonstrates is that the federal tax system, taken as a whole, shows a moderately progressive structure, in which tax burdens steadily rise as a percentage of incomes, at least for those earning more than $20,000/year. The average (effective) tax rate imposed on individuals fortunate

Table 12.1 JCT Baseline Distribution of Income and Federal Taxes (2013)

	Baseline Distribution of Income and Taxes (2013)			
	Number of Returns (thousands)	Expanded Income ($ millions)	Tax Liability ($ millions)	Average Tax Rate
0 to 10,000	18,506	80,476	6,513	8.1
10,000 to 20,000	18,328	277,369	7,879	2.8
20,000 to 30,000	20,427	503,472	34,666	6.9
30,000 to 40,000	15,853	554,348	56,225	10.1
40,000 to 50,000	14,654	657,243	82,227	12.5
50,000 to 75,000	24,357	1,503,844	213,051	14.2
75,000 to 100,000	16,860	1,459,798	237,769	16.3
100,000 to 200,000	24,334	3,303,188	682,788	20.7
200,000 to 500,000	6,094	1,708,978	439,925	25.7
500,000 to 1,000,000	743	497,484	148,679	29.9
Over 1,000,000	362	1,173,450	375,042	32.0
Total	160,518	11,719,650	2,284,763	19.5

Source: Staff Joint Committee on Taxation, *Modeling the Distribution of Taxes*, table 9.

enough to earn over $1 million/year is 32 percent, which based on my random polling is far lower than most people imagine.

As previously observed, the results for the second-lowest income class in particular are skewed by effects of the large "making work pay" subsidies made available through the income tax, particularly in the form of the earned income tax credit and the child tax credit. Both the CBO and the JCT staff treat the portions of these credits that reduce income tax liabilities as tax reductions, thereby pulling down the average tax rates of lower-income Americans. The JCT staff treats cash income tax refunds (credits that exceed tax liabilities, and that result in cash grants to taxpayers) as reductions in total taxes paid by the relevant income group, rather than as income subsidies, while the CBO does the opposite for general budget accounting purposes (but then reverses field and follows the JCT practice in its recent series of household income and tax distributional studies). All these social expenditures delivered through the tax system should be accounted for consistently as spending programs, whether they reduce tax liabilities or result in the receipt of a check. Here again we see how tax expenditures occlude our understanding of the size and functions of government.

"Distributionally Neutral" Tax Law Changes

To summarize to this point, the United States today has a progressive overall tax structure. The staff of the Joint Committee on Taxation's 2013 "baseline" tax distribution table (Table 12.1) shows that, when all federal taxes are considered, every income level pays taxes, and effective (average) tax burdens follow a rational progressive rate path. The federal personal income tax when viewed in isolation appears even more progressive, but that misses the point that the personal income tax is only one of a suite of taxes that individuals ultimately bear.

The staff of the Joint Committee on Taxation's "baseline" 2013 tax distribution table is unusual, in that most JCT staff distributional work is done in the context of proposed *changes* in tax law. Distribution tables are prepared in this second setting to answer the invariable question asked by members of Congress, which is, are we sharing the benefits of this overall tax cut (more rarely in recent years, are we sharing the burdens of this overall tax increase) in a "distributionally neutral" fashion? Most distributional analysis therefore focuses on the distributional consequences of incremental changes in law, not the baseline.

It turns out that the concept of distributional neutrality in respect of changes in overall tax revenues is much more elusive than one might expect. Putting to one side all the issues discussed in chapter 4 of what is the right unit to measure (family, household, tax return), and what is the right measure of economic income, the preparation of JCT staff distributional tables in this specific context requires a difficult judgment to be made, which is, are we trying to show the incremental change in the distribution of tax *revenues,* or of tax *burdens?*[16] The two measures are very different in some important cases, like gains from sales of stock or other investments (capital gains).

The problem in every case is that changes in tax law induce changes in behavior, and one therefore must decide which new behaviors reflect new economic burdens, and which reflect new economic opportunities; surprisingly, toting up changes in tax collections can mask whether a taxpayer's economic burdens have gone up or down. To make things even more difficult, if a change in tax law adds to budget deficits, those deficits must ultimately be financed through higher taxes at some future date; how should those indefinite future liabilities be reflected in current-year distributional tables?[17]

Imagine that the capital gains tax rate is slashed for a two-year period from current law (20 percent) to 10 percent. Capital gains of course are very top-heavy in their distribution—one of the many disadvantages of poverty being that one does not have a large portfolio of investment assets—so the change in law would be interesting only to the rich. Affluent investors might rush to sell all the appreciated investment assets they could, and in fact sell so many investments in the tax holiday period that for those two years tax revenues from capital gains go up, not down. (This is not the same, by the way, as saying that tax cuts pay for them-selves: the phenomenon posited in the example is real, but is a one-time response to the new tax environment—an acceleration into the current year of capital gains that otherwise would be harvested in future years. As a result, even if the new rate continued in perpetuity, long-term steady state capital gains tax collections would be lower in the 10 percent tax rate environment than under current law.)

If in this example incremental distributional tables followed tax revenues, then the rich would be shown as assuming a larger share of the total tax pie, and as a result the cut in capital gains taxes would be paraded as "highly progressive." If, on the other hand, sober-minded economists had their way, and the incremental distributional tables followed the change in tax *burdens*, then in that case the rich obviously were made better off, not worse, as evidenced by the way they rushed to sell their investments, and the distributional tables would show the most affluent taxpayers' tax burdens *decreasing*.

It is not fruitful to describe here the internal debates within Congressional staff over the years regarding how this issue should be resolved. The short version is that the sober-minded economists had their say,[18] but were quickly reversed. The main incremental distributional tables prepared by the JCT staff for use in debating actual tax legislation simply distribute the incremental changes in tax revenues. The effective tax rate columns are the only signal as to whether the distribution of tax revenues accurately tracks economic changes in tax burdens.

Now put this important question to one side, and assume that the distribution of changes in tax revenues parallels the distribution of changes in tax burdens. (Once one moves away from capital gains taxes in particular, this assumption often is good enough for government work.) Imagine that it has been decided that personal income tax collections must rise in the aggregate, but that the tax hike will be allocated among individual taxpayers in a "distributionally neutral" man-ner. What do those words actually mean? The answer is that a change in overall tax collections is treated as distributionally neutral when every income tier has its tax bill increased (or decreased) by the same percentage.[19]

Here is a simple example. Imagine a typical progressive income tax system comprising three individuals, A, B, and C.[20] The "baseline" distribution is as follows:

	INCOME	TAX	EFF. TAX RATE
A	$100	$10	10%
B	$500	$100	20%
C	$1,000	$300	30%
TOTALS:	$1,600	$410	25.6%

It is decided that total tax revenues need to be $500, not $410. This $90 increase in tax revenues represents a 22 percent overall tax hike (500/410 = 1.22).

A "distributionally neutral" allocation of that $90 is understood to mean that everyone's effective tax rate goes up by 22 percent. (Alternatively, you can say that A gets a tax increase of his share of the old total tax bill—$10/$410—multiplied by the tax increase—$90.) As a result, A will now pay $12.20 in tax, not $10; B will pay $121.95, not $100, and C will pay $365.85, not $300. The overall tax bill of course will be $500. In graphical terms, if you imagine prior law's tax rate progression as a curve, then a distributionally neutral tax increase or decrease will move the whole curve straight up or down, without changing its shape.

A distributionally neutral increase in tax revenues thus requires C in my example to pay a new effective tax rate of 36.6 percent (122 percent of his old rate of 30 percent), while A will pay 12.2 percent (122 percent of his old rate of 10 percent). C and his apologists will demand to know why his tax burden has gone up by 6.6 percentage points, while A's has only gone up by 2.2 points. The answer is, that is what is required to keep C's share of the overall tax burden constant. But the critical point to note is how much C's tax rate needs to increase in terms of percentage points, not percentage of total tax burdens: a full 6.6 percentage points.

When confronting a large tax increase in the real world, rather than in my hypothetical example, it may not always be possible, because of economic efficiency concerns or political economy realities, to raise top income taxpayers' rates as much as would be required to preserve distributional neutrality—that is, to retain the shape of the current tax progression curve. It is as if a pin is stuck into the curve at the top rate, and the rest of the curve must pivot around that point. When that happens, distributional neutrality is lost, and more particularly as the curve pivots around the fixed top rate, the curve becomes flatter, which is to say, less progressive.

This is the inevitable result of the collision between the need for more tax revenues and the fundamental stickiness (whether for reasons of theory or practice) of top tax rates. The next section reviews some of these stickiness constraints.

How Much Tax Progressivity Should We Have?

The earlier discussion in this chapter argued that the original impetus behind the progressive rate structure of the income tax ("ability to pay," recognizing of course the term's complete indeterminacy in actual application) was more constructive than the inequality remediation impulses that came to the fore in the New Deal. That discussion also suggested that progressive income tax rate structures could be justified along several margins, such as the declining marginal utility of income (as filtered through the value judgment that this is an appropriate aspirational norm for a society to adopt), and the consistency of progressive income taxation with social insurance goals.

Finally, as a reminder, we have a progressive income tax today. While increasing its progressivity at the top end would be deeply controversial, the United States is not currently enmeshed in a full bore "flat tax" war of words. To the contrary, when introducing his tax reform initiatives in 2013, Dave Camp, the chairman of the House Ways and Means Committee, was explicit that tax reform should not upset the current distribution of tax liabilities—that is, the progressive tax liabilities achieved under current law.

But all of this begs the question, how much progressivity in tax rate structure is the right amount? This is the sort of question best resolved through the give and take of rational political discourse, as intermediated by Congress. Nonetheless, there are some outer limits to plausible possible outcomes.

One approach to answering this question might be through the lens of history. When I began practicing tax law, the maximum tax rate on "unearned" income (essentially, capital income other than capital gains) was 70 percent, and on "earned income" (labor income) 50 percent, if that labor income qualified for the so-called "maxi-tax." The corporate income tax was 48 percent. A few years later, for two brief years following the Tax Reform Act of 1986, the maximum tax rate on all forms of capital income (including capital gains) and of labor income was the same—28 percent, and the corporate income tax was reduced to 34 percent. Individual top marginal tax rates increased during the 1990s, until they reached 39.6 percent. Today, most forms of capital income (other than interest income) are taxed at effective marginal rates well below those of labor income, and the top marginal rate imposed on the highest-income individuals is again 39.6 percent— or 43.4 percent, if one includes the Medicare tax on labor income.[21]

All of this suggests that history offers no clear guidance as to what the top rate should be. You can find historical precedent to support any intuition, and if you choose you can draw causal relationships between economic growth in a period and the progressive rate schedule you prefer. But those purported causal relationships are completely unreliable, because they are swamped by omitted variables—exogenous shocks (oil, financial overleveraging, or terrorism for example), demographic factors, large-scale economic developments (the Internet revolution), and the like. Moreover, no amount of inference along these lines can prove the negative—that is, what economic growth would have looked like under a different tax regime.

What I draw from history is that tax law is not like the Ring carried by Frodo— it does not rule us all. History suggests that we all get on with the business of living, and of doing business, under very different tax structures. That is not to say that we should be recklessly indifferent to tax system design, but only that we should not assume that lower tax rates, always, are unequivocably necessary and sufficient conditions to economic growth.

Another approach to dialing in the right amount of income tax progressivity is to start with economic models developed in the theoretical optimal tax literature and then to apply to those models empirical research into individuals' real-world sensitivity to tax rates, to come up with a considered opinion as to how much progressivity is the right amount. In a very important paper published in 2011, Nobel laureate Peter Diamond and his coauthor Emmanuel Saez did just that.[22]

More specifically, Diamond and Saez set out to calculate the "optimal" tax rate on the top one percent or so of the income distribution—individuals whose incomes averaged about $1.4 million in 2007, before deductions. By "optimal," Diamond and Saez meant the tax rate on top incomes that maximizes tax revenues, after taking into account the negative incentive effects of taxation on economic activity. A higher tax rate would reduce economic activity so much that tax collections would go down, not up. A lower rate would mean that lower-income individuals would be required to fund the resulting revenue shortfall. Diamond and Saez effectively embraced the declining marginal utility of income as a social norm; in fact, their specification of the "social welfare function" apparently put a value of zero on the last dollar earned by the most affluent American. As a result, a lower than "optimal" tax rate on the most affluent Americans, and a concomitant shifting of the burden to lower-income Americans, would reduce overall social welfare.

Putting matters differently, regardless of the level of revenues that government requires, Diamond and Saez would argue that one should develop an optimal tax rate progression by starting from the optimal (i.e., revenue-maximizing) rate on the very top of the income distribution. With that number fixed in every case, one then could scale tax rates further down the income ladder to satisfy government's budget needs.

Diamond and Saez concluded that the "optimal" tax rate on the top one percent of the income distribution is 73 percent (including state and local taxes). This estimate was not greeted with universal enthusiasm across the entire political spectrum.

Diamond and Saez's core estimate that the optimal tax rate on very high incomes is 73 percent is sensitive to the porosity of the tax base—that is, the ease with which higher taxes can be avoided. Using a different set of tax elasticity estimates than their preferred specifications and current law's definitions, deductions, and exclusions, Diamond and Saez nonetheless computed an optimal rate of 54 percent, including state and local taxes, or about 48 percent for federal income taxes only. This rate is still higher than the top tax rate imposed from January 1, 2013, onward, although not by as much as was true when Diamond and Saez published their paper in 2011. At the low end, Diamond and Saez essentially concluded that subsidizing low-income wage earners—as we do today, through the earned income tax credit—was logically consistent with optimal tax theory.

Finally, Diamond and Saez concluded that taxing capital income was not such a bad idea after all.[23] This last conclusion responds to a large body of theoretical literature arguing that it is a mistake to impose any tax on the basic ("normal") returns to capital. This debate is extremely interesting to theorists, but as a political economy matter the entire purpose of the income tax from the time of its adoption was to tax capital income. Moreover, to my knowledge no country wholly exempts capital income from its income tax base, and as Diamond and Saez point out (here following rather than leading the lawyers in their analysis), in many practical cases it is very difficult to tease apart capital from labor income. For all these reasons, this book does not develop this debate in any detail.[24]

Diamond and Saez's paper does not definitively resolve the practical application of optimal tax theory to real-world behaviors; that is not how empirical research in the social sciences works. Nor are the premises of optimal tax theory universally accepted—in particular, its reliance on utilitarian social welfare norms that have at their core a theory of the declining marginal utility of income. The market triumphalists described earlier in this book might argue, for example, that individual liberty is the overriding social norm, which would in turn lead to different conclusions about top tax rates. Finally, others might specify a different "social welfare function" than that adopted by Diamond and Saez, with its steeply declining marginal utility of income, which again would change their results.

The critical point, however, is that the work of these two highly regarded academics is roughly congruent with both the overall character and the actual numbers employed in the construction of our current progressive income tax rate structure. We are not required fully to embrace Diamond and Saez's invitation to try a little more progressivity at the top to take some comfort from that fact. A progressive income tax looking roughly like the one we have today may not have the same status as Newton's laws of gravity, but contrary to the rhetoric of market triumphalists, it is a principled place to be.

The third leg in triangulating our progressive income tax rate structure is to benchmark the United States against other countries. Table 8.4 in chapter 8 did that. What it showed was, first, that most peer countries impose marginal personal income tax rates on their highest-income citizens at levels hovering just below 50 percent, or in a few cases a bit above that figure. Second, many countries begin to impose that top rate at incomes far lower than in the United States. By both standards, the United States is nowhere near the top of the heap in taxing its highest-income citizens.

To summarize, the top marginal personal income tax rate draws support from history (but then again, so does most any top rate one can imagine). Following the January 1, 2013, "fiscal cliff" deal, our top marginal rate is not terribly different from that of other peer countries, although we reserve that top rate for incomes at a higher level than do many other jurisdictions. And finally, academic research into both optimal tax theory and real-world responsiveness to increasing tax rates argues that the top marginal personal income tax rate is well within the envelope of revenue- and welfare-enhancing possibilities. That top rate could drift a little higher and still satisfy both standards—but only a little higher, under the more conservative of the specifications employed by Diamond and Saez or under the political economy pressures evident everywhere in the world that turning the tax odometer past 50 percent is very difficult to accomplish.

The tax progressivity well is simply not as deep as progressives like to imagine. Adverse incentive effects start to erode the revenue pickup from higher rates, and incurring the hatred of the rich paralyzes the political process. There is a reason that most every peer country finds that its top marginal personal income tax rate should be a two-digit number beginning with a 4! So long as we allow the political debate to be shaped solely in terms of preserving (or increasing) the progressivity of the tax system at the top, we inadvertently are capping the size of government well below its optimal level.

And this in turn has major implications for tax rate progressivity in the context of changes in overall tax collections. If (as chapter 6 argued) we need to find additional revenues on the order of 2 percent of GDP per annum, or perhaps a bit more, it will be very difficult to do so by raising taxes on the highest-income Americans alone. And if tax rates at the highest income levels cannot go up very much further, then any substantial increase in total tax revenues collected through the income tax will reduce, not increase, overall progressivity. The tax distribution curve will rotate around a pin stuck at a top rate not very different from current law's top rate, as explained in the prior section of this chapter.

Raising more tax revenues reasonably efficiently necessarily points in the direction of increasing tax burdens on Americans with incomes well below the top. But as the next section shows, doing so can still be consistent with progressive values, because the resulting net fiscal system can be materially more progressive than our current fiscal environment.

TWO LEVERS OF PROGRESSIVITY

Tax revenues must rise. We can huff and puff about this until we faint from exhaustion, but it is an inescapable fact, in light of our painfully inadequate current revenue base, as documented by the Congressional Budget Office, our surging population of elderly Americans, our commitment to a military that spends roughly 45 percent of the world's aggregate defense budgets, and our collective waste of almost $1 trillion every year in excess healthcare spending, both before and after the implementation of the Affordable Care Act. And all this is before considering the productive investments and social insurance that government can buy, which opportunities are inexcusable as a straightforward business matter to leave unfunded.

In turn, because top tax rates are sticky, the inevitable conclusion is that as tax revenues increase, the tax system will grow less progressive. To argue that our future tax system will be somewhat less progressive than current law's distribution of burdens does not mean, however, that the personal income tax should be abandoned, or that a consumption tax (for example, a value added tax of the sort employed elsewhere in the world) necessarily must be adopted. To the contrary, as the next chapter demonstrates, a great deal of revenue can be raised without introducing new taxes or raising the top marginal rate materially. But doing so does require raising marginal rates on lower-income tax brackets—for example, by restoring the bulk of the pre-2001 tax rate structure.

The unavoidable conclusion that the collision of higher tax revenues and sticky top rates means that our future tax system will be less progressive leads many progressive pundits to despair, but this despondency is largely the result of an inappropriate fixation on the tax side of things, to the exclusion of the goods that government delivers to its citizens. *The important question is not the progressivity of our tax system, but rather the progressivity of our country's fiscal system—the net of its spending and taxing.* Once we free ourselves from our fixation on taxation as the entirety of fiscal policy, we discover that we can in fact fund a more progressive fiscal system.

Debating the progressivity of a tax system in the abstract thus is a meaningless distraction from serious discourse. Yet in every aspect of our fiscal debates, we compartmentalize the tax and spending functions and wrangle over each separately. Different committees in Congress handle each, economists and pundits alike analyze the structure of each separately, and no institution is charged with presenting a holistic picture of the net distributional consequences of our combined taxing and spending programs.

Distributional Analyses of the Fiscal System

Measuring the progressivity of a fiscal system is a much more difficult concept than standard tools capture. Taxing and spending each have distributional consequences, and the two are bound to each other by the fact that taxing funds spending.

To present a more complete picture of the distributional consequences of government intervention, we need to capture three variables: the progressivity of the tax system in the abstract, the size of the tax system, and how the resulting revenues are spent. In turn, determining how money is spent for purposes of a fiscal system distributional analysis means that we must determine who are the beneficiaries of each program.

Some spending can be associated with specific recipients, but a large fraction of government spending (military, roads, education, and so on) falls into the category of "public goods"—goods that are generally available to everyone (technically, "non-excludable" goods), and that generally can be used by one person without precluding their use by others ("non-rivalrous" goods). Once a new public road is built, anyone can drive on it, and one person's driving on it does not preclude another from doing so too. Nonetheless, a comprehensive fiscal system distributional analysis requires assigning the value of the government investment in that road to someone, on some basis. In November 2013 the Congressional Budget Office estimated that about 40 percent of all government spending in 2006—some $1.1 trillion—fell into the category of public goods.[25]

Finally, once we move from the distribution of tax burdens to a complete picture of the "gives" and "gets" of our fiscal system, in the broadest sense, we no longer are tied to comparative incomes as our metric. When the subject is the distribution of tax burdens, income and wealth are the obvious ways of ordering people: it does not make much sense to distribute tax burdens according to our heights. But when we look at the totality of government spending and taxing, we in fact might want to see distributional consequences by reference to attributes other than income. We might, for example, want to know how the elderly are making out relative to younger Americans, and so on. Implementing all this requires answering questions that official scorekeepers have not previously had to face.

As a first cut, we could look at the distributional consequences of the sum of our tax and transfer systems. The Reynolds–Smolensky progressivity index described in chapter 8 can be used for this purpose, provided it is applied starting from a base of market incomes, and ending with a base that is after taxes and transfer/benefits payments. (The CBO measure of "after-tax" income does capture the latter.) By doing so, we would be comparing the Gini index (the standard measure of inequality) of pure market outcomes in the economy to the Gini index of where we actually end up, after all the taxes and highly targeted transfer payments that are intermediated through government.

For several years, the Congressional Budget Office has extended its distributional work on the tax side of the equation to include direct transfer and entitlements benefits (that is, spending that can be traced to benefits received by a specific individual). This category includes not just transfer programs like SNAP or housing benefits for the poor, but also Social Security payments, and the value to participants of the Medicare or Medicaid coverage they enjoy. This measure still excludes public goods, however.

The trend has been for targeted transfer and entitlements spending to become less progressive over time; as a result, their impact in reducing income inequality materially decreased from 1979 to 2007.[26] The reasons are twofold: first, poverty-related transfer payments in fact have been on a long-term downward trajectory as a percentage of GDP (interrupted, of course, by the economic and jobs crisis in which the United States is still mired), and, second, Medicare and Social Security benefits, which are not means-tested, have taken a larger fraction of total targeted benefits spending. The increased spending for Medicare and Social Security thus has not been as effective as are programs like SNAP or the earned income tax credit at reducing inequality.

You can see from Figure 12.1, which covers the period from 1979 through 2007 (that is, just before the economic collapse of the Great Recession), how the lowest-income quintile of Americans obtained a substantially declining share of entitlements benefits, while the other quintiles, including the highest-income group, all increased their shares. The principal reason is that the largest entitlements (Social Security and Medicare) are not means-tested, and have consumed an ever-increasing share of the total entitlements pie.

Most transfer payments and entitlements benefits have always gone to the elderly, whose benefits are largely not means-tested, and their share has been on a steady upward trajectory for decades. Many of the elderly are low-income households, but some are not. In any event, elderly childless households now absorb roughly 70 percent of all entitlements spending (see Figure 12.2).

The net effect has been that transfers and entitlements benefits, taken as a whole, had in 2007 a materially smaller impact on mitigating income inequality

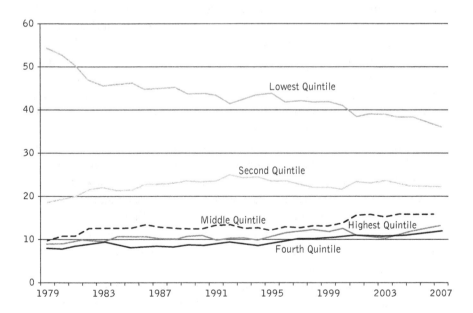

FIGURE 12.1 Share of Total Transfers, by Market Income Group

Source: CBO, *Trends in the Distribution of Household Income*, 24.

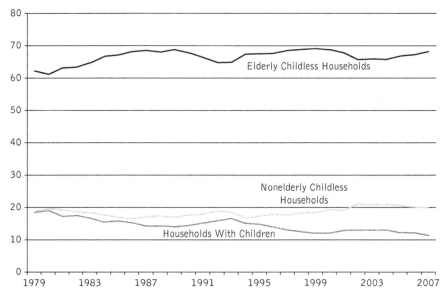

FIGURE 12.2 Share of Total Transfers, by Type of Household

Source: CBO, *Trends in the Distribution of Household Income*, 24.

than was true in 1979. Focusing on tax progressivity alone (which, as it happens, displayed the same long-term trend of doing less and less to mitigate income inequality) misses the larger of the two government instruments that affect income inequality, and distracts from the important story of how entitlements programs have become increasingly devoted to the elderly, regardless of need.

Figure 12.3 presents another way of visualizing how our fiscal policies have been redirected over time from helping the lowest-income Americans to subsidizing those in the middle.[27] Using data from 1979 to 2009, I observed households ranked by their market income and then split into five equal groups (quintiles). I followed each quintile before and after government involvement by calculating its share of pre-tax market income and comparing that to its share of income after both taxes and transfers. The two most affluent quintiles typically had lower shares of total national income after taxes and transfers than they had of total pre-tax market income; the reverse was true for the lower three quintiles. This is expected in a progressive fiscal system: higher earners are taxed more, and some of those proceeds are invested in lower earners.

Figure 12.3 goes a step further, by showing what percentage of the share of national income surrendered by the two highest income quintiles was captured by each of the lower quintiles. Figure 12.3 does not reflect the absolute size of the shares of national income given up by the upper two quintiles, but does show

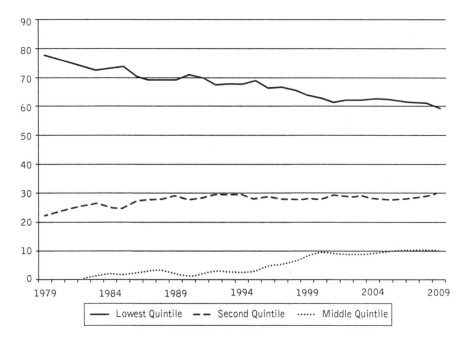

FIGURE 12.3 Income Capture by Lower Quintiles (1979–2009)

Source: CBO, *Trends in the Distribution of Household Income*, supplemental tables.

how much of the pie (whatever its size) each of the lower three quintiles has been consuming over time.

Since the 1980s the lowest income quintile has gone from capturing almost 80 percent of the fraction of national income given up by the two highest quintiles to less than 60 percent. Because the shares captured by all three of the lower quintiles must add up to 100 percent of what is given up by the upper two quintiles, the lowest quintile necessarily lost at the hands of the second and middle quintile. Why as a society do we choose to use fiscal policies to subsidize the middle class, and to do so more extensively than in the past? The middle class is not doing as well as it might, were government to seize the opportunities to invest in Americans more comprehensively, but most of those households have reasonably adequate resources. That is not the case for many households in the lowest quintile.

Very little empirical work has been done to date on measuring the distributional consequences of the entirety of our fiscal system, and in particular incorporating the large fraction of government spending that goes toward acquiring public goods. The OECD has attempted to do this from time to time, by including the value of public education and other public services in their calculations of after-tax and transfer inequality, but the OECD does not regularly publish such data.[28] Nonetheless, this approach would paint a fairer picture of the progressivity of our overall fiscal system than we have available today.

The Congressional Budget Office released its first tentative effort along these lines only in November 2013, in the form of a distributional analysis of substantially all federal spending and taxes for 2006.[29] That effort raised as many questions as it answered, but it is an important first step, and should be encouraged.

The CBO in this new study divided government spending into three categories: "cash and near-cash transfers" (both income support transfers and Social Security benefits), health care transfers (Medicare, Medicaid, etc.), and "spending on other goods and services" (public goods). Given the large size of the third category (40 percent of spending), the first question is, who benefits from it? The CBO here wisely punted, and offered two scenarios: one in which the benefits of public goods are shared per capita, and one where those benefits are shared in proportion to market incomes.[30]

The idea behind the second distribution method is that the affluent drive more than do the poor, have more stuff to be protected by the military, and so on. More empirical work here might narrow the range of plausible assumptions. My own intuition is that the right answer is probably somewhere between the two cases modeled by the CBO. In this regard, recall an earlier discussion in chapter 4 of how the CBO assumes that the cost of running a household increases by the square root of household size, so that a family of four is thought to have twice the needs of a family of one. That rule of thumb is based on research conducted in that specific context, but nonetheless might be as useful a place as any other to start. That is, the household with four times the income of another probably calls on public goods more than does the poorer household, but under my suggested starting point, would be treated with receiving twice the distributional benefits of spending on public goods as the poorer household, not four times as much. This reflects the idea that, for example, the affluent might use public roads more, but surely that greater utilization does not expand linearly with income.

For the CBO, distributing tax burdens of course is old hat, but in this new context it actually raises important questions that previously had been ignored in distributional analyses. For example, the CBO presents a chart showing the distribution of the $480 billion in federal healthcare transfer payments in 2006, measured by type of household (elderly/non-elderly), as well as a separate chart showing the distribution of the $175 billion in healthcare transfer payments received by non-elderly households, measured by income quintiles.[31] But those charts simply ignore the $250 billion or so in federal transfer payments baked into the tax code, in the form of the tax expenditure for employer-sponsored healthcare, as discussed in chapter 9. That spending is top-heavy in its income distribution, and would if included lead to a dramatically different picture of the distribution of healthcare transfer payments to the non-elderly, ordered by income quintiles, than that shown in the CBO study. Here again we see how tax expenditures distort almost every effort to grasp what government does, and who pays for it.

The CBO has already developed the methodologies to distribute the benefits of tax expenditures across the population of taxpayers, and doing so here for the largest tax expenditures would materially improve the accuracy of the CBO's analysis of government's total distributional effects on our lives.[32] A complete effort would require essentially unbundling the tax code, to start with "gross" (pre-hidden spending) tax revenues, and then to distribute as spending programs the various major tax expenditures. The resulting presentation would not tie in directly with official budget line items, but the purpose of this distributional analysis is to communicate a different kind of information; the budget line items follow Congressional authorization procedures, which are just not relevant to communicating the relative net burdens or benefits received from the sum of all government spending and taxing.

The CBO's preliminary work is summarized in Figure 12.4 and Table 12.2. Figure 12.4 is a standard tax distribution table for 2006, showing the average tax burden per non-elderly household for each income quintile (so elderly households

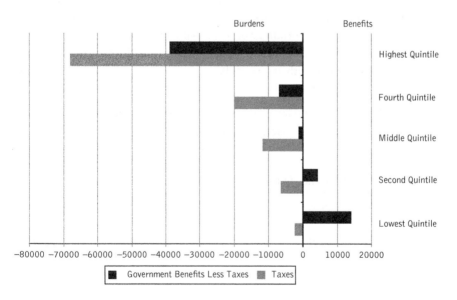

FIGURE 12.4 Taxes Paid and Net Benefits Received per Non-elderly Household, by Incomes
Source: CBO, The Distribution of Federal Spending and Taxes, exhibit 23, supplemental tables.

are ignored), but with a new set of data side by side: the combined effect of government spending for the benefit of such households, allocated according to market incomes, minus the taxes paid by those households.

Figure 12.4 graphically illustrates what we already knew, which is that the average household in the lowest income quintile receives a share of total government spending, net of taxes paid, that exceeds that household's small stand-alone tax liability. This of course is exactly what one would expect in any country that has social insurance programs. What is more surprising is the top end. There we see that the average household in the highest income quintile receives an effective rebate of 43 percent of the taxes it pays, in the form of its share of government spending on its behalf.

The CBO presentation contains only five data points, but it nonetheless is possible to use the CBO's innovative work here to construct rough and ready Gini indexes that sketch how government intervention affects inequality among non-elderly Americans. Table 12.2's rightmost column does just this.

What Table 12.2 suggests is that within the non-elderly population, tax burdens have only a small effect on income inequality—the Gini indexes of the population based on their pre-tax market incomes, and on their after-tax market incomes, are very close. It is the spending side of things (market income, plus benefits, minus taxes) that introduces some real progressivity relative to the starting point of pre-tax market incomes. Within the population of the non-elderly, it is the spending side of things that is the principal driver of progressive outcomes. This is consistent with the theme of this chapter that focusing on progressive taxation simply misses the more important lever of government intervention.

Figure 12.5 is a similar summary to Figure 12.4, but this time the relevant metric is elderly versus non-elderly households.

Table 12.2 Effect of Government on Gini Indexes of Non-elderly Household Incomes

	Lowest Quintile	Second Quintile	Middle Quintile	Fourth Quintile	Highest Quintile	Gini Index
Average Market Income	12,600	36,100	59,500	89,900	240,800	46.50
Market Income Minus Taxes	10,000	29,600	47,700	70,200	172,700	44.34
Market Income Plus Benefits Minus Taxes	26,600	40.300	58,100	82,900	201,900	38.38

Source: CBO, The Distribution of Federal Spending and Taxes, and author's calculations.

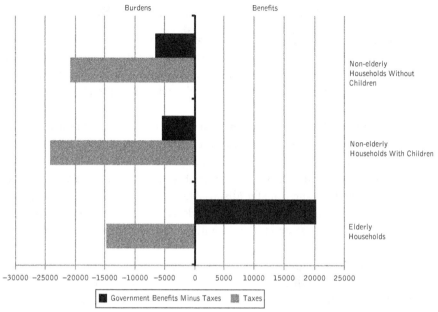

FIGURE 12.5 Taxes Paid and Net Benefits Received per Household, by Household Types

Source: CBO, *The Distribution of Federal Spending and Taxes*, exhibit 12, supplemental tables.

Figure 12.5 confirms that points made a little earlier, that the elderly are the overwhelming winners in any analysis of the combined effects of government taxes and spending on behalf of households.

Notwithstanding its methodological difficulties, the holistic perspective evident in the CBO's first attempt to distribute almost all government spending and taxes is important, because our current fixation on the progressivity of the tax system in the abstract fundamentally distorts policy options. This myopic focus leads to claims from market triumphalists that the highest income tax rates should come down, because our tax system is "very progressive," without any understanding of how small our total tax burdens in fact are, or the net progressivity of the entire taxing and spending function of government. This misbegotten focus further means that we pay inadequate attention to how entitlement benefits spending has become less progressive over time, and the relative sharing of burdens and benefits between the elderly and non-elderly populations. And finally, this misplaced emphasis on tax progressivity by itself leads policymakers from a progressive point of view to rule as unacceptable facially regressive tax instruments that can in fact be employed to advance progressive agendas.

Regressive Taxes Fund Progressive Fiscal Systems

It is common in the OECD for regressive taxes to fund progressive overall government systems. In particular, European value added taxes are regressive when viewed in the abstract, but they also raise huge sums of money. European countries spend those revenues in highly progressive ways, and thereby achieve progressive overall systems.[33]

Figure 12.6 uses OECD data from the first decade of the 2000s to show the correlation between the progressivity of a country's tax rate structure and its impact on reducing after-tax inequality. Inequality reduction is measured by the percentage decrease in the Gini index between pre-tax and transfer (market) income inequality and post-tax and transfer (disposable) income inequality. Progressivity is measured by the Kakwani index, which as described earlier measures the progressivity of a tax in the abstract (that is, without regard to how much money the tax raises).

Surprisingly, the progressivity of a tax system's rate structure is *negatively* correlated with the overall reduction in inequality that a country achieves. The United States has the most progressive income tax rate structure, viewed in the abstract, yet it has by far the smallest overall impact on income inequality.

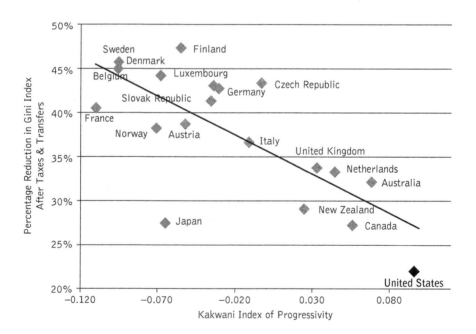

FIGURE 12.6 Effect of Tax System on Reducing Inequality

This trend remains constant when including publicly provided services, such as public health care and education. Figure 12.7 is the same as Figure 12.6, except that the effect of the overall tax and transfer system is measured by the percentage decrease in the Gini index after taxes, transfers, and the imputed value of public services. This is the closest OECD analogue to the new CBO work summarized a few paragraphs earlier.[34]

By contrast, there is a clear positive correlation between the overall size of a country's tax collections and its success at reducing inequality through the inter-mediation of government. Figure 12.8 again uses OECD data from the first decade of the 2000s to make this point. As in Figure 12.6, this figure charts the percent-age decrease in the Gini index for income inequality between pre-tax and transfer income and post-tax and transfer income, but this time as a function, not of the abstract progressivity of the tax system, of the overall amount of revenue collected, measured as a percentage of each country's GDP.

The United States is the lowest-tax country among the countries surveyed, but achieves by far the smallest reduction in income inequality.

Both as a matter of political economy and of economic theory, there are limi-tations on how much tax revenue can be raised by highly progressive taxes, because at some point (although economists disagree as to exactly where that point is) the deadweight losses associated with high marginal tax rates make further attempts at progressivity self-defeating, and because the squawks of the

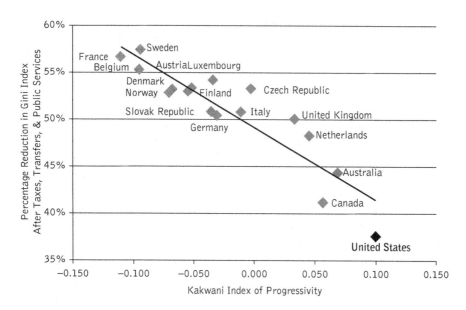

FIGURE 12.7 Effect of Tax System on Reducing Inequality (after Public Services)

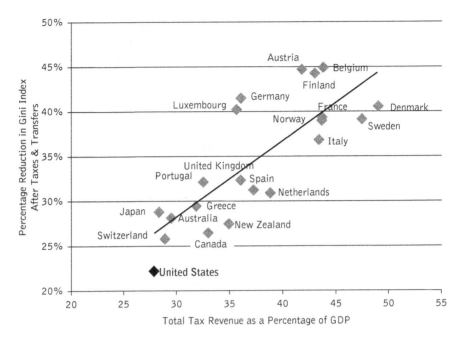

FIGURE 12.8 Reduction in Inequality as Function of Size of Tax System

affluent geese as they are being plucked become intolerable. As a matter of practical necessity, therefore, every country sooner or later discovers that a high level of tax collections requires a less progressive overall tax system, as Figure 12.9 shows.

In sum, advocates for more progressive tax rates are wrong to assume that progressive rates, alone, in practice will lead to greater reductions in inequality.[35] The figures above make clear that the overall size of a tax system is much more important in achieving a substantial change in levels of inequality, after all aspects of a fiscal system are considered. The observation that the size, not the progressivity of the rate structure, is the most important characteristic of a tax system from the standpoint of reducing inequality has an important implication: government spending, not the manner in which revenue is raised, decreases inequality. This explains why countries with regressive taxes, including the European countries that rely heavily on value added taxes (economically the same as sales tax) achieve the most redistribution. In these countries, taxes are not particularly redistributive by themselves, but large revenues are raised, allowing governments to lower inequality through significant social investment and insurance programs.

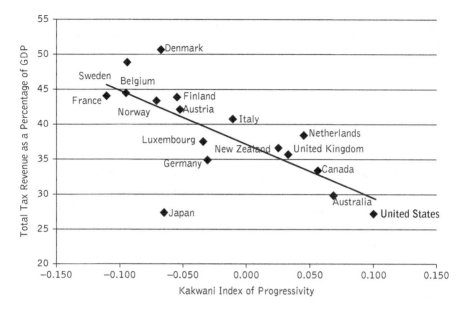

FIGURE 12.9 Total Tax Revenues versus Tax System Progressivity

PROGRESSIVE FISCAL SYSTEMS AND HAPPINESS

As Adam Smith reminded us, the purpose of inquiries such as this book is to increase the happiness of society. It is therefore appropriate to pause for a moment and ask whether there is any evidence suggesting a correlation between progressive fiscal systems (with their attendant larger tax demands) and the happiness of the societies that have embraced those systems.

The answer is yes. The body of research in this area actually is very large, and includes important contributions by Nobel laureate Daniel Kahneman, Richard Easterlin, Jeffrey Sachs, and many other highly regarded social scientists. The research considers all the obvious impediments to reaching robust conclusions, like cultural differences, changing incomes over time, and other potential obstacles to interpersonal comparisons. (Can anyone expect the dour Germans ever to say they are happy? That sort of thing.) In the end, this is a serious and important area of social science research, not a touchy-feely invitation to tune in and drop out.[36]

My colleague at the University of Southern California, Thomas Griffith, conducted a careful review of the relationship between progressive taxation and happiness a few years ago.[37] His review of the happiness research concluded that, among wealthy nations, equality of outcomes was more important to overall happiness in a society than was the rate of a country's economic growth. From a happiness perspective, rapidly increasing inequality unfortunately plays directly against human nature, even if incomes rise in absolute terms, because of our rapid adaptation to whatever income level we experience (assuming that it is well above subsistence levels) and our wants for "positional goods." Were Griffith to repeat that work today looking at the distribution of the entirety of the fiscal system, rather than just the tax structure, my intuition is that his results would be even more dramatic.

Benjamin Radcliff, an academic at Notre Dame, has recently published a book reflecting his substantial empirical research in this area, *The Political Economy of Human Happiness: How Voters' Choices Determine the Quality of Life*.[38] In it he explicitly addresses the issue underlying this chapter, and indeed this book, which is, does a larger government, with its progressive spending and higher tax burdens, lead to greater or lesser well-being (the more inclusive term for happiness, in its most meaningful sense)?

Radcliff's book analyzes surveys and other data from industrialized economies generally, and separately from the United States. Radcliff concludes that public investments in important goods like education, and well-functioning social insurance, lead to higher overall reported levels of happiness, in the meaningful sense of life satisfaction, not momentary jolliness:[39]

> In the argument between Left and Right over the size of the state, I demonstrate that "big government" is more conducive to human well-being, controlling for other factors. Indeed the single most powerful individual- or national-level determinant of the degree to which people positively evaluate the quality of their lives is the extent to which they live in a generous and universalistic welfare state. Put differently, the greater the "social wage" that society pays its members, the happier people tend to be.... Overall, it is clear that the quality of human life improves as more of the productive capacity of society comes under political—which is to say...democratic—control. The subordination of the market to democracy thus appears to promote human happiness....
>
> It is equally important to note that all of the factors...contribute to greater well-being without particular regard to socioeconomic status. While some of the relationships are indeed stronger for working- and middle-class citizens, in every case, higher-status persons also benefit.

The thrust of my book is to emphasize the complementary role of government to private markets in two areas where private markets fail—investment in public goods and social insurance. I therefore shy away from broader invocations of the virtues of "political control" over the market. But I think it plain that Radcliff's research is entirely consistent with my more modest claims for restoring the role of government as a partner in those areas where private markets have demonstrated that they cannot go it alone.

Many other papers reach similar conclusions. For example, in a recent large-scale review published by the United Nations (although the work of private experts, not a UN agency), the United States placed 17th in overall self-reported subjective well-being, which if you think about it is a remarkably unimpressive showing for the richest large economy in the world. What is more, subjective well-being fell more in the United States than it did in most other countries during the Great Recession.[40] Denmark, Norway, and Switzerland were the top medalists, but the Netherlands, which actually is a more diverse society than outsiders sometimes suspect, finished fourth, followed by Sweden and Canada. Canada's materially higher subjective well-being score is particularly relevant, given its many similarities to the United States, but its commitment to a much larger role for government.

In another recent paper, researchers relying on a large-scale survey concluded that, looking only at the United States (so as to avoid any possible cross-country cultural differences), Americans on average were happier in years with less rather than more income inequality, even where the greater inequality years were also years with higher GDP. The researchers concluded that the reason was not the rise in income inequality itself, but rather the erosion of perceived fairness and general trust that survey respondents identified as correlated with higher inequality in our society.[41]

The overall thrust of the research is more or less what you would expect, had you chosen to listen to your mother: money is important, but it does not buy all forms of happiness. Caring for others enriches your soul. Mental health is critically important, even if roundly ignored by much public and private health insurance.[42] Being out of work stinks. Opportunities for life satisfaction must themselves be meaningful to change long-term perceptions of life satisfaction. Participating in a society where the rules of life seem to be fair leads to greater satisfaction, regardless of one's particular outcomes. And so on.

I have chosen not to emphasize any of this research in this book. Instead, I have tried to make the affirmative business case for public investment, where the economic and social returns on our money are conspicuously high, and the business case for social insurance, because sensible business people buy insurance against the perils they cannot control, in order to concentrate more fully on the risks that they want to take on. I have done this because in my view it is pointless to try to convince anyone that the United States should be more like Denmark, or even Canada, because those countries score higher on life satisfaction surveys than we do.

As proof, I point you to an excellent column written by Michael Hiltzik of the *Los Angeles Times* reviewing Benjamin Radcliff's new book in this area, but more particularly to the comments posted under it in the online edition.[43] Those comments fall into three predictable buckets: the Nordic countries are small and homogeneous, so of course they are happy; the United States was founded on the single principle that we are promised the freedom to pursue our own happiness by government getting out of our way, because that is what "freedom" means; and finally, all that government can do is guarantee the pursuit of happiness, not its attainment. This of course is a bowdlerized summary: the most telling actual comment was that we should repeal Obamacare promptly so that we can get on with the business of thinning the herd.

The difference between climate change denial and happiness research is that most people are at least dimly aware that there is something called climate change science, even if they are not so sure about its conclusions, given that it was cold out just the other day. The happiness research seems to be rejected at a deeper, more troubling level, as simply impossible to contemplate. The rejection does not even rise to the level of a conscious repudiation of a body of work susceptible of analysis or criticism.

Franklin Delano Roosevelt had it right when he implied that freedom is a more nuanced word than most Americans appreciate. Both freedom and the pursuit of happiness are distant aspirations when one starts the adventure of life far behind one's counterparts, because of the accident of your parents' poverty, and the greater social enrichment and education to which the children of the affluent are exposed. So long, however, as millions of Americans think that absolute atomism is all that "freedom" can mean, there is no point spitting into this headwind.

It may be that my emphasis on returns to social investment and on the desirability of insurance to address the unavoidable perils encountered in the adventure of life is a similarly doomed enterprise, but it has the virtue of couching matters in terms drawn from our everyday commercial experience, without any explicit moralizing. And should through some alignment of the planets a bit of common sense seeps into our political discourse, and we begin to take advantage of the investment and insurance opportunities that surround us, it is good to know that as best as the researchers can tell, we are indeed likely to move our society a little bit further along the happiness spectrum.

PROGRESSIVE FISCAL SYSTEMS AND EFFICIENCY

At every turn in this book I have tried to develop the economic efficiency case for government investment in public goods and for social insurance as value-generating activities, both from a narrow GDP perspective and when a broader view of social returns is considered. These activities complement private markets in arenas where private markets invariably are incomplete. Why imagine a world where private markets magically fill vacuums they have left empty for generations, when a more immediate and straightforward market participant is at hand?

Similarly, I have reviewed at several points the economic research on how individuals respond to taxation, and have shown that the more extreme descriptions of allergies to taxation are based on political propagandizing to defend an obvious interest group (the rich) or represent slightly pathological behavior, like severe agoraphobia or other anxiety disorders. In every case we try to help those who suffer, but we do not structure the entirety of our society around their idiosyncratic reactions. I further have argued for a moderate approach to the taxation of top incomes that falls well short of the outer limits suggested by the work of Diamond and Saez.

Combining the two strands essentially changes nothing, except that it becomes easier to apply traditional cost-benefit analysis when both the cost of funding a collective investment or social insurance program and its financial and social returns can be considered together. When we do, we see a grand tableau of opportunities spreading out before us. We could enhance our wealth as well as our happiness were only we to appreciate that government performs useful work when it complements markets in areas that private participants habitually leave incomplete.

CHAPTER 13

THE BETTER BASE CASE

All those different orders and societies [that comprise a state] are dependent upon the state to which they owe their security and protection. That they are subordinate to that state, and established only in subserviency to its prosperity and preservation, is a truth acknowledged by the most partial member of every one of them. It may often, however, be hard to convince him that the prosperity and preservation of the state require any diminution of the powers, privileges, and immunities of his own particular order or society.

—ADAM SMITH, *The Theory of Moral Sentiments*,
Part VI, Sec. II, Chap. II.

FOCUS OF THE BETTER BASE CASE

This chapter offers a way forward for our country's fiscal policy over the next decade or thereabouts, which I call the Better Base Case. The Better Base Case contemplates unwinding the Budget Control Act's spending corsets, adding incremental infrastructure programs, and raising tax revenues sufficient to keep those revenues within hailing distance of the recalibrated outlays. The ideas do not involve grand bargains or unprecedented tax reform, but nonetheless would fundamentally reorient fiscal policy for the better.

The Better Base Case essentially puts the country on a fiscal path closer to where we were at the end of the Clinton administration than where we are today. Spending would be somewhat higher than our current trends, due in part to the repeal of the sequestration and other Budget Control Act constraints, and tax revenues would be significantly higher, due principally to the readoption of Clinton-era tax rate schedules. (The Better Base Case then makes a number of surgical adjustments around this new base, described at length below.) The 2013 fiscal cliff tax deal did just this, but only for the very highest-income taxpayers; what I am proposing here is to raise taxes throughout the income distribution by returning to pre-2001 tax rate schedules more generally.

The spending side of the Better Base Case follows from points developed in earlier chapters. We cannot run a government that delivers core services that support the rule of law and basic norms of decency, supervises the largest economy in the world, marshals a military almost as large as the rest of the world's put together, and indulges itself in the most inefficient healthcare system ever invented, all while spending less on government resources as a percentage of our GDP than any other developed economy. Pundits on the right of the political spectrum are quick to tote up the efficiency costs of more taxes, but ignore the welfare costs to our society as a whole from allowing basic functions of government to wither from lack of funding.

In turn, we know how to raise almost enough revenues without fundamentally rethinking our tax system. The pre-2001 personal income tax rate tables that would apply today, were it not for the American Taxpayer Relief Act of 2012, were in fact commensurate with our ongoing revenue needs. There are some efficiency costs to these higher tax rates when viewed in the abstract, but there are many reasons to believe that on balance this move is welfare-enhancing, because those efficiency costs are not overwhelmingly large, and the public goods purchased with the resulting revenues will have large and important positive welfare implications.

As developed in chapters 5 and 8, an extensive body of economic research suggests that a return to pre-2001 personal income tax policies would have only a modest effect on the decisions and effort level of taxpayers.[1] High-ability US taxpayers will not be taxed at high rates by worldwide norms.[2] And most research suggests that labor effort (particularly of the primary wage earner in a household) is relatively inelastic to changes in tax rates of the magnitudes at stake when crossing from 2013's tax rate structure to pre-2001 rates—particularly given that the highest-income taxpayers, who presumably have particular sensitivity to tax rate changes, already face the pre-2001 top rate, thanks to the January 1, 2013, compromise.[3]

The Congressional Budget Office in fact investigated this very question in 2012. It concluded that a return to the pre-2001 personal income tax rate structure

> would raise tax rates on capital income and labor earnings, which would decrease private saving and the supply of labor; those responses, by themselves, would reduce future output. However, the effects of those responses would probably be outweighed by the impact of the substantial decrease in budget deficits, which, by itself, would increase future output by a growing amount over time. Hence, by CBO's estimates, the policy changes scheduled [as of 2012] to occur under current law [i.e., the return

to pre-2001 rates] would, on balance, have a *positive* medium- and long-term effect on the economy.[4]

In other words, the net effect of the higher tax revenues contemplated by the Better Base Case will be good for the economy, not a drag on future economic progress. This point is made even more persuasive by the fact that we already have absorbed whatever deadweight losses were incurred in raising the top tax rates on the highest income Americans, as a result of the American Taxpayer Relief Act of 2012.

The Better Base Case presented here emphasizes a medium-term time horizon—a decade or thereabouts—for four reasons. First, I have found that terrifying readers about what the fiscal environment will look like in 50 or 75 years tends only to elicit existential despair and disengagement. Second, relatively modest steps taken today can make the long-term picture much more easily addressed. It is simply an artifact of the compounding of money—or in this case, the absence of money, in the form of deficits—over time that some measurable contributions to a more robust fiscal path in the medium term will greatly mitigate our fiscal problems in the long term.

Third, the medium term should serve as the on-ramp to more sustainable long-term mandatory spending pathways, because whenever important "entitlement" programs are changed, those changes must be phased in slowly. This is not code for slashing Social Security, or turning Medicare into a voucher system, but rather a marker that we need to rethink comprehensively how we deliver healthcare in the United States. Medicare actually points in the right direction, in that it is single-payer system with low administrative costs. It is an extremely indulgent single payer, of course, which is a significant part of the problem, but the largest problem is that healthcare for the *non-elderly* is delivered through a crazy patchwork of overlapping systems in which national affordability, administrative efficiency, and health outcomes are all the losers.

The fourth reason to focus on a reasonably foreseeable time horizon is that I do not believe that there is such a thing as a steady state fiscal policy. Our economy rapidly evolves, our national security needs evolve, and so do our needs and wants as citizens. Fiscal policy must also evolve to suit the exigencies of the times.

My medium-term time horizon base case does not rely on a political "grand bargain," or on new tax instruments. One reason is that, having watched Congress in action from the inside, I do not believe that the institution can digest that large a meal. The other is that a grand bargain is unnecessary as a first step, and insisting on developing a grand bargain before moving forward on any other front is simply a promise of paralysis. The next decade or so should serve as the ramp to a different mix of fiscal instruments, but, again, whenever major changes are contemplated to our large spending programs, like Social Security or Medicare, those changes must be phased in slowly, so as to be fair to settled expectations. What we need in the meantime is to finance the government we have, and to do so in ways that do not starve our own future, whether through excessive deficits or through failure to invest in ourselves.

By the same token, I fully appreciate why some economists might like to see a value added tax (VAT) (basically, a national sales tax) replace at least some of the revenues collected by the income tax, and I understand the economic logic behind a large-scale carbon tax to address the externalities of pollution and global warming, while raising significant revenues. But large-scale tax programs again are so politically paralyzing as to guarantee only stasis.

The reality is that our fiscal problems are not unprecedented, and they do not require fundamental revamping of our basic fiscal instruments, at least for a decade or more. What we do need is to put to one side our culture of fiscal narcissism, in light of the demographic and other realities described earlier, and accept tax burdens that we ourselves—not our grandparents, but most of the readers of this book—found completely unexceptional 15 years ago.

RIGHT-SIZING SPENDING

As chapter 6 summarized, as recently as 2012 our fiscal future looked almost rosy, at least over the medium term. In February 2012, the Congressional Budget Office estimated that the fiscal year 2021 deficit would be only 1.2 percent of GDP; overall, in the 2017–2022 period, deficits would have been sufficiently small to lead to a paydown every year of total federal debt outstanding as a percentage of GDP.

One year later, CBO forecast that the fiscal year 2021 deficit would be triple the 2012 estimate, at 3.6 percent of GDP, and debt held by the public would climb as a percentage of GDP in every year after 2018. Chapter 6 further demonstrated that the decline and fall of our medium-term fiscal forecast was entirely due to the January 1, 2013, "fiscal cliff" tax deal (the American Taxpayer Relief Act).

At the same time, CBO's 2012 and 2013 budget forecasts for 2021 were unrealistically optimistic in respect of their deficit predictions. Most urgently, those forecasts assumed (as CBO is required to do) that all of the strictures of the Budget Control Act of 2011 on the size of the federal discretionary budget would continue in force. (The Budget Control Act also imposes some significantly smaller caps on Medicare-related payments.)

I begin with the opposite assumption, which is that, for all the reasons developed in Part II of this book, we are throttling our own future prosperity and the happiness of our society if we allow the sequestration and other constraints of the Budget Control Act to continue. So for purposes of my Better Base Case, I assume that government spending will grow at the rate of inflation from its 2012 base, so as to stay flat in real terms over time. In 2012, CBO calculated that the difference between fiscal year 2021 projected discretionary spending, determined by assuming that 2012 spending would grow at the rate of inflation, and the maximum permitted under the Budget Control Act, would be about $165 billion. Over the 10-year period 2014–2023, eliminating those constraints will cost roughly $1.5 trillion. This additional spending will need to be financed, which is why the other side of the Better Base Case is a higher level of tax revenues.

If we as a country can agree on government spending reductions that make sense to us, then taxes can be lower than those I suggest in this section. As it happens, I do not believe that this can or should happen, because of the demographic headwinds we face, our inability to rethink healthcare delivery systems (at least in the short run), and all our pressing opportunities for collective investment and social insurance. Nonetheless, if there are pots of money now being spent by government that we do not need to spend, I am all for taxing myself less rather than more. But to argue for lower taxes because that will lead to lower spending is like arguing that by buying clothes that are too small, one is sure to lose weight.[5]

Chapter 10 made the case for a much more substantial commitment to public investment in infrastructure. The restored levels of spending made possible by unshackling ourselves from the Budget Control Act's self-imposed constraints contemplate more infrastructure investment than that possible under the Budget Control Act's constrictions, but would fall short of an optimal long-term target. Public nondefense investments at all levels of US government combined are now at the lowest levels, as a percentage of GDP, since World War II.[6]

The American Society of Civil Engineers and a report prepared in 2010 by Our Fiscal Security, a joint venture among Demos, the Economic Policy Institute, and the Century Foundation,[7] both recommended *incremental* public investment in infrastructure in the range of $200–$250 billion per year. (By way of context, the federal government in 2012 spent $126 billion on nondefense physical capital investments and $64 billion on nondefense research and development; total government spending (mostly at the state and local government level) on surface transportation projects, which are the largest segment of public physical capital infrastructure investments, runs about $200 billion per year.[8]) This figure is aspirational, of course, but gives a sense of the opportunities currently being forgone. As chapter 10 demonstrated, those increased investments in turn will lead to higher welfare, both through increased employment opportunities for millions of Americans not destined to engineer the next big mobile app and through the positive economic returns generated by those investments.[9]

Some of this incrementally higher public investment can come from reshufflings within the resuscitated federal budget, but investment at these levels will require new financing sources and a national infrastructure bank, as described in chapter 10. A plan by which the federal government invests an incremental

$50 billion per year directly and indirectly in infrastructure should be sufficient to fund infrastructure investments at the right order of magnitude. Amounts at this level would enable the federal government to increase somewhat its direct infrastructure funding, including grants to sub-national government, and to subscribe over time to the stock of a new national infrastructure bank, in a total commitment of $200 billion (roughly the same book value equity capitalization as JP Morgan Chase). The national infrastructure bank in turn can provide significant additional financing for public projects by accessing the private debt capital markets.

The CBO's 2013 forecast of all government outlays in fiscal year 2021 was $5.2 trillion ($5,200 billion). My two spending suggestions above would bring that total to a little over $5.4 trillion. That gives us a revenue target to shoot for, as opposed to the usual Procrustean process in Washington, of starting from an arbitrary revenue level and cutting spending to suit. And like a game of horseshoes, we do not need to hit the target precisely to declare ourselves winners; a deficit in the range of 1 to 1.5 percent of GDP ($235 billion to $355 billion in 2021) is close enough for purposes of my rough-cut illustrations.

RIGHT-SIZING REVENUES

We need to size our revenues to the inescapable realities of the demands properly placed on the government of the world's richest and most powerful large economy, which means that our government must spend at the levels suggested in the preceding section.

To finance this spending, the inescapable conclusion is that we need higher revenues than those we can collect under our current tax system. The most straightforward way to do this is to revert to the personal income tax rate schedules in effect before 2001, which is exactly what would have happened on January 1, 2013, but for the fiscal cliff tax deal, which allowed the 2001 temporary tax rate schedule to expire only for the most affluent taxpayers. In 2012, CBO estimated that this level of collections (about 21 percent of GDP in fiscal year 2021, prior to taking into account the recent restatement of GDP described in chapter 6) was sufficient to bring projected revenues close to projected spending, leaving a projected deficit of 1.2 percent of GDP. In turn, we need to top up that level of revenues a bit to accommodate my suggested incremental programs of loosening of the Budget Control Act's shackles, and a larger commitment to infrastructure investment.

The conclusion that revenue collections must rise significantly sits badly with some. They like to point out that high taxes impede economic growth and job creation. It is true that, all things being equal, lower taxes are better than higher taxes, and lower marginal tax rates are better than higher marginal tax rates. But these sorts of nostrums have as much policy utility as the old adage that, all other things being equal, it is better to be rich and healthy than poor and sick. Tax revenues need to increase not because higher taxes are desirable as an independent goal, but because there is no other choice as part of a transition from current policies, which in turn have been shaped by both political parties over many decades.

In fact, we begin with such a low level of taxation in the United States (chapter 8) that we have plenty of room to increase tax revenues without materially affecting efficiency goals. And while recourse to history always is fraught, because at any point in time many things are going on beyond fiscal policy, it is the case that in the last years of the 1990s the economy was very robust, and this country ran government surpluses. We cannot guarantee that future economic performance will mirror those years, but we can fairly assume that human beings have not evolved very much in the last 15 years or so. Since labor market participation and savings were strong in the 1990s, it is not realistic to maintain that a reversion to comparable tax rates today will lead Americans to pack it all in and become a nation of beachcombers.

Research and history alike, including the Congressional Budget Office analysis quoted at the outset of this chapter, suggest that the deadweight losses associated with moving to pre-2001 across the board tax rates would not be terribly large, especially given the very low rates from which we would move, and the fact that the highest-income Americans already face pre-2001 rates on their last dollars of income. Indeed, the CBO analysis concluded that the move would be welfare enhancing, because higher tax revenues would reduce the economic costs of increasing government borrowings crowding out private investment. Moreover, in this setting, where the alternative is to starve government at levels unprecedented in our own recent history or in the experience of other developed economies, any residual private efficiency losses would be swamped by the welfare gains from the government spending programs that could be funded at rational levels.

It turns out, however, that there are good reasons beyond a simple aversion to higher taxes to be unenthusiastic about the return of the specific tax system that was in place before 2001. That tax system had several conspicuous design defects. The individual alternative minimum tax (AMT) was one; by (perverse) design, it was not indexed to inflation, and so applied to more and more taxpayers with every passing year. But there were other major flaws as well.

In response, the Better Base Case contemplates some surgical nips and tucks to deliver about the same level of revenues as would have been the case had we on January 1, 2013, simply reverted to pre-2001 tax law, while correcting the flaws of that older law. In 2012, a co-author and I published a paper analyzing the revenue consequences of this package of improvements, using the Tax Policy Center's microsimulation tax model, similar to that used by the staff of the Joint Committee on Taxation to produce the official revenue estimates on which Congress relies.[10] (The CBO incorporates JCT tax projections when the CBO produces its overall budget forecasts.) The Better Base Case is approximately revenue neutral over a 10-year time horizon, relative to the 2012 "baseline"—that is, the assumption that on January 1, 2013, all the temporary personal income and estate tax rules had lapsed, and we had turned back the clock to pre-2001 law. This means that the Better Base Case delivers about the same level of revenues for fiscal year 2021 as the CBO contemplated when it prepared its 2012 baseline projections.

Specifically, the Better Base Case begins by reintroducing all the tax rate brackets that applied before 2001. It then addresses the principal structural flaws in pre-2001 tax law by proposing the following revisions to those rules:

1. Permanently repeal the individual alternative minimum tax. The American Taxpayer Relief Act of 2012 (ATRA, the January 1, 2013, fiscal cliff tax deal) instituted a permanent AMT "patch," but under this half-solution tens of millions of Americans would still be subject each year to the AMT. The Better Base Case goes further and eliminates the AMT entirely.
2. Retain the child tax credit at its 2012 level. (ATRA did this as well.) The child tax credit is extremely important to most middle class families; moreover, like the earned income tax credit, the refundable portion of the child tax credit is a "making work pay" incentive, in that it is only available to the extent taxpayers have earned income. The pre-2001 credit was half as large and had more limited refundability.
3. Keep the tax rate on dividends the same as the tax rate on capital gains (20 percent) rather than reverting to a system where dividends are taxed at full ordinary income rates. (ATRA did this as well.)
4. Reinstate 2009's estate tax rules, which means a $3.5 million exclusion (permanently indexed for inflation) and a 45 percent maximum tax rate. This is much more generous than the pre-2001 estate tax laws assumed in the CBO's 2012 baseline revenue projections; those rules provided a non-indexed $1 million exemption and a top rate of 55 percent. (ATRA was still more generous: it enacted a $5 million exclusion, indexed for inflation, and a 40 percent top rate.)

The estate tax is extremely important to ensuring over the long term an open society not dominated by vast concentrations of dynastic family wealth. Pre-2001 law missed this point, and hit families that saw themselves as decidedly middle class. The 2009 levels of taxation allow for a reasonable amount of wealth to pass tax-free on the death of the second-to-die spouse (estate tax basically is not imposed on the death of the first-to-die of a married couple).

Since the right focus of the estate tax should be on dynastic wealth, safeguards against estate tax avoidance actually are more important than the exclusion amount. These avoidance opportunities abound under current law, and are reflected in the JCT and CBO revenue forecasts for the estate tax under all its recent permutations. A comprehensive cleanup of the estate tax (not reflected in the Better Base Case's revenue projections) would raise significant revenue and reorient the tax toward accomplishing its purpose. Those revenue pick-ups were not reflected in the estimates in our 2012 paper, but could be substantial, particularly in light of some of the large Internet-spawned fortunes created in the last two decades.

These four tax tweaks all cost the government money relative to the CBO 2012 baseline—that is, relative to pre-2001 tax law. Even the estate tax proposal I just made costs money relative to that baseline; while it is true that the Better Base Case's estate tax rates and exclusions are less favorable than 2013 law, they are more generous than pre-2001 law, and as a result score as revenue losers against the CBO 2012 baseline.

The Better Base Case therefore acknowledges that our ongoing tax revenue needs require collections comparable to the revenues that would be raised under unimproved pre-2001 law. This means that the four tax tweaks must be paid for through a new revenue stream—one totaling about $1.5 trillion over 10 years (as of our 2012 estimate). Eliminating the AMT and the other improvements listed above are costly.

One way to scrounge up the $1.5 trillion needed to correct the structural flaws of pre-2001 tax law would be to raise marginal tax rates beyond those that prevailed before 2001. This is a poor idea, if one's goal is to have a prayer of actually effecting change. First, as a matter of political economy, a narrative grounded in reverting to the same tax brackets under which we all prospered in the 1990s has resonance; marginal rates higher than those would abandon this compelling narrative. Second, the sticker shock relative to 2013-level tax brackets would be too great for any electorate to absorb, no matter how articulate the explanation.

Third, there are always efficiency costs to higher marginal tax rates in particular (see chapters 5 and 8).[11] As explained in those earlier chapters, economists believe that it is the marginal tax rate—the tax on the next dollar of income—that most directly influences our behavior. If the government forgoes $1.5 trillion in potential tax revenues over 10 years to correct the four structural flaws listed above, and then raises marginal tax rates on top of the move to pre-2001 rates sufficiently to restore total tax collections by that same $1.5 trillion, there would be no apparent net effect on tax revenues (or in Congressional jargon, we would have found a "pay for" to cover the taxes forgone), but beneath the surface society would have suffered a new incremental deadweight loss.

While the deadweight losses attributable to the higher tax rates contemplated by pre-2001 tax law might not have been visible or disabling, when netted against the deficit reduction welfare gains and welfare gains from government spending programs that those higher taxes would fund, these deadweight losses did exist. Adding still higher marginal tax rates on top of the pre-2001 structure would exacerbate those (modest) deadweight losses, but because deadweight loss increases *more* than linearly with tax rate hikes, this second layer of tax rate hikes would incur materially more deadweight loss, per dollar of revenue raised, than did the move to the pre-2001 tax rate structure.[12]

As a result, the better path to raising the $1.5 trillion to fix pre-2001 tax law is to find *inframarginal* tax revenue streams—techniques to increase the average taxes, to compensate for the tax forgone through the four tweaks outlined above, without raising the marginal tax bracket rates. Inframarginal revenues introduce less deadweight loss than do marginal tax rate hikes. For example, the Congressional Budget Office has written that:

> increasing revenues by raising marginal tax rates on labor (the rates that would apply to an additional dollar of a taxpayer's income from work) would reduce people's incentive to work and therefore reduce the amount of labor supplied to the economy, whereas increasing revenues to a similar extent by broadening the tax base would probably have a smaller negative effect, or even a positive effect, on the amount of labor supplied.[13]

Fortunately, there is an important inframarginal revenue stream waiting to be tapped, through the curbing of personal itemized deductions.[14] Along with our disjointed subsidies for healthcare, these are the largest and least defensible tax expenditures, which were the subject of chapter 9.[15] There is a widespread bipartisan consensus that the current personal itemized deductions are perverse, inefficient, and unaffordable.[16] For example, the subsidies for investment in one's home profoundly distort individuals' investment decisions and home prices.[17] Scaling back these existing distortions is welfare-enhancing (reduces deadweight loss baked into current law), because by doing so the tax system would no longer put its thumb on the scale of an individual's decisions as to how to invest her money.

The Better Base Case therefore contemplates paying for the four tax tweaks to pre-2001 tax law outlined above by raising $1.5 trillion, or thereabouts, over 10 years through capping both personal itemized deductions and the standard deduction to a 15 percent tax rate benefit. The standard deduction invariably gets a free pass when tax expenditures are examined, but the standard deduction has all the same "upside-down subsidy" characteristics as do itemized deductions, and has no greater justification as a normative income tax matter.

Imagine that you are a high-income taxpayer facing a marginal personal income tax rate of 39.6 percent. If you deduct $100 in mortgage interest expense, you save $39.60 in federal income tax. Under the Better Base Case, you would get a $15 tax savings from this deduction—just as would taxpayers in the 15, 25, 28, 33, or 35 percent tax rate brackets. The Better Base Case thus addresses the upside-down nature of the current deduction structure by capping those personal deductions at a constant 15 percent tax rate benefit, so that wealthy Americans are not subsidized disproportionately compared to middle-income taxpayers.[18] At the same time, a 15 percent benefit cap leaves in place more than one-half aggregate value of the personal itemized deductions under pre-2001 rate tables, which minimizes transition concerns.

Curbing personal itemized deductions along these lines raises revenues without raising statutory tax rates. By happy coincidence, this move independently addresses the fact that the most expensive of the personal itemized deductions— those relating to subsidizing homeownership—are themselves particularly distortionary subsidies that have had clear negative effects on the allocation of investment capital in the United States.[19] Doing so also moderates the inefficiencies by which we provide these subsidies to those who would have bought their homes (or made charitable contributions, or chosen to live in high-tax states) regardless of the tax incentives.[20] Capping the tax preferences for these items also will add to the progressivity of the tax system, because itemizers generally have higher pre-tax incomes than do taxpayers claiming the standard deduction.[21] (Only about one-third of tax return filers are eligible to claim itemized deductions today.)

The reason to curb *all* the personal itemized deductions is that it is impossible to choose among them. Each can be defended as an incentive for one desirable goal or another. Our only practical hope is to round up and corral all these sacred tax cows at once.

As discussed in chapter 9, I recognize the appeal of the charitable contribution deduction, and the argument that this deduction in fact serves useful policy goals, by subsidizing in an open and democratic fashion welfare-enhancing activities that in other countries are entirely state-financed. By subsidizing donations, the charitable contribution deduction no doubt induces more charitable giving than otherwise would be the case. One recent review of the economic literature, however, concluded that the forgone tax revenues from operating the subsidy exceed the amount of this induced giving, and that observed responses in charitable giving to changes in tax rates are largely transitory timing effects.[22] This would mean that scaling back the charitable contribution deduction would have some immediate transition effects (accelerating large contributions into the year before the effective date of any change and artificially depressing giving in the following year), and probably would dampen charitable giving somewhat in the long term, but would be more than made up in increased tax revenues.

The debate on the charitable contribution deduction often is conducted against the background of an imaginary ideal. In fact, the charitable contribution deduction has significant design flaws in common with the other personal item-ized deductions, in the upside-down nature of the subsidy and in the fact that much of the subsidy goes to charitable giving that would have occurred regard-less of the deduction. The upside-down structure of the subsidy is particularly apparent in this setting, because the charitable contribution deduction is the most top-heavy of the personal itemized deductions. What is more, the charitable con-tribution deduction has its own unique set of problems, including exotic gaming of the rules (donor-advised funds, charitable remainder unitrusts), outright fraud (inflating values of contributions of tangible property, like art), and thinly veiled vanity projects (the Kleinbard Museum of String). The charitable contribution deduction is not the blushing bride of personal itemized deductions.[23]

At bottom, the personal itemized deductions, as the name implies, are all *per-sonal* expenses. Scaling them back to a uniform 15 percent tax benefit would make the tax system more progressive, more efficient, less distortive, and simpler. (The first three of these reasons apply as well to converting the standard deduction to a 15 percent tax credit.) Doing so also would raise a great deal of money without adding unduly to the deadweight loss from taxation, and raising a great deal of tax revenue in general is something that we have no choice but to embrace.

ADDITIONAL REVENUES

The presentation of the Better Base Case in the preceding section demonstrated how we can resuscitate government from its incipient near-death experience, without recourse to novel tax policies or crushing burdens. The restored levels of spending will enable sensible policies to proceed, and the revised tax system, including the elimination of the hated Alternative Minimum Tax, is fairer and more efficient than current law.

Incremental infrastructure investment of the magnitude suggested here can be funded through the gasoline excise tax; this makes particular sense, given that surface transportation projects account for such a large share of total public infrastructure investment. As currently structured, the gasoline excise tax is a fixed tax per gallon of gasoline, and therefore is neither tied to increasing prices at the gas pump nor indexed to inflation more generally. As a result, the tax has effectively grown smaller and smaller with every passing year. An increase in the gasoline tax by 35 cents per gallon and indexation of the tax going forward from there would by itself raise over $450 billion over the next 10 years—around $50 billion in fiscal year 2021.[24]

One of the reasons for the deterioration in our deficit projections at the end of the 10-year period on which this chapter concentrates is that spending on Social Security is projected to outstrip Social Security payroll taxes and other trust fund revenue sources. The most effective response is to phase out completely the cap on taxable earnings; even allowing benefits accordingly to rise under the current schedule, this step alone assures Social Security solvency for the next 70 years.[25] What is more, doing so improves the overall progressivity of the tax system; as described in chapter 12, that is not our only goal in fiscal policy, but it makes achieving a progressive fiscal system all the easier.

Looking just at fiscal year 2021, this move would bring in almost $130 billion in new net revenue in that year—almost enough to completely fund the repeal of the Budget Control Act's constraints for that year.[26] The resulting assets would belong to the trust funds and would entitle taxpayers to increased benefits (which have been reflected in the net revenue figure just suggested), but as described in chapter 6, trust fund assets indirectly fund current-year spending, because those assets are lent to the Treasury's general fund. Public Treasury debt outstanding is affected by revenues in, and cash outlays out, so these additional revenues would have exactly the same deficit reduction consequences as an increase in any other tax revenue stream.

It is true, of course, that removing the cap on taxable wages for Social Security purposes would add to the tax burden on labor income at the top end of the scale, but given that the remainder of the package has no effect on the top end, this might be forgiven. Moreover, the resulting trust fund assets will ensure that, under current law, the trust fund can continue to pay current levels of benefits for the indefinite future to all workers, regardless of their pre-retirement wages. Finally, a labor income tax is a consumption tax by another name, and arguably this might be a less economically inefficient move than materially increasing capital income tax burdens.

There are a number of important technical problems in current law in distinguishing labor income from capital income; basically, the great sport among the affluent is to disguise labor income as capital income, because the latter is more lightly taxed. If we properly characterized labor income in the first place, rather than allowing it to masquerade as capital gains in particular, the Social Security base would be greatly enhanced, and we could lower payroll tax rates a bit to reflect that. The last section of this chapter talks about how one might do this, but it is not a trivial technical exercise.

Healthcare remains our greatest fiscal and ethical dilemma. The Congressional Budget Office has assembled a long list of possible fiscal patches,[27] but none of the proposals by itself makes the problem disappear, and some popular ideas (e.g., tort reform) actually have derisorily small fiscal consequences. What is needed, of course, is to abandon the current tax subsidies for employer-provided healthcare (amounting to roughly $3 trillion in income and payroll tax costs over the coming decade), to abandon the Affordable Care Act's Byzantine layering of insurers upon insurers, and to do what every other country does, which is to run a single-payer system.

We could save roughly $10 *trillion* over the next decade if only we were to bring down our national private and public healthcare spending to the same level as the second-most profligate country in the world. Not even the United States is rich enough to throw away this much money every year. But this issue is extraordinarily fractious, and our commitment at both ends of the political system to magical thinking about it runs very deep. In the absence of any consensus as to even the cardinal point of the compass toward which we should head, I think it best for the prospects of the Better Base Case that this sensible package of proposals not be mired in a bottomless pit of angry healthcare debates. Perhaps in a couple of years the environment will be less poisonous, and we then can get to work on this urgent project.

There is nothing particularly "fundamental" about the Better Base Case, or even corporate tax reform of the sort summarized in the next section. Both are classic exercises in base broadening, in the individual case accompanied by higher income tax revenue collections, and in the corporate case accompanied by lower rates. Tax policy wonks are much too quick to describe incremental maintenance work to the tax code as fundamental tax reform.

Some might criticize this presentation for being too quick to rely on old taxes, in particular the income tax, rather than looking to a major new revenue source, either as a replacement for existing taxes or in addition to them. For example, a tax on greenhouse emissions used to finance a payroll tax reduction might make good sense, because it directly addresses a negative externality—the long-term cost to society of greenhouse gases—and because it lowers the immediate tax wedge on labor. (More formally, this is largely an illusion, in that payroll taxes ultimately burden consumption, and so do taxes on various greenhouse gases, albeit over a narrower range of consumption goods, but illusion is a more powerful force in determining how taxes actually affect behavior than is sometimes appreciated.) A value added tax—basically, a sales tax—used to finance healthcare under a single payer system would be another example.[28]

I have shied away from new taxes deliberately, however. Old taxes have two great virtues. One is that they are well understood; the other is that they are baked into prices and behaviors. Moving to large-scale new taxes can alter relative prices or change behaviors in ways that are profoundly unsettling. Given that new taxes are not necessary to accomplish our fiscal objectives over the next decade, I do not rely on them for the Better Base Case, notwithstanding their appeal. Over a longer-term horizon, of course, the analysis might be different.

Every other developed economy in the world relies on a national VAT (a sales tax by another name) to fund government. VATs can raise great sums of money, and to a first order approximation are thought to be more efficient than income taxes, because VATs do not burden the day-to-day ("normal") returns to saving, and therefore do not distort the intertemporal decision of whether to consume today or to consume tomorrow.

In the United States, however, a VAT is viewed as a sort of Fiscal Sauron. Larry Summers has a VAT joke that he has deployed at so many talks that it can now safely be recorded in print without depriving him of the element of surprise. Whenever he speaks, Summers is asked when the United States will have a VAT. He responds that the problem with a VAT is that the Democrats fear that it is highly regressive, while Republicans object that it is a money machine for the government. But, Summers continues, once the Democrats figure out that the VAT is a money machine, and the Republicans tumble onto the fact that the VAT is regressive, why *then* we'll get a VAT!

As chapter 12 developed, this clever syllogism turns out to be false: in fact regressive VATs fund progressive fiscal systems elsewhere in the world. A VAT therefore actually can play an important role in a real-life progressive construction of government. But VATs remain mired in bipartisan disdain. Every now and then the Senate approves, by truly overwhelming margins, a nonbinding resolution that the United States will never have a VAT. It is comforting to see senators reaching across the aisle in this manner, but by the same token there seems to be little point in my advocating truly doomed causes.

FUNDAMENTAL TAX REFORM—NICE BUT UNNECESSARY

There is a school of thought inside the Beltway that, whatever the problem, fundamental tax reform (always spoken in the solemnest tones) must be the solution. Because I am by training a tax law specialist, I should be a disciple of this school of thought, but as the outline of the Better Base Case just demonstrated, there is no need to invoke anything terribly fundamental to restore government and our budget alike to good health. Nonetheless, there are two areas of tax reform that deserve more comment. The discussion that follows gets a little technical.

Corporate Tax Reform

Corporate income tax revenues are about one-quarter as large as personal income tax collections, but nonetheless are important in absolute terms ($5 trillion over the next 10 years), and impose large economic efficiency costs. There is a surprising amount of consensus as to what needs to be done to improve matters in this area.

The federal corporate tax rate—nominally, 35 percent—is much too high, relative to world norms. The right corporate rate is in the range of 25–28 percent. Most economists agree that the corporate income tax is the tax most likely to succeed at introducing significant deadweight loss into the tax system, so reducing the statutory tax rate without sacrificing total tax revenues should be a high priority. What this implies is "revenue neutral" corporate tax reform: the tax rate should be lowered, and the base—the measure of taxable income to which the tax applies—should be broadened.

Every country that has reduced its corporate tax rate (as many have in the last decade or so) has done so by scaling back its business tax expenditures, starting with accelerated tax depreciation. Under current US law, the combination of accelerated tax depreciation on new equipment purchases and the deductibility of interest expense on debt incurred to purchase that equipment actually yields a *negative* effective tax rate. This means that we collectively pay companies to make those investments.[29] In addition, the tax code is stacked to the rafters with other business tax subsidies, each resting on a more dubious policy justification than the last. If we throw all these business tax expenditures into the pot, we can get into the right range for corporate tax rates. And if the rate itself falls squarely in the middle of world norms, the political case for all these distortive incentives dissolves.

The largest issue in corporate tax reform is what to do about international taxation. American multinational firms have established themselves as world leaders in global tax avoidance strategies, through the generation of what I have termed "stateless income."[30] The result is that many well-known US multinationals today enjoy single-digit effective tax rates on their foreign income.

Stateless income planning is not just about shifting profits from the United States to foreign tax havens, thereby depriving the United States of the tax revenues that should be associated with the value added work of US firms performed in the United States; it also (and this was underappreciated until recently) is about shifting profits from high-tax foreign jurisdictions to low-tax foreign jurisdictions. Business lobbyists like to present stateless income tax planning as required for "competitiveness" and similar buzzwords, but the fact is that there are no countries in the world where US multinationals both face significant numbers of real customers and have tax rates hovering around 5 percent. More important, there are large efficiency costs to a tax system that unintentionally encourages US firms to prefer investing in high-tax foreign jurisdictions over investing in the United States, because it turns out that for technical reasons it is easier to shift profits from high-tax foreign countries to tax havens than it is to shift profits from the United States to tax havens.[31]

The problem of stateless income planning is not unique to US multinationals, but we can take a perverse pride in the knowledge that US firms have been world leaders in developing the requisite tax technologies. The situation is now so out of control that in 2012 the G-20 group of countries deputized the Organisation for Economic Co-operation and Development to propose on an extremely accelerated timetable a concrete set of action plans to address what the OECD calls "Base Erosion and Profit Shifting" (BEPS) problems.

At the same time, US tax law (but not that of most other countries) effectively induces US multinational firms to keep their surplus low-taxed foreign profits in their foreign subsidiaries, because the US parent would be required to pay full US tax on the "repatriation" of those earnings (less a credit for any foreign income taxes already paid). As a result, by late 2013 US firms held about $2 trillion in so-called "permanently reinvested" offshore earnings.

It is a great overstatement, popular in the business press, to claim that this rule leads to "trapped cash," or that the repeal of current law would lead to a wave of business reinvestment in the United States. First, a US multinational's offshore cash hoard invariably is invested in the US economy, in the form of investments in dollar assets (US Treasury obligations, money market funds, commercial paper, and bank deposits). Second, as Apple Inc. demonstrated in 2013, there are ways of accessing offshore earnings without incurring a tax cost, starting with simply borrowing in the United States and using the earnings on offshore cash to pay the interest costs. Third, we in fact held a corporate offshore tax amnesty in 2004; more than $300 billion over and above the usual level came back to the United States from foreign subsidiaries of US firms. Most studies, however, have concluded that the cash went to prop up stock prices through stock buy-backs or dividends, not to invest in productive capacity (as the law nominally required). Nonetheless, there are efficiency costs to suboptimal allocations of offshore earnings, and as a result there is a bipartisan consensus that a revised corporate tax system should eliminate this defect.

What is needed, then, is a tax system that eliminates any US tax incentives to retain foreign profits in foreign subsidiaries, if the optimal uses of the funds are back in the United States, but that also addresses stateless income planning. My goals in my academic work in this area, and the OECD's goals in its BEPS project, simply stated, are that firms should report income in the jurisdiction to which that income has the strongest economic nexus. Such a rule would lead to a superior allocation of resources around the world, because tax planning would not drive the location of physical or financial assets, and because in the tug of war between multinational firms and fiscal authorities around the world, multinational firms would not keep all the marbles. In this regard, it is important to remember that corporate profits that end up being taxed nowhere require that the resulting tax revenue shortfalls must be shouldered by ordinary individuals in all the affected jurisdictions. Once a jurisdiction has decided that a corporate income tax makes sense (as basically all major jurisdictions have done), then it is important that the corporate tax system in fact reach the income it was nominally designed to burden.

There are two basic strategies for accomplishing these objectives. One is to adopt a "territorial" tax system, where a multinational group's genuine business profits earned outside the parent company's jurisdiction are not taxed again by the domicile of the parent company when the profits are repatriated; this model in turn must be accomplished with powerful anti-abuse measures. I summarize this approach as "territorial with teeth." The other strategy is for the domicile of a multinational group's parent firm to impose a reasonably low corporate tax rate, tax the worldwide profits of multinational groups on a consolidated basis (just as the public financial statements of those firms are prepared), and grant a tax credit against parent country tax liabilities for the income taxes paid by foreign subsidiaries. I call this a "full inclusion" method.

The territorial-with-teeth strategy is most consonant with world norms, but it is extremely difficult to implement anti-abuse rules that accomplish their intended purpose, and no more. The full inclusion method is closer to traditional US norms, is easier to implement, and is much more robust to creative tax planning shenanigans. Its "competitiveness" standing, however, rests entirely on the domicile of a multinational group choosing a moderate tax rate, by world norms. (One implication of this is that a jurisdiction that follows the full inclusion model effectively loses some control over where it sets its corporate tax rate.)

This is a classic Hobson's choice. Either approach, if taken seriously, would be a large step forward from current (2013) US corporate tax law. On balance, I have advocated the full inclusion approach, for the reasons developed in my academic papers referenced in the notes.

One encouraging development in this area—which, to emphasize, lies at the heart of corporate tax reform—came in late 2011, when Congressman Dave Camp, chairman of the House Ways and Means Committee, released a "discussion draft" for international corporate tax reform legislation. The release of a discussion draft was important as a process matter, because it meant that these technically complex proposals could be aired and debated by interested parties in an orderly manner, as opposed to the House Ways and Means Committee's prior penchant for releasing full-blown legislation essentially immediately before voting on it.[32] It was also important as a substantive matter, because while the draft (as expected) embraced a territorial tax regime, the draft disappointed many in the business community by recognizing that a territorial tax system must be accompanied by anti-abuse rules, and by proposing some. Those anti-abuse rules (known as Options A, B, and C) were not sufficiently robust in the form originally proposed, but the fact that serious anti-abuse rules were proposed at all was to my thinking the first signal that comprehensive bipartisan corporate tax reform was a realistic aspiration.

In late 2013, Senator Max Baucus, then the chairman of the Senate Finance Committee, responded with his own detailed and ambitious package of possible corporate international tax reforms. Chairman Baucus's proposal also was drafted in the alternative; apparently anxious to have the last word, he denominated his options as Option Y and Option Z. Option Y contemplated a territorial tax system, but relied on a relatively high US minimum (or "soak-up") tax on foreign income, under which foreign income would always be taxed at a rate no less than 80 percent of the US rate. Option Z was a variant on a full-inclusion system, except that only 60 percent of the income from bona fide foreign business activities directly conducted by foreign subsidiaries through their own personnel would be taxed in the United States.[33]

The United States is unique among major developed countries in that more than half of all US business income is earned by non-corporate business entities, such as partnerships and limited liability companies. This business income is treated as earned by, and therefore is taxed to, the owners of these unincorporated businesses. (By contrast, corporate profits are taxed to the corporation, and shareholders pay tax again—albeit at a preferential 20 percent rate—when corporate profits are distributed as dividends.) As a rule of thumb, publicly owned companies (US and foreign) must be treated for US tax purposes as corporations, so the unincorporated sector basically comprises private businesses—some of which can be very large.[34]

The existence of the large unincorporated domestic business sector has greatly complicated the politics of corporate tax reform. The problem has been the premise that, if Congress "does something" for corporations, it must do something by way of tax cuts for the unincorporated business sector as well. It is not difficult to see the logical errors in this claim. First, the reason to do something about corporate tax reform is that the corporate rate is too high relative to the world norms, and our international tax system is perverse, by anyone's measure. As a result, the United States is a less attractive environment for inbound investment than it should be, and we endure all the distortions attendant on our bizarre international tax system that were briefly summarized above. These issues are not particularly relevant to the domestic unincorporated business sector.[35] Second, the corporate tax is a two-stage tax: a corporate tax rate of 25 percent, and a dividend tax rate of 20 percent applied to after-corporate tax profits (i.e., 20 percent x 75 percent), yields a combined tax rate on currently distributed profits of 40 percent—just about the same as the tax rate on unincorporated businesses.

Third, if unincorporated firms wake up one morning and find that Congress has bestowed on corporations an attractive new tax regime, the unincorporated sector has a remedy—incorporate! It is tax-free to do so.

It is true that none of my logical objections responds to the political realities of the moment. I would turn this on its head, though, and observe that if we live in a world where political demands as conspicuously fatuous as these gain currency, we collectively need to invest a great deal more in educating ourselves about these issues, and in hiring a better class of legislator.

REALLY FUNDAMENTAL INCOME TAX REFORM

Capital Income Is the Problem

The other direction for fundamental reform, and the one more interesting to me in terms of my professional work, is to think about genuinely fundamental *income* tax reform.

There are only two important kinds of income: returns from labor and returns from capital. When tax law professors teach Tax 1, we like to discuss cases involving cash stuffed into a piano bought at a secondhand shop, or treasure trove, but these are not important contributors to economic output.

It turns out that we know a good deal about how to tax labor income, and in general do a pretty good job of it. But when it comes to taxing capital income, we perform very poorly. We are inconsistent in how we measure capital income, depending on the formal labels that different investments take, and we likewise are inconsistent in the tax rates we apply to that capital income that does come to our attention. More fundamentally, we do not have a coherent underlying theory of what we are trying to accomplish.

As described earlier in this book, "capital income" comprises all returns to capital, in the narrow, traditional sense of the term "capital."[36] The term is not synonymous with "capital gain"; the latter is just one instance of capital income. Capital income includes, by way of example, interest and dividend income, property rental income, and royalties, as well as capital gains.

Capital income also includes most net business income. Business firms of course bring both labor and capital to bear in generating net income; at least in the case of publicly held corporations, however, the labor component is fully compensated and deducted from the business tax base. As a result, the remaining business tax base contains only capital income. (The problem of the closely held business, where an owner-entrepreneur puts both her own capital and her labor to work, and where the net income of the firm cannot through simple inspection be divided into labor and capital income components, is considered below.)

Simply measuring capital income is famously difficult in theory, and nearly impossible in contemporary practice. To do so requires uprooting at least four deeply engrained practical hurdles in our tax system.

First, we must confront the "realization doctrine." This is the rule under which we tax profits from the sale of investments only in the year of sale, even though in an economic sense those profits accrue every day, and even though the remainder of our income tax is calculated on an annual basis. The realization doctrine in practice means that the taxation of capital gain—a very important instance of capital income—is essentially optional on the part of the taxpayer.

Second, we must deal with the different conceptual cubbyholes into which tax law places debt instruments (bonds, debentures, loans), on the one hand, and equity instruments (stock), on the other. By virtue of this largely artificial distinction, completely different income measurement tools apply to financial instruments that might be economically similar, but that give rise to different formal legal rights and obligations.

In essence, our rules for taxing investments fall into two categories: debt, and everything else. Returns on debt generally are measured fairly accurately and are taxed annually, regardless of whether paid out in cash. Moreover, interest expense is deducted by the obligor and included in income by the investor, so that the business profits of a firm used to service its debt are not taxed to the firm at all, but only to the investor (which in turn might well be a tax-exempt institution, so that the business income used to service that interest expense might in the end escape all taxation). Returns on many other investments (raw land, corporate stock) are not measured and taxed annually, except to the extent that cash is received (land rents or dividends). In turn, we do not coordinate at all the taxation of stock investors and the firms in which they invest.

This leads to the third challenge, which is that we must address the (non)coordination of firm- and investor-level measures of the same real incomes. Economists traditionally equate capital (and therefore the measurement of returns to capital) with "real" assets employed in a business, by which they mean investments in tangible, greasy machinery, or buildings, or land, or even intangible assets like patents, trademarks, or goodwill, but *not* financial assets such as stocks and bonds. In a more quotidian sense, however, capital income is earned in respect of investments in both real assets and financial assets that, in the broadest sense, are indirect claims on those real assets. Coordinating the taxation of returns to real and financial assets is one of the great challenges in designing a practical income tax on capital; progress here has not been helped by many economists' breezy dismissal of financial assets as unimportant to our thinking about capital income.

Fourth, we must address our arbitrary tax depreciation and expense capitalization rules. This sounds excessively tedious, even by the standards of this section of the book, but depreciation and capitalization go to the heart of whether capital income, in the form of net business profits on firm income tax returns, is accurately measured. The next section elaborates.

Even if we were to overcome the capital income measurement issues outlined above, we still would not have a complete approach to capital income tax reform. We would need to establish a theory to explain the rate(s) at which capital income is to be taxed. And, assuming that capital and labor incomes will be taxed at different rates (as is the case today, sometimes), we would face a new and important question: How do we distinguish the two? For example, an entrepreneurial chef decides to open a new restaurant. She invests her life's savings of $500,000, and works there 16 hours a day, six days a week, taking out no salary. Five years later, the restaurant is a great success, due in part to her culinary skill. What fraction of the current annual profits is attributable to her labor contributions and what to the capital she has invested?

This last point was particularly underappreciated until the controversy surrounding the taxation of "carried interest" received by investment fund managers forced our collective attention to the issue. (This refers to the shares of an investment partnership's capital gains that are awarded to fund managers in return for their agreement to run the investment partnership.) We need an administratively reliable means to distinguish labor from capital income in cases where the two are hopelessly intermingled.

Carried interest turns out not to be a difficult case; despite all the huffing and puffing on the issue, carried interest plainly is just labor income earned by investment managers for managing other people's capital; the fund manager's capital income, properly construed, is the income from his investment in developing his own management company. But the problem is pervasive in small businesses, where an owner–manager earns net business income attributable to the combination of her personal effort and the capital she puts at risk. So long as we apply different tax rules to labor income and capital income, this indissolubly intermingled income is likely to be characterized by taxpayers in whichever way minimizes their tax liabilities (these days, as capital income).

Fundamental income tax reform thus must accomplish two objectives. First, it must introduce what I call a "labor–capital income centrifuge," to tease apart labor and capital income when they are commingled in the hands of the small business owner–manager (or other cases). Second, a reform package must adopt a coherent theory of capital income taxation, and then measure returns to capital consistently, no matter the form of the business organization through which they are earned or the label of the financial instrument through which an investor holds her claim.

Decomposing Capital Income

Relatively recent academic work has brought new clarity to the understanding of the components of capital income. In turn, these academic insights can usefully be employed in designing a capital income tax base as part of genuinely fundamental income tax reform. In other words, the place to begin is by adopting a coherent theory of the economic components of capital income—not the formal labels we attach to returns on investment—and then developing administrable means to identify and tax those economic components at tax rates consistent with our economic theory.

Modern economic literature basically divides the returns to capital into three categories.[37] First are time-value-of-money returns (termed "normal" returns), which represent the core risk-free return from postponing consumption of one's wealth. To an economist, all capital earns this normal return. Second are risky returns, the higher returns that one expects to obtain for accepting the risk of uncertain rewards. (Actual risky returns, of course, may be negative in individual cases.) Finally, taxpayers also can earn what economists call "economic rents" or "inframarginal returns"—the supersized returns that come from a unique and exclusive market position or asset, such as a valuable patent or trade name.[38]

Rental income from renting an undeveloped lot for use as a parking lot typically would represent a normal return on one's capital; economic rents, by contrast, are jumbo returns that are not attributable simply to taking on lots of risk.

A well-designed *income* tax should systematically measure and tax normal returns—the dull, plodding, interest-like returns that one might expect to earn, for example, by investing in a savings account or a Treasury bond. Indeed, this is the key difference between a well-designed income tax and a consumption tax: by design, the former taxes time-value-of-money returns, whereas the latter exempts them from the tax base.[39]

In theory, both income taxes and consumption taxes burden economic rents, because in one case they are taxed as income and in the other those returns fund consumption (which is all that money is supposed to be good for). It is the normal return to savings—the compensation received for the delay in consumption from today until tomorrow—that an ideal income tax reaches but an ideal consumption tax does not.

And even more surprising, in theory neither an ideal income tax nor an ideal consumption tax imposes any burden on pure risk-taking. The theory is that you can always scale up your bet to reflect the tax hit (assuming losses are fully refundable). Many counterexamples might leap to mind (if I am already working full-time to run one restaurant, I can't just open a second one), but these counter-examples often in fact demonstrate a confusion between labor and capital income, not a bona fide example of being unable to increase an investment wager.

It turns out that the current tax code does an absolutely terrible job measuring normal returns, perhaps reflecting the modest understanding of the importance of taxing these returns when the tax model was first constructed some 100 years ago. More surprisingly, however, systematically measuring and taxing these time-value returns are much more difficult than they appear. Much of the complexity of any business income tax stems from this fact.

If one focuses exclusively on real assets and economic concepts of income, then, by definition, an investment in a "marginal" asset is one that generates net economic income each year equal to the normal return applied to the investor's unrecovered investment.[40] This almost self-evident observation means that, in a world consisting entirely of direct equity-funded investments in real assets, one would calculate normal returns on investment—and taxable business income—solely through economically accurate depreciation schedules. This thought in turn is surprising to many non-economists, who associate time-value-of-money concepts exclusively with financial instruments, and who think of depreciation as some arbitrary allowance that is wholly unrelated to measuring an investor's normal returns.

An income tax system will properly measure and tax time-value-of-money (normal) returns on real assets only if two conditions are satisfied. First, the tax system must develop comprehensive rules to capitalize, rather than deduct, expenditures that create or enhance the value of a real asset (for example, expenditures to build a factory or to establish a brand name). This problem is pervasive in the current tax system, where, for example, all advertising expenses are currently deductible, even if they are incurred to develop a valuable brand name.

Second, the tax system must permit recovery of the cost of such investments through economic depreciation schedules—that is, schedules that comport with the actual depreciation in value of those assets from year to year. Viewed from this perspective, accelerated depreciation systems "encourage" overinvestment in real assets for the simple reason that, by design, they undertax the returns from those investments relative to economic measures of income.[41]

Unfortunately for this simple presentation, taxpayers do not invest their capital exclusively in real assets; they also acquire financial assets, such as stocks, bonds, options, and other, more obscure instruments. As described earlier, economists sometimes ignore financial assets as background noise, on the theory that financial assets in the aggregate are simply indirect claims against all the real capital invested in business. No practical income tax system, however, ignores financial assets. The current tax code therefore taxes businesses on the returns derived from capital invested in real assets (through capitalization and depreciation rules) and taxes households on the income derived from capital invested in financial assets.[42]

As briefly described above, one very difficult challenge in designing an income tax system that properly measures capital income is to coordinate and allocate tax liabilities at these two different levels—the financial investor holding financial capital instruments and the business enterprise investing in real assets and earning net business income—to advance the fundamental objective of imposing a single comprehensive and constant tax burden on normal returns. The current tax system fails utterly in this critical exercise.

There is no simple answer to the coordination and allocation dilemma, although virtually every possible permutation has been explored. Yet the exercise of coordination and allocation between investors holding financial assets and business enterprises holding real assets is critically important if the resulting system is to be economically neutral—that is, if it is to impose a comparable tax burden on all returns to capital, regardless of the form in which an investment is made.

As a starting point, whatever the tax rate structure that may be agreed on, a coherent capital income tax would burden all "normal" returns (the basic "return to waiting," or the time value of money) at a consistent rate, regardless of the legal form in which that income is earned. For risky returns, economists argue that the most important consideration is to treat losses as symmetrically as possible with gains, so as to avoid a systematic bias in the tax law against risk-taking. The actual rate here is less important, because again investors can just scale up their bets (in theory) to put themselves in the same after-tax position as if the tax had not been imposed. And finally, supersized returns also must all be taxed at a consistent rate, regardless of the legal form in which that income is earned. As a logical matter, however, that rate need not be the same as the rate imposed on normal returns.

But at What Rate?

The foregoing discussion decomposed capital income into three constituent elements (normal returns, risky returns, and economic rents), but did not answer the obvious question, at what rate should they be taxed? And how should that rate relate to tax rates on labor income? Put risky returns to one side, on the theory that symmetry between gains and losses is more important than nominal rate. That leaves us with normal returns and economic rents.

Economists are surprisingly cheerful about high taxes on economic rents. The theory is very simple—these are supersized returns not generally available in the market. They are neither replicable nor scalable. An owner is thrilled to receive economic rents, and so long as she is left after taxes with more than she could get by way of normal returns, the theory goes, why should she complain?

From the other direction, and although the consensus is not quite as complete here, most economists are uncomfortable with taxing normal returns at high rates, including rates as high as the rates imposed on labor income. At the same time, risk-adjusted normal returns should form the bulk of returns on capital, so getting the rate on normal returns right is arguably even more important than squeezing the last dollar of tax revenues out of economic rents.

For a great many reasons of administrative efficiency and political economy, I believe that the right place to begin in designing an income tax on capital is by adopting a "dual income tax" of the sort actually employed by some of the Nordic countries at one point or another in the recent past. Dual income tax systems are income taxes that explicitly reject the ideal of a single rate of tax on all income from whatever source derived, and instead impose different rates on capital income, on the one hand, and all other income (principally, labor income), on the other. Typically, a dual income tax adopts a relatively low flat rate of tax on capital income, and progressive rates on labor income, where the highest labor income rate is materially greater than the flat capital income rate, but other rate structures are possible.

The hallmark of a "dual income tax" is its two-pronged schedular design, under which all capital income (or at least any normal return) is taxed more lightly than is labor income.[43] Norway has been the leader in designing dual income taxes; it has implemented different systems that alternatively have taxed all capital income at one flat rate, or that more recently have taxed normal returns at a low rate while endeavoring to tax economic rents at basically the top rate on labor income.[44]

There are good reasons to adopt what might be thought of as "first generation" dual income tax principles. Under this approach, all returns to capital
would be taxed at one low flat rate, while labor income would be taxed at increasing marginal rates to a top rate considerably higher than the capital income
tax—say, 25 percent in one case and 40 percent in the other. (Technically, capital income of taxpayers whose marginal tax bracket is lower than 25 percent
would be taxed at the lower rate, but it turns out that capital income, because it
appertains to capital, is highly concentrated among the affluent.) By doing so,
the dual income tax implements a tolerable compromise that avoids drawing
a line between normal returns and rents. The theory of normal returns, risky
returns, and rents is beguiling, but telling one from another in practice is a difficult undertaking.

Many economists believe that the income tax itself is a flawed norm, and
that economic efficiency can be enhanced (without impairing equity concerns)
by adopting a progressive consumption tax as the US model.[45] As previously
explained, a consumption tax does not burden normal returns (the basic returns
on investment that compensate for deferring consumption from today to the
future). A low flat-rate income tax on normal returns can be understood as moving in the direction of a consumption tax, even if such a system does not fully
achieve all the purported efficiency ends of a consumption tax. Importantly, a low
flat-rate tax on normal returns does so while largely avoiding the extraordinarily
difficult transition issues that would be raised by the replacement of our capital
income tax with a consumption tax.[46]

A low flat-rate tax on normal returns might cynically be described as a
Solomonic compromise between two warring camps divided over whether a positive tax on normal returns to capital is desirable. It is fairer, however, to see the
underlying principle at work as a recognition that capital and labor income are
sufficiently different that a desirable tax scheme for one is not necessarily optimal
for the other, and that the best evidence to date argues in general for moderation
in the taxation of capital income.[47]

The logical alternative is to argue that economic rents, like labor income, in fact
can bear a higher tax rate than normal returns, and that the right move here is to
ensure that economic rents are exposed to full labor-income marginal rates. This
alternative is consistent with economic logic, and in fact was the basis for the most
recent (2006) revision of the Norwegian dual income tax system, but raises many
difficulties.[48] Among other problems, it inadvertently would lose some efficiency,
by exposing risky returns to asymmetrical after-tax outcomes, as when years of
small losses lead to one hugely successful investment, and it would greatly complicate the novel but perfectly feasible approach to taxing capital income that I outline below. Such a move also has obvious political economy problems, in light of
global trends in headline corporate rates.

We start from a place where capital income often is untaxed, or taxed at wildly different effective rates. To move to a world where all capital income is taxed consistently would be an enormous accomplishment; if doing so required undertaxing economic rents somewhat, I would argue that the result still would be good enough for government work.

THE DUAL BUSINESS ENTERPRISE INCOME TAX

Because capital income taxation long ago fell out of academic favor, very little work has been done in recent decades in rethinking how we might better define the capital income tax base. Moreover, some of the leading capital income tax reform ideas that have been proposed, such as the Comprehensive Business Income Tax (CBIT) proposed by the US Treasury Department in 1992, assume away the problem by assuming that the tax base (e.g., corporate net income) is accurately measured and presenting the issue as simply one of coordination between firms and investors.

It is possible to do better. That is the purpose of the Dual Business Enterprise Income Tax (Dual BEIT).[49] The "dual" part of the name reflects the proposal's debt to Nordic dual income taxes. As just described, their fundamental insight was that there is no economic or policy reason to assume that an ideal income tax would burden labor income and capital income under the identical rate schedule. The Business Enterprise Income Tax, or BEIT (pronounced "bite," like a tax bite) part, is the mechanism I developed to introduce a feasible system for taxing capital income at that flat rate in a consistent manner.

A dual income tax, in which capital income is taxed more lightly than labor income, brings squarely to the front the necessity of developing a new tax tool, the labor–capital income centrifuge, to tease apart labor and capital income when they are commingled in the hands of a small business owner–manager (or other cases). Having done so, a dual income tax must be implemented in a way that measures returns to capital consistently, no matter the form of the business organization through which they are earned or the label of the financial instrument through which an investor holds her claim.

Nordic dual income tax systems point toward one answer to the question of tax rates, and further resolve a specific element in defining the capital income tax base, which is the separation of capital income from the labor–capital matrix in which it often is found in nature. But dual income tax systems do not assure that capital income is measured accurately.[50] That is, other than in the one area of segregating capital from labor income, dual income tax systems by themselves do not define the capital income base. That is the purpose of the BEIT part of things.

A Labor–Capital Income Centrifuge

An explicit dual income tax—that is, any regime that taxes capital income at one rate and labor income at another—requires a labor–capital income centrifuge to divide business income between labor and capital components in those cases where the suppliers of labor and capital cannot be relied on to specify those returns accurately by themselves. Given the shoddy work we have made of the issue in the past, a mechanical solution of the sort adopted (at least for a period of time) by the Nordic countries, in which a reasonable return to capital is imputed and the remaining income treated as labor income, can hardly be faulted as inexcusably imprecise.[51] Moreover, the solution is self-assessable and universally applicable.

The idea of the labor–capital income centrifuge is straightforward. In those cases where markets cannot be expected reliably to separate labor from capital income—that is, in the case of closely held private companies—an owner–manager of a firm determines the portion of her total returns that are attributable to her capital invested in the firm by multiplying that capital by a fraction (which typically could be determined by a formula tied to one-year government securities); the result would be deemed the return to capital, and the remainder deemed the return to her labor. Actual Nordic implementations rapidly grew more complex, for example to deal with whether the asset base should be a net or gross asset concept and how to determine when a company was sufficiently closely held as to invoke the labor–capital income centrifuge, but as these questions have been considered in great detail elsewhere, they will not be repeated here.[52]

A New Measure of the Capital Income Base

The BEIT is a novel proposal for measuring capital income much more accurately than has been true in the past, but it has only a handful of new components, built on top of existing income tax concepts.

Here is a high-level view of how the BEIT would work. For simplicity, I present the BEIT as it would apply to a public company in which, by hypothesis, labor and capital income have already been teased apart through market pricing of labor inputs. The principles can be extended to closely held private firms as well, with the introduction of a labor–capital income centrifuge and other adaptations.

The BEIT adopts two novel strategies. First, unlike other comprehensive income tax proposals, the BEIT splits the taxation of returns to capital by taxing time value of money (normal) returns only at the *investor* level, while taxing extraordinary returns at the *business enterprise* level. By doing so, the BEIT sidesteps the problems that plague CBIT and similar comprehensive entity-only income tax proposals, all of which accurately tax normal returns only if they get economic depreciation precisely right.

Second, the BEIT seeks to reduce the realization principle to its smallest possible component. By taxing normal returns to investors rather than business enterprises, the BEIT takes advantage of the intuition that financial investments turn over more rapidly than do noninventory real assets, so that the *base* for determining normal returns is closer to the economic ideal. For the same reasons, the BEIT repeals numerous exceptions to the recognition of income and requires mandatory income accruals with respect to normal returns. The result is a system where reported taxable income tracks economic income much more closely than under current law.

The BEIT requires only a few new operative rules to accomplish these results. First, all business enterprises are taxed as entities. Second, firm-level interest deductions are disallowed and replaced by a new Cost of Capital Allowance (COCA). The annual COCA rate is set by statute at a formula rate that varies with one-year Treasury rates. A firm's annual COCA deduction is simply its adjusted basis in its assets multiplied by the COCA rate. Thus, the COCA deduction is available regardless of whether a firm's real assets are financed with debt or equity.

The effect of the COCA allowance is that the BEIT at the *firm* level operates as a consumption tax, in which normal returns are tax-free and only net risky returns and economic rents are taxed. The BEIT operates as a consumption tax because the COCA deduction in respect of a firm's unrecovered investment in its assets (its tax basis in those assets) has the same present value as an immediate deduction for capital investment (assuming the COCA rate is set properly). This means in turn that the value of the COCA deduction is unaffected by tax depreciation schedules; Congress can meddle as much as it chooses without changing the economic burden of the tax to a firm. A similar economic result could be achieved by simply allowing the expensing of all capital investment, but the COCA mechanism has a number of practical advantages over that approach.

Third, investors include in income annually an amount equal to the same COCA rate multiplied by *their* adjusted tax basis in their investments (the Includible Amount). They do so regardless of whether they receive cash returns from their investment in a given year. Includible Amounts function much like the rules governing original issue discount for debt instruments under current tax law: the investor's tax basis goes up by the amount of her Includible Amount and down in respect of cash received on her investment (e.g., dividends or interest). Cash returns thus are relevant only insofar as they affect an investor's remaining adjusted tax cost in her investment.

The COCA inclusion at the investor level means that investors are taxed on the normal returns to their investments every year. In more formal terms, the BEIT is designed to tax economic rents and risky returns from business enterprises at the firm level and "normal" returns to capital at the investor level. The aggregate result is that all the components of capital income are taxed once, and only once.

In other words, the BEIT adds an investor-level tax on normal returns on top of a firm-level consumption tax. The combination of the two amounts to a unified income tax on capital (which by definition burdens normal returns as well as economic rents and risky returns). It is this allocation of returns (normal returns only to investors; rents and risky returns to firms) and the use of the COCA mechanism to accomplish these results that are the novel contributions of the BEIT.

In comparative tax law terms, the BEIT can be explained at the firm level as a superior implementation of an Allowance for Corporate Equity (ACE) system of the sort actually adopted by some European countries, because unlike ACE systems, the BEIT offers the same deduction (the COCA) regardless of whether real assets are financed with debt or equity.[53] The BEIT thus removes the temptation to issue equity-flavored debt instruments, which still remains in ACE systems where the "interest" rate on the hybrid instrument exceeds the ACE allowance.

The BEIT achieves neutrality in other dimensions as well. It taxes all business operations identically (by taxing enterprises, regardless of legal form, consistently). Second, it renders tax objectives irrelevant to the choice of an issuer's capital structure because the capital the issuer employs, not the security issued, determines its cost of capital allowance. Similarly, the tax liabilities of investors are driven by the capital they invest and the cash returns they earn, not the label of the instruments they hold.

Finally, the BEIT, although an income tax, offers corporate managers a consumption tax environment in which to conduct business. This in turn can be used to advantage in integrating the BEIT with a worldwide tax consolidation approach to business enterprise taxation going forward. This should resonate with managers who today express concern about international "competitiveness," and further means that those managers will be able to pursue acquisitions and divestitures without regard to substantial tax consequences. (The papers referenced in the notes elaborate on these themes.)

The BEIT is exactly the right move for making the United States an attractive place for foreign as well as domestic investors to invest. Because foreign investors in US corporations will face a domestic corporate consumption tax, those investors will enjoy the benefits of the reduction in business tax burdens. And at the same time, US resident investors will bear the full burden of capital income tax on the normal returns to all their investments, wherever located. Since the capital of multinational firms is generally held to be much more mobile than the residence of individual citizens of the United States, the result will be a more attractive environment for investment in the United States and a reduction in the impetus to move capital out of the United States.[54]

To summarize, for a tax system that purports to tax capital income and that could in fact be implemented in a large modern economy, the BEIT does a remarkably good job. Most fundamentally, it taxes all capital income once, and only once, without cumbersome (and frequently abused) integration schemes or the like. Economic rents are taxed to the enterprise and normal returns to investors. By definition, the BEIT eliminates the debt–equity distinction, neutralizes the importance of different depreciation or capitalization regimes, automatically coordinates firm-level and investor-level incomes, and mitigates (but does not wholly eliminate) the consequences of the realization doctrine. What is more, the BEIT moves a large fraction of capital income to the level of investors, rather than firms, a development that has important helpful ramifications in light of the relative international mobility of capital compared to people. For all these reasons, the BEIT is an extremely attractive vehicle for imposing a successful capital income tax.

At the same time, the BEIT by itself is largely agnostic about tax rates. The concept originally was conceived primarily as a vehicle for the accurate measurement of capital income, and it can be adjusted to tax normal returns, on the one hand, and rents and risky returns, on the other, at the same or different rates, which rates in turn can be the same as, or different from, those applied to labor income. Dual income tax principles and the BEIT thus are complementary. The former offer a device for accurately teasing apart labor and capital income in those cases where they otherwise form an indissoluble matrix and a theoretical hook from which to hang a reasoned view of the appropriate tax burden on all capital income. The BEIT picks up from there, and ensures that all capital income is taxed once, and only once, through its consistent and comprehensive design of the tax base.

CHAPTER 14

WE ARE BETTER THAN THIS

In this [last part of my] book I have endeavored to show, first, what are the necessary expences of the sovereign, or commonwealth; which of those expences ought to be defrayed by the general contribution of the whole society; and which of them, by that of some particular part only, or of some particular members of it: secondly, what are the different methods in which the whole society may be made to contribute towards defraying the expences incumbent on the whole society, and what are the principal advantages and inconveniencies of each of those methods: and, thirdly and lastly, what are the reasons and causes which have induced almost all modern governments to mortgage some part of this revenue, or to contract debts, and what have been the effects of those debts upon the real wealth, the annual produce of the land and labour of the society.

—ADAM SMITH, *The Wealth of Nations*, Introduction and Plan of the Work.

MOVING FORWARD

Readers may be disappointed by the modesty of my substantive recommendations. I contemplate tax revenues and federal government spending levels roughly commensurate with those at the end of the Clinton administration, which most readers of this book lived through and emerged unscathed. I do not propose replacing the income tax with a value added tax, or anything else. I do not have in my back pocket a 10-point plan to reform the delivery of healthcare services in the United States, recommendations on the number of nuclear aircraft carriers the Navy should deploy, or proposals to rewrite any of our income support programs. What is the explanation for this uncharacteristic modesty in expression and ambition?

One answer is that I am not an expert simultaneously in military strategy, healthcare institutions, and all the other topics to which this book has adverted. I respect the work of genuine experts in the field, and defer to them on technical questions of how government's work in their respective disciplines can be enhanced. The more fundamental answer, however, is that the United States of America is not broken. Our fundamental fiscal health is not in crisis. Our challenges are real, but highly tractable. What we collectively require are, first, better information; second, a more holistic approach to public debates on fiscal policy, by which I mean that our emphasis should be on the consequences of fiscal policies in the aggregate; and third, a broader understanding of the obligations and opportunities to which government can respond on behalf of the entirety of the citizenry of the United States.

The United States remains the largest and most dynamic economy in the world. Our outstanding federal debt grew substantially during the Great Recession, but that is exactly what our fiscal automatic stabilizers were designed to do. Our national income is more than adequate to service that debt, and to begin paying it back down. Our only crises in this regard are those we choose to artificially impose on ourselves through a political process dominated by fear, sloganeering, and misinformation.

Our current wealth and future prosperity are driven primarily by private markets. No sensible person disagrees with that. But markets are not perfectly complete everywhere, all the time, and as a result government has critically important complementary roles to play, as an investor in our infrastructure and our fellow citizens, and as an insurer against the worst vicissitudes of life.

This book has examined how we are doing in investing in ourselves, and in offering coherent social insurance programs. The answer is not very well. We starve ourselves of investment in infrastructure, and we underinsure ourselves in many respects. The result is a less happy society, to return to Adam Smith's injunction to us, and also a less prosperous one. Well-designed social insurance programs increase our appetite for economic risk, rather than depress it, and public infrastructure investments yield positive economic returns, just as private investments do. These are the functions that our government is good at and to which this book has been addressed. Once one moves beyond police powers and the like, what we call government spending and taxing in many respects is really investing and insuring, with those investments and insurance premiums collected through the mechanism of taxation.

The book has further considered whether we have reached some natural limit on our ability to finance collective investment and insurance through the intermediation of government. The answer is no. We face budget deficit issues today because we have chosen systematically to undertax ourselves since 2001, not because the engine of our economy cannot supply any more revenues than those we currently collect.

In short, for the last decade or more we have allowed the existence of deficits to determine the contours of our government spending—the uses to which we put our government. This is backward. What this book has urged is that the right way to think about things is to ask this question: What investment and insurance opportunities are there for all of us, acting together, to advance the happiness of our society? In answering this question, we need to be mindful of a great many dynamics—the frustration and unhappiness that comes with paying taxes, the deadweight loss of taxation, the estimated positive economic and social returns on that collective spending, the limited competencies of government agencies, and so on. But the starting point in every case should not be determined by establishing an arbitrarily small amount of tax to collect, and then treating government like an institutional Procrustes, whose only responsibility it is to amputate the welfare of our fellow citizens to suit that amount.

We cannot embrace every generous impulse, because in many cases the return on investment, in the broadest sense, is too low, relative to its social and economic costs. But by looking at the actual state of economic health of millions of Americans (not to mention their physical health), by comparing the US experience to the mix of public goods furnished by other developed economies, and by reviewing the economic literature on the deadweight loss of taxation, the inescapable conclusion emerges that we can do better for our fellow citizens, which in the long run also means doing better for ourselves.

There is an important predicate underlying this conclusion that compilations of data and economic research cannot teach, because it is a point of elementary civics. This predicate is that all of us who are citizens of this great country are in it together, and that our national policies must reflect the understanding that the happiness of our society depends on the collective happiness of all of us. Our political liberties generally are secure and unthreatened, except in the off-kilter imaginations of some or in the impulse to suppress the political rights of those Americans who are thought to be inadequately propertied to exercise their constitutional political rights. What is more generally threatened is the recognition that all of us stand on equal footing as citizens.

This book has argued that the contrary view, encapsulated as market triumphalism, is a flawed pastiche of abstract economic nostrums and unhealthy political claims. It is the marriage of a belief in the infallibility of private market outcomes and the claim that our political liberties depend on laissez-faire economic policies. But markets are not always perfect, market freedoms and political freedoms are not identical, and political liberties can exist without the most fundamentalist sort of laissez-faire policies as a prerequisite.

Market triumphalists' imaginations run riot, in directions that are simultaneously paranoid and self-centered. They see around the corner the impending collapse of social order, always predicated on the same anti-democratic instinct: the shirtless and rootless masses (all of whom happen to be fellow citizens) will fasten on the taxing power as the way to take from the rich and give to themselves, thereby killing the golden goose while grabbing a few eggs. This is why market triumphalist rhetoric is so fixated on taxation, to the exclusion of the goods that taxation purchases. But as billionaire philanthropist Eli Broad recently pointed out, "We are the only country in the developed world without large national labor or socialist parties, and it's unlikely that many Americans ever are going to be converted to the notion that it's sinful to be wealthy. What we all need to continue to believe, and to act on, is the conviction that it's wrong and socially destructive for the rich to forget those who still can use a hand up."[1]

At every turn, market triumphalists seek to impugn the genuine political rights and liberties of others and to paint themselves as the intended victims of self-defeating "leveling down." The result is that they are quick to sacrifice their fellow citizens' claims to genuine equality of opportunity, as reflected, for example, in comparable levels of investment in their children's health and education. They do this by denying the legitimacy of government investment or insurance in general and by claiming that all existing programs are marked by irredeemable design flaws, administrative incompetence, and participant fraud.

Very recently, for example, Richard Epstein, some of whose views have already been described, wrote an extraordinary commentary effectively claiming that the Constitution prohibits public investment or insurance programs. As discussed in chapter 2, the Constitution provides that "[t]he Congress shall have Power to lay and collect Taxes,... to pay the Debts and provide for the common Defence and general Welfare of the United States." Epstein wrote:

> The clause is not a catchall that sweeps in every objective under the sun. Federal taxes are meant to fund only a short list of public—i.e. nonexcludable—goods that only the central government can provide....
>
> The proper interpretation of the clause raises thorny questions about whether, for example, the United States could provide disaster relief that benefits some but not all states. President Grover Cleveland thought that the answer was an emphatic "no" in 1887 when he vetoed the Texas Seed Bill, which allocated $10,000 for Texas drought relief. Under the Constitution, he did "not believe that the power and duty of the General Government ought to be extended to the relief of individual suffering which is in no manner properly related to the public service or benefit."
>
> Indeed, the vital element in this clause is that it prohibits any transfer payment from one group of individuals to another, as those cannot serve the "general welfare of the United States."[2]

Grover Cleveland is not often proffered as a paragon of constitutional interpretive genius, and in the period since 1887 we have witnessed hundreds of disaster relief acts and similar legislation that have contradicted his claims. But more fundamentally, Epstein misapprehends both the taxing power and the meaning of the "general welfare of the United States."

People like Epstein recoil at the taxing power because it is in fact constitutionally unconstrained, within the bounds of rationality (and a few trivial limits), and the only remedy for oppressive taxation is to vote the rascals out. The Supreme Court made this point, for example, in 1888—the year following Grover Cleveland's veto of the Texas Seed Bill:

> The judicial department cannot prescribe to the legislative department limitations upon the exercise of its acknowledged powers. The power to tax may be exercised oppressively upon persons; but the responsibility of the legislature is not to the courts, but to the people by whom its members are elected.[3]

Many other cases since have made essentially the same point.

No one's welfare is enhanced by having resources simply taken away (the tax side in the abstract). As a result, there is no general welfare advanced through taxation viewed in the abstract, other than the oddball Pigovian tax case (that is, a tax aimed at curing a market negative externality, like pollution). Moreover, money is fungible: tax A cannot logically be said to fund Spending B, because taxes all flow into one pot, whence funds are disbursed on spending programs. (Even the so-called trust funds operate in this manner, as chapter 6 explained.) The Constitution's reference to the "general welfare of the United States" therefore logically describes its third power enumerated in the quoted sentence, which is to spend the money raised by taxes in ways that provide for the country's general welfare.[4]

Epstein claims that the Constitution's grant of Congressional power "prohibits any transfer payment from one group of individuals to another, as those cannot serve the 'general welfare of the United States.'" But to write this is to deny both Supreme Court jurisprudence and the meaning of "insurance," unless his only point is the trivial one of reminding readers that taxes must first flow into the Treasury, and then out to a group of individuals, rather than being forcibly paid directly from one group to another.[5] Only some insureds have insurance claims in any given year, but *every* insured benefits from the existence of that insurance. This is why Grover Cleveland was wrong in 1887, and why there was so much well-deserved anger at those members of Congress who sought to block the Hurricane Sandy relief bill: the federal government of the United States offers, through disaster relief and similar measures, de facto disaster insurance to all regions of the United States. And more directly, the "transfer payments" that

Epstein finds offensive in fact are social insurance programs from which all of us, even Epstein, benefit, because the programs exist for all of us, should our circumstances change.

So, too, government investment enhances the welfare of all, regardless of its geographic location. Does anyone seriously claim that the Hoover Dam did not enhance the general welfare of the entire country, even though most of us do not live in Nevada or Arizona, which it straddles? Similarly, Congress determined that the investments in the financial sector at the height of the financial crisis, or the investments in the automobile sector, would advance the welfare of the entire United States; having made that good faith determination, at that point the constitutional criteria were satisfied.

Market triumphalists lie awake nights waiting for the mobs to tax them into penury—and yet it has never happened. Our democracy is in this respect more functional than market triumphalists give it credit for. And by the same token, the market triumphalist agenda is fundamentally more anti-democratic than is generally perceived. It is their success in disguising their self-centered, slightly paranoid, and anti-democratic impulses behind the garb of concerned deficit hawks or protectors of our moral backbones from the siren call of cushy unemployment benefits that make them the villains in the story I have told.

THE PURSUIT OF HAPPINESS

I began this book by summarizing the moral philosophy of Adam Smith, a man who has become the adopted mascot of a contemporary social movement that would disgust him. As chapter 2 developed, Smith understood the human inclination to strive for more things, but also understood the ultimate futility of this as an ordering principle for a life well led. To Smith, "happiness" was the goal of life, a sentiment shared generally with other eighteenth-century Enlightenment scholars.[6] But happiness did not mean whatever floats your boat, to put things in a more modern idiom. To Smith, happiness was a long-term state of tranquility, obtained "through moral education, habituation in moral rules, and a reasonable arrangement of social institutions and life,"[7] which when generally practiced yielded a society dominated by "the general prevalence of wisdom and virtue."[8]

Closer to home, Thomas Jefferson worked squarely within this then-contemporary focus on happiness as an ordering principle of life, and incorporated it into our Declaration of Independence, when he wrote, "We hold these truths to be self-evident: that all men are created equal; that they are endowed by their creator with unalienable rights; that among these are . . . the pursuit of happiness." The Declaration continued, that "it is the Right of the People . . . to institute new Government, laying its foundation on such principles and organizing its powers in such form, as to them shall seem most likely to effect their Safety and Happiness."

Jefferson did not choose the term "happiness" at random. Among other sources, he appears to have read *The Theory of Moral Sentiments* closely, and in fact recommended Smith's book in a famous reading list that Jefferson prepared for his brother-in-law, Robert Skipwith, in 1771.[9] And his emphasis that a new government should be constituted so as to be most likely to effect its citizens' happiness certainly echoes Smith's statement in *The Theory of Moral Sentiments* that governments "are valued only in proportion as they tend to promote the happiness of those who live under them. That is their sole use and end."[10]

Many scholars have considered the influence of *The Wealth of Nations* on post-Revolutionary American thinkers, including Jefferson.[11] (That book, of course, was first published in London in 1776, and therefore had no influence on Jefferson's worldview at the time of the Declaration.) *The Theory of Moral Sentiments* has not received as much attention. Nonetheless, the book was widely known in pre-Revolutionary America. For example, a New York bookseller listed it for sale in 1761 (two years after its first publication in England), and a comprehensive survey of American libraries found the book in 17 out of 92 pre-Revolutionary booklists.[12] This might not sound like a very broad dissemination, but in fact only a handful of contemporary moral philosophy books were more widely held; Hume's *Essays* appeared in only a few more lists; Hutcheson's *A System of Moral Philosophy* in a few less.

Perhaps the best window into the importance of *The Theory of Moral Sentiments* to pre-Revolutionary American thinkers is a strange pamphlet published in 1764 by Arthur Lee, one of six American patriot brothers from Virginia.[13] Lee lived a large portion of his life in Europe; he earned a medical degree at Edinburgh and a law degree in London. Lee was a well-known advocate in England for the colonies' rights before the Revolution, and was one of three American commissioners (along with Benjamin Franklin) representing the interests of the United States in Paris during the Revolutionary War, where in the standard accounts he proved himself to be thoroughly disagreeable and unable to work with Franklin.

Lee's 1764 pamphlet, written while he lived in London, was titled *An Essay in Vindication of the Continental Colonies of America from the Censure of Mr Adam Smith, in His Theory of Moral Sentiments.*[14] It was a response to a passage in *The Theory of Moral Sentiments* in which Smith described African slaves in the colonies as possessing "a degree of magnanimity, which the soul of his sordid master is scarce capable of conceiving. Fortune never exerted more cruelly her empire over mankind, than when she subjected those nations of heroes to the refuse of the jails of Europe...." In response, Lee penned an argument that was intended to defend the honor of Americans of European descent; in doing so, Lee produced a document that was simultaneously vilely racist and a call for the elimination of slavery (on the theory that slavery corroded the moral fiber of the slave owner).

What is interesting about Lee's otherwise rightly forgotten pamphlet is that Lee begins by apologizing for having taken so long to respond to Smith, whose book had first been published four years earlier: this speaks to the importance generally accorded to *The Theory of Moral Sentiments*. More directly, Lee writes of Smith's book: "[Smith's] ingenious theory of morals has, very deservedly, gained the world's esteem; and I am sorry it should contain anything so unworthy of its general character. I am sorry, because I admire it, and wish I could have esteemed its author."[15] In short, *The Theory of Moral Sentiments* was a book that educated Americans read in the 1760s and 1770s, and it is perfectly plausible to imagine that Jefferson, among others, found in it some inspiration for his own applied moral philosophy.[16]

It often is claimed that Jefferson's famous phrase in the Declaration of Independence guarantees only the right to "pursue" happiness—rather like chasing a butterfly—not to obtain it, and therefore that the Constitution guarantees only equality of opportunity. From this, the conclusion somehow is drawn that modern social insurance programs are unnecessary, apparently because they create too much undeserved happiness. This common claim is an anachronism, of course, as Jefferson's sentiment did not appear in the Constitution at all. More important, and as this book has been at pains to develop, equality of opportunity often does not exist in our society, as when we inexplicably make public investments in the education of children in direct rather than inverse proportion to their family's affluence. But it nonetheless is worth considering for a minute what Jefferson might have been driving at, as a way of connecting the American political tradition back to Smith's important work on moral philosophy.

The academic "pursuit of happiness" literature is vast, and includes at least two books dedicated entirely to the phrase's history and explication.[17] It turns out that the phrase is straightforward to interpret, except for the words "pursuit" and "happiness." Actually, that oversimplifies matters—in Jefferson's context, scholars also disagree about "we hold" and "self-evident."[18] The literature is complicated by a larger debate over the extent to which Jefferson's Declaration is inspired almost entirely by John Locke's emphasis on natural rights and the political philosophy of "liberalism"—meaning respect for an individual's autonomous decisions—or whether there is also a flavor of classical "republicanism" at work—meaning the state as a paramount entity, in whose governance citizens participate, whose civic values are inculcated through education and social mores, and through which citizens realize their full potential.[19] I wish only to make two points.

First, "pursuit" does not have to mean a chase for an ethereal will-o'-the-wisp. When we play the game Trivial Pursuit, we use the word in its alternative meaning, of a current avocation (or in this context, a pastime)—a path or practice on which we currently are embarked. Arthur Schlesinger, among others, through careful consideration of then-contemporary uses of the word, convincingly argued that Jefferson used "pursuit" in this sense of a current practice, not a distant hope.[20] As Schlesinger points out, the same long sentence in the Declaration in which the phrase "the pursuit of happiness" appears concludes with the statement that it is a government's present duty to the governed "to effect their safety and happiness." If your guru tells you to "follow your bliss," she is sending you on a voyage of self-discovery, in which the voyage is the point. So, perhaps, also with "pursuit."

Second, Jefferson probably used "happiness" in ways close to Smith's use of the term, as a state of tranquility reached through a life of virtue. In 1819, Jefferson wrote to a friend and neighbor, William Short, of his admiration for the philosophy of Epicurus ("I too am an Epicurean"), and attached to that letter a distillation of what he took to be the essence of Epicureanism, which he identified as having been prepared around 1789—admittedly, after the Declaration, but nonetheless at a time that sheds some light on his thinking. His bullet-point summary of the moral philosophy of Epicurus began:

Moral [Philosophy] —

- Happiness is the aim of life.
- Virtue the foundation of happiness.
- Utility the test of virtue.[21]

One modern scholar summarized the moral foundations of Jefferson's construct of happiness as follows:

> [B]y defining freedom as "freedom in all just pursuits," ... Jefferson was emphasizing that freedom was license to do not anything at all in order to attain one's "greatest happiness" but only what was consistent with the moral sense of justice.... This emphasis on freedom in the context of morality in the pursuit of greatest happiness demonstrates that morality was an essential ingredient in Jefferson's idea of happiness.... [M]oral behavior fulfilled the moral nature of man, and Jefferson expressed this idea when he said, "And if the Wise [would] be the happy man, as these sages say, he must be virtuous too; for, without virtue, happiness cannot be."[22]

Jefferson, of course, did not mean to impute any particular religious code to the word "virtue." He was famously opposed to imposing his religious views on others, and as it happens he saw the Bible as a "tradition" rather than the literal word of God.[23] But "virtue" did imply education and socialization along the same lines that Smith outlined: that is, our happiness rests on virtue, and virtue in turn is a learned skill. Jefferson thus did not limit us to one mode of expression. Our unalienable right to the pursuit of happiness means the right to pursue our own bliss, as guided by our internal guru, *provided* that we have a well-developed moral compass to point the way.

For this reason, public education was for Jefferson an essential component of good government, and the only basis on which democracy could prosper. Henry Steele Commager neatly summed up the relationship in Jefferson's thought between happiness, virtue, and education:

> How odd that the term enlightenment in Europe should refer to a program imagined by philosophers. . ., while in America it meant popular education. "Enlighten the people generally," said Jefferson, and . . . "no other sure foundation can be devised for the preservation of freedom and happiness. . . . Preach a crusade against ignorance; establish and improve the law for educating the common people. Let our countrymen know that the people can protect us against the evils of misgovernment."
>
> All the founding fathers were educators. . . . Greatest of them all was Jefferson, who planned a complete educational system for Virginia, wrote educational provisions into the ordinances governing the West, and built the University of Virginia. . . . where else in the western world do you find anything like this?[24]

The sad answer to Commager's rhetorical question is, not necessarily in the United States, any more. In 2013 the Kansas state legislature slashed public spending on education 16.5 percent below 2008 levels, while passing an income tax cut benefiting mostly higher income residents. A state trial court ruled that the current level of funding violates Kansas's constitutional requirement that the state make "suitable provision" for public education, and ordered Kansas to raise its per-student spending from $3,838 to $4,492, but in response the governor appealed. News accounts at the time reported that, if the trial court's decision were to be upheld, "legislators are threatening to amend the state's Constitution by removing the requirement for 'suitable' school funding and to strip Kansas courts of jurisdiction to hear school finance cases altogether."[25]

Fiscal policy—the objects of our collective spending and how we choose to finance those activities—is a window into our fiscal soul, and the view right now is disquieting. Homo Economicus struts across center stage of our public discourse, declaiming that science commands that unalloyed market outcomes cannot help but be optimal. The Growth Fairy hovers over the scene, threatening that efforts to increase investments in ourselves will force her to withdraw to a more hospitable land, never to return. When the pope observes that perhaps that trickle-down economics stuff doesn't seem to be working, he is attacked as a know-nothing Marxist. And poor Adam Smith, professor of moral philosophy, remains a captive of those on whom life has showered affluence, and who revel in confusing their good fortune with great virtue.

We all are Americans. We all deserve to pursue our own happiness, but this promise that binds us as a country requires as a precondition more than simply being neither incarcerated nor a serf. We can afford to do better. We can afford to be better citizens to one another.

When will we honor Adam Smith and Thomas Jefferson? When will we choose to govern ourselves in ways that are most likely to effect the happiness of our whole society?

NOTES

INTRODUCTION

1. Christopher Flavelle, "Obamacare Shows How Americans Are Becoming Jerks," *Bloomberg.com*, November 19, 2013, http://www.bloomberg.com/news/2013-11-19/obamacare-shows-how-americans-are-becoming-jerks.html.

2. Robert H. Frank and Philip J. Cook, *The Winner-Take-All Society: Why the Few at the Top Get So Much More Than the Rest of Us* (New York: Penguin Group, 1995).

3. Adam Smith, *The Theory of Moral Sentiments*, 6th ed. (New York: Penguin Group, 2010), Part III, chap. 3, 159.

CHAPTER 1

1. I use "fiscal policy" in its broadest sense as encompassing all government spending and taxing, not in the narrower sense of what Richard Musgrave called the "stabilization function" of government, which is concerned with managing employment, price stability, and economic growth. A debt-financed government-spending package designed to assist the economy in recovering from a recession is an example of the "stabilization function" of government in operation. Richard A. Musgrave and Peggy B. Musgrave, *Public Finance in Theory and Practice*, 5th ed. (New York: McGraw-Hill, 1989), 11–13.

2. The federal TARP program was a justifiable exception, because it operated only to put a floor on firms' market risks for a very limited amount of time in the most difficult economic circumstances that this country had faced in three generations. The adverse follow-on effects from a collapse of the entire financial sector, or of the entire automobile industry, rightly were judged to be too enormous to allow. The good judgment of the Bush and Obama administrations in implementing TARP is evidenced by the fact that, when the program's remaining General Motors investment is sold, the government will have turned a profit on the entire intervention. As of June 2013, the federal government had $28.58 billion in TARP funds outstanding, most of which remained invested in the automotive industry (including about $7.3 billion in GM common stock).

Its investments in the financial sector have already been liquidated at a significant profit. U.S. Treasury, *Troubled Asset Relief Program: Monthly Report to Congress* (June 2013).

3. Mark Kelman, *Strategy or Principle?: The Choice Between Regulation and Taxation* (Ann Arbor: University of Michigan Press, 1999), is an excellent overview of the economic and constitutional issues inherent in this decision.

4. Economic texts typically distinguish between an individual's *utility* and a society's *welfare*, but this book uses the latter term consistently for both contexts.

Welfare economics is the branch of economics that ponders the normative consequences of policies. For example, would we be better off as a society with a flat tax or a progressive income tax, assuming that the two raised the same revenue? Part of the answer depends on economic efficiency questions in the narrow sense (which kind of tax distorts market behaviors less?). But part depends on what the resulting society looks like, and how we feel about that—in particular, with respect to the issue of economic inequality.

Welfare economics typically does not set out to prove that one set of trade-offs between efficiency and equality logically must be normatively superior to all others. Indeed, a famous proposition by Kenneth Arrow basically demonstrates that, even if we know a great deal about every individual's preferences, we cannot transform that information into a society's preferred set of trade-offs. See Allen M. Feldman's entry in *The New Palgrave Dictionary of Economics*, s.v. "welfare economics" ("There is no logically infallible way to solve the problem of distribution.").

This is the arena in which political processes are uniquely competent to furnish an answer.

Instead, welfare economics assumes one or more plausible sets of a society's preferences for economic equality (or inequality)—each called a social welfare function—and considers which policies are most consistent with those assumed preferences and efficiency. Welfare economics in turn might be criticized for including only one normative criterion to balance against efficiency goals—inequality, as reflected in a society's appetite for "redistribution."

As this country's political discourse in recent years has demonstrated, "freedom" itself might be viewed as an independent normative criterion not fully captured in the standard efficiency vs. redistribution trade-off model. That is, redistribution is shorthand for one mechanism to address inequality, which in turn implicates a specific attitude about the intersection of political and economic freedoms. A different mechanism (minimum wage, earned income tax credit) might be viewed as having different resonance along the freedom continuum, and therefore might lead to a different set of social preferences. In short, the mechanism by which values are articulated matters.

For all the above reasons, this book therefore treats welfare economics as illuminating but not dispositive when it comes to formulating actual policies.

5. Milton Friedman, *Capitalism and Freedom* (Chicago: University of Chicago Press, 1962), chap. 2.

6. Ibid., 31.

7. John Kay, "Scrap the Jubilee? Why Not Christmas Too?" *Financial Times*, May 29, 2012.

8. Gardiner Harris, "Index of Happiness? Bhutan's New Leader Prefers More Concrete Goals," *New York Times*, October 4, 2013, http://www.nytimes.com/2013/10/05/world/asia/index-of-happiness-bhutans-new-leader-prefers-more-concrete-goals.html.

9. Hypervigilant know-it-alls will note that I have folded into my characterization of the NIPAs the BEA's "Input-Output Accounts."

10. Charlotte Ann Bond et al., "Integrated Macroeconomic Accounts for the United States," *Survey of Current Business* 87 (February 2007): 14.

11. Joseph E. Stiglitz, "GDP Fetishism," *Economist's Voice* 6, no. 8 (September 2009): 1–3.

12. Benjamin Bridgman et al., "Accounting for Household Production in the National Accounts, 1965–2010," *Survey of Current Business* 92 (May 2012): 23.

13. Economists usually distinguish among consumption, savings, and investment. Consumption is the money we spend on ourselves, within the personal sphere of our lives. Consumption is not necessarily fun spending; medical expenses, for example, are treated as consumption. For reasons of historical convenience, spending on "consumer durables" like automobiles and refrigerators is treated as consumption in the current year. When individuals put money in the bank, they are saving. The word "investment" is reserved for acquisitions of means of production, like new greasy machinery for a factory. So, in general, individuals save and firms invest. Consistent with the make-believe landlord-tenant relationship inside every homeowner, economists classify home-ownership as the one form of investment, in this technical sense, that individuals who are not directly engaged in their own trade or business make.

14. Francois Lequiller and Derek Blades, *Understanding National Accounts* (OECD, 2006), 37–38.

15. Bureau of Economic Analysis, "Preview of the 2013 Comprehensive Revision of the National Income and Product Accounts," *Survey of Current Business* (March 2013): 13–39; Robin Harding, "US Economy Takes Olympic Leap to Add 3% to GDP," *Financial Times*, July 28, 2013; Robin Harding, "US Economy Gets a Hollywood Makeover," *Financial Times*, April 21, 2013.

16. Cass R. Sunstein, "Well Being and the State," *Harvard Law Review* 107, no. 6 (1994): 1303–1327.

17. Ibid.

18. Compare Alan B. Krueger and David A. Schkade, "The Reliability of Subjective Well-Being Measures," *Journal of Public Economics* 92, nos. 8–9 (2008): 1833–1845, with Michael E. DeBow and Dwight R. Lee, "Happiness and Public Policy: A Partial Dissent (or Why a Department of Homeland Happiness Would be a Bad Idea)," *Journal of Law and Politics* 22 (2006): 283–301, and Will Wilkinson, "In Pursuit of Happiness Research: Is It Reliable? What Does It Imply for Policy?" *Policy Analysis* 590 (2007): 1–41.

19. The ISEW is also known as the Genuine Progress Indicator. John Talberth, Clifford Cobb, and Noah Slattery, "The Genuine Progress Indicator 2006: A Tool for Sustainable Development," *Redefining Progress* (February 2007): 1–31.

20. For example, I do not discuss very much the welfare implications of national parks or wilderness areas, notwithstanding that I think the case for them is easily made.

21. Anandi Mani et al., "Poverty Impedes Cognitive Function," *Science* 341, no. 6149 (August 30, 2013): 976–980.

22. The figure of speech comes from Emily Badger, "How Poverty Taxes the Brain," *The Atlantic Cities*, August 29, 2013, http://www.theatlanticcities.com/jobs-and-economy/2013/08/how-poverty-taxes-brain/6716/. See also Cardiff Garcia, "Poor Choices," *Financial Times Alphaville*, November 27, 2013, http://ftalphaville.ft.com/2013/11/27/1622532/poor-choices/.

23. Save the Children Foundation, *Food for Thought: Tackling Child Nutrition to Unlock Potential and Boost Prosperity*, by Liam Crosby, Daphne Jayasinghe, and David McNair (2013), 1.

24. Improvements in nutrition and education during childhood benefit more than just wages. A recent study found that preventing vascular morbidity and providing for higher levels

of education contribute to lower levels of dementia in advanced age. Fiona E. Matthews et al., "A Two-Decade Comparison of Prevalence of Dementia in Individuals Aged 65 Years and Older from Three Geographical Areas of England: Results of the Cognitive Function and Ageing Study I and II," *The Lancet* 382, no. 9902 (2013): 1406.

Worldwide, the cost of dementia in 2010 was estimated at $604 billion, a third of which was borne in North America. That figure represents a real cost to society—productivity lost by the victims of dementia, wages unearned by family members caring for aging parents, and money spent on professional care and medical bills. Altogether that adds up to about one percent of the world's GDP. Alzheimer's Disease International, *World Alzheimer Report 2010: The Global Economic Impact of Dementia*, by Anders Wimo and Martin Prince (September 2010), 4.

25. US Department of Agriculture, *Household Food Security in the United States in 2012*, by Alisha Coleman-Jensen, Mark Nord, and Anita Singh (Economic Research Report No. 155, September 2013).

26. Bruce Stokes, "U.S. Stands Out as a Rich Country Where a Growing Minority Say They Can't Afford Food," *Pew Research Center*, May 24, 2013, http://www.pewresearch.org/fact-tank/2013/05/24/u-s-stands-out-as-a-rich-country-where-a-growing-minority-say-th ey-cant-afford-food/.

27. Center for American Progress, *Hunger in America: Suffering We All Pay For*, by Donald S. Shepard, Elizabeth Setren, and Donna Cooper (October 2011).

28. Sheryl Gay Stolberg, "On the Edge of Poverty, at the Center of a Debate on Food Stamps," *New York Times*, September 4, 2013, http://www.nytimes.com/2013/09/05/us/as-debate-reopens-f ood-stamp-recipients-continue-to-squeeze.html.

29. Victoria Stilwell, "Bodies Double as Cash Machines with U.S. Income Lagging," *Bloomberg News*, October 15, 2013, http://www.bloomberg.com/news/2013-10-15/bodies-double-as-cash-machines-with-u-s-income-lagging-economy.html.

30. Stolberg, "On the Edge of Poverty, at the Center of a Debate on Food Stamps."

31. House Appropriations Committee Democrats, *Report on Sequestration* (February 13, 2013), 19–20.

32. US Government Accountability Office, *Early Intervention: Federal Investments Like WIC Can Produce Savings*, GAO/HRD-92-18 (Washington, DC: US Government Printing Office, 1992); US Department of Agriculture, Food and Nutrition Service, *Infant Mortality among Medicaid Newborns in Five States: The Effects of Prenatal WIC Participation*, by Barbara Devaney and Allen Schirm (Washington, DC: US United States Government Printing Office, 1993), v.

33. Larry M. Bartels, *Unequal Democracy: The Political Economy of the New Gilded Age* (Princeton, NJ: Princeton University Press, 2010).

34. Carter C. Price and Christine Eibner, "For States That Opt Out of Medicaid Expansion: 3.6 Million Fewer Insured and $8.4 Billion Less in Federal Payments," *Health Affairs* 32, no. 6 (June 2013): 1030–1036.

35. Paul Krugman, "The Spite Club," *New York Times*, June 7, 2013, http://www.nytimes.com/2013/06/07/opinion/krugman-the-spite-club.html.

36. Abby Goodnough, "Tennessee Race for Medicaid: Dial Fast and Try, Try Again," *New York Times*, March 25, 2013, http://www.nytimes.com/2013/03/25/us/tennessee-holds-health-c are-lottery-for-the-poor.html.

CHAPTER 2

1. George J. Stigler, "The Successes and Failures of Professor Smith," *Journal of Political Economy* 84, no. 6 (December 1976): 1199–1213, 1212.

2. Ibid.

3. Adam Smith, *The Wealth of Nations* (London: Methuen & Co., 1776), chap. 2.

4. A technically correct formulation of a "Pareto-optimum" allocation of resources, according to the First Fundamental Theorem of Welfare Economics, would be phrased in terms of "marginal rates of substitution" of production and consumption, but this is not an economics text.

5. Gary S. Becker, *The Economic Approach to Human Behavior* (Chicago: University of Chicago Press, 1976), 14.

6. Stigler, "Successes and Failures of Professor Smith," 1200–1201.

7. Donald Winch, "Adam Smith: The Prophet of Free Enterprise?" *History of Economics Review* 16 (Summer 1991): 104 ("What makes the choice of Smith for the role of liberal capitalist ideologue so inappropriate is his scepticism and moderation.").

8. Recent biographies include: James Buchan, *The Authentic Adam Smith: His Life and Ideas* (New York: W.W. Norton, 2006); and Nicholas Phillipson, *Adam Smith: An Enlightened Life* (New Haven, CT: Yale University Press, 2010). Monographs touching on his moral philosophy and its relationship to his economic thinking include: Jerry Evensky, *Adam Smith's Moral Philosophy: A Historical and Contemporary Perspective on Markets, Law, Ethics and Culture* (Cambridge, UK: Cambridge University Press, 2005); Samuel Fleischacker, *On Adam Smith's Wealth of Nations: A Philosophical Companion* (Princeton, NJ: Princeton University Press, 2004); Charles L. Griswold Jr., *Adam Smith and the Virtues of Enlightenment* (Cambridge, UK: Cambridge University Press, 1999); Ryan Patrick Hanley, *Adam Smith and the Character of Virtue* (Cambridge, UK: Cambridge University Press, 2009); Leonidas Montes, *Adam Smith in Context: A Critical Reassessment of Some Central Components of His Thought* (New York: Palgrave Macmillan, 2004); D. D. Raphael, *The Impartial Spectator: Adam Smith's Moral Philosophy* (Oxford, UK: Oxford University Press, 2007); Emma Rothschild, *Economic Sentiments: Adam Smith, Condorcet, and the Enlightenment* (Cambridge, MA: Harvard University Press, 2001); and Jeffrey T. Young, *Economics as a Moral Science: The Political Economy of Adam Smith* (Cheltenham, UK: Edward Elgar, 1997).

9. Adam Smith, *The Theory of Moral Sentiments*, 6th ed. (London: A. Millar, 1790), part I, sec. I, chap. 1.

10. Ibid., part II, sec. II, chap. 3. See also Fleischacker, *On Adam Smith's Wealth of Nations: A Philosophical Companion*, 46 ("Smith shows how deeply our happiness depends on our living up to moral standards, how we aspire to and are made happy by the internalization of standards of virtue that we initially regard as imposed on us by our society. . . . No one will be truly happy who is not also truly virtuous: Happiness consists, for social beings like us, in winning the love of others by living up, internally as well as externally, to their expectations of us.").

11. Smith, *Theory of Moral Sentiments*, part III, chap. 1.

12. Smith, *The Wealth of Nations*, book I, chap. 2.

13. Smith, *Theory of Moral Sentiments*, part II, sec. II, chap. 2.

14. Ibid., part I, sec. III, chap. 1.

15. Ibid., part IV, chap. 1.

16. Fleischacker, *On Adam Smith's* Wealth of Nations: *A Philosophical Companion*, 68–69; Griswold, *Adam Smith and the Virtues of Enlightenment*, 217–227.

17. Smith, *Theory of Moral Sentiments*, part IV, chap. 1.

18. Ibid., part IV, chap. 2.

19. Ibid., part III, chap. 3.

20. Ibid., part I, sec. I, chap. 5.

21. Ibid., part III, chap. 5.

22. Smith, *Wealth of Nations*, book V, chap. I, part III, art. II.

23. Ibid., book I, chap. VIII.

24. Evensky, *Adam Smith's Moral Philosophy*, chap. 1.

25. Smith, *Wealth of Nations*, book IV, chap. II. To be clear, Smith violently opposed the prevailing "mercantilist" policies of the time, under which a nation's prosperity lay in exporting as much as possible, and importing as little as possible, so as to accumulate the greatest possible store of gold. But by the same token he did believe that the "domestic circuit" of money from investment through production to sales was more valuable to a society than was the "foreign circuit."

26. Evensky, *Adam Smith's Moral Philosophy*, 163 ("The invisible hand is not, as the modern discourse generally suggests, the magic of a market economy at work. That is but one of its handiworks. This invisible hand is for Smith the hand of the deity that designed the 'economy of nature' and those invisible 'connecting principles' that guide humankind's evolution.").

27. Smith, *Theory of Moral Sentiments*, part IV, chap. 1.

28. Ibid., part VI, sec. III, conclusion.

29. Daniel Stedman Jones, *Masters of the Universe: Hayek, Friedman, and the Birth of Neoliberal Politics* (Princeton, NJ: Princeton University Press, 2012), 113–115. David Harvey's *A Brief History of Neoliberalism* (New York: Oxford University Press, 2005) is a more polemical history.

30. Jones, *Masters of the Universe*, 116–117.

For a modern retelling of the same theory, seeRichard A. Epstein, *Forbidden Grounds: The Case Against Employment Discrimination* (Cambridge, MA: Harvard University Press, 1992). Epstein argues that discrimination laws are poor policy, not just because they are unnecessary to prevent discrimination in modern, competitive employment markets, but because they interfere with the right to contract: "An antidiscrimination law is the antithesis of freedom of contract, a principle that allows all persons to do business with whomever they please for good reason, bad reason, or no reason at all." Ibid., 3. But as others have pointed out, Epstein's argument is largely dependent on his assumptions of perfectly competitive markets and perfectly equal and rational agents contracting with each other. It just as easily justifies repealing laws that prohibit drug use, sodomy, pornography, prostitution, gambling, or dueling.John J. Donohue III, "Advocacy versus Analysis in Assessing Employment Discrimination Law," *Stanford Law Review* 44, no. 7 (1992): 1586–1614. Yet prohibitions on discriminatory hiring practices today, like those on dueling in the Revolutionary era, are a justified reflection of our collective moral sentiments.

31. Cf. Shira B. Lewin, "Economics and Psychology: Lessons for Our Own Day from the Early Twentieth Century," *Journal of Economic Literature* 34 (September 1996): 1293–1323.

For example, George J. Stigler and Gary S. Becker disparage the idea that it might be appropriate to look to "psychologists? anthropologists? phrenologists?" to explain anything about human tastes.George J. Stigler and Gary S. Becker, "De Gustibus Non Est Disputandum," *The American Economic Review* 67, no. 2 (March 1977): 76. Instead, they argue that a rational utility maximization model can explain all tastes, that tastes do not differ importantly across people, and that all differences in behavior can be explained as the result of differences in prices or incomes.

32. See, for example, Paul Krugman's observation, "the economics profession went astray because economists, as a group, mistook beauty, clad in impressive-looking mathematics, for truth." Paul Krugman, "How Did Economists Get It So Wrong?" *New York Times*, September 2, 2009, http://www.nytimes.com/2009/09/06/magazine/06Economic-t.html. See also "The Other-Worldly Philosophers," *The Economist*, July 16, 2009, http://www.economist.com/node/14030288. ("Economists can become seduced by their models, fooling themselves that what the model leaves out does not matter. It is, for example, often convenient to assume that markets are 'complete'—that a price exists today, for every good, at every date, in every contingency.").

33. Wendy Brown, "American Nightmare: Neoliberalism, Neoconservatism, and De-Democratization," *Political Theory* 34, no. 6 (2006): 690–714.

34. John Rawls, *Justice as Fairness: A Restatement*, 2nd ed. (New York: Belknap Press, 2001).

35. *United States v. Butler*, 297 U.S. 1 (1936).

36. Ibid., at 65.

37. Ibid., at 66. See also *South Dakota v. Dole*, 483 U.S. 203, 207 (1987), where Chief Justice Rehnquist reaffirmed this central point (and indeed moved beyond the Butler court in some respects) ("In considering whether a particular expenditure is intended to serve general public purposes, courts should defer substantially to the judgment of Congress.").

The Court in Butler went on to hold that the particular exercise of the spending power at issue there did violate the Constitution, on the grounds that the tax in question was channeled directly from one group of taxpayers to fund distributions to others. This technical defect was quickly solved by rewriting the legislation to cause the tax to flow to the general fund of the Treasury, and to separately subsidize the second group of taxpayers. See *McCray v. United States*, 195 U.S. 27 (1904).

38. *National Federation of Independent Businesses v. Sebelius, Secretary of Health and Human Services*, 132 S. Ct. 2566, 2579 (June 28, 2012) (citations omitted).

39. Financial Crisis Inquiry Commission, *The Financial Crisis Inquiry Report: Final Report of the National Commission on the Causes of the Financial and Economic Crisis in the United States*, dissenting statement by Peter J. Wallison (Washington, DC: US Government Printing Office, 2011). The claims are rejected, for example, in the main body of the report; in the Dissenting Statement to that report of Keith Hennessey, Douglas Holtz-Eakin, and Bill Thomas; in Jason Thomas and Robert Van Order, "A Closer Look at Fannie Mae and Freddie Mac: What We Know, What We Think We Know and What We Don't Know" (working paper, George Washington University, March 2011), http://business.gwu.edu/creua/research-papers/files/fannie-freddie.pdf; and in David Min, "Faulty Conclusions Based on Shoddy Foundations: FCIC Commissioner Peter Wallison and Other Commentators Rely on Flawed Data from Edward Pinto to Misplace the Causes of the 2008 Financial Crisis," *Center for American Progress*, February 2011, http://www.americanprogress.org/issues/2011/02/pdf/pinto.pdf.

40. M. Todd Henderson and Frederick Tung, "Paying Bank Examiners for Performance: Should Regulators Receive Bonuses for Effectively Guarding the Public Interest?" *Regulation* 35, no. 1 (Spring 2012): 32–38.

41. This heading is a play on the phrase "Soup kitchens caused the Depression!" which comes from an online commentor on John Quiggin, "Food Stamps Cause Global Depression?" *Crooked*

Timber, November 2, 2012, http://crookedtimber.org/2012/11/02/26429/. It was the source of the title of Paul Krugman, "Soup Kitchens Caused the Great Depression," *New York Times*, November 3, 2012, http://krugman.blogs.nytimes.com/2012/11/03/soup-kitchens-caused-the-great-depression/.

42. Jonathan S. Masur and Eric A. Posner, "Regulation, Unemployment, and Cost-Benefit Analysis," *Virginia Law Review* 98 (May 2012): 610. To be clear, the authors disclaim the idea that this model is necessarily descriptive of reality. On the other hand, the authors basically rely on this model, with the addition of a single new constraint, in considering how unemployment should figure into regulatory cost-benefit analysis. (As one example, they argue that employees in industries at risk of layoffs are overpaid, as a form of implicit unemployment insurance; this claim fits nicely with the model, but does it describe accurately workers in a small town with a handful of large employers?) If the model is a poor description of reality, it might be the case that methodologies premised on that model also might poorly fit with reality.

43. Casey B. Mulligan, *The Redistribution Recession: How Labor Market Distortions Contracted the Economy* (New York: Oxford University Press, 2012); *Hearing on More Spending, Less Real Help: How Today's Fragmented Welfare System Fails to Lift Up Poor Families, Before the Subcommittee on Human Resources of the Committee on Ways and Means, U.S. House of Representatives*, 113th Cong. (June 18, 2013) (testimony of Casey B. Mulligan, "Work Incentives, Accumulated Legislation, and the Economy").

Another example is testimony from a year earlier before the same subcommittee offered by Clifford F. Thies, who, as the Eldon R. Lindsey Chair of Free Enterprise at Shenandoah University, signals his perspective in his job title. *Joint Hearing on How Welfare and Tax Benefits Can Discourage Work, Before the Subcommittee on Human Resources and Subcommittee on Select Revenue Measures of the Committee on Ways and Means, U.S. House of Representatives*, 112th Cong. 38 (June 27, 2012) (testimony of Clifford F. Thies, "The Implicit Tax Rate on Low Income Americans"). One difference is that Thies recounts the history of the negative income tax—a flat dollar grant to every citizen regardless of need—as an alternative to the "making work pay" ameliorations described below.

44. Mulligan, *Redistribution Recession*, 272 ("opt to earn less").

45. For example, the nonpartisan Congressional Budget Office concluded that "[t]he primary reason for the increase in the number of participants [in the 2007–2011 period] was the deep recession from December 2007 to June 2009 and the subsequent slow recovery; there were no significant legislative expansions of eligibility for the program during that time." Congressional Budget Office, *The Supplemental Nutrition Assistance Program* (April 2012), 4.

46. In one example, Mulligan estimated that post-2007 SNAP policy changes increased SNAP enrollment by 20.3 percent, but a recent National Bureau of Economic Research working paper calculated that those policy changes accounted for only 7.5 percent of enrollment. Peter Ganong and Jeffrey B. Liebman, "The Decline, Rebound, and Further Rise in SNAP Enrollment: Disentangling Business Cycle Fluctuations and Policy Changes" (NBER Working Paper 19363, National Bureau of Economic Research, August 2013), 29–30.

47. Marios Michaelides and Peter R. Mueser, "Recent Trends in the Characteristics of Unemployment Insurance Recipients," *Monthly Labor Review* (July 2012), 28, http://www.bls.gov/opub/mlr/2012/07/art3full.pdf.

48. David R. Henderson, "Encouraging Joblessness," *Regulation* 36, no. 1 (Spring 2013): 68–69.

49. Ben Steverman, "The Job Market Has a Senior Moment," *Bloomberg.com*, June 21, 2013, http://www.bloomberg.com/news/2013-06-21/the-job-market-has-a-senior-moment.html.

50. Federal Reserve Bulletin, *Changes in U.S. Family Finances from 2007 to 2010: Evidence from the Survey of Consumer Finances* (June 2012), 17, 30.

51. Mulligan, *Redistribution Recession*, 267 (unemployment benefits account for 67 percent of the additional benefits).

52. Catherine Rampell, "Companies Spend on Equipment, Not Workers," *New York Times*, June 9, 2011, http://www.nytimes.com/2011/06/10/business/10capital.html; Paul Gomme and Peter Rupert, "Measuring Labor's Share of Income," *Policy Discussion Papers* (Federal Bank of Cleveland, November 2004), 7, http://clevelandfed.org/research/policydis/no7novo4.pdf.

53. Edward J. McCaffery, *Taxing Women: How the Marriage Penalty Affects Your Taxes* (Chicago: University of Chicago Press, 1997); Edward J. McCaffery, "Americans' 90% Tax Rate," *CNN. com*, February 8, 2013, http://www.cnn.com/2013/02/08/opinion/mccaffery-marginal-tax-rates.

54. Milton Friedman, *Capitalism and Freedom: Fortieth Anniversary Edition* (Chicago: University of Chicago Press, 2002), 191–195.

55. For a good review of the problem see *Joint Hearing on How Welfare and Tax Benefits Can Discourage Work, Before the Subcommittee on Human Resources and Subcommittee on Select Revenue Measures of the Committee on Ways and Means, U.S. House of Representatives,* 112th Cong. 49 (June 27, 2012) (testimony of C. Eugene Steuerle, "Marginal Tax Rates, Work, and the Nation's Real Tax System").

56. Mulligan, *Redistribution Recession*, 95 (arguing that only changes in the EITC are relevant to his analysis).

57. See Nicholas Eberstadt, *A Nation of Takers: America's Entitlement Epidemic* (West Conshohocken, PA: Templeton Press, 2012).

58. I am not arguing here about divisive social issues that are expressed primarily in non-economic terms (such as issues pertaining to gay marriage), but rather those issues whose first order consequence is to impose an apparent efficiency cost in service of a more intangible value that adds to our collective welfare.

59. Margaret Thatcher, "There Is No Such Thing as Society," interview with Douglas Keay, *Women's Own Magazine*, October 31, 1987, http://www.margaretthatcher.org/document/106689.

60. Eberstadt, *Nation of Takers*, 43, 47, 73.

61. Richard A. Epstein, "In Praise of Income Inequality," *Defining Ideas: A Hoover Institutional Journal* (February 19, 2013), http://www.hoover.org/publications/defining-ideas/article/140746.

62. Rampell, "Companies Spend on Equipment, Not Workers."

63. Harvey Golub, "My Response to Buffett and Obama: Before You Ask for More Tax Money from Me, Raise the $2.2 Trillion You Already Collect Each Year More Fairly and Spend It More Wisely," *Wall Street Journal*, August 22, 2011, http://online.wsj.com/article/SB10001424053111903 639404576516724218259688.html.

64. Rawls, *Justice as Fairness*.

CHAPTER 3

1. Jesse Bricker et al., "Changes in U.S. Family Finances from 2007 to 2010: Evidence from the Survey of Consumer Finances," *Federal Reserve Bulletin* 98, no. 2 (June 2011): 1–80 (hereinafter "*SCF Survey*").

2. To be precise: "The components of income in the SCF are wages; self-employment and business income; taxable and tax-exempt interest; dividends; realized capital gains; food stamps and other, related support programs provided by government; pensions and withdrawals from retirement accounts; Social Security; alimony and other support payments; and miscellaneous sources of income for all members of the primary economic unit in the household." *SCF Survey*, 5, n. 5.

3. They do not tell the identical story because different government agencies define key concepts like "family" or "household" differently, because of differences in how data are collected or recorded, or in calculating the effects of inflation, and so on. Economists all over the country are kept busy trying to figure out how to merge one government database with another to get a comprehensive picture of our economic condition; it is considered a day for ordering beer along with pizza when one set of data can be "imputed" into another database. (Chapter 4 has more to say about this particular issue.)

SCF Survey, 5, n. 5, outlines some of the reasons why the Federal Reserve's data are not strictly comparable to the Census Bureau's similar-sounding statistics.

4. US Census Bureau, *Statistical Abstract of the United States 2012: Income, Expenditures, Poverty and Wealth* (2011), table 696, http://www.census.gov/prod/2011pubs/12statab/income.pdf. The data for "households" are worse—a 4.5 percent increase over 19 years. In Census Bureau lingo, a household includes all the persons who occupy a housing unit as their usual place of residence. A family comprises the members of a household who are related by blood or marriage. Cohabitating adults or adult roommates comprise a household, but not a family.

5. For the period in question, men's wages rose 7 percent, and women's 15 percent, from their respective 1990 base levels. The number of full-time, year-round male workers increased by 14 percent, and the number of women, 36 percent. US Census Bureau, *Income, Poverty, and Health Insurance Coverage in the United States: 2010*, by Carmen DeNavas-Walt, Bernadette D. Proctor, and Jessica C. Smith, Pub. P60–239 (September 2011), table A-5 (hereinafter "*Income and Poverty: 2010*").

6. US Bureau of Labor Statistics, *Establishment Data: Table B-2, Average Hours and Earnings of Production and Nonsupervisory Employees on Private Nonfarm Payrolls by Major Industry Sector* (August 2013), http://www.bls.gov/news.release/empsit.t18.htm.

7. *SCF Survey*, 76, provides inflation indices for the years in question.

8. *Income and Poverty: 2010*, table A-5.

9. Congressional Budget Office, *Changes in the Distribution of Workers' Annual Earnings Between 1979 and 2007* (October 2009), table 8. The median male worker's hourly wage moved from $19.50/hour to $19.60/hour.

The CBO analysis combines part-time and full-time workers, and excludes self-employment income.

10. Ibid., 12. (The women participation rate for ages 25 to 54 actually increased from 66 to 76 percent between 1979 to 2000, but fell to 74 percent by 2007.)

11. Ibid., table 8.

12. Emmanuel Saez, *Striking It Richer: The Evolution of Top Incomes in the United States (Updated with 2012 Preliminary Estimates)* (September 3, 2013), http://elsa.berkeley.edu/~saez/saez-UStopincomes-2012.pdf.

13. *SCF Survey*, table 12; Sylvia A. Allegretto, "The State of Working America's Wealth, 2011: Through Volatility and Turmoil, the Gap Widens," *Economic Policy Institute* (March 22, 2011): 21–26.

14. While the middle class has seen historically slow economic growth, taxes on the middle class are also at historical lows. The latter stems from the former in two ways: the middle class has earned a declining share of income (resulting in a smaller tax burden) and policy makers have sought to ease the pain endured by the middle class due to stagnant growth. The Bush-era tax cuts and their subsequent extension in 2013 are examples of this policy in action. While this sort of tax relief has its benefits, the fact that it has often been accompanied by even lower relative burdens for high-income earners has lessened its ability to improve outcomes for the middle class. Kirk J. Stark and Eric M. Zolt, "Tax Reform and the American Middle Class," *Pepperdine Law Review* 40, no. 5 (May 2013): 1211.

15. *SCF Survey*, 17.

16. Congressional Budget Office, *Changes in the Distribution of Workers' Annual Earnings Between 1979 and 2007*, table 2.

17. Organisation for Economic Co-operation and Development, *StatExtracts: Average Annual Hours Actually Worked Per Worker* (2013), http://stats.oecd.org/Index.aspx?DataSetCode=ANHRS.

18. Congressional Budget Office, *How CBO Projects Income* (July 2013), 4, http://www.cbo.gov/sites/default/files/cbofiles/attachments/44433-IncomeProjection.pdf.

19. Susan Fleck, John Glaser, and Shawn Sprague, "The Compensation-Productivity Gap: A Visual Essay," *Monthly Labor Review* (Bureau of Labor Statistics, January 2011): 63, http://www.bls.gov/opub/mlr/2011/01/art3full.pdf. The US Bureau of Economic Analysis calculated that employee compensation share of gross domestic income declined from 55.7 percent in 2002 to 53 percent in 2012. US Bureau of Economic Analysis, *National Income and Products Accounts Tables* (last revised, August 7, 2013), table 1.11.

20. US Bureau of Labor Statistics, "The Unemployment Rate and Beyond: Alternative Measures of Labor Underutilization," *Issues in Labor Statistics* (June 2008), http://www.bls.gov/opub/ils/pdf/opbils67.pdf.

21. US Bureau of Labor Statistics, *Labor Force Participation Rate—25–54 Yrs* (accessed 2013), http://data.bls.gov/timeseries/LNU01300060.

22. Alina Tugend, "Unemployed and Older, and Facing a Jobless Future," *New York Times*, July 27, 2013, B4.

23. H. Luke Shaefer and Kathryn Edin, "Rising Extreme Poverty in the United States and the Response of Federal Means-Tested Transfer Programs," *National Poverty Center Working Paper Series #13–06* (working paper, May 2013).

24. Ibid.

25. US Census Bureau, *Income, Poverty, and Health Insurance Coverage in the United States: 2011*, by Carmen DeNavas-Walt, Bernadette D. Proctor, and Jessica C. Smith, Pub. P60–243 (September 2012), Appendix B, http://www.census.gov/prod/2012pubs/p60-243.pdf (hereinafter "*Income and Poverty: 2011*").

26. US Census Bureau, *Statistical Abstract of the United States: 2012* (2012), table 711, http://www.census.gov/compendia/statab/2012/tables/12s0711.pdf.

27. *Income and Poverty: 2011*, Appendix B.

28. Ibid., 17.

29. US Census Bureau, *The Research Supplemental Poverty Measure 2011*, by Kathleen Short, Pub. P60–244 (November 2012), http://www.census.gov/hhes/povmeas/methodology/supplemental/research/Short_ResearchSPM2011.pdf.

When compared to the official poverty measure, the SPM shows fewer children living in poverty, but somewhat more working Americans and many more elderly Americans.

30. US Census Bureau, *Historical Income Tables: Income Inequality* (2011), table A-3, http://www.census.gov/hhes/www/income/data/historical/inequality/IE-1.pdf.

31. Congressional Budget Office, *The Distribution of Household Income and Federal Taxes, 2008 and 2009* (July 2012), table 1, http://www.cbo.gov/publication/43373.

32. Organisation for Economic Co-operation and Development, *OECD Factbook 2011–2012: Economic, Environmental and Social Statistics.*

33. The charts and specific numbers come from Congressional Budget Office, *Trends in the Distribution of Household Income Between 1979 and 2007*, and the supplemental data posted online at: http://www.cbo.gov/publication/42729.

34. Emmanuel Saez, *Striking It Richer: The Evolution of Top Incomes in the United States (Updated with 2012 Preliminary Estimates),*" http://elsa.berkeley.edu/~saez/saez-UStopincomes-2012.pdf.

35. *Income and Poverty: 2011*, table A-2.

36. Congressional Budget Office, *The Distribution of Household Income and Federal Taxes, 2008 and 2009* (July 2012), supplemental table 9.

37. James M. Poterba, Steven F. Venti, and David A. Wise, "Were They Prepared for Retirement? Financial Status at Advanced Ages in the HRS and AHEAD Cohorts," *National Bureau of Economic Research Working Paper Series* (working paper no. 17824, February 2012), http://www.nber.org/papers/w17824.pdf.

38. The Ukraine also edges us out, but it is a country with a population 1/10 that of the United States.

39. Peter Gottschalk, "Inequality, Income Growth, and Mobility: The Basic Facts," *Journal of Economic Perspectives* 11, no. 2 (Spring 1997): 37; Eric Zolt, "Inequality in America: Challenges for Tax and Spending Policies," *Tax Law Review* 66, no. 1101 (2013).

40. Gerald Auten and Geoffrey Gee, "Income Mobility in the United States: New Evidence from Income Tax Data," *National Tax Journal* 62, no. 2 (June 2009): 301–328; Gerald Auten, Geoffrey Gee, and Nicholas Turner, "Income Inequality, Mobility and Turnover at the Top in the US, 1987–2010," *American Economic Review: Papers and Proceedings* 103, no. 3 (May 2013): 168–172, doi:10.1257/aer.103.3.168.

41. Katharine Bradbury and Jane Katz, "Trends in U.S. Family Income Mobility, 1967–2004," *Federal Reserve Bank of Boston Working Paper No. 09-07* (August 20, 2009).

42. Wojciech Kopczuk, Emmanuel Saez, and Jae Song, "Earnings Inequality and Mobility in the United States: Evidence from Social Security Data since 1937," *Quarterly Journal of Economics* 125, no. 1 (February 2010), 91–128, doi:10.1162/qjec.2010.125.1.91.

43. More specifically, income inequality displayed a U-shaped pattern, declining until about 1953, then increasing dramatically from the early 1950s to about 1990, and then climbing much more slowly until the study's end date of 2000.

44. Internal Revenue Service, Statistics of Income Division, *The 400 Individual Income Tax Returns Reporting the Largest Adjusted Gross Incomes Each Year, 1992–2009*, http://www.irs.gov/pub/irs-soi/09intop400.pdf.

45. Raj Chetty et al., "The Economic Impacts of Tax Expenditures: Evidence from Spatial Variation Across the U.S." US Treasury Department (January 2014), http://www.irs.gov/pub/irs-soi/14rptaxexpenditures.pdf. The paper is summarized by David Leonhardt, "In Climbing Income Ladder, Location Matters," *New York Times*, July 22, 2013.

46. Sean F. Reardon, "The Widening Academic Achievement Gap Between the Rich and the Poor: New Evidence and Possible Explanations," chap. 5 in *Whither Opportunity? Rising Inequality, Schools, and Children's Life Chances*, ed. Greg J. Duncan and Richard Murnane (New York: Russell Sage Foundation, 2011).

47. Neeraj Kaushal, Katherine Magnuson, and Jane Waldfogel, "How Is Family Income Related to Investments in Children's Learning?" chap. 9 in *Whither Opportunity? Rising Inequality, Schools, and Children's Life Chances*, ed. Greg J. Duncan and Richard Murnane.

48. Miles Corak, "Income Inequality, Equality of Opportunity, and Intergenerational Mobility," *Journal of Economic Perspectives* 27, no. 3 (2013): 79–102.

49. The annual Forbes/Center for College Affordability and Productivity rankings of US undergraduate programs includes "post-graduate success" as a major factor in its methodology. Center for College Affordability and Productivity, *Compiling the 2013 Forbes/CCAP Rankings* (2013), http://centerforcollegeaffordability.org/uploads/2013_Methodology.pdf. The total scores assigned to different colleges vary widely. The highest ranked civilian public school in 2013 was the University of California, Berkeley, in 22nd place.

50. Ibid., 20.

51. Thomas D. Griffith, "Progressive Taxation and Happiness," *Boston College Law Review* 45, no. 5 (2004): 1363–1398.

CHAPTER 4

1. A good summary is Center on Budget and Policy Priorities, *A Guide to Statistics on Historical Trends in Income Inequality*, by Chad Stone, Danilo Trisi, and Arloc Sherman (revised April 17, 2014), http://www.cbpp.org/files/11-28-11pov.pdf.

2. Economic Policy Institute, *CEO Compensation and CEO-to-Worker Compensation Ratio, 1965–2011 (2011 dollars)* (updated June 18, 2012), http://stateofworkingamerica.org/chart/swa-wages-table-4-43-ceo-compensation-ceo/.

3. N. Gregory Mankiw, "Defending the One Percent," *Journal of Economic Perspectives* 27, no. 3 (2013): 21–34, doi:10.1257/jep.27.3.21.

4. Thomas Piketty and Emmanuel Saez, "Income Inequality in the United States, 1913–1998," *Quarterly Journal of Economics* 118, no. 1 (February 2003): 1–39.

5. Joseph E. Stiglitz, *The Price of Inequality: How Today's Divided Society Endangers Our Future* (New York: W. W. Norton, 2012).

6. Smith, *Wealth of Nations*, book I, chap. XI, part III.

7. Thomas Piketty, Emmanuel Saez, and Stefanie Stantcheva, "Optimal Taxation of Top Labor Incomes: A Tale of Three Elasticities," *National Bureau of Economic Analysis* (working paper no. 17616, November 2011).

8. Josh Bivens and Lawrence Mishel have further extended this work in a recent article that addresses some objections raised to the Piketty, Saez, and Stantcheva paper. Josh Bivens and Lawrence Mishel, "The Pay of Corporate Executives and Financial Professionals as Evidence of

Rents in Top 1 Percent Incomes," *Journal of Economic Perspectives* 27, no. 3 (2013): 57–78, doi:10.1257/jep.27.3.57.

9. Smith, *Wealth of Nations*, book I, chap. II.

10. N. Gregory Mankiw, "Spreading the Wealth Around: Reflections Inspired by Joe the Plumber," *Eastern Economic Journal* 36, no. 3 (2010): 285–298.

11. Smith, *Theory of Moral Sentiments*, part I, chap. III.

12. Richard V. Burkhauser, Jeff Larrimore, and Kosali I. Simon, "A 'Second Opinion' on the Economic Health of the American Middle Class," *National Tax Journal* 65, no. 1 (March 2012): 7–32.

13. Jeff Larrimore, Richard Burkhauser, Shuaizhang Feng, and Laura Zayatz, "Consistent Cell Means for Topcoded Incomes in the Public Use March CPS (1976–2007)," *Journal of Economic and Social Measurement* 33 (2008): 89–128.

14. Ibid., 111.

15. Thomas Edsall, "The Fight over Equality," *New York Times*, April 22, 2012, http://campaign-stops.blogs.nytimes.com/2012/04/22/the-fight-over-inequality/.

16. Congressional Budget Office, *Trends in the Distribution of Household Income Between 1979 and 2007*, 33.

17. Alvaredo, Atkinson, Piketty, and Saez, *The World Top Incomes Database*.

18. It is tempting to read this presentation (essentially copied in format from the Burkhauser group's paper) additively from left to right, but doing so technically is incorrect. For example, size-adjusted household income might theoretically have grown at a faster rate, but started from a lower base, than tax unit income. As a result, the difference in growth rates does not directly inform you about the absolute size of either.

For example, column (3), which is pre-tax and post-transfer, grew at a slower rate than column (4), which is post-tax and post-transfer, but one ordinarily would expect the absolute sizes of the pre-tax incomes in column (3) to be larger than the post-tax incomes in column (4). There actually is a further wrinkle here, which is how the refundable portion of the earned income tax credit and the child credit are treated—as negative taxes or as additional transfer payments. Median incomes should generally fall outside the range of the earned income tax credit, but would often qualify for the child credit.

19. Catherine Rampell, "Millenials, in Their Parents' Basements," *New York Times*, August 1, 2013, http://economix.blogs.nytimes.com/2013/08/01/millennials-in-their-parents-basements/. In 2012 a record 36 percent of Americans aged 18–31 lived in their parents' homes.

20. Burkhauser, Larrimore, and Simon, 8: "[T]he apparent failure of the median American to benefit from economic growth can largely be explained by the use of an income measure for this purpose [the income tax records relied on by Piketty and Saez] that does not fully capture what is actually happening to the resources available to middle class individuals"; and 29: "[O]nce broadening the income definition to post-tax, post-transfer, size-adjusted household...income, middle class Americans are found to have made substantial gains...."

21. Congressional Budget Office, *The Distribution of Household Income and Federal Taxes, 2008 and 2009*, 2.

22. The presentation here compares two terminal points, 1979 and 2007, and does not allocate year-by-year income growth to different income levels.

23. Congressional Budget Office, *Trends in the Distribution of Household Income Between 1979 and 2009* (2012).

24. Congressional Budget Office, *Changes in the Distribution of Workers' Annual Earnings Between 1979 and 2007*. The text draws from tables 2 and 8.

25. Richard A. Epstein, "In Praise of Income Inequality," *Defining Ideas*, February 19, 2013, http://www.hoover.org/publications/defining-ideas/article/140746/.

26. Robert H. Frank, *Falling Behind: How Rising Inequality Harms the Middle Class* (Berkeley: University of California Press, 2007).

27. Kevin Hassett and Aparna Mathur, "Consumption and the Myths of Inequality," *Wall Street Journal*, October 24, 2012.

28. Smith, *Wealth of Nations*, book I, chap. VIII.

29. Eryn Brown, "Diaper Crisis among Poor Families Endangers Children, Study Finds," *Los Angeles Times*, July 30, 2013.

30. Smith, *Wealth of Nations*, book I, chap. VIII.

31. Mark Perry, "Yes, the Middle Class Has Been Disappearing, but They Haven't Fallen into the Lower Class, They've Risen into the Upper Class," *AEIdeas*, July 12, 2013, http://www.aei-ideas.org/2013/07/yes-the-middle-class-has-been-disappearing-but-they-havent-fallen-into-the-lower-class-theyve-risen-into-the-upper-class/.

32. The data are most conveniently available at table A-1 of the 2010 edition of the Census Bureau's annual publication, *Income, Poverty, and Health Insurance Coverage in the United States: 2009*, by Carmen DeNavas-Walt, Bernadette D. Proctor, and Jessica C. Smith, Pub. P60-238 (September 2010).

33. Smith, *Theory of Moral Sentiments*, book I, sec. III, chap. III.

CHAPTER 5

1. John Harwood, "Don't Dare Call the Health Law 'Redistribution,'" *New York Times*, November 23, 2013.

2. "The welfare economist wishes to determine the desirability of a particular policy—not in terms of his or her own values, but in terms of some explicitly stated ethical criteria." Robin W. Boadway and Neil Bruce, *Welfare Economics* (Oxford: B. Blackwell, 1984), 1.

3. Gareth D. Myles, "Taxation and Economic Growth," *Fiscal Studies* 21, no. 1 (2000): 141–168.

4. A good overview of the issues is found in Eric Engen and Jonathan Skinner, "Taxation and Economic Growth," *National Tax Journal* 49, no. 4 (December 1996): 617–642.

5. Martin Feldstein, "How Big Should Government Be?" *National Tax Journal* 50, no. 2 (1997): 197–213.

6. Cf. Institute for Fiscal Studies, *Tax by Design: The Mirrlees Review*, by Sir James Mirrlees et al. (Oxford: Oxford University Press, September 2011), 29, http://www.ifs.org.uk/mirrleesreview/design/taxbydesign.pdf, which points out that revenue neutral tax legislation in particular has no net meaningful income effect. The passage in question does not explicitly consider the income effect of government spending, which presumably would extend the point it makes to a broader range of fiscal policies.

7. Jonathan Gruber, *Public Finance and Public Policy*, 4th ed. (New York: Worth Publishers, 2007), 620.

8. Arthur Okun is credited with first using this metaphor. Arthur M. Okun, *Equality and Efficiency: The Big Trade Off* (Washington, DC: Brookings Institution, 1975).

The leaky bucket metaphor is an example of the "common-sense" understanding of dead-weight loss, which differs from the modern economic sense.Hans Lind and Roland Granqvist, "A Note on the Concept of Excess Burden," *Economic Analysis & Policy* 40, no. 1 (March 2010): 63–73. Economists more technically refer to the "common-sense" usage as one that looks to uncompensated rather than compensated elasticities. The authors argue that if actual behavior in the real world is unchanged—if when examining a proposed labor income tax the income and substitution effects precisely cancel each other out—then the "common-sense" understanding (which they attribute to Pigou) would be that the excess burden is zero.

By contrast, the technical modern economic usage would compare the income tax to an entirely hypothetical and nonimplementable lump sum tax to show that, by reference to that benchmark, the income tax introduces an efficiency loss. The authors question whether a benchmark that exists only in economists' models is a useful guide to actual policymaking; they suggest instead that the relevant benchmark in any case might be the least distortive implementable tax.

In turn, Harvey S. Rosen and Ted Gayer in *Public Finance*, 9th ed. (Boston: McGraw-Hill/ Higher Education, 2010), 336, describe the "common-sense" use of the term as "fallacious."

I find the Lind and Granqvist distinction of two uses of the term "deadweight loss" to be quite helpful in reading the literature in this area, and their larger point about what constitutes a fair benchmark is an interesting metaphysical question for real-world policymaking. Nonetheless, this chapter is written by a nonspecialist for nonspecialists, and the points I make do not turn on this distinction. I therefore make no great effort to distinguish the two uses.

9. This example, and many published economic studies, actually measure "common-sense" deadweight loss, as described in note 8, because they focus on actual visible responses to taxation. Gruber, *Public Finance and Public Policy*, 620.

10. For the sake of clarity, this mental experiment ignores other taxes; the basic point is unaffected, however, by including them.

11. Similarly, the 2012–2013 jump in the capital gains tax rates from 15 percent to 20 percent reduced the after-tax returns to capital gains by only 5/85, or 5.9 percent.

12. OECD, *Economic Outlook Annex Tables* (2013), http://www.oecd.org/eco/outlook/economi-coutlookannextables.htm.

13. Rosen and Gayer, *Public Finance*, 343.

14. Following the earlier notes, these studies could be said to adopt the common-sense view of deadweight loss.

15. For a very recent and accessible summary of the economic literature, see Center on Budget and Policy Priorities, *Recent Studies Find Raising Taxes on High-Income Households Would Not Harm the Economy: Policy Should Be Included in Balanced Deficit-Reduction Effort*, by Chye-Ching Huang (April 24, 2012), http://www.cbpp.org/cms/index.cfm?fa=view&id=3756.

16. Congressional Research Service, *Tax Rates and Economic Growth*, CRS Pub. R42111 (Washington, DC: Office of Congressional Information and Publishing, December 5, 2011).

17. Ibid.; Peter Diamond and Emmanuel Saez, "The Case for a Progressive Tax: From Basic Research to Policy Recommendations," *Journal of Economic Perspectives* 25, no. 4 (2011): 172 ("A number of studies have shown large and quick responses of reported [taxable] incomes along the tax avoidance margin at the top of the distribution, but no compelling study to date has shown substantial responses along the real economic responses margin among top earners.").

The Diamond and Saez study concludes that, under plausible assumptions, the optimal highest marginal tax rate should be greater than 70 percent. (Optimal tax theory seeks to "maximize a [given] social welfare function subject to a government budget constraint, taking into account that individuals respond to taxes and transfers. Social welfare is larger when resources are more equally distributed, but redistributive taxes and transfers can negatively affect incentives to work, save, and earn income in the first place. This creates the classical trade-off between equity and efficiency which is at the core of the optimal income tax problem." Ibid., 165.)

18. Joel Slemrod and Jon Bakija, *Taxing Ourselves: A Citizen's Guide to the Debate over Taxes*, 4th ed. (Cambridge, MA: MIT Press, 2008), 146.

19. Retirement assets such as 401(k)s and IRAs were 14.5 percent of all US household assets in 2010. Congressional Research Service, *U.S. Household Savings for Retirement in 2010* (2013), 21, http://www.fas.org/sgp/crs/misc/R43057.pdf.

20. Eric M. Engen and William G. Gale, "The Effects of Fundamental Tax Reform on Saving," chap. 3 in *Economic Effects of Fundamental Tax Reform*, ed. Henry J. Aaron and William G. Gale (Washington, DC: Brookings Institution Press, 1996), 35, argues that these asset allocation efficiency losses are not very large.

21. Congressional Budget Office, *A Review of Recent Research on Labor Supply Elasticities* (Working Paper, October 2012), http://www.cbo.gov/publication/43675/.

22. Congressional Budget Office, *How the Supply of Labor Responds to Changes in Fiscal Policy* (October 2012), http://www.cbo.gov/sites/default/files/cbofiles/attachments/10-25-2012-Labor_Supply_and_Fiscal_Policy.pdf.

23. Beginning in 2013, an additional 3.8 percent tax on net investment income enacted as part of the 2010 health reform legislation applies to certain high-income taxpayers.

24. I am old enough to have practiced tax law when the maximum individual tax rate was 70 percent, and taxpayers were thrilled by the prospect of qualifying for the 50 percent "maxi-tax" on labor income, yet even in that environment I observed individuals working and striving for more.

25. Martin A. Feldstein, "Tax Avoidance and the Deadweight Loss of the Income Tax," *Review of Economics and Statistics* 81, no. 4 (November 1999): 674–680. An excellent plain-English summary of Feldstein's work in this area is Martin A. Feldstein, "The Effect of Taxes on Efficiency and Growth," *Tax Notes* 111, no. 6 (May 8, 2006): 679–684. A more recent review of the literature is Emmanuel Saez, Joel Slemrod, and Seth H. Giertz, "The Elasticity of Taxable Income with Respect to Marginal Tax Rates: A Critical Review," *Journal of Economic Literature* 50, no. 1 (March 2012): 3–50.

26. Seth Giertz, "The Elasticity of Taxable Income: Influences on Economic Efficiency and Tax Revenues, and Implications for Tax Policy," in *Tax Policy Lessons from the 2000s*, ed. Alan D. Viard (Washington, DC: AEI Press, 2009); Raj Chetty, "Is the Taxable Income Elasticity Sufficient to Calculate Deadweight Loss? The Implications of Evasion and Avoidance," *American Economic Journal: Economic Policy* 1, no. 2 (2009): 31–52, doi:10.1257/pol.1.2.31; Saez, Slemrod, and Giertz, "The Elasticity of Taxable Income with Respect to Marginal Tax Rates: A Critical Review."

27. Firms rely principally on retained earnings, not sales of new shares of stock, to finance business investment, but the increase in share value represented by the retention of earnings is an implicit form of additional savings by the shareholder.

28. Feldstein, "The Effect of Taxes on Efficiency and Growth," points out that observing the response of the supply of savings to taxation does not measure the deadweight loss from taxing savings: what ultimately matters from a deadweight loss perspective is the extent to which taxation reduces future consumption paid for by those savings. When the analysis pivots to the effect of taxation on growth, however, the supply of savings takes precedence, because savings (including savers' shares of retained earnings) are the ultimate funding for business investments.

29. A start-up could organize itself as a partnership or LLC, or perhaps incorporate in a low-tax jurisdiction, but few start-ups choose to do so because of the limited tax benefits, liquidity constraints, and substantial legal benefits of US incorporation. Susan C. Morse, "Startup LTD: Tax Planning and Initial Incorporation Location," *Florida Tax Review* 14, no. 8 (2013): 319–360.

30. Engen and Skinner, "Taxation and Economic Growth," 617–642.

31. This tripartite division follows Alan J. Auerbach, *Testimony of Alan J. Auerbach, Robert D. Burch Professor of Economics and Law Director, Burch Center for Tax Policy and Public Finance, University of California, Berkeley, Before the House Ways and Means Committee: Tax Reform, Growth and International Competitiveness* (June 8, 2005) ("*Auerbach Testimony*").

32. Yuri Vanetik, "For More Jobs, Fix the Corporate Tax Code," *Los Angeles Times*, July 3, 2013, http://articles.latimes.com/2013/jul/03/opinion/la-oe-vanetik-tax-reform-growth-20130703.

33. General Accountability Office, *Corporate Income Tax: Effective Tax Rates Can Differ Significantly from the Statutory Rate*, GAO Pub. GAO-13-520 (May 2013).

34. *Auerbach Testimony*.

35. For reasons relating to the time value of money, it is not responsive to argue that future earnings will in fact be taxed.

36. Congressional Budget Office, *Taxing Capital Income: Effective Rates and Approaches to Reform* (October 2005).

37. Slemrod and Bakija, *Taxing Ourselves: A Citizen's Guide to the Debate over Taxes*, 146.

38. Since the low point of the Great Recession in 2008, when before-tax corporate profit was $517.9 billion, profit has tripled to $1,754.2 billion. Private nonresidential fixed investment—investment in fixed capital assets excluding real estate and inventory—reached a low point in 2009 at $1,285.4 billion but has since rebounded to $1,670.9 billion. US Bureau of Economic Analysis, *National Income and Product Accounts* (accessed 2013), http://www.bea.gov/national/.

39. Alan J. Auerbach, "Tax Reform, Capital Allocation, Efficiency, and Growth," chap. 2 in *Economic Effects of Fundamental Tax Reform*, ed. Henry J. Aaron and William G. Gale, 35, argues that these asset allocation efficiency losses are not very large.

40. Edward D. Kleinbard, "Stateless Income," *Florida Tax Review* 11, no. 9 (2011), 699–773.

41. Anthony B. Atkinson, "The Welfare State and Economic Performance," *National Tax Journal* 48, no. 2 (June 1995): 179; Engen and Skinner, "Taxation and Economic Growth," 617–642.

42. Congressional Research Service, *Tax Rates and Economic Growth*; Congressional Research Service, *Taxes and the Economy: An Economic Analysis of the Top Tax Rates since 1945*, CRS Pub. R42729 (Washington, DC: Office of Congressional Information and Publishing, December 12, 2012).

43. Christina D. Romer and David H. Romer, "The Macroeconomic Effects of Tax Changes: Estimates Based on a New Measure of Fiscal Shocks," *American Economic Review* 100, no. 3 (June 2010): 763–801.

44. The baseline is briefly outlined at ibid., 780.

45. Carlo A. Favero and Francesco Giavazzi, "How Large Are the Effects of Tax Changes?" *National Bureau of Economic Research Working Paper Series* (working paper No. 7439, August 2009), http://www.nber.org/papers/w15303.

46. See, for example, the dueling lists of research in William McBride, "What Is the Evidence on Taxes and Growth?" *Tax Foundation Special Report No. 207* (December 18, 2012), and Center on Budget and Policy Priorities, *Academic Research Lacks Consensus on the Impact of State Tax Cuts on Economic Growth: A Reply to the Tax Foundation*, by Michael Mazerov (June 17, 2013).

47. Myles notes that at the time of his paper, "Taxation and Economic Growth" (2000), economic models that incorporated the growth effects of tax policies ("endogenous growth models") were "recent" developments.

48. See, for example, Alex Rosenberg and Tyler Curtain, "What Is Economics Good For?" *New York Times*, August 24, 2013, http://opinionator.blogs.nytimes.com/2013/08/24/what-is-economics-good-for/.

49. US Department of the Treasury, Office of Tax Analysis, *A Dynamic Analysis of Permanent Extension of the President's Tax Relief* (July 25, 2006), 4.

An important feature of this type of model is that a permanent reduction in taxes, as compared to the baseline, would lead to an unsustainable accumulation of government debt relative to GNP and the model will not converge without an offsetting change to stabilize the debt-to-GNP ratio. In this type of model, the tax relief is typically financed by an offsetting change in taxes or spending, which can occur in the future or contemporaneously with the initial policy change and can take a multitude of forms. In this analysis it is assumed that the government's financing requirement is satisfied by either cutting future government spending or raising future taxes, in part to illustrate the sensitivity of the results to the financing assumption.

50. Shu-Chun Susan Yang, "Do Capital Income Tax Cuts Trickle Down?" *National Tax Journal* 60, no. 3 (September 2007): 551–567.

CHAPTER 6

1. R. Glenn Hubbard and Tim Kane, "Republicans and Democrats Both Miscalculated," *New York Times*, August 11, 2013, http://www.nytimes.com/2013/08/12/opinion/republicans-and-democrats-both-miscalculated.html.

2. See, for example, Bain & Company, Inc., *A World Awash in Money: Capital Trends Through 2020* (2012), 3 ("Our analysis leads us to conclude that for the balance of the decade, markets will generally continue to grapple with an environment of capital superabundance.").

3. Congressional Budget Office, *The Budget and Economic Outlook: Fiscal Years 2002–2011* (January 2001), xiv.

4. For probably the shortest complete summary, see Congressional Research Service, *The Congressional Budget Process: A Brief Overview*, CRS Report RS20095 (Washington, DC: Office of Congressional Information and Publishing, August 22, 2011). For a more complete summary, see Congressional Research Service, *Introduction to the Federal Budget Process*, CRS Report 7-5700 (Washington, DC: Office of Congressional Information and Publishing, December 3, 2012). Standard texts include Stanley E. Collender, *The Guide to the Federal Budget: Fiscal 2000* (New York: Century Foundation Press, 1999); Walter J. Oleszek, *Congressional Procedures and*

the Policy Process, 8th ed. (Washington, DC: CQ Press, 2011); and Allen Schick, *The Federal Budget: Politics, Policy, Process*, 3rd ed. (Washington, DC: The Brookings Institution, 2007).

5. The text here ignores niceties like the differences between "authorizations" and "appropriations," as well as the Congressional procedures for considering the Budget.

6. Congressional Budget Office, *The Supplemental Nutrition Assistance Program* (April 2012), 7.

7. Congressional Budget Office, *Social Security Policy Options* (July 2010), 3.

8. The United States measures its outstanding debt in two different ways, to reflect the conventions surrounding Social Security and other "trust fund" programs. The meaningful measure is debt held by the public. When the Social Security Trust Fund runs a current surplus, it effectively funds current government spending by investing the surplus in Treasury bonds. The Treasury debt held by the Social Security Trust fund is money owed by government's left pocket to its right pocket, and really is nothing more than a notation of a moral commitment to tax future generations enough to transfer cash back to the Trust Fund when required to continue benefit payouts at promised levels.

9. Bruce Bartlett, "The Bush Tax Cuts: 10 Years Later," *Tax Notes* 131, no. 11 (June 13, 2011): 1195–1197.

10. Congressional Budget Office, *The 2013 Long-Term Budget Outlook* (September 2013), 77–80.

11. Organisation for Economic Co-operation and Development, "Medium and Long-Term Scenarios for Global Growth and Imbalances," chap. 4, in *OECD Economic Outlook* 2012, no. 1 (June 19, 2012), 194.

12. Congressional Budget Office, *Updated Budget Projections: Fiscal Years 2013 to 2023* (May 2013), 1.

13. The executive branch's abilities to operate in the absence of appropriations are described in detail in Congressional Research Service, *Shutdown of the Federal Government: Causes, Processes, and Effects*, by Clinton T. Brass, CRS Pub. RL34680 (Washington, DC: Office of Congressional Information and Publishing, August 6, 2013).

14. This discussion is drawn from Edward D. Kleinbard, "The Debt Ceiling's Escape Hatch," *New York Times*, January 9, 2013, http://www.nytimes.com/2013/01/10/opinion/an-escape-hatch-for-the-debt-ceiling.html.

15. For a discussion of how automatic stabilizers operate, see, for example, Congressional Budget Office, *The Budget and Economic Outlook: Fiscal Years 2012–2022* (January 2012), appendix C.

16. Congressional Budget Office, *Letter to the Honorable Nancy Pelosi Providing an Estimate of H.R. 4872* (March 20, 2010), 2–4.

17. Congressional Budget Office, *Estimated Impact of American Recovery and Reinvestment Act on Employment and Economic Output from October 2012 through December 2012* (February 2013).

18. More specifically, using CBO data, I calculated that the unweighted average debt-to-GDP ratio for the 20 years 1988–2007, and for the 30-year period 1978–2007, was 18.3 percent. For the 40-year period 1968–2007, it was 18.2 percent.

19. My calculation of forgone revenues in the 2008–2012 period is not a general equilibrium calculation; that is, it does not take into account the effect on GDP of collecting higher taxes in a recession.

20. Congressional Budget Office, *Updated Budget Projections: Fiscal Years 2013 to 2023*, 1.

21. Congressional Budget Office, *Budget and Economic Outlook: Fiscal Years 2013 to 2023*, 4.

22. William G. Gale and Alan J. Auerbach, "Fiscal Fatigue: Tracking the Budget Outlook as Political Leaders Lurch from One Artificial Crisis to Another," *Brookings*, February 28, 2013, http://www.brookings.edu/research/papers/2013/02/28-fiscal-fatigue-budget-outlook-gale.

23. Congressional Budget Office, *Budget and Economic Outlook: Fiscal Years 2013 to 2023*, 1.

24. This is an important fact, given that the CBO's 2012 baseline projections for economic life after the expiration of the Bush tax cuts had baked into them any and all adverse macroeconomic effects stemming from the jump in tax rates—the "fiscal shock" that we all were told would assuredly follow were we to have fallen off the "fiscal cliff" on January 1, 2013. These macroeconomic effects were measurable in the early years of the 2012 projections, because of the economy's fragility, but the net consequence would have been much higher tax collections, and an equally robust economy, by the end of the period. In other words, the CBO's economic models implied that the dreaded fiscal shock in fact would not have had any measurable long-term adverse consequences for economic growth. Of course, we could have had an even better outcome than that analyzed by the CBO in 2012 by phasing out the Bush tax cuts over two or three years—a fiscal slope rather than a fiscal cliff.

25. Congressional Budget Office, *The 2013 Long-Term Budget Outlook* (September 2013), 13.

26. Ibid., chap. 7.

27. Congressional Budget Office, *Options for Reducing the Deficit: 2014 to 2023* (November 2013).

28. The tax revenue figure comes from CBO, *2013 Long-Term Budget Outlook*, 13. The interest cost differential reflects a comparison of the 2013–2022 projections for interest expense in the 2013 and 2012 *Budget and Economic Outlooks*.

29. Congressional Budget Office, *2013 Long-Term Budget Outlook*.

30. Congressional Budget Office, *The Budget and Economic Outlook: Fiscal Years 2013 to 2023* (February 2013), 24–25.

31. Martin Feldstein, "A Simple Route to Major Deficit Reduction: A 2% Cap on Tax Deductions and Exclusions Would Reduce the National Debt by $2 Trillion over a Decade," *Wall Street Journal*, February 20, 2013, http://online.wsj.com/article/SB1000142412788732488050457829692027892 1676.html.

32. Suzanne Gamboa, "Budget Cuts Mean Fewer Children at Head Start," *Associated Press*, August 19, 2013, http://bigstory.ap.org/article/budget-cuts-mean-fewer-children-head-start.

33. Thom Patterson, "The Most Important Jet You Can't See," *CNN.com*, July 19, 2013, http://www.cnn.com/2013/07/19/travel/air-force-one-sam-26000-sequestration.

34. Gabriel Muller, "Budget Cuts Put Low-Income Americans in Homes Squeeze," *Financial Times*, August 18, 2013, http://www.ft.com/intl/cms/s/0/5bad680c-0674-11e3-ba04-00144feab7de.html.

35. Michael D. Shear and Ron Nixon, "U.S. Workers are Grounded by Deep Cuts," *New York Times*, August 18, 2013, http://www.nytimes.com/2013/08/19/us/us-workers-are-grounded-by-deep-cuts.html.

36. Sam Stein, "Sequestration Forces Scientist to Euthanize His Genetically Modified Rabbits," *Huffington Post*, August 16, 2013, http://www.huffingtonpost.com/2013/08/16/sequestration-science_n_376877.html.

37. International Monetary Fund, *United States: Staff Report for the 2013 Article IV Consultation*, IMF Country Report No. 13/236 (Washington, DC: IMF, July 9, 2013).

38. Congressional Budget Office, *Letter to the Honorable Chris Van Hollen Regarding How Eliminating the Automatic Spending Reductions Specified by the Budget Control Act Would Affect the U.S. Economy in 2014* (July 25, 2013).

39. Ibid., 56.

40. Congressional Budget Office, *The Budget and Economic Outlook: Fiscal Years 2013 to 2023*, 27, 30–31.

41. Alan J. Auerbach and William G. Gale, "The Federal Budget Outlook: No News Is Bad News," *Brookings Institution* (April 2012). Auerbach and Gale take a longer-term perspective than I do in this chapter; my focus is principally on the next decade, and theirs on several decades further into the future.

42. Douglas W. Elmendorf, *Federal Health Care Spending: Why Is It Growing? What Could Be Done about It?* (November 13, 2013), 5.

43. Cf. "Boiling Frog," *Wikipedia*, last modified December 21, 2013, http://en.wikipedia.org/wiki/Boiling_frog.

44. Congressional Budget Office, *CBO's 2011 Long-Term Budget Outlook* (June 2011), 45–47.

CHAPTER 7

1. See chapter 4 and Bureau of Economic Analysis, *Preview of the 2013 Comprehensive Revision of the National Income and Product Accounts: Changes in Definitions and Presentations* (March 2013), http://www.bea.gov/scb/pdf/2013/03%20March/0313_nipa_comprehensive_revision_preview.pdf.

2. Douglas W. Elmendorf, "Choices for Federal Spending and Taxes" (presentation to the National Association for Business Economics, Congressional Budget Office, March 26, 2012), 6, http://www.cbo.gov/sites/default/files/cbofiles/attachments/PresentationNABE_3-26-12.pdf.

3. This is particularly the case if veterans' benefits and services are properly recharacterized as a component of defense spending, rather than as nondefense discretionary spending (the current budget presentation).

4. Congressional Budget Office, *Updated Budget Projections: Fiscal Years 2013–2023* (May 2013), 16, 24.

5. Ibid., 24.

6. Organisation for Economic Co-operation and Development, Social Expenditure Database [Data Chart EQ 5.1].

7. Organisation for Economic Co-operation and Development, Public Social Expenditure as Percentage of GDP, Social Expenditure Database [chart Social Spending 1960-2012].

8. Organisation for Economic Co-operation and Development, *Economic Outlook, Analysis and Forecasts* (May 2013), Annex Table 25, http://www.oecd.org/eco/outlook/economicoutlookannextables.htm.

9. Organisation for Economic Co-operation and Development, Public Social Expenditure as Percentage of GDP, Social Expenditure Database [chart Social Spending 1960-2012].

10. Stockholm International Peace Research Institute, *SIPRI Yearbook 2011: Armaments, Disarmament and International Security* (Solna, Sweden: SIPRI, 2011), Table 4.2 (and author's calculation).

11. Stockholm International Peace Research Institute, *Military Expenditure Database*, http://www.sipri.org/research/armaments/milex/milex_database (and author's calculation based on published population estimates for 2012).

12. Congressional Budget Office, *An Analysis of the Navy's Fiscal Year 2014 Shipbuilding Plan* (October 2013), 19–21.

13. This is a universal phenomenon in developed countries. See, for example, Organisation for Economic Co-operation and Development, *OECD in Figures 2009* (Paris: OECD Publishing, 2009), 6–7.

14. Congressional Budget Office, *The 2013 Long-Term Budget Outlook* (September 2013), 51.

15. Ibid.

16. This sum roughly accords with how much more we spend per capita than does the next most lavish country in the world (Norway), as described later in this section.

17. Organisation for Economic Co-operation and Development, *OECD Health Data 2013: How Does the United States Compare* (2013).

18. Ibid.

19. Organisation for Economic Co-operation and Development, *Why Is Health Spending in the United States So High?* (2011).

20. Thomas Bodenheimer, "Coordinating Care—A Perilous Journey Through the Health Care System," *The New England Journal of Medicine* 358, no. 10 (March 6, 2008): 1064–1071; Elizabeth A. McGlynn et al., "The Quality of Healthcare Delivered to Adults in the United States," *The New England Journal of Medicine* 348, no. 26 (June 26, 2003): 2635–2645; National Academy, *Best Care at Lower Cost: The Path to Continuously Learning Healthcare in America* (Washington, DC: The National Academies Press, 2013), Table 3-1.

21. Organisation for Economic Co-operation and Development, *Public Expenditures on Health Per Capita at Current Prices and PPPs* (June 27, 2013).

22. Congressional Budget Office, *CBO's 2011 Long-Term Budget Outlook* (June 2011), 45–47.

23. Council of Economic Advisors, *Trends in Health Care Cost Growth and the Role of the Affordable Care Act* (November 2013), http://www.whitehouse.gov/sites/default/files/docs/healthcostreport_final_noembargo_v2.pdf.

24. The Henry J. Kaiser Family Foundation, *Assessing the Effects of the Economy on the Recent Slowdown in Health Spending* (August 22, 2013), http://kff.org/health-costs/issue-brief/assessing-the-effects-of-the-economy-on-the-recent-slowdown-in-health-spending-2/.

25. Social Security Administration, *Social Security Basic Facts* (July 26, 2013), http://www.ssa.gov/pressoffice/basicfact.htm.

26. For an interesting alternative conceptualization of Social Security, see Daniel Shaviro, "Should Social Security and Medicare Be More Market-Based?" *Elder Law Journal* 21 (2013): 87–148.

27. Doubters are encouraged to read Francine J. Lipman and James E. Williamson, "Social Security Benefits Formula 101: A Practical Primer," *ABA Section of Taxation NewsQuarterly* 29, no. 4 (Summer 2010): 15–17, http://www.mwe.com/info/pubs/aba_summer2010.pdf; or Social Security Administration, *Social Security: Understanding the Benefits 2013* (February 2013), http://www.ssa.gov/pubs/EN-05-10024.pdf.

28. Congressional Budget Office, *Social Security Policy Options* (July 2010), ix.

29. Ibid., 3.

30. Congressional Research Service, *Social Security Reform: Legal Analysis of Social Security Benefit Entitlement Issues*, CRS Report RL32822 (Washington, DC: Office of Congressional Information and Publishing, June 7, 2013).

31. For discussions of some other Social Security policy options, see Congressional Budget Office, *Social Security Policy Options*; Congressional Budget Service, *Increasing the Social Security Payroll Tax Base: Options and Effects on Tax Burdens*, CRS Report RL33943 (Washington, DC: Office of Congressional Information and Publishing, February 5, 2013).

32. Congressional Budget Office, *Social Security Policy Options*, 18–19.

33. See chapter 8.

34. A useful summary of the principal terms of all the major federal healthcare programs is Congressional Budget Office, *The 2012 Long-Term Budget Outlook* (June 2012), chap. 3.

35. Congressional Budget Office, *Rising Demand for Long-Term Services and Supports for Elderly People* (June 2013).

36. Congressional Budget Office, *Health Care Reform and the Federal Budget* (June 16, 2009). See also Congressional Budget Office, *Budget Options Volume I: Health Care* (December 2008).

37. Ibid. For a recent set of proposals, see The Henry J. Kaiser Family Foundation, *Policy Options to Sustain Medicare For the Future* (February 20, 2013), http://kff.org/medicare/report/policy-options-to-sustain-medicare-for-the-future/.

38. C. Eugene Steuerle and Caleb Quackenbush, "Social Security and Medicare Taxes and Benefits over a Lifetime: 2012 Update," *The Urban Institute*, 2012, http://www.urban.org/UploadedPDF/412660-Social-Security-and-Medicare-Taxes-and-Benefits-Over-a-Lifetime.pdf. The methodology is explained in "Q&A with C. Eugene Steuerle: Estimating Social Security and Medicare Taxes and Benefits over a Lifetime," *The Urban Institute*, last accessed December 25, 2013, http://www.urban.org/retirees/Estimating-Social-Security.cfm.

39. C. Eugene Steuerle, "Are You Paying Your Fair Share for Medicare?" *The Urban Institute*, January 6, 2011, http://www.urban.org/publications/901397.html.

40. Douglas Elmendorf, Director, Congressional Budget Office, to Honorable John Boehner, 24 July 2012, http://cbo.gov/sites/default/files/cbofiles/attachments/43471-hr6079.pdf.

41. Congressional Budget Office, *CBO's Estimate of the Net Budgetary Impact of the Affordable Care Act's Health Insurance Coverage Provisions Has Not Changed Much over Time* (May 14, 2013).

42. Paul N. Van de Water, "Medicare Is Not 'Bankrupt': Health Reform Has Improved Program's Financing," *Center on Budget and Policy Priorities*, June 3, 2013, http://www.cbpp.org/cms/?fa=view&id=3532.

43. The programs are summarized in Congressional Budget Office, *Growth in Means-Tested Programs and Tax Credits for Low-Income Households* (February 2013).

44. Staff of Joint Committee on Taxation, *Estimates of Federal Tax Expenditures for Fiscal Years 2012–2017*, JCS-1-13 (Washington, DC: U.S. Government Printing Office, February 1, 2013), table 1, footnote 4.

45. Congressional Budget Office, *The Budget and Economic Outlook: Fiscal Years 2013 to 2023* (February 2013), 24.

46. Congressional Budget Office, *Growth in Means-Tested Programs*, 18.

47. Ibid., 10.

48. United States Department of Agriculture, *Official USDA Food Plans: Cost of Food at Home at Four Levels, U.S. Average, July 2013* (August 2013).

49. United States Department of Agriculture, Center for Nutrition Policy and Promotion, *Thrifty Food Plan, 2006*, CNPP-19 (April 2007).

50. Congressional Budget Office, *Growth in Means-Tested Programs*, 18.

51. Ibid.

52. Ezra Klein, "Peggy Noonan Attacks Obamacare for Doing What Peggy Noonan Wants Obamacare to Do," Wonkblog, *Washington Post*, August 20, 2013, http://www.washingtonpost.com/blogs/wonkblog/wp/2013/08/20/peggy-noonan-attacks-obamacare-for-doing-what-peggy-noonan-wants-obamacare-to-do/?wpisrc=nl_wnkpm.

53. Congressional Budget Office, *Growth in Means-Tested Programs*, 13.

54. The Henry J. Kaiser Family Foundation, *Analyzing the Impact of State Medicaid Expansion Decisions*, by Robin Rudowitz and Jessica Stephens (July 17, 2013), http://kaiserfamilyfoundation.files.wordpress.com/2013/07/8458-analyzing-the-impact-of-state-medicaid-expansion-decisions2.pdf.

55. Ibid.

CHAPTER 8

1. Martin A. Sullivan, "Busting Myths about Rich People's Taxes," *Tax Notes* 135, no. 3 (April 16, 2012): 251–254; Edward D. Kleinbard, "The Role of Tax Reform in Deficit Reduction," *Tax Notes* 133, no. 9 (November 28, 2011): 1108–1113.

2. Organisation for Economic Co-operation and Development, *Economic Outlook Annex Tables* (accessed August 2013), 26, http://www.oecd.org/eco/outlook/economicoutlookannextables.htm.

3. Organisation for Economic Co-operation and Development, *Taxing Wages 2013* (Paris: OECD Publishing, 2013), 14 (explains the concept in more detail).

4. OECD data sometimes distinguish between "Consumption Taxes," which include sales taxes, value added taxes, excise taxes, and the like, and "Taxes on Goods and Services," which is a slightly broader concept that includes all consumption taxes. Organisation for Economic Co-operation and Development, *OECD Revenue Statistics 2012* (Paris: OECD Publishing, 2012), Annex A (providing a formal definition). For purposes of this book the differences are immaterial.

5. Organisation for Economic Co-operation and Development, *Economic Surveys: United States 2012* (Paris: OECD Publishing, June 2012), 30.

6. More technically, a labor income tax imposes the same burdens as a sales or other consumption tax if three conditions are satisfied: (1) tax rates do not change; (2) all investments yield a normal return (that is, I do not earn supersized returns on my investment—formally, "economic rents"); and (3) the tax system can easily distinguish one's (taxable) labor income from one's (tax-exempt) capital income. Edward D. Kleinbard, "Paul Ryan's Roadmap to Inequality," *Tax Notes* 136, no. 10 (September 3, 2012): 1199.

7. Edward D. Kleinbard, "Herman Cain's 999 Tax Plan," *Tax Notes* 133, no. 4 (October 24, 2011): 469–480.

8. Harvey Golub, "My Response to Buffett and Obama," *Wall Street Journal*, August 22, 2011, http://online.wsj.com/news/articles/SB10001424053111903639404576516724218259688.

9. Josh Voorhees, "Mitt Romney Is Still Trying, Failing to Explain Away His '47 Percent' Remarks," *Slate*, July 29, 2013, http://www.slate.com/blogs/the_slatest/2013/07/29/mitt_romney_on_mojo_s_47_percent_tape_actually_i_didn_t_say_that_about_personal.html.

10. *Harper v. Virginia State Board of Elections*, 383 U.S. 663, 668 (1966) ("Wealth, like race, creed, or color, is not germane to one's ability to participate intelligently in the electoral process.").

11. Chuck Marr and Chye-Ching Huang, "Misconceptions and Realities about Who Pays Taxes," *Center on Budget and Policy Priorities*, September 17, 2012, http://www.cbpp.org/files/5-26-11tax.pdf.

12. Staff of the Joint Committee on Taxation, *Present Law and Background Data Related to the Federal Tax System in Effect for 2010 and 2011*, JCX-19-10 (March 22, 2010), table 11. The tables for 2011 should not be relied on at all, because they reflect the assumption (then embedded in law) that all of the "Bush tax cuts" would expire at the end of 2010. This did not come to pass; instead, all the Bush tax cuts were extended through 2012, and all the cuts other than the tax rates on the highest-income Americans were made permanent as of 2013. The JCT data for 2010 also are not perfectly accurate, because Congress reduced the 2010 alternative minimum tax burden on higher-income Americans at the very end of 2010, after the publication had been issued. As a result, the report overstates somewhat the tax burdens on more affluent Americans.

13. Congressional Budget Office, *The Distribution of Household Income and Federal Taxes, 2008 and 2009* (July 2012).

14. Staff of the Joint Committee on Taxation, *Modeling the Distribution of Taxes on Business Income*, JCX-14-13 (October 16, 2013), table 9, 25.

15. Edward D. Kleinbard, "Reading JCT Staff Distribution Tables: An Introduction to Methodologies and Issues," Keynote address to the 21st Annual Institute on Current Issues in International Taxation (Washington, DC: Joint Committee on Taxation, December 9, 2008).

16. These figures treat the federal tax savings available to affluent Americans who itemize their personal deductions as rebates of state and local taxes.

17. Tax Policy Center, *Why Some Tax Units Pay No Income Tax*, by Rachel M. Johnson et al. (Urban Institute and Brookings Institution, July 27, 2011), http://www.taxpolicycenter.org/Uploa dedPDF/1001547-Why-No-Income-Tax.pdf. For a summary chart, see http://www.taxpolicycenter. org/taxtopics/federal-taxes-households.cfm.

18. For a summary chart, see "Tax Topics: Who Doesn't Pay Federal Taxes?" *Tax Policy Center, Urban Institute and Brookings Institution*, accessed December 25, 2013, http://www.taxpolicycenter.org/taxtopics/federal-taxes-households.cfm. Updated data from 2013 show that the number of households that pay no federal income tax has now gone down to 43.3 percent; it will continue to decline as the economy recovers.

19. Marr and Chye-Ching, "Misconceptions and Realities about Who Pays Taxes," n19.

20. Ibid.

21. A few important recent contributions include Alan J. Auerbach, "Who Bears the Corporate Tax? A Review of What We Know," *Tax Policy and the Economy* 20 (Cambridge, MA: MIT Press, 2006): 1–40; US Department of the Treasury, Office of Tax Analysis, *A Review of the Evidence on the Incidence of the Corporate Income Tax*, OTA Paper 101, by William M. Gentry (December 2007); Kimberly A. Clausing, "In Search of Corporate Tax Incidence," *Tax Law Review* 65, no. 3 (2012): 433–472; Jennifer C. Gravelle, "Corporate Tax Incidence: Review of General Equilibrium Estimates and Analysis," *National Tax Journal* 66, no. 1 (March 2013): 185–214.

22. Congressional Budget Office, *Distribution of Household Income and Federal Taxes*, 16–18.

23. Staff of the Joint Committee on Taxation, *Modeling the Distribution of Taxes*, table 9, 25.

24. Patrick Driessen, "What Conditions Tax Distribution and Dynamic Scoring Are In," *Tax Notes* 141, no. 4 (October 28, 2013): 425–430.

25. The process and some of the important issues are described in Kleinbard, "Reading JCT Staff Distribution Tables."

26. Edward D. Kleinbard, "Mitt Romney's Marvelously Unburdened Income," *Huffington Post*, January 27, 2012, http://www.huffingtonpost.com/edward-d-kleinbard/mitt-romney-taxes_b_1235218.html.

27. Edward D. Kleinbard, "Stateless Income," *Florida Tax Review* 11, no. 9 (2011): 699–773.

28. CBO, *Distribution of Household Income and Federal Taxes*, 22, n34.

29. Ari Fleischer, "The Latest News on Tax Fairness," *Wall Street Journal*, July 22, 2012, http://online.wsj.com/news/articles/SB10000872396390444873204577537250318931044.

30. The most common measures of progressivity and inequality are summarized in Appendix B of Congressional Budget Office, *Trends in the Distribution of Household Income Between 1979 and 2007*. Longer treatments are John Creedy, "Taxation, Redistribution and Progressivity: An Introduction," *Australian Economic Review* 32, no. 4 (1999): 410–422; Paul D. Allison, "Measures of Inequality," *American Sociological Review* 43, no. 6 (December 1978): 865–880; Frank A. Cowell, *Measuring Inequality*, 3rd ed. (New York: Oxford University Press, 2011).

31. Nanak Kakwani, "Measurement of Tax Progressivity: An International Comparison," *Economic Journal* 87, no. 345 (March 1977): 71–80.

32. Congressional Budget Office, *Trends in the Distribution of Household Income Between 1979 and 2007*, 20.

CHAPTER 9

1. Much of this chapter is based on Edward D. Kleinbard, "The Congress within the Congress: How Tax Expenditures Distort Our Budget and Our Political Processes," *Ohio Northern University Law Review* 36 (2010): 1–29, and Edward D. Kleinbard, "The Hidden Hand of Government Spending," *Regulation* 33, no. 3 (Fall 2010): 18–22.

2. Internal Revenue Service, "Notice 2009-23: Qualifying Gasification Project Program," *Internal Revenue Bulletin* 2009-16 (April 20, 2009), http://www.irs.gov/irb/2009-16_irb/ar06.html; Internal Revenue Service, "Notice 2009-24: Qualifying Advanced Coal Project Program," *Internal Revenue Bulletin* 2009-16 (April 20, 2009), http://www.irs.gov/irb/2009-16_irb/ar07.html.

3. Eric J. Toder, "Tax Cuts or Spending—Does It Make a Difference?" *National Tax Journal* 53, no. 3 (September 2000): 361–372.

4. Edward D. Kleinbard, "Tax Expenditure Framework Legislation," *National Tax Journal* 63, no. 2 (June 2010): 353–382.

5. Organisation for Economic Co-operation and Development, *Tax Expenditures in OECD Countries* (2010), 234, fig. II.1.1.

6. Organisation for Economic Co-operation and Development, *Restoring Fiscal Sustainability in the United States: Economics Department Working Paper No. 806*, by Patrick Lenain, Robert Hagemann, and David Carey (October 25, 2010), 15, http://www.oecd.org/eco/46258004.pdf.

7. For reasons suggested in the text, this does not mean that the United States is a high-tax country by world norms, because other countries also employ tax expenditures, and comparability

across countries is difficult to measure. Nonetheless, in light of our tax expenditure addiction, it probably is the case that the United States in practice is effectively a higher-taxed country than the official statistics suggest. But by the same token, the United States also is unusual in rebating those higher taxes to high-income taxpayers, rather than lower-income ones, through the most expensive of the tax expenditure programs.

8. Congressional Budget Office, *The Distribution of Major Tax Expenditures in the Individual Income Tax System* (May 2013), 6.

9. Ibid., 15.

10. Staff of the Joint Committee on Taxation, *Estimates of Federal Tax Expenditures for Fiscal Years 2012-2017*, Pub. JCS-1-13 (Washington, DC: U.S. Government Printing Office, February 1, 2013), 38.

11. Congressional Budget Office, *The Distribution of Major Tax Expenditures in the Individual Income Tax System*, 6; Staff of the Joint Committee on Taxation, *Tax Expenditures for Healthcare*, Pub. JCX-66-08 (Washington, DC: U.S. Government Printing Office, July 30, 2008).

12. Congressional Budget Office, *The Distribution of Major Tax Expenditures in the Individual Income Tax System*, 12.

13. Daniel N. Shaviro, "Rethinking Tax Expenditures and Fiscal Language," *Tax Law Review* 57 (Winter 2004): 187–231.

14. Ibid.

15. David A. Weisbach and Jacob Nussim, "The Integration of Tax and Spending Programs," *Yale Law Journal* 113 (2004): 955–1028; Toder, "Tax Cuts or Spending—Does It Make a Difference?"

16. Staff of the Joint Committee on Taxation, *A Reconsideration of Tax Expenditure Analysis*, Pub. JCX-37-08 (Washington, DC: U.S. Government Printing Office, May 12, 2008).

The JCT staff's 2009 retreat from the analysis proposed therein to its traditional presentations of tax expenditure analysis was a mistake, not only for the reason mentioned in the text, but also because reverting to an excessive reliance on a "normal tax" as the analytical starting point weakens the case for bipartisan agreement on the central importance of tax expenditure reform.

17. Ibid., 49–50.

18. Congressional Research Service, *Tax Expenditures: Compendium of Background Material on Individual Provisions*, S. Prt. 112-45 (December 2012) (prepared for the Senate Budget Committee).

19. One study looked at some of the major individual tax expenditures as a group and concluded that their repeal would raise more money than the simple sum of the revenues forgone from each. Leonard E. Burman, Christopher Geissler, and Eric J. Toder, "How Big Are Total Individual Income Tax Expenditures, and Who Benefits from Them?" *The American Economic Review* 98, no. 2 (May 2008): 83.

20. Kleinbard, "Congress within the Congress."

21. Congressional Budget Office, *The Distribution of Major Tax Expenditures in the Individual Income Tax System*.

22. Adam J. Cole, Geoffrey Gee, and Nicholas Turner, "The Distributional and Revenue Consequences of Reforming the Mortgage Interest Deduction," *National Tax Journal* 64, no. 4 (2011): 977–1000.

23. Robert Carroll, John F. O'Hare, and Phillip L. Swagel, *Costs and Benefits of Housing Tax Subsidies* (The Pew Charitable Trusts, June 2011), http://www.pewtrusts.org/uploadedFiles/wwwpewtrustsorg/Reports/Economic_Mobility/Pew_Housing_Report.pdf; Evridiki Tsounta,

Home Sweet Home: Government's Role in Reaching the American Dream (International Monetary Fund Working Paper Wp/11/191, August 2011), http://www.imf.org/external/pubs/ft/wp/2011/wp11191.pdf.

24. For example, Tsounta, *Home Sweet Home*, 28, table 8, finds that Canada's tax subsidies for homeownership are perhaps one-fifth as large as a percentage of GDP as those of the United States, yet Canada has a higher rate of homeownership.

25. Edward D. Kleinbard and Joseph W. Rosenberg, "The Better Base Case," *Tax Notes* 135, no. 10 (June 4, 2012): 1237–1247. See also Lily L. Batchelder, Fred T. Goldberg Jr., and Peter R. Orzag, "Efficiency and Tax Incentives: The Case for Refundable Tax Credits," *Stanford Law Review* 59, no. 23 (2006): 44–48. Batchelder and her co-authors recommended that credits be refundable; for revenue reasons, I believe that they should not be.

26. See, for example, Center on Budget and Policy Priorities, *Testimony of Robert Greenstein President, Center of Budget and Policy Priorities Before the Senate Committee on Budget* (March 9, 2011), table 1 (listing distributional consequences of itemized deductions by income quintiles).

27. This discussion is drawn from Edward D. Kleinbard, "3 Ways to Relieve Our Tax Hangovers," *CNN*, April 22, 2013, http://www.cnn.com/2013/04/20/opinion/kleinbard-tax-burden/index.html.

CHAPTER 10

1. Robin Harding, Richard McGregor, and Gabriel Muller, "US Public Investment Falls to Lowest Level since War," *Financial Times*, November 3, 2013, http://www.ft.com/intl/cms/s/0/f0e71a16-4487-11e3-a751-00144feabdco.html. An earlier study came to essentially the same conclusion. Manasi Deshpande and Douglas W. Elmendorf, *An Economic Strategy for Investing in America's Infrastructure, The Hamilton Project* (Washington, DC: The Brookings Institution, July 2008), 7, http://www.brookings.edu/~/media/research/files/papers/2008/7/infrastructure%20elmendorf/07_infrastructurestrat_elmendorf.pdf.

2. Joseph E. Stiglitz, Justin Yifu Lin, and Célestin Monga, "The Rejuvenation of Industrial Policy" (Policy Research Working Paper No. 6628, World Bank, September 2013).

3. American Society of Civil Engineers, *2013 Report Card for America's Infrastructure* (March 2013), http://www.infrastructurereportcard.org/a/browser-options/downloads/2013-Report-Card.pdf.

4. Ibid., 65.

5. Dan Weikel, "Completed Colton Crossing Overpass to Eliminate Rail Bottleneck," *Los Angeles Times*, August 28, 2013, http://articles.latimes.com/2013/aug/28/local/la-me-colton-crossing-20130829.

6. Yonah Freemark, "What Is Moynihan Station?" *Friends of Moynihan Station*, August 24, 2005, http://www.moynihanstation.org/newsite/2005/08/moynihan_station_animation.html.

7. US Government Accountability Office, *Commuter Rail: Potential Impacts and Cost Estimates for the Cancelled Hudson River Tunnel Project*, GAO-12-344, report to the Chairman, Subcommittee on Surface Transportation and Merchant Marine Infrastructure, Safety, and Security, Committee on Commerce, Science, and Transportation, US Senate (March 2012); Kate Zernike, "Christie Stands by His Decision to Cancel Train Tunnel," *New York Times*, April 10, 2012, http://www.nytimes.com/2012/04/11/nyregion/christie-stands-by-his-decision-to-cancel-trans-hudson-tunnel.html.

8. Bill Wichert, "Amtrak to Construct 'Tunnel Box' for Hudson River Rail Project to Cross Manhattan Development," *NJ.com*, March 5, 2013, http://www.nj.com/somerset/index.ssf/2013/03/amtrak_to_construct_tunnel_box.html.

9. Richard Dobbs et al., *Infrastructure Productivity: How to Save $1 Trillion a Year* (McKinsey & Company, January 2013), 49.

10. Ibid., 16, 49.

11. "Life in the Slow Lane: America's Transport Infrastructure," *Economist*, April 28, 2011, http://www.economist.com/node/18620944.

12. American Society of Civil Engineers, *2013 Report Card for America's Infrastructure*, 6, 14, 46.

13. "The World's Top 100 Airports," *World Airport Awards* (2013), http://www.worldairportawards.com/Awards_2013/top100.htm. Other American notables that cracked the top 50 were the Denver International Airport (36) and the San Francisco International Airport (40).

14. Alex Davies, "11 Incredibly Fast Trains That Leave America in the Dust," *Business Insider*, November 26, 2012, http://www.businessinsider.com/the-10-fastest-trains-in-the-world-2012-11 (China has broken the 300 miles per hour barrier).

15. Deshpande and Elmendorf, *Economic Strategy for Investing*.

16. Steven Weinberg, "The Crisis of Big Science," *The New York Review of Books*, May 10, 2012, http://www.nybooks.com/articles/archives/2012/may/10/crisis-big-science/.

17. Congressional Budget Office, *An Analysis of the Navy's Fiscal Year 2014 Shipbuilding Plan* (October 2013), 19–21.

18. US Government Accountability Office, *High-Risk Series: An Update*, GAO-13-283 (February 2013), 24.

19. Ibid.

20. International Transportation Forum, *Understanding the Value of Transport Infrastructure: Guidelines for Macro-level Measurement of Spending and Assets* (Paris: OECD, 2013), 7.

21. World Economic Forum, *Global Competitiveness Report 2013–2014*, edited by Klaus Schwab (Geneva: World Economic Forum, 2013), http://www.weforum.org/issues/global-competitiveness.

22. Susan Lund et al., *Game Changers: Five Opportunities for US Growth and Renewal* (McKinsey & Company, July 2013), exhibit 21.

23. Josh Bivens, *Public Investment: The Next "New Thing" for Powering Economic Growth*, EPI Briefing Paper No. 338 (Washington, DC: Economic Policy Institute, 2012), http://www.epi.org/publication/bp338-public-investments/; Deshpande and Elmendorf, *Economic Strategy for Investing*.

24. Diane Cardwell, "Cities Weigh Taking Over from Private Utilities," *New York Times*, March 13, 2013, http://www.nytimes.com/2013/03/14/business/energy-environment/cities-weigh-taking-electricity-business-from-private-utilities.html?pagewanted=all&_r=2&; Matthew Yglesias, "Municipal Utilities Are about as Good (or Bad) as the Other Options," *Slate.com*, March 22, 2013, http://www.slate.com/blogs/moneybox/2013/03/22/municipally_owned_utilities_about_as_good_or_bad_as_the_other_options.html.

25. A closely related concept is that of "merit goods"—goods that cost money to deliver to the marginal user, but which would be systematically underconsumed in the absence of government intervention, because of a consumer's budget constraint or imperfect information. Government-subsidized fresh vegetables are merit goods.

26. Ronald H. Coase, "The Lighthouse in Economics," *Journal of Law and Economics* 17, no. 2 (1974): 357–376.

27. One example is Francis M. Bator, "The Anatomy of Market Failure," *Quarterly Journal of Economics* 72, no. 3 (August 1958): 351–379.

28. Elodie Bertrand, "The Coasean Analysis of Lighthouse Financing: Myths and Realities," *Cambridge Journal of Economics* 30, no. 3 (May 2006): 389–402; David E. van Zandt, "The Lessons of the Lighthouse: 'Government' or 'Private' Provision of Goods," *Journal of Legal Studies* 22, no. 1 (January 1993): 47–72.

29. Smith, *The Wealth of Nations*, Book I, chap. II, Conclusion.

30. Van Zandt, "The Lessons of the Lighthouse."

31. Jeff Tan, "Infrastructure Privatisation: Oversold, Misunderstood and Inappropriate," *Development Policy Review* 29, no. 1 (2011): 47–74.

32. James Meeks, "In the Sorting Office," *London Review of Books*, April 28, 2011, http://www.lrb.co.uk/v33/no9/james-meek/in-the-sorting-office.

33. David Parker, "The UK's Privatisation Experiment: The Passage of Time Permits a Sober Assessment" (working paper no.1126, CESifo, February 2004), http://www.cesifo-group.de/ifoHome/publications/working-papers/CESifoWP/CESifoWPdetails?wp_id=14559571 (summarizes the UK experience through the mid-1990s, and considers some of the difficulties in measuring the impact of these programs on national welfare).

34. "The Economist Explains: Why Is the Royal Mail Being Privatised?" *Economist*, October 10, 2013, http://www.economist.com/blogs/economist-explains/2013/10/economist-explains-9/; Peter Orszag, "The Best Fix for Postal Service Is to Take It Private," *Bloomberg.com*, July 24, 2012, http://www.bloomberg.com/news/2012-07-24/best-fix-for-postal-service-is-to-take-it-private.html.

35. David Alan Aschauer, "Is Public Expenditure Productive?" *Journal of Monetary Economics* 23 (1989): 177–200.

36. David Alan Aschauer, "How Big Should the Public Capital Stock Be?: The Relationship between Public Capital and Economic Growth," *The Jerome Levy Economics Institute of Bard College, Public Policy Brief*, no. 43 (1998): 11.

37. Henry J. Aaron, "Discussion of David A. Aschauer, *Why Is Infrastructure Important?*" (Federal Reserve Bank of Boston Conference Series Proceedings, 1990), http://ideas.repec.org/a/fip/fedbcp/y1990p21-68n34.html.

38. Cesar Calderon, Enrique Moral-Benito, and Luis Serven, *Is Infrastructure Capital Productive? A Dynamic Heterogeneous Approach* (Policy Research Working Paper no. 5682, World Bank, June 2011); US Department of the Treasury and Council of Economic Advisors, *A New Economic Analysis of Infrastructure Investment* (March 23, 2012) http://www.treasury.gov/resource-center/economic-policy/Documents/20120323InfrastructureReport.pdf.

39. Pedro Duarte Bom and Jenny E. Ligthart, *How Productive Is Public Capital?: A Meta-analysis* (CESifo Working Paper no. 2206, January 2008). Some of the early papers are summarized in Edward M. Gramlich, "Infrastructure Investment: A Review Essay," *Journal of Economic Literature* 32, no. 3 (September 1994): 1176–1196. Gramlich's paper introduces a separate theme, which is how infrastructure investment should be financed—through general revenues or user fees?

40. Bom and Ligthart, *How Productive Is Public Capital?*, 31.

41. Josh Bivens, *Public Investment: The Next "New Thing" for Powering Economic Growth*, 9.

42. David Alan Aschauer, "Why Is Infrastructure Important?" (Boston: Federal Reserve Bank of Boston, 1990), 31–32.

43. A good summary of existing programs is William A. Galston and Korin Davis, *Setting Priorities, Meeting Needs: The Case for a National Infrastructure Bank* (Washington, DC: The Brookings Institution, December 13, 2012).

44. Ibid., 3–4.

45. A typical consideration (and rejection) of capital budgeting is contained in Kathleen Brown and Jon S. Corzine, Chairs, *Report of the President's Commission to Study Capital Budgeting* (Washington, DC: US Government Printing Office, February 1999).

46. Congressional Research Service, *Federal Budget Process Reform in the 111th Congress: A Brief Overview*, R40113 (May 20, 2010), 14.

47. Gramlich, *Infrastructure Investment*, 1176–1196.

48. Timo Henckel and Warwick McKibbin, *The Economics of Infrastructure in a Globalized World: Issues, Lessons and Future Challenges* (Washington, DC: The Brookings Institution, June 4, 2010), http://www.brookings.edu/research/papers/2010/06/04-infrastructure-economics-mckibbin (summarizing research by Frederic Blanc-Brude).

49. Frederic Blanc-Brude and Omneia R.H. Ismail, *Who Is Afraid of Construction Risk?: Infrastructure Debt Portfolio Construction* (EDHEC-Risk Institute, July 2013), http://www.edhec-risk.com/edhec_publications/all_publications/RISKReview.2013-03-28.1327/attachments/EDHEC_Publication_Who_is_Afraid_of_Construction_Risk_F.pdf.

50. Galston and Davis, *Setting Priorities, Meeting Needs*.

51. Organisation for Economic Co-operation and Development, *PISA 2009 Results: What Students Know and Can Do—Student Performance in Reading, Mathematics and Science (Volume I)* (OECD, 2010), http://www.oecd.org/pisa/pisaproducts/48852548.pdf.

52. Ibid., Table I.A: Comparing Countries' Performance.

53. Organisation for Economic Co-operation and Development, *OECD Economic Surveys: United States* (OECD, June 2012), 69, http://www.keepeek.com/Digital-Asset-Management/oecd/economics/oecd-economic-surveys-united-states-2012_eco_surveys-usa-2012-en#page1.

54. For an example, visit the *WJEC* site at http://www.wjec.co.uk/students/past-papers/.

55. Organisation for Economic Co-operation and Development, *OECD Skills Outlook 2013: First Results from the Survey of Adult Skills* (OECD, October 2013), http://skills.oecd.org/skillsoutlook.html.

56. National Center for Education Statistics, *Digest of Education Statistics 2011* (Washington, DC: US Department of Education, June 2012), table 28, 53.

57. A 2011 study analyzing the correlation between teacher compensation and student performance found that a 10 percent increase in teachers' pay would give rise to a 5 to 10 percent increase in student performance. Peter Dolton and Oscar Marcenaro-Gutierrez, "If You Pay Peanuts Do You Get Monkeys? A Cross Country Comparison of Teacher Pay and Student Performance," *Economic Policy* 26, no. 65 (January 2011): 5–55.

58. Michael Greenstone, Adam Looney, Jeremy Patashnik, and Muxin Yu, *Thirteen Economic Facts about Social Mobility and the Role of Education*, The Hamilton Project (Washington, DC: The Brookings Institution, June 2013), 8.

59. Ibid., 9.

60. Organisation for Economic Co-operation and Development, *Strong Performers and Successful Reformers in Education: Lessons from PISA for the United States* (OECD, 2011), 34.

61. National Center for Education Statistics, *Revenues and Expenditures for Public Elementary and Secondary School Districts: School Year 2009–10 (Fiscal Year 2010)* (Washington, DC: Department of Education, 2012), Table 2, 6.

62. Ibid., 32.

63. Martin Carnoy and Richard Rothstein, "What Do International Tests Really Show about U.S. Student Performance?" Economic Policy Institute Report (January 28, 2013), http://s2.epi.org/files/2013/EPI-What-do-international-tests-really-show-about-US-student-performance.pdf.

64. National Center for Education Statistics, *Digest of Education Statistics: 2011*, table 64.

65. Tommy Unger, "Affording a House in a Highly Ranked School Zone? It's Elementary," *Redfin.com* (September 25, 2013), http://blog.redfin.com/blog/2013/09/paying-more-for-a-house-with-a-top-public-school-its-elementary.html#.UlNhrhaE7ww.

66. In Los Angeles, for example, a house in a top-tier school district costs on average 79 percent more than a comparable house in an average school district. Adrian Glick Kudler, "Homes are 79% More Expensive in LA's Top School Districts," *Curbed LA*, September 25, 2013, http://la.curbed.com/archives/2013/09/homes_are_79_more_expensive_in_las_top_school_districts.php.

67. Organisation for Economic Co-operation and Development, *OECD Economic Surveys: United States*, 30.

68. Anne Fernald, Virginia A. Marchman, and Adriana Weisleder, "SES Differences in Language Processing Skill and Vocabulary Are Evident at 18 months," *Developmental Science* 16, no. 2 (2013): 234–248. The paper is summarized by Motoko Rich, "Language-Gap Study Bolsters a Push for Pre-K," *New York Times*, October 21, 2013, http://www.nytimes.com/2013/10/22/us/language-gap-study-bolsters-a-push-for-pre-k.html.

69. Raj Chetty et al., "How Does Your Kindergarten Classroom Affect Your Earnings? Evidence from Project STAR," *Quarterly Journal of Economics* 126, no. 4 (November 2011): 1593–1660. The authors also have published a short non-technical summary, available at http://www.hks.harvard.edu/fs/jfriedm/STAR_Kappan.pdf.

70. Miles Corak, "Income Inequality, Equality of Opportunity, and Intergenerational Mobility," *Journal of Economic Perspectives* 27, no. 3 (2013): 20.

71. Greenstone, Looney, Patashnik, and Yu, *Thirteen Economic Facts*, 12.

72. Christopher A. Lubienski and Sarah Theule Lubienski, *The Public School Advantage: Why Public Schools Outperform Private Schools* (Chicago: University of Chicago Press, 2014).

73. Diane Ravitch, *Reign of Error: The Hoax of the Privatization Movement and the Danger to America's Public Schools* (New York: Alfred A. Knopf, 2013).

74. Organisation for Economic Co-operation and Development, *Strong Performers and Successful Reformers in Education*, 38.

CHAPTER 11

1. Florence Edler de Roover, "Early Examples of Marine Insurance," *Journal of Economic History* 5, no. 2 (November 1945): 172–200; Peter Spufford, *Power and Profit: The Merchant in Medieval Europe* (New York: Thames & Hudson, 2003), 30–43.

2. *The New Palgrave Dictionary of Economics*, s.v. "insurance."

3. Emmett J. Vaughan and Therese M. Vaughan, *Fundamentals of Risk and Insurance*, 8th ed. (New York: John Wiley & Sons, 1999), chap. 2.

4. Edward D. Kleinbard, "Competitive Convergence in the Financial Services Markets," *Taxes* 81, no. 3 (March 2003): 225–261.

5. Ibid.

6. Michael J. Graetz and Jerry L. Mashaw, *True Security: Rethinking American Social Insurance* (New Haven, CT: Yale University Press, 1979), 282.

7. That is, you could invest 2,000 florins risk-free, and earn 200 florins from that investment, for a total of 2,200 florins. Alternatively, you could send out 20 ships, each representing an investment of 100 florins, with an expected return of 121 florins (the amount invested plus a 21% return) 19 times, and a loss of 100 florins once when that ship sinks. [(19 x 121 florins) – 100 florins] is about 2,200.

8. This subsection has benefited enormously from the assistance and advice of Samuel Sessions, M.D., of UCLA. Doctor Sessions is unique in the country in having served as deputy assistant secretary of the Treasury for Tax Policy prior to his conversion to medical practice. Doctor Sessions publishes extensively in the field of healthcare delivery and budget policies.

9. Ashley Parker, "A Wife Committed to Cruz's Ideals, but a Study in Contrasts to Him," *New York Times*, October 23, 2013, http://www.nytimes.com/2013/10/24/us/politics/a-wife-committed-to-cruzs-ideals-but-a-study-in-contrasts-to-him.html.

10. Agency for Healthcare Research and Quality, *Statistical Brief #421: Differentials in the Concentration in the Level of Health Expenditures across Population Subgroups in the U.S., 2010*, by Steven B. Cohen and Namrata Uberoi (August 2013), http://meps.ahrq.gov/mepsweb/data_files/publications/st421/stat421.shtml.

11. Ezra Klein, "The Two Most Important Numbers in American Health Care," *Washington Post WonkBlog*, September 19, 2013, http://www.washingtonpost.com/blogs/wonkblog/wp/2013/09/19/the-two-most-important-numbers-in-american-health-care/.

It is no surprise that unhealthy poor Americans ultimately bear such high costs. In many regards, the US healthcare system is the most or one of the most unequal among our peers. For example, the income disparity as to the probability of a doctor visit in the past year is the highest in the United States among OECD peers. Organisation for Economic Co-operation and Develpment, *Income-Related Inequalities in Health Service Utilisation in 19 OECD Countries, 2008–2009*, by Marion Devaux and Michael de Looper (OECD Health Working Paper, 2012), 17–18, doi:10.1787/5k95xd6stnxt-en.

12. Germany's private plans described in the text below are not really exceptions, because participants are required to maintain the policies for life, premiums do rise with overall medical costs, and the prices of medical services and products are government-regulated.

13. Erika C. Ziller, Andrew F. Coburn, Timothy D. McBride, and Courtney Andrews, "Patterns of Individual Health Insurance Coverage, 1996–2000," *Health Affairs* 23, no.6 (2004): 219.

14. America's Health Insurance Plans, *Individual Health Insurance 2009: A Comprehensive Survey of Premiums, Availability, and Benefits* (October 2009), http://www.ahip.org/Individual-Health-Insurance-Survey-2009/. AHIP is the trade association of private health insurers. Some individuals withdrew from the underwriting process before completing it; they are included in the number in the text.

15. Sabrina Corlette, JoAnn Volk, and Kevin Lucia, *Real Stories, Real Reforms* (Georgetown University Center on Health Insurance Reforms and the Robert Wood Johnson Foundation, September 2013), http://www.rwjf.org/content/dam/farm/reports/issue_briefs/2013/rwjf407972.

16. For a review of the healthcare systems in our peer countries see Sarah Thomson, Robin Osborn, David Squires, and Miraya Jun, eds., *International Profiles of Health Care Systems, 2013* (The Commonwealth Fund, November 2013).

17. Elizabeth A. McGlynn et al., "The Quality of Healthcare Delivered to Adults in the United States," *The New England Journal of Medicine* 348, no. 26 (June 26, 2003): 2643.

18. National Research Council, *U.S. Health in International Perspective: Shorter Lives, Poorer Health* (Washington, DC: National Academies Press, 2013).

19. Ibid., 38, table 1–2.

20. George C. Halvorson, *Health Care Reform Now!: A Prescription for Change* (San Francisco: Wiley 2007), x.

21. Bruce C. Vladeck and Thomas Rice, "Market Failure and the Failure of Discourse: Facing Up to the Power of Sellers," *Health Affairs* 28, no. 5 (2009): 1305–1315, doi:10.1377/hlthaff.28.5.1305.

22. Reed Abelson, Katie Thomas, and Jo Craven McGinty, "Health Care Law Fails to Lower Prices for Rural Areas," *New York Times*, October 23, 2013, http://www.nytimes.com/2013/10/24/business/health-law-fails-to-keep-prices-low-in-rural-areas.html.

23. Robert Pear, "U.S. Plans to Unveil New Insurance Options," *New York Times*, September 29, 2013, http://www.nytimes.com/2013/09/30/us/politics/us-plans-to-unveil-new-insurance-options.html.

24. Tina Rosenberg, "The Cure for the $1,000 Toothbrush," *New York Times*, August 13, 2013, http://opinionator.blogs.nytimes.com/2013/08/13/the-cure-for-the-1000-toothbrush/.

25. Shannon Brownlee, Joseph Colucci, and Thom Walsh, *Productivity and the Health Care Workforce* (New America Foundation, October 2013), 10–11.

26. Lawrence P. Casalino et al., "What Does It Cost Physicians to Interact with Health Insurance Plans?" *Health Affairs* 28, no. 4 (2009): 533–543. The study surveyed solo and group physician practices and did not include doctors working for the federal government, HMOs, or hospitals.

27. National Academy, *Best Care at Lower Cost: The Path to Continuously Learning Healthcare in America* (Washington, DC: The National Academies Press, 2013), 101.

28. Elisabeth Rosenthal, "In Need of a New Hip, but Priced Out of the U.S.," *New York Times*, August 3 2013, http://www.nytimes.com/2013/08/04/health/for-medical-tourists-simple-math.html; Elisabeth Rosenthal, "The Growing Popularity of Having Surgery Overseas," *New York Times*, August 6, 2013, http://www.nytimes.com/2013/08/07/us/the-growing-popularity-of-having-surgery-overseas.html.

29. Nina Bernstein, "How to Charge $546 for Six Liters of Saltwater," *New York Times*, August 25, 2013, http://www.nytimes.com/2013/08/27/health/exploring-salines-secret-costs.html.

30. Organisation for Economic Co-operation and Development, *Why Is Health Spending in the United States So High?* (2011), 3, http://www.oecd.org/unitedstates/49084355.pdf. While it is true that rich countries spend more on healthcare than do poor countries, the United States is an outlier. We spend nearly $3,000 more per person per year than do the Swiss, even though we have similar GDPs per capita. Ibid., 2.

31. Gerard F. Anderson, Uwe E. Reinhardt, Peter S. Hussey, and Varduhi Petrosyan, "It's the Prices, Stupid: Why the United States Is So Different from Other Countries," *Health Affairs* 22, no.3 (2003): 89–105.

32. National Academy, *Best Care at Lower Cost*, 92. These figures are likely to be underestimated given that a recent study found that 86 percent of adverse events were not reported in hospital records. Ibid.

33. T. Bodenheimer, "Coordinated Care—A Perilous Journey Through the Health Care System," *The New England Journal of Medicine* 358, no. 10 (2008): 1064–1071.

34. Elisabeth Rosenthal, "The Soaring Cost of a Simple Breath," *New York Times*, October 13, 2013, http://www.nytimes.com/2013/10/13/us/the-soaring-cost-of-a-simple-breath.html.

35. G. Michael Allan, Joel Lexchin, and Natasha Wiebe, "Physician Awareness of Drug Cost: A Systematic Review," *PLoS Medicine* 4, no. 9 (2007): 1486–1496.

36. Drugs.com, *U.S. Pharmaceutical Sales—2012* (accessed 2013), http://www.drugs.com/stats/top100/2012/sales.

37. Sean P. Keehan et al., "National Health Spending Projections Through 2020: Economic Recovery and Reform Drive Faster Spending Growth," *Health Affairs* 30, no. 8 (August 2011): n14.

38. National Academy, *Best Care at Lower Cost*, 99 ("For 31 out of the last 40 years, health care costs have increased at a greater rate than the economy as a whole, and health care spending is expected to continue increasing more rapidly than the total economy, growing 4 to 8 percent per year through 2020.").

39. Congressional Budget Office, *Updated Budget Projections: Fiscal Years 2013 to 2023* (May 2013), 7.

40. Congressional Budget Office, *The Budget and Economic Outlook: Fiscal Years 2013 to 2023* (February 2013), 24.

41. Daniel Shaviro, *Making Sense of Social Security Reform* (Chicago: University of Chicago Press, 2001), offers a helpful overview of the structure and fiscal consequences of Social Security. See also Graetz and Mashaw, *True Security*.

42. The programs and their fiscal costs are summarized in Congressional Budget Office, *Growth in Means-Tested Programs and Tax Credits for Low-Income Households* (February 2013). The CBO has also published more detailed examinations of many of the individual programs.

43. Rick Ungar, "GOP Congressman Stephen Fincher on a Mission from God-Starve the Poor While Personally Pocketing Millions in Farm Subsidies," *Forbes*, May 22, 2013, http://www.forbes.com/sites/rickungar/2013/05/22/gop-congressman-stephen-fincher-on-a-mission-from-god-starve-the-poor-while-personally-pocketing-millions-in-farm-subsidies/. For more on Congressman Fincher's theological confusion, see Jack Jenkins, "Congressman's Misuse of Bible Verse Belies Bad Theology and Ideology on Food Stamps," *Think Progress*, May 23, 2013, http://thinkprogress.org/economy/2013/05/23/2053081/congressmans-misuse-of-bible-verse-belies-bad-theology-and-ideology-on-food-stamps/.

44. James Oliphant, "Love It or Hate It, Obamacare Redistributes Americans' Wealth," *National Journal*, November 21, 2013.

45. Amia Srinivasan, "Questions for Free-Market Moralists," *New York Times*, October 20, 2013, http://opinionator.blogs.nytimes.com/2013/10/20/questions-for-free-market-moralists/.

46. Sheryl Gay Stolberg, "On the Edge of Poverty, at the Center of a Debate on Food Stamps," *New York Times*, September 4, 2013, http://www.nytimes.com/2013/09/05/us/as-debate-reopens-food-stamp-recipients-continue-to-squeeze.html.

47. Steve Miller, "Steve Southerland's Campaign Paid for Upkeep and Rent on Congressman's Home," *Florida Center for Investigative Reporting*, September 16, 2013, http://fcir.org/2013/09/16/

steve-southerlands-campaign-paid-for-upkeep-and-rent-on-congressmans-home/. The Congressman's arrangements apparently do not violate campaign finance laws, but that is not the point here: the point is that outcomes to some extent are determined by forces outside our control—in this case, choosing one's parents wisely.

48. I recognize that my simplistic variant on Rawls's edifice has as a postulate the view that we choose to be born, but any other axiom seems to lead to moral philosophies too gloomy to contemplate.

49. Congressional Budget Office, *The Supplemental Nutrition Assistance Program* (April 2012).

50. Michael McAuliff, "Food Stamps: Military Families Redeem $100 Million a Year in SNAP Benefits," *Huffington Post*, June 19, 2013, http://www.huffingtonpost.com/2013/06/19/food-stamps-military_n_3462465.html.

51. Victoria Stilwell, "The American Body (as Cash Machine)," *Bloomberg News*, October 15, 2013, www.bloomberg.com/news/2013-10-15/bodies-double-as-cash-machines-with-u-s-income-lagging-economy.html.

52. "WATCH: Unabashed Surfer Receiving Food Stamps to Buy Sushi and Avoid Work," *Fox News*, August 12, 2013, http://nation.foxnews.com/2013/08/12/watch-unabashed-surfer-receiving-food-stamps-buy-sushi-and-avoid-work.

CHAPTER 12

1. Ajay K. Mehrotra, *Making the Modern American Fiscal State: Law, Politics, and the Rise of Progressive Taxation, 1877–1929* (New York: Cambridge University Press, 2013).

2. Ibid., 12.

3. Louis Kaplow, "Taxation and Redistribution: Some Clarifications," *Tax Law Review* 60, no. 2 (2007): 57–81. Kaplow's joke is that the most progressive tax imaginable (ignoring the incentive effects of taxation) would be a flat tax of 100 percent, combined with equal "demogrants" (cash awards) to all taxpayers, because it would achieve a complete equalization of after-tax incomes.

4. I do not mean to suggest that there was no debate at all along these lines, only that it was a secondary point. The principal battle line was drawn over the idea of an income tax, not whether it should be proportional or progressive. For a brief summary of the Congressional debate surrounding the first income tax after the passage of the Sixteenth Amendment, see Joseph J. Thorndike, "Original Intent and the Revenue Act of 1913," *Tax Notes* 140 (September 30, 2013): 1490–1492. Thorndike quotes some New York newspapers that took issue with the moral basis of progressive taxation, but what is more directly on point is that Elihu Root, senator from New York, former secretary of state, and a senior statesman of the time, acknowledged that he did not object to the concept, so long as it was applied in moderation. The versions of the Revenue Act of 1913 passed by each chamber of Congress contained a progressive rate structure.

5. Edwin Robert Anderson Seligman, *Progressive Taxation in Theory and Practice*, 2nd ed. (Princeton, NJ: American Economic Association, 1908), 209–210.

6. Joseph J. Thorndike, "Four Things That Everyone Should Know about New Deal Taxation," *Tax Notes* 121, (November 24, 2008): 973–975.

7. Joseph J. Thorndike, *Their Fair Share: Taxing the Rich in the Age of FDR* (Washington, DC: Urban Institute Press, 2013), 133.

8. Robert H. Frank, *Luxury Fever: Weighing the Cost of Excess* (Princeton, NJ: Princeton University Press, 2010).

9. Walter J. Blum and Harry J. Kalven, Jr., *The Uneasy Case for Progressive Taxation* (Chicago: University of Chicago Press, 1953).

10. Kaplow, "Taxation and Redistribution," 78 n42. Kaplow offers a scathing analysis of the weaknesses in Blum and Kalven's monograph, starting from the fundamental observation that Blum and Kalven, in attacking the case for progressive taxation, fail to make a positive case for proportional taxation.

In retrospect, Blum and Kalven's monograph is better understood as an iterative step in the history of ideas rather than as compelling economics. Their contribution was to disrupt what had become a largely unexamined consensus assumption regarding the desirability of progressive taxes, implemented through increasing marginal tax brackets. This assumption had crystallized from the work of progressive taxation enthusiasts dating back to Seligman, and continuing through the New Deal extension of the purposes of progressive taxation to include a quasi-sumptuary function.

11. Daniel N. Shaviro, "Replacing the Income Tax with a Progressive Consumption Tax," *Tax Notes* 103, no. 1 (April 5, 2004): 91–113; Joseph Bankman and David A. Weisbach, "The Superiority of an Ideal Consumption Tax over an Ideal Income Tax," *Stanford Law Review* 58, no. 5 (2006): 1413–1456.

12. This (without any invocation of geese) is the justification suggested in Bruce Bartlett, *The Benefit and the Burden: Tax Reform—Why We Need It and What It Will Take?* (New York: Simon and Schuster, 2012), 61–66.

13. Joseph Bankman and Thomas Griffith, "Social Welfare and the Rate Structure: A New Look at Progressive Taxation," *California Law Review* 75, no. 6 (1987): 1905–1967. There have been many technical contributions in the field of optimal tax analysis since the publication of Bankman and Griffith's work, but this paper has the twin virtues of explaining how optimal tax analysis works, and relating it closely to moral philosophy.

14. Kaplow, "Taxation and Redistribution," makes this point several times in passing (see p. 69), but does not tease out what its implications might be for tax system design.

15. Staff of the Joint Committee on Taxation, *Modeling the Distribution of Taxes on Business Income*, JCX-14-13 (Washington, DC: US Government Printing Office, October 16, 2013), 25, table 9.

16. Staff of Joint Committee on Taxation, *Reading JCT Staff Distribution Tables: An Introduction to Methodologies and Issues*, by Edward D. Kleinbard, Chief of Staff (December 9, 2008).

17. Douglas W. Elmendorf, Jason Furman, William G. Gale, and Benjamin H. Harris, "Distributional Effects of the 2001 and 2003 Tax Cuts: How Do Financing and Behavioral Responses Matter?" *National Tax Journal* 61, no. 3 (September 2008): 365–380.

18. Staff of the Joint Committee on Taxation, *Methodology and Issues in Measuring Changes in the Distribution of Tax Burdens*, JCS-7-93 (Washington, DC: US Government Printing Office, June 14, 1993). That monograph argued that a "static" analysis of proposed tax changes—that is, without considering behavioral reactions to the change in law—in general got closer to an accurate measure of changing tax burdens than do official revenue estimates, which do take tax-induced behavioral effects into consideration. Elmendorf et al. argue for a "dynamic" distributional analysis of tax law changes, but it is not clear how their analysis would capture the capital gains conundrum posed in the text.

19. Martin A. Sullivan, "How to Read Tax Distribution Tables," *Tax Notes* 90, no. 13 (March 26, 2001): 1747–1755.

20. Cf. Stephen Leacock, "A, B and C: The Human Element in Mathematics," in *Literary Lapses* (Montreal: Gazette Printing Company, 1910).

21. As of 2013, a new 3.8 percent tax applies to the "unearned" income of high-income individuals; this basically extends to capital income a tax analogous to the Medicare tax paid on labor income. As a result, those forms of capital income that are taxed at the maximum marginal rates applicable to individuals (e.g., interest income) also face a marginal tax rate of 43.4 percent.

The text ignores all the demonstrations in the literature of much higher marginal rates at lower income levels, attributable to one program or another phasing out, for the reasons explained earlier—these marginal rates are correct in a technical sense, but often apply only to a few hundred or at most a few thousand dollars of incremental income, after which an individual returns to the normal progression of published marginal rates. I view these high marginal rates as relatively thin clouds through which one climbs on the income ladder. They are artifacts of offering income support programs that unsurprisingly are withdrawn as income rises, and as such are very difficult to design around. It also is not at all clear that these high marginal rates have great salience with taxpayers; most empirical work concludes that taxpayers in fact are poor estimators of their own marginal tax situations.

22. Peter Diamond and Emmanuel Saez, "The Case for a Progressive Tax: From Basic Research to Policy Recommendations," *Journal of Economic Perspectives* 25, no. 4, (2011): 165–190.

23. Another important contribution along the same lines, and with an overlapping co-author, is James Banks and Peter Diamond, "The Base for Direct Taxation," in *Dimensions of Tax Design: The Mirrlees Review* (Oxford: Oxford University Press, 2010), chap. 6, 548–648.

24. In my own work, I argue for a middle ground of low but consistent rates on capital income. Chapter 13 offers a very quick summary of my reasoning.

25. Congressional Budget Office, *The Distribution of Federal Spending and Taxes in 2006* (November 2013).

26. Congressional Budget Office, *Trends in the Distribution of Household Income Between 1979 and 2007* (October 2011), 20–21. See also Arloc Sherman, Robert Greenstein, and Kathy Ruffing, "Contrary to 'Entitlement Society' Rhetoric, over Nine-Tenths of Entitlement Benefits Go to Elderly, Disabled, or Working Households," *Center on Budget and Policy Priorities*, February 10, 2012, http://www.cbpp.org/files/2-10-12pov.pdf.

27. I thank my research assistant Richard Bohm for developing this mode of visual presentation.

28. Organisation for Economic Co-operation and Development, *Divided We Stand: Why Inequality Keeps Rising* (Paris, OECD Publishing, 2011), chap. 8.

29. Congressional Budget Office, *The Distribution of Federal Spending and Taxes in 2006* (November 2013).

30. Ibid, 45. Kaplow, "Taxation and Redistribution," 71 n24, also briefly reviews some of the arguments on each side of this coin.

31. Congressional Budget Office, *The Distribution of Federal Spending and Taxes in 2006*, 16, 28.

32. Congressional Budget Office, *The Distribution of Major Tax Expenditures in the Individual Income Tax System* (May 2013).

33. The remainder of this chapter relies on research originally undertaken by a student in my tax policy seminar at the USC Gould School of Law, Ashley Elnicki, now in private practice. The OECD has since discontinued the dataset featuring the Kakwani index data used here.

34. Because of data constraints, the Gini index information is from the late 2000s, and the Kakwani index data are from the mid-2000s.

35. John Creedy, "Taxation, Redistribution and Progressivity: An Introduction," *Australian Economic Review* 32, no. 4 (1999): 410–422, doi:10.1111/1467-8462.00130.

36. The literature is reviewed, as of a decade ago, in Bruno S. Frey and Alois Stutzer, "What Can Economists Learn from Happiness Research?" *Journal of Economic Literature* 40, no. 2 (June 2002): 402–435.

37. Thomas D. Griffith, "Progressive Taxation and Happiness," *Boston College Law Review* 45, no. 5 (September 2004): 1363–1398.

38. Benjamin Radcliff, *The Political Economy of Human Happiness: How Voters' Choices Determine the Quality of Life* (New York: Cambridge University Press, 2013).

39. Ibid., 7–8.

40. John Helliwell, Richard Layard, and Jeffrey Sachs, eds., *World Happiness Report 2013* (New York: Sustainable Sustainable Development Solutions Network, 2013), 3.

41. Shigehiro Oishi, Selin Kesebir, and Ed Diener, "Income Inequality and Happiness," *Psychological Science* 22, no. 9 (2011): 1095–1100.

42. Helliwell, Layard, and Sachs, eds., *World Happiness Report 2013*, chap 3.

43. Michael Hiltzik, "How Much Are We Willing to Pay for the Pursuit of Happiness?" *Los Angeles Times*, November 3, 2013, http://www.latimes.com/business/la-fi-hiltzik-20131103,0,901196.column#axzz2kU4ECPpy.

CHAPTER 13

1. Center on Budget and Policy Priorities, *Recent Studies Find Raising Taxes on High-Income Households Would Not Harm the Economy: Policy Should Be Included in Balanced Deficit-Reduction Effort* (April 24, 2012).

2. Martin A. Sullivan, "Busting Myths about Rich People's Taxes," *Tax Notes* 135, no. 3 (April 16, 2012): 251–254. Phil Gramm and Steve McMillin argued to the contrary in the *Wall Street Journal* ("The Real Causes of Income Inequality," April 6, 2012, A-13) but Sullivan demonstrated the inaccuracies and logical fallacies in their arguments.

3. Peter Diamond and Emmanuel Saez, "The Case for a Progressive Tax: From Basic Research to Policy Recommendations," *Journal of Economic Perspectives* 25, no. 4 (2011): 172, doi:10.1257/jep.25.4.165 ("A number of studies have shown large and quick responses of reported [taxable] incomes along the tax avoidance margin at the top of the distribution, but no compelling study to date has shown substantial responses along the real economic responses margin among top earners.").

4. Congressional Budget Office, *Choices for Deficit Reduction* (November 2012), 25 (emphasis added).

5. For an empirical rejection of the hypothesis that tax cuts can drive spending reductions, see Christina D. Romer and David H. Romer, "Do Tax Cuts Starve the Beast? The Effect of Tax Changes on Government Spending," *Brookings Papers on Economic Activity* (Spring 2009): 139–200.

6. Robin Harding, Richard McGregor, and Gabriel Muller, "US Public Investment Falls to Lowest Level since War," *Financial Times*, November 3, 2013.

7. American Society of Civil Engineers, *2013 Report Card for America's Infrastructure* (March 2013), 65; Our Fiscal Security, *Investing in America's Economy: A Budget Blueprint for Economic Recovery and Fiscal Responsibility* (November 29, 2010), http://www.ourfiscalsecurity.org/storage/Blueprint_OFS.pdf.

8. Congressional Budget Office, *Federal Investment* (December 2013); Congressional Budget Office, *Infrastructure Banks and Surface Transportation* (July 12, 2012).

9. See, for example, in addition to the extended discussion in chapter 10, Josh Bivens, "Public Investment: The Next 'New Thing' for Powering Economic Growth," *Economic Policy Institute Briefing Paper* (April 18, 2012), http://www.epi.org/publication/bp338-public-investments.

10. Edward D. Kleinbard and Joseph Rosenberg, "The Better Base Case," *Tax Notes* 135, no. 10 (June 4, 2012): 1237–1247.

11. For example, Congressional Budget Office, *The 2013 Long-Term Budget Outlook*, 80–82, lays out the CBO's modeling of the efficiency costs of higher tax rates. Based on its reading of the empirical literature, the CBO assumes that if after-tax wages go down as a result of higher taxes, then the average tax "income effect"—the reaction to having less money—will point taxpayers in the direction of working harder, not less hard, but that the "substitution effect"—the reaction to a higher tax on the next dollar of income—will dominate, and lead to a decrease in the labor supply. This implies that moderate inframarginal tax rate hikes should not have materially negative effects on labor supply.

12. Jonathan Gruber, *Public Finance and Public Policy*, 596–597.

13. Congressional Budget Office, *Choices for Deficit Reduction*, 24 (footnote omitted).

14. Admittedly, scaling back personal itemized deductions has some marginal consequences. Ibid., 24 n29.

If, for example, you are a taxpayer near the top of the 25 percent rate bracket, then the loss of your personal itemized deductions might propel you into the 28 percent rate bracket on your last few dollars of income. The difference is that across the board tax rate hikes are marginal moves for *all* taxpayers, while curbing personal itemized deductions has marginal consequences only for some taxpayers, depending on their exact income level and quantum of such deductions. In addition, curbing personal itemized deductions mitigate deadweight losses—through distortions in capital investment decisions.

15. Douglas W. Elmendorf, *Confronting the Nation's Fiscal Policy Challenges* (September 13, 2011), 46.

16. See, for example, Michael M. Gleeson and Michael Beller, "Ryan Budget Calls for Top Tax Rates of 25 Percent," *Tax Notes* 134, no. 13 (March 26, 2012): 1595–1597. Both Rep. Paul Ryan, R-Wis., and Rep. Patrick J. Tiberi, R-Ohio, have argued that tax expenditures must be scaled back, but neither has made specific proposals.

17. William G. Gale, Jonathan Gruber, and Seth Stephens-Davidowitz, "Encouraging Homeownership Through the Tax Code," *Tax Notes* 115, no. 12 (June 18, 2007): 1171–1189.

18. Cf. Lily L. Batchelder, Fred T. Goldberg Jr., and Peter R. Orszag, "Efficiency and Tax Incentives: The Case for Refundable Tax Credits," *Stanford Law Review* 59, no. 23 (2006): 44–48.

19. Robert Carroll, John F. O'Hare, and Phillip L. Swagel, *Costs and Benefits of Housing Tax Subsidies* (Pew Charitable Trusts, June 2011).

20. For example, Evridiki Tsounta, "Home Sweet Home: Government's Role in Reaching the American Dream," *IMF Working Paper* (working paper no. Wp/11/191, August 2011), table 8, finds that Canada's tax subsidies for homeownership are perhaps one-fifth as large as a percentage of GDP as those of the United States, yet Canada has a higher rate of homeownership.

21. See, for example, Center on Budget Policy and Priorities, *Testimony of Robert Greenstein President, Center on Budget and Policy Priorities Before the Senate Committee on Budget* (March 9, 2011), table 1 (listing distributional consequences of itemized deductions by income quintiles).

22. Congressional Research Service and Senate Budget Committee, *Tax Expenditures: Compendium of Background Material on Individual Provisions*, S. Prt. 112–45 (December 2012), 695–696.

23. Bruce Bartlett, *The Benefit and the Burden: Tax Reform—Why We Need It and What It Will Take* (New York: Simon & Schuster, 2012), chap. 14.

24. Congressional Budget Office, *Options for Reducing the Deficit: 2014 to 2023* (November 2013), 168 (Option 31).

25. Congressional Budget Office, *Social Security Policy Options* (July 2010), 18.

26. Congressional Budget Office, *Options for Reducing the Deficit: 2014 to 2023*, 141 (Option 18) gives the year-by-year breakdown for the net incremental revenues that would be collected were the ceiling on taxable payroll tax wages lifted from today's level, which covers about 83 percent of all wages, to a higher ceiling that would cover 90 percent of all wages, a 7 percentage point increase. Multiplying that estimate by 17/7 gives a rough estimate of the revenues that would be raised by eliminating the ceiling entirely.

27. Congressional Budget Office, *Options for Reducing the Deficit: 2014 to 2023*, chap. 5.

28. Leonard E. Burman, "A Blueprint for Tax Reform and Health Reform," *Virginia Tax Review* 28 (2009): 287–323.

29. Congressional Budget Office, *Taxing Capital Income: Effective Rates and Approaches to Reform* (October 1, 2005).

30. Edward D. Kleinbard, "Stateless Income," *Florida Tax Review* 11, no. 9 (2011): 699–774; Edward D. Kleinbard, "The Lessons of Stateless Income," *Tax Law Review* 65 (2011): 99–171. A very short overview is Edward D. Kleinbard, "The Global Tax Avoidance Dance," *Huffington Post*, March 31, 2011, http://www.huffingtonpost.com/edward-d-kleinbard/the-global-tax-avoidance-_b_843318.html.

31. Ibid.

32. Edward D. Kleinbard, "Three Cheers for Dave Camp," *Tax Notes* 138, no. 5 (February 4, 2013): 619–620.

33. Jonathan Weisman, "Senator Offers Overhaul of Corporate Tax Code," *New York Times*, November 19, 2013, http://www.nytimes.com/2013/11/20/business/senator-baucus-offers-bill-to-overhaul-corporate-tax-code.html.

34. For example, the largest private business in the United States, Cargill, had annual revenues in excess of $133 billion in 2012, and the top five combined for $346 billion. "America's Largest Private Companies," *Forbes*, 2012, http://www.forbes.com/largest-private-companies/list/.

35. See, for example, Staff of the Joint Committee on Taxation, *Modeling the Distribution of Taxes on Business Income*, Pub. JCX-14-13 (October 16, 2013), for a discussion of the relative importance of international activities to the two sectors.

36. Thus, at least in this context, the term "capital" does not include human capital.

37. David A. Weisbach, "The (Non)Taxation of Risk," *Tax Law Review* 58 (2004): 1–64; Edward D. Kleinbard, "Designing an Income Tax on Capital," chap. 4 in *Taxing Capital Income* (Washington, DC: Urban Institute Press, 2007).

38. Robert H. Wessel, "A Note on Economic Rent," *American Economic Review* 57, no. 5 (1967): 1223 ("The traditional rent concept also allows to divide, conceptually at least, factor compensation into two parts, payments which induce factors to work and surplus which only confers a greater reward for work which would have been done anyway.").

Economists like to confuse the rest of us by using "inframarginal" actually to mean greater than marginal, when discussing returns to investment, and smaller than marginal, when discussing tax rates.

39. Edward McCaffery has shown that the combination of a postpaid consumption tax and progressive rates of tax on the amount consumed in a year can be viewed as taxing normal returns in a year of outsized consumption, when compared with the results reached under a "steady state" consumption model, in which savings are used to smooth lifetime consumption, rather than to finance a single year of consumption run riot. Edward J. McCaffery, "A New Understanding of Tax," *Michigan Law Review* 103 (2005): 807–938.

40. To take the two extremes, if the normal return is 5 percent, an investor that invests $100 in a perpetual machine can expect to receive cash flow (and net income) each year of $5. An investor in a machine that is worthless after one year must receive $105 in cash flow from that machine, which, after application of $100 in depreciation, leaves the investor with the same $5 of income—and $100 to invest in a new machine.

41. This discussion ignores for this purpose the distorting effects of inflation.

42. Businesses also can hold financial assets, but that does not change the basic thrust of the argument.

43. Wolfgang Eggert and Bernd Genser, *Dual Income Taxation in EU Member Countries* (CESifo DICE Report 2005, no. 1, January 2005), 41–47 ("The [dual income tax] is a schedular tax regime which divides total income into capital and labour income and regards them as different tax bases."). In practice, a dual income tax can be implemented in such a manner that there is no risk of some unspecified type of income failing to be taxed under either schedule.

44. See Edward D. Kleinbard, "An American Dual Income Tax: Nordic Precedents," *Northwestern Journal of Law and Social Policy* 5, no. 1 (2010): 41–86.

45. Joseph Bankman and David A. Weisbach, "The Superiority of an Ideal Consumption Tax over an Ideal Income Tax," *Stanford Law Review* 58, no. 5 (2006): 1413–1456; Edward J. McCaffery, "A New Understanding of Tax"; Daniel N. Shaviro, "Replacing the Income Tax with a Progressive Consumption Tax," *Tax Notes* 103, no. 1 (2004): 91–113.

46. See, for example, Ronald A. Pearlman, "Transition Issues in Moving to a Consumption Tax: A Tax Lawyer's Perspective," in *Economic Effects of Fundamental Tax Reform*, 393 (describing these transition issues in detail).

47. Sijbren Cnossen, "Taxing Capital Income in the Nordic Countries: A Model for the European Union?" in *Taxing Capital Income in the European Union: Issues and Options for Reform*, ed. Sijbren Cnossen (Oxford: Oxford University Press, 2000), 187 (explaining that it "should be possible to tax capital income positively but that moderation is advisable"). It should be remembered that well-designed standard consumption tax proposals, in fact, tax returns to capital when

those returns constitute rents. See, for example, McCaffery, "A New Understanding of Tax," 812–816; Shaviro, "Replacing the Income Tax with a Progressive Consumption Tax," 98–103.

48. Ibid., 67–79.

49. Edward D. Kleinbard, "Corporate Capital and Labor Stuffing in the New Tax Rate Environment," http://papers.ssrn.com/sol3/papers.cfm?abstract_id=2239360, develops the Dual BEIT in a bit more detail, but a comprehensive restatement of the proposal is overdue.

An early conceptual presentation of the BEIT was Kleinbard, "Designing an Income Tax on Capital." I considered its detailed implementation issues in *Rehabilitating the Business Income Tax* (Hamilton Project, June 2007), http://www.hamiltonproject.org/papers/rehabilitating_the_business_income_tax1. In both cases I included for reasons of perceived political economy a feature (an extra tax on "excess returns") that was both complicated and logically unnecessary. This presentation does not repeat that tactical error.

50. Ibid.

51. This is a principal theme of Kleinbard, "An American Dual Income Tax: Nordic Precedents."

Daniel Halperin, "Mitigating the Potential Inequity of Reducing Corporate Rates," *Tax Notes* 126, no. 5 (February 1, 2010): 641–658, also briefly raises the possibility of solutions along these lines.

52. Kleinbard, "An American Dual Income Tax: Nordic Precedents."

53. The term "Allowance for Corporate Equity" (ACE) was proposed by the Institute for Fiscal Studies in 1991, and Michael Devereux and Harold Freeman, Institute for Fiscal Studies, *Equity for Companies: A Corporation Tax for the 1990s* (1991); Michael P. Devereux and Harold Freeman, "A General Neutral Profits Tax," *Fiscal Studies* 12, no. 3 (1991): 1–15. The BEIT and ACE systems have different agendas. ACE was conceived as an alternative mechanism for implementing a *consumption* tax: corporations would receive a tax deduction equal to a notional cost of equity, calculated in a manner similar to the COCA deduction (applied, however, to "shareholders' funds," not all assets), and continue to deduct actual interest expense. Distributions to shareholders would in some fashion be exempt from tax; like the drafters of CBIT, however, the proponents of ACE became a bit vague when discussing how preference items would be handled, and capital gains taxed.

Like CBIT, ACE did not advance the taxation of financial derivatives at all. Like COCA, however, ACE deductions for notional capital charges corrected for errors in company-level depreciation practices. Devereux and Freeman, "A General Neutral Profits Tax," 5.

Unlike both CBIT and COCA, ACE applied only to corporations and retained a distinction between debt and equity: actual interest expense on the former would be deductible, while notional capital charges could be deducted in respect of the latter. The limitation of ACE to one class of business entities and the preservation of the debt–equity distinction seem to be fundamental weaknesses of the proposal.

54. Organisation of Economic Co-ordination and Development, *Economic Survey of Norway 2012* (2012), 87; Rosanne Altshuler, Benjamin H. Harris, and Eric Toder, *Capital Income Taxation and Progressivity in a Global Economy* (Washington, DC: Tax Policy Center, April 26, 2011), expand on this important point.

For the sake of brevity this chapter does not discuss the BEIT's international dimensions, beyond this one observation as to its effects on inbound investment and capital mobility.

CHAPTER 14

1. Richard Riordan and Eli Broad, "It Isn't a Sin to Be Rich," *Los Angeles Times*, December 27, 2013, http://articles.latimes.com/2013/dec/27/opinion/la-oe-1227-riordan-broad-wealth-20131227.

2. Richard A. Epstein, "The Constitution's Vanishing Act," *Defining Ideas*, December 16, 2013, http://www.hoover.org/publications/defining-ideas/article/163681.

3. *Spencer v. Merchant*, 125 U.S. 345, 355 (1888).

4. Chapter 2 discussed in a bit more detail the debate between the Hamilton and Madison camps as to the meaning of the taxing and spending clause; suffice it to say that there are 200 years of history on the side of the view summarized in the text.

5. *United States v. Butler*, 297 U.S. 1 (1936), discussed in chapter 2.

6. Gary Wills, *Inventing America: Jefferson's Declaration of Independence* (New York: Houghton Mifflin, 1978), chap. 18; Henry Steele Commager, *Jefferson, Nationalism and the Enlightenment* (New York: George Braziller, 1978), chap. 4; Darrin M. McMahon, *Happiness: A History* (New York: Grove Press, 2006), chap. 6.

7. Charles L. Griswold, Jr., *Adam Smith and the Virtues of Enlightenment* (Cambridge, UK: Cambridge University Press, 1999), 225.

8. Smith, *Theory of Moral Sentiments*, part IV, chap. 2.

9. Allen Jayne, *Jefferson's Declaration of Independence: Origins, Philosophy and Theology* (Lexington: University Press of Kentucky, 1998), 76.

10. Smith, *Theory of Moral Sentiments*, part IV, chap. I.

11. For example, Samuel Fleischacker, "Adam Smith's Reception among the American Founders, 1776–1790," *William and Mary Quarterly*, Third Series, 59, no. 4 (October 2002): 897–924.

12. David Lundberg and Henry F. May, "The Enlightened Reader in America," *American Quarterly* 28, no. 2 (Summer 1976): 262–293.

13. For a sympathetic biography, see Louis W. Potts, *Arthur Lee: A Virtuous Revolutionary* (Baton Rouge: Louisiana State University Press, 1981).

14. The pamphlet is available online at http://babel.hathitrust.org/cgi/pt?id=mdp.3901503926 1972;view=1up;seq=11.

15. Ibid., 31.

16. As described further in the text below, there is an enormous literature in this area. Traditionally, scholars have emphasized John Locke's *Two Treatises of Government* as foundational to Jefferson's political philosophy at the time he drafted the Declaration. In response, Wills, *Inventing America*, argued that Jefferson was not following Locke, but rather was inspired by Francis Hutcheson, a Scottish moral philosopher and the teacher of Smith. Wills's thesis has not always met a kind reception. Ronald Hamowy, "Jefferson and the Scottish Enlightenment: A Critique of Garry Wills's Inventing America: Jefferson's Declaration of Independence," *William and Mary Quarterly*, Third Series, 36, no. 4 (October 1979): 503–523. It is odd that *The Theory of Moral Sentiments* plays such a modest role in these spirited debates, given that it had quickly "gained the world's esteem," to quote Arthur Lee again, and was widely held in colonial libraries.

17. Darrin McMahon, *The Pursuit of Happiness: A History from the Greeks to the Present* (New York: Penguin Press, 2006); Howard Mumford Jones, *The Pursuit of Happiness* (Cambridge, MA: Harvard University Press, 1953), 99.

18. Michael P. Zuckert, *The Natural Rights Republic: Studies in the Foundation of the American Political Tradition* (Notre Dame, IN: University of Notre Dame Press, 1996), chap. 2.

19. Alan Gibson, *Understanding the Foundation: The Crucial Questions*, 2nd ed. (Lawrence: University Press of Kansas, 2010), chap. 4, is a helpful summary of the historiography.

20. Arthur M. Schlesinger, "The Lost Meaning of the 'Pursuit of Happiness,'" *William and Mary Quarterly* 21, no. 3 (1964): 326–327.

21. Thomas Jefferson to William Short, October 31, 1819, http://www.csun.edu/~hcfll004/jef-flet.html.

22. Jayne, *Jefferson's Declaration of Independence: Origins, Philosophy and Theology*, 136.

23. Wills, *Inventing America*, 248–255.

24. Commager, *Jefferson, Nationalism and the Enlightenment*, 113–114.

25. David Sciarra and Wade Henderson, "What's the Matter with Kansas' Schools?" *New York Times*, January 7, 2014, http://www.nytimes.com/2014/01/08/opinion/whats-the-matter-with-kansas-schools.html.

BIBLIOGRAPHY

Aaron, Henry J. *Discussion of David A. Aschauer, Why Is Infrastructure Important?* Federal Reserve Bank of Boston Conference Series Proceedings, 1990. http://ideas.repec.org/a/fip/fedbcp/y1990p21-68n34.html.

Aaron, Henry J., and William G. Gale, ed. *Economic Effects of Fundamental Tax Reform.* Washington, DC: Brookings Institution Press, 1996.

Aaron, Henry J., Leonard E. Burman, and C. Eugene Steuerle, eds. *Taxing Capital Income.* Washington, DC: Urban Institute Press, 2007.

Agency for Healthcare Research and Quality. *Statistical Brief #421: Differentials in the Concentration in the Level of Health Expenditures across Population Subgroups in the U.S., 2010.* By Steven B. Cohen and Namrata Uberoi. August 2013. http://meps.ahrq.gov/mepsweb/data_files/publications/st421/stat421.shtml.

Allan, G. Michael, Joel Lexchin, and Natasha Wiebe. "Physician Awareness of Drug Cost: A Systematic Review." *PLoS Medicine* 4, no. 9 (2007): 1486–1496.

Allegretto, Sylvia A. "The State of Working America's Wealth. 2011: Through Volatility and Turmoil, the Gap Widens." *Economic Policy Institute*, Briefing Paper #292 (March 22, 2011). http://www.epi.org/publication/the_state_of_working_americas_wealth_2011/.

Allison, Paul D. "Measures of Inequality." *American Sociological Review* 43, no. 6 (December 1978): 865–880.

Altshuler, Rosanne, Benjamin H. Harris, and Eric Toder. *Capital Income Taxation and Progressivity in a Global Economy.* Washington, DC: Tax Policy Center, April 26, 2011.

Alvaredo, Facundo, Anthony B. Atkinson, Thomas Piketty, and Emmanuel Saez. *The World Top Incomes Database.* Accessed July 2013. http://topincomes.g-mond.parisschoolofeconomics.eu/.

Alzheimer's Disease International. *World Alzheimer Report 2010: The Global Economic Impact of Dementia.* By Anders Wimo and Martin Prince. September 2010. http://www.alz.co.uk/research/files/WorldAlzheimerReport2010.pdf.

America's Health Insurance Plans. *Individual Health Insurance 2009: A Comprehensive Survey of Premiums, Availability, and Benefits.* October 2009. http://www.ahip.org/Individual-Health-Insurance-Survey-2009/.

American Society of Civil Engineers. *2013 Report Card for America's Infrastructure.* March 2013. http://www.infrastructurereportcard.org/a/browser-options/downloads/2013-Report-Card.pdf.

Anderson, Gerard F., Uwe E. Reinhardt, Peter S. Hussey, and Varduhi Petrosyan. "It's the Prices, Stupid: Why the United States Is So Different from Other Countries." *Health Affairs* 22, no. 3 (2003): 89–105.

Aschauer, David Alan. "Is Public Expenditure Productive?" *Journal of Monetary Economics* 23 (1989): 177–200.

Aschauer, David Alan. *Why Is Infrastructure Important?* Boston: Federal Reserve Bank of Boston, 1990.

Aschauer, David Alan. "How Big Should the Public Capital Stock Be?: The Relationship between Public Capital and Economic Growth." *The Jerome Levy Economics Institute of Bard College, Public Policy Brief,* no. 43 (1998): 5–31.

Atkinson, Anthony B. "The Welfare State and Economic Performance." *National Tax Journal* 48, no. 2 (June 1995): 171–198.

Auerbach, Alan J. "Who Bears the Corporate Tax? A Review of What We Know." *Tax Policy and the Economy* 20 (Cambridge, MA: MIT Press, 2006): 1–40.

Auerbach, Alan J., and William G. Gale. "The Federal Budget Outlook: No News Is Bad News." *Brookings Institution.* April 2012. http://www.urban.org/UploadedPDF/1001589-The-Budget-Outlook-No-News-Is-Bad-News.pdf.

Auten, Gerald, and Geoffrey Gee. "Income Mobility in the United States: New Evidence from Income Tax Data." *National Tax Journal* 62, no. 2 (June 2009): 301–328.

Auten, Gerald, Geoffrey Gee, and Nicholas Turner. "Income Inequality, Mobility and Turnover at the Top in the US, 1987–2010." *American Economic Review: Papers and Proceedings* 103, no. 3 (May 2013): 168–172. doi:10.1257/aer.103.3.168.

Bain & Company, Inc. *A World Awash in Money: Capital Trends Through 2020.* 2012. http://www.bain.com/Images/BAIN_REPORT_A_world_awash_in_money.pdf.

Bankman, Joseph, and David A. Weisbach. "The Superiority of an Ideal Consumption Tax over an Ideal Income Tax." *Stanford Law Review* 58, no. 5 (2006): 1413–1456.

Bankman, Joseph, and Thomas Griffith. "Social Welfare and the Rate Structure: A New Look at Progressive Taxation." *California Law Review* 75, no. 6 (1987): 1905–1967.

Banks, James, and Peter Diamond. "The Base for Direct Taxation," in *Dimensions of Tax Design: The Mirrlees Review.* Oxford: Oxford University Press, 2010.

Bartels, Larry M. *Unequal Democracy: The Political Economy of the New Gilded Age.* Princeton, NJ: Princeton University Press, 2010.

Bartlett, Bruce. "The Bush Tax Cuts: 10 Years Later." *Tax Notes* 131, no. 11 (June 13, 2011): 1195–1197.

Bartlett, Bruce. *The Benefit and the Burden: Tax Reform—Why We Need It and What It Will Take.* New York: Simon and Schuster, 2012.

Batchelder, Lily L., Fred T. Goldberg Jr., and Peter R. Orszag. "Efficiency and Tax Incentives: The Case for Refundable Tax Credits." *Stanford Law Review* 59, no. 23 (2006): 44–48.

Bator, Francis M. "The Anatomy of Market Failure." *Quarterly Journal of Economics* 72, no. 3 (August 1958): 351–379.

Becker, George. *The Economic Approach to Human Behavior.* Chicago: University of Chicago Press, 1976.

Bertrand, Elodie. "The Coasean Analysis of Lighthouse Financing: Myths and Realities." *Cambridge Journal of Economics* 30, no. 3 (May 2006): 389–402.

Bivens, Josh. "Public Investment: The Next 'New Thing' for Powering Economic Growth." *Economic Policy Institute Briefing Paper* (April 18, 2012). http://www.epi.org/publication/bp338-public-investments.

Bivens, Josh, and Lawrence Mishel. "The Pay of Corporate Executives and Financial Professionals as Evidence of Rents in Top 1 Percent Incomes." *Journal of Economic Perspectives* 27, no. 3 (2013): 57–78. doi:10.1257/jep.27.3.57.

Blanc-Brude, Frederic, and Omneia R. H. Ismail. *Who Is Afraid of Construction Risk?: Infrastructure Debt Portfolio Construction*. EDHEC-Risk Institute, July 2013. http://www.edhec-risk.com/edhec_publications/all_publications/RISKReview.2013-03-28.1327/attachments/EDHEC_Publication_Who_is_Afraid_of_Construction_Risk_F.pdf.

Blum, Walter J., and Harry J. Kalven Jr. *The Uneasy Case for Progressive Taxation*. Chicago: University of Chicago Press, 1953.

Boadway, Robin W., and Neil Bruce. *Welfare Economics*. Oxford: B. Blackwell, 1984.

Bodenheimer, Thomas. "Coordinating Care—A Perilous Journey Through the Health Care System." *New England Journal of Medicine* 358, no. 10 (March 6, 2008): 1064–1071.

Bom, Pedro Duarte, and Jenny E. Ligthart. *How Productive Is Public Capital?: A Meta-analysis*. CESifo Working Paper no. 2206, January 2008.

Bond, Charlotte Ann, Teran Martin, Susan Hume McIntosh, and Charles Ian Mead. "Integrated Macroeconomic Accounts for the United States." *Survey of Current Business* 87 (February 2007): 14–31.

Bradbury, Katharine, and Jane Katz. "Trends in U.S. Family Income Mobility, 1967–2004." *Federal Reserve Bank of Boston Working Paper* No. 09-7 (August 20, 2009).

Bricker, Jesse, Arthur B. Kennickell, Kevin B. Moore, and John Sabelhaus. "Changes in U.S. Family Finances from 2007 to 2010: Evidence from the Survey of Consumer Finances." *Federal Reserve Bulletin* 98, no. 2 (June 2011): 1–80.

Bridgman, Benjamin, Andrew Dugan, Mikhael Lal, Matthew Osborne, and Shaunda Villones. "Accounting for Household Production in the National Accounts, 1965–2010." *Survey of Current Business* 92 (May 2012): 23–36.

Brown, Kathleen, and Jon S. Corzine, Chairs. *Report of the President's Commission to Study Capital Budgeting*. Washington, DC: US Government Printing Office, February 1999.

Brown, Wendy. "American Nightmare: Neoliberalism, Neoconservatism, and De-democratization." *Political Theory* 34, no. 6 (2006): 690–714.

Brownlee, Shannon, Joseph Colucci, and Thom Walsh. *Productivity and the Health Care Workforce*. New America Foundation, October 2013. http://growth.newamerica.net/sites/newamerica.net/files/policydocs/Brownlee_Colucci_Walsh_ProductivityNAF_10.2013_2.pdf.

Buchan, James. *The Authentic Adam Smith: His Life and Ideas*. New York: W.W. Norton, 2006.

Burkhauser, Richard V., Jeff Larrimore, and Kosali I. Simon. "A 'Second Opinion' on the Economic Health of the American Middle Class." *National Tax Journal* 65, no. 1 (March 2012): 7–32.

Burman, Leonard E. "A Blueprint for Tax Reform and Health Reform." *Virginia Tax Review* 28 (2009): 287–323.

Burman, Leonard E., Christopher Geissler, and Eric J. Toder. "How Big Are Total Individual Income Tax Expenditures, and Who Benefits from Them?" *The American Economic Review* 98, no. 2 (May 2008): 79–83.

Calderon, Cesar, Enrique Moral-Benito, and Luis Serven. *Is Infrastructure Capital Productive? A Dynamic Heterogeneous Approach.* Policy Research Working Paper no. 5682, World Bank, June 2011.

Carnoy, Martin, and Richard Rothstein. "What Do International Tests Really Show about U.S. Student Performance?" Economic Policy Institute Report. January 28, 2013. http://s2.epi.org/files/2013/EPI-What-do-international-tests-really-show-about-US-student-performance.pdf.

Carroll, Robert, John F. O'Hare, and Phillip L. Swagel. *Costs and Benefits of Housing Tax Subsidies.* The Pew Charitable Trusts, June 2011. http://www.pewtrusts.org/uploadedFiles/wwwpewtrustsorg/Reports/Economic_Mobility/Pew_Housing_Report.pdf.

Casalino, Lawrence P., Sean Nicholson, David N. Gans, Terry Hammons, Dante Morra, Theodore Karrison, and Wendy Levinson. "What Does It Cost Physicians to Interact with Health Insurance Plans?" *Health Affairs* 28, no. 4 (2009): 533–543.

Center for American Progress. *Hunger in America: Suffering We All Pay For.* By Donald S. Shepard, Elizabeth Setren, and Donna Cooper. October 2011. http://www.americanprogress.org/issues/2011/10/pdf/hunger_paper.pdf.

Center for College Affordability and Productivity. *Compiling the 2013 Forbes/CCAP Rankings.* 2013. http://centerforcollegeaffordability.org/uploads/2013_Methodology.pdf.

Center on Budget and Policy Priorities. *A Guide To Statistics on Historical Trends in Income Inequality.* By Chad Stone, Danilo Trisi, and Arloc Sherman. October 23, 2012. http://www.cbpp.org/files/11-28-11pov.pdf.

Center on Budget and Policy Priorities. *Academic Research Lacks Consensus on the Impact of State Tax Cuts on Economic Growth: A Reply to the Tax Foundation.* By Michael Mazerov. June 17, 2013. http://www.cbpp.org/files/6-17-13sfp.pdf.

Center on Budget and Policy Priorities. *Recent Studies Find Raising Taxes on High-Income Households Would Not Harm the Economy: Policy Should Be Included in Balanced Deficit-Reduction Effort.* By Chye-Ching Huang. April 24, 2012. http://www.cbpp.org/cms/index.cfm?fa=view&id=3756.

Center on Budget and Policy Priorities. *Testimony of Robert Greenstein President, Center of Budget and Policy Priorities Before the Senate Committee on Budget.* March 9, 2011. http://www.cbpp.org/files/2-13-13pov-test.pdf.

Chetty, Raj, John N. Friedman, Nathaniel Hilger, Emmanuel Saez, Diane Whitmore Schanzenbach, and Danny Yagan. "How Does Your Kindergarten Classroom Affect Your Earnings? Evidence from Project STAR." *The Quarterly Journal of Economics* 126, no. 4 (November 2011): 1593–1660.

Chetty, Raj, Nathaniel Hendren, Patrick Kline, and Emmanuel Saez. "The Economic Impacts of Tax Expenditures: Evidence from Spatial Variation across the U.S." US Treasury Department (January 2014). http://www.irs.gov/pub/irs-soi/14rptaxexpenditures.pdf.

Chetty, Raj. "Is the Taxable Income Elasticity Sufficient to Calculate Deadweight Loss? The Implications of Evasion and Avoidance." *American Economic Journal: Economic Policy* 1, no. 2 (2009): 31–52. doi:10.1257/pol.1.2.31.

Clausing, Kimberly A. "In Search of Corporate Tax Incidence." *Tax Law Review* 65, no. 3 (2012): 433–472.

Cnossen, Sijbren. "Taxing Capital Income in the Nordic Countries: A Model for the European Union?" in *Taxing Capital Income in the European Union: Issues and Options for Reform*, ed. Sijbren Cnossen. Oxford: Oxford University Press, 2000.

Coase, Ronald H. "The Lighthouse in Economics." *Journal of Law and Economics* 17, no. 2 (1974): 357–376.

Cole, Adam J., Geoffrey Gee, and Nicholas Turner. "The Distributional and Revenue Consequences of Reforming the Mortgage Interest Deduction." *National Tax Journal* 64, no. 4 (2011): 977–1000.

Collender, Stanley E. *The Guide to the Federal Budget: Fiscal 2000*. New York: Century Foundation Press, 1999.

Commager, Henry Steele. *Jefferson, Nationalism and the Enlightenment*. New York: George Braziller, 1978.

Congressional Budget Office. *Taxing Capital Income: Effective Rates and Approaches to Reform*. October 2005. http://www.cbo.gov/sites/default/files/cbofiles/ftpdocs/67xx/doc6792/10-18-tax.pdf.

Congressional Budget Office. *Budget Options Volume I: Health Care*. December 2008. http://www.cbo.gov/sites/default/files/cbofiles/ftpdocs/99xx/doc9925/12-18-healthoptions.pdf.

Congressional Budget Office. *Health Care Reform and the Federal Budget*. June 16, 2009. http://www.cbo.gov/sites/default/files/cbofiles/ftpdocs/103xx/doc10311/06-16-healthreformandfederalbudget.pdf.

Congressional Budget Office. *Changes in the Distribution of Workers' Annual Earnings Between 1979 and 2007*. October 2009. http://www.cbo.gov/sites/default/files/cbofiles/ftpdocs/105xx/doc10527/10-02-workers.pdf.

Congressional Budget Office. *Letter to the Honorable Nancy Pelosi Providing an Estimate of H.R. 4872*. March 18, 2010. http://www.cbo.gov/sites/default/files/cbofiles/attachments/hr4872_0.pdf.

Congressional Budget Office. *Social Security Policy Options*. July 2010. http://www.cbo.gov/sites/default/files/cbofiles/ftpdocs/115xx/doc11580/07-01-ssoptions_forweb.pdf.

Congressional Budget Office. *CBO's 2011 Long-Term Budget Outlook*. June 2011. http://www.cbo.gov/sites/default/files/cbofiles/attachments/06-21-Long-Term_Budget_Outlook.pdf.

Congressional Budget Office. *Trends in the Distribution of Household Income Between 1979 and 2007*. October 2011. http://www.cbo.gov/sites/default/files/cbofiles/attachments/10-25-HouseholdIncome.pdf.

Congressional Budget Office. *The Budget and Economic Outlook: Fiscal Years 2012 to 2022*. January 2012. http://www.cbo.gov/sites/default/files/cbofiles/attachments/01-31-2012_Outlook.pdf.

Congressional Budget Office. *The Supplemental Nutrition Assistance Program*. April 2012. http://www.cbo.gov/sites/default/files/cbofiles/attachments/04-19-SNAP.pdf.

Congressional Budget Office. *The 2012 Long-Term Budget Outlook*. June 2012. http://www.cbo.gov/sites/default/files/cbofiles/attachments/06-05-Long-Term_Budget_Outlook_2.pdf.

Congressional Budget Office. *Infrastructure Banks and Surface Transportation*. July 12, 2012. http://www.cbo.gov/sites/default/files/cbofiles/attachments/07-12-12-InfrastructureBanks.pdf.

Congressional Budget Office. *The Distribution of Household Income and Federal Taxes, 2008 and 2009*. July 2012. http://www.cbo.gov/sites/default/files/cbofiles/attachments/43373-06-11-HouseholdIncomeandFedTaxes.pdf.

Congressional Budget Office. *A Review of Recent Research on Labor Supply Elasticities.* Working Paper, October 2012.

Congressional Budget Office. *How the Supply of Labor Responds to Changes in Fiscal Policy.* October 2012. http://www.cbo.gov/sites/default/files/cbofiles/attachments/10-25-2012-Labor_Supply_and_Fiscal_Policy.pdf.

Congressional Budget Office. *Choices for Deficit Reduction.* November 2012. http://www.cbo.gov/sites/default/files/cbofiles/attachments/43692-DeficitReduction_print.pdf.

Congressional Budget Office. *Estimated Impact of American Recovery and Reinvestment Act on Employment and Economic Output from October 2012 Through December 2012.* February 2013. http://www.cbo.gov/sites/default/files/cbofiles/attachments/43945-ARRA.pdf.

Congressional Budget Office. *Growth in Means-Tested Programs and Tax Credits for Low-Income Households.* February 2013. http://www.cbo.gov/sites/default/files/cbofiles/attachments/43934-Means-TestedPrograms.pdf.

Congressional Budget Office. *The Budget and Economic Outlook: Fiscal Years 2013 to 2023.* February 2013. http://www.cbo.gov/sites/default/files/cbofiles/attachments/43907-BudgetOutlook.pdf.

Congressional Budget Office. *The Distribution of Major Tax Expenditures in the Individual Income Tax System.* May 2013. http://www.cbo.gov/sites/default/files/cbofiles/attachments/43768_DistributionTaxExpenditures.pdf.

Congressional Budget Office. *Updated Budget Projections: Fiscal Years 2013 to 2023.* May 2013. http://www.cbo.gov/sites/default/files/cbofiles/attachments/44172-Baseline2.pdf.

Congressional Budget Office. *CBO's Estimate of the Net Budgetary Impact of the Affordable Care Act's Health Insurance Coverage Provisions Has Not Changed Much over Time.* May 14, 2013. http://www.cbo.gov/publication/44176.

Congressional Budget Office. *Rising Demand for Long-Term Services and Supports for Elderly People.* June 2013. http://www.cbo.gov/sites/default/files/cbofiles/attachments/44363-LTC.pdf.

Congressional Budget Office. *How CBO Projects Income.* July 2013. http://www.cbo.gov/sites/default/files/cbofiles/attachments/44433-IncomeProjection.pdf.

Congressional Budget Office. *Letter to the Honorable Chris Van Hollen Regarding How Eliminating the Automatic Spending Reductions Specified by the Budget Control Act Would Affect the U.S. Economy in 2014.* July 25, 2013. http://www.cbo.gov/sites/default/files/cbofiles/attachments/44445-SpendReductions_1.pdf.

Congressional Budget Office. *The 2013 Long-Term Budget Outlook.* September 2013. http://www.cbo.gov/sites/default/files/cbofiles/attachments/44521-LTBO2013_0.pdf.

Congressional Budget Office. *An Analysis of the Navy's Fiscal Year 2014 Shipbuilding Plan.* October 2013. http://www.cbo.gov/sites/default/files/cbofiles/attachments/44655-Shipbuilding.pdf.

Congressional Budget Office. *Options for Reducing the Deficit: 2014 to 2023.* November 2013. http://www.cbo.gov/sites/default/files/cbofiles/attachments/44715-OptionsForReducingDeficit-2_1.pdf.

Congressional Budget Office. *The Distribution of Federal Spending and Taxes in 2006.* November 2013. http://www.cbo.gov/sites/default/files/cbofiles/attachments/44698-Distribution_11-2013.pdf.

Congressional Research Service. *Federal Budget Process Reform in the 111th Congress: A Brief Overview.* Pub. R40113. May 20, 2010.

Congressional Research Service. *Increasing the Social Security Payroll Tax Base: Options and Effects on Tax Burdens.* CRS Pub. RL33943. Washington, DC: Office of Congressional Information and Publishing, February 5, 2013. http://www.fas.org/sgp/crs/misc/RL33943.pdf.

Congressional Research Service. *The Congressional Budget Process: A Brief Overview.* CRS Pub. RS20095. Washington, DC: Office of Congressional Information and Publishing, August 22, 2011.

Congressional Research Service. *Tax Rates and Economic Growth.* CRS Pub. R42111. Washington, DC: Office of Congressional Information and Publishing, December 5, 2011.

Congressional Research Service. *Tax Expenditures: Compendium of Background Material on Individual Provisions.* S. Prt. 112-45. December 2012.

Congressional Research Service. *U.S. Household Savings for Retirement in 2010.* 2013.

Congressional Research Service. *Social Security Reform: Legal Analysis of Social Security Benefit Entitlement Issues.* CRS Pub. RL32822. Washington, DC: Office of Congressional Information and Publishing, June 7, 2013.

Congressional Research Service. *Shutdown of the Federal Government: Causes, Processes, and Effects.* CRS Pub. RL34680. Washington, DC: Office of Congressional Information and Publishing, August 6, 2013.

Congressional Research Service. *Tax Expenditures: Compendium of Background Material on Individual Provisions.* S. Prt. 112–45. December 2012. http://archive.org/stream/taxexpoounit/taxexpoounit_djvu.txt.

Congressional Research Service. *Introduction to the Federal Budget Process.* CRS Pub. 7-5700. Washington, DC: Office of Congressional Information and Publishing, December 3, 2012.

Congressional Research Service. *Taxes and the Economy: An Economic Analysis of the Top Tax Rates since 1945.* CRS Pub. R42729. Washington, DC: Office of Congressional Information and Publishing, December 12, 2012.

Corak, Miles. "Income Inequality, Equality of Opportunity, and Intergenerational Mobility." *Journal of Economic Perspectives* 27, no. 3 (2013): 79–102.

Corlette, Sabrina, JoAnn Volk, and Kevin Lucia. *Real Stories, Real Reforms.* Georgetown University Center on Health Insurance Reforms and the Robert Wood Johnson Foundation, September 2013. http://www.rwjf.org/content/dam/farm/reports/issue_briefs/2013/rwjf407972.

Council of Economic Advisors. *Trends in Health Care Cost Growth and the Role of the Affordable Care Act.* November 2013. http://www.whitehouse.gov/sites/default/files/docs/healthcostreport_final_noembargo_v2.pdf.

Cowell, Frank A. *Measuring Inequality.* 3rd ed. New York: Oxford University Press, 2011.

Creedy, John. "Taxation, Redistribution and Progressivity: An Introduction." *Australian Economic Review* 32, no. 4 (1999): 410–422.

DeBow, Michael E., and Dwight R. Lee. "Happiness and Public Policy: A Partial Dissent (or Why a Department of Homeland Happiness Would Be a Bad Idea)." *Journal of Law and Politics* 22 (2006): 283–301.

Deshpande, Manasi, and Douglas W. Elmendorf. *An Economic Strategy for Investing in America's Infrastructure, The Hamilton Project.* Washington, DC: The Brookings Institution, July 2008. http://www.brookings.edu/~/media/research/files/papers/2008/7/infrastructure%20elmendorf/07_infrastructurestrat_elmendorf.pdf.

Devereux, Michael P., and Harold Freeman. "A General Neutral Profits Tax." *Fiscal Studies* 12, no. 3 (1991): 1–15.

Diamond, Peter, and Emmanuel Saez. "The Case for a Progressive Tax: From Basic Research to Policy Recommendations." *Journal of Economic Perspectives* 25, no. 4, (2011): 165–190.

Dobbs, Richard, Herbert Pohl, Diaan-Yi Lin, Jan Mischke, Nicklas Garemo, Jimmy Hexter, Stefan Matzinger, Robert Palter, and Rushad Nanavatty. *Infrastructure Productivity: How to Save $1 Trillion a Year.* McKinsey & Company, January 2013. http://www.mckinsey.com/insights/engineering_construction/infrastructure_productivity.

Dolton, Peter, and Oscar Marcenaro-Gutierrez. "If You Pay Peanuts Do You Get Monkeys? A Cross Country Comparison of Teacher Pay and Student Performance." *Economic Policy* 26, no. 65 (January 2011): 5–55.

Donohue, John J., III. "Advocacy versus Analysis in Assessing Employment Discrimination Law." *Stanford Law Review* 44, no. 7 (1992): 1583–1614.

Driessen, Patrick. "What Conditions Tax Distribution and Dynamic Scoring Are In." *Tax Notes* 141, no. 4 (October 28, 2013): 425–430.

Drugs.com. *U.S. Pharmaceutical Sales—2012.* Accessed 2013. http://www.drugs.com/stats/top100/2012/sales.

Duncan, Greg J., and Richard Murnane, eds., *Whither Opportunity? Rising Inequality, Schools, and Children's Life Chances.* New York: Russell Sage Foundation, 2011.

Eberstadt, Nicholas. *A Nation of Takers: America's Entitlement Epidemic.* West Conshohocken, PA: Templeton Press, 2012.

Economic Policy Institute. *CEO Compensation and CEO-to-Worker Compensation Ratio, 1965–2011 (2011 dollars).* Updated June 18, 2012. http://stateofworkingamerica.org/chart/swa-wages-table-4-43-ceo-compensation-ceo/.

Edler de Roover, Florence. "Early Examples of Marine Insurance." *Journal of Economic History* 5, no. 2 (November 1945): 172–200.

Eggert, Wolfgang, and Bernd Genser. "Dual Income Taxation in EU Member Countries." *CESifo DICE Report* 2005, no. 1 (January 2005): 41–47. http://www.cesifogruppe.de/pls/guestci/download/CESifo%20DICE%20Report%202005/CESifo%20DICE%20Report%201/2005/dicereport105-rr1.pdf.

Elmendorf, Douglas W. *Confronting the Nation's Fiscal Policy Challenges.* September 13, 2011. http://www.cbo.gov/publication/42761.

Elmendorf, Douglas W. "Choices for Federal Spending and Taxes." Presentation to the National Association for Business Economics. Congressional Budget Office, March 26, 2012. http://www.cbo.gov/sites/default/files/cbofiles/attachments/PresentationNABE_3-26-12.pdf.

Elmendorf, Douglas W, Director, Congressional Budget Office, to Honorable John Boehner. 24 July 2012. http://cbo.gov/sites/default/files/cbofiles/attachments/43471-hr6079.pdf.

Elmendorf, Douglas W. *Federal Health Care Spending: Why Is It Growing? What Could Be Done about It?* November 13, 2013. http://www.cbo.gov/sites/default/files/cbofiles/attachments/45144-Williams.pdf.

Elmendorf, Douglas W., Jason Furman, William G. Gale, and Benjamin H. Harris. "Distributional Effects of the 2001 and 2003 Tax Cuts: How Do Financing and Behavioral Responses Matter?" *National Tax Journal* 61, no. 3 (September 2008): 365–380.

Engen, Eric, and Jonathan Skinner. "Taxation and Economic Growth." *National Tax Journal* 49, no. 4 (December 1996): 617–642.

Epstein, Richard A. *Forbidden Grounds: The Case against Employment Discrimination.* Cambridge, MA: Harvard University Press, 1992.

Epstein, Richard A. "In Praise of Income Inequality." *Defining Ideas: A Hoover Institutional Journal* (February 19, 2013). http://www.hoover.org/publications/defining-ideas/article/140746.

Evensky, Jerry. *Adam Smith's Moral Philosophy: A Historical and Contemporary Perspective on Markets, Law, Ethics and Culture.* Cambridge, UK: Cambridge University Press, 2005.

Favero, Carlo A., and Francesco Giavazzi. "How Large Are the Effects of Tax Changes?" *National Bureau of Economic Research Working Paper Series* (working paper no. 7439, August 2009). http://www.nber.org/papers/w15303.

Feldstein, Martin. "How Big Should Government Be?" *National Tax Journal* 50, no. 2 (1997): 197–213.

Feldstein, Martin. "Tax Avoidance and the Deadweight Loss of the Income Tax." *Review of Economics and Statistics* 81, no. 4 (November 1999): 674–680.

Feldstein, Martin. "The Effect of Taxes on Efficiency and Growth." *Tax Notes* 111, no. 6 (May 8, 2006): 679–684.

Fernald, Anne, Virginia A. Marchman, and Adriana Weisleder. "SES Differences in Language Processing Skill and Vocabulary Are Evident at 18 months." *Developmental Science* 16, no. 2 (2013): 234–248.

Financial Crisis Inquiry Commission. *The Financial Crisis Inquiry Report: Final Report of the National Commission on the Causes of the Financial and Economic Crisis in the United States.* Dissenting statement by Peter J. Wallison. Washington, DC: Government Printing Office, 2011. http://www.gpo.gov/fdsys/pkg/GPO-FCIC/pdf/GPO-FCIC.pdf.

Fleck, Susan, John Glaser, and Shawn Sprague. "The Compensation-Productivity Gap: A Visual Essay." *Monthly Labor Review* (Bureau of Labor Statistics, January 2011). http://www.bls.gov/opub/mlr/2011/01/art3full.pdf.

Fleischacker, Samuel. "Adam Smith's Reception among the American Founders, 1776–1790." *William and Mary Quarterly*, Third Series, vol. 59, no. 4 (October 2002): 897–924.

Fleischacker, Samuel. *On Adam Smith's Wealth of Nations: A Philosophical Companion.* Princeton, NJ: Princeton University Press, 2004.

Frank, Robert H. *Falling Behind: How Rising Inequality Harms the Middle Class.* Berkeley: University of California Press, 2007.

Frank, Robert H. *Luxury Fever: Weighing the Cost of Excess.* Princeton, NJ: Princeton University Press, 2010.

Frey, Bruno S., and Alois Stutzer. "What Can Economists Learn from Happiness Research?" *Journal of Economic Literature* 40, no. 2 (June 2002): 402–435.

Friedman, Milton. *Capitalism and Freedom.* Chicago: University of Chicago Press, 1962.

Gale, William G., and Alan J. Auerbach. "Fiscal Fatigue: Tracking the Budget Outlook as Political Leaders Lurch from One Artificial Crisis to Another." *Brookings*, February 28, 2013. http://www.brookings.edu/research/papers/2013/02/28-fiscal-fatigue-budget-outlook-gale.

Gale, William G., Jonathan Gruber, and Seth Stephens-Davidowitz. "Encouraging Homeownership Through the Tax Code." *Tax Notes* 115, no. 12 (June 18, 2007): 1171–1189.

Galston, William A., and Korin Davis. *Setting Priorities, Meeting Needs: The Case for a National Infrastructure Bank.* Washington, DC: The Brookings Institution, December 13, 2012.

Ganong, Peter, and Jeffrey B. Liebman. "The Decline, Rebound, and Further Rise in SNAP Enrollment: Disentangling Business Cycle Fluctuations and Policy Changes." NBER Working Paper 19363. National Bureau of Economic Research, August 2013.

Gibson, Alan. *Understanding the Foundation: The Crucial Questions.* 2nd ed. Lawrence: University Press of Kansas, 2010.

Gleeson, Michael M., and Michael Beller. "Ryan Budget Calls for Top Tax Rates of 25 Percent." *Tax Notes* 134, no. 13 (March 26, 2012): 1595–1597.

Gomme, Paul, and Peter Rupert. "Measuring Labor's Share of Income." *Policy Discussion Papers* (Federal Bank of Cleveland, November 2004). http://clevelandfed.org/research/policydis/no7novo4.pdf.

Gottschalk, Peter. "Inequality, Income Growth, and Mobility: The Basic Facts." *Journal of Economic Perspectives* 11, no. 2 (Spring 1997): 21–40.

Government Accountability Office. *Corporate Income Tax: Effective Tax Rates Can Differ Significantly from the Statutory Rate.* GAO Pub. GAO-13-520. May 2013. http://www.gao.gov/assets/660/654957.pdf.

Graetz, Michael J., and Jerry L. Mashaw. *True Security: Rethinking American Social Insurance.* New Haven, CT: Yale University Press, 1979.

Gramlich, Edward M. "Infrastructure Investment: A Review Essay." *Journal of Economic Literature* 32, no. 3 (September 1994): 1176–1196.

Gravelle, Jennifer C. "Corporate Tax Incidence: Review of General Equilibrium Estimates and Analysis." *National Tax Journal* 66, no. 1 (March 2013): 185–214.

Greenstone, Michael, Adam Looney, Jeremy Patashnik, and Muxin Yu. *Thirteen Economic Facts about Social Mobility and the Role of Education*, The Hamilton Project. Washington, DC: The Brookings Institution, June 2013.

Griffith, Thomas D. "Progressive Taxation and Happiness." *Boston College Law Review* 45, no. 5 (2004): 1363–1398.

Griswold, Charles L., Jr. *Adam Smith and the Virtues of Enlightenment.* Cambridge, UK: Cambridge University Press, 1999.

Gruber, Jonathan. *Public Finance and Public Policy.* 4th ed. New York: Worth Publishers, 2013.

Halperin, Daniel. "Mitigating the Potential Inequity of Reducing Corporate Rates." *Tax Notes* 126, no. 5 (February 1, 2010): 641–658.

Halvorson, George C. *Health Care Reform Now!: A Prescription for Change.* San Francisco: Wiley 2007.

Hamowy, Ronald. "Jefferson and the Scottish Enlightenment: A Critique of Garry Wills's Inventing America: Jefferson's Declaration of Independence." *William and Mary Quarterly*, Third Series, vol. 36, no. 4 (October 1979): 503–523.

Hanley, Ryan Patrick. *Adam Smith and the Character of Virtue.* Cambridge, UK: Cambridge University Press, 2009.

Harper v. Virginia State Board of Elections, 383 U.S. 663 (1966).

Harvey, David. *A Brief History of Neoliberalism.* New York: Oxford University Press, 2005.

Hearing on More Spending, Less Real Help: How Today's Fragmented Welfare System Fails to Lift Up Poor Families, Before the Subcommittee on Human Resources of the Committee on Ways and Means, U.S. House of Representatives. 113th Cong. June 18, 2013. Testimony of Casey B. Mulligan, "Work Incentives, Accumulated Legislation, and the Economy."

Hearing on Tax Reform, Growth, and International Competitiveness, Before the Committee on Ways and Means, U.S. House of Representatives. 109th Cong. June 9, 2005. Testimony of Alan J. Auerbach, Robert D. Burch Professor of Economics and Law Director, Burch Center for Tax Policy and Public Finance, University of California, Berkeley.

Helliwell, John, Richard Layard, and Jeffrey Sachs, eds. *World Happiness Report 2013*. New York: Sustainable Sustainable Development Solutions Network, 2013.

Henckel, Timo, and Warwick McKibbin. *The Economics of Infrastructure in a Globalized World: Issues, Lessons and Future Challenges*. Washington, DC: The Brookings Institution, June 4, 2010. http://www.brookings.edu/research/papers/2010/06/04-infrastructure-economics-mckibbin.

Henderson, David R. "Encouraging Joblessness." *Regulation* 36, no. 1 (Spring 2013): 68–72.

Henderson, M. Todd, and Frederick Tung. "Paying Bank Examiners for Performance: Should Regulators Receive Bonuses for Effectively Guarding the Public Interest?" *Regulation* 35, no. 1 (Spring 2012): 32–38.

Henry J. Kaiser Family Foundation, The. *Policy Options to Sustain Medicare for the Future*. February 20, 2013. http://kff.org/medicare/report/policy-options-to-sustain-medicare-for-the-future/.

Henry J. Kaiser Family Foundation, The. *Analyzing the Impact of State Medicaid Expansion Decisions*. By Robin Rudowitz and Jessica Stephens. July 17, 2013. http://kaiserfamilyfoundation.files.wordpress.com/2013/07/8458-analyzing-the-impact-of-state-medicaid-expansion-decisions2.pdf

Henry J. Kaiser Family Foundation, The. *Assessing the Effects of the Economy on the Recent Slowdown in Health Spending*. August 22, 2013. http://kff.org/health-costs/issue-brief/assessing-the-effects-of-the-economy-on-the-recent-slowdown-in-health-spending-2/.

House Appropriations Committee Democrats. *Report on Sequestration*. 2013. http://www.npaf.org/files/Sequestration%20full%20report.pdf.

WJEC. "GCE Past Papers." Accessed December 2013. http://www.wjec.co.uk/students/past-papers/.

Institute for Fiscal Studies. *Equity for Companies: A Corporation Tax for the 1990s*. 1991. http://www.ifs.org.uk/comms/comm26.pdf.

Institute for Fiscal Studies––. *Tax by Design: The Mirrlees Review*. By Sir James Mirrlees, Stuart Adam, Timothy Besley, Richard Blundell, Stephen Bond, Robert Chote, Malcolm Gammie, Paul Johnson, Gareth Myles, and James Poterba. Oxford: Oxford University Press, September 2011. http://www.ifs.org.uk/mirrleesreview/design/taxbydesign.pdf.

Internal Revenue Service, Statistics of Information Division. *The 400 Individual Income Tax Returns Reporting the Largest Adjusted Gross Incomes Each Year. 1992–2009*. http://www.irs.gov/pub/irs-soi/09intop400.pdf.

Internal Revenue Service. "Notice 2009-23: Qualifying Gasification Project Program." *Internal Revenue Bulletin* 2009-16 (April 20, 2009). http://www.irs.gov/irb/2009-16_irb/ar06.html.

Internal Revenue Service. "Notice 2009-24: Qualifying Advanced Coal Project Program." *Internal Revenue Bulletin* 2009-16 (April 20, 2009). http://www.irs.gov/irb/2009-16_irb/ar07.html.

International Labour Organization. *Global Wage Report 2012/13*. 2013. http://www.ilo.org/global/research/global-reports/global-wage-report/2012/lang--en/index.htm.

International Monetary Fund. *United States: Staff Report for the 2013 Article IV Consultation*. IMF Country Report No. 13/236. Washington, DC: IMF, July 9, 2013.

International Transportation Forum. *Understanding the Value of Transport Infrastructure: Guidelines for Macro-level Measurement of Spending and Assets*. Paris: OECD, 2013.

Jayne, Allen. *Jefferson's Declaration of Independence: Origins, Philosophy and Theology*. Lexington: University Press of Kentucky, 1998.

Joint Hearing on How Welfare and Tax Benefits Can Discourage Work, Before the Subcommittee on Human Resources and Subcommittee on Select Revenue Measures of the Committee on Ways and Means, U.S. House of Representatives. 112th Cong. 38. June 27, 2012. Testimony of Clifford F. Thies, "The Implicit Tax Rate on Low Income Americans."

Joint Hearing on How Welfare and Tax Benefits Can Discourage Work, Before the Subcommittee on Human Resources and Subcommittee on Select Revenue Measures of the Committee on Ways and Means, U.S. House of Representatives. 112th Cong. 49 (June 27, 2012). Testimony of C. Eugene Steuerle, "Marginal Tax Rates, Work, and the Nation's Real Tax System."

Jones, Daniel Stedman. *Masters of the Universe: Hayek, Friedman, and the Birth of Neoliberal Politics.* Princeton, NJ: Princeton University Press, 2012.

Jones, Howard Mumford. *The Pursuit of Happiness.* Cambridge, MA: Harvard University Press, 1953.

Kakwani, Nanak. "Measurement of Tax Progressivity: An International Comparison." *Economic Journal* 87, no. 345 (March 1977): 71–80.

Kaplow, Louis. "Taxation and Redistribution: Some Clarifications." *Tax Law Review* 60, no. 2 (2007): 57–81.

Keehan, Sean P., Andrea M. Sisko, Christopher J. Truffer, John A. Poisal, Gigi A. Cuckler, Andrew J. Madison, Joseph M. Lizonitz, and Sheila D. Smith. "National Health Spending Projections Through 2020: Economic Recovery and Reform Drive Faster Spending Growth." *Health Affairs* 30, no. 8 (August 2011): 1594–1605.

Kelman, Mark. *Strategy or Principle?: The Choice Between Regulation and Taxation.* Ann Arbor: University of Michigan Press, 1999.

Kleinbard, Edward D. "Competitive Convergence in the Financial Services Markets." *Taxes* 81, no. 3 (March 2003): 225–261.

Kleinbard, Edward D. *Rehabilitating the Business Income Tax.* Hamilton Project, June 2007. http://www.hamiltonproject.org/papers/rehabilitating_the_business_income_tax1.

Kleinbard, Edward D. "Reading JCT Staff Distribution Tables: An Introduction to Methodologies and Issues." Keynote address to the 21st Annual Institute on Current Issues in International Taxation. Washington, DC: Joint Committee on Taxation, December 9, 2008.

Kleinbard, Edward D. "An American Dual Income Tax: Nordic Precedents." *Northwestern Journal of Law and Social Policy* 5, no. 1 (2010): 41–86.

Kleinbard, Edward D. "The Congress within the Congress: How Tax Expenditures Distort Our Budget and Our Political Processes." *Ohio Northern University Law Review* 36 (2010): 1–29.

Kleinbard, Edward D. "Tax Expenditure Framework Legislation." *National Tax Journal* 63, no. 2 (June 2010): 353–382.

Kleinbard, Edward D. "Stateless Income." *Florida Tax Review* 11, no. 9 (2011): 699–773.

Kleinbard, Edward D. "The Lessons of Stateless Income." *Tax Law Review* 65 (2011): 99–171.

Kleinbard, Edward D. "Herman Cain's 999 Tax Plan." *Tax Notes* 133, no. 4 (October 24, 2011): 469–480.

Kleinbard, Edward D. "The Role of Tax Reform in Deficit Reduction." *Tax Notes* 133, no. 9 (November 28, 2011): 1108–1113.

Kleinbard, Edward D. "Paul Ryan's Roadmap to Inequality." *Tax Notes* 136, no. 10 (September 3, 2012): 1195–1205.

Kleinbard, Edward D. "Three Cheers for Dave Camp." *Tax Notes* 138, no. 5 (February 4, 2013): 619–620.

Kleinbard, Edward D., and Joseph Rosenberg. "The Better Base Case." *Tax Notes* 135, no. 10 (June 4, 2012): 1237–1247.

Kopczuk, Wojciech, Emmanuel Saez, and Jae Song. "Earnings Inequality and Mobility in the United States: Evidence from Social Security Data since 1937." *Quarterly Journal of Economics* 125, no. 1 (February 2010): 91–128. doi:10.1162/qjec.2010.125.1.91.

Krueger, Alan B., and David A. Schkade. "The Reliability of Subjective Well-Being Measures." *Journal of Public Economics* 92, no. 8–9 (2008): 1833–1845.

Larrimore, Jeff, Richard V. Burkhauser, Shuaizhang Feng, and Laura Zayatz. "Consistent Cell Means for Topcoded Incomes in the Public Use March CPS (1976–2007)." *Journal of Economic and Social Measurement* 33 (2008): 89–128.

Leacock, Stephen. "A, B and C: The Human Element in Mathematics," in *Literary Lapses*. Montreal: Gazette Printing Company, 1910.

Lequiller, Francois, and Derek Blades. *Understanding National Accounts.* Paris: OECD, 2006.

Lewin, Shira B. "Economics and Psychology: Lessons for Our Own Day from the Early Twentieth Century." *Journal of Economic Literature* 34 (September 1996): 1293–1323.

Lind, Hans, and Roland Granqvist. "A Note on the Concept of Excess Burden." *Economic Analysis & Policy* 40, no. 1 (March 2010): 63–73.

Lipman, Francine J., and James E. Williamson. "Social Security Benefits Formula 101: A Practical Primer." *ABA Section of Taxation NewsQuarterly* 29, no. 4 (Summer 2010): 15–17. http://www.mwe.com/info/pubs/aba_summer2010.pdf.

Lubienski, Christopher A., and Sarah Theule Lubienski. *The Public School Advantage: Why Public Schools Outperform Private Schools.* Chicago: University of Chicago Press, 2014.

Lundberg, David, and Henry F. May. "The Enlightened Reader in America." *American Quarterly* 28, no. 2 (Summer 1976): 262–293.

Lund, Susan, James Manyika, Scott Nyquist, Lenny Mendonca, and Sreenivas Ramaswamy. *Game Changers: Five Opportunities for US Growth and Renewal.* McKinsey & Company, July 2013. http://www.mckinsey.com/insights/americas/us_game_changers.

Mani, Anandi, Sendhil Mullainathan, Eldar Shafir, and Jiaying Zhao. "Poverty Impedes Cognitive Function." *Science* 341, no. 6149 (August 30, 2013): 976–980.

Mankiw, N. Gregory. "Spreading the Wealth Around: Reflections Inspired by Joe the Plumber." *Eastern Economic Journal* 36, no. 3 (2010): 285–298.

Mankiw, N. Gregory. "Defending the One Percent." *Journal of Economic Perspectives* 27, no. 3 (2013): 21–34. doi:10.1257/jep.27.3.21.

Marr, Chuck, and Chye-Ching Huang. "Misconceptions and Realities about Who Pays Taxes." *Center on Budget and Policy Priorities*, September 17, 2012. http://www.cbpp.org/files/5-26-11tax.pdf.

Masur, Jonathan S., and Eric A. Posner. "Regulation, Unemployment, and Cost-Benefit Analysis." *Virginia Law Review* 98 (May 2012): 610–634.

Matthews, Fiona E., Antony Arthur, Linda E. Barnes, John Bond, Carol Jagger, Louise Robinson, and Carol Brayne. "A Two-Decade Comparison of Prevalence of Dementia in Individuals Aged 65 Years and Older from Three Geographical Areas of England: Results of the Cognitive Function and Ageing Study I and II." *The Lancet* 382, no. 9902 (October 2013): 1405–1412. doi:10.1016/S0140-6736(13)61570-6.

McBride, William. "What Is the Evidence on Taxes and Growth?" *Tax Foundation Special Report* No. 207 (December 18, 2012).

McCaffery, Edward J. *Taxing Women: How the Marriage Penalty Affects Your Taxes.* Chicago: University of Chicago Press, 1997.

McCaffery, Edward J. "A New Understanding of Tax." *Michigan Law Review* 103 (2005): 807–938.

McCall, John J. "Insurance." in *The New Palgrave Dictionary of Economics*, ed. John Eatwell, Murray Milgate, and Peter Newman. Palgrave Macmillan, 1987. http://www.dictionaryofeconomics.com/article?id=pde1987_X001146&goto=I&result_number=1777.

McCray v. United States, 195 U.S. 27 (1904).

McGlynn, Elizabeth A., Steven M. Asch, John Adams, Joan Keesey, Jennifer Hicks, Alison DeCristofaro, and Eve A. Kerr. "The Quality of Healthcare Delivered to Adults in the United States." *The New England Journal of Medicine* 348, no. 26 (June 26, 2003): 2635–2645.

McMahon, Darrin M. *Happiness: A History.* New York: Grove Press, 2006.

McMahon, Darrin M. *The Pursuit of Happiness: A History from the Greeks to the Present.* New York: Penguin Press, 2006.

Mehrotra, Ajay K. *Making the Modern American Fiscal State: Law, Politics, and the Rise of Progressive Taxation, 1877–1929.* New York: Cambridge University Press, 2013.

Michaelides, Marios, and Peter R. Mueser. "Recent Trends in the Characteristics of Unemployment Insurance Recipients." *Monthly Labor Review* (July 2012). http://www.bls.gov/opub/mlr/2012/07/art3full.pdf.

Miller, Steve. "Steve Southerland's Campaign Paid for Upkeep and Rent on Congressman's Home." *Florida Center for Investigative Reporting*, September 16, 2013. http://fcir.org/2013/09/16/steve-southerlands-campaign-paid-for-upkeep-and-rent-on-congressmans-home/.

Min, David. "Faulty Conclusions Based on Shoddy Foundations: FCIC Commissioner Peter Wallison and Other Commentators Rely on Flawed Data from Edward Pinto to Misplace the Causes of the 2008 Financial Crisis." *Center for American Progress*, February 2011. http://www.americanprogress.org/issues/2011/02/pdf/pinto.pdf.

Montes, Leonidas. *Adam Smith in Context: A Critical Reassessment of Some Central Components of His Thought.* New York: Palgrave Macmillan, 2004.

Morse, Susan C. "Startup LTD: Tax Planning and Initial Incorporation Location." *Florida Tax Review* 14, no. 8 (2013): 319–360.

Mulligan, Casey B. *The Redistribution Recession: How Labor Market Distortions Contracted the Economy.* New York: Oxford University Press, 2012.

Musgrave, Richard A., and Peggy B. Musgrave. *Public Finance in Theory and Practice.* 5th ed. New York: McGraw-Hill, 1989.

Myles, Gareth D. "Taxation and Economic Growth." *Fiscal Studies* 21, no. 1 (2000): 141–168.

National Academy. *Best Care at Lower Cost: The Path to Continuously Learning Healthcare in America.* Washington, DC: The National Academies Press, 2013.

National Center for Education Statistics. *Revenues and Expenditures for Public Elementary and Secondary School Districts: School Year 2009–10 (Fiscal Year 2010).* Washington, DC: US Department of Education, 2012.

National Center for Education Statistics. *Digest of Education Statistics 2011.* Washington, DC: US Department of Education, June 2012.

National Federation of Independent Businesses v. Sebelius, Secretary of Health and Human Services, 132 S. Ct. 2566 (June 28, 2012).

National Research Council. *U.S. Health in International Perspective: Shorter Lives, Poorer Health.* Washington, DC: National Academies Press, 2013.

Oishi, Shigehiro, Selin Kesebir, and Ed Diener. "Income Inequality and Happiness." *Psychological Science* 22, no. 9 (2011): 1095–1100.

Okun, Arthur M. *Equality and Efficiency: The Big Trade Off.* Washington, DC: Brookings Institution, 1975.

Oleszek, Walter J. *Congressional Procedures and the Policy Process.* 8th ed. Washington, DC: CQ Press, 2011.

Organisation for Economic Co-operation and Development. *Divided We Stand: Why Inequality Keeps Rising.* Paris: OECD Publishing, 2011.

Organisation for Economic Co-operation and Development. *Economic Outlook Annex Tables.* Accessed August 2013. http://www.oecd.org/eco/outlook/economicoutlookannextables.htm.

Organisation for Economic Co-operation and Development. *Economic Outlook, Analysis and Forecasts.* May 2013. http://www.oecd.org/eco/outlook/.

Organisation for Economic Co-operation and Development. *Economic Survey of Norway 2012.* 2012. http://www.oecd.org/norway/economicsurveyofnorway2012.htm.

Organisation for Economic Co-operation and Development. *Economic Surveys: United States 2012.* June 2012. http://www.oecd.org/eco/surveys/economic-survey-united-states.htm.

Organisation for Economic Co-operation and Development. *Growing Unequal.* 2008. http://www.oecd.org/els/soc/growingunequalincomedistributionandpovertyinoecdcountries.htm.

Organisation for Economic Co-operation and Development. *Income-Related Inequalities in Health Service Utilisation in 19 OECD Countries, 2008–2009.* By Marion Devaux and Michael de Looper. OECD Health Working Paper, 2012. http://www.oecd-ilibrary.org/social-issues-migration-health/income-related-inequalities-in-health-service-utilisation-in-19-oecd-countries-2008-2009_5k95xd6stnxt-en.

Organisation for Economic Co-operation and Development. "Medium and Long-Term Scenarios for Global Growth and Imbalances," chap. 4, in *OECD Economic Outlook* 2012, no. 1. June 19, 2012. http://www.oecd-ilibrary.org/economics/oecd-economic-outlook-volume-2012-issue-1_eco_outlook-v2012-1-en.

Organisation for Economic Co-operation and Development. *OECD Employment Outlook 2013.* 2013. http://www.oecd.org/employment/emp/oecdemploymentoutlook.htm.

Organisation for Economic Co-operation and Development. *OECD Factbook 2009: Economic, Environmental and Social Statistics.* 2009. http://www.oecd-ilibrary.org/content/book/factbook-2009-en.

Organisation for Economic Co-operation and Development. *OECD Factbook 2011–2012: Economic, Environmental and Social Statistics.* 2012. http://www.oecd-ilibrary.org/content/book/factbook-2011-en.

Organisation for Economic Co-operation and Development. *OECD Health Data 2013: How Does the United States Compare.* 2013. http://www.oecd.org/unitedstates/Briefing-Note-USA-2013.pdf.

Organisation for Economic Co-operation and Development. *OECD in Figures 2009.* Paris: OECD Publishing, 2009. http://www.oecd-ilibrary.org/economics/oecd-in-figures-2009_oif-2009-en.

Organisation for Economic Co-operation and Development. *OECD Revenue Statistics 2012.* Paris: OECD Publishing, 2012. http://www.oecd-ilibrary.org/taxation/revenue-statistics-2012_rev_stats-2012-en-fr.

Organisation for Economic Co-operation and Development. *OECD Skills Outlook 2013: First Results from the Survey of Adult Skills.* Paris: OECD Publishing, October 2013. http://skills.oecd.org/OECD_Skills_Outlook_2013.pdf.

Organisation for Economic Co-operation and Development. *PISA 2009 Results: What Students Know and Can Do—Student Performance in Reading, Mathematics and Science (Volume I).* OECD, 2010. http://www.oecd.org/pisa/pisaproducts/48852548.pdf.

Organisation for Economic Co-operation and Development. *Public Expenditures on Health Per Capita at Current Prices and PPPs.* June 27, 2013. http://www.oecd-ilibrary.org/social-issues-migration-health/public-expenditure-on-health-per-capita-2013-1_pubexhltcap-table-2013-1-en.

Organisation for Economic Co-operation and Development. *Restoring Fiscal Sustainability in the United States: Economics Department Working Paper No. 806.* By Patrick Lenain, Robert Hagemann, and David Carey. October 25, 2010. http://www.oecd.org/eco/46258004.pdf.

Organisation for Economic Co-operation and Development. *Revenue Statistics: Comparative Tables.* 2010. http://www.oecd-ilibrary.org/taxation/data/revenue-statistics/comparative-tables_data-o 0262-en;jsessionid=7loc322d8lbqi.delta.

Organisation for Economic Co-operation and Development. *Society at a Glance 2011.* 2011. http://www.oecd-ilibrary.org/social-issues-migration-health/society-at-a-glance-2011_soc_glance-2011-en.

Organisation for Economic Co-operation and Development. *Strong Performers and Successful Reformers in Education: Lessons from PISA for the United States.* OECD, 2011. http://www.oecd.org/edu/school/programmeforinternationalstudentassessmentpisa/strongperformersandsuccessfulreformersineducationlessonsfrompisafortheunitedstates.htm.

Organisation for Economic Co-operation and Development. *Tax Expenditures in OECD Countries.* 2010. http://www.oecd.org/gov/budgeting/taxexpendituresinoecdcountries-oecdpublication.htm.

Organisation for Economic Co-operation and Development. *Taxing Wages 2013.* Paris: OECD Publishing, 2013. http://www.oecd-ilibrary.org/taxation/taxing-wages-2013_tax_wages-2013-en.

Organisation for Economic Co-operation and Development. *Why Is Health Spending in the United States So High?* 2011. http://www.oecd.org/unitedstates/49084355.pdf.

Our Fiscal Security. *Investing in America's Economy: A Budget Blueprint for Economic Recovery and Fiscal Responsibility.* November 29, 2010. http://www.ourfiscalsecurity.org/storage/Blueprint_OFS.pdf.

Parker, David. "The UK's Privatisation Experiment: The Passage of Time Permits a Sober Assessment." Working paper no. 1126, CESifo, February 2004. http://www.cesifo-group.de/ifoHome/publications/working-papers/CESifoWP/CESifoWPdetails?wp_id=14559571.

Phillipson, Nicholas. *Adam Smith: An Enlightened Life.* New Haven, CT: Yale University Press, 2010.

Piketty, Thomas, and Emmanuel Saez. "Income Inequality in the United States, 1913–1998." *Quarterly Journal of Economics* 118, no. 1 (February 2003): 1–39.

Piketty, Thomas, Emmanuel Saez, and Stefanie Stantcheva. "Optimal Taxation of Top Labor Incomes: A Tale of Three Elasticities." *National Bureau of Economic Analysis* (working paper no. 17616, November 2011).

Poterba, James M., Steven F. Venti, and David A. Wise. "Were They Prepared for Retirement? Financial Status at Advanced Ages in the HRS and AHEAD Cohorts." *National Bureau of Economic Research Working Paper Series* (working paper no. 17824, February 2012). http://www. nber.org/papers/w17824.pdf.

Price, Carter C., and Christine Eibner. "For States That Opt Out of Medicaid Expansion: 3.6 Million Fewer Insured and $8.4 Billion Less in Federal Payments." *Health Affairs* 32, no. 6 (June 2013): 1030–1036.

"Q&A with C. Eugene Steuerle: Estimating Social Security and Medicare Taxes and Benefits over a Lifetime." *The Urban Institute* (accessed December 25, 2013). http://www.urban.org/retirees/ Estimating-Social-Security.cfm.

Radcliff, Benjamin. *The Political Economy of Human Happiness: How Voters' Choices Determine the Quality of Life*. New York: Cambridge University Press, 2013.

Raphael, D. D. *The Impartial Spectator: Adam Smith's Moral Philosophy*. Oxford, UK: Oxford University Press, 2007.

Ravitch, Diane. *Reign of Error: The Hoax of the Privatization Movement and the Danger to America's Public Schools*. New York: Alfred A. Knopf, 2013.

Rawls, John. *Justice as Fairness, A Restatement*. 2nd ed. New York: Belknap Press, 2001.

Romer, Christina D., and David H. Romer. "Do Tax Cuts Starve the Beast? The Effect of Tax Changes on Government Spending." *Brookings Papers on Economic Activity* (Spring 2009): 139–200.

Romer, Christina D., and David H. Romer. "The Macroeconomic Effects of Tax Changes: Estimates Based on a New Measure of Fiscal Shocks." *American Economic Review* 100, no. 3 (June 2010): 763–801.

Rosen, Harvey S., and Ted Gayer. *Public Finance*. 9th ed. Boston: McGraw-Hill/Higher Education, 2010.

Rothschild, Emma. *Economic Sentiments: Adam Smith, Condorcet, and the Enlightenment*. Cambridge, MA: Harvard University Press, 2001.

Saez, Emmanuel, Joel Slemrod, and Seth H. Giertz. "The Elasticity of Taxable Income with Respect to Marginal Tax Rates: A Critical Review." *Journal of Economic Literature* 50, no. 1 (March 2012): 3–50.

Saez, Emmanuel. *Striking It Richer: The Evolution of Top Incomes in the United States (Updated with 2012 Preliminary Estimates)*. September 3, 2013. http://elsa.berkeley.edu/~saez/ saez-UStopincomes-2012.pdf.

Save the Children Foundation. *Food for Thought: Tackling Child Nutrition to Unlock Potential and Boost Prosperity*. By Liam Crosby, Daphne Jayasinghe, and David McNair. 2013. http://www. savethechildren.org/atf/cf/%7B9def2ebe-10ae-432c-9bd0-df91d2eba74a%7D/FOOD_FOR_ THOUGHT.PDF.

Schick, Allen. *The Federal Budget: Politics, Policy, Process*. 3rd ed. Washington, DC: The Brookings Institution, 2007.

Schlesinger, Arthur M. "The Lost Meaning of the 'Pursuit of Happiness.'" *William and Mary Quarterly* 21, no. 3 (1964): 325–327.

Seligman, Edwin Robert Anderson. *Progressive Taxation in Theory and Practice*. 2nd ed. Princeton, NJ: American Economic Association, 1908.

Shaefer, H. Luke, and Kathryn Edin. "Rising Extreme Poverty in the United States and the Response of Federal Means-Tested Transfer Programs." *National Poverty Center Working Paper Series #13–06* (working paper, May 2013).

Shaviro, Daniel. *Making Sense of Social Security Reform*. Chicago: University of Chicago Press, 2001.

Shaviro, Daniel. "Replacing the Income Tax with a Progressive Consumption Tax." *Tax Notes* 103, no. 1 (April 5, 2004): 91–113.

Shaviro, Daniel. "Rethinking Tax Expenditures and Fiscal Language." *Tax Law Review* 57 (Winter 2004): 187–231.

Shaviro, Daniel. "Should Social Security and Medicare Be More Market-Based?" *Elder Law Journal* 21 (2013): 87–148.

Sherman, Arloc, Robert Greenstein, and Kathy Ruffing. "Contrary to 'Entitlement Society' Rhetoric, over Nine-Tenths of Entitlement Benefits Go to Elderly, Disabled, or Working Households." *Center on Budget and Policy Priorities*, February 10, 2012. http://www.cbpp.org/files/2-10-12pov.pdf.

Slemrod, Joel, and Jon Bakija. *Taxing Ourselves: A Citizen's Guide to the Debate over Taxes*. 4th ed. Cambridge, MA: MIT Press, 2008.

Smith, Adam. *The Theory of Moral Sentiments*. 6th ed. London: A. Millar, 1790.

Smith, Adam. *An Inquiry into the Nature and Causes of the Wealth of Nations*. London: Methuen & Co., 1776.

Social Security Administration. *Social Security: Understanding the Benefits 2013*. February 2013. http://www.ssa.gov/pubs/EN-05-10024.pdf.

Social Security Administration. *Social Security Basic Facts*. July 26, 2013. http://www.ssa.gov/pressoffice/basicfact.htm.

South Dakota v. Dole, 483 U.S. 203 (1987).

Spencer v. Merchant, 125 U.S. 345 (1888).

Spufford, Peter. *Power and Profit: The Merchant in Medieval Europe*. New York: Thames & Hudson, 2003.

Staff of the Joint Committee on Taxation. *Methodology and Issues in Measuring Changes in the Distribution of Tax Burdens*. Pub. JCS-7-93. Washington, DC: US Government Printing Office, June 14, 1993.

Staff of the Joint Committee on Taxation. *A Reconsideration of Tax Expenditure Analysis*. Pub. JCX-37-08. Washington, DC: US Government Printing Office, May 12, 2008.

Staff of the Joint Committee on Taxation. *Tax Expenditures for Healthcare*. Pub. JCX-66-08. Washington, DC: US Government Printing Office, July 30, 2008.

Staff of the Joint Committee on Taxation. *Reading JCT Staff Distribution Tables: An Introduction to Methodologies and Issues*. By Edward D. Kleinbard, Chief of Staff. December 9, 2008. https://www.jct.gov/publications.html?func=startdown&id=1253.

Staff of the Joint Committee on Taxation. *Present Law and Background Data Related to the Federal Tax System in Effect for 2010 and 2011*. Pub. JCX-19-10. March 22, 2010. https://www.jct.gov/publications.html?func=startdown&id=3674.

Staff of the Joint Committee on Taxation. *Estimates of Federal Tax Expenditures for Fiscal Years 2012–2017*. Pub. JCS-1-13. Washington, DC: US Government Printing Office, February 1, 2013.

Staff of the Joint Committee on Taxation. *Modeling the Distribution of Taxes on Business Income*. Pub. JCX-14-13. Washington, DC: US Government Printing Office, October 16, 2013.

Stark, Kirk J., and Eric M. Zolt. "Tax Reform and the American Middle Class." *Pepperdine Law Review* 40, no. 5 (May 2013): 1209–1234.

Steuerle, C. Eugene, and Caleb Quackenbush. "Social Security and Medicare Taxes and Benefits over a Lifetime: 2012 Update." *The Urban Institute*, 2012. http://www.urban.org/UploadedPD F/412660-Social-Security-and-Medicare-Taxes-and-Benefits-Over-a-Lifetime.pdf.

Stigler, George J. "The Successes and Failures of Professor Smith." *Journal of Political Economy* 84, no. 6 (December 1976): 1199–1213.

Stigler, George J., and Gary S. Becker. "De Gustibus Non Est Disputandum." *The American Economic Review* 67, no. 2 (March 1977): 76–90.

Stiglitz, Joseph E. "GDP Fetishism." *Economist's Voice* 6, no. 8 (September 2009): 1–3.

Stiglitz, Joseph E. *The Price of Inequality: How Today's Divided Society Endangers Our Future*. New York: W. W. Norton, 2012.

Stiglitz, Joseph E., Justin Yifu Lin, and Célestin Monga. "The Rejuvenation of Industrial Policy." Policy Research Working Paper No. 6628, World Bank, September 2013.

Stockholm International Peace Research Institute. *Military Expenditure Database*. http://www. sipri.org/research/armaments/milex/milex_database.

Stockholm International Peace Research Institute. *SIPRI Yearbook 2011: Armaments, Disarmament and International Security*. Solna, Sweden: SIPRI, 2011.

Sullivan, Martin A. "How to Read Tax Distribution Tables." *Tax Notes* 90, no. 13 (March 26, 2001): 1747–1755.

Sullivan, Martin A. "Busting Myths about Rich People's Taxes." *Tax Notes* 135, no. 3 (April 16, 2012): 251–254.

Sunstein, Cass R. "Well Being and the State." *Harvard Law Review* 107, no. 6 (1994): 1303–1327.

Talberth, John, Clifford Cobb, and Noah Slattery. "The Genuine Progress Indicator 2006: A Tool for Sustainable Development." *Redefining Progress* (February 2007): 1–31.

Tan, Jeff. "Infrastructure Privatisation: Oversold, Misunderstood and Inappropriate." *Development Policy Review* 29, no. 1 (2011): 47–74.

Tax Policy Center. *Why Some Tax Units Pay No Income Tax*. By Rachel M. Johnson, James Nunns, Jeffrey Rohaly, Eric Toder, and Roberton Williams. Urban Institute and Brookings Institution, July 27, 2011. http://www.taxpolicycenter.org/UploadedPDF/1001547-Why-No-Income-Tax.pdf.

Thomas, Jason, and Robert Van Order. "A Closer Look at Fannie Mae and Freddie Mac: What We Know, What We Think We Know and What We Don't Know." Working paper, George Washington University, March 2011. http://business.gwu.edu/creua/research-papers/files/fannie-freddie. pdf.

Thomson, Sarah, Robin Osborn, David Squires, and Miraya Jun, eds. *International Profiles of Health Care Systems, 2013*. The Commonwealth Fund, November 2013. http://www. commonwealthfund.org/~/media/files/publications/fund-report/2013/ nov/1717_thomson_intl_profiles_hlt_care_sys_2013_v2.pdf.

Thorndike, Joseph J. "Four Things That Everyone Should Know about New Deal Taxation." *Tax Notes* 121, no. 8 (November 24, 2008): 973–975.

Thorndike, Joseph J. "Original Intent and the Revenue Act of 1913." *Tax Notes* 140, no. 14 (September 30, 2013): 1490–1492.

Thorndike, Joseph J. *Their Fair Share: Taxing the Rich in the Age of FDR.* Washington, DC: Urban Institute Press, 2013.

Toder, Eric J. "Tax Cuts or Spending—Does It Make a Difference?" *National Tax Journal* 53, no. 3 (September 2000): 361–372.

Tsounta, Evridiki. "Home Sweet Home: Government's Role in Reaching the American Dream." *IMF Working Paper.* Working paper no. Wp/11/191, August 2011.

Tsounta, Evridiki. *Home Sweet Home: Government's Role in Reaching the American Dream.* International Monetary Fund Working Paper Wp/11/191, August 2011. http://www.imf.org/external/pubs/ft/wp/2011/wp11191.pdf.

US Bureau of Economic Analysis. "Preview of the 2013 Comprehensive Revision of the National Income and Product Accounts." *Survey of Current Business* (March 2013): 13–39.

US Bureau of Economic Analysis. *National Income and Products Accounts Tables.* Last revised, August 7, 2013. http://www.bea.gov/iTable/index_nipa.cfm

US Bureau of Economic Analysis. *Preview of the 2013 Comprehensive Revision of the National Income and Product Accounts: Changes in Definitions and Presentations.* March 2013. http://www.bea.gov/scb/pdf/2013/03%20March/0313_nipa_comprehensive_revision_preview.pdf.

US Bureau of Economic Analysis. *National Economic Accounts.* Accessed 2013. http://www.bea.gov/national/Index.htm.

US Bureau of Economic Analysis. *National Income and Product Accounts.* http://www.bea.gov/national/.

US Bureau of Labor Statistics. "The Unemployment Rate and Beyond: Alternative Measures of Labor Underutilization." *Issues in Labor Statistics* (June 2008). http://www.bls.gov/opub/ils/pdf/opbils67.pdf.

US Bureau of Labor Statistics. *Charting International Labor Comparisons 2012.* 2012. http://www.bls.gov/fls/chartbook/2012/chartbook2012.pdf.

US Bureau of Labor Statistics. *International Comparisons of Annual Labor Force Statistics, 1970–2012.* June 7, 2013. http://www.bls.gov/fls/flscomparelf/lfcompendium.pdf.

US Census Bureau. *Historical Income Tables: Income Inequality.* 2011. http://www.census.gov/hhes/www/income/data/historical/inequality/IE-1.pdf.

US Census Bureau. *Income, Poverty, and Health Insurance Coverage in the United States: 2010.* By Carmen DeNavas-Walt, Jessica L. Semega, and Melissa A. Stringfellow. Pub. P60-239. September 2011. http://www.census.gov/prod/2011pubs/p60-239.pdf.

US Census Bureau. *Statistical Abstract of the United States 2012: Income, Expenditures, Poverty and Wealth.* 2011. http://www.census.gov/prod/2011pubs/12statab/income.pdf.

US Census Bureau. *The Research Supplemental Poverty Measure 2011.* By Kathleen Short. Pub. P60-244. November 2012. http://www.census.gov/hhes/povmeas/methodology/supplemental/research/Short_ResearchSPM2011.pdf.

US Department of Agriculture. Food and Nutrition Service. *Infant Mortality among Medicaid Newborns in Five States: The Effects of Prenatal WIC Participation.* By Barbara Devaney and Allen Schirm. Washington, D.C.: US Government Printing Office, 1993.

US Department of Agriculture, Center for Nutrition Policy and Promotion. *Thrifty Food Plan, 2006*, CNPP-19. April 2007. http://www.cnpp.usda.gov/publications/foodplans/miscpubs/tfp2006report.pdf.

US Department of Agriculture. *Official USDA Food Plans: Cost of Food at Home at Four Levels, U.S. Average, July 2013*. August 2013. http://www.cnpp.usda.gov/Publications/FoodPlans/2013/CostofFoodJul2013.pdf.

US Department of Agriculture. *Household Food Security in the United States in 2012*. By Alisha Coleman-Jensen, Mark Nord, and Anita Singh. Economic Research Report No. 155, September 2013. http://www.ers.usda.gov/publications/err-economic-research-report/err155.aspx#.U4TP5V7irwI.

US Department of the Treasury, Office of Tax Analysis. *A Dynamic Analysis of Permanent Extension of the President's Tax Relief*. July 25, 2006. http://www.treasury.gov/resource-center/tax-policy/Documents/Dynamic-Analysis-of-Permanent-Extension-of-Presidents-Tax-Relief-7-25-2006.pdf.

US Department of the Treasury, Office of Tax Analysis. *A Review of the Evidence on the Incidence of the Corporate Income Tax*, OTA Paper 101. By William M. Gentry. December 2007. http://www.treasury.gov/resource-center/tax-policy/tax-analysis/Documents/ota101.pdf.

US Department of the Treasury, Office of Tax Analysis. *Troubled Asset Relief Program: Monthly Report to Congress*. June 2013. http://www.treasury.gov/initiatives/financial-stability/reports/Documents/June%202013%20Monthly%20Report%20to%20Congress.pdf.

US Department of the Treasury and Council of Economic Advisors. *A New Economic Analysis of Infrastructure Investment*. March 23, 2012. http://www.treasury.gov/resource-center/economic-policy/Documents/20120323InfrastructureReport.pdf.

US Government Accountability Office. *Early Intervention: Federal Investments Like WIC Can Produce Savings*. Pub. GAO/HRD-92-18. Washington, DC: US Government Printing Office, 1992.

US Government Accountability Office. *Commuter Rail: Potential Impacts and Cost Estimates for the Cancelled Hudson River Tunnel Project*. Pub. GAO-12-344. Report to the Chairman, Subcommittee on Surface Transportation and Merchant Marine Infrastructure, Safety, and Security, Committee on Commerce, Science, and Transportation, US Senate. March 2012.

US Government Accountability Office. *High-Risk Series: An Update*. Pub. GAO-13-283. February 2013. http://www.gao.gov/assets/660/652133.pdf.

United States v. Butler, 297 U.S. 1 (1936).

van Zandt, David E. "The Lessons of the Lighthouse: 'Government' or 'Private' Provision of Goods." *Journal of Legal Studies* 22, no. 1 (January 1993): 47–72.

Vaughan, Emmett J., and Therese M. Vaughan. *Fundamentals of Risk and Insurance*. 8th ed. New York: John Wiley & Sons, 1999.

Viard, Alan D., ed. *Tax Policy Lessons from the 2000s*. Washington, DC: AEI Press, 2009.

Vladeck, Bruce C., and Thomas Rice. "Market Failure and the Failure of Discourse: Facing Up to the Power of Sellers." *Health Affairs* 28, no. 5 (2009): 1305–1315. doi:10.1377/hlthaff.28.5.1305.

Weisbach, David A.o "The (Non)Taxation of Risk." *Tax Law Review* 58 (2004): 1–64.

Weisbach, David A., and Jacob Nussim, "The Integration of Tax and Spending Programs." *Yale Law Journal* 113 (2004): 955–1028.

Wessel, Robert H. "A Note on Economic Rent." *American Economic Review* 57, no. 5 (1967): 1223.

West-Shore Fuel, Inc. v. United States, 598 F.2d 1236 (2d Cir. 1979).

Wilkinson, Will. "In Pursuit of Happiness Research: Is It Reliable? What Does It Imply for Policy?" *Policy Analysis* no. 590 (2007): 1–41.

Wills, Gary. *Inventing America: Jefferson's Declaration of Independence.* New York: Houghton Mifflin, 1978.

Winch, Donald. "Adam Smith: The Prophet of Free Enterprise?" *History of Economics Review* 16 (Summer 1991): 102–106.

World Economic Forum. *Global Competitiveness Report 2013–2014.* Edited by Klaus Schwab. Geneva: World Economic Forum, 2013. http://www.weforum.org/issues/global-competitiveness.

Yang, Shu-Chun Susan. "Do Capital Income Tax Cuts Trickle Down?" *National Tax Journal* 60, no. 3 (September 2007): 551–567.

Young, Jeffrey T. *Economics as a Moral Science: The Political Economy of Adam Smith.* Cheltenham, UK: Edward Elgar, 1997.

Ziller, Erika C., Andrew F. Coburn, Timothy D. McBride, and Courtney Andrews. "Patterns of Individual Health Insurance Coverage, 1996–2000." *Health Affairs* 23, no. 6 (November 2004): 210–221.

Zolt, Eric. "Inequality in America: Challenges for Tax and Spending Policies." *Tax Law Review* 66 (2013): 1101–1153.

Zuckert, Michael P. *The Natural Rights Republic: Studies in the Foundation of the American Political Tradition.* Notre Dame, IN: University of Notre Dame Press, 1996.

INDEX

Page numbers followed by *f* and *t* indicate figures and tables, respectively. Numbers followed by n indicate notes.